The Art of Captain Cook's Voyages

The publication of *The Art of Captain Cook's Voyages* has been assisted by
The Australian Government
The New Zealand Government
The Australia–New Zealand Foundation
The Royal Society
The Utah Foundation
The Visual Arts Board of the Australia Council

Rüdiger Joppien and
Bernard Smith

The Art of Captain Cook's Voyages

Volume Three   Catalogue

The Voyage of the *Resolution* and *Discovery* 1776-1780

with a
Descriptive Catalogue
of all known original drawings and
paintings of peoples, places, artefacts
and events and original engravings
associated with the Voyage

Published for the
Paul Mellon Center for Studies
in British Art by
YALE UNIVERSITY PRESS,
New Haven and London, 1988

in association with the
AUSTRALIAN ACADEMY
OF THE HUMANITIES

Designed by Derrick I. Stone Design
Typeset by Meredith Typesetting
Printed by Owen King Printers Australia Pty Ltd

Library of Congress catalog card number 84-52812
ISBN 0-300-04105-5 (v.111)

TO THE MEMORY OF

J. C. Beaglehole and R. A. Skelton

CONTENTS

DESCRIPTIVE INVENTORY OF COLLECTIONS

This inventory lists all works catalogued according to their present location. It is arranged alphabetically by (1) city or province and (2) institution. Private collections preferring anonymity are listed under the appropriate country. The names of commercial houses, such as auctioneers and dealers, are followed by the year, in brackets, in which the items were sold or offered for sale. For all multi-item collections possessing a common location (e.g., PXX 2, Dixson Library, State Library of New South Wales, Sydney) a description of the collection is given first, then the provenance to the extent that it is known with a note on watermarks where relevant, and lastly a concordance is provided between the identification number normally used by the relevant institution (to the left) when there is one and the number given in this catalogue (to the right).

Existing Collections

ASHFORD, Kent, England
Knatchbull Collection
Brabourne Estate, Smeeth

A water-colour drawing by John Webber

Provenance
The drawing is of the same provenance as three drawings by John James Barralet listed in Volume One: 1.5A, 1.113A 1.122A. All four undoubtedly derive from the original collection of Sir Joseph Banks. When Banks died on 20 June 1820 he left his property to his wife, Lady Banks, for life. In two codicils to his will he proposed that his natural history library should go to his librarian Robert Brown (1773-1858) and hence to the British Museum, and that his papers and manuscripts should be looked after and where appropriate disposed of by his relative Sir Edward Knatchbull (1781-1849), a nephew of Lady Banks. In 1849 Sir Edward Knatchbull was succeeded by his first son from his second marriage: Sir Edward Knatchbull-Hugessen (1829-1893) (Hugessen being the surname of his mother), who in 1880 became Lord Brabourne. After the Banks's papers had been unsuccessfully offered to the British Museum in the early 1880s Lord Brabourne arranged for two auctions at Sotheby's, on 11 March 1886 and 14 April 1886. A third auction with new Banks material from the Knatchbull family occurred in 1928. It was due to these auctions that the Banks papers became widely distributed. (For their history see Banks (1962): Beaglehole's textual introduction, I, 127-39.) As Beaglehole pointed out, certain items did not pass through the sale rooms, but were sold individually, and doubtless some were retained. There seems little doubt that the four drawings were a part of Banks's papers and have remained in the Knatchbull family until the present day.

3.15

AUSTRALIA
Private Collection

One oil painting of Captain Cook by John Webber from Trinity House, Hull, Yorkshire.
3.452

Two water-colour drawings by William Ellis from the Rhona Townley Searle collection (q.v.).
3.8
3.97

BERKELEY, California, U.S.A.
Farquhar Collection

Collection of fourteen drawings by John Webber in pencil and wash.

Provenance
This set was advertised in catalogue 551 by the London bookseller Francis Edwards in 1932 — together with 8 volumes of 'Capt. James Cook, Three voyages round the World, maps, charts and plates . . . 1773-85', George Forster 'Voyage round the World in the *Resolution*, 1772-75, folding map, 2

vols. 1777', John R. Forster 'Observations made during the Voyage round the World, 1778', Sydney Parkinson 'Journal of a Voyage to the South Seas in H.M.S. the *Endeavour* with portrait, map and 26 plates, 1784', 'The plates to Cook and Parkinson in 3 vols, folio.'

Concordance
The drawings as listed by Edwards is as follows:

1. Woman of Kamtschatka		3.351
2. Native of Kamtschatka		3.349
3. Man of Kamtschatka		3.343
4. Woman of Kamtschatka		3.344
5. Kamtskadales		3.345
6. Inside of a winter habitation, Kamtschatka		3.363
7. & 8. Natives of Cook's River (2)	3.238,	3.267
9. Woman of Cook's River		3.246
10. Native of Nootka		3.222
11. Canoe of Nootka and Natives on their first approach to the ship		3.227
12. Woman of Nootka Sound		3.225
13. Native of the Island of Mangea		3.180
14. Native of Utowi, Sandwich Islands, signed 'J. Webber, 1778'		3.186

The list is followed by the remark: 'With the exception of No. 1 these drawings are unpublished, and are entirely different versions from the engravings in Cook's Third Voyage.'

According to Mrs Farquhar, no watermarks can be discovered in the drawings, since all drawings are mounted. The drawings are very lightly numbered in pencil on their verso in Mr Farquhar's hand. Mrs Farquhar explains that 'these numbers do not match the numbers used by Edwards . . .' (*in litt.* 11 May 1985).

BERN, Switzerland
Kunstmuseum

A drawing by John Webber from the collection of Niklaus Friedrich von Mülinen (1760-1833), collector, historian and politician, 'Schultheiss' (burgermaster) of Bern from 1814-1827.
Inv. no. 6436   3.145

CAMBRIDGE, England
Fitzwilliam Museum

Two oil paintings by J. Webber

Concordance
Inv. no. 276   3.411
Inv. no. 454   3.114

CAMBRIDGE, Massachusetts, U.S.A.
Peabody Museum of Archaeology and Ethnology, Harvard University

Thirteen water-colour drawings of the American north-west coast subject matter by John Webber.

Provenance
Received from the Estate of David I. Bushnell Jr who bought twelve of them from Francis Edwards, London, in 1925 (see Campbell/Edwards Collection). When Bushnell published his collection in 1928, he referred to them as '12 drawings' (p. 2). The thirteenth drawing within this collection (3.252) is an almost exact copy of one of them and was omitted from Bushnell's article. Where and when it was acquired is not known.

Ref: Bushnell, Jr (1928).

Concordance
41 — 72 — 10 / 496	3.215
41 — 72 — 10 / 497	3.220
41 — 72 — 10 / 498	3.223
41 — 72 — 10 / 499	3.201
41 — 72 — 10 / 500	3.204
41 — 72 — 10 / 501	3.247
41 — 72 — 10 / 502	3.236
41 — 72 — 10 / 503	3.286
41 — 72 — 10 / 504	3.265

41 — 72 — 10 / 505	3.256
41 — 72 — 10 / 506	3.252
41 — 72 — 10 / 507	3.251
41 — 72 — 10 / 508	3.275

CANBERRA, A.C.T., Australia
National Library of Australia

1. Rex Nan Kivell Collection
For Sir Rex de Charambac Nan Kivell, see Vol.2, p.118.

i. Oil painting by John Webber
NK 1   3.313

ii. Fifteen water-colour drawings by J. Webber.
The drawings include portraits, figure studies, and drawings of boats and animals from Tahiti and Hawaii to the north-west coast of America, the Arctic, Kamchatka and South East Asia. They are of varying sizes, both signed and unsigned, inscribed and uninscribed.

The Webber drawings are inventoried, NK 52 A — O. Three further drawings 52 P — R formerly ascribed to Webber are here attributed to A.W. Devis, who accompanied Captain Henry Wilson in his voyage on the *Antelope* (1783). They are of course not included in this catalogue.

Provenance
Drawings 52A, 52C, 52D, 52E, 52F, 52H, 52K, 52L, 52M appear to have been purchased from the London bookseller Francis Edwards, in 1921 or some time after. They are listed in Edwards's *Catalogue* 416, July 1921, no. 769, p. 48. Several of them have 'Capt. Campbell' endorsed on them, indicating that they originally came from the Campbell Collection (See Campbell/Edwards Collection). The provenance of the other drawings is not known, but they may also have passed through Edwards's hands, since the inscriptions on the back of some and the general character and condition of the drawings suggest that they were once part of the Campbell collection.

Concordance
NK 52A	3.439
NK 52B	3.253
NK 52C	3.336
NK 52D	3.440
NK 52E	3.347
NK 52F	3.350
NK 52G	3.332
NK 52H	3.333
NK 52I	3.435
NK 52J	3.178
NK 52K	3.442
NK 52L	3.402
NK 52M	3.399
NK 52N	3.131
NK 52O	3.413

iii. Four works by Webber of unknown or doubtful provenance.
NK 2185	3.74
NK 5192	3.150
NK 5929	3.154
R 3631	3.456

iv. Three water-colour drawings (after Webber) by an unknown artist.
NK 6788A	3.397f
NK 6788B	3.410d
NK 6788C	3.362c

v. Seventeen water-colour drawings by William Ellis.
Including views, motifs of landscape scenery, and habitations, from Kerguelen's Land to Kamchatka.

All drawings are signed, dated and inscribed in black or brown ink. Most are inscribed along the lower margin, others on verso, in a careful, even hand. It seems that the style of the inscription is similar to those on the drawings in the Alexander Turnbull Library, Wellington. With them they also share an occasional reference to Captain D. or Dixon.

The majority of the drawings show small, brown numbers mostly on the face of the drawing, ranging from 4 to 84; these however do not follow the chronology of the voyage. This apparently random way of numbering has not yet been explained.

The character of the drawings as finished works is underlined by the fact that almost all drawings possess framing lines. They give the appearance of presentation copies. The frames consist of double sepia lines, ink and pencil lines, but are not uniform.

Various watermarks occur, that also appear on paper used by J. Webber: the lily-in-a-shield under crown, with the letters 'G R' or 'W' below, is the most frequent one (nine examples). Two other drawings have J. WHATMAN, and I H S I. VILLEDARY respectively. The rest is unmarked or indecipherable.

Provenance
Sixteen of the drawings have consecutive numbers running from 53A-53P; these formed one portfolio on receipt from Rex Nan Kivell (see his picture catalogue 63A-P). These can be traced to the Museum Book Store, London, where they seem to have been bought after 1941 (see the Museum Book Store Collection).

Concordance

NK 53A	3.207
NK 53B	3.192
NK 53C	3.243
NK 53D	3.364
NK 53E	3.211
NK 53F	3.334
NK 53G	3.206
NK 53H	3.208
NK 53I	3.355
NK 53J	3.197
NK 53K	3.235
NK 53L	3.274
NK 53M	3.255
NK 53N	3.258
NK 53O	3.121
NK 53P	3.5

The seventeenth drawing by William Ellis in the Rex Nan Kivell Collection seems to be of a different provenance altogether.

NK 6577	3.84

vi. NK 7402

A copy of Captain George Dixon, *A Voyage Round the World*, London 1789. Tipped into the book are eight drawings in pencil, wash or water-colour; seven relate to Cook's voyages, the eighth is a drawing by Dixon himself. The drawings are inscribed in brown ink in neat writing, which is also characteristic of inscriptions on Ellis drawings at the La Trobe Library, Melbourne and the Alexander Turnbull Library, Wellington. None of the drawings is signed, and unlike the drawings in Melbourne and Wellington they lack numbers on rectos or versos. Watermarks, where present, vary between 'GR' under a crown surrounded by wreaths in a circle, 'EB/I' surrounded by leaves in a circle and a lily in a shield. One drawing (fp. 102) is a copy of a portrait of the 'Man of Caledonia' as drawn by Hodges, engraved by Aliamet and published in Cook's account of the second voyage as pl. 39 (see 2.M11). It is noteworthy that the drawing is mistakenly inscribed in ink as a third voyage document: 'Priest of Sandwich Isles' and in pencil 'This was the Friendly priest, ment^d in Ellis's Voyage. Capt. D.'

The six drawings relating to Cook's third voyage have been traditionally ascribed to Ellis. Two of these are here attributed on the basis of style to Webber. The other four drawings, executed in pencil, are in a style which would relate them to the pencil drawings in the Alexander Turnbull Library (A.264).

Provenance
The provenance of the drawings is unknown. The drawing by Dixon is a view of 'Hippah Island, Queen Charlotte Isles'. It was apparently tipped in opposite the engraving after the drawing; when the other seven drawings were placed into the book after 1789, possibly by Dixon himself, or a person who had access to his material. The fact that the drawing of the 'Man of Caledonia' is inscribed with 'Capt. D' seems to suggest someone acting on the authority of Dixon.

Concordance

fp. 68	3.242
fp. 128	3.101
fp. 154	3.239
fp. 308	3.368

238

fp. 309   3.407
fp. 311   3.422

2. Petherick Collection
E.A. Petherick (1847-1917), bookseller, bibliographer and collector (see *Australian Dictionary of Biography*, 5, 438).
Wash drawing attributed to John Webber.
R. 6879   3.217

3. Gift of The Public Archives of Canada
Two drawings by John Webber of Tongan views, formerly in the Public Archives of Canada, Ottawa and presented to the National Library of Australia, on the occasion of its opening in 1968 (see also under Ottawa).
Acc. no. 3994   3.60
Acc. no. 3995   3.61

Miscellaneous items
4. Water-colour drawing attributed to William Ellis, acquired from Aquarius Fine Arts, Hamilton, New Zealand.
R. 7595   3.196

5. Atlas of engravings of Cook's third voyage with book-plate of Thomas Philip Earl de Grey (1781-1859). Thomas Philip became Earl de Grey on 4 May 1833 on the death of his maternal aunt, Amabel Hume Campbell, Countess de Grey of Wrest, Bedfordshire. De Grey was a Fellow of the Royal Society and a Fellow of the Society of Antiquaries (see also DNB, viii, p. 651).

6. Atlas of engravings of Cook's third voyage, representing proof-states, annotated in Webber's hand, with a book-plate referring to the former owner, the Skottowe Hall Library.

The volume is part of a bigger collection of plates and original drawings which appeared at Sotheby's on 10 May 1949 (lot. 419), which was described as follows: 'A Unique Collection of 317 plates to illustrate the three voyages of Captain Cook' and 'of 17 coloured wash drawings of costumes, many originals (portraits and charts included) in 4 vols half cow-hide gilt, from the Skottowe Hall Library . . . ' The seventeen costumes drawings mentioned were produced for P.J. de Loutherbourg's pantomime 'Omai or, a Trip round the world' first staged at Covent Garden Theatre on 20 December 1785; many of them are based on original drawings and plates after drawings by John Webber, who collaborated on the show (see Joppien, (1979)).

The Skottowe family lived in Great Ayton (Ayton Hall), south of Middlesbrough, Yorkshire, from about 1725 until the early years of the nineteenth century. Thomas Skottowe is known to have paid for the schooling of the young James Cook, who was educated together with his own children. One of them and a near-contemporary to Cook was John Skottowe, Thomas's second son. He later became governor of St Helena from 1764 to 1782 and Cook visited that island both during the first and the second voyage.

Cook sustained a warm relationship with Thomas Skottowe. From his first voyage he brought back various gifts for Skottowe, including two Maori clubs, and went to deliver these on New Year's Day of 1772, only to find that Skottowe had died but recently. Among these gifts may have been the *Wahaika* and *patu onewa* from New Zealand, which are now in the Auckland Museum. They were given to the Museum by Miss Beverly M. Sanders, a descendant of Thomas Skottowe's, in 1953 (Kaeppler, 1978a, 188 no.11 and 191 no.14). Personal connections with the two other sons of Thomas Skottowe, Coulson and Nicholas Skottowe, are not recorded. However, against this background it is not inconceivable that some member of the Skottowe family formed a collection of Cook memorabilia possibly extending this after 1825, as might be gathered from Sotheby's sale catalogue of 1949, where the provenance of the print volumes is explained as: 'From the collection of George Baker; sale at Sotheby's June 26 1825, lots 592-3, 595-7 and 600-602'. The name Skottowe Hall Library is curious, and we have not been able to identify its location.

ref: Kitson (1907) 4-5; Skottowe (1963) 20.
We owe much useful information on this subject to Ms Emma Hicks, London.

DUBLIN, Ireland

National Gallery of Ireland

One water-colour drawing by Webber.
Inv. no. 2303   3.130

DUNEDIN, New Zealand
The Hocken Library, University of Otago

Two water-colour drawings by an unknown artist.

PaA 372(6585)   3.129

PaB 372(6584)   3.319

EDINBURGH, Scotland
National Gallery of Scotland

Two pencil drawings of Nootka by John Webber.

Provenance
Transferred to the National Gallery of Scotland in 1910 from the Royal Scottish Academy, to whom they had been bequeathed in 1878 by David Laing, an antiquarian and bookseller of Edinburgh.

Concordance
D 1452   3.200
D 1453   3.203

ENGLAND
Private Collection (I)
One oil painting and two water-colour drawings by John Webber.
3.27
3.346
3.409

Private Collection (II)
Six drawings in pencil and sepia wash by John Webber, 1976 exhibited in the art gallery of Hartnoll and Eyre (subsequently Eyre and Hobhouse) London.

Provenance
The six drawings belong to a larger group of ethnographical portraits (see also 3.11), of which one is a copy after a drawing by John Webber (3.181A), and four are copies after drawings by or engravings after William Hodges (see vol.II, 257-8). It is believed that the Webber drawings were acquired by George Forster during his visit to London in March 1790 as visual material intended for his projected history of the South Sea Islands. Forster's history however, remained unfinished. After Forster's death the drawings were probably sold by his widow Therese to the Duke Ernst II of Saxe-Gotha-Altenburg, who already owned a set of thirty-two natural history drawings by G. Forster from Cook's second voyage; these had been purchased in 1781 (now in the Forschungsbibliothek Gotha, Codex Gothanus Membranatius I 131). In 1936 two of the thirty-two natural history drawings were sold from the (then) Schlossmuseum Gotha and were acquired by the London dealer N. Sinelnikov of the Orion bookshop. The fact that these reappeared in 1976 together with the ethnographic drawings by Webber (and after Hodges) seems to indicate that all drawings were disposed of at the same time and by the same source.

Ref: Steiner/Baege (1971) 53-66; Joppien (1976a)

Concordance
3.181
3.182
3.378
3.379
3.400
3.403
3.181a (after Webber)

Private Collection (III)
Five drawings in pencil by Webber, in preparation for his softground etchings of South Sea views, offered for sale by Eyre and Hobhouse, London (1984). Their provenance is unrecorded.
3.21
3.73
3.133
3.146
3.340

Private Collection (IV)
Three pencil drawings by John Webber of unclear provenance. It is said that these once formed a

240

collection with the Ellis drawings in the Alexander Turnbull Library (A.264) but were separated prior to the sale.

3.209
3.210
3.365

Private Collection (V)
Pen and wash drawing by John Webber of unknown provenance.
3.27

FRANCE
Private Collection
Oil painting by John Webber.
3.151

HOBART, Tasmania, Australia
The Allport Library and Museum of Fine Arts, State Library of Tasmania
One portrait drawing by Webber

For provenance see ENGLAND, Private Collection (II)
3.11

HONOLULU, Hawaii, U.S.A.
Bernice P. Bishop Museum

1. Eight drawings by John Webber of Hawaiian subject matter.

Provenance
From the Campbell Collection; listed in Francis Edwards *Catalogue* 416, London July 1921, no. 769, 47, purchased by Spencer Bickerton, from whom they were acquired in 1922. Bickerton acted as agent for the museum (see Campbell/Edwards Collection).

Concordance

1922.129	3.179
1922.129	3.188
1922.129	3.294
1922.129	3.297
1922.129	3.300
1922.129	3.302
1922.129	3.308
1922.129	3.317

2. A water-colour drawing by J. Webber.

Presented by Mrs A.W.F. Fuller in 1963 (see Fuller Collection).
1963.254   3.184

3. Two water-colour drawings by W. Ellis.

Together with two others by Ellis representing coastal views of Oneehow and Owhaow, the drawings were purchased by George R. Carter from the Museum Book Store, London in 1928 (catalogue 107, nos. 8, 9, 17 and 18). No. 9 was a short time later exchanged for no. 2 (see the Museum Book Store Collection).

George R. Carter (1866-1933), governor of the territory of Hawaii from 1903 to 1907, was also a bibliophile and a collector. He is remembered for two collections of rare Hawaiiana. One was donated to the Hawaiian Mission Children's Society in Honolulu, the other was given to the Bernice P. Bishop Museum by his son in 1955.
1928.167   3.83
Neg. 935   3.296

4. One water-colour drawing by W. Ellis from the Rhona Townley Searle collection (see under Searle Collection).
1984.122   3.65

Honolulu Academy of Arts

One oil painting by Webber.
Acc. no. 4268   3.90

LONDON, England
Admiralty House, Whitehall

Three oil paintings by John Webber.

Webber painted these and possibly some others (which are either unlocated or which the Admiralty might have disposed of later on) while he was under contract to the Admiralty from 1784 to 1785.
3.280
3.372
3.410

British Library, Department of Manuscripts

1. Add. MS 15513
A volume of 30 drawings in water-colour by J. Webber: comprising 16 views, 5 historical events relating to the voyage, 4 portraits, 2 figure drawings and 3 drawings of artefacts, mainly from the earlier part of the voyage. All drawings, except for two (f.1 and f.2 showing coastal views) are listed here.

Provenance
Lodged with the Admiralty by the artist as a part of the fulfilment of his commission, and presented by the Lords Commissioners of the Admiralty to the British Museum on 13 June 1843.
(*Catalogue of Additions to the MSS in the British Museum in the years MDCCCXLI-MDCCXLV*, London, 1850.) First sent to the Print Room, but on 5 April 1845 transferred to the Department of Manuscripts.

Concordance
The following folios are listed in this volume:

f.3	3.3	f.17	3.106
f.4	3.10	f.18	3.111
f.5	3.13	f.19	3.102
f.6	3.16	f.20	3.135
f.7	3.38	f.21	3.139
f.8	3.45	f.22	3.140
f.9	3.47	f.23	3.122
f.10	3.48	f.24	3.160
f.11	3.57	f.25	3.152
f.12	3.64	f.26	3.124
f.13	3.86	f.27	3.171
f.14	3.93	f.28	3.175
f.15	3.119	f.29	3.165
f.16	3.99	f.30	3.168

2. Add. MS 15514
A volume of 61 folios with drawings by John Webber, including many coastal views, 19 general views, 10 portraits of Pacific people, 3 figure drawings, 5 of inhabitants and 10 of artefacts. Folios with coastal views are the following: f.1, f.2 (a,b), f.3 (a,b), f.4 (a-j), f.12, f.13 (a,b), f.14, f.17, f.33, f.34, f.39, f.59, f.60. Except for f.2b these drawings are not included in this catalogue but will be published in *The Charts and Views of Captain Cook's Voyages*, Cambridge University Press for the Hakluyt Society (forthcoming).

f.58 is not included in this volume. This is a water-colour drawing representing Table Mountain at the Cape of Good Hope; it is signed and dated 'S. Davis 1780' (or 1786). We have no reason to believe that the drawing relates to Cook's voyages.

Provenance
Lodged with the Admiralty by the artist as a part of the fulfilment of his commission. Presented by the Lords Commissioners of the Admiralty to the British Museum on 13 June 1843. (*Catalogue of Additions to the MSS in the British Museum in the years MDCCCXLI-MDCCXLV* London, 1850.) First sent to the Print Room, but on 5 April 1845 transferred to the Department of Manuscripts.

Concordance
The following folios are listed in this volume

f.2b	3.234	f.9	3.232
f.5	3.230	f.10	3.190
f.6	3.248	f.11	3.244
f.7	3.198	f.15	3.263
f.8	3.240	f.16	3.270

f.18	3.283	f.40	3.371
f.19	3.285	f.41	3.374
f.20	3.292	f.42	3.375
f.21	3.259	f.43	3.369
f.22	3.262	f.44	3.389
f.23	3.314	f.45	3.390
f.24	3.185	f.46	3.387
f.25	3.316	f.47	3.384
f.26	3.310	f.48	3.380
f.27	3.325	f.49	3.381
f.28	3.326	f.50	3.408
f.29	3.338	f.51	3.415
f.30	3.352	f.52	3.412
f.31	3.330	f.53	3.396
f.32	3.341	f.54	3.418
f.35	3.348	f.55	3.405
f.36	3.360	f.56	3.420b
f.37	3.362	f.57	3.420a
f.38	3.331	f.61	3.335

3. Add MS 17277

A miscellaneous collection of 51 folios containing 53 drawings by Webber in pencil, wash and colour relating to the third voyage, many are field sketches and studies from which Webber composed his more developed drawings. Folios 52-85 are devoted to European subjects. The Cook drawings comprise: 13 portraits of Pacific people, 12 views, 5 of habitations including a Chinese temple, 5 of European vessels including 2 of *Resolution*, 3 of artefacts, 3 of canoes, 2 figure drawings, and 1 of an historical event. Two drawings of birds, nos 9 and 23, are also included in this catalogue. No 6 is a portrait of a young man in pencil; because its relationship to third voyage material is unclear, it has been omitted from the catalogue, but is reproduced at plate 197.

Provenance

A ms note on p. 1 reads 'Purchased of H. Bohn 13 Nov 1847' (probably Henry George Bohn, 1796-1884, collector, publisher and bookseller). Another note reads: 'All the drawings in this book are by Mr Webber, July 26 1793.' followed by indecipherable initials. It is possible that the volume was, or parts of it were, bought at Christie's sale of Webber's drawings and prints held on 14 and 15 June 1793.

Concordance

no.1	3.446	no.28	3.289
no.2	3.442	no.29	3.261
no.3	3.448	no.30	3.307
no.4	3.449	no.31	3.306
no.5	3.450	no.32r	3.312
no.7	3.18	no.32v	3.299
no.8	3.19	no.33	3.327
no.9	3.436	no.34	3.366
no.10	3.161	no.35	3.329a
no.11	3.116	no.36	3.329b
no.12	3.128	no.37	3.357
no.13	3.125	no.38	3.358
no.14	3.123	no.39	3.367
no.15	3.170	no.40	3.370
no.16	3.177	no.41	3.388
no.17	3.219	no.42r	3.383
no.18r	3.169	no.42v	3.416
no.18v	3.173	no.43	3.373
no.19	3.231	no.44	3.395
no.21r,v	3.194a,b	no.45	3.401
no.22	3.24	no.46	3.404
no.23	3.438	no.47	3.183
no.24	3.288	no.48	3.417
no.25	3.254	no.49	3.421
no.26	3.273	no.50	3.443
no.27	3.272	no.51	3.430

British Museum, Department of Prints and Drawings

1. Miscellaneous drawings by John Webber

Concordance

1859-7-9-102	3.212
1909-7-3-2	3.391
1914-5-20-689	3.445
1914-5-20-692	3.444
1957-7-5-54	3.414

2. 199˙ b.2
Album of 46 natural history drawings by John Webber.
Folio size, 38 drawings of birds, 7 of fish and one of a lizard. All drawings stuck to the page, mostly two on one sheet. Formerly in the collection of Sir Joseph Banks, already in Jonas Dryander's catalogue of Banks's Library. The album is incomplete and seems to be broken up from a bigger series of natural history drawings. The drawings have pencil numbers in their u.r. corners, ranging consecutively from 98-143.

When the Banks collection of books and manuscripts was transferred from the British Museum in Bloomsbury to the new building of the British Museum (Natural History) in Cromwell Road in 1881, this volume was mistakenly left behind and sent to the Department of Prints and Drawings in 1913. (1914-5-20-358 . . . 403.)

3.431

Ref: Lysaght (1959) for the birds.

3. 246˙ a.2
John Webber's *Views in the South Seas*, album of oblong folio size measuring 425 × 597mm. It has no impression but was bound up later. Acquired by the British Museum in 1917. It bears the book-plate of Thomas Philip Earl de Grey, Wrest Park. (For the Earl de Grey, see also under Canberra, National Library of Australia.)

4. C.6˙
Collection of softground etchings and hand-coloured etchings from the South Seas by John Webber.

British Museum (Natural History), Zoological Library

Album of 115 natural history drawings in pencil and water-colour by William Ellis, representing 90 birds (ff. 7-96), 15 fishes (ff. 97-111) and 10 drawings of mammals, crustaceans and mollusca (ff.1-3, 5-6 and 112-115).

The album, which measures 12 13/16 × 8 15/16 : 325 × 227 is bound in leather. Almost all drawings are rendered in water-colour (an exception, for example, is the buffalo from Pulau Condore, f.6), the water-colour however applied with various finish. The size of the sheets differs greatly in height and width, some drawings, like f.107 only measure 2 ½ (64) in height, suggesting that the album was made up from a body of diverse drawings. Smaller drawings were probably cut out from bigger sheets, the sheets having a standard size of about 12 3/16 × 7 ½ (310 × 190), that is foolscap size. Most of them have watermarks which appear in other drawings by Ellis as well, showing Britannia in a palisade ('Pro Patria') and the 'GR' under a crown surrounded by wreaths in a circle. Additional watermarks comprise 'I. VILLEDARY', 'S.I. AY', 'LVG'. All drawings are numbered in blackish ink in u.r. corner. The bird drawings are also numbered in pencil on verso in u.l. corner. The ink numbers are consecutive but do not follow the course of the voyage. Neither do the pencil numbers follow the voyage. The majority of the drawings are neatly framed with black lines in ink.

Some drawings are signed 'W. Ellis' or 'W. Ellis del.' in brownish ink, while others are signed more carefully, also in ink 'W: W: Ellis ad. viv: delin! et pinx 1779'. Almost all drawings are inscribed according to their location, sometimes personal observations or remarks about the circumstances from which the drawing resulted, are added.

A note by R.A. Skelton (23 March 1954) stuck on to the first page reads: 'The MS notes pencilled in sloping hand on the verso of the drawings may with reasonable confidence be assigned to Ellis' hand. Every form of letter formed in these pencil notes can be paralleled in the two pages of MS (f.4), the hand of which can be identified with that of the signatures on the drawings. The argument from handwriting is reinforced by the wording of some of the endorsements which (e.g. "Flew on board off Japan") could hardly derive from anyone but the artist.'

f.4 is a sheet from Ellis's notebook in very fluent hand, in brown ink on LVG watermarked paper; f.4 r begins with a reference to Pulau Condore and deals mostly with birds; f.4 v discusses other animals either observed or heard of, monkeys, amphibia, lizards, snakes etc., as well as fruit. The last paragraph deals with the inhabitants of Pulau Condore. (No continuation of Ellis's notebook is known elsewhere.)

Provenance

The drawings seem to be the ones which Ellis made over to Banks in 1782 (see p. 204). They are mentioned in Jonas Dryander's *Autograph manuscript catalogue of the drawings of animals in the library of Sir J. Banks arranged in systematic order*, in the British Museum (Natural History), Zoology Library, 89 fd. After Banks's death they were inherited (together with Banks's books and manuscripts) by his librarian Robert Brown, and in 1827 by the British Museum; they were transferred from the British Museum (Bloomsbury) in 1881 to the newly founded British Museum (Natural History) in South Kensington.

Ref: Lysaght (1959) for the birds; Sawyer (1971) 125.
3.432

British Museum (Natural History), Botanical Library

Ref: Sawyer (1971) 125, 197.

One water-colour drawing of a plant by John Webber from the Banksian Collection.
3.426a

Two water-colour drawings of flowers by John Webber in a 'Collection of Drawings by Francis Masson'.
3.429

Two water-colour drawings of plants by William Ellis.
3.428

National Maritime Museum

John Webber
1. Oil painting from the Admiralty collection.
3.149

2. Three large water-colour drawings from the Admiralty collection.
3.14
3.189
3.269

These drawings can be identified from Webber's Catalogue, submitted to the Admiralty in 1780; they were listed under 'roll-size'. Because of their considerable format, they may have been separated from the rest and thus escaped transfer with the other Webber drawings from the Admiralty to the British Museum in 1843.

3. Collection of miscellaneous drawings, many of which are sketches of Polynesian and Chinese vessels. Two sheets have drawings on verso.

The drawings are bound up in a volume of folio size together with plates from Cook's first voyage (Hawkesworth), from Vancouver's voyage as well as from James Wilson's *Missionary Voyage to the Southern Pacific Ocean* (London, 1799). The album is imprinted on the spine 'Plates to Cook's Voyages. Voyage I'. The album is said to derive from the Admiralty's collection, but its date of accession by the National Maritime Museum is unknown. The drawings are in the character of field studies, it can thus be assumed that they did not belong to the group of drawings which Webber officially submitted to the Admiralty in 1780. The collection may have been formed by an individual collector.

Concordance

3.56	3.318
3.71	3.382
3.132	3.385
3.148	3.386
3.153	3.392
3.159	3.393
3.250	3.406
3.260	3.419
3.264	3.394

4. Two water-colours from the collection of Captain A.W.F. Fuller.
3.144
3.155

5. Three water-colour drawings after John Webber of unknown provenance.
3.92c
3.138c
3.276c

William Ellis (after ?)
6. Three water-colours, from the collection of Captain A.W.F. Fuller.
Three drawings have been selected for this catalogue out of a number of ten, being almost identical versions of three water-colours by Ellis which were formerly in the Rhona Townley Searle collection (see under Searle collection). Like the Searle drawings, from which they seem to have been copied, they are inscribed in ink along lower margin in a smallish but often fluent hand, referring to the location represented. Like the Searle drawings they are signed and dated. Their paper is partly watermarked with a lily in a shield with 'G.R.' below and a crown above. The other seven drawings show coastal views and profiles; they are not included in this catalogue.
3.9
3.66
3.98

Naval Library, Ministry of Defence, West Brompton

A pencil, pen and wash drawing by John Webber, which probably Webber submitted to the Admiralty in 1780 and which since then became separated from the main bulk of drawings. No history of this drawing is recorded by the Naval Library.
3.12

National Portrait Gallery

One oil painting by John Webber of Captain Cook.
3.451

Public Record Office, Chancery Lane
Wash and water-colour drawing by William Ellis.
MPM 44   3.303

Royal Academy of Arts

One oil painting by Webber.
3.91

Sir John Soane's Museum

One water-colour by Webber.
3.191

Victoria and Albert Museum, Print Room.

Two water-colour drawings by John Webber.
Gift of John Sheepshanks 1857 to the South Kensington Museum.
F.A. 481   3.376
F.A. 482   3.157

MELBOURNE, Victoria, Australia
The La Trobe Library, State Library of Victoria

William Ellis: four sheets of drawings in pencil or water-colour, drawn on recto and verso. Various inscriptions in ink and pencil, also numbers. Two of the drawings signed and dated. The watermarks used represent 'GR' under a crown, surrounded by wreaths in a circle, 'I. VILLEDARY' and an incomplete one of a lily in a shield under a crown. It is evident from the type of drawing, its size, watermark and character of inscription that H.5402 belongs to the same group of drawings as those in the Alexander Turnbull Library, Wellington.

Provenance
Gift of Walter Astley, Colac, Victoria on 23 September 1913 to the State Library. According to family tradition the drawings had come into the family collection through Thomas Astley of Liverpool, England. (On the Astley family see under provenance of the Ellis drawings in the Alexander Turnbull Library.)
Ref: Lewis (1970).

Concordance
H.5402r   3.62
H.5402v   3.69
H.5403   3.25
H.5404   3.7
H.5405   3.427

NELSON, New Zealand
The Bishop Suter Art Gallery

One oil painting by Webber.
3.20

NEW HAVEN, Connecticut, U.S.A.
Yale Center for British Art, Paul Mellon Collection

1. Three oil paintings by John Webber.
3.2
3.174
3.398

2. Four pencil drawings by John Webber in preparation of his softground etchings of the South Seas.
3.44
3.276
3.377
3.397

3. One water-colour drawing after John Webber.
3.146c

Yale University Art Gallery, Yale University

One oil painting by Webber.
3.213

NORTHRIDGE, California, U.S.A.
Mrs. Carl Schaefer Dentzel Collection

One water-colour drawing by John Webber.
3.214

Carl S. Dentzel, who died in 1980, was a collector and director of the Southwest Museum, Los Angeles, Cal. 90042. He is said to have possessed at least six drawings by John Webber of north-west American content, however, except for this one, it has not been possible to identify their subject matter.

OTTAWA, Canada
The Public Archives of Canada

Six drawings by John Webber. Together with a drawing by N. Dance, one by G. B. Cipriani and five by Hodges (see vol. 2, 122) these drawings derive from the third volume of a collection of prints and drawings relating to Cook's voyages. The history of the collection is not known. It is believed that they were acquired around 1930 by Sir Arthur Doughty, Dominion Archivist from 1904 to 1935 (Dr Douglas Schoenherr, *in litt.* 20 May 1982).

Dr Schoenherr has provided a detailed description of the three volumes: 'Three folio volumes with red marbled covers and black leather spine and corners. On the spine of each is stamped in gold letters: *COOKS / VOYAGES* and below this, **1, 2,** and **3** on each of the respective volumes. This binding is clearly not the original one, for in places where the black leather has come loose along the spine, one can see the remains of an earlier binding underneath, of light brown leather stamped with gold. On one volume, enough of the black spine has come loose to read *Vol. / II.* stamped in gold between gold bands on the light brown leather. The three folios are not exactly the same size, the pages of the first measuring 66.6 × 45.4 cm, those of the third measuring 67.0 × 49.7 cm. The first volume contains 80 folio pages, the second 69, and the third 64.

'The contents of the volumes may be summarized as follows.

Vol. I   — engraved portraits of Cook after Dance, Webber, etc.
          — a set of proofs before letters of the prints from the First Voyage, many with inscriptions in pencil across the bottom, sometimes cropped off at the bottom edge and usually beginning with the words "First Voyage . . ." and followed by the title and the corresponding volume and page number in the text. The proofs are usually mounted on the recto, once or twice on a verso, and are sometimes accompanied by another state of the print.
          — an engraved portrait of Cook after Hodges.
          — a set of proofs, usually after letters but before numbers, from the Second Voyage. Most are mounted on a recto; some on larger sheets appear to be sewn into the binding. There are some earlier states before letters with inscriptions in pencil across the bottom, usually beginning with the words "Second Voyage . . . " and often with the corresponding volume and page number.

Vol. II — proofs of the oval engraved portraits of Cook and King after Webber, printed in sepia and both inscribed in pen and grey ink, along bottom of platemark: *Publis'd as the Act directs by J. Webber N° 312 Oxford S! June* ᵗʰ *4* ᵗʰ *1784.*
 — a set of proofs before letters from the Third Voyage, with pencil inscriptions along the bottom beginning "Last Voyage . . . ". Only occasionally is there more than one state of the same print.
 — an unfinished state of the Death of Cook after Webber.
 — a proof of the same print before letters.

Vol. III — engraved portraits of Cook after Webber and Dance.
 — Fols. 2-8 contained the original drawings, mounted on both rectos and versos (5 by Hodges, 8 by Webber, 1 by Cipriani and 1 by Dance [2 of our Webbers were given to the National Library, Canberra, in 1968]). The drawings have all been removed from the folio pages, but in certain cases one can see where a drawing was formerly mounted from its offset on the opposite page. It also appears that at least two folio pages were removed from the volume, perhaps at the same time the drawings were removed, with the result that one cannot completely reconstruct the original order of the drawings in the folio. No list was made when they were removed, an operation that occurred at an unknown date.
 — two copies of the Death of Cook, after Webber.
 — a proof set of the Maps and Charts from the three voyages, some with pencil inscriptions along the bottom.'

Two additional drawings by John Webber which also belonged to the album (I-8 and I-14) were presented to the National Library of Australia on the occasion of its opening in 1968 (3.60 and 3.61).

Concordance

I-10 (c.2620)	3.281
I-11 (c.2621)	3.282
I-12 (c.2821)	3.205
I-13 (c.2822)	3.216
I-1 (c.13415)	3.221
I-15 (c.13424)	3.42

OXFORD, England
Ashmolean Museum, Department of Prints and Drawings

One pencil, wash and water-colour drawing by John Webber.
3.120

SALEM, Massachusetts, U.S.A.
Peabody Museum

1. Four drawings by John Webber, three views and one of the *Resolution* and *Discovery* in the ice. Gift of Stephen W. Phillips, 1947.
 The drawing of *The Resolution and Discovery among the Ice* (3.277) bears a note by Phillips referring to Francis Edwards, London, as the vendor of the drawing in 1921. Since this and the other three drawings can be tentatively identified with items listed in Webber's Catalogue it is possible that all four drawings once belonged to the Campbell Collection and were sold by Edwards in 1921 (see Campbell/Edwards Collection).

M.12463	3.277
M.12464	3.81
M.12465	3.137
M.12466	3.354

2. One oil painting by John Webber.

M.15651	3.72

SAN MARINO, California, U.S.A.
The Huntington Library and Art Gallery

One water-colour drawing by John Webber.
3.1

SEATTLE, Washington State, U.S.A.
University of Washington, Suzallo Library, Edward W. Allen Collection

Two drawings by John Webber, presented by Edward W. Allen in 1968.

Provenance
The provenance of 3.268 is not clear. For the provenance of 3.278 see Campbell/Edwards Collection.
3.268
3.278

SYDNEY, New South Wales, Australia
Art Gallery of New South Wales

One oil painting by Webber.
Acc no. 4.1976   3.87

Dixson Galleries, State Library of New South Wales

Five water-colour views and one oil painting by Webber.

Provenance
Presented by Sir William Dixson in 1929 when his collection was given to the State Government of New South Wales.

Concordance
DG23	3.156
DG24	3.136
DG26	3.305
DG27	3.89
DG28	3.94
DG189	3.88

Dixson Library, State Library of New South Wales

1. PXX2
Drawings by John Webber.

Guard book, measuring 74.5 × 57.0 cm, breadth, 6.5 cm, bound in green morocco gilt, stamped in gilt on the spine 'Illustrations of Cooke's Voyages. Original Drawings by Webber'.

The volume comprises 46 drawings of which 40 are by John Webber. These are well developed water-colours and include: 9 views, 3 interiors, 7 historical events, 7 portraits, 3 figure drawings, 2 habitations, 6 drawings of cult practices, 2 canoes and 1 artefact. 5 drawings by J. Barralet (fols. 15.43.44.45.46) and one by G.B. Cipriani (fol. 14) relate to Cook's first voyage (see vol. 1, 71).

The first page has the book plate and coat of arms of Sir William Dixson 'Fortes Fortuna Juvat'. On lower left imprinted 'Colnaghi Cockspur Street' and '204' (in pencil).

The 46 drawings are laid on folios mostly one drawing per folio. They are surrounded by brown enframing lines drawn on the folios. The titles are written in pencil below the lines by a later (modern) hand in accordance with the inscriptions to the atlas of the official account. Underneath Cipriani's drawing of the 'Dance in Otaheite' (f. 14) it has been remarked 'not engraved' because this engraving does not appear in the atlas of the third voyage, though it was engraved for Hawksworth's Voyages. Other peculiarities of the inscriptions suggest that the inscriber was not familiar with Cook material, and it seems possible that the mounting of the drawings and their arrangement was carried out by Colnaghi's in the middle or the second half of the nineteenth century. At this time the drawings were possibly bound up into this one volume. Thirty-eight of the drawings are reduced in scale and in many cases altered versions of larger originals by Webber in the British Library: Add. MSS 15513 and 15514. They served as models for the engravers and were thus executed between 1781-1783 on the basis of earlier drawings, and studies which Webber had brought home.

Provenance
The drawings probably entered the collection of Sir Joseph Banks after they were used by the engravers. This seems to be corroborated by the fact that the volume also contains several drawings by J. Barralet after drawings by Sydney Parkinson of Cook's first voyage. There are other drawings by Barralet for Banks among the Banks manuscripts in the British Library.

The history of these drawings can be followed after they were purchased by Colnaghi's and resold either at the end of the nineteenth or at the beginning of the twentieth century. In 1920 the drawings were in the possession of the London booksellers Maggs Bros. and listed in their catalogues: *cat.* 398 (1920), item 712; *cat.* 413 (1921), item 582a; *cat.* 491 (1927), item 127.

A note in the Mitchell Library accession cards under J. Webber indicates that the album was in the possession, if not in the ownership of the State (then the Public) Library of New South Wales in September 1929. It thus seems likely that the album was acquired from Maggs Bros. by Sir William

Dixson in (or shortly after) 1927 and handed over to the library with Sir William Dixson's collection in 1929.

Ref: Joppien (1978), 58.

Concordance

no. 1	3.4	no. 23	3.199
no. 2	3.17	no. 24	3.202
no. 3	3.39	no. 25	3.241
no. 4	3.46	no. 26	3.237
no. 5	3.51	no. 27	3.245
no. 6	3.49	no. 28	3.287
no. 7	3.55	no. 29	3.266
no. 8	3.59	no. 30	3.249
no. 9	3.58	no. 31	3.271
no. 10	3.100	no. 32	3.279
no. 11	3.110	no. 33	3.284
no. 12	3.107	no. 34	3.257
no. 13	3.103	no. 35	3.298
no. 16	3.141	no. 36	3.301
no. 17	3.172	no. 37	3.309
no. 18	3.176	no. 38	3.311
no. 19	3.167	no. 39	3.293
no. 20	3.166	no. 40	3.339
no. 21	3.218	no. 41	3.328
no. 22	3.224	no. 42	3.361

2. Pe 210-216, Pf. 50-56
Drawings by John Webber.

Fourteen drawings in water-colour, well finished: 3 portraits of Pacific people, 4 of canoes, 2 of cult practices and 1 each of a girl dancing, an animal, a bird, a view and an historical event. Most drawings are discoloured through exposure to light. They are laid down on card and most are endorsed both by lot and other kinds of numbers and inscribed 'Captain Campbell'.

Provenance
From the collection of Sir William Dixson. Most of the drawings can be identified as items listed in Webber's Catalogue and have therefore in all probability once belonged to the Admiralty collection. In the late eighteenth or early nineteenth century they come into the possession of a member of the Campbell family and were probably sold to Dixson by the London bookseller Francis Edwards in the early twentieth century (see Campbell/Edwards Collection).

Concordance

Pe210	3.37	Pf.50	3.109
Pe211	3.43	Pf.51	3.127
Pe212	3.31	Pf.52	3.70
Pe213	3.115	Pf.53	3.437
Pe214	3.22	Pf.54	3.50
Pe215	3.158	Pf.55	3.434
Pe216	3.104	Pf.56	3.143

3. Q 77/37
The following drawings by Webber are interleafed into Thomas Pennant's copy of Cook/King, *Voyage to the Pacific Ocean.* 2nd edn (London, 1785) vol. III.

Concordance

fp. 226	3.342
fp. 252	3.441

4. MS Q. 151-152 Log by Henry Roberts in two volumes.
Volume 1 of the log contains a number of illustrations in water-colour by Henry Roberts, mostly of coastal views (f.7, f.32, f.43, f.61, f.65, f.72, f.147, a,b, f.249), of which two have an added human interest, showing Cook islanders in their canoes (f.61 and f.65).

Volume 1 (Q.151) bound in brown smooth calf, the title folio inscribed: 'A Log / of the Proceedings/ of His Majesties Sloop Resolution / on Discoveries, towards the / North Pole. / James Cook Esq.ᵣ Commander / by / Henry Roberts. Mate / ' (to which is added in the hand of Henry Roberts's son

David Roberts) ' / from Decem! 1, 1776 to October 3rd 1778', / Captain Henry Roberts deid (sic) in the West Indies of Yellow fever, while / in Command of His Maj. Ship Undaunted also his Eldest Son Henry / This Journal has been in my possession forty years prior in / my mothers Maddalana Sardenia 1 May 1859 / David Roberts / Son to Henry Roberts and a retired Captain in the Royal Navy / '.

Volume 2 (Q.152) in brown rough calf, begins on 4 October 1778 and ends on 30 November 1779 with the words: '. . . we made the coast of China, when the Journals, Charts and Papers etc, were demanded by the Captain through order of the Lords of the Admiralty from the Officers and People' (f.146). Volume 2 has no drawings except for charts. The paper used for both volumes is that of 'J. WHATMAN'.

Provenance
Volume 1 was purchased by Sir William Dixson from Maggs Bros. London in 1938.

Volume 2 was found in a London bookshop in 1928 during the Bicentenary Celebrations of the birth of Captain Cook (Beaglehole in Cook, *Journals* III (1967), 1, p. clxxxv). It was listed in Francis Edwards's *Catalogue of the Library of the late James Edge Partington*, 1934, no. 569, but it is not known when and where Partington acquired it. It was purchased by Sir William Dixson from Edwards in September 1934.

Concordance
vol 1, f.61	3.28
vol 2, f.65	3.32

Mitchell Library, State Library of New South Wales

1. PXD 59⁻¹
One drawing by John Webber. Four other drawings by J. Webber and William Ellis (?) which originally belonged to this album, are now filed under PXD 59⁻²(qv). In addition the volume holds one drawing from Cook's second voyage: Cipriani/Hodges *The Landing at Middleburgh* (vol. 2,181; 2.73).

An album of 122 folio pages, measuring 62.0 × 45.0 cm and comprising a complete set of engravings of the three voyages of Captain Cook, among them many in proof-stage, with additional prints of Omai by F. Bartolozzi, after N. Dance (f.56), of J. Webber's Death of Cook (f.2), and of Webber's portraits of Cook (f.4a,b). Early print impressions of engravings from the second and the third voyage include 'A Man of Caledonia' (f.40b), 'A Man of Mallicolo' (f.47a), a 'Portrait of Potatow' (f. 54a), 'A Man of Van Diemens Land' (f. 64b) and 'A Woman of Eaoo' (f.74a).

The folio is bound in brown leather with gilt impressed lettering on the spine. The pages were trimmed when bound. On the inside front cover a book-plate with a coat-of-arms (Knight of the Garter). According to Mr Thomas Woodcock, College of Arms, London, the book-plate probably belonged to a Duke of Hamilton. The book-plate of the 10th Duke, who succeeded in 1819 and died in 1852, in the Franks Collection (13420) shows an 'Armorial shield in a garter on a mantle'. On the inside back cover is the book-plate of 'Sir William Augustus Fraser of Ledeclune and Morar Baronet'. Sir William, 4th Baronet (1826-1898) was a historian, writer, politician, and 'one of the Queen's body-guard for Scotland' (The *Times* — obituary — 16 March 1898).

The album has a number of peculiarities that may be described as follows:
 (i) Most prints have a black stamp of a fleur-de-lis attached in the lower centre. Its significance is unknown.
 (ii) Several recto and verso pages bear inscriptions. On many of the versos are inscriptions apparently referring to plates of the first and second voyage, which suggests that the plates referred to were removed at one stage and arranged differently. The pages were then re-used for plates of the third voyage. Lack of chronological order of the verso inscriptions makes it evident that the earlier arrangement was broken up and the volume rebound.
(iii) Folios 18a, 100 and 109v are mounted with engravings by George Cooke (1781-1834) for Pinkerton's *Collection of Voyages and Travels* in seventeen volumes, after illustrations of Cook's third voyage and of J.J. de Labillardière's *Relation du Voyage à la Recherche de la Pérouse* (Paris 1800). Since Pinkerton's edition was published only between 1808-1814, it would seem therefore that the album was not bound up before 1814.

Provenance
There is no evidence as to who formed this collection of engravings, proof engravings and original drawings. However, it is important to note that the volume contains the greatest number of cancelled plates from the second and third voyage that is known. The fact that the cancelled plates were available only to a few people suggests that these could only have been procured by a person who was involved in the production of the official account. Probably someone associated with Banks or Sandwich.

Stuck into the flyleaf of the album is a label of Bernard Quaritch, the London bookseller, addressed to 'David S. Mitchell Esq., Sydney NSW', further below 'Agent Genl. for New South Wales'. This suggests that the album was sent to Sydney first 'on inspection'. A cutting containing a description of the item, presumably from the Quaritch catalogue, is attached, reading: 'Cook (Capt. Ja.) Three voyages Round the World. A complete Set of the Plates to the three voyages (unfolded), comprising fine proofs of the engravings in 2 states, including the large and small plates by Bartolozzi of the Death of Captain Cook, with the ORIGINAL DRAWING by Webber, the landing at Middleburgh by Sherwin, with the original drawing by Hodges; Man of Kamtschatka travelling in Winter with ORIGINAL DRAWING by Webber; full-length portrait of Omai, 2 cancelled plates and 3 UNPUBLISHED DRAWINGS, ALL NEATLY MOUNTED ON CARTRIDGE PAPER AND BOUND IN OLD RUSSIA WITH BROAD INLAID ORNAMENTAL BORDERS . . ." ATLAS FOLIO 1773-77-85.

Ref: Cook, Bibliography (1970), item 1844

Concordance
f.115   3.337

2. PXD 59^{-2}
Four drawings by J. Webber and William Ellis (?), which were originally contained in the album PXD 59^{-1} (see above) but which have since been stored seperately.

Concordance
f.1   3.304
f.6   3.353
f.7   3.82
f.8   3.195

3. Log of James Burney   Safe 1/64
Two drawings in pencil, pen and water-colour, the first by Webber, the second by an unknown artist (James Burney?).

The log of James Burney under Safe 1/64 is divided into three volumes, dealing with the voyage from 10 February 1776 to 11 October 1777, 12 October 1777 to 24 July, 25 July 1778 to 14 February 1779 and from 15 February to 24 August 1779, and entitled 'Journal of the Proceedings of his Maj^{ys} Sloop, the Discovery Chas Clerke Commander, in company with the Resolution Captn James Cook'.

The drawings are contained in volumes 1 and 2.

Provenance
After the purchase of volume 4 in Sydney in 1921, volumes 1-3 were acquired in London eighteen months later. No previous sources are known.

Concordance
vol 1 f.12   3.426b
vol 2 f.91   3.142

TAUNTON, Somerset, England
Hydrographic Department of the Admiralty, Ministry of Defence

Harbour view of St Peter and St Paul on Edward Riou's 'Plan of the Bay of Avatch'ka'.
HD 524 / 1   3.356

TORONTO, Ontario, Canada
Royal Ontario Museum

One water-colour by Webber.
957.261   3.233

WELLINGTON, New Zealand
Alexander Turnbull Library

1. A 264
Seventy-two drawings by William Ellis on 49 separate sheets, drawn in pencil, ink and wash, mixed media. They include material related to Kerguelen Land, New Zealand, the Cook Islands, the Friendly Islands, the Society Islands, the north-west coast of America, the Aleutians, the Sandwich Islands, Alaska, Kamchatka and Siberia.

Many of the drawings have been titled and signed in ink some time after they were drawn, and after Ellis's *Authentic Narrative of a Voyage Performed by Captain Cook and Captain Clerke in his Majesty's Ships Resolution and Discovery . . .*, (London, 1782) had been published, since annotational references to the book, in the same ink and hand are provided on many of the drawings. Most of the drawings are on similar paper and bear inscriptions and numbers in either one or two (the second in pencil) hands.

The papers used for 10 drawings are watermarked 'GR' under a crown, surrounded by wreaths in a circle; 16 drawings have the watermark 'Pro Patria' with Britannia (or the maid of Holland) seated within a palisade. None of these sheets of paper exceed the size of 315 × 199 and are of foolscap format = standard size for writing paper since the beginning of the seventeenth century. In his standard work on watermarks, Churchill says about the English foolscap paper: 'One of the marks used to distinguish English foolscap size paper is the Britannia watermark. It seems incredible that we had to go to Holland for our Britannia watermark, but it seems that this was the case. The British watermark appears to have been evolved from one of the Pro Patria watermarks representing the maid of Holland seated within a pallisade and holding a hat on the point of a spear' (43-4).

The paper represented here could have been used by Ellis both for his diary as well as for the description of natural history specimens. The same watermarks 'GR' and 'Pro Patria' appear among Ellis drawings in the British Museum, Natural History, in the La Trobe Library and in the National Library of Australia (on sheets tipped into G. Dixon's *Voyage round the world*). One can therefore assume, that Ellis preferred this paper for (most of) his field sketches.

In a few other instances where bigger paper was used, either different watermarks or no watermarks at all are to be noticed. It should be noted that Ellis's more developed water-colour drawings which were probably executed in the later part of the voyage under the influence of Webber, bear watermarks of 'I. TAYLOR', 'J. WHATMAN and 'I. VILLEDARY' — paper which Webber also used.

Provenance
According to information passed on with the drawings, they originate from the Astley family of Liverpool, who in the eighteenth and nineteenth century were a family of engravers. A member of that family was the portrait painter John Astley (1730-1787) a pupil of Hudson. Another Astley was Sir Edward Astley (1729-1802), an important collector of prints, particularly of Rembrandt; his collection was sold in 1816 (see Wilson/Borrow (1973), 22). It is not known however, how the Astleys acquired the Ellis drawings. The drawings share a common provenance with the Ellis drawings in the La Trobe Library, Melbourne, which were a gift of Walter Astley of Colac, Victoria made on 23 September 1913, who was a member of the Australian branch of the Astley family. It is recorded that the La Trobe Collection came from Thomas Astley of Liverpool.

A present member of the Australian branch of the Astley family, living in Melbourne, has supplied the baptism certificate of his ancestor, William Astley, born 27 October 1829, baptized 16 November 1829, son of William and Mary Astley of Hale Street, Engraver in Liverpool. *Gore's Liverpool Street Directories* mention in 1821 a William Astley, engraver in 15 Hale Street. He lived at that address until 1837, but in 1841 and 1843 his address is given as 8 Hale Street. He could have been the son of Thomas Astley, who is listed in the *Liverpool Street Directories* as early as 1787, as watch engraver, engraver and copper plate printer, living in Stanley Street, and who is still listed in that street as late as 1837. He could still be identical with Thomas Astley of 8 Hale Street, recorded in 1841 or be the son of the former. William Astley (1885-1911) second son of Thomas Astley, jeweller of Liverpool, was brought to Australia in 1855 by his family. He later became well known as the writer 'Price Warung'. It was probably through this branch of the family that the La Trobe Ellis drawings came to Australia.

Then, after sixty years, more Astley family Ellis drawings appeared at a sale at Phillips, Son & Neale, Blenheim St, New Bond Street London on 3 June 1974 and were bought by K.L. Young, Brunswick Gardens, London W.8, who in turn sold them in 1976 to the South Sea Library, London and Wellington. They were then acquired by the Alexander Turnbull Library in 1976. (For the relevant checks in the *Liverpool Street Directories* we are indebted to Ms Mary Bennett, Keeper of British Art in the Walker Art Gallery, Liverpool.)

Eight sheets of bird drawings and a drawing of a walrus are not specifically catalogued: birds: 32, 33, 34, 35, 38, 40, 42, 48, walrus: 14B (see cat. no. 3.433). Entirely omitted from this catalogue are coastal views and profiles: 7B, 8B, 12 (now preserved at B 41/44), 21B, 37B, 43A, 43B, 46B. Drawing 39 though a coast view has been included here, because it served as a model for one of Ellis's more accomplished drawings.

In accordance with the inventory list by Murray-Oliver (1977) the recto of each sheet is described as A, the verso as B.

Ref: Murray-Oliver (1977), 28-37, together with articles by Hoare (1977), Davidson (1977) and Medway (1977).

Concordance

1	3.6	20B	3.164
2	3.23	21A	3.321
3	3.26	22A-23A	3.96
4	3.30	22B	3.162
5A	3.29	23B	3.118
5B	3.35	24	3.108
6A	3.34	25	3.105
6B	3.36	26A	3.163
7A	3 33	26B	3.423
8A	3.40	27A	3.147
9A	3.63	27B	3.126
9B	3.52	28	3.295
10A	3.54	29A	3.134
10B	3.53	29B	3.324
11	3.67	30	3.229
13A+14A	3.41a,b	31	3.228
13B	3.68	36	3.291
14B	3.433	37A	3.226
15A	3.77	39	3.193
15B	3.424	41	3.290
16A	3.78	44A	3.315
16B	3.79	44B	3.425
17A	3.80	45	3.187
17B	3.75	46A	3.322
18	3.76	47A	3.320
19A	3.112	47B	3.323
19B	3.85	49A	3.359
20A	3.117		

2. One oil painting by John Webber.
3.113

3. Three drawings by John Webber in preparation of his softground etchings of the South Seas.
B91/4   3.92
B91/5   3.95
B91/6   3.138

4. Copy of a portrait of Captain J. King.
3.456a

WELLINGTON, New Zealand
National Art Gallery, Portrait Collection

One oil painting by John Webber of Captain Cook.
3.453

Four early collections, now redistributed

1. The Museum Book Store Collection, London

In 1924 the Museum Book Store, 45 Museum Street, London, W.C.1 offered ten water-colour drawings by William Ellis (*catalogue* 94, item 562), but these remained unsold. The drawings, plus another nine drawings by Ellis were re-advertised in *catalogue* 107 of the Museum Book Store, (1928), item 41. From this group Governor George R. Carter of Hawaii chose four drawings, nos. 8, 9, 17 and 18. When it was discovered that no. 9 had been wrongly titled and did not represent Kealakekua Bay (but Avacha Bay instead), the drawing was returned and exchanged for no. 2. The four drawings were donated to the Bernice P. Bishop Museum in 1955.

The remaining drawings were acquired by the London collector Rex Nan Kivell who later gave them to the National Library of Australia. The only drawing that cannot be located is no. 19 in the Museum Book Store list: 'View of Part of the East Side of Japan . . .'. It might have been bought by Nan Kivell but lost later.

The following list of drawings is quoted from the 1928 catalogue. Bernice P. Bishop Museum, Honolulu:
  2. View in Oitapeeah Bay in the Island of Otaheite   3.83
  8. View of a Priest's House at Owyhee   3.296
 17. View of Oneehow, one of the Sandwich Islands, South Sea
 18. Part of the West Side of Owhaow (Owhyhee), one of the Sandwich Islands . . .

254

National Library of Australia, Rex Nan Kivell Collection:
1. Christmas Harbour in the Island of Desolation, or Kerguelan's Land   3.5
3. View of Ship-Cove, in King George's Sound, on the N.W. Coast of America: where
   the tents are fixed was called Astronomers' Rock   3.197
4. View in King George's Sound, N.W. Coast of America   3.207
5. View in King George's Sound, on the North-West Coast of America   3.192
6. Prince Williams Sound in Sandwich Sound, on the N.-W. Coast of America   3.243
7. View of Snug Corner Harbour, Sandwich Sound, N.-W. Coast of America   3.235
9. View of part of the beach in Kealakeakua Bay, Hawaii (without title)   3.355
10. Winter View of Kamtschatka   3.334
11. A Russian Hut in the Harbour of St. Peter and St. Paul in Kamtschatka   3.364
12. Outside of the Huts at Unalaska, N.-W. Coast of America   3.255
13. A Rock and a Distant View in King George's Sound, N.-W. Coast of America   3.206
14. View of the Huts at Tschutschi Noss, Asia   3.274
15. The Entrance into Ship Cove, King George's Sound, N.-W. Coast of America   3.208
16. View of the Singular Tree in King George's Sound, N.-W. Coast   3.211

As this book went to press, John Maggs, London, supplied us with a copy of a Museum Book Store catalogue of 1941 (no. 125) which again lists the above mentioned drawings in the National Library of Australia (entry 453, pp. 69-70). It also includes two other Ellis drawings which had not been part of the 1928 collection: 3.121 and 3.258. It does not, however, mention 3.84, nor is there another reference to the 'View of Part of the East Side of Japan' which had been included in the 1928 edition.

The provenance of the Ellis drawings beyond the Museum Book Store is unknown. They might be — if only in part — identical with the Ellis drawings which appeared in Exeter during the nineteenth century, and may relate to a peculiar inscription which is on the back of a drawing, apparently representing the coast of Kamchatka, which is presently kept in an Australian private collection. The drawing is by D. or Dr Childe, and though the inscription is confused in some points, it might still be useful to quote it at length: 'About 40 of these drawings depicting various scenes in the south seas & other parts visited by Capt. Cook's expedition 1787 (sic), were sold at Mr. Selton's sale at Exmouth by Crews & Son. Most of them were original drawings in colour by W. Ellis, signed and dated, & others by the above [Childe] both of whom accompanied the expedition.

'Twenty-five were purchased by the late Mr. Drayton of Exeter (Bookseller) who catalogued & sold to a London Dealer 24 of them for £5. I bought the remainder & sold all except this for £14. Later Mr. Drayton found an odd one & having heard they were of value obtained £4 for this one, which at this rate would have made the price of the lot somewhere about £100. S.M.' (in. litt. Ms Trish Middleton, Canberra).

M. M. Rowe, County Archivist at the Devon Record Office informs us that 'Draytons were a booksellers who operated in Exeter from the early nineteenth century and a William Drayton from this family died, according to one source, in 1879' (in litt. 12 July 1984). Nothing is known about Mr Selton or Crews & Son. Thus the provenance of the Ellis drawings must presently remain unsolved.

2. The Campbell/Edwards Collection
In his *Catalogue* 416 (July 1921), the London bookseller Francis Edwards of 83 High Street, Marylebone, London W.1, offered a 'Collection of Thirty-Three Original Water-Colour Drawings relating to the Sandwich Islands, Nootka Sound (Vancouver), Prince William's Sound, Alaska, and Kamtschatka . . . many of which are unpublished' (item no. 769, pp. 47-8). Thirty of these can be followed almost without any doubt to four different institutions: the National Library of Australia, Rex Nan Kivell Collection, Canberra; the Peabody Museum, Harvard University, Cambridge, Massachusetts; the Bernice P. Bishop Museum, Honolulu and the Suzzallo Library, University of Washington, Seattle. They can be identified as follows:

National Library of Australia:
— The Inside of a Winter Habitation in Kamtschatka   3.333
— Native Man and Woman (2 drawings)   3.399 + 3.402
— A Man of Kamtschatka travelling in Winter   3.336
— A Woman of Kamtschatka   3.350
— A White Bear   3.440
— A Sea Otter   3.439
— A Man of Kamtschatka   3.347
— An Animal of the Deer Tribe   3.442

Peabody Museum, Harvard University:
— Inside of a House in Oonalashka   3.256
— Natives of Oonalashka and their Habitations   3.251
— A Woman of Oonalashka   3.265
— A Man of Prince William Sound   3.236

The drawings which cannot be satisfactorily identified are 'Three Drawings of Canoes of Oonalashka'. Their title responds only in part to another drawing in the Suzallo Library (3.268), so they may not as yet have come to light.

Concerning the provenance of these drawings two documents, relating to the drawings at the Peabody Museum, and to the Bernice P. Bishop Museum are illuminating. After Spencer Bickerton had bought the eight drawings of Hawaiian subject matter, Francis Edwards wrote about them: 'Sir Archibald Campbell (1st Baronet), Governor of New Brunswick, acquired these pictures during his Governorship of N.B. 1831-37. They were brought home to Gibliston, Fifeshire, the Scottish home of the Campbell Family, and there they remained till recently, when Sir Everard im Thurn, who was visiting Sir Wm. Campbell (4th Baronet) pointed out to him their value and suggested that I would be a proper person to buy them' (Mrs C. Timberlake, Bernice P. Bishop Museum, *in litt.* 13 May 1977).

David I. Bushnell Jr who had bought the twelve drawings relating to the north-west coast of America was informed by Francis Edwards concerning the drawings' provenance, 'They came from Sir William Campbell of Ava, 3rd Bart., and originally belonged to his grandfather, Sir William Campbell, Governor of New Brunswick, 1831-1837, who bought them in New Brunswick together with some drawings by Capt. Samuel Wallis . . . It is not known how they came to New Brunswick, but it is suggested that the Admiralty here dispersed some of their collections some time before 1830.' Edwards to Bushnell, 13 February 1925.

The drawings belonged at one stage to the main body of drawings which Webber, in fulfilment of his contract, had left with the Admiralty in 1780. The majority of these, or rather what was still left of them, the Lords Commissioners of the Admiralty presented to the British Museum in 1843.

There is no information as to why a member of the Campbell family should have taken an interest in these drawings, however, it might be suggested, that the memory of Cook in the family was responsible for this. Captain, later Vice-Admiral John Campbell (1720?-1790), an 'excellent practical seaman and a man of science' (Beaglehole in Cook, *Journals* III (1967), 1, 38) had introduced Cook to the Council of the Royal Society in 1768. Campbell himself had at one time been suggested to sail to the South Seas and to look for a North-West Passage (Beaglehole, ibid, p. LI). That Cook had a high regard for Campbell is apparent from his letters to Dr Douglas, the editor of the official account of the second voyage of 26 April and 23 June 1776: 'C. Campbell will look over the Nautical part' and 'When Captain Campbell has looked over the MS. it will be put into the hands of Mr. Strahan [the printer]'. (British Museum, Egerton 2180, f.9, 17.) Campbell was appointed Vice-Admiral in 1779 and governor of Newfoundland in 1782. In 1786 he returned to London. His attachment to Cook and his close relationship to Lord Keppel, may have suggested Campbell as a suitable recipient of the Webber drawings (provided that they were disposed of in this way). The drawings may equally have been acquired (as stated by Edwards) by Sir Archibald Campbell. Lot numbers at the back of several of the drawings also suggest that the Admiralty may have disposed of them by sale.

The history of this collection is further complicated by the fact that the Campbell Collection did not consist of only thirty-three drawings. There is very good reason to believe that Francis Edwards held more drawings from the same source, and that he either did not choose to advertise them, or advertised them in some catalogue we have not seen. John Webber's drawing the *The Resolution and Discovery among the Ice* in the Peabody Museum, Salem (3.277) provides some information to this point. Two labels on the back of the drawing read: 'Hawaiian Collection 379 of Stephen W. Phillips. Bt. in London 1921 of Francis Edwards T×24, Cook's ships in the Ice an unpublished sketch by James Webber

. . .' and '. . . these original sketches by Webber were sold in London 1920-1, for very large prices. I was able to get this one but couldn't get the Hawaiian ones as they were sold together'.

The drawing is not mentioned in the catalogue by Edwards. The drawing of similar subject matter *The Resolution beating through the Ice . . .* was in fact bought by Bushnell and differs widely in size from the Phillips drawing. Phillips's label can therefore only mean that Edwards had more drawings in stock.

Many of the drawings mentioned above which we had the chance to inspect have 'Capt. Campbell' written on their back and thus verify the history of their provenance. This characteristic is also true of seven water-colour drawings by Webber which are now in the Dixson Library in Sydney and which might have been acquired by Sir William during the 1920s, or early 1930s, when he bought much other material relating to the Pacific. The drawings endorsed 'Capt. Campbell' in the Dixson Library are here catalogued as: 3.31; 3.37; 3.43; 3.50; 3.104; 3.115 and 3.437. Since Francis Edwards must be regarded as the agent of the Campbell drawings it seems logical to assume that these also went through his hands.

3. The Rhona Townley Searle Collection

On 26 January 1984 Sotheby's London auctioned a group of ten pen and water-colour drawings, signed and dated by W. Ellis, showing Pacific scenery and coastal profiles from Adventure Bay in Van Diemen's Land to Avacha Bay, Kamchatka and Sulphur Island. The drawings are remarkable for being more spirited but near to identical versions of ten drawings, also signed and dated in the National Maritime Museum, London, Fuller Collection.

The Searle drawings were originally preserved in an album but were split up for auction. The following table shows their lot nos, their title and their present location:

86 View of the Rock at the Entrance of the Bay of Awatschka — Private Collection, England, on loan to the Cook Museum, Whitby
87 View of Adventure Bay, Van Diemen's Land, New Holland — Private Collection, Australia (3.8)
88 Continuation of the Coast from Providence Harbour, in the Island Unalaschka — Private Collection, England, on loan to the Cook Museum, Whitby
89 View of Atowa, Sandwich Islands — Bernice P. Bishop Museum, Honolulu
90 View of Atowa, Sandwich Islands — Bernice P. Bishop Museum, Honolulu
91 View of Middleburgh, Friendly Isles — Bernice P. Bishop Museum, Honolulu (3.65)
92 Schumagin's Isles — Bernard Quaritch Ltd, London
93 Sulphur Island, Two Views — Bernard Quaritch Ltd London — Private Collection, Australia
94 The Harbour of Sangoonoodha, in the Island of Unalaschka — The Public Archives of Canada
95 View of Matavai Bay, in the Island Otaheite — Private Collection, Australia (3.97)

The drawings of lot nos. 87, 91 and 95 have been selected for inclusion into this volume: they show a pronounced interest in landscape representation, ethnographic subject matter and in historic moments of the voyage. The others are more topographical in character.

The drawings are inscribed in ink along the lower margin in a small, neat hand, referring to the location represented. They are enframed by single ink lines. Their paper is watermarked 'I. TAYLOR' or 'J. WHATMAN'. The two Hawaiian views — not listed in this catalogue — are numbered '9' and '10' the only two to be numbered. The views are inscribed 'Captn D.' Two drawings, the View of Schumagin Isles and the View of Sulphur Island, refer to Ellis's *Narrative* (1782). (For a discussion of the whole group of drawings as part of Ellis's œuvre see pp. 210.)

The provenance of these drawings is unclear. A book-plate in the inside front cover gives the names of the previous owners as Rhona Townley Searle and Howard Palmer. Nothing is known about Searle. Palmer was a business man from New London, Connecticut. During the 1920s he worked as a treasurer to the family firm of Palmer Brs. Mills; he died about 1932. He was also a prominent explorer. His brother George was a book collector whose collection is now housed in the Connecticut College Library. From Palmer, the album of the Ellis drawings came to a friend, and his widow donated it to the Lyman Allyn Museum in New London. The drawings were offered for sale to the National Maritime Museum, London in 1983 and sold by auction subsequently (information partly based on communication by Mr Edgar de N. Mayhew of the Lyman Allyn Museum to Mrs Cynthia Timberlake of the B.P. Bishop Museum, Hawaii, *in litt.* 23 August 1984).

The album itself, in which the Ellis drawings had been pasted, was also offered for sale as lot no. 96. It contained prints relating to Cook's second and third voyage, 34 after W. Hodges, 28 after John Webber, plus one other, altogether 63 folios. The album was bought by Maggs Bros., London and subsequently sold to The Public Archives of Canada. Dr Douglas Schoenherr of the Picture Division of The Public Archives of Canada has kindly examined the album for us: 'The cover measures 54.1 × 36.7 cm and is bound in purplish brown leather spine and corners over marbled boards. Glued to the spine is a brown leather label with the following title stamped in gold: PLATES/TO/COOKS/VOYAGE. The inside front cover bears the bookplate of Rhona Townley Searle. The volume begins with 'A Chart of the Southern Hemisphere; showing the Tracks of some of the most distinguished Navigators: By Captain James Cook . . .' There follow 63 folios each bearing prints of generally poor quality from the 2nd and 3rd voyages usually trimmed within the platemark. In some instances a sheet of tissue has been glued to the verso of the folio facing the print on the recto. Some of the prints bear inscriptions in pen and brown ink referring to page numbers apparently in Cook's *Voyages*. At the conclusion of the album may be clearly seen the stubs of the folios which contained the Ellis drawings. Two watermarks are found on the album pages, which are of laid paper (53.2 × 35.3 cm): the first consisting of an elaborate coat-of-arms bearing a fleur de lis and with a crown at the top and the initials GR at the bottom. The other watermark reads: I TAYLOR.' (*In. litt.*, 24 July 1984.)

4. The Fuller Collection

Captain Alfred Walter Francis Fuller (29 March 1882-13 December 1961) was a well-known British collector of ethnographica and of visual material from the Pacific. His collection of ethnographica is now in the Field Museum, Chicago. His paintings, drawings and prints, many of which he annotated in pencil, he left to other institutions. His collection relating to Cook's third voyage, which he presented to the National Maritime Museum, comprise 2 drawings by John Webber, 10 by (or after) William Ellis, as well as 3 paintings after John Cleveley. In addition Fuller gave the Maritime Museum a painting of Cook's *Landing at Middleburg* (after Hodges) and a number of drawings by Peircy Brett taken during Captain Anson's Voyage around the world. Fuller's collection was donated to the museum in December 1961 through the National Art Collections Fund. Other works of art from his collection were donated to the Bernice P. Bishop Museum, Honolulu. His library was acquired by that institution in 1964. (On Fuller see Force and Force (1971).)

DESCRIPTIVE CATALOGUE

General Comments

ARRANGEMENT

The catalogue has been arranged so that it can be conveniently used as a visual supplement to the progress of each of the voyages, so in listing items chronology has been the first consideration. All items that can be related to a specific place, and by inference if need be to a specific time, are placed in chronological order. Professor Beaglehole's edition of the journals of Cook has been used for this purpose, and for this reason a date is normally added after a citation from the journals, when it provides evidence for the position of the item in the catalogue. To avoid confusion we have not attempted to convert from ship's time in Cook's journals.

Dates or approximate dates are provided at the extreme right of the title of each item, in the following forms:

[Mar 1777], where it has been concluded that the work was begun and completed in the month specified;
[Mar-Jun 1777], where the work was completed between the months specified;
[Mar 1777-], where the work was completed in the month specified or later.

Where it was not possible to place an item in a chronological sequence precisely, it has been grouped towards the end of the relevant landfall, e.g. Tonga, Society Islands, Hawaii. The arrangement adopted has meant in practice that items have been assembled for each major landfall according to two sequences: (1) by chronology and version, (2) by subject, for all items for which a precise chronology has not been established. For precise references to subjects, however, the index should be used.

Where no signatures, dates or watermark are given in an item's description it may be assumed that none has been noticed, or in the case of watermarks, is not visible because of the mounting technique and so on adopted.

As for Volumes 1 and 2, drawings, paintings and engravings relating to the same subject matter are brought together as version sequences within the overall chronological sequence. For Volume 3 however the material as a whole tends to fall more firmly into successive version sequences. Therefore, in this volume we have decided to mark the beginning of each version sequence by placing, so far as this is possible, the earliest known *finished* drawing of a sequence first, instead of beginning a new sequence with field studies, as in Volumes 1 and 2. In each sequence wherever possible, we follow this finished drawing with field studies. Then follow developed works (often executed after the end of the voyage) and finally engravings from both the official account of the voyage, and from Ellis's *Narrative* (1782). Because Webber was official artist to the voyage we have also included his portraits of Cook, King and Gore in a final section at the end of the catalogue. Webber's *Views in the South Seas* are included. They sometimes provide scenes for which there is no other visual evidence, the original drawings having been lost. Where Ellis's drawings have been found to be similar to or modelled on those of Webber we have listed them along with Webber's relevant work.

A summary survey of the natural history drawings by Webber and Ellis is included for convenience. It is to be hoped that one day a fully-illustrated catalogue of all their work in this field will be published.

Eighteenth and early nineteenth century copies that have sometimes been mistaken for originals are listed beside relevant originals. We have not attempted to illustrate later copies but occasionally mention them in the text when they have been known to cause confusion.

SYSTEM OF NUMBERING

3.	refers to Cook's third voyage to the Pacific.
3.1	refers to an original drawing or painting made on the voyage, or a drawing of an artefact collected on the voyage but drawn after the voyage.
3.1A,B,C etc.	refers to a print (engraving, aquatint etc.) based on an original drawing made on the voyage.
3.1a,b,c etc.	is used as a subdivision in items in this catalogue, and sometimes also to indicate hand copies of engravings.

TITLES AND INSCRIPTIONS

Titles have been drawn from inscriptions on the item itself, wherever considered accurate or at least not misleading, or from the earliest known reliable source, e.g. the title of a related engraving. This practice has been adopted in order to establish, so far as is possible, acceptable traditional titles and avoid the needless creation of new titles — even when they might appear to be of greater accuracy or precision. Where new titles have been considered desirable the title is enclosed within square brackets. Original spelling and capitalization are preserved, with modern spelling added in square brackets where considered desirable. But it is obviously unnecessary to add Tahiti after every use of Otaheite, and there are many such parallel cases. In citing inscriptions *sic* has normally been avoided.

DIMENSIONS

Height precedes width, first in inches, then in millimetres. If drawings are not enclosed within framing lines the actual size of the sheet is given, otherwise the area enclosed by the lines.

VERSIONS

= *ver.* Cross-references are here given to other related drawings, engravings, etc., cited in the catalogue.

REFERENCES

= *ref.* Includes references both to books, periodicals and exhibition catalogues.

TENERIFE

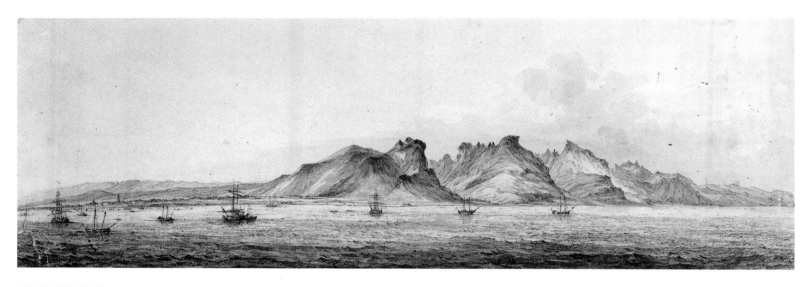

JOHN WEBBER

3.1   **Tenerife**   **[Aug 1776]**
        pen and water-colour, $8^{5}/_{16} \times 25^{1}/_{4}$: 211×642
        on old mount $11^{15}/_{16} \times 26$: 303×660.

Inscribed on old mount: 'No 2 A View of the port of the Island
of Teneriffe'.

Panoramic view of the Island of Tenerife.

'At 8 AM Anchored in the Road of St Cruz on the SE side of
the Island of Teneriffe in 23 fathom Water the bottom sand and
owse; Punta de Nago, the east point of the road bore N 64° E,
St Frances Church, remarkable by having a high Steeple, WSW
the Pico S 65° W and the SW point of the road on which stands
a fort or castle s 39° W. In this situation we moored NE & SW
a cable each way, being near half a mile from the Shore. Found
riding here La bousole a French Frigate commanded by M. Baur-
dat, two brigs of the same Nation, an English Brig from London
bound to Senegal and fourteen sail of Spanish Vessels.' Cook,
Journals III, 1, 9.
ref: *Colnaghi Exh. Cat.* (1936) (27).

     Colnaghi and Co. (1936), in 1962 still in the collection
     of Sir Bruce Ingram, London. Sold to Huntington Library,
     5 September 1962.

Huntington Library and Art Gallery, San Marino, California.

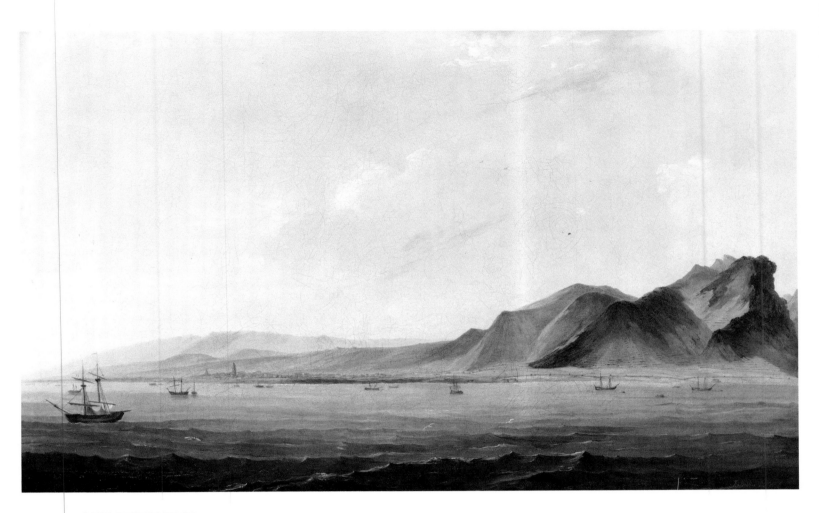

JOHN WEBBER [?]

3.2   **Tenerife [plate 1]**   [1776]
      oil on canvas, 26½ × 43¾ : 673 × 1112, signed and
      dated 'J. Webber pinx 1776' (l.r.).

The painting represents the left section of 3.1; it has moved the
three ships at centre further towards the left and omitted other
boats.

The picture, though it has long been attributed to Webber, does
not seem to represent the artist's mature style. The picture lacks
atmosphere, is feeble in the representation of waves and uncon-
vincing in the depiction of the ships. However, since the signature
appears to be in Webber's hand, the picture may be taken as an
early and not quite successful exercise in the representation of
harbour views. We have no information that, prior to this painting, Webber had ever painted maritime subject matter.

ref: Richmond (1963) 1, 60 (47) and 2, repr. 201.

        Sabin Galleries, London, Collection of Mr and Mrs Paul
        Mellon.

Yale Center for British Art, Paul Mellon Collection, New Haven.

CAPE OF GOOD HOPE

18 October to 1 December 1776

There are no known drawings of local subject-matter for the first stay at the Cape. Webber probably spent most of his time on the portrait of Cook now in the National Portrait Gallery, London (3.451).

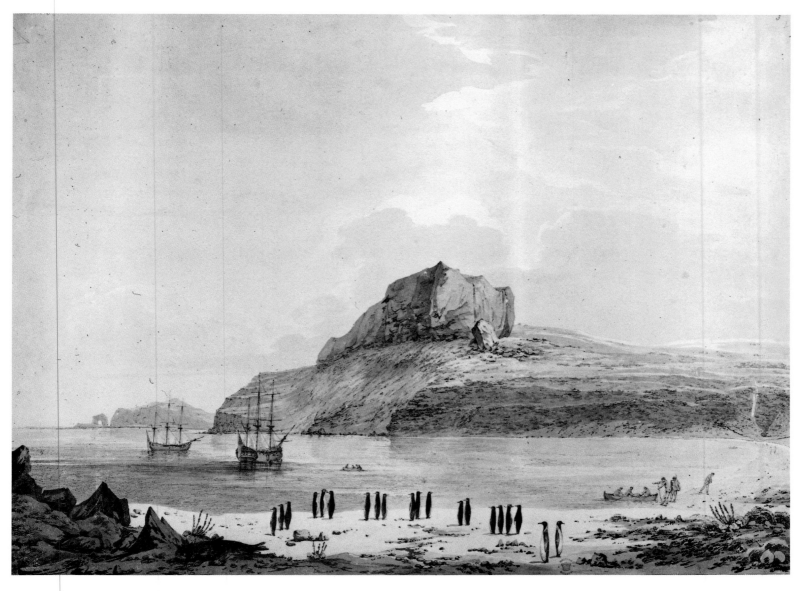

JOHN WEBBER

3.3   **A View of Christmas Harbour [plate 2]**
                                          [Dec 1776–]
           pen, wash and water-colour, 19⅜ × 25⅞ : 492 × 657,
           unsigned.

Inscribed no '2' in u.r. corner, identifying it with that listed as
'2. A View of Christmas Harbour' in Webber's Catalogue.

The *Resolution* and *Discovery* in the harbour, two ship's boats out,
one landing with seamen on the shore. In the central foreground
a flock of twenty penguins disposed in groups. A sea-lion in the
left foreground near rocks. In the background a cliff surmounted
by a large rock.

'I found the shore in a manner covered with Penguins and other birds and Seals, but these were not numerous, but so fearless that we killed as ma(n)y as we chose for the sake of their fat or blubber to make Oil for our lamps and other uses.' Cook, *Journals* III, 1, 29.

'Here I display'd the British flag and named the harbour Christmas harbour as we entered it on that Festival.' Ibid., 32.

ver: For a later version, see 3.4. Two studies of penguins by Webber are kept in the British Museum, Department of Prints and Drawings, 199* b.2 (see 3.431). For the plant of the Kerguelen cabbage see Webber's drawings at 3.426 a, b.

ref: Cook, *Journals* III, 1, pl. 10; Begg (1969) pl. 167, 137; Cobbe (1979) pl. II (col.).

British Library, London, Add. MS 15513, f.3.

JOHN WEBBER

3.4   **A View of Christmas Harbour**   [c. 1781-3]
water-colour, 8¾ × 14⅞ : 222 × 378, unsigned.

Title as above in pencil in a later hand on folio below drawing.

ver: A similar view to 3.3, with human interest added. Almost identical in size and subject with the engraving (3.4A).

Dixson Library, State Library of New South Wales, Sydney. PXX 2, 1.

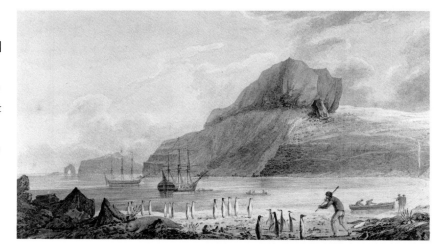

JOHN WEBBER (after)

3.4A   **A View of CHRISTMAS HARBOUR, in KER-GUELEN'S LAND.**
Engraving. 'J. Webber del.' — 'Newton sculp.'

Published in Cook/King (1784) pl. 4, I, 62-7.

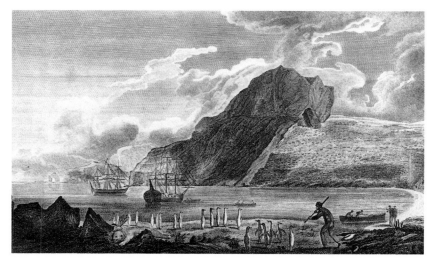

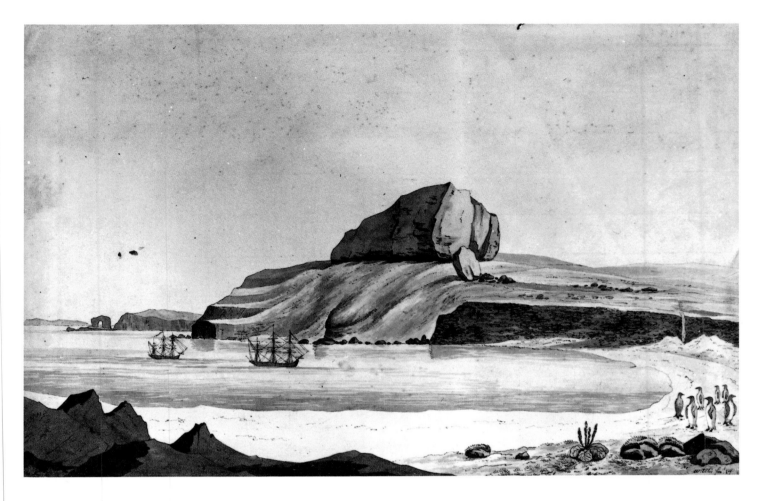

WILLIAM ELLIS

3.5 **Christmas Harbour in the Island of Desolation**
[plate 3] [Dec 1776–]
pen, wash and water-colour, 12¹¹⁄₁₆ × 19⅜ : 322
× 492. Signed 'W. Ellis fec! 1776' in black ink'. (76
is rubbed and may have been corrected.) W/m: 'J.
WHATMAN'.

Inscribed 'Christmas Harbour, in the Island of Desolation, on
Kerguelan's Land' in brown ink below the drawing. Inscribed '44
[?]' in brown ink in u.l. corner, greatly faded.

The *Resolution* and *Discovery* in the harbour. Behind them a cliff
surmounted by a huge rock. An arched rock in the distance near
the harbour entrance. A group of seven penguins on the shore
at right.

'. . . at eight in the evening anchored in a small bay, about half
a mile from shore. The rocks were almost covered with penguins,
and numbers of shags flew round us. Captain Cook immediately
ordered out one of the boats, to see if they could discover a
convenient watering-place, and to make likewise some observations upon the produce of the place.' Ellis, *Narrative* (1782), I,
6-7.

'It [Kerguelen Is.] is easily to be known by a remarkable pierced
rock on its eastern side, which is like the gateway of some old
castle. The harbour is very secure, and is surrounded by high
land. If we may judge of the general produce of this place, from
what we saw of it at Christmas Harbour, it is certainly as rocky,
barren, and desolate an island as can be conceived, which induced
Captain Cook to call it the Island of Desolation.' Ellis, ibid, 12.

ver: For what appears to be an earlier version, see 3.6.
ref: Rienits (1968) 115; Beaglehole (1974) pl. 31.

Museum Book Store, London 1928, *Cat.* 107 (1928) (41/1) and
Cat. 125 (1941) 453.

National Library of Australia, Canberra. Rex Nan Kivell Collection, 53/P.

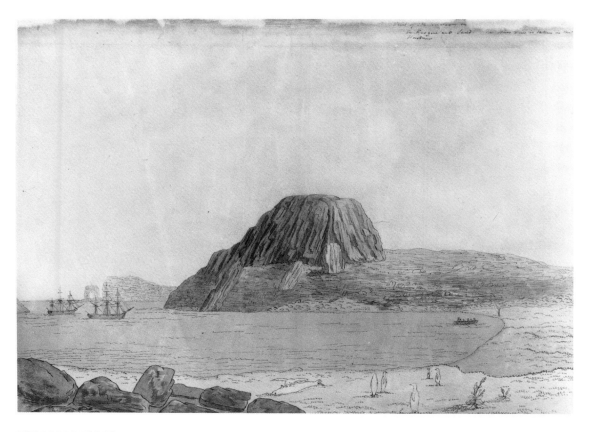

WILLIAM ELLIS

3.6   **A View of the Entrance in [Christmas Harbour] in Kerguelan's Land.**   **[Dec 1776]**
pen, wash and water-colour, 9⁷⁄₁₆ × 13¾ : 240 × 353, unsigned.

Inscribed in ink (u.r.) 'View of the entrance in . . . in Kerguelan's Land', the paper torn removing probably the words 'Christmas Harbour'. Following the title, in the same hand 'The Other View is taken in the Harbour'. On verso 'Vol I p. 12' referring to Ellis (1782). For the passage in Ellis (1782), to which the inscription refers, see 3.5.

The *Resolution* and *Discovery* are anchored at the harbour mouth, an arched rock between and behind them; at right, near the shore, a boat and a man standing on shore nearby; in the foreground a dead seal and five penguins.

'The other view' may refer to the view from which the engraving 3.6A was made, which was taken from a vantage point, somewhat different from that of this drawing.

ver: for a developed version, see 3.5.
ref: Murray-Oliver (1977), 29, pl. II.

Alexander Turnbull Library, Wellington. A264.1.

WILLIAM ELLIS (after)

3.6A   **A View of the Island of Desolation**
Engraving. 'W. Ellis del.' — 'Scott sculp'.
'Published Dec.ʳ 14th 1781, by G. Robinson.'

Published in Ellis (1782) I, fp. 12.

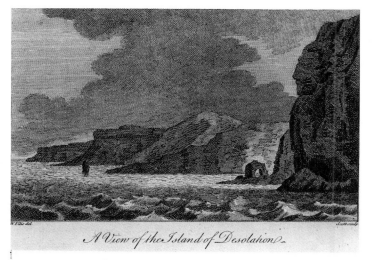

A View of the Island of Desolation.

For this engraving no drawing is known; the same view is represented in Webber's coastal profile (British Library Add. MS 15513 f. 1b) inscribed 'Kerguelen's Land' and engraved in Cook/King (1784) I, pl. fp. 83.

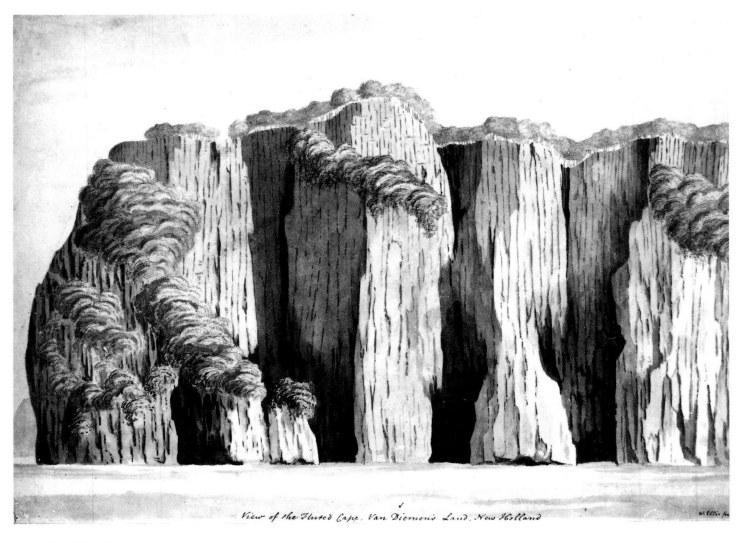

View of the Fluted Cape, Van Diemen's Land, New Holland

WILLIAM ELLIS

3.7 **View of the Fluted Cape, Van Diemen's Land, New Holland [plate 10]**   [Jan 1777]
pencil and water-colour, $10\frac{5}{8} \times 14\frac{3}{4}$: 270×375.

Signed and dated 'W. Ellis fecit 1777' (l.r.).

The title inscribed as above in ink below, also in pencil '1.15' (u.c.) and '64' in ink (u.l.), on verso in brown ink '5' (l.r.); w/m: upper part of a lily in a shield under crown.

There are two different inscriptions in pencil on verso, both in the same hand: 'This Cape is composed of Columns like the Giants Causway Capt D[ixon]' and 'There are several places on the N.W. Coast of America which are also similar to the Giants Causway. At one place on the said Coast the Rocks resembled Columns supporting Arches, resembling Ancient Ruins, through some of which a ship might have sailed. This account I had from Capt. Dixon who says he saw also a wonderful large Cave, the Roof of which was curiously arched in perspective, resembling

a Theatre. Into this Cave the Sea flowed, and it afforded Shelter for Thousands of Birds. This is not mentioned in his Voyage G.H. 6 Oct. 88.'

There is a crude drawing of a cave in perspective added to the text.

Fluted Cape is in Lat 43.22 Long 147.22 on Bruny Island and named on William Blight's chart of V.D.L. showing the track of the *Resolution* and *Discovery* 24-30 January 1777. [HO 497/2]. Anderson wrote in his Journal on 25 January 1777 'in the forenoon we open'd fluted Cape which forms one boundary of Adventure Bay. In the evening a gentle breeze sprang up from ENE, and we stood pretty close in shore . . .' Cook, *Journals* III, 2, 783.

'Its [Adventure Bay] exact situation is in [blank] s Latitude [blank] E Longitude from London and may be known from a headland call'd fluted Cape, from the oblong perpendicular stripes with which it is mark'd, form'd by a whitish stone which makes the

268

cliffs towards the sea and has a very picturesque appearance when you pass near it.' Ibid., 789-90.

Ellis mentions Fluted Cape in his *Narrative* (1782): 'We traced the coast, passing Storm Bay and the Fluted Cape, till the 27th, and at two in the afternoon the Discovery anchored in Adventure Bay in 13 fathom of water, sandy bottom . . .' Ellis (1782), I, 15.

The drawing is of particular interest not only for its representation which is unique among the body of Cook drawings and paintings but also for its inscription on the back, which indicates an earlier collector whose monogram was G.H. (probably George Humphrey) who had discussed the drawing with 'Captain Dixon', probably George Dixon, formerly armourer on the *Discovery* and later a Captain in the Merchant Navy. Dixon's name is referred to a number of times on drawings by William Ellis (see pp. 208-13).

ref: Lewis (1970) 6, 9.

La Trobe Library, State Library of Victoria, Melbourne. H.5404.

WILLIAM ELLIS

3.8   **View of Adventure Bay, Van Diemen's Land, New Holland**   **[Jan 1777]**
pen, brown ink and water-colour over traces of pencil, 7¼ × 18⅜ : 195 × 465, signed and dated 'W. Ellis fec! 1777' [l.r.].

Inscribed in ink as above along lower margin. The drawing is pasted on to a mount.

The two ships are anchored in the bay. In the left foreground trees and shrubs, at right a sandy beach, in the distance rounded hills.

'We traced the coast, passing Storm Bay and the Fluted Cape, till the 27th, and at two in the afternoon the Discovery anchored in Adventure Bay in 13 fathom of water, sandy bottom. The Resolution at this time was in the offing and did not arrive till past four.' Ellis (1782), I, 15.

'Adventure Bay (so called last voyage by Captain Furneaux of the *Adventure*) lies in lat. 43 deg. 14 min. S. and long 147 deg. 28 min. E. The land surrounding it is moderately high, and covered with variety of trees to the very tops. They are in general tall and straight; some afford an agreeable spice, and others abound with gums. The under-wood is so thick as almost to render travelling impracticable in the valleys . . .' Ibid., 21.

'. . . a design I had formed of puting into Adventure Bay to get a little Wood and some grass for our Cattle both of which we were in great want of. We therefore stood for the Bay, in which we anchored at 4 in the afternoon in 12 fathom Water over a bottom of Sand and owse' Cook, *Journals* III, 1, 50.

Compare also Anderson's extensive description of the bay. Ibid., 2, 783-4.

ver: This view may correspond to a similar view by Webber listed in his Catalogue (no. 7) as 'The S.E. part of Adventure Bay', the location of which is unknown. A similar view of the South side of Adventure Bay is reproduced as an engraving in Cook/King (1784), I, fp. 117. For what is possibly a copy of 3.8 see 3.9.

ref: Sotheby's *Cat.* 26 Jan. 1984, lot 87 (col.).

Rhona Townley Searle collection.

Private collection, Australia.

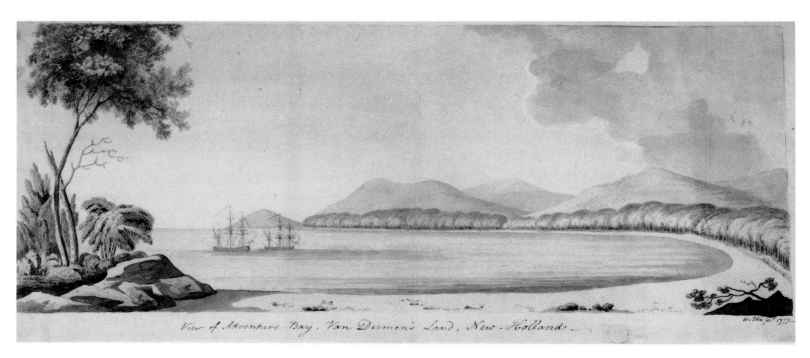

View of Adventure Bay, Van Diemen's Land, New-Holland.

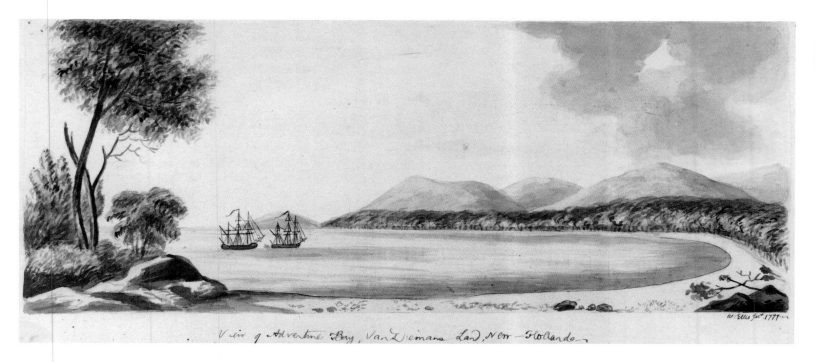

View of Adventure Bay, Van Diemans Land, New Holland (handwritten inscription)

WILLIAM ELLIS (after)

3.9   View of Adventure Bay, Van Diemans Land, New Holland   **[Dec 1777]**
pen and water-colour over pencil, 8⅛ × 18⅝ : 206 × 472, signed and dated 'W.: Ellis fec! 1777' (l.r.); w/m: 'GR' under a lily in a shield with crown above.

The title as above inscribed in ink across lower margin.

Fuller's notes on the back: 'It is no doubt a pure coincidence, but many of the letters, and in fact [. . . ?] are similar to the handwriting of Joseph Gilbert, Master of the Resolution on the 2nd voy', 'see Cook's 3rd Voyage, vol. 1, pl. 9, p. 117, where a plan of Adventure Bay is given and a sketch of the East side of the Bay which may possibly have been taken from this drawing'.

ver: For another version see 3.8.
ref: Cook, *Journals* III, 1, pl. 11; Rienits (1968) 132 (col.); Murray-Oliver (1969a) pl. 95 (col.)

Collection of Captain A.W.F. Fuller.

National Maritime Museum, London.

JOHN WEBBER

3.10   A Man of New Holland [plate 14]   **[Jan 1777–]**
pencil, with the hair coloured in red crayon, 18⅝ × 12¾ : 473 × 324, signed and dated 'J. Webber. 1777' in pencil (l.l.)

Inscribed 'A Man of New Holland' in pencil on the mount, and '5' in corner (u.r.) of drawing identifying it with the one so listed and titled, as above, in Webber's Catalogue.

The head and torso show cicatrized incisions.

'The keloid scars so typical of the Australian aboriginal adult male; they came from cuts incised with a flint or other sharp stone knife, which were often rubbed with ashes or clay to enlarge the effect. They denoted initiation into manhood, but other functions were totemistic and aesthetic. Banks noticed them on the first voyage, *Endeavour Journal* II, p.126.' Beaglehole's note in Cook, *Journals* III, 1, 52.

First contact with the natives was made on 28 January when Cook met a party of natives: 'Eight men and a boy'. 'They were quite naked & wore no ornaments except the large punctures or ridges raised on the skin, some in straight and others in curved lines . . . they were of the common stature but rather slender; their skin was black and also their hair which was as woolly as any Native of Guinea, but they were not distinguished by remarkable thick lips nor flat noses, on the contrary their features were far from disagreeable; they had pretty good eyes and their teeth were tolerable even but very dirty; most of them had their hair and beards anointed with red ointment and some had their faces painted with the same composition.' Cook, *Journals* III, 1, 52.

ver: For an engraving of the bust only see 3.10A.
ref: Cook *Journals* III, 1, pl. 12a; Rienits (1968) 116; Murray-Oliver (1969a) pl. 97.

British Library, London. Add MS 15513, f.4.

4

15.513.4

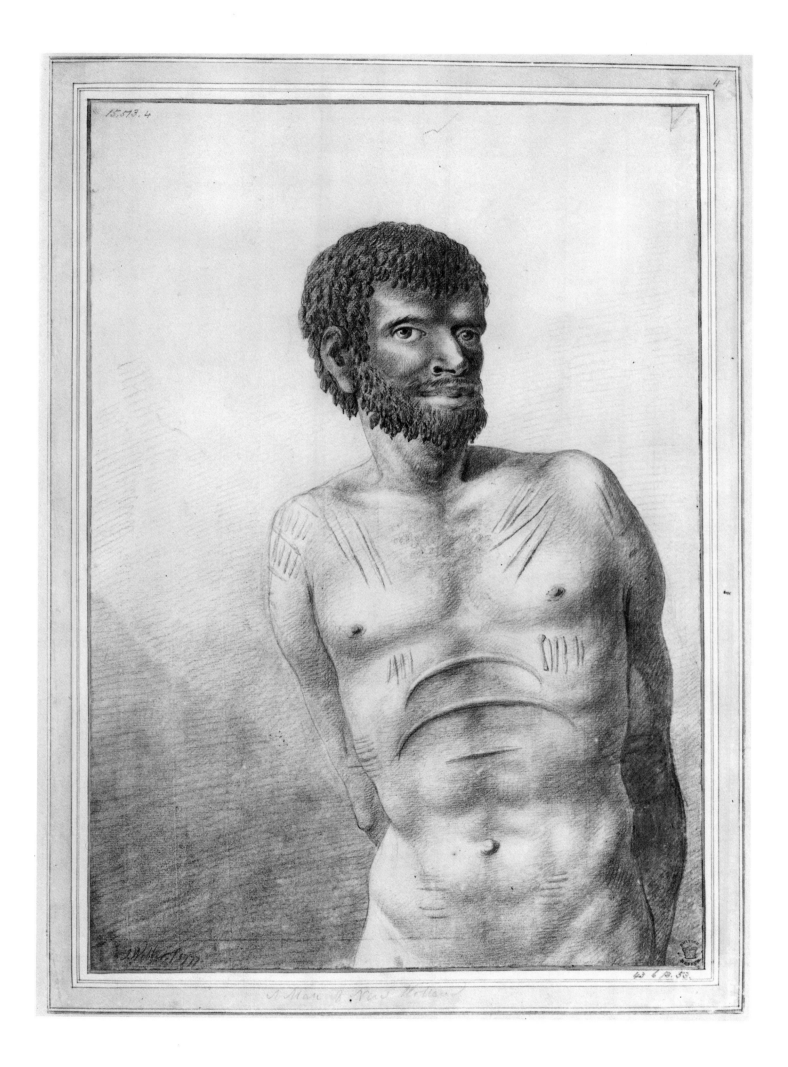

JOHN WEBBER (after)

3.10A   A MAN of VAN DIEMEN'S LAND
Engraving. 'J. Webber del.' — 'J. Caldwall sc.'

Cook/King (1784) pl. 6, I, 96-7.

A proof-state inscribed in pencil 'A man of Van Diemens land. New Holland' by Webber and 'Caldwall' is kept in the National Library of Australia, Canberra, in a folio of plates from the Skottowe Hall Library.

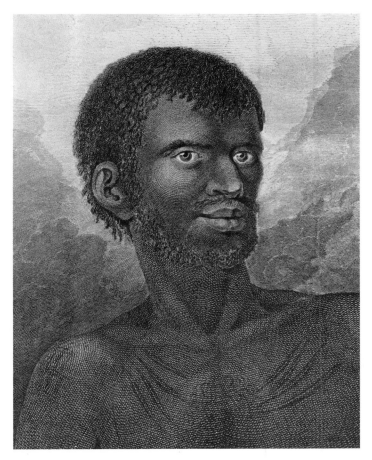

3.10B
Another version of a plate of 'A Man of Van Diemen's Land' is kept at the Mitchell Library, Sydney (PXD 59^{H1}, fol. 64 b). It is a cancelled plate and is inscribed 'J. Webber del' — 'J.W. Hüllmann Sculp, Schultze direxit'. The native is looking towards the left. The engraving is stamped by a lily and seems to be of eighteenth century origin. It is not, as the names of the engravers might suggest, a German copy after the Caldwall engraving, for it is also titled 'A Man of Van Diemen's Land'.

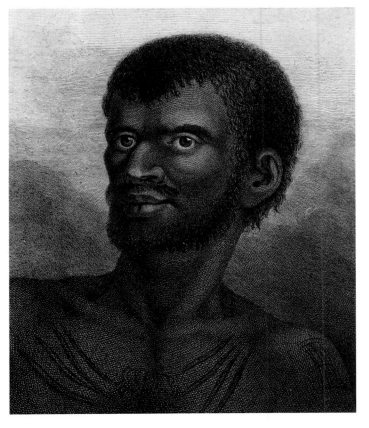

JOHN WEBBER

3.11   A Native of Van Dieman's Land.   [Jan 1777]
sepia wash over pencil, 14 × 11½ : 355 × 292, unsigned.

Inscribed 'A native of Van Diemans Land. New Holland' in the artist's hand in pencil and numbered '5' in corner (u.l.). On back in a recent hand 'by Webber' and an innacurate inscription 'Similar to pl.2 in Cook's Atlas of the first (sic.) voyage'.

Head and shoulders of a Tasmanian Aborigine in three-quarter view, looking left. Short curly hair and woolly beard, and cicatrized scars on chest and left arm.

The same man appears to have been used again in 3.12, standing at the right of the front group holding his arm.

ref: Joppien (1976a) 43, repr. 4.

Hartnoll and Eyre (1976). Purchased by the Tasmanian Library Board with Allport Bequest funds.

Allport Library and Museum of Fine Arts, State Library of Tasmania, Hobart.

5

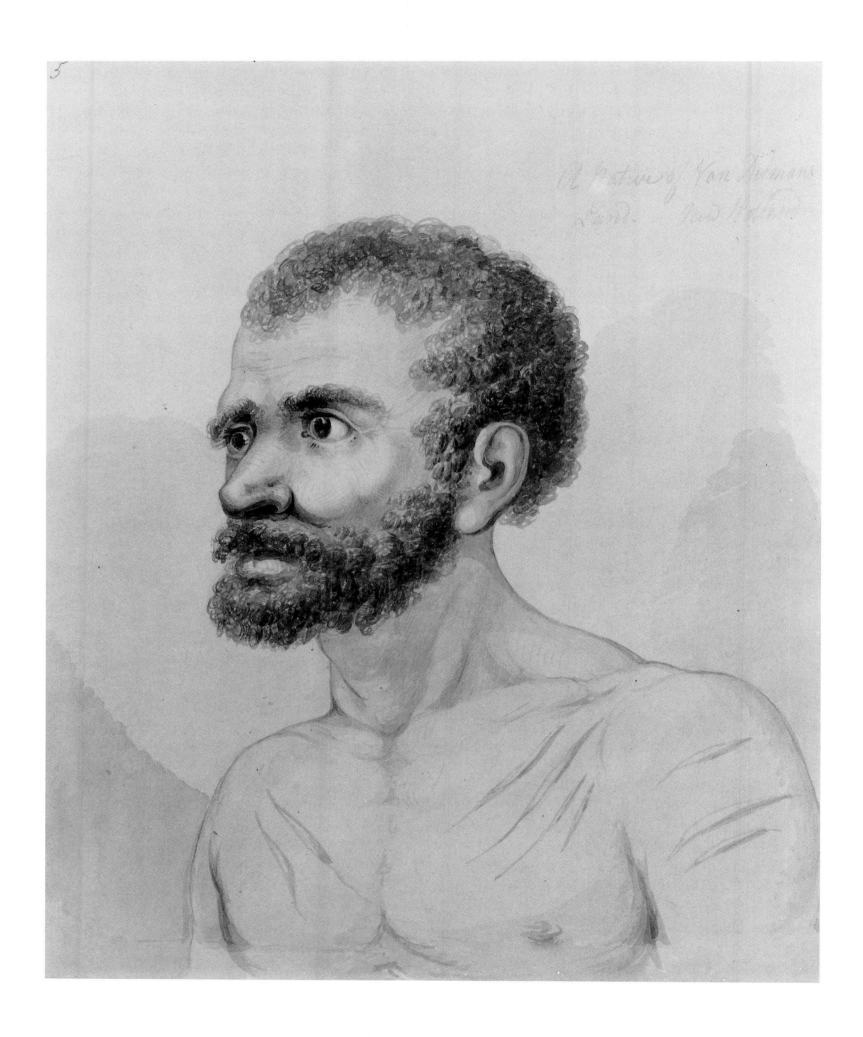

A Native of Van Diemans
Land. New Holland

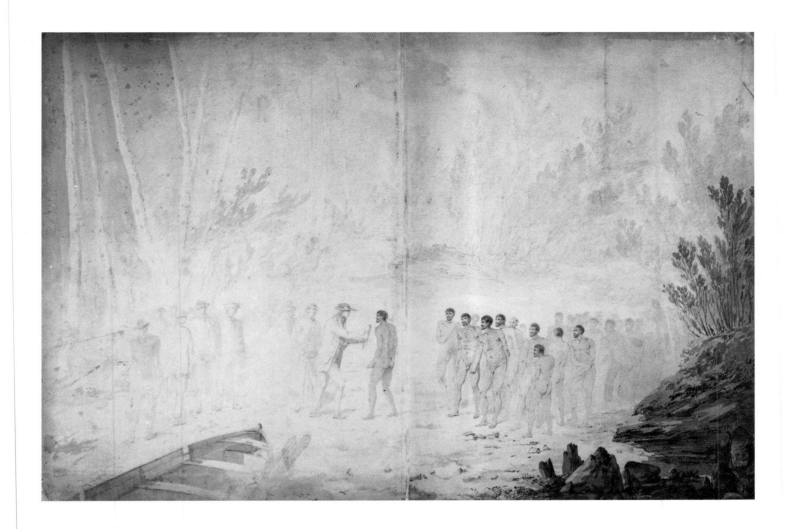

JOHN WEBBER

3.12   **An Interview between Captain Cook and the Natives
[plate 12]**   **[Jan 1777–]**
pencil, pen and wash, 26 × 38¼ : 660 × 972, un-
signed. This drawing is probably the one referred to
as no. 8 in Webber's Catalogue, in his section for 'Van
Dieman's Land', with the title as above.

On the back of the linen support a sheet of paper has been pasted
down on which is inscribed in ink in an unknown hand 'Capt.
Cook's Interview with Natives in Adventure Bay — Van Diemen's
Land. January 29-1777'.

Cook advances to meet a naked Tasmanian and seems to be
offering a string of beads; the others in a group on the right, with
a humpbacked man in the foreground, ninth from the left. On
the far left a party of Cook's men. In the foreground a rowing
boat has been pulled on to the shore.

The drawing most probably represents Cook's second meeting
with the natives on 29 January, about which he gives the following
report: 'We had not be[en] long landed before about twenty of
them men and boys joined us without expressing the least fear
or distrust, some of them were the same as had been with us the
day before, but the greatest part were strangers. There was one
who was much deformed, being humpbacked, he was not less
distinguishable by his wit and humour, which he shewed on all
occasions and we regreted much that we could not understand
him for their language was wholy unintilligible to us: it is different
from that spoken by the inhabitants of the more Northern parts
of this Country, which is not extraordinary sence they differ in
many other respects. Some of these men wore loose round the
neck 3 or 4 folds of small Cord which was made of the fur of

some animal, and others wore a narrow slip of the Kanguroo skin
tied round the ankle; these were all the ornaments I saw any of
them wear. I gave each of them a string of Beads and a Medal,
which I thought they received with some satisfaction.' *Journals*
III, 1, 54.

ref: Beaglehole (1974) pl. 32; Smith (1979a) pl. 31.

Naval Library, Ministry of Defence, London.

274

3.13   **A Woman of New Holland [plate 15]   [Jan 1777–]**
pencil, 18⅝ × 12⅝ : 457 × 321, signed 'J. Webber.
1777' in pencil (l.l).

Inscribed 'Woman of New Holland' in pencil on mount below
drawing. 'No 4' inscribed in corner (u.r.), identifying it as that
so listed and titled, as above, in Webber's Catalogue.

A Tasmanian carrying a child on her back, with a skin slung from
her left shoulder about her middle.

After staying with the wooding party, Cook returned to the ships,
but shortly afterwards a party of several women and children
appeared, as King reported to Cook afterwards: 'The Women wore
a Kanguroo skin in the same shape as it came from the animal,
tied over the shoulder and round the waist, but it was evidently
intended for no other purpose than for the conveniency of carrying
the child, for in all other respects they [are] as naked as the men,
and as black, with hair of the same Colour & texture. Some had
their heads wholy shaved, some only on one side, while others
again shaved all the upper part and leaving a circle of hair round
the head as is the custom with some Fryers'. Cook, *Journals* III,
1, 55. (29 January 1777.)
'They [the women] carried their children in a manner that show'd
some degree of tenderness but suffer'd them to hang backwards
and sleep expos'd to the heat of the sun. The breasts of those
who had born children were loose and pendulous . . . ' Anderson
in ibid., 2, 788.

ver: For engraving (half-length only) see 3.13A
ref: Cook, *Journals* III, 1, pl. 12b; Rienits (1968) 116; Murray-
Oliver (1969a) pl. 98 (col.).

British Library, London. Add MS 15513, f.5.

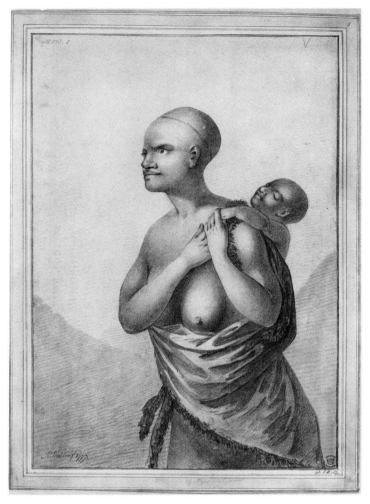

JOHN WEBBER (after)

3.13A   **'A WOMAN of VAN DIEMEN'S LAND'**
Engraving. 'J. Webber del.' — 'J. Caldwall sc.'

Cook/King (1784) pl. 7, I, 101-2.

A proof-state inscribed in pencil 'A Woman of New Holland',
'J. Webber del' and 'Calwall [sic] sc' all in Webber's hand is kept
in the National Library of Australia, Canberra, in a folio of plates
from the Skottowe Hall Library.

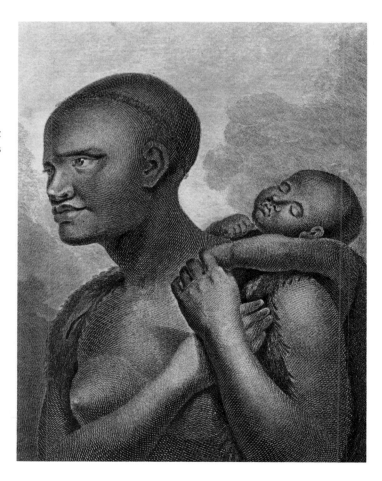

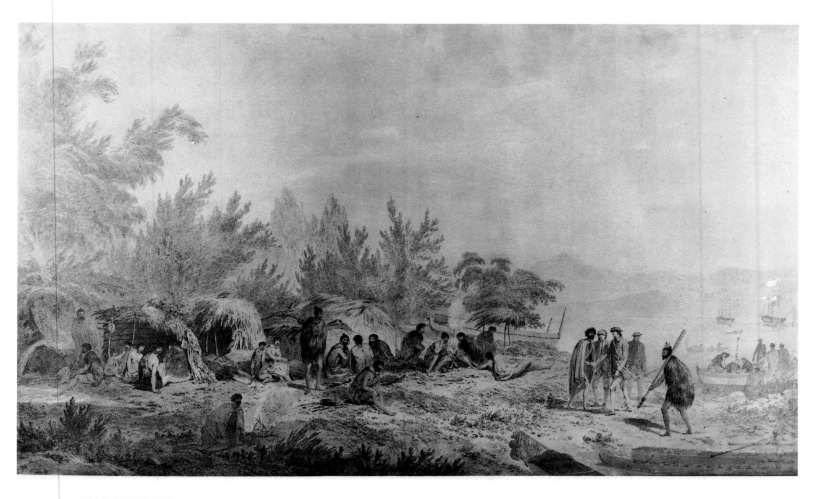

JOHN WEBBER

3.14   [Captain Cook in Ship Cove, Queen Charlotte Sound]
        [plate 17]   [Feb 1777–]
        pen, wash and water-colour, 23⅞ × 38¾ : 607 × 985,
        signed and dated 'John Webber del. 1777' (l.r.).

The drawing is listed in Webber's Catalogue, either as no. 12 'A General view of Queen Charlotte Sound' or no. 13 'A representation of the Natives in their temporary habitations', more likely it is the latter. In the list of 'Drawings omitted in the list selected for Publication referred to by Capt. Cook', National Library of Australia, Department of Manuscripts, MS 9/29, this drawing is referred to, 'Febr. 13. 1777', as 'A Drawing of a New Zeeland Village'.

At left and centre, a large group of Maoris mostly seated in and near their habitations, one standing; at extreme right, the *Resolution* and *Discovery* in the bay and two ship's boats landing. Cook has landed with two of his party and is greeting a chieftain. Another Maori stands nearby holding a *taiaha* over his shoulder. The view is as looking over from Ship Cove to Long Island and Hippa Island.

'It is curious to see with what facility they build these little temporary habitations: I have seen above twenty of them erected on a spot of ground that not an hour before was covered with shrubs & plants . . . These temporary habitations are abundantly sufficient to shelter them from the wind and rain, which is the only purpose's they want them for . . . Mr. Webber has made a drawing of one of these Villages that will convey a better idea of them than any written discription.' Cook, *Journals* III, 1, 60-1. (13 February 1777.)

ref: Cook, *Journals* III, 1, pl. 13; Rienits (1968) 120; Begg (1969) f/piece and pl. 170, 139 (col.); Murray-Oliver (1969a) pl. 101 (col.); Skelton (1969) pl. X; Beaglehole (1974) pl. 33.

National Maritime Museum, London, on loan from the Admiralty.

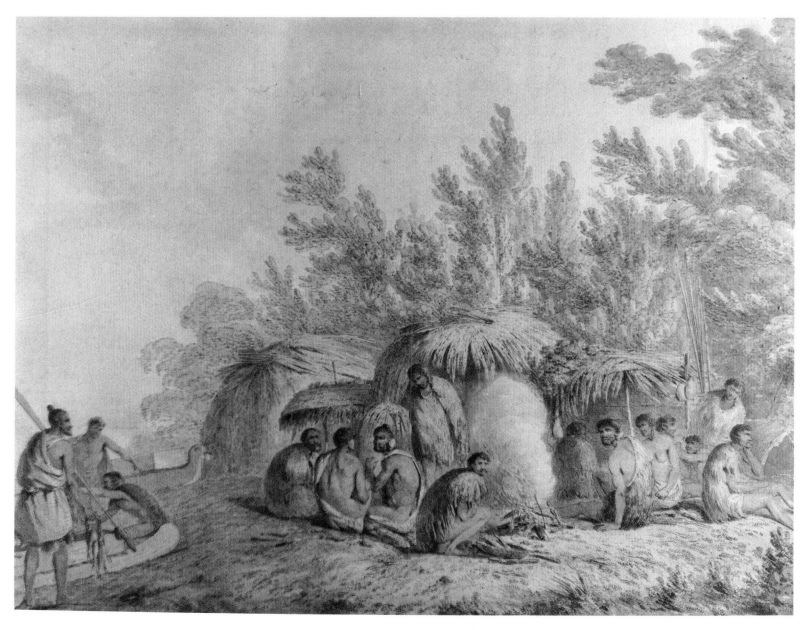

JOHN WEBBER

3.15   **Maori Huts [plate 18]**   [Feb 1777–]
          pen, wash and water-colour, 10¾ × 15½ : 273 × 394,
          signed 'J. Webber del' (l.r.).

Maori men and women squatting next to their huts, in the centre
a crouching native, roasting fish in an open fire. On the left
three natives engaged with their canoes.

Among the various groups of natives, several figures correspond
to 3.14. The similarity is particularly close between the right half
of this drawing and the left of 3.14.

prov: Probably from the collection of Sir Joseph Banks, by descent
        to the present owner.

Knatchbull Collection, Ashford, Kent.

277

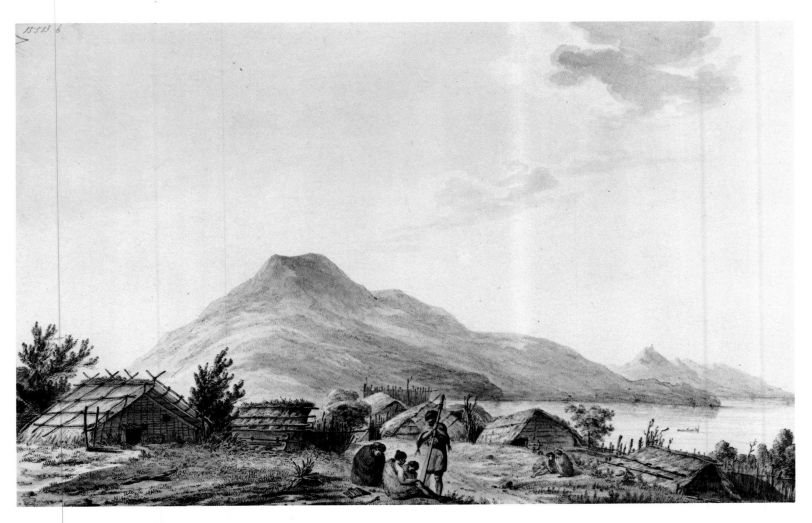

JOHN WEBBER

3.16   **The Hippah [plate 19]**   [Feb 1777–]
pen, wash and water-colour, 12½ × 19½ : 317 × 495,
signed and dated 'John Webber fc drawn from nature
in 1777' (l.r.). Inscribed 'New Zealand. Inside of a
Hippah or Fort' in pencil on mount below drawing.

Inscribed in pencil 'no 11' in corner (u.l.), corresponding to '11
The Hippah' in Webber's Catalogue. Numbered '13' in corner
(u.r.).

Maori habitations within a stockade of stakes to be seen at l.r.
and in central background. A small group of Maoris by a pathway
in central foreground, and two others seated further back to the
right. 'Hippah Island' is to the South of Motuara Island and
opposite Ship Cove in Queen Charlotte Sound. The view is taken
looking north with Motuara in the background.

The drawing may have resulted from Cook's visit to a *pa* on 15
February: 'On the 15th [Feb 1777] I made an excursion in my
boat to look for grass, and visited the Hippah or fortified Village
at the SW point of Motuara, and the places w[h]ere our Gardens
were on that island. There were no people at the former but the
houses and pallisades were rebuilt and in good order and had been
inhabited not long before. A description of this Hippah is unnecessary now as it is mention[ed] in my first Voyage page 395
[Hawkesworth] . . . and the drawings No—&— the first represents a part of the inside of the village . . .' Cook, *Journals* III,
1, 62. The *pa* is marked on the chart by Richard Pickersgill on
Cook's first voyage, 'A Plan of Queen Charlo: Sound . . . ' held
in the Hydrographic Office, Taunton.

ver: For studies for the huts for this drawing see 3.18 and 3.19.
For another version of this composition but later executed
see 3.17.

ref: *Exh. Cat.* Auckland (1964) pl. 32; Cook, *Journals* III, 1,
pl. 14; Rienits (1968) 133; Begg (1969) pl. 172, 142 (col.);
Spencer (1985) 9; Kaeppler (1978a) fig. 393; Starzecka
(1979) pl. 51.

British Library, London. Add MS 15513, f.6.

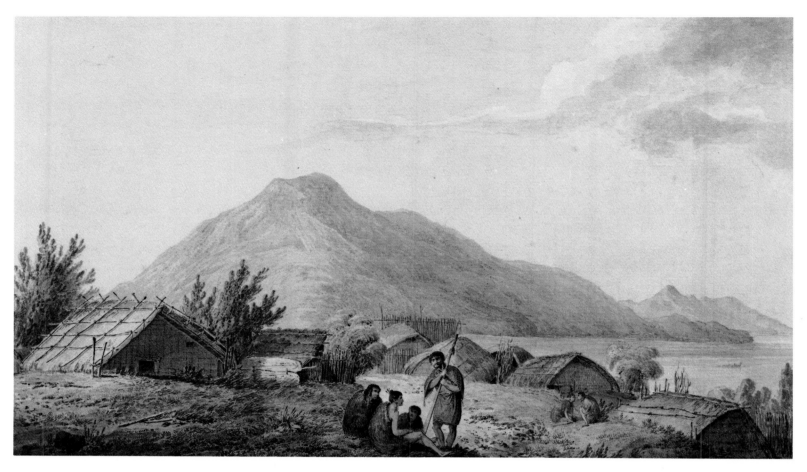

JOHN WEBBER

3.17 **The Inside of a Hippah** [c. 1781-3]
water-colour, 8¾ × 15 : 222 × 381, unsigned. The
title as above in pencil by a later hand on folio below
the drawing, followed by 'in New Zeeland'.

A group of natives at centre foreground, two others on the other
side of the pathway at right; native habitations in the middle
distance, a mountainous landscape, waters of Queen Charlotte
Sound at right.

ver: Similar to 3.16 but smaller; prepared for the engraving
3.17A.

Dixson Library, State Library of New South Wales, Sydney,
PXX 2, 2.

JOHN WEBBER (after)

3.17A **'The INSIDE of a HIPPAH in NEW ZEELAND'**
Engraving. 'J. Webber del.' - 'B.T. Pouncy sculp.'

Published in Cook/King (1784) pl. 10, I, 156-7.

A proof-state which was touched up with white for correction is
in the Mitchell Library, Sydney. PXD 59⁻¹, fol. 66 verso.

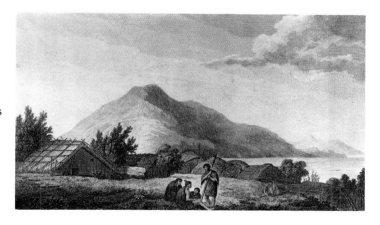

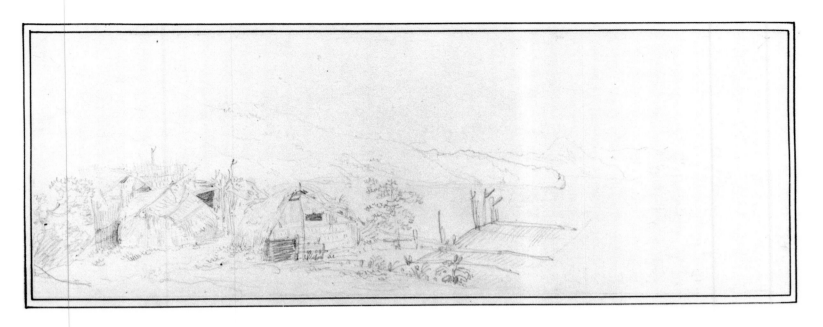

JOHN WEBBER

3.18   A drawing of a *pa*   **[Feb 1777]**
pencil, 5⁵⁄₁₆ × 15⅛ : 135 × 384, unsigned.

A study for 3.16 and 3.17.

British Library, London. Add MS 17277, no. 7.

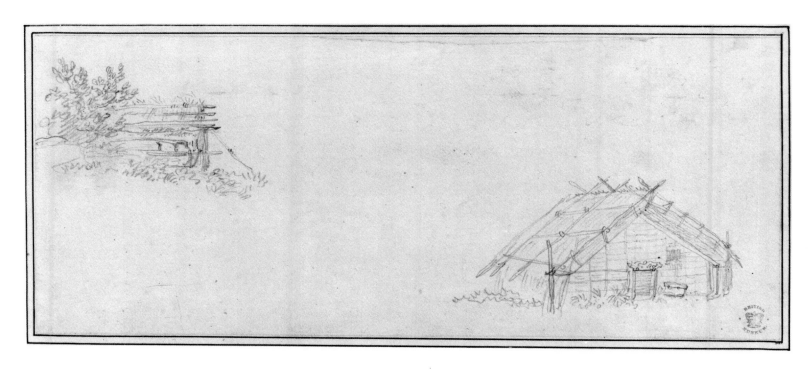

JOHN WEBBER

3.19   **[Two Maori huts]**   **[Feb 1777]**
        pencil, 5¾ × 14 : 146 × 350, unsigned.

Study for 3.16 and 3.17; one of the houses has a carved lintel.

The hut on the right corresponds closely to a description given
by Anderson: 'The best [hut] I ever saw was about thirty feet
long, fifteen broad and six high, built exactly in the manner of
one of our country barns. . . . At one end was a small square
hole which served as a door to creep in at, and near it another
much smaller whose use seem'd to be for letting out the smoke
. . . This however ought to be considered as one of the best and
probably the residence of some principal person.' Cook, *Journals*
III, 2, 810-11.

ref: Kaeppler (1978a) fig. 392 (a detail of the drawing, one
      house only).

British Library, London. Add MS 17277, no. 8.

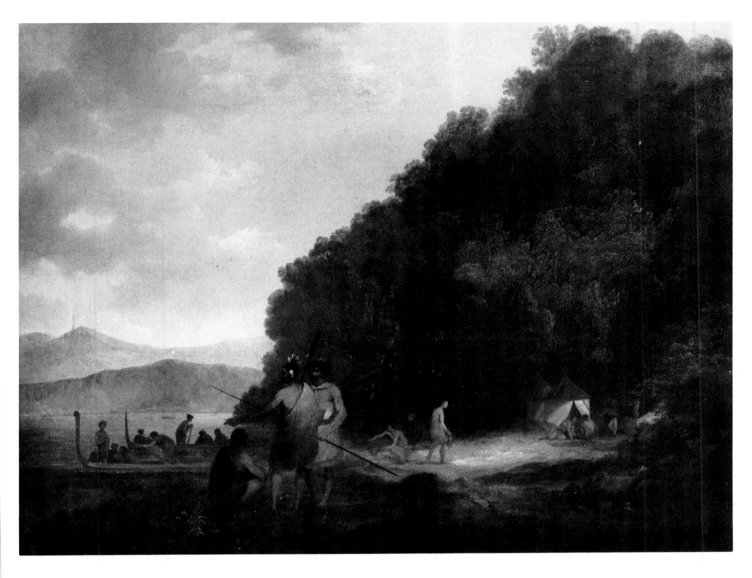

JOHN WEBBER

3.20   **Ship Cove, Queen Charlotte Sound**   [c. 1788]
oil on canvas, 23⁹⁄₁₆ × 30⁷⁄₈ : 605 × 784.

Two Maori canoes in the left foreground near the shore; in the distance a third canoe; to the right a ship's boat, with two sailors; in the foreground a group of three Maoris; one in back view seated looking towards the canoes, another in profile standing holding a paddle in the right hand while pointing towards the water with the left; a third, full-face holding a spear. To the right, and on the other side of a small stream flowing in from the right, two Maoris bringing fish towards the astronomer's tents, before which two other Maoris are seated, and to whom the seamen appear to be speaking; on the path, further to the right, another figure.

A painting of 'View of Queen Charlotte's Sound, New Zealand' was exhibited at the RA 1789 (212); this may be the same picture.

Possibly the place referred to by Anderson (13 February 1777): 'The people employ'd in fixing tents by a rivulet which runs into the largest cove here & which has formerly been occupy'd for the same purpose by Captⁿ Cook and Captⁿ Furneaux.' Cook, *Journals*, III, 2, 797.

ver: For Webber's print of this composition see 3.21A.
ref: *Exh. Cat.* Auckland (1964) no. 29; Murray-Oliver (1969a) pl. 99 (col.); Docking (1971) pl. 3 (col.).

Presented to the Suter Gallery by Sir Francis Dillon Bell KB, in July 1931.

Bishop Suter Art Gallery, Nelson, New Zealand.

JOHN WEBBER

3.21   **View in Queen Charlotte Sound, New Zealand**
[c. 1790]
pencil, 11⅛ × 16¹⁄₁₆ : 282 × 408; w/m: PORTAL & BRIDGES.

The drawing is squared for transfer and is likely to be a preparatory study for Webber's softground etching of the above title, published on 1 October 1790 (3.21A).

Comparison between the drawing and Webber's print reveals some small but significant differences: for example, part of the tent on the right in Webber's print, almost hidden by bushes, is lacking entirely from the drawing; the crouching native in front of the tent in the print has his legs crossed, whereas in the drawing one leg is out-stretched; there are also differences of delineation within the barrel on the right; on the left of the softground etching the two ships are placed together, while in the drawing they are separated with the bow of the native canoe in the middle; there are differences in the natives' hair style as well as in the position of the English seamen in the boat in the back. All these variations as well as the slightly different measurements between the drawing and the softground etching suggest that the drawing is an original work by Webber and not a copy after the print.

It seems likely that this drawing and 3.21A were preceded by his oil painting of the same subject (3.20).

Eyre and Hobhouse, London (1984).

Private collection, England.

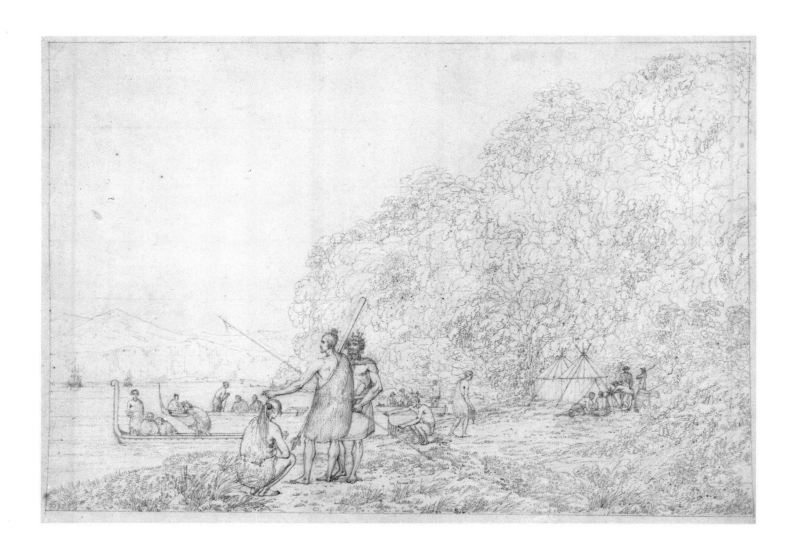

JOHN WEBBER

3.21A   **a. View in Queen Charlottes Sound, New Zealand** [1790]
softground etching, tinted in brown and grey wash, or hand-coloured, 12¾ × 17⅝ : 325 × 447 (11⁹⁄₁₆ × 16⅜ : 293 × 416). 'J. Webber fecit'; 'London Pub.ᵈ Oct.ʳ 1 1790 by J. Webber N.º 312 Oxford Street'; 'Vide Cook's last Voyage, Vol. 1 Chap. 7'.

ref: Kaeppler (1978a) fig. 44 (101) in col.; British Museum, Department of Prints and Drawings, London, 246˙ a.2. and C. 6˙; also Bernice P. Bishop Museum, Honolulu, (Fuller Collection) and Alexander Turnbull Library, Wellington. The examples in 246˙ a.2. and C.6˙ are signed 'J. Webber fecit R.A.'.

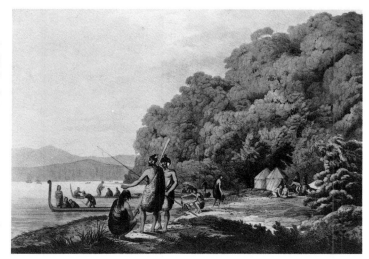

   b. A View in Queen Charlotte Sound, New Zealand [1809]
coloured aquatint. 'J. Webber fecit. R.A.'; 'London. Pub.ᵈ April 1 1809 by Boydell & Comp.ʸ N.º 90 Cheapside'; 'Vide Cook's last Voyage, Vol. I Chap 7'.

Issued by J. Boydell, *Views in the South Seas*, London 1808, pl. I.

National Maritime Museum, London; Bernice P. Bishop Museum, Honolulu.

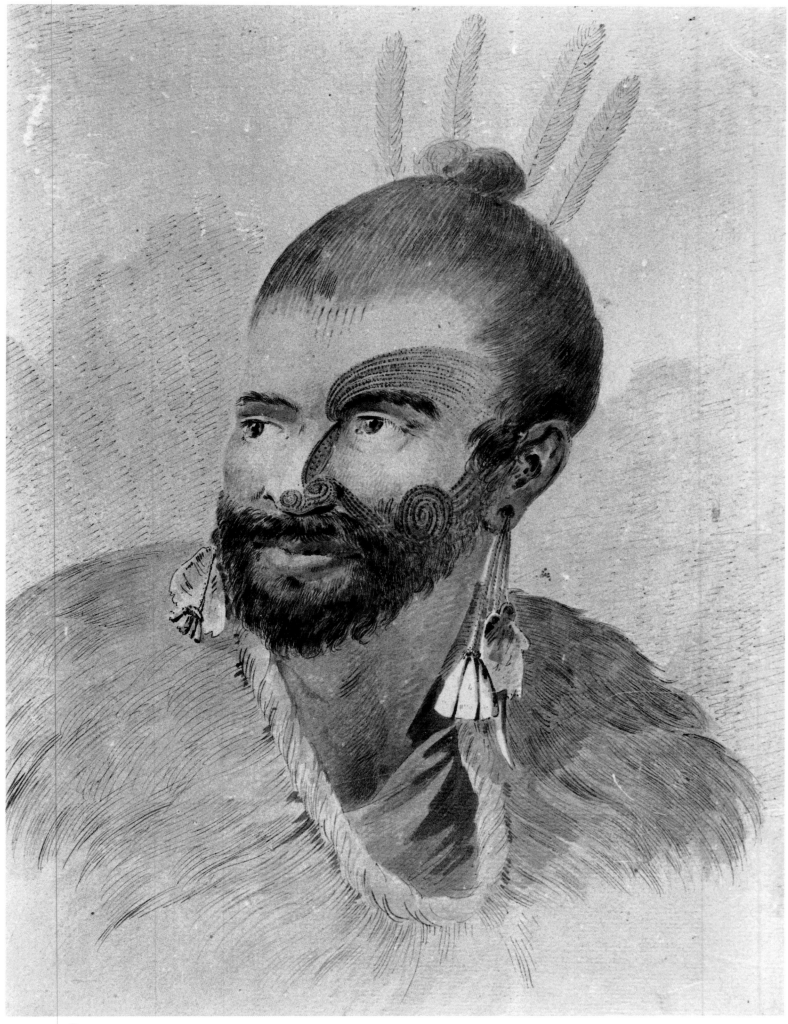

284

JOHN WEBBER

3.22   A Portrait of the Chief Kahura [Kahoura]
[plate 20]   **[Feb 1777–]**
pen and wash, with faint tints of water-colour, 17¼
× 12¼ : 438 × 313, unsigned.

The sheet has been cut down removing the lined frames, varnished
and mounted on card, lot 'no 12' endorsed in ink. The light
edges around the picture suggests that at one stage it was framed.
The drawing may be tentatively identified with 'A Portrait of a
Chief', which is no. 9 in Webber's Catalogue as the only portrait
of a New Zealand chief.

That this drawing was among Webber's drawings for the Admiralty, is made even more likely by a reference to the publication
of the official account. A list of 'Drawings omitted in the list
selected for Publication referred to by Capt. Cook' (National
Library of Australia, Department of Manuscripts, MS 9/29) mentions under 'Febr. 13.1777', 'A Drawing of [the] Chief of the
Party who murdered Capt. Furneaux's Men'. The date thus given
allows the chief to be identified as Kahura, whom Cook indeed
mentions on 13 February and on the following days. On 25
February Cook reports Kahura sat to Mr Webber for his portrait
(Cook, *Journals* III, 1, 69). Webber also did an oil portrait of
Kahura, which is listed in his Catalogue (no. 8 among his portraits
in oil— 'Kahowra a Chief').

A view of head and shoulders. He looks towards the left, wearing
a *pake*, pendant ear-ornaments, a top-knot and four feathers in
his hair. Tattoo markings on forehead, on nose and left cheek.
See Anderson's description of Maori dress and adornment in
Cook, *Journals* III, 2, 809 f.

ref: *Exh. Cat.* Auckland (1964) pl. 30; Murray-Oliver (1969a)
        pl. 100; *Exh. Cat.* Portland (1974) 138a.

Dixson Library, State Library of New South Wales, Sydney.
Pe 214.

WILLIAM ELLIS

3.23   A New Zealand Warrior   [Feb 1777–]
pencil, 11¾ × 7¼ : 298 × 181, unsigned; w/m: 'GR'
under crown surrounded by wreaths in a circle.

The title as above inscribed in black ink (u.r.). On verso inscribed
in ink '16' (l.l.) and 'p' (l.r.).

Back view of a naked warrior with a light fringed beard wearing
a top-knot and two feathers, brandishing a *patu*.

ref: Murray-Oliver (1977) 29.

Alexander Turnbull Library, Wellington. A264.2.

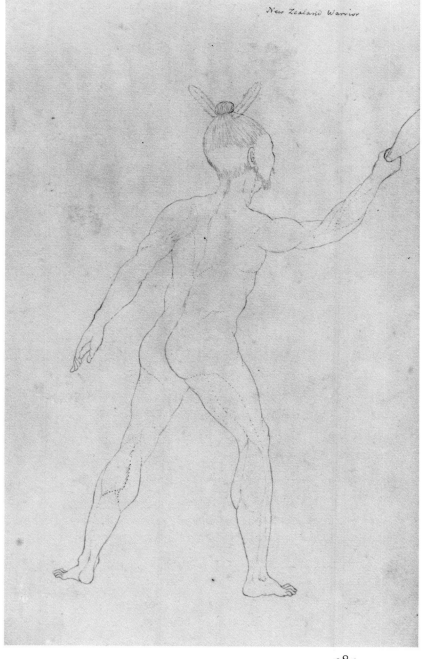

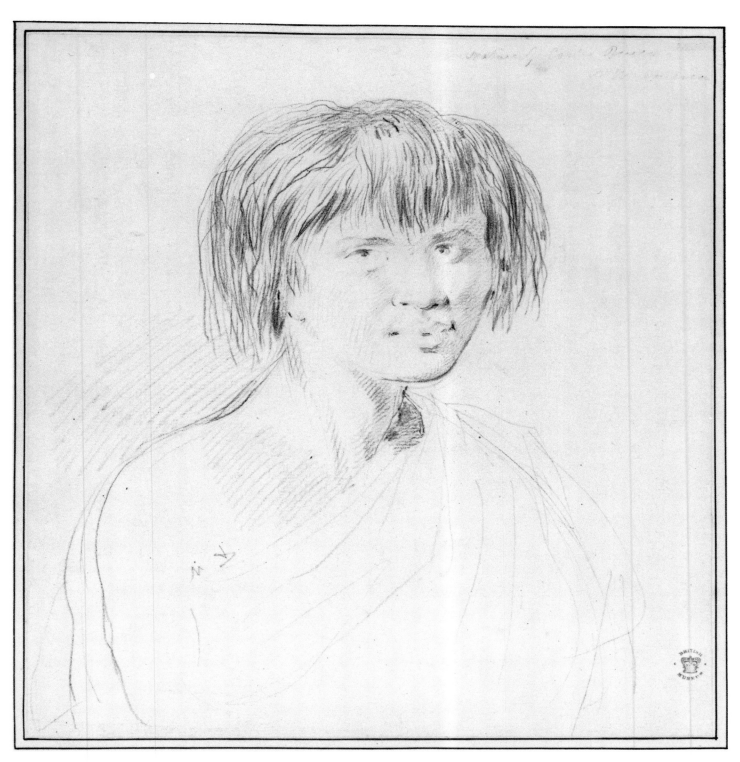

JOHN WEBBER

3.24   **A Portrait of a Maori Woman (?)**   [Feb 1777?]
pencil, 12⁵⁄₁₆ × 11¹¹⁄₁₆ : 313 × 297, unsigned.

The drawing is entitled in pencil 'Native of Cook's River N.W. America', and numbered '27' (u.r.).

Three-quarter portrait of a native woman with broad nose and loose, straight hair. She is draped over her left shoulder and wears no ornament. Her light dress and the expression of her face make it very unlikely that she is from the north-west coast of America. She is certainly Polynesian and may be a Maori. For a similar drawing of a woman of New Zealand by Ellis see 3.25.

British Library, London. Add MS 17277, no 22.

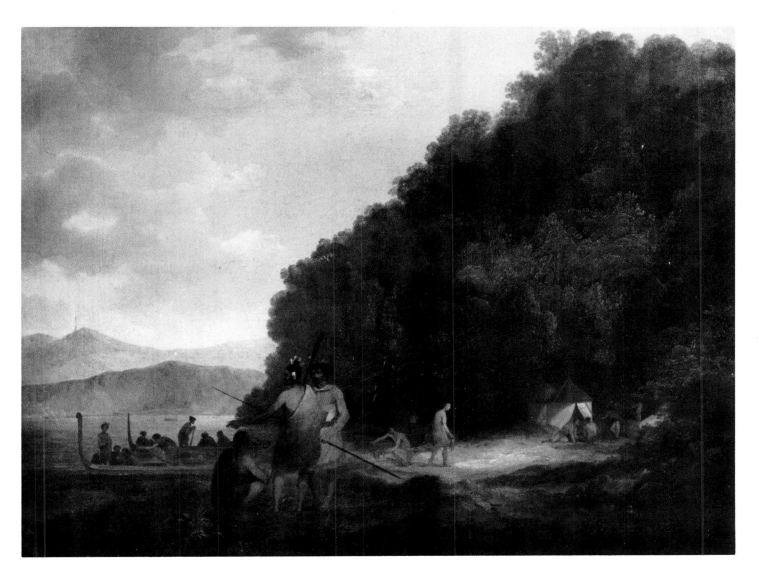

JOHN WEBBER

3.20   Ship Cove, Queen Charlotte Sound   [c. 1788]
oil on canvas, 23⁹⁄₁₆ × 30⅞ : 605 × 784.

Two Maori canoes in the left foreground near the shore; in the distance a third canoe; to the right a ship's boat, with two sailors; in the foreground a group of three Maoris; one in back view seated looking towards the canoes, another in profile standing holding a paddle in the right hand while pointing towards the water with the left; a third, full-face holding a spear. To the right, and on the other side of a small stream flowing in from the right, two Maoris bringing fish towards the astronomer's tents, before which two other Maoris are seated, and to whom the seamen appear to be speaking; on the path, further to the right, another figure.

A painting of 'View of Queen Charlotte's Sound, New Zealand' was exhibited at the RA 1789 (212); this may be the same picture.

Possibly the place referred to by Anderson (13 February 1777): 'The people employ'd in fixing tents by a rivulet which runs into the largest cove here & which has formerly been occupy'd for the same purpose by Captⁿ Cook and Captⁿ Furneaux.' Cook, *Journals*, III, 2, 797.

ver: For Webber's print of this composition see 3.21A.

ref: *Exh. Cat.* Auckland (1964) no. 29; Murray-Oliver (1969a) pl. 99 (col.); Docking (1971) pl. 3 (col.).

Presented to the Suter Gallery by Sir Francis Dillon Bell KB, in July 1931.

Bishop Suter Art Gallery, Nelson, New Zealand.

282

JOHN WEBBER

3.21   View in Queen Charlotte Sound, New Zealand
[c. 1790]
pencil, 11⅛ × 16¹⁄₁₆ : 282 × 408; w/m: PORTAL & BRIDGES.

The drawing is squared for transfer and is likely to be a preparatory study for Webber's softground etching of the above title, published on 1 October 1790 (3.21A).

Comparison between the drawing and Webber's print reveals some small but significant differences: for example, part of the tent on the right in Webber's print, almost hidden by bushes, is lacking entirely from the drawing; the crouching native in front of the tent in the print has his legs crossed, whereas in the drawing one leg is out-stretched; there are also differences of delineation within the barrel on the right; on the left of the softground etching the two ships are placed together, while in the drawing they are separated with the bow of the native canoe in the middle; there are differences in the natives' hair style as well as in the position of the English seamen in the boat in the back. All these variations as well as the slightly different measurements between the drawing and the softground etching suggest that the drawing is an original work by Webber and not a copy after the print.

It seems likely that this drawing and 3.21A were preceded by his oil painting of the same subject (3.20).

Eyre and Hobhouse, London (1984).

Private collection, England.

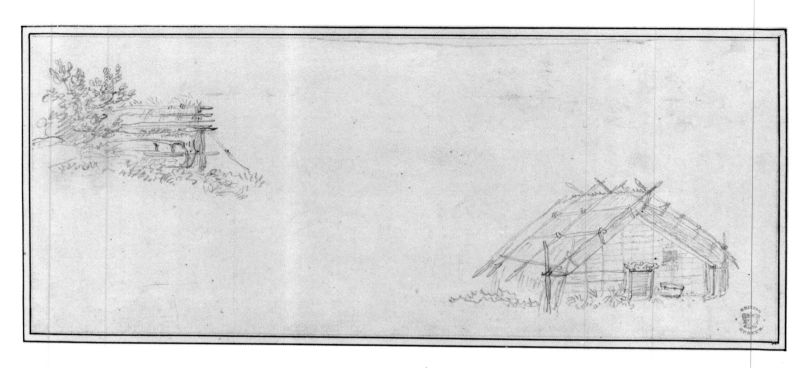

JOHN WEBBER

3.19   [Two Maori huts]   [Feb 1777]
pencil, 5¾ × 14 : 146 × 350, unsigned.

Study for 3.16 and 3.17; one of the houses has a carved lintel.

The hut on the right corresponds closely to a description given by Anderson: 'The best [hut] I ever saw was about thirty feet long, fifteen broad and six high, built exactly in the manner of one of our country barns. . . . At one end was a small square hole which served as a door to creep in at, and near it another much smaller whose use seem'd to be for letting out the smoke . . . This however ought to be considered as one of the best and probably the residence of some principal person.' Cook, *Journals* III, 2, 810-11.

ref: Kaeppler (1978a) fig. 392 (a detail of the drawing, one house only).

British Library, London. Add MS 17277, no. 8.

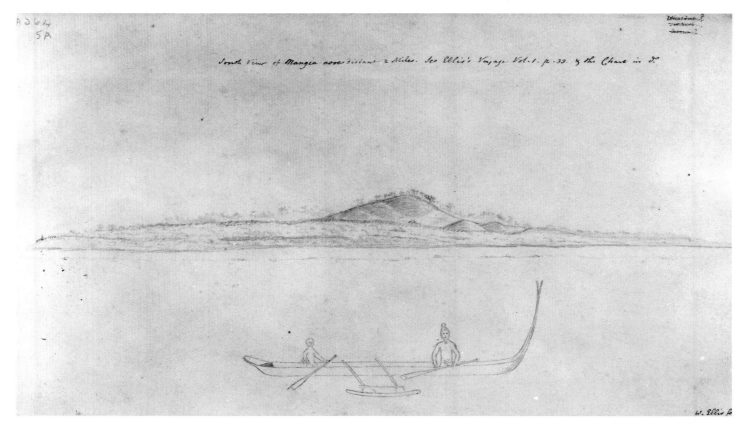

WILLIAM ELLIS

3.29 **[Two Men in a Canoe off Mangaia] [30 Mar 1777]** pencil, 7¼ × 11⅞ : 180 × 302, signed 'W. Ellis fecit' in ink (l.r.).

Inscribed across the upper part of the drawing 'South View of [in black ink] Mangia-nooe, [in brown ink] distant 2 Miles' [in black ink] followed by 'See Ellis's Voyage Vol. I. p. 33 & the Chart in d.°' both inscriptions in brown ink by the same hand. 'Whatdue? / see back / Atowi?' is inscribed (u.r.) in black ink but crossed out in brown ink. On verso inscribed in ink '9'. On verso three studies of heads of natives of Atiu (3.35).

Two men paddling an outrigger canoe before an island fringed with thick vegetation.

'At four we were running along the south-side, at about the distance of four miles, which, as the sun was just rising, afforded a most pleasing prospect. The interior parts rose in moderately high hills, upon the tops of which were trees of various kinds. The sides next the sea were very woody, and we could plainly distinguish coco nut and plantain trees in abundance. — Upon our nearer approach to the shore, we saw many of the natives running along the beach, and, by the help of our glasses, found that some had large clubs upon their shoulders, and that others were armed with long spears. As we proceeded, the Indians followed us, shouting and hollowing, their number increasing very fast. Soon after two of them put off in a canoe (the only one we saw) and came within fifty or sixty yards of the ships, but would not venture nearer, though we made all the friendly signs we could think of . . . Their complexion appeared to be of the dark olive cast, their hair was fastened to the top of their heads something in the New Zeeland fashion: one of them had a large pearl oyster-shell suspended from his neck, and something round his middle; the other was naked. — The canoe was neatly made and furnished with an outrigger; the stern was high for so small a boat, and terminated in a kind of fork.' Ellis (1782) I, 33-4.

ver: The drawing is similar in composition to 3.30 but may represent an earlier state.

ref: Murray-Oliver (1977) 29.

Alexander Turnbull Library, Wellington. A264.5A.

WILLIAM ELLIS

3.30 **[Two Men in a Canoe off Mangaia]** **[Mar 1777–]** pen, wash and water-colour, 7¾ × 13½ : 197 × 337, signed 'W. Ellis fecit' (l.r.); w/m: part of shield with initials LVG = Lubertus van Gerrevink.

Inscribed 'South View of Mangia-nooe, distant two Miles' followed by 'See Ellis's Voyage, Vol. I. p. 33, and the Chart in Vol. I' in brown ink. On verso inscribed '8' in brown ink (l.r.).

A more accomplished version of 3.29 in ink and water-colour giving light and shade to the island and indicating waves. The figures, though still poor, are better rendered than in 3.29.

ref: Murray-Oliver (1977) 29, pl. III; *Exh. Cat.* Auckland, (1977), cat. 36 repr.

Alexander Turnbull Library, Wellington. A264.4.

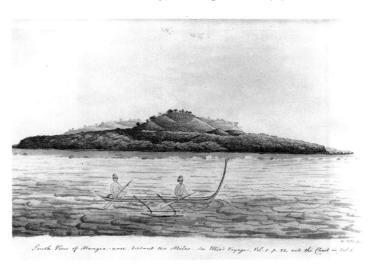

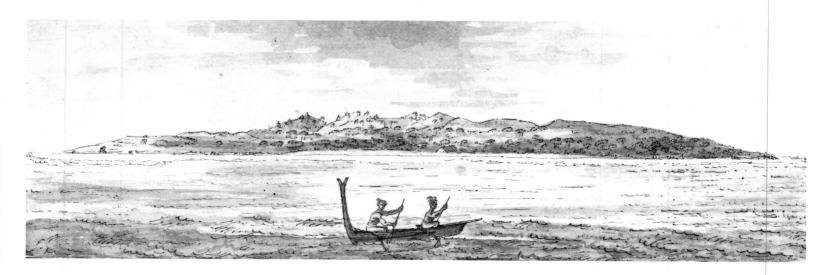

HENRY ROBERTS

3.28   **[Two Men in a Canoe off Mangaia]**   **[Mar 1777]**
pen, wash and water-colour, $2^{15}/_{16} \times 9^{1}/_{4}$: 74 × 235.

Two natives in canoe, with the island in the background. Below the drawing on the page there is a map showing Mangaia and its geographical position.

For Roberts's account of Mangaia see his Log, ff. 60-1.

Dixson Library, State Library of New South Wales, Sydney. Henry Robert's Log, MS Q 151-2, f. 61.

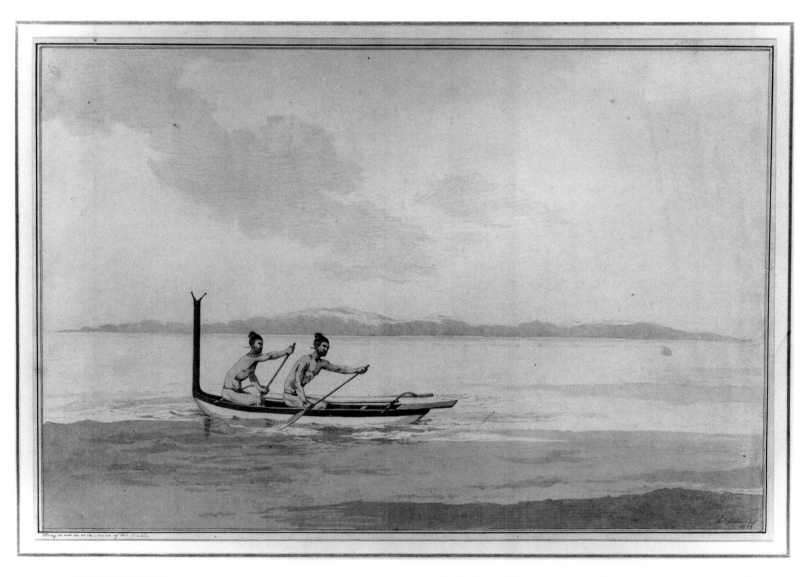

JOHN WEBBER

3.27   **[Two Men in a Canoe off Mangaia]**   **[Mar 1777–]**
pen and wash, 12¾ × 18½ : 324 × 470 signed and
dated 'Jnᵒ Webber del 1777'; w/m: 'IHS I VILLEDARY'.

Inscribed in ink (l.l.) 'Mony ne nou ne neva, name of this Island'.
Inscribed no. '61' (u.l.), identifying it with that listed as '61 A
Canoe with a view of the Island [Monyneneva]' in Webber's
Catalogue.

Two natives in a narrow outrigger canoe rowing. The stern rises
vertically. The island in the background. The island also known
as Discovery's Island.

'As we drew near the shore two men launched a small Canoe,
and paddled towards us.' Cook, *Journals* III, 1, 78.

'The Canoe we saw at *Mangia nooe nai naiwa* . . . had a flat board
or piece of wood projecting out at the fore part like the small

Ivahahs at Otaheite, but it had a high upright stern like some
in New Zealand: the upper end of this stern post was forked. The
drawings which Mr. Webber made of these Canoes will convey
the best idea of them.' Cook, *Journals* III, 1, 88.

'We saw only one Canoe which was exceeding narrow, a flat
board projected about a foot from one end from which was a
perpendicular piece of about six feet long the uppermost end of
which was shaped like the figure V. It had an outrigger and was
neatly made.' King's Journal 30 March, quoted in Cook, *Journals*
III, 1, 78, 3n.

A similar description is offered by Anderson in Cook, *Journals*
III, 2, 828. For the type of canoe see Haddon and Hornell (1936),
I, 159-62.

ref: Christie's Sale *Cat.*, 14 June 1977 (lot 3) 3 top.

Private collection, England.

WILLIAM ELLIS

3.25   **A Woman of New Zealand**   **[1777]**
pencil, 15 × 10¾ : 381 × 273, signed and dated 'W.
Ellis fecit 1777' (l.r.); w/m: 'VILLEDARY'.

The title as above, in ink below the drawing. '68' inscribed in
brown ink (l.l.), also numbered on verso in brown ink ('3'.

Head and shoulders of a young woman with dishevelled hair,
draped to reveal most of her breasts.

In his *Narrative* (1782) Ellis gives no description of the New Zealand women.

ref: Lewis (1970) 6, repr. 7.

La Trobe Library, State History of Victoria, Melbourne. H 5403.

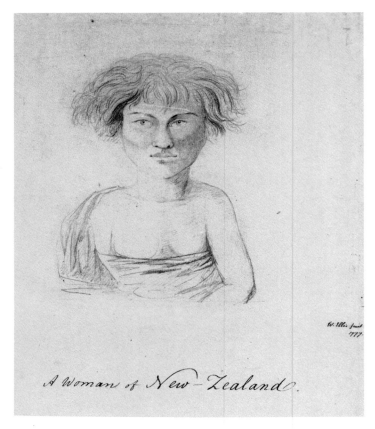

A Woman of New-Zealand.

WILLIAM ELLIS

3.26   **A Woman of New Zealand (?)**   **[1777?]**
pencil, 10¼ × 7¼ : 261 × 181, signed and dated in
pencil 'W. Ellis fec. 1777' (l.r.).

The title as above inscribed in pencil across lower edge of the
drawing. On verso inscribed in ink '14' (l.l.), 'n' (l.r.).

A full-face portrait of a young woman with curly hair, she wears
an ornament of feather balls in her left ear and a cloak over her
right shoulder.

The hair-style and the facial expression is different from the
woman portrayed in 3.25, and bears more resemblance to Webber's
portrait of a native girl of Tahiti (3.115 and 3.116). Webber's
Tahitian girl also wears pendant ear ornaments. It therefore seems
possible that the inscription on Ellis's drawing is mistaken.

ref: Murray-Oliver (1977) 29.

Alexander Turnbull Library, Wellington. A264.3.

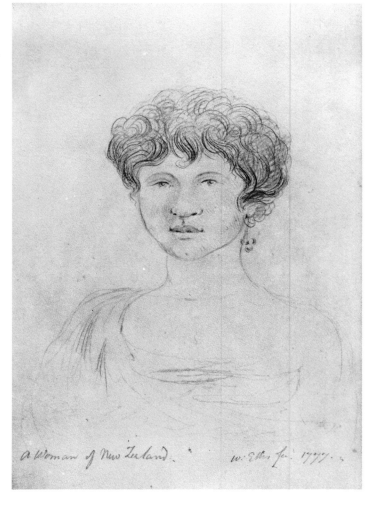

A Woman of New Zealand.   w. Ellis fec. 1777.

JOHN WEBBER

3.31   [A Man of Mangaia] [plate 21]   [Mar 1777]
        pen over pencil, 17¼ × 12¼ : 438 × 311, unsigned.

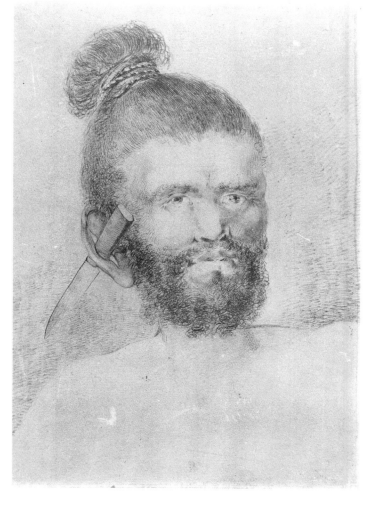

Across the lower edge of the drawing a strongly faded inscription
'Native of Man . . . [rest illegible]. Endorsed in ink 'Lot no 14'
(blotted out) then '13' and in pencil 'maple frame' and also 'Capt
Campbell'. The original sheet had pen frame lines which have
mostly been cut off. Light 'frames' around the picture, where the
varnish was not exposed to the sun and did not darken, suggests
that the picture was long kept in a frame, perhaps in a 'maple
frame'.

The drawing may be identified tentatively as the 'Portrait of a
Native', no. 60 in the Monyneneva section of Webber's Catalogue.

A bearded man with top-knot almost full-face, looking slightly
to the right. A European knife is held in an insertion in his right
ear.

The man represented is the one who transferred into Cook's boat,
when Cook reconnoitred the reef off Mangaia. 'At length when
they perceived we were going to the Ships they all left us except
the man we had in the boat, he tho not without evident signs
of fear, accompanied us on board' (Cook, *Journals* III, 1, 79; see
also Anderson in ibid., 2, 828). From Anderson we hear that
the native's name was Mou'rooa [Mourua]. In describing two of
the natives who had come out in a canoe to meet the ships, he
says that 'the lobe of their ears was pierc'd or rather slit, in which
one of them stuck a knife and some Beads'. Ibid; 2, 827.

ver: For the related engraving see 3.31A.

Dixson Library, State Library of New South Wales, Sydney.
Pe 212.

JOHN WEBBER (after)

3.31A   'A MAN of MANGEA'
        Engraving. 'J. Webber del.' — 'W. Sharp sculp.'

Published in Cook/King (1784) pl. 11, I, 173.

A proof-state inscribed in pencil 'Sharp' and 'Mangea-noe-nai-
nai Man' apparently in an old hand and numbered in pencil 'N°
11' (u.r.) is kept in the National Library of Australia, Canberra,
in a folio of plates from the Skottowe Hall Library.

Sharp's engraving was one of the earliest to be printed, as can
be gleaned from a letter of Lord Sandwich to Dr Douglas on 19
November 1782. Asking whether the title 'Man of mangea' would
be correct, Sandwich writes: 'now it is suggested that Mangea is
not the name of the Island but that it was allways denominated
Mangeanoenaiva by the natives'. (Egerton MS 2180, f.55-6.)

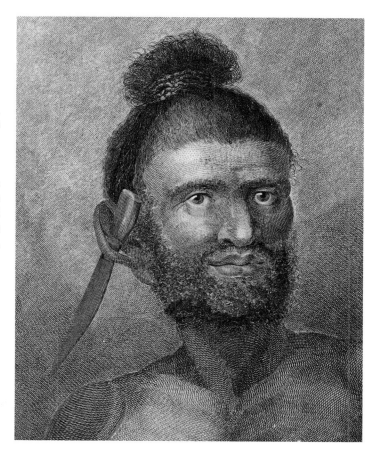

ATIU

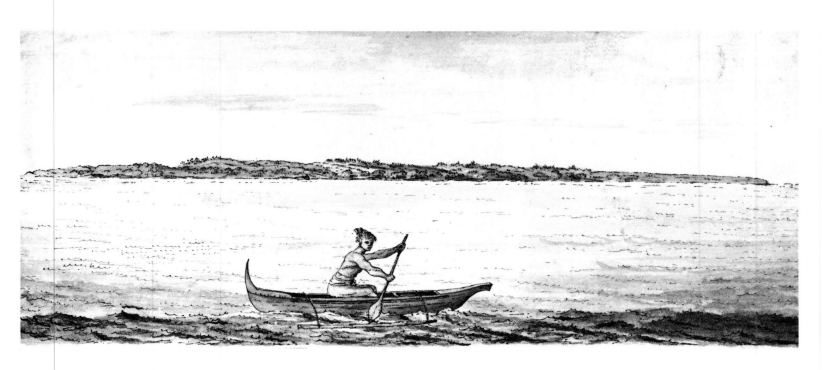

HENRY ROBERTS

3.32   [A Man of Atiu in his Canoe]   [Apr 1777]
pen, wash and water-colour, 3¾ × 9¼ : 98 × 230.

Showing a native in an outrigger canoe, behind the coastal-profile of Atiu. The drawing is on the same folio as Roberts's chart of 'Watieu', 'Mangea' and 'Hervey's Isles'.

The representation may refer to the scene which Cook describes: 'Just as the Boats were puting off, we observed several Canoes coming of from the shore; they went first to the Discovery she being the nearest Ship, soon after three came to the Resolution, each conducted by one man, with a little persuasion one of them made his Canoe fast to the Ship and came aboard and he was soon after followed by the others'. Cook, *Journals* III, 1, 81-2.

'The canoes of this island, at least as came off to the Ships, are but small, long and narrow and supported by out riggers, that is such as are single. The stern is elevated about 3 or 4 feet something like a ships stern post, the head is flat above, but prow-like below and turns down at the extremity like the end of a fidle.' Ibid., 87-8. For the types of canoe see Haddon and Hornell (1936) I, 161ff.

Dixson Library, State Library of New South Wales, Sydney. Henry Roberts's Log, MS Q 151-2, f.65.

WILLIAM ELLIS

3.33   [Natives of Atiu in their Canoes]   [Apr 1777]
pencil, 6¾ × 9¾ : 169 × 248, unsigned.

Inscribed in brown ink 'Canoes of Whatdue, or Watieu. See Ellis's Voyage Vol. I. page 45' across the top of the drawing. On verso inscribed in ink 'II' (l.l.). On verso faint outline of a hilly island, not identified.

At left a figure with a turban-like headdress paddling an outrigger canoe of the same type as in 3.32; at right, another canoe with a figure seated, the paddle across his knees; fruit or coconuts in the bottom of the canoe. At left, in the distance, the outline of an island.

The ships were visited by several canoes on 2 April 1777: 'As the ships were standing in, many of the natives put off, some in single, others in double canoes; the single have seldom room enough to contain more than one person, the double ones will hold eight or ten.' Ellis (1782) I, 38.

On the type of canoe depicted see Haddon and Hornell (1936) I, 156-70.

ref: Murray-Oliver (1977) 30.

Alexander Turnbull Library, Wellington. A264.7A.

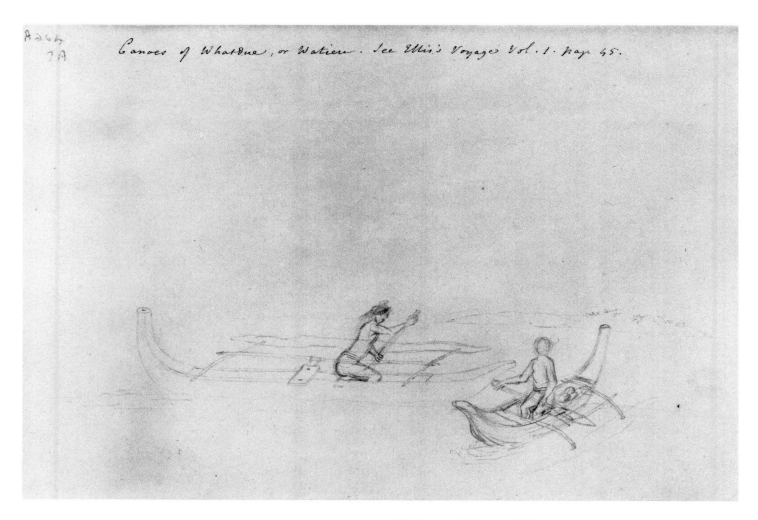

WILLIAM ELLIS

3.34   **[A Canoe of Atiu]**   **[Apr 1777]**
pencil, 8 × 6⁹⁄₁₆ : 203 × 167, unsigned; w/m: 'GR'
under crown, surrounded by wreaths in a circle.

Inscribed on the sheet above the canoe in pencil 'Whatdue', and
immediately above 'Whatdue' or 'Watieu' in black ink followed
by 'See Ellis's Voyage Vol 1. p.45' in brown ink. Inscribed in
brown ink '10' (l.l.).

A drawing in outline of an outrigger canoe. On verso is the
drawing of a fan (3.36).

The reference to vol. I, 45, refers to Ellis's identification of that
island: 'The Indian name of this island is Watieu . . . '.

On the type of canoe depicted see Haddon and Hornell (1936)
I, 156-66.

ref: Murray-Oliver (1977) 30.

Alexander Turnbull Library, Wellington. A264.6A.

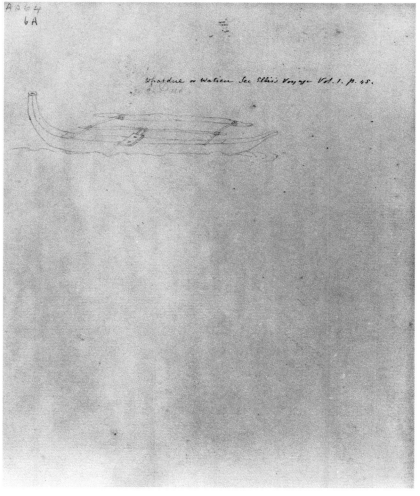

3.35 [Portraits of Natives of Atiu (?)] **[Apr 1777]**
pencil and wash, 7 × 11¾ : 179 × 301, unsigned.

Inscribed in pencil 'Whatdue' at top of the drawing, also 'Whatdue [in black ink] or Watieu' [in brown ink] in corner (u.r.) followed by 'Ellis's Voyage Vol. I. p.45' also in brown ink. Numbered '9' in brown ink in corner (l.l.). On verso is the drawing of two natives in a canoe off Mangaia (3.29).

Three studies of heads on one sheet: (a) above, a woman facing three-quarter left, with long hair held by a clip at the back of the neck, (b) centre, profile of a man facing left, (c) below, woman full-face: each has the hair treated differently, (b) wears a turban or head-band, compare the paddler at left in 3.33, (c) a turban or head-band pierced by up-standing hair or perhaps feathers.

The reference to Ellis, 45 is in general terms: 'Both the men and women were clothed much in the Otaheitee manner . . . The Indian name of this island is Watieu . . . '. More appropriate is a quote from 38: 'Their size was above the middle standard, and they were stout well-made people, with fine open countenances; their colour of the olive cast, with a mixture of brown. Their hair was black; in some long, in others short, and wore in a variety of forms, just as convenience or fancy directed.'

'In general they had the hair ty'd on the crown, long, black and of a most luxuriant growth.' Anderson in Cook, *Journals* III, 2, 840. However neither in Anderson nor Cook is there a reference to the turban-like head-bands. It must therefore remain open, whether the heads represent natives of Atiu.

ref: Murray-Oliver (1977) 30.

Alexander Turnbull Library, Wellington. A264. 5B.

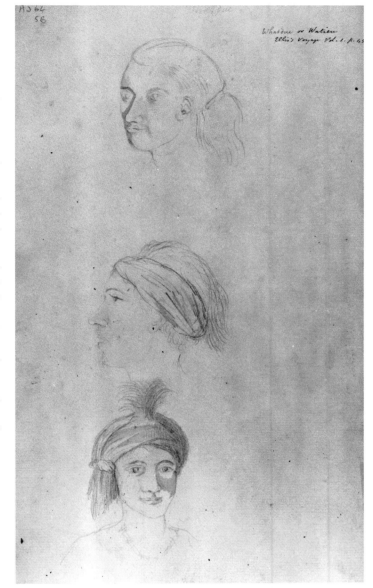

3.36 A Fan **[c. 1777]**
pencil, 7¾ × 6¾ : 200 × 168, unsigned.

Inscribed 'Whatdue?' in black ink (u.r.). On verso numbered '10' in brown ink. On verso is the drawing of a canoe of Atiu (3.34).

A detailed drawing with cross hatching and neatly carved handle, with a hole in the middle.

A reference to a fan is made by Anderson, describing his visit to the island of Atiu, when he was accompanied by Gore, Burney and Omai: ' . . . we found a person who seem'd a chief sitting on the ground cross legg'd, cooling himself with a sort of triangular fan made from a leaf of the cocoa palm with a polished handle of black wood fix'd to one point'. Cook, *Journals* III, 2, 834.

ref: Murray-Oliver (1977) 30.

Alexander Turnbull Library, Wellington. A264.6B.

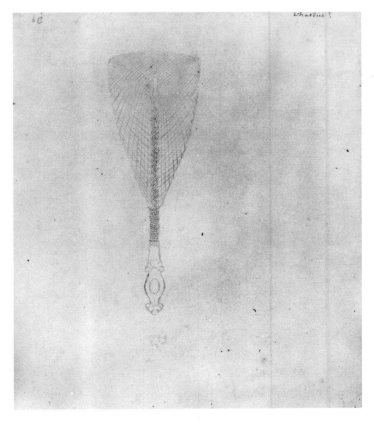

MANUAE (Hervey Island)

6 April 1777

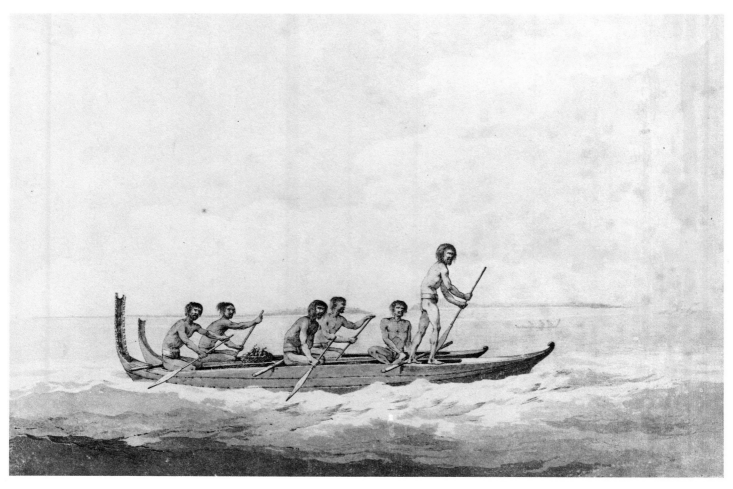

JOHN WEBBER

3.37   [Six Men in a Canoe off Manuae]
        [plate 22]   [Apr 1777]
pen and wash, 12¼ × 18 : 311 × 457, signed and
dated 'Jnº Webber 1777' (but the signature and date
partly scratched out and almost indecipherable).

Mounted on card. On verso erroneously inscribed 'Canoe, Mangaia', possibly in Dixson's hand with lot 'no 18' and '3' in ink
and in pencil 'Captain Campbell' in an eighteenth century hand.
Originally mounted on card.

The drawing can be identified as Webber's drawing 'A canoe with
Natives and a distant view of the Island (Herveys Island)', no.
64 in Webber's Catalogue.

Six natives in a double canoe, one standing near the prow; another
canoe containing three, in the mid-distance, the shoreline of the
island behind.

Describing the canoes of Manuae, Cook says: 'Their canoes are
larger than those we saw at the other islands but like them not
distinguished by any remarkable workmanship. The construction
of the stern bore some resemblance to those of Wautieu and the

tead [head?] projected out nearly in the same manner, but the
extremity turned up instead of down. See the drawing.' Cook,
Journals III, 1, 90.

Cook's reference to Webber's drawing most probably points to
the one which was omitted later from the drawings selected for
publication (see the list 'Drawings omitted in the list selected for
Publication referred to by Capt. Cook', National Library of Australia, Department of Manuscripts, MS 9/29). Under 'Apr. 6.
1777' a 'Drawing of Harvey's Island' is listed, which seems to be
identical with the one represented here.

The coast line in the drawing is split by an opening. This accords
with Anderson's observation: 'In the mean time we stood towards
the SW part of the island and being now past noon we had gone
so far as to see it was two islands join'd by a broad reef which
runs under water.' Cook, *Journals* III, 2, 847.

For similar types of double canoes of the Cook Islands see Haddon
and Hornell (1936) I, 170-4.

Dixson Library, State Library of New South Wales, Sydney.
Pe 210.

NOMUKA (Annamooka)

1 to 14 May 1777   3.38–3.44B

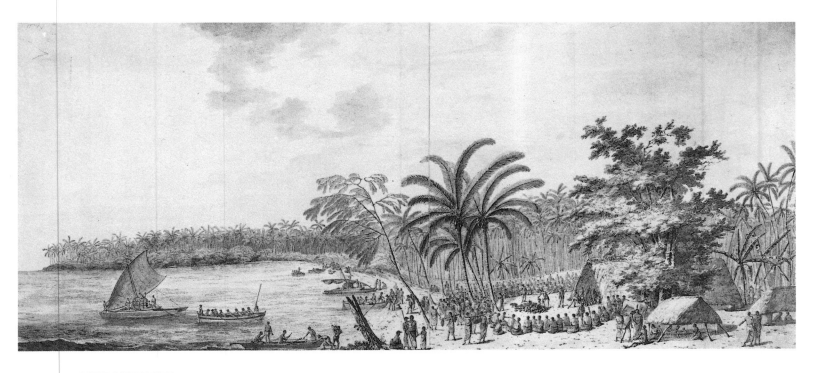

JOHN WEBBER

3.38   **The Harbour of Annamooka**
           [plate 25]   [May 1777–]
pen, wash and water-colour on two sheets, stuck
together, 17⅝ × 39⅜ : 448 × 1000, signed and dated
'John Webber del 1777' (l.r.).

The title as above in pencil on the mount below the drawing.
A number in corner (u.r.) is illegible, but it is likely that this
drawing is the one listed as no 25 in Webber's Catalogue. On
the mount at right also: 'See Atlas pl. 13'.

Men of Cook's company and many natives on shore and in boats
and canoes nearby.

'Capt Cook went on shore in the Bay & fixed upon a House
which he hired of the Indians for our Use during our Stay, which
saved us the Trouble of erecting the Tents. The Astronomers
lived on shore tho' they did not fix their Observatories here. The
Horses, Cattle, Sheep &c were sent on shore with two Men to
look after them . . . The different Parties on shore were under
the Command of the second Lieut, & a Market was established
before the House under the Management of the Gunners of each
ship, who were the sole Persons employed to Traffick with the
Indians for Provisions, all other trade being strictly prohibited;
a large Ring was made before the House where those who had
any thing for market exposed them to sale.' Samwell in Cook,
Journals III, 2, 1013.

About this place in general see also ibid., 1, 96-102, as well as
Ellis, (1782) I, 58-60.

ver: For a later version see 3.39.

ref: Cook, *Journals* III, 1, pl. 15.

British Library, London. Add MS 15513, f.7.

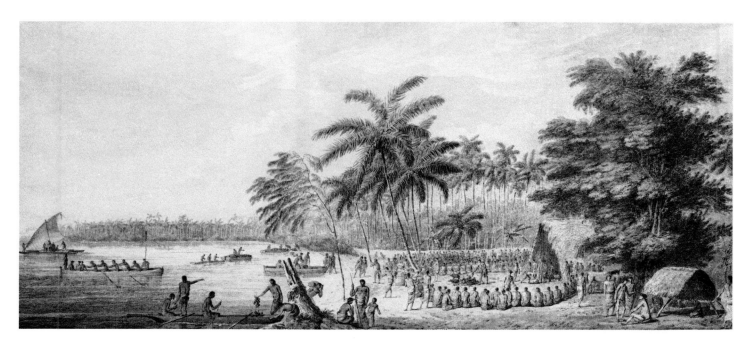

JOHN WEBBER

3.39   A View of Anamooka   [c. 1781-3]
        water-colour, 8⅝ × 19¾ : 219 × 498, unsigned.

Inscribed in pencil 'A view of Anamooka' by a later hand on folio
below drawing.

ver: A similar view to 3.38 but smaller. The engraving 3.39A
        is virtually identical except that it lacks the two standing
        figures at the extreme right.

Dixson Library, State Library of New South Wales, Sydney.
PXX2, 3.

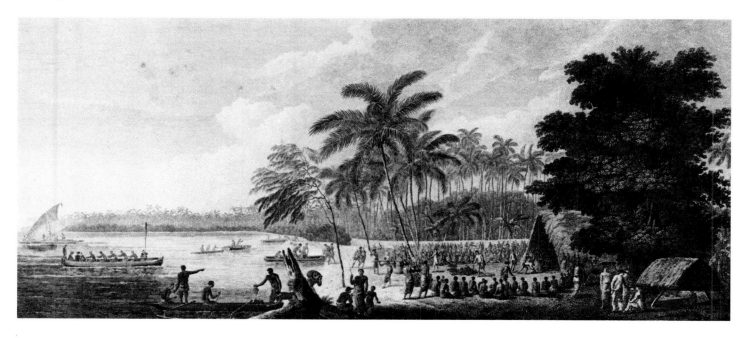

JOHN WEBBER (after)

3.39A   'A VIEW at ANAMOOKA'
        Engraving. 'J. Webber del.' — 'W. Byrne sc.'

Published in Cook/King (1784) pl. 13, I, 230.

A proof-state incribed in pencil 'View of the Harbour of Anamooka. Rotterdam, — Friendly Isles' in Webber's hand is kept
in the National Library of Australia, Canberra, in a folio of plates
from the Skottowe Hall Library.

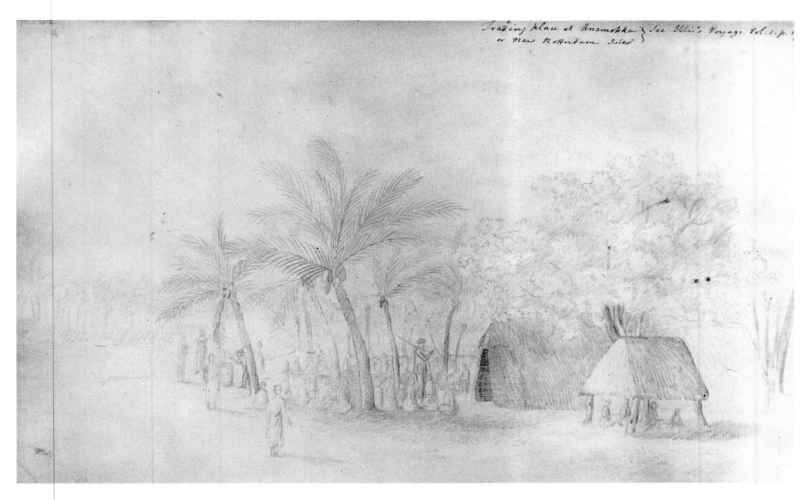

WILLIAM ELLIS

3.40   **The Trading Place at Annamooka**   **[May 1777]**
pencil, 7⁹⁄₁₆ × 12¼ : 192 × 310, unsigned; w/m:
'GR' under crown, surrounded by wreaths in a circle.

Inscribed in brown ink 'Trading Place at Anamokka or New
Rotterdam Isles See Ellis's Voyage Vol I. p. 59' (u.r.). On verso
numbered in brown ink '15' in corner (l.r.). On verso a coastal
profile of Amatafoa (A 264.8B).

Sailors trading with islanders in a coconut grove; three native
huts at right, four figures beneath the foremost hut, a marine,
at centre, surrounded by natives, guarding a tent, a cooper at
work at left.

'The next day (May 3d) the astronomers tents, instruments,
&c. were got on shore, together with the coopers, the empty
casks, &c. and the marines. The chief of the island furnished
us with a large hut for our reception on shore, in the front of
which the market was held; a line was drawn between the natives
and us, at some distance from the hut, to prevent their crowding
too near, and none of them were permitted to come within it.
We were abundantly supplied with hogs, fowls, yams, plantains,
breadfruit, and coconuts, and in short fared sumptiously every
day.' Ellis, (1782) I, 59-60.

ver: The location and the two huts at right appear to be the
same as in 3.38. For the motif of the hut on the right with
figures see 3.40A.

ref: Murray-Oliver (1977) pl. V, 30.

Alexander Turnbull Library, Wellington. A264.8A.

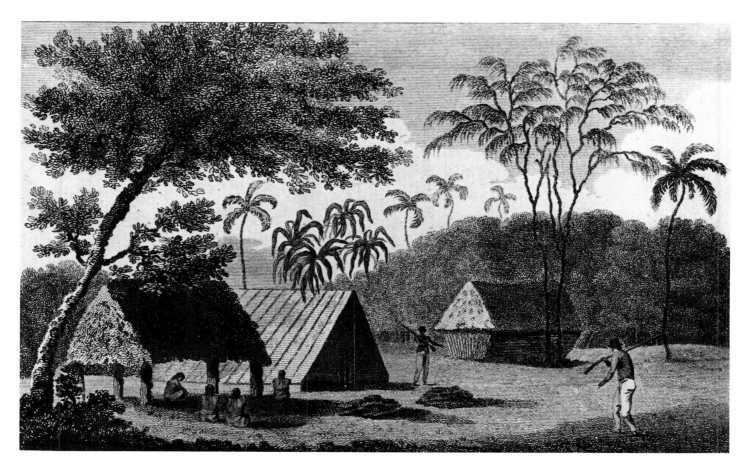

WILLIAM ELLIS (after)

3.40A   **'A View of the Market Place at Amsterdam, or Tongataboo'**
Engraving. 'W. Ellis del.' — 'J. Heath sculp.' 'Publish'd Dec.' 14 1781 by G. Robinson'.

Published in Ellis (1782) I, f. 72.

The engraving echoes Ellis's drawing of the trading place at Anamooka (3.40) but is laterally reversed. The drawing seems to
have been made at Anamooka, but the name of the engraving
changed to 'Market-place at Tongataboo'. That however was only
established on 11 June 1777.

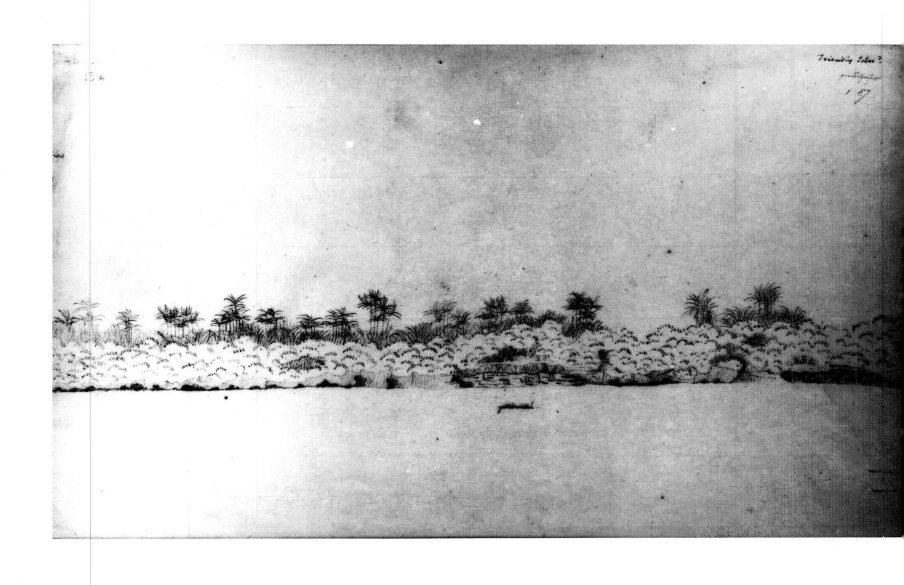

300

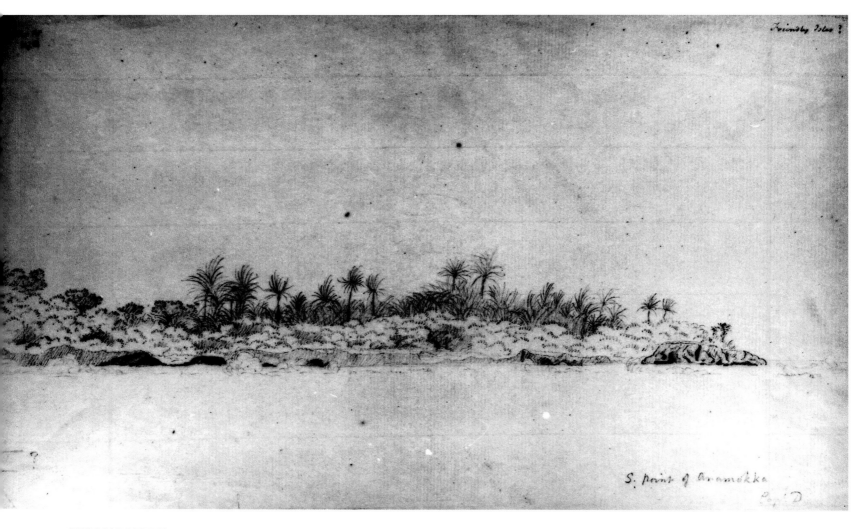

WILLIAM ELLIS

3.41a, b [Annamooka]   **[2 May 1777]**
pencil, 7¼ × 12¼ : 184 × 310, unsigned; w/m: 'GR'
under crown surrounded by wreaths in a circle.

Inscribed 'Friendly Isles?', in black ink (u.r.) of 13A and 14A,
also inscribed 'yellowish' in ink beneath rock in central foreground
of 13A. Numbered '1.87' (u.r.) of 13A (as a reference at Ellis's
Narrative). Inscribed in pencil 'S. point of Anamokka' (l.r.) and
below is 'Capt.D.', both on 14A.

A coastal view which also indicates the character of the vegetation
of Nomuka. On verso a drawing of a double canoe (3.68) and
of a walrus (3.433).

The probable reference to Ellis (1.87) seems incorrect, since that
page does not refer to Nomuka, but rather to 'Happi islands'
('Lefoogo'), 'Tongataboo or Amsterdam' and 'Middleburg, or
Eaoowe'. This view however is not of any of those places.

'At noon the extremes of Anamooka bore S.E. by S. and S. ½
W distant from the nearest shore three miles. At four in the
afternoon, both vessels anchored, and soon after were moored
a cable each way, the best bower of the Discovery being in seventeen fathom . . . her distance from the reef about three cables
length.' Ellis (1782) I, 57-8.

'Anamooka, or Rotterdam, lies in lat. 20 deg. 14 min. S. it is
almost surrounded by a reef of coral rock, and affords no good
harbour. The soil is rich and fertile, except when you approach
the shore, where it becomes sandy: it is of a very moderate ele-
vation, and well clothed with trees of various kinds . . .' Ibid.,
I, 86.

Alexander Turnbull Library, Wellington. A 264.13A, 14A.

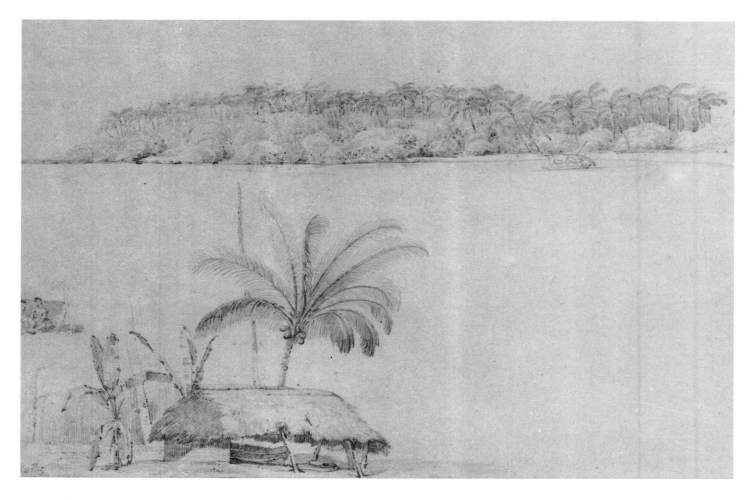

JOHN WEBBER

3.42   **Three Nomukan Sketches [plate 27]**   **[May 1777]**
pencil, 12¾ × 19¾ : 324 × 502, unsigned; w/m: 'IHS/
I. VILLEDARY'.

Three drawings on one sheet
a. a low-lying peninsula thickly covered with vegetation and to
   the right a sandy beach with Tongan canoe nearby.
b. below a Tongan hut; nearby plantains and palms.
c. two figures seated within the entrance to a grass hut.

'The Houses of these people are of various sizes and like those
of Otaheite consists chiefly of a thatched roof supported by pillars
and rafters desposed in a very judicious manner and the workmanship in many extremely neat, the floor is raised with earth smoothed
and covered with strong thick Matting and kept very clean;
. . . The most of them are inclosed on the weather Side and
some more than two thirds round, with strong Mats or the branches
of the Cocoanut tree plated or woven one into a nother; these
they fix up edgeways and reach from the eaves to the ground and
answers the purpose of a wall. A thick strong Mat about 2½ or
3 feet broad, bent into the form of a semi-circle and set up upon
its edge with the ends against the wall, like unto the fender of
a fire hearth, incloses a place for the Master and Mistress of the
family to sleep in . . .' Cook, *Journals* III, 1, 168.

ver: a. is a study for the left hand section of 3.38; b. and c. are
        studies for the hut at the right of 3.38 and of 3.43. The
        motif of the hut in b. is related to E. Scott's engraving 'A
        View of a Hut and Plantation at Amsterdam, or Tonga-
        Taboo' in Ellis, (1782) I, opp. 95. It thus seems possible
        that Ellis made a copy of Webber's sketch.

The Public Archives of Canada, Ottawa. I-15 (C 13424).

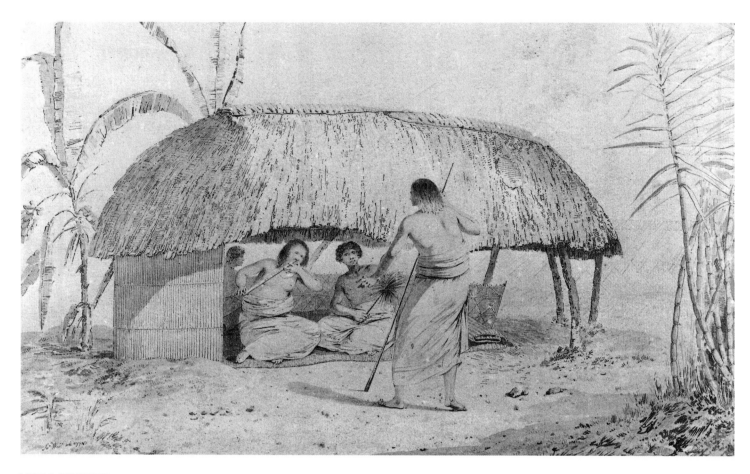

JOHN WEBBER

3.43 **A View in Annamooka [plate 46]** **[1777/78]**
pencil, pen and wash, 12¼ × 18 : 311 × 457, signed
and dated 'Jnº Webʳ del 1778' in ink [l.l.]. The drawing
has been varnished and mounted on cardboard and is
framed by two black lines.

Inscribed on verso in pencil 'Captain Campbell' in an eighteenth
century hand and lot no '4' in ink partly erased. This drawing
may be tentatively identified as 'A conversation', no. 16 in
Webber's Catalogue.

The date 1778 next to Webber's signature indicates that this
drawing was completed, or reworked, some considerable time after
the event, perhaps from an earlier study which has not survived.

Back view of a Tongan standing before a hut holding a stick,
behind which are seated three others, one playing a nose flute,
one holding a palm frond. The fourth figure behind in the interior
of the hut. Banana plants at left; bamboo at right.

The scene echoes Samwell's observation: 'About sunset they play
upon their Flutes, sing or sit in discourse with their Women before
their Houses.' Cook, *Journals* III, 2, 1036. Regarding the nose
flute see Anderson's and Samwell's comment, ibid., 940 and
1038-9.

ver: For another version of this composition see 3.44.

ref: *Cook-Bibl.* (1970), no. 1818, there titled 'Hut and Three
Natives of Tonga', from an old inscription on the back of
the drawing (now erased).

Dixson Library, State Library of New South Wales, Sydney.
Pe 211.

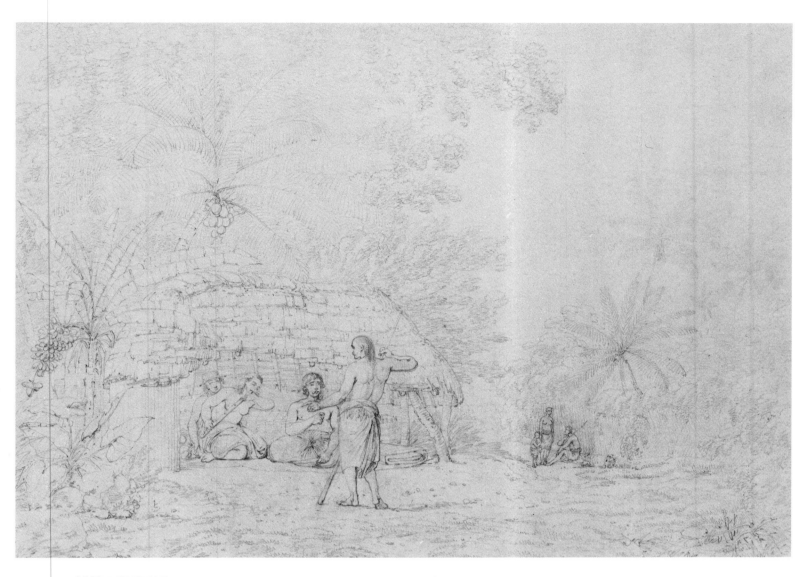

JOHN WEBBER

3.44   A View in Annamooka   [c. 1781]
pencil, 10¹⁵⁄₁₆ × 15¹⁵⁄₁₆ : 278 × 400; w/m:
'J. WHATMAN'.

The drawing is squared for transfer, and is likely to be a preparatory
study for 3.44A.

In comparing the drawing with its print versions (3.44A) a number of differences are revealed. The drawing shows the woman
playing the nose flute crouching on her knees whereas in the
prints her knees are covered with cloth. There seems to be another
native in the back of the hut in the print versions, which is
omitted from the drawing. There are also considerable differences
in the hairstyle of the standing native. Very noticeably, the
branches along the upper edge of the drawing extend beyond the
middle of the sheet, reaching over the family on the ground; in
the print versions this branch is much shorter. Finally, the coconut tree in the drawing shows many more nuts than in the prints.
Such differences suggest that the drawing is an original by Webber
rather than a copy after either of the prints.

ver: developed from 3.43.

Yale Center for British Art, Paul Mellon Collection, New Haven.

304

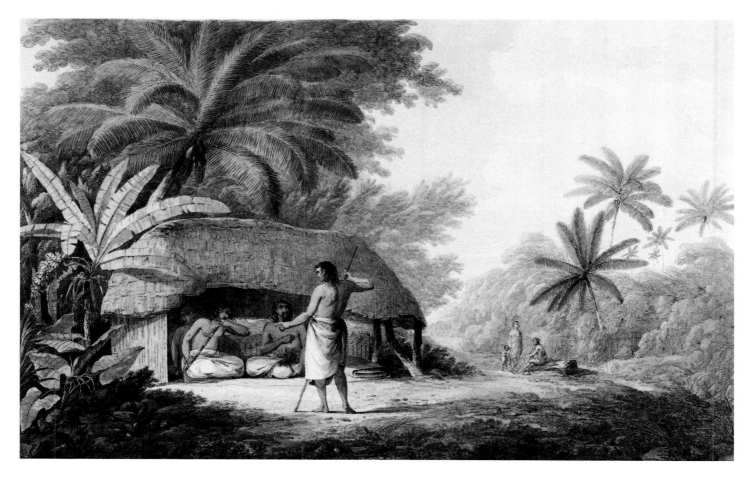

JOHN WEBBER

3.44A   **a. 'A View in Annamooka, one of the Friendly Isle's'** [1787]
coloured etching, $11^5/_{16} \times 16^{11}/_{16}$: 287×424 $(9^{15}/_{16} \times 15^5/_8$: $252 \times 397)$. 'Drawn & Etch'd by J. Webber'. On the right a reference to M.C. Prestel visibly erased, probably by Webber himself. 'London Pub^d. [Feby. 1] (inserted by hand in pencil) 1787 by J. Webber N°. 312 Oxford Street'. 'Vide Cooks last Voy. Vol I Chap. IV'.

British Museum, Department of Prints and Drawings, London
C. 6˙.

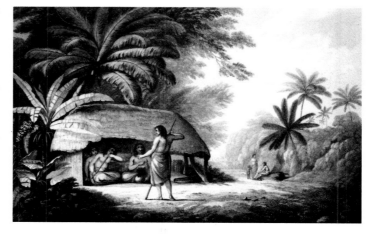

    b. 'A View in Annamooka, one of the Friendly Isle's' [1787]
uncoloured aquatint, $11^5/_8 \times 17$: 296×432 $(10 \times 15^{13}/_{16}$: $255 \times 402)$.
'Drawn & Etch'd by J. Webber'. 'Aquatinta by M.C. Prestel'. 'London Pub^d . . . (blank) 1787 by J. Webber N°. 312 Oxford Street'. 'Vide Cooks last Voy. Vol. I, Chap. IV'.

ref: Murray-Oliver (1969b) pl. 1 illustrating a print in the Alexander Turnbull Library, and Kaeppler (1978a) fig. 45 (102) showing a version from the Fuller Collection, Bernice P. Bishop Museum, Honolulu.

Hartnoll and Eyre, London (1978); Alexander Turnbull Library, Wellington. Coloured copies with the same inscriptions are kept in the Fuller Collection, Bernice P. Bishop Museum, Honolulu, and in the National Library of Australia, Canberra. Another copy but with the publication line 'London Pub^d. Feby. 1 1788 by J. Webber N°. 312 Oxford Street' is in the British Museum, Department of Prints and Drawings, London. C. 6˙.

This subject was not included in the later series of Webber's *Views*. No other versions are known to exist.

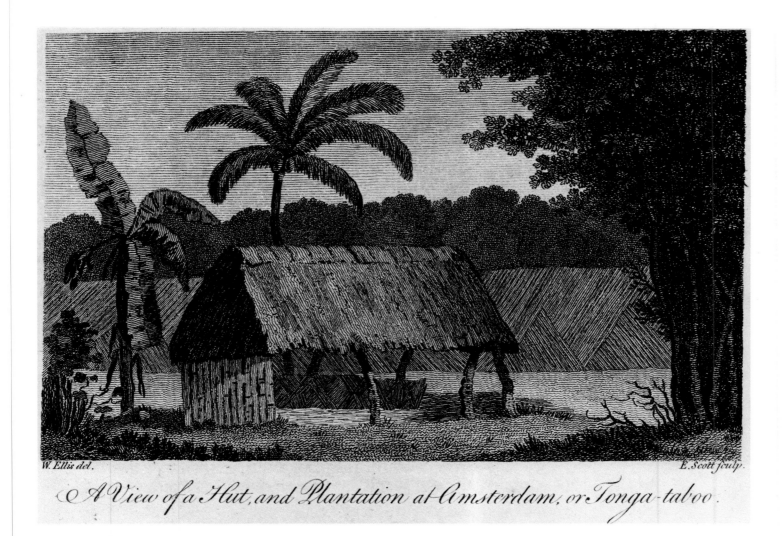

W. Ellis del. — E. Scott sculp.

A View of a Hut, and Plantation at Amsterdam, or Tonga-taboo.

WILLIAM ELLIS (after)

3.44B **'A View of a Hut, and Plantation at Amsterdam, or Tonga-taboo'**
Engraving. 'W. Ellis del.' — 'E. Scott sculp.'. 'Published 14 Dec. 1781 by G. Robinson'.

Published in Ellis (1782) I, f.95.

No drawing by Ellis of this engraving is known. The hut, however, shows some similarity to Webber's drawing of 3.42.

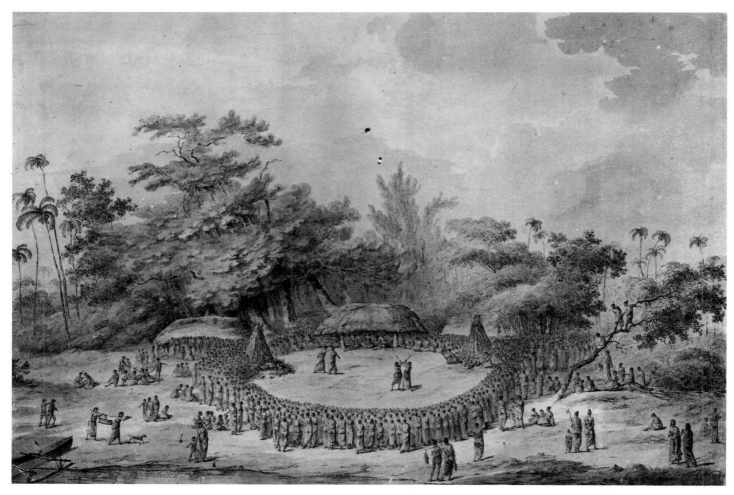

JOHN WEBBER

3.45   The Reception of Captain Cook at Hapaee
        [plate 28]   [May 1777–]
        pen, wash and water-colour, 17⁵⁄₁₆ × 25¹⁄₁₆ : 448
        × 636, signed 'drawn from nature by J. Webber' (l.r.).

The title as above in pencil on the mount below drawing with
additional inscription in same hand 'see atlas pl. 16'. Also inscribed 'No 22' (?) in pencil [u.r.] which would identify this
drawing as the one listed and titled '22 The manner of receiving,
entertaining and making Captain Cook a present of the produc-
tions of the Island, on his Arrival at the Happi', in Webber's
Catalogue.

Two pairs of combatants, one pair boxing, the other pair fighting
with clubs, within a large circle of spectators. Some men of Cook's
company to the left on the fringe of the crowd. In the left
foreground a dog with pointed ear.

'Presently after a number of men entered the Circle or Area before
us, armed with Clubs made of the green branches of the Cocoanut
tree, these paraded about for a few minutes and then retired the
one half to one side and the other half to the other, and seated
themselves before the spectators: but soon after went to single

Combat, one or two steping forward from the one side and chal-
lenging those on the other which was done more by actions than
words; if the Challenge was expected, which was generally the
case, each put himself in a proper attitude and began to engage
and continued till one or the other gave out or their weapons
were broke . . . This entertainment was now and then suspended
for a few minutes, at these intervals there were Wristling and
Boxing matches; the first were performed in the same m[an]ner
as at Otahiete, and the second very little different from the
method practiced in England.' Cook, *Journals* III, 1, 107.

For a general description of the scene see ibid, 106-8. Another
description of Cook's reception is given by Samwell, ibid. 2,
1016-19, which refers also to the setting of the scene: 'A prodigious
Number of the Natives were collected together on the Beach
& a large Space was left clear for our People. Captn. Cook with
some of the officers of each Ship sat in a House at the upper end
of the open Area along with Phenow & the Chiefs of the Island'
(1016).

ver: For a smaller version see 3.46.
ref: *Exh. Cat.* Auckland (1964) pl.33; Cook, *Journals* III, 1,
        pl.16; Kaeppler (1978a) fig.505.

British Library, London. Add MS 15513, f.8.

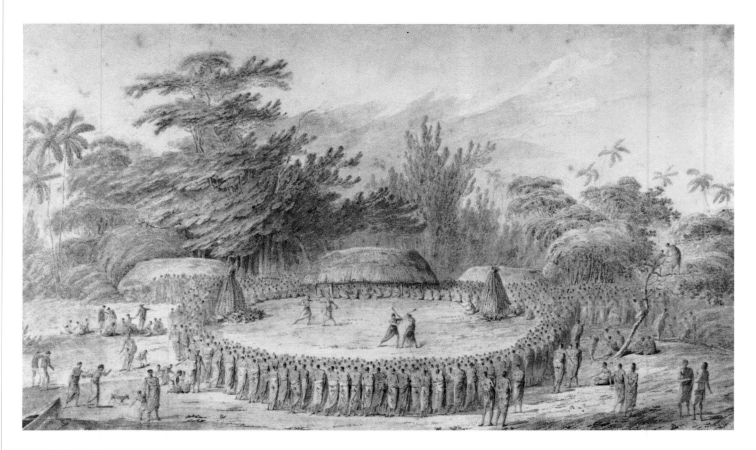

JOHN WEBBER

3.46 **The Reception of Captain Cook in Hapaee**
[c. 1781-3]
water-colour, 8¹³⁄₁₆ × 15 : 224 × 381, unsigned.

The title as above in pencil by a later hand on the folio beneath the drawing.

ver: A smaller version of 3.45. The model for and almost identical with the engraving 3.46A.

ref: Murray-Oliver (1969a) pl. 105 (col.).

Dixson Library, State Library of New South Wales, Sydney. PXX2, 4.

JOHN WEBBER (after)

3.46A **'The RECEPTION of CAPTAIN COOK in HAPAEE'**
Engraving. 'J. Webber del.' — 'Heath sculp.'

Published in Cook/King (1784) pl. 14, I, 245.

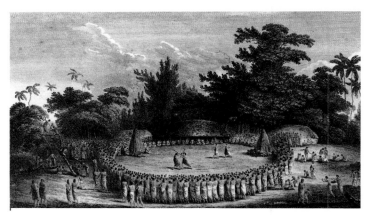

A proof-state inscribed in pencil 'Reception at Hapai one of the Friendly Isles' in Webber's hand and numbered in pencil 'Nº 14' (u.r.) is kept at the National Library of Australia, Canberra, in a folio of plates from the Skottowe Hall Library.

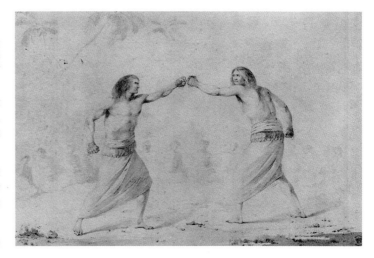

3.47 **A Boxing Match, Friendly Islands [plate 29] [1778]**
pen, pencil and wash, 12¼ × 17¾ : 311 × 451, signed
and dated 'Jnº Webber del 1778' (l.l.).

Inscribed 'Boxers at the Friendly Islands' in pencil on the mount
below drawing, inscribed no. '20' faintly in pencil (u.r.). 'A
Boxing Match' is listed under 'The Friendly Islands' in Webber's
Catalogue as no 14.

The date 1778 next to Webber's signature indicates that this
drawing was completed, or reworked some considerable time after
the event, perhaps from an earlier study which however has not
survived.

Two boxers with spectators seated in a semicircle and palm trees
sketched faintly in background.

Cook and his men witnessed boxing matches in Tonga on 18 May
and 18 June 1777, Cook, *Journals* III, 1, 107 and Anderson in
ibid., 2, 899-901.

Another detailed description of a boxing match is given by Samwell in ibid., 2, 1027-8, who begins with the following remark:
'The first step taken in this Exercise is to bind the clenched fist
with a small Chord so that it cannot be opened'. (1027.)

For the description in Cook's official account see Cook/King
(1784) I, 302.

The drawing may have served for I. Taylor's engraving of the
same title (3.47A).

ver: The two figures are related to the boxers depicted in 3.45
and 3.46.

ref: Cook, *Journals* III, 1, pl. 19; Murray-Oliver (1969a) pl.
104.

British Library, London. Add MS 15513, f.9.

JOHN WEBBER (after)

3.47A **'A BOXING MATCH in HAPAEE'**
Engraving. 'J. Webber del.' — 'I. Taylor sc.'

Published in Cook/King (1784) pl. 15, I, 246, 302.

A proof-state inscribed in pencil 'A Boxing Match friendly Isles
Amsterdam' in Webber's hand, also 'Taylor' and 'The Plate re-
touched . . .(?) this was printed off' in another hand is kept in
the National Library of Australia, Canberra, in a folio of plates
from the Skottowe Hall Library.

The plate for this engraving was ready in November 1782; this
is attested by Lord Sandwich's letter to Dr Douglas, asking whether
the title 'a boxing match in Happee' . . . 'should not be written
Happi' (letter of 19 November 1782, British Library, Egerton MS
2180, f.55-6).

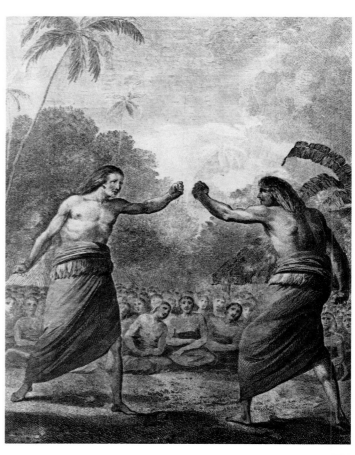

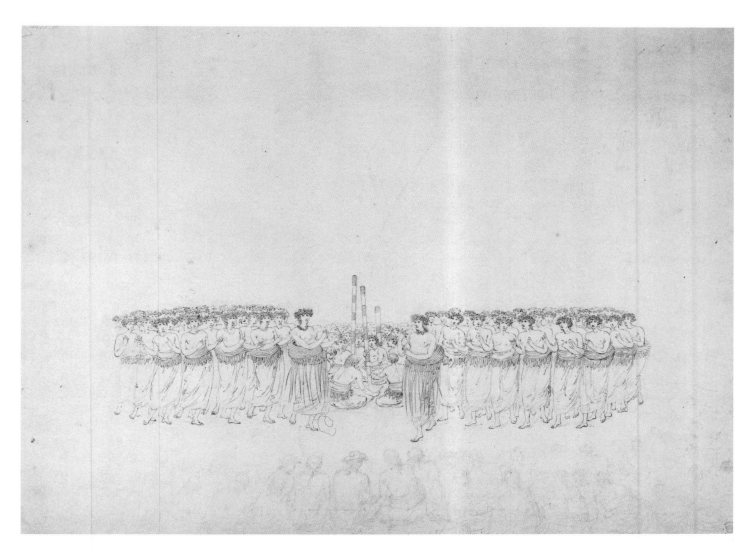

JOHN WEBBER

3.48   **A Night Dance by Women in Hapaee**
        [plate 32]   [20 May 1777—]
        pen and pencil (unfinished), 19¼ × 26 : 489 × 660,
        unsigned.

The drawing is probably referred to in Webber's Catalogue, no.
24: 'A night Heiva or Dance, by Women.'

For 20 May 1777 Cook recorded: 'A number of men seated themselves in a circle before us and began a Song not one word of
which we understood; the musick was in the middle of the circle
and consisted simply of two large pieces of bamboo with which
they struck the ground end-ways and produced a dead hollow
sound, each was managed by one man, who held it nearly in a
Virtical position, the upper end was open but the other was closed
by one of the joints. In a short time a number of Women, dressed
better than Common, came and encircled the men in a kind of
dance and joined in the Song; thus they continued for a full half
hour, when two elderly women (one on each side, and who
seemed to have the management of the whole) brough[t] the
others up, dancing, two by two and ranged them before the chief,
which ended the dance and the assembly broke up.' Cook, *Journals*
III, 1, 110. An extensive description of the Heiva is given by
Anderson (ibid., 2, 875) and by Samwell (ibid., 2, 1019-20).
For the dresses of the dancing women see Williamson's account
(ibid., 1, 110.3n). Cook and his party were also entertained by
night dances on 17 June 1777 on Tongataboo, which were similar
to those experienced at Ha'apai.

Of such Tongan dances in general Cook wrote, 'These dances
vary perhaps much more than we were able to discover, however

there appeared a sort of sameness throughout the whole, and so
would, I apprehend the most of our Country dances to people as
inacquainted with them as we were with theirs. The drawings
which M.ʳ Webber has made of these performances will give a
very good idea of the order in which they range themselves but
neither pen nor pencil can describe the numerous actions and
motions they observe, which as I have before observed are easy
and graceful and many of them extremely so.' Cook, *Journals* III,
1, 131.

On the other hand Dr John Douglas, the editor of the official
account of the voyage wrote (in the name of Cook): 'The drawings
which Mr. Webber made of the performances at Hapaee, and
which are equally applicable to those exhibited now will serve
much to illustrate the account here given of the order in which
the actors range themselves.' Cook/King, (1784) I, 297.

ver: A larger and probably an earlier version of 3.49.

British Library, London. Add MS 15513, f.10.

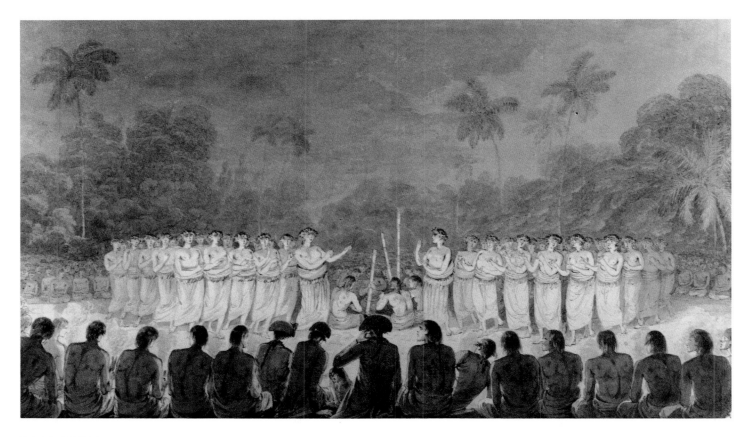

JOHN WEBBER

3.49   **A Night Dance by Women in Hapaee**
        [plate 33]   [c. 1781-3]
        pen and wash and tints of blue water-colour, 8⅞ ×
        15 : 225 × 381, unsigned. The title as above in pencil
        by a later hand on the folio beneath the drawing.

Cook and his men are seated in the foreground with their backs
to the viewer, the dancers in a line before them.

ver: Almost same composition as in 3.48 but executed with
        greater accomplishment. Engraved by W. Sharp (3.49A).

Dixson Library, State Library of New South Wales, Sydney.
PXX 2, 6.

JOHN WEBBER (after)

3.49A   **'A NIGHT DANCE by WOMEN in HAPAEE'**
        Engraving. 'J. Webber del.' — 'W. Sharp sculp.'

Published in Cook/King (1784) pl. 17, I, 250-1.

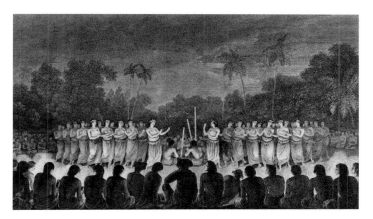

A proof-state inscribed in pencil 'Night Dance by Women —
Friendly Isles' in Webber's hand is kept in the National Library
of Australia, Canberra, in a folio of plates from the Skottowe
Hall Library.

This plate was the last one of the figure subjects to be printed.
On 29 April 1784, G. Nicol, the publisher wrote to Dr Douglas
the editor: 'Mr. Nicol . . . sends him by the Bearer the four
remaining plates of the voyage viz N°. 17, 85, 86 & 87 [the latter
ones being plates of the views of headlands] which compleates
that part of the work.' (British Library, Egerton MS 2180, f.205.)

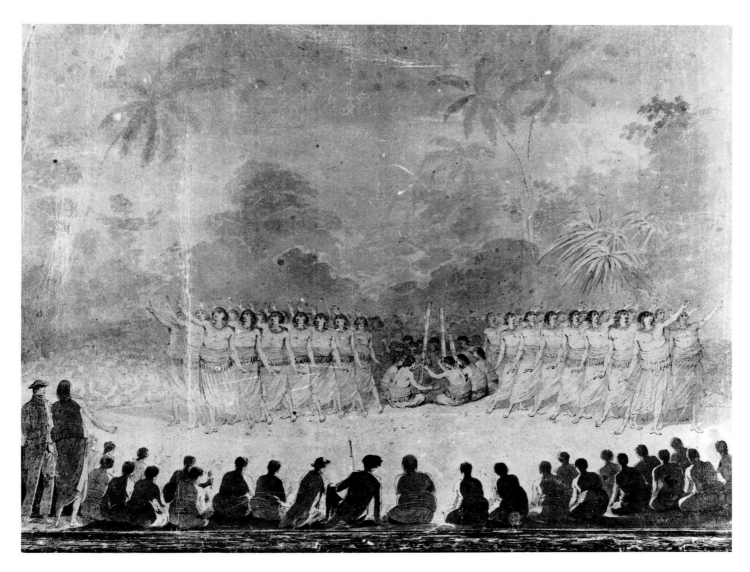

JOHN WEBBER

3.50   **A Night Dance by Men in Hapaee**
        [plate 34]   **[20 May 1777–]**
        pen and wash, 19½ × 26½ : 495 × 660, unsigned.

Endorsed in pencil in an eighteenth century hand (Webber's?), much faded 'Night Heava by Men at the Friendly Isles' and 'Captain Campbell' in pencil. In ink 'Lot No. 17' crossed out and 'Lot No 1' substituted.

The surface of the drawing has been varnished and scratched and damaged in places; the sheet has frame line in black ink and has been mounted on board [perhaps by Webber himself]. Some of the edges are lighter which would suggest that the drawing was framed for some time. It is probably the version referred to in Webber's Catalogue, no. 23 as 'A night Heiva or Dance, performed by Men'.

'Both men and Women accompanied the Song with a variety of motions of the hands and snaping of the fingers, which seems to be an essential part of their singing.' Cook, *Journals* III, 1, 110. Anderson's description is more detailed: 'To these [the women] succeded fifteen men . . . They were dispos'd in a sort of circle divided at the front . . . They sometimes sung slowly in conjunction with the chorus during which they made several very fine motions with their hands but different from those of the women, at the same time inclining the body to either side alternately by raising one leg which was stretch'd outwards and resting on the other, the arm of the same side being also stretch'd fully upwards.' Ibid., 2, 876.

ver: A larger version of 3.51, with minor differences. It is less finished and appears to be the earlier version.

Dixson Library, State Library of New South Wales, Sydney. Pf. 54.

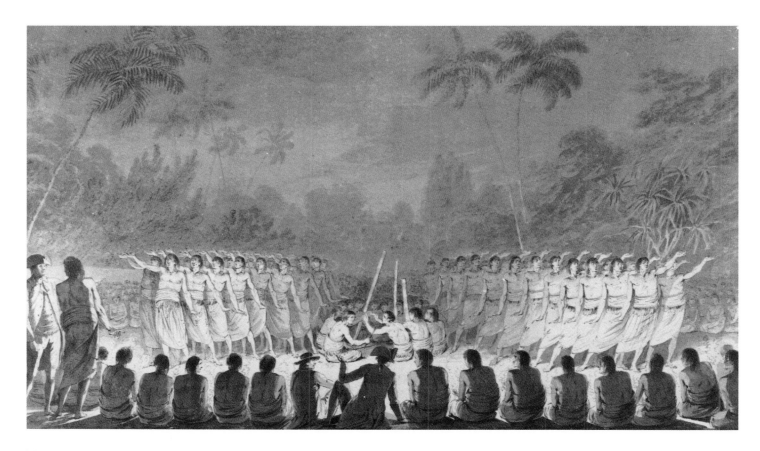

JOHN WEBBER

3.51   A Night Dance by Men in Hapaee   [c.1781-3]
pen and blue and grey wash, tints of water-colour, 8¾
× 15¼ : 223 × 388, unsigned.

The title as above in pencil by a later hand on the folio beneath
the drawing.

Cook and some of his men seated in the foreground with their
backs to viewer. In front of them are two rows of dancers who
are divided by the musicians.

ver: See 3.50 for a larger version of the subject with minor
         differences. Similar in size and prepared for the engraving
         (3.51A).

Dixson Library, State Library of New South Wales, Sydney.
PXX 2, 5.

JOHN WEBBER (after)

3.51A   'A NIGHT DANCE by MEN in HAPAEE'
Engraving. 'J. Webber del' — 'W^m. Sharp sculp.'

Published in Cook/King (1784) pl. 16, I, 251-2.

A proof-state inscribed in pencil 'Night Dance, by Men' in Webber's hand and numbered in pencil 'N°. 19' (u.r.) is kept in the
National Library of Australia, Canberra, in a folio of plates from
the Skottowe Hall Library.

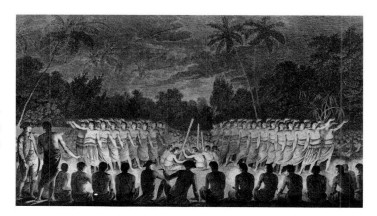

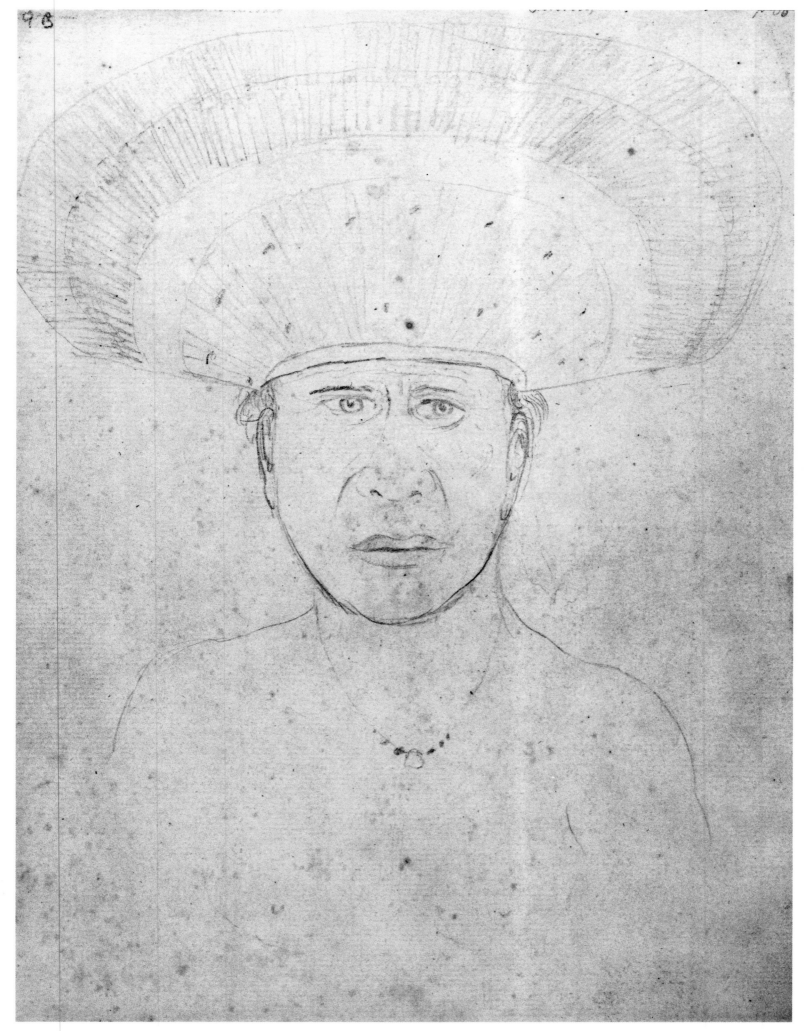

WILLIAM ELLIS

3.52   [Portrait of a Tongan Chief]   [May 1777]
pencil, 11⁷⁄₁₆ × 7½ : 290 × 190, unsigned.

Inscribed 'Feenow' in pencil (u.r.), then crossed out, followed by 'Vol I p. 66', referring to Ellis (1782). Numbered '14' in brown ink in l.l.; w/m: 'GR' under a crown, surrounded by wreaths in a circle. On verso a drawing of a young woman (3.63).

Murray-Oliver (1977) 30-1, considers it to be a portrait of Fatafehi Paulaho, the Tu'i Tonga, or 'King'. The feathered head dresses (*fae*) 'could be worn only by the highest of chiefs — and perhaps only by the Tui Tonga himself', Kaeppler (1971) 213, and Paulaho is certainly wearing the *fae* in 3.52A.

On the other hand it must be admitted that the head in this drawing does not closely resemble that in 3.52A. Moreover Finau gave Cook to believe that he was Tu'i Tonga when they first met and undertook to go to Vava'u and 'get some red feathered caps for me'. Cook, *Journals* III, 1, 112. Finau did not return with any *fae* and acknowledged, in a state of dejection, upon his return, that Paulaho was Tu'i Tonga.

The fact remains however that the pencilled inscription 'Feenow' is likely to be the earliest and probably therefore a correct one in Ellis's hand. The hand that crossed it out also drew attention to Ellis's account of Paulaho, *Narrative* (1782) 1, 66, as 'the real King of Tonga'. But this attempt at correction may have itself been mistaken. Finau may well have worn a *fae* in passing himself off as Tu'i Tonga to Cook and Ellis may have drawn his portrait when wearing it at that time. Cook had certainly seen *fae* before he met Paulaho.

On the present evidence it is not possible to decide conclusively whether the portrait is of Paulaho or Finau, but it slightly favours the latter.

ref: Murray-Oliver (1977) 30-31; Kaeppler (1971) 213.

Alexander Turnbull Library, Wellington. A264.9B.

JOHN WEBBER (after)

3.52A   'POULAHO, KING of the FRIENDLY ISLANDS'
[plate 48]   [May 1777]
Engraving. 'J. Webber del.' — 'J. Hall sculp.'

Published in Cook/King (1784) pl. 18, I, 264-5 and 267-8.

A proof-state inscribed in pencil 'King Poulehou. friendly Isles' in Webber's hand and numbered in pencil 'N°. 20' (u.r.) is kept in the National Library of Australia, Canberra, in a folio of plates from the Skottowe Hall Library.

No original drawing or painting of Fatafehi Paulaho has survived. Cook made the acquaintance of the Tongan king on 27 May 1777. On the 28th, as Cook was about to leave Ha'apai Paulaho came on board 'and brought me one of their Caps made or at least covered with red feathers: these Caps were much sought after by us from knowing they would be highly valued at Otaheite. . . . These Caps or rather bonnets are made of the tail feathers of the Tropic bird with the red feathers of the Paroquets worked upon them or in along with them, they are made so as to tie upon the forehead without any Crown, and have the form of a Semi-circle whose radis is 18 or 21 Inches; but a painting which Mr. Webber has made of Fattafee Polaho dressed in one of these bonnets will convey the best idea of them.' Cook, *Journals* III, 1, 117.

Webber's portrait of Paulaho is listed in Webber's Catalogue as no. 1 of the 'Portraits in Oyl Colours' as 'Powlehow King of the Friendly Islands wearing a Cap of Ceremony'.

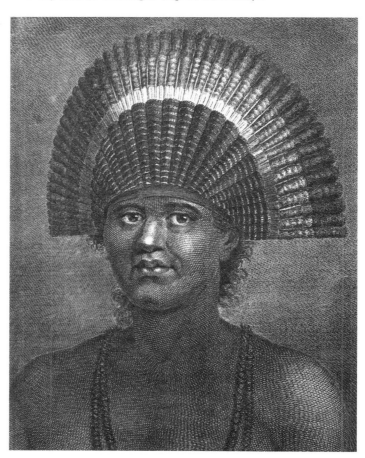

Royal Canoe of Anamooka or Rotterdam, one of the Friendly Isles in the South-Seas, see Ellis's Voyage Vol. 1. page 70.

WILLIAM ELLIS

3.53 **The Royal Canoe of Anamooka**   **[May 1777]**
pencil, 12 × 7½ : 305 × 190, signed in brown ink
'W. Ellis fecit' (l.r.).

Inscribed in brown ink 'Royal Canoe of Anamooka, or Rotterdam, one of the Friendly Isles in the South-Seas' below drawing and followed by 'see Ellis's Voyage Vol. I. page 70' in the same hand; numbered '16' (l.l.). On verso is the drawing of the canoe of the King of Anamooka (3.54).

A rough pencil drawing of a large double canoe (*tongiaki*) containing many small figures in outline. For the type of canoe represented see Haddon and Hornell (1936) I, 265-72.

'About Noon (27 May 1777) a large sailing Canoe came under our Stern in which the Indians on board told us was Fattafee Polaho King of all the Isles.' Cook *Journals* III, 1, 115.

'In the afternoon we got up our anchors and made sail, attended by Powlahow and Feenow, in their canoes, which went at a great rate, and a number of smaller ones. The royal canoe was distinguished from the rest by a small bundle of grass, of a red colour, fastened to the end of a pole, and fixed in the stern of the canoe in the same manner as our ensign staffs.' Ellis (1782) I, 70.

ref: Murray-Oliver (1977) 31.

Alexander Turnbull Library, Wellington. A264.10B.

316

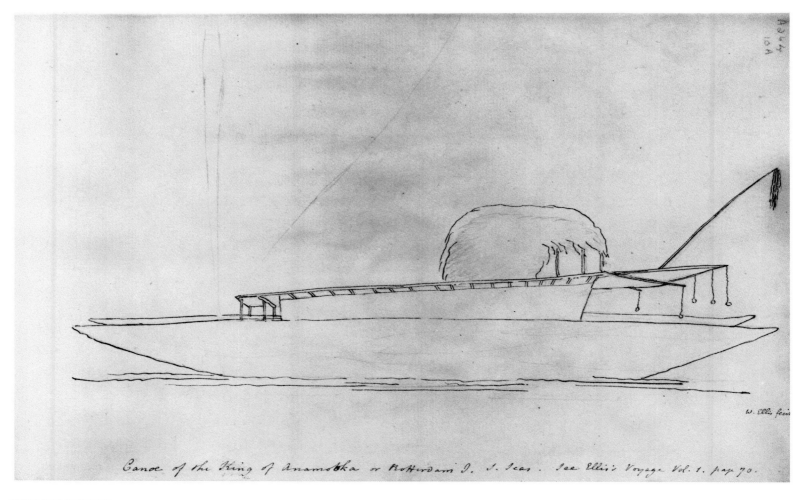

Canoe of the King of Anamooka or Rotterdam I. S. Seas. See Ellis's Voyage Vol. 1. pag 70.

WILLIAM ELLIS

3·54   **Canoe of the King of Anamooka**   [May 1777]
pen and pencil, 7½ × 12 : 190 × 305, signed in brown
ink 'W. Ellis fecit' (l.r.); w/m 'GR' under crown, surrounded by wreaths in a circle.

Inscribed 'Canoe of the King of Anamooka or Rotterdam I. S.
Seas' in brown ink below drawing and followed by 'See Ellis's
Voyage Vol I page 70' in the same hand. On verso the drawing
of the Royal Canoe of Anamooka (3.53), and numbered '16' in
brown ink.

An outline drawing of a large double canoe (*tongiaki*), with a
deck-house and triangular sail lightly sketched in pencil. A raking
flag-pole at rear (see Ellis's description, 3.53).

ref: Murray-Oliver (1977) 31.

Alexander Turnbull Library, Wellington. A264.10A.

10 June 1777 to 10 July 1777   3.55–3.63

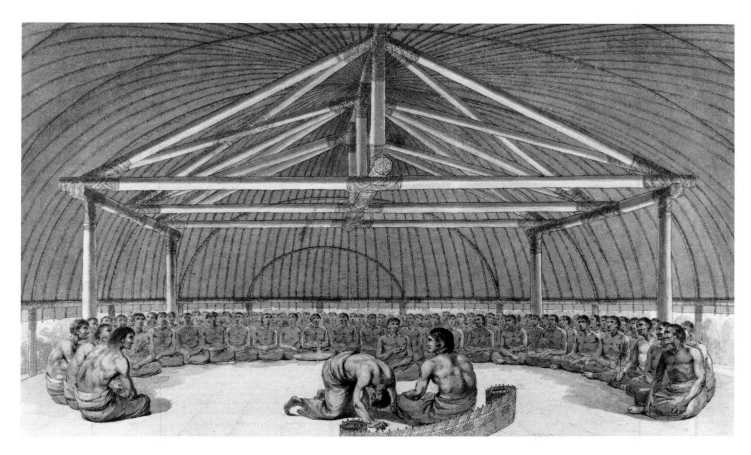

JOHN WEBBER

3.55   **Poulaho, King of the Friendly Islands, drinking Kava [plate 40]**   **[c. 1781-3]**
pen and water-colour, 9⅛ × 15¼ : 232 × 388, unsigned.

The title as above in pencil by a later hand on the folio below the drawing.

A drawing of this subject (which probably preceded this version but has not been located) is mentioned in Webber's Catalogue as no. 15 'King Pawlehow drinking his Cava, and attended by the Principal Chiefs of the Island'. 3.55 was probably developed from that lost original for the engraving, 3.55A.

A semicircle of natives, seated in a large house, watching a man prostrate before the 'King' in the foreground. The 'King' is Fatafei Poulaho, 36th Tu'i Tonga, c. 1770-84.

Cook and his men took part or witnessed kava ceremonies a few times: on 10 June subsequent to Cook's landing on Tonga-taboo, on 26 and 27 June, on 8 July and on 9 July 1777. The ceremony on 27 June took place in a house with 'hundred or upwards' people attending. Webber probably had this scene in mind when he made his original drawing, Cook *Journals* III, 1, 140-1. Samwell reports that touching the foot of a chief with one's head, as depicted in this scene, was a sign of reverence. Ibid., 2, 1027.

Engraved by W. Sharp (3.55A).

Dixson Library, State Library of New South Wales, Sydney. PXX 2, 7.

318

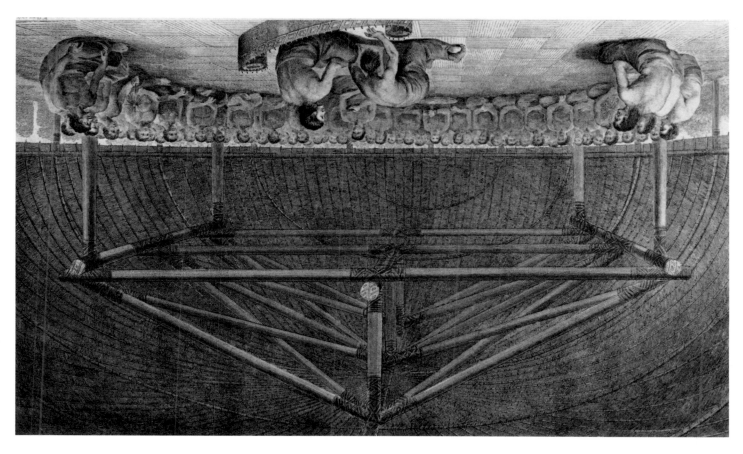

JOHN WEBBER (after)

3.55A   'POULAHO, KING of the FRIENDLY ISLANDS, **drinking KAVA'**

Engraving, 'J. Webber del.' — 'W. Sharp sculp.'

Published in Cook/King (1784) pl. 20, I, 279, 312, 316.

A proof-state inscribed in pencil 'King Pouhehoo drinking Cava. Happae. Friendly Isles' in Webber's hand is kept in the National Library of Australia, Canberra, in a folio of plates from the Skottowe Hall Library.

3.56   **[A Tongan Dance]**   [probably 21 Jun 1777]
pencil, wash and water-colour, 12⅜ × 19⅜ : 314 ×
492, unsigned.

A large crowd of spectators seated in a semicircle watching groups
of two dancers; in the central foreground, a circle of musicians.

The dance to which Cook was invited by Poulaho was probably
witnessed on 21 June 1777. Cook's description of the yam posts
which are situated in the back of the drawing is revealing: 'After
breakfast I attended him a shore and found his people very busy
in two places in the front of our area, fixing in an upright and
square position four very long posts, near two feet from each
other. The space between the post[s] were afterwards filled up
with yams, and as they went on seized sticks a cross from post
to post, at the distance of about every four feet to prevent the
posts from seperating by the weight of the yams. When they got
to the top of these post[s] they fastened others to them and so
continued till each pile was the height of 30 feet or upwards'
Cook, *Journals* III, 1, 135. See also Anderson's description of the
same in *ibid.*, 2, 901.

ref: Cook, *Journals* III, 1, pl. 17, Rienits (1968) 136 (col.);
Beaglehole (1974) pl. 34.

National Maritime Museum, London. (In volume of plates to
Cook's Voyages.)

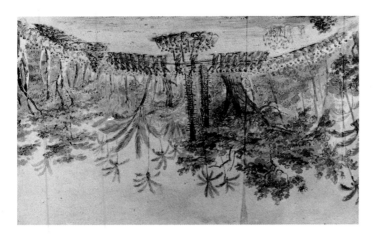

3.57   **A View of a *fa'itoka*, or Burying Ground**   [Jun 1777—]
pen, wash and water-colour, 17⅜ × 24¾ : 411 × 629,
signed and dated in ink 'Jn Webber del 1777' (l.r.).

Inscribed 'View of a Fiatooka or Morai in Tongataboo' in pencil
on the mount below the drawing and 'atlas pl. 21'. This drawing
is probably that listed as no. 26 in Webber's Catalogue, 'The
Burying place for a family of a Chief at Amsterdam'.

At left a native group beside a hut; at centre right a man carrying
bananas on a stick slung across his shoulder, in the middle distance
the mount of the *fa'itoka*.

'The Places set apart for burying the dead are raised with Gravel
about a foot or two above the level of the Ground, on which
stand two or three Houses which are constantly shut up but
contain nothing in them; these Cemeteries called in their Language
Dano are kept very neat & clean & the Indians are generally
displeased at our approaching them. Besides these there are others
raised of Stones which are the burying places of the Chiefs & are
called Fyntocka.' Samwell in Cook, *Journals* III, 2, 1037.

Cook visited a royal *fa'itoka* in the village of Mu'a on 26 June,
but the description he gives of the scene varies in several details
from Webber's representation. *Ibid.*, 1, 138-9. However, the
fa'itoka depicted seems to be identical with the one Webber saw,
for in the official account of the voyage, in which Cook's observations are expanded by reports from other members of the expedition, an explicit reference is made to Webber: 'Mr. Webber's
drawing of this fiatooka will supply the defects of any description.'
Cook/King (1784) I, 314. As Webber played an active part in
the publication of the official account, the identification of the
scene seems beyond doubt.

Webber's drawing also echoes Anderson's description of the landscape of Tonga, which is worth quoting in part:

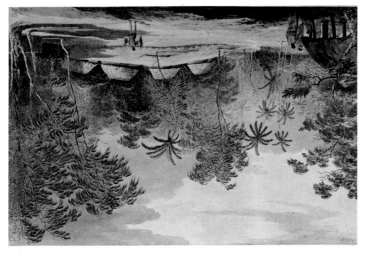

'It ought also to be observed that though the materials for forming
grand Landscapes are wanting [i.e. at Tongatapu] there are many
of what might at least be called neat prospects about the cultivated
grounds and dwelling places, but more especially about the Fy-
atokkas or burying grounds, where nature sometimes art, sometimes
nature has done much to please the eye.' Anderson in Cook,
Journals III, 2, 920.

ver: 3.60 is a preparatory drawing for this view; 3.58 and 3.59
are later versions.

ref: Cook, *Journals* III, 1, pl. 18.

British Library, London. Add MS 15513, f.11.

JOHN WEBBER

3.59   A View of a *fa'itoka*, or Burying Ground [c. 1783]
pen, wash and water-colour, 8¾ × 15⁵/₁₆ : 223 × 382, unsigned.

Inscribed 'A Fiatooka, or Morai in Tongataboo' in pencil on the folio beneath the drawing by a later hand.

ver: Same composition as 3.57 and 3.58. It corresponds both in size and composition to 3.59A and was probably done in preparation for the engraving. For a landscape study of the subject see 3.60.

ref: Murray-Oliver (1969a) pl. 108 (col.).

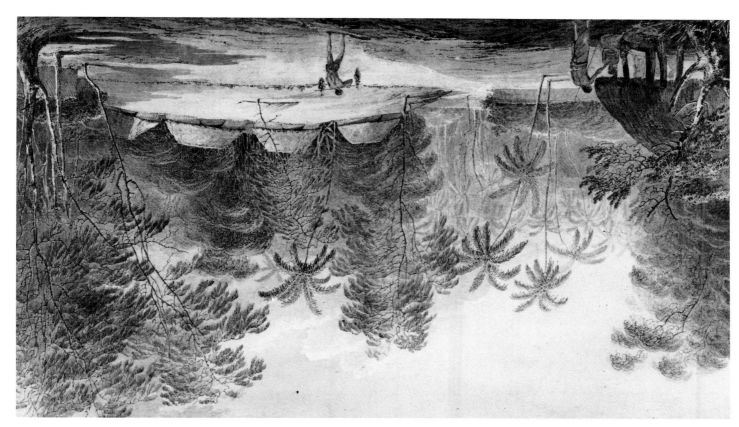

ver: The drawing depicts the same scene as 3.57 and 3.59 but varies in details of the trees and in the figures. It is larger than the latter and its colours are fresher and lighter, particularly in the sky and the earth. The drawing has the quality of a presentation work which might also explain its later date.

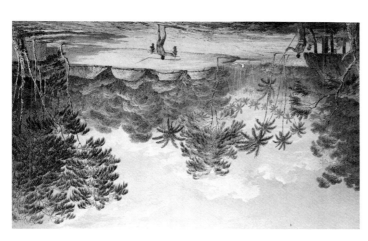

Inscribed 'A Fiatooka, or Morai in Tongataboo' in pencil by a later hand on the folio beneath the drawing.

3.58   A View of a *fa'itoka*, or Burying Ground   [1778]
[plate 43]
pen, wash and water-colour, 16 × 25⁵/₈ : 406 × 651, signed and dated 'J. Webber del 1778' (l.r.).

JOHN WEBBER

JOHN WEBBER (after)

3·59A 'A FIATOOKA, or MORAI in TONGATABOO'
Engraving. 'J. Webber del.' — 'W. Ellis sculp.'

Published in Cook/King (1784) pl. 21, I, 312-14.

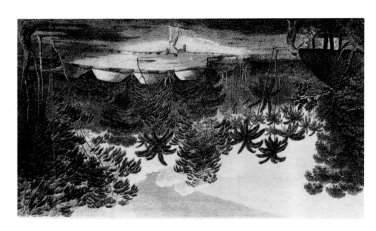

A proof-state with no letter-press nor pencil inscription, which has been touched up with grey wash for correction is kept in the National Library of Australia, Canberra, in a folio of plates from the Skottowe Hall Library.

Concerning the proper title of this engraving which was finished in November 1782, Lord Sandwich passed on the following consideration to Dr Douglas, the editor: 'The third doubt is upon the inscription a Fiatoka or Morai in Tongataboo. Is it proper to explain one Indian term by an Indian term of another country & would it not be more accurate to describe it by an English appellation calling it a Fiatoka or burial place, or perhaps a place of worship?' Letter of 19 November 1782, British Library, Egerton MS 2180, f.56.

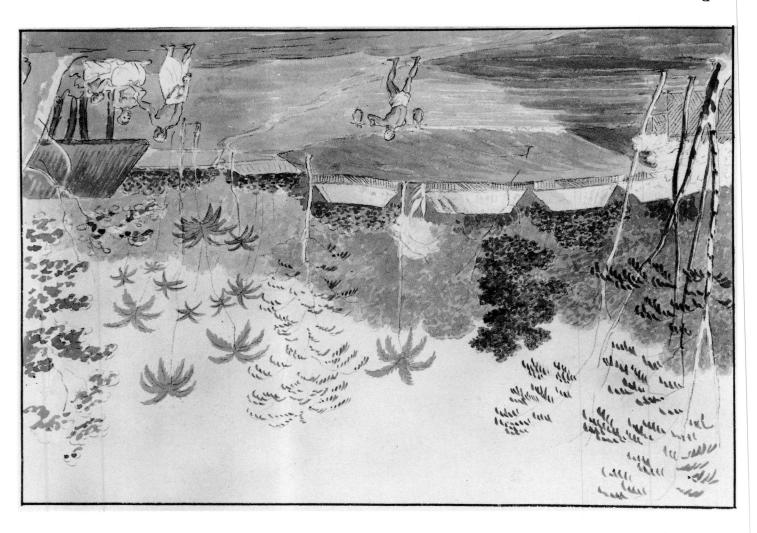

3·59B
A copy of the engraving rendered in pencil and water-colour, titled 'A Fiatoka or Morai in Tongataboo' in ink at centre below drawing is kept at the Alexander Turnbull Library, Wellington (B. 91/1). Its signature was recently identified by Ms Moira M. Long as that of Charles Hamilton Smith (1776-1859) 'an English artist who copied published engravings and lithographs' (in litt. 7 May 1984).

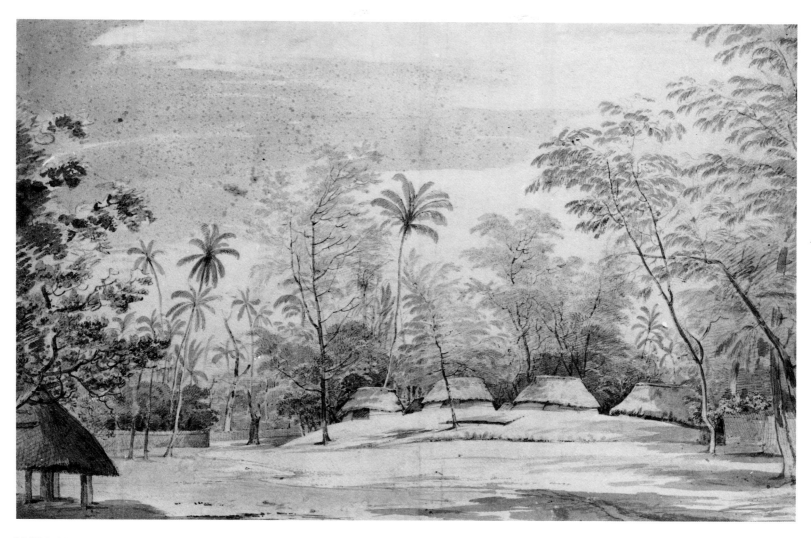

JOHN WEBBER

3.60   **A View of a fa'itoka, or Burying Ground**
                                                    [Jun 1777]
        pencil and sepia wash, 16½ × 25⅛ : 419 × 638,
        unsigned; w/m: 'J. WHATMAN'.

On verso the coastal profile of an island which is unfinished, also
some brush strokes.

ver: A preparatory drawing for 3.57, but without figures. The
         drawing may well be a field-drawing, made on the spot.

Formerly in The Public Archives of Canada, Ottawa, and presented to the National Library of Australia, on the occasion of
its opening in 1968.

National Library of Australia, Canberra. Acc. no. 3994.

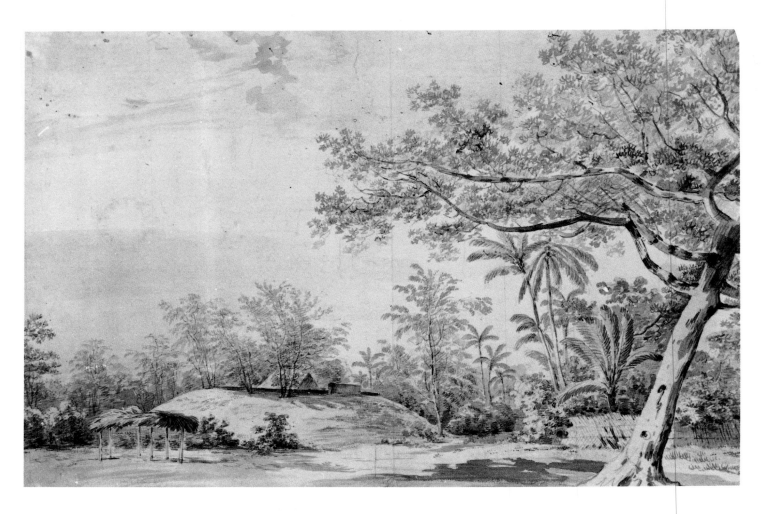

JOHN WEBBER

3.61   **[A Ceremonial Ground in Tongataboo]**
[plate 42]   **[8-9 Jul 1777]**
pencil, sepia and wash, 16½ × 25 : 419 × 635,
unsigned.

An open space with a mount and an enclosed structure in the
back. At left an open hut with thatched roof resting on six poles.
On the right a tree, and a fence. Palm trees and other trees in
the background.

The place depicted can be identified from the engraving 'The
Natche, a Ceremony in Honour of the King's son, in Tongataboo' in Cook/King (1784) pl. 22. This ceremony, called *inasi*,
took place in the village of Mua on 8 and 9 July. Anderson in
his description of the place of action speaks of a 'single fya'tocka
on the mount', Cook, *Journals* III, 2, 914 (8 July 1777) and of
'a small shade or roof near the middle of the space' or 'a royal
Canopy', ibid., 915.

Cook also refers to the ceremony, ibid., 1, 145-54.

ver: The drawing is a preparatory study to a composition which
Webber refers to in the Admiralty catalogue as no. 29: 'The
Annache or Ceremony of Inauguration of the Heriditary
Prince at Amsterdam' and which led to the engraving 3.61A.

Formerly in The Public Archives of Canada, Ottawa, and presented to the National Library of Australia, on the occasion of
its opening in 1968.

National Library of Australia, Canberra. Acc. no. 3995.

JOHN WEBBER (after)

3.61A   **'The NATCHE, a CEREMONY in HONOUR of the
KING'S SON, in TONGATABOO'**   **[plate 41]**

Engraving. 'J. Webber del.' — 'Landscape by S. Middiman' — 'Figures by J. Hall'.

Published in Cook/King (1784) pl. 22, I, 337-43.

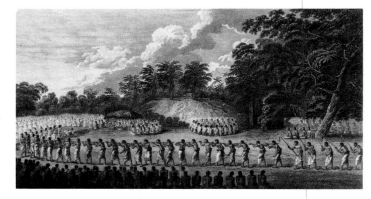

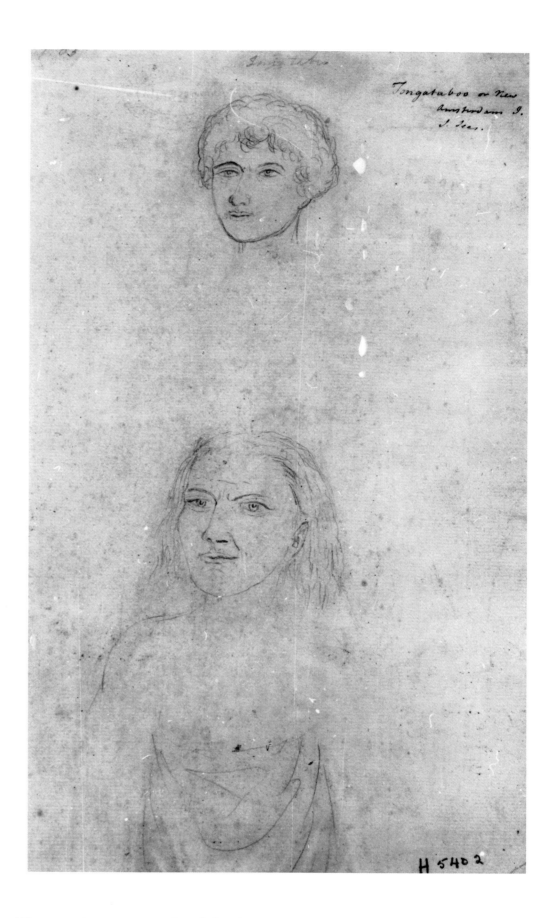

WILLIAM ELLIS

3.62   [Head Studies of Natives of Tongatapu]
[Jun, Jul 1777]
pencil, 11⅞ × 7¼ : 302 × 184, unsigned; w/m: 'GR'
under crown, surrounded by wreaths in a circle.

Inscribed 'Tongataboo' in pencil [u.c.], and 'Tongataboo [in black
ink] or New Amsterdam I. S.Seas' in brown ink (u.r.). Also
inscribed '1.03' at u.l. in pencil. On verso a pencil drawing of
a Tongan sailing canoe, see. no. 3.69. On verso inscribed '13'
(l.l.).

Pencil sketches of (a) a young man or young woman with curly
hair, of the head only, (b) of an older man, half-length, with
longish, straight hair.

Page 103 in Ellis (1782) gives no description of individual natives,
but refers to the heiva dance and to wrestling matches.

ref: Lewis (1970) 6.

La Trobe Library, State Library of Victoria, Melbourne. H. 5402.

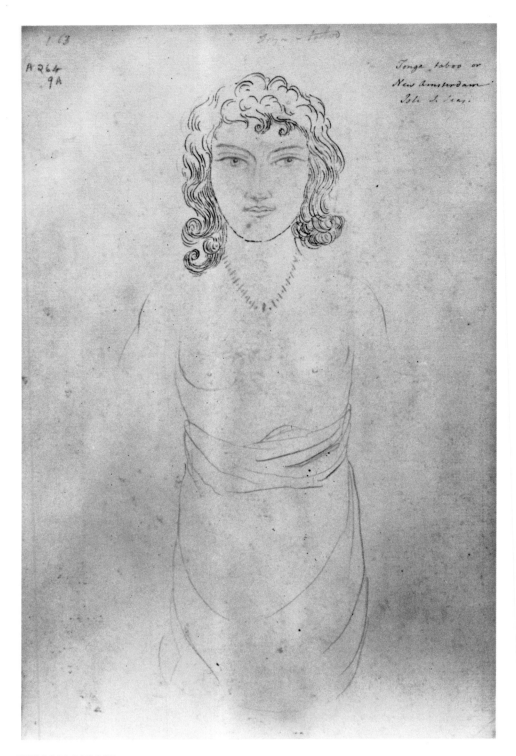

WILLIAM ELLIS

3.63   **[A Young Woman of Tongatapu]   [Jun, Jul 1777?]**
pencil and pen, 11⁷⁄₁₆ × 7½ : 290 × 190, unsigned.

Inscribed 'Tonga taboo [in black ink] or New Amsterdam Isle
S.Seas' in brown ink (u.r.), also in pencil 'Tonga-Taboo' and
(u.l.) '1.63' — a reference to Ellis (1782). On verso numbered
'14' in brown ink (l.l.). On verso is a drawing of a Tongan chief
(3.52).

A three-quarter standing figure in frontal pose; the face and hair
in ink, the body in pencil; wearing a necklace and curly hair to
the neck; bare breasts, draped from the waist.

'Long hair is a mark of distinction, and none are permitted to
wear it but the principal people. The agee* girls and women let
it hang in ringlets down to their waists, and the men likewise
wear it in the same form.' Ellis, *Narrative* (1782) I, 92. 'Round
their necks they frequently put a kind of ruff or necklace of flowers,

or leaves of various kinds which are generally chosen for their
fragrance or colour', ibid., 94. Ellis's observations appear to echo
those by Clerke, ibid., 2, 1308-9.

The reference to p.63 is puzzling, for here Ellis's *Narrative* reports
on Cook's ships leaving Anamooka and going to Ha'apai on the
suggestion of Finau. There is yet no reference of Tongatapu.

*agee: Scottish and dialect — on or to one side, awry, off from
the straight line. (Oxford English Dictionary.) Perhaps
Ellis is here referring to the Tongan dancing girls, the
movements of whom he describes in considerable detail
a little later (98-104). Compare Samwell: 'These Agee
Girls as we called them'. Cook, *Journals* III, 2, 1042.

ref: Murray-Oliver (1977) 30.

Alexander Turnbull Library, Wellington. A264.9A.

JOHN WEBBER

3.64   [A Woman of Eua] [plate 49]   [Jul 1777]
       pencil and wash, 17¾ × 12¹⁄₁₆ : 451 × 306, un-
       signed. Inscribed erroneously in pencil on the mount
       below drawing 'Woman of Sandwich Island'.

Traces of the number '18' in pencil are just decipherable (u.r.).
The drawing thus corresponds to no. 18 in Webber's Catalogue
'A Portrait of a Woman' in the section 'Friendly Isles'.

A young woman with freely flowing hair; draped beneath bare
breasts. She wears a double necklace.

Speaking about the women of the Friendly Islands, Samwell gives
the following description: 'The Women are in general handsome
tho' many among them somewhat masculine . . . They wear
much the same kind of Clothing as the men & wear necklaces
of Shells and the Legs of Fowls & some made of a small black
Seed. They are clothed from the Waist to the Knees & all the
other parts are exposed. The lower Class of young women have
their Hair cut short, while those of the Agee order wear it long
& flowing down their Shoulders which had a graceful and a truly
elegant Appearance . . .' Cook, *Journals* III, 2, 1042. But concerning the people of Eua Samwell also has this to say: 'Consid-
ering the small Distance between this Island and Tongataboo the
difference between the Natives is remarkable, these being a small
sized mean-looking People in comparison with the others & the
women in general are not so handsome'. Ibid., 2, 1050-1.

To King we owe some illuminating remarks about the head dress
of the women of the Friendly Isles: 'they are still more various
in their fashion of wearing it [their hair], being cut short on some
parts & others left long, yet as they seem to admire fine long hair,
we rather suppose that when it is even partially cut & we know
it to be the case when all short, that is in memory of some deceas'd
friend'. Ibid., 2, 1365.

ver: Engraved in reverse (3.64A). A copy of this drawing of the
       late nineteenth century is in the Bernice P. Bishop Museum,
       Honolulu, titled erroneously 'Woman of Sandwich Islands
       (Webber 1793)'.

British Library, London. Add MS 15513 f.12.

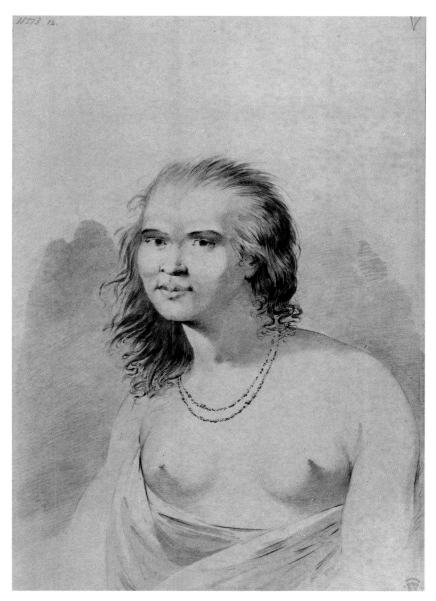

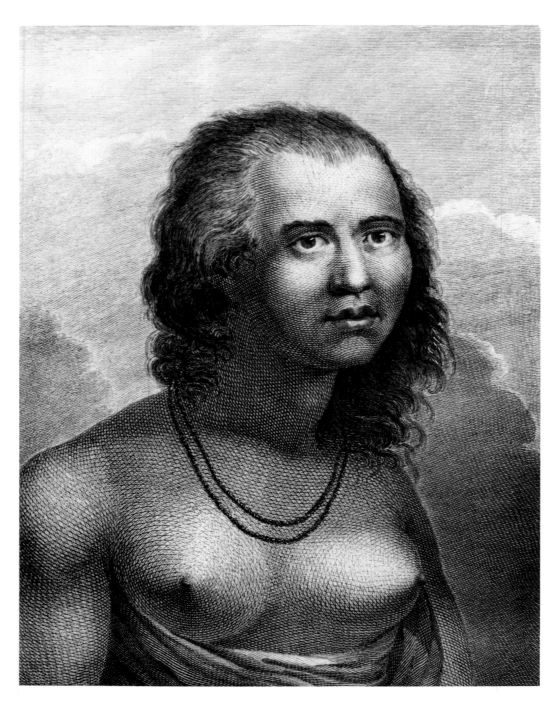

JOHN WEBBER (after)

3.64A 'A WOMAN of EAOO'
Engraving. 'J. Webber del.' — 'J. Hall sculp.'

Published in Cook/King (1784) pl.23.

ver: A proof-state inscribed in pencil 'A Woman — friendly
Isles. Eoao' in Webber's hand, numbered in pencil 'N°. 17'
(u.r.) with the letter-press 'John Hall Sculp 1783' and
'Drawn by John Webber' is kept in the National Library
of Australia, Canberra, in a folio of plates from the Skottowe
Hall Library.

Another copy thus inscribed and dated is preserved in the
Mitchell Library, Sydney. PXD 59⁻ⁱ, f.74a.

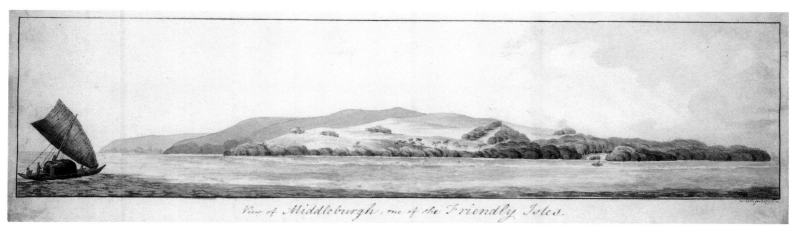

View of Middleburgh, one of the Friendly Isles.

WILLIAM ELLIS

3.65 **View of Middleburgh, one of the Friendly Isles**

[1777]

pen and brown ink and water-colour, 5⅞ × 20¾ : 15 × 52.5. Signed and dated (l.r.) 'W. Ellis fect. 1777'.

Inscribed in ink as above along lower margin. The drawing is pasted to a mount, w/m '[I.TA]YLOR'.

A view of Eua (Middleburg), one of the Friendly or Tongan Islands. A native canoe on the left, manned by four figures. A reef along the island coast, with a small native boat at a distance.

'Middleburg, or Eaoowe, is to the northward of Amsterdam, in lat. 21 degr. 21 min. S. This island is by far the most pleasant of the whole, and is interspersed with lawns, hills and dales, as beautiful as can be conceived. The soil upon the hills is nearly of the colour of red-oker, that in the vallies black and rich.' Ellis, (1782) I, 87-8.

ver: In his Catalogue Webber lists 'A View of the Island of Middleburg' (no. 28). That drawing has not been identified, but could be identical with a coastal view in water-colour in the Alexander Turnbull Library, Wellington (B. 41/44). It was hitherto attributed to William Ellis, as part of the Ellis group of drawings in the Alexander Turnbull Library, but its free and fluent water-colour style suggests an attribution to John Webber. See the forthcoming volume of *Charts and Views of Captain Cook's Voyages*, III.

Both 3.65 and 3.66 are heavily indebted to the view in the Alexander Turnbull Library. The sailing boat corresponds closely with a drawing by Ellis (3.67).

For a slightly larger version of this view see 3.66. Both versions are similarly inscribed except for the 'h' in 'Middelburgh' (3.65).

ref: Sotheby's *Cat.* 26 January 1984, lot 91.

Rhona Townley Searle Collection

Bernice P. Bishop Museum, Honolulu. Inv. no. 1984.122.

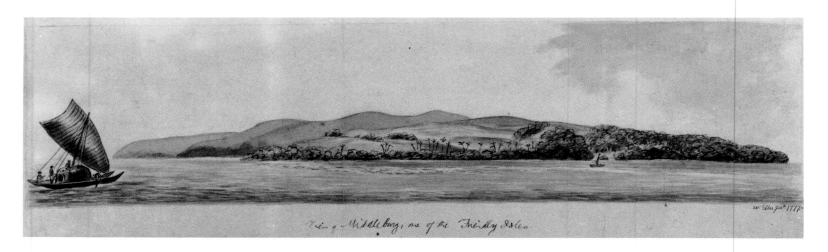

View of Middelburg, one of the Friendly Isles.

WILLIAM ELLIS (after)

3.66   **View of Middelburg, one of the Friendly Isles**

[1777]

water-colour over pencil, 6¼ × 20⅞ : 159 × 530, signed and dated 'W. Ellis fec^t 1777'. The title as above inscribed in ink across lower margin; w/m: shield and crown [cut off].

ver: For another version see 3.65.

Collection of Captain A.W.F. Fuller.

National Maritime Museum, London.

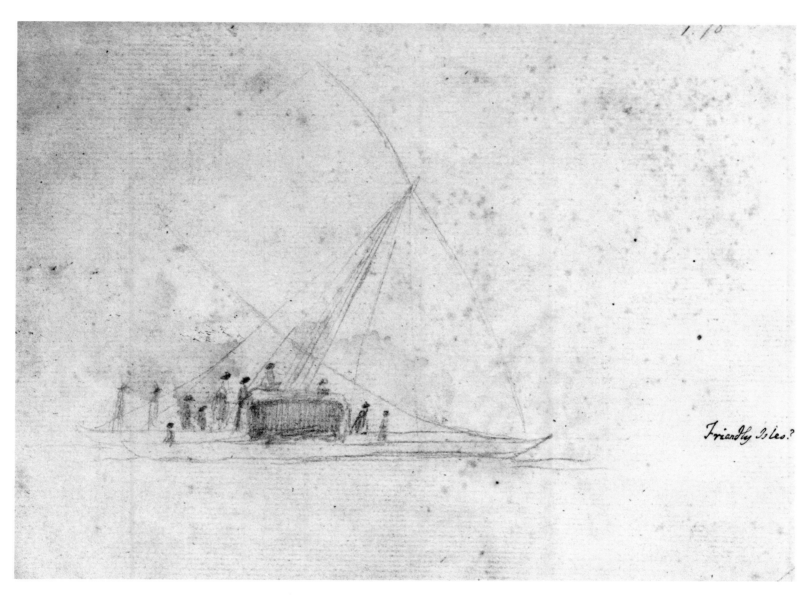

WILLIAM ELLIS

3.67   [A Double Canoe]   [Jun, Jul 1777]
        pencil, 5½ × 7½ : 140 × 190, unsigned,

Inscribed 'Friendly Isles?' in black ink at right hand side, numbered in pencil '1.70' (u.r.), referring to Ellis (1782). On verso inscribed in ink '17' in corner (l.l.).

A slight sketch of a large double canoe containing eleven figures, some seated, some standing. The canoe (*tongia*) may represent the same as 3.69, but seen from the other side. For the type of canoe depicted see Haddon and Hornell (1936) I, 265-72. The canoe is similar to the one incorporated in Ellis's drawing of a 'View of Middleburgh' (3.65).

'The canoes of these islands are without exception the best we ever saw: the double ones are made large enough to carry fifty or sixty people, and sail at a great rate. Upon them they generally fix or erect a hut or shed which is for the reception of the master and his wives and family.' Ellis (1782) I, 110.

ref: Murray-Oliver (1977) 31.

Alexander Turnbull Library, Wellington. A264.11.

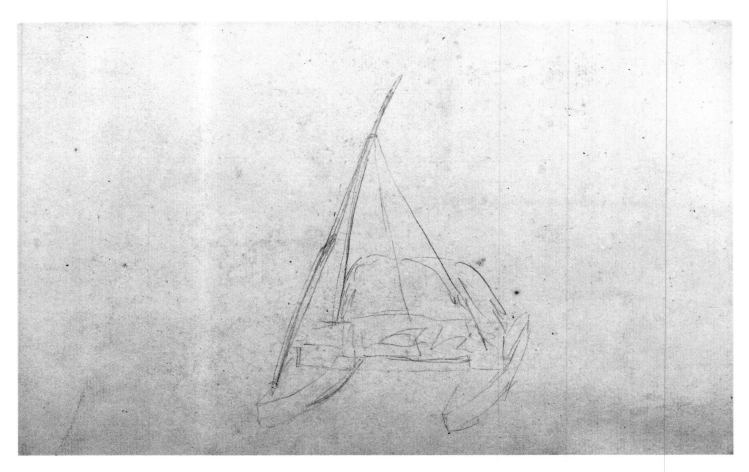

WILLIAM ELLIS

3.68 **[A Double Canoe]** **[Jun, Jul 1777]**
pencil, 7¼ × 12³⁄₁₆ : 184 × 310, unsigned; w/m:
'GR' under crown, surrounded by wreaths in a circle.

Inscribed in ink '26' in corner (u.l.). On verso is a drawing of part of the coast-line of Anamooka (3.41a).

A slight field-sketch of the same type of canoe as represented in 3.54, seen from the front.

ref: Murray-Oliver (1977) 31.

Alexander Turnbull Library, Wellington. A264.13B.

WILLIAM ELLIS

3.69 **[A Sailing Canoe]** **[Jun, Jul 1777]**
pencil, 11⅞ × 7¼ : 302 × 184, unsigned.

An erroneous inscription 'New Zealand' (u.l.), 'by W. Ellis' (u.r.), both in pencil. Inscribed no '13' in brown ink (l.l.).

On verso is a drawing of two natives of Tongataboo, see 3.62.

A large sailing canoe with a house or stage in the middle, crowded with figures. It appears to be a *tongiaki* with Kalia features similar to the one in 3.67, but seen from the other side. For the squid-like design on the sail compare a drawing by Hodges 2.78. For a canoe of this type see Haddon and Hornell (1936) I, 271, also 266 where the figure of a cock on the sail is discussed.

ref: Lewis (1970) 6.

La Trobe Library, State Library of Victoria, Melbourne. H 5402.

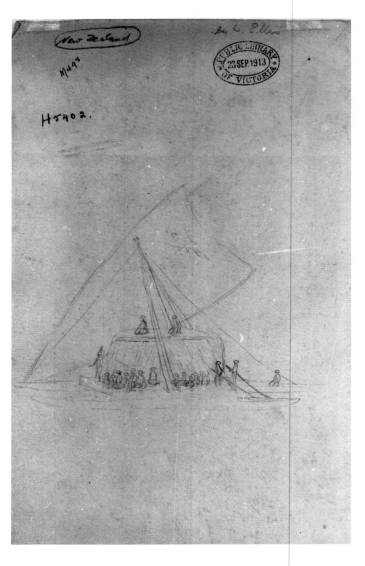

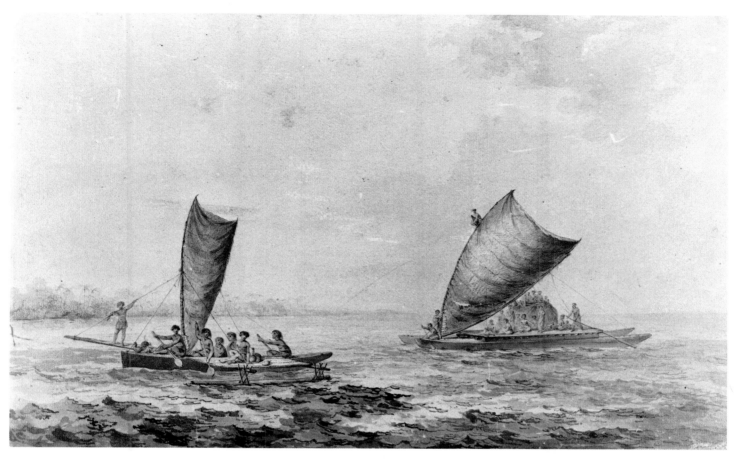

JOHN WEBBER

3.70   **Canoes of the Friendly Islands**   [1777]
pen and wash, 12¼ × 19¼ : 311 × 489, a signature,
possibly 'Webber 1777' has been scratched out at l.r.
and is now indecipherable.

This drawing may be the one referred to in Webber's Catalogue
under 'The Friendly Islands' as '19. Sailing Canoes'. The sheet
has been cut down, leaving only the inner edge of the ink framing
lines, and mounted on card. The surface has been varnished,
leaving lighter edges which suggest that the drawing was once
framed. Endorsed twice in ink 'Lot No 3'.

Two sailing canoes manned by natives, some paddling. The canoe
at right has a grass hut built on it. There is a man on a lookout
at the top of the mast. A palm-lined shore in the distance at left.

Samwell describes the two kinds of canoes of the Friendly Isles:
'Their canoes are of two Sorts, double & single and of a very
curious construction & well finished & must cost them much
Labour, they consist of several pieces of plank very ingeniously
adapted to each other & sewed together on the inside of the
Canoe; the single ones are in general large enough to hold six
people, have an outrigger to them & are covered over with a deck
at the Head and Stern under which they stow the different articles
they carry in them. On these decks they fasten 10 or a dozen
white Shells as ornaments & at the stern there is a Support for
a fishing rod which they generally carry along with them. The
double or sailing Canoes are built large & strong with a Stage,
on which a Hut is built. Some of them are capable of carrying
80 or 100 Men & can keep the Sea a long time in these Latitudes.
Their Sails are made of strong Matting & have generally the
Image of a Cock upon them.' Cook, *Journals* III, 2, 1038.

For the types of canoes represented see Haddon and Hornell
(1936) I, 265-72.

ver: For a field-sketch of the left canoe see 3.71.

Dixson Library, State Library of New South Wales, Sydney.
Pf. 52.

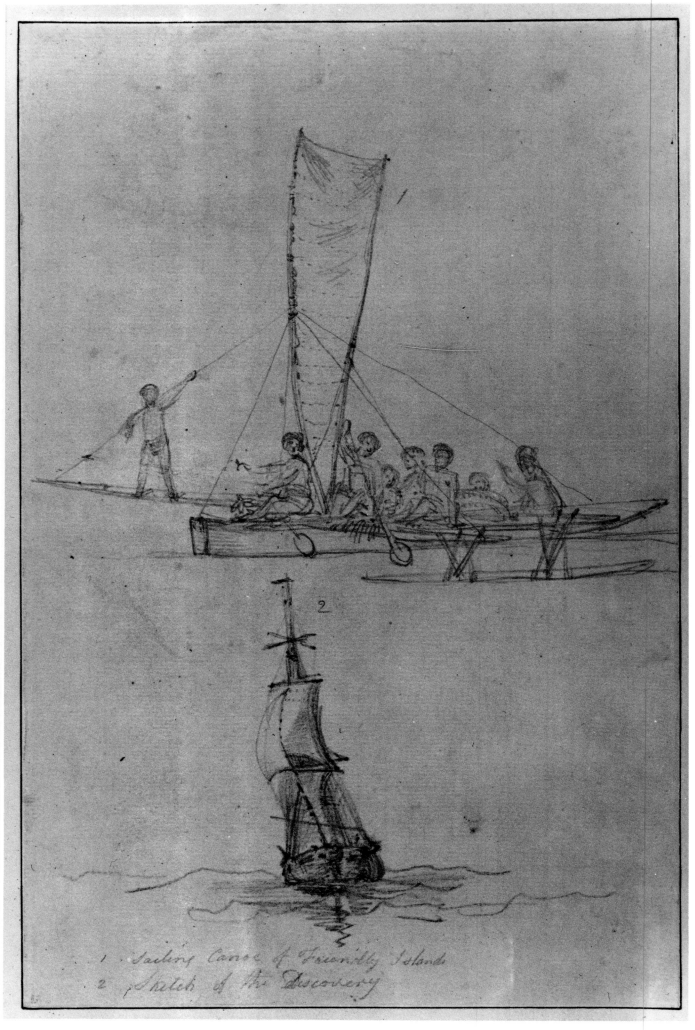

1 Sailing Canoe of Friendly Islands
2 Sketch of the Discovery

334

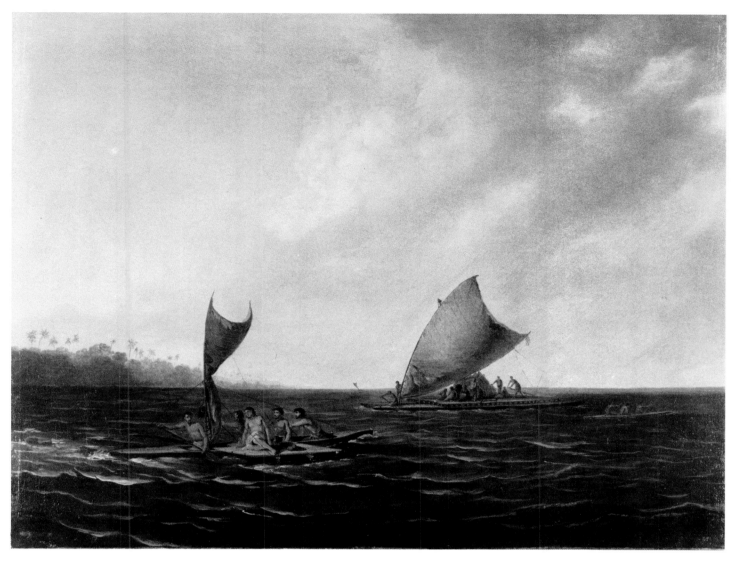

JOHN WEBBER

3.71   **Sailing Canoe of [the] Friendly Islands [and] Sketch of the *Discovery***   **[c. May-Jul 1777]**
pencil, 10⅞ × 7⅛ : 276 × 181, unsigned; w/m; 'GR' under crown.

The title as above inscribed in pencil along the lower edge of the sheet. On verso some quick sketches of sails and riggings.

ver: For a more finished version of the canoe see 3.70.

National Maritime Museum, London. (In volume of plates to Cook's voyages.)

JOHN WEBBER

3.72   **Boats of the Friendly Islands**   **[c. 1791]**
oil on canvas, 19 × 25 : 482 × 635.

Two Tongan sailing canoes in open water, view of an island to the left. The front canoe is manned by five people, one is a woman.

For the types of canoes see Haddon and Hornell (1936), I, 260-1, 271 (where 3.73A is reproduced).

ver: For other versions of this subject see 3.70 and 3.73.

The Earl of Portsmouth, Barton House, 1937 (Christie's 18 June 1971 (27)); resold Sotheby's Belgravia 20 March 1973 (20), purchased by Roy Miles, Fine Paintings Ltd, London, in the late 1970s sold to present owner.

Peabody Museum, Salem.

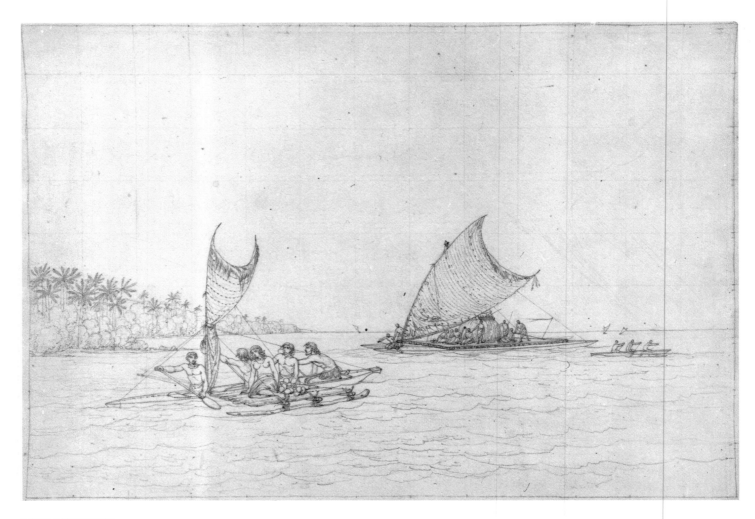

JOHN WEBBER

3.73 **Boats of the Friendly Islands** [c. 1791]
pencil, 12¼ × 17 : 311 × 432 (sheet-size); 11¼ × 16⁷⁄₁₆ : 287 × 418 (image-size); w/m: lily in shield under crown, below 'W' = Whatman.

The drawing is squared for transfer and most likely a preparatory study for Webber's softground etching of the above title, published on 1 August 1791 (3.73A).

Close comparison between this drawing and Webber's print reveals a number of small but significant differences, for example, variations in the grouping of the figures in the second boat; in the drawing there are more figures and more fruit in the boat.

There also is a little boat in the offing left of the big canoe at the back, and diagonal pencil lines in the sky which seem to suggest rain or sun rays. These differences suggest that the drawing is an original work by Webber and not a copy after the print.

Eyre and Hobhouse, London (1984).

Private collection, England.

JOHN WEBBER

3.73A **a. 'Boats of the Friendly Islands'**
softground etching, tinted in brown and grey wash, or hand-coloured, 12¾ × 17⅝ : 324 × 447 (11⅜ × 16⁷⁄₁₆ : 288 × 417) 'J. Webber R.A. fecit'. 'Publish'd Aug.ᵗ 1 1791 by J. Webber H.ᵒ 312 Oxford Street'. 'Vide Cook's last voyage Vol. II [sic. for I] Bk II Chap. IV'.

British Museum, Department of Prints and Drawings, London, 246˙ a.2. and C.6.˙.

336

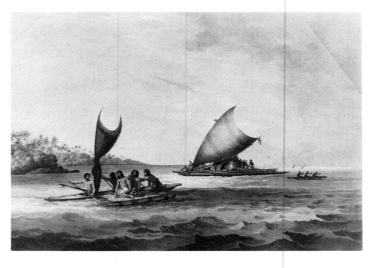

b. 'Boats of the Friendly Islands'
coloured aquatint. 'J. Webber R.A. fecit'. 'London Pub.ᵈ April 1 1809 by Boydell & Comp.ʸ N.ᵒ 90, Cheapside'. 'Vide Cooks last Voyage Vol. II [sic. for I] Bk II Chap. IV'.

Issued by J. Boydell, *Views in the South Seas*, London 1808, pl. II.

National Maritime Museum, London; Bernice P. Bishop Museum, Honolulu.

JOHN WEBBER (or after)

3.74   **Canoes of the Friendly Islands**   [May, Jul 1777]
        pen and water-colour on cardboard, 10⅝ × 16⅛ : 270
        × 410, unsigned.

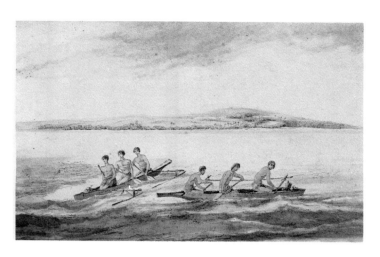

On verso in ink 'Mr [?] Archdeacon' and in pencil 'J. Archdeacon'
as well as 'of an island in the Pacific Ocean taken from an outline
lent me by Capt.ⁿ D. Roberts RN' in ink (apparently cut off to
the left).

Two outrigger canoes, each paddled by three natives. The coast-
line of an island in the background. The canoes may be related
to the *tafa'anga* type used for inshore fishing, see Haddon and
Hornell (1936) I, 259-61.

'Capt.ⁿ D. Roberts' probably refers to Captain David Roberts,
son of Henry Roberts, who inscribed Henry Roberts's log in the
Dixson Library on 1 May 1859 as 'a retired Captain in the Royal
Navy'. The inscription on verso reads as if the drawing was done
(in the nineteenth century) from an outline lent by Captain
Roberts. However the drawing gives very much an eighteenth
century impression and at first sight seems to resemble the works
of John Webber, particularly the rowers. Also some parts of the
island's landscape are rendered with some delicacy, especially the
slopes. On the other hand the drawing is executed on cardboard
which is unusual for Webber's working method, some of the
colours, like those of the sky and those for the waves are somewhat
smudgy and not quite in Webber's style. Is then the drawing a
nineteenth century copy of a Webber drawing, which had remained in Roberts's family? The copyist, if he can be termed as
such, Mr Archdeacon, is not known as an artist, and the circumstances which led to this drawing presently remain unknown.
Because of the type of the canoes depicted the scene is tentatively
identified as in the Friendly Isles.

National Library of Australia, Canberra. Rex Nan Kivell Collection. NK 2185.

WILLIAM ELLIS

3.75   **[A Canoe with two Tongans.]**   [c. May-Jul 1777]
        pencil and pen, 6⁷⁄₁₆ × 7⁹⁄₁₆ : 164 × 192, un-
        signed; w/m: 'GR' under crown, surrounded by wreaths,
        in a circle.

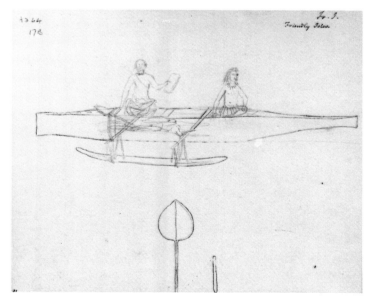

Inscribed 'Fr.I. Friendly Isles' in black and brown ink; numbered
'21' in brown ink (l.l.). On verso the portrait drawing of a native
woman (3.80).

Two figures in an outrigger canoe of the *tafa'anga* type, one holding
a rectangular object; below the blade of a paddle.
For the type of canoe see Haddon and Hornell (1936) I, 259-61.

ver: The canoe is of a similar type as the canoe in 3.74. For
          the same boat laterally reversed see 3.75A.

ref: Murray-Oliver (1977) 32.

Alexander Turnbull Library, Wellington. A264.17B

WILLIAM ELLIS (after)

3.75A   **'A Canoe of the Friendly Islands'**
        Engraving. 'W. Ellis del.' — 'W. Walker sculp.' 'Pub-
        lished Dec.ʳ 14 1781, by G. Robinson'.

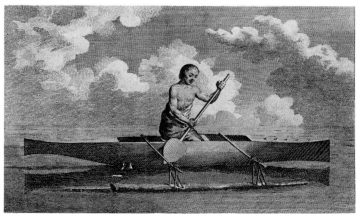

Published in Ellis (1782) I, f.p. 110.

No drawing for this engraving is known but it may have been
based on 3.75 and 3.76.

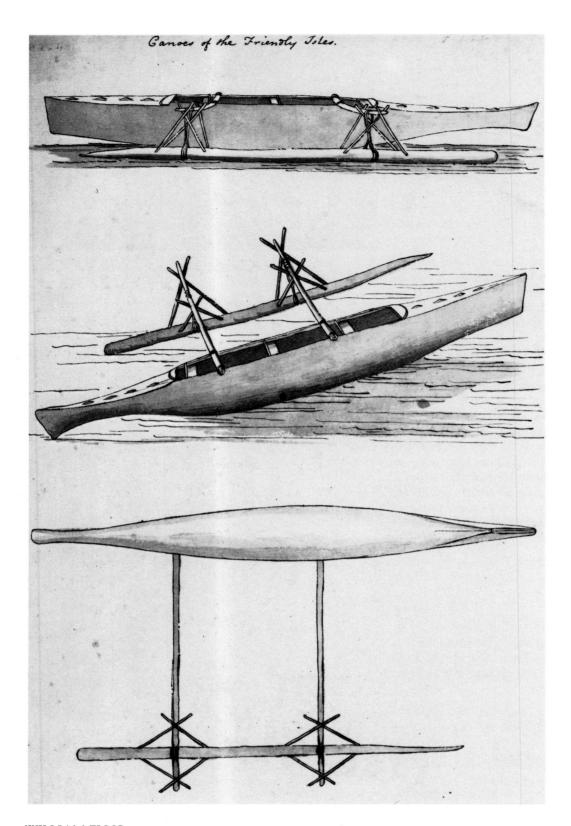

WILLIAM ELLIS

3.76   Canoes of the Friendly Isles   [May–Jul 1777–]
pen and wash, $11^5/_8 \times 7^9/_{16}$: 295 × 192, unsigned;
w/m: 'Pro Patria' with Britannia.

The title as above inscribed in brown ink across the upper edge of the sheet. Numbered in pencil (u.r.) '1.59.70' crossed out, '1.110' substituted; referring to Ellis (1782). On verso inscribed '29' in brown ink in corner (l.l.).

Showing the mode of construction of an outrigger canoe, (a) side view, (b) from above and to side, (c) in plan, when inverted.

'The canoes of these islands are without exception the best we ever saw: They are all made of the breadfruit-tree, which is an exceeding light wood: the workmanship is very neat, and they appear on the outside as if composed of one solid piece: but upon closer inspection, you find that they consist of a great number, which fit exactly one with the other, and by means of a ledge on the inside are secured together with coconut line. The single ones are furnished with an outrigger.' Ellis, (1782) I, 110.

ver: The canoe represented is of the same kind as in 3.75 and 3.75A.

ref: Murray-Oliver (1977) 32, pl. 4.

Alexander Turnbull Library, Wellington. A 264.18.

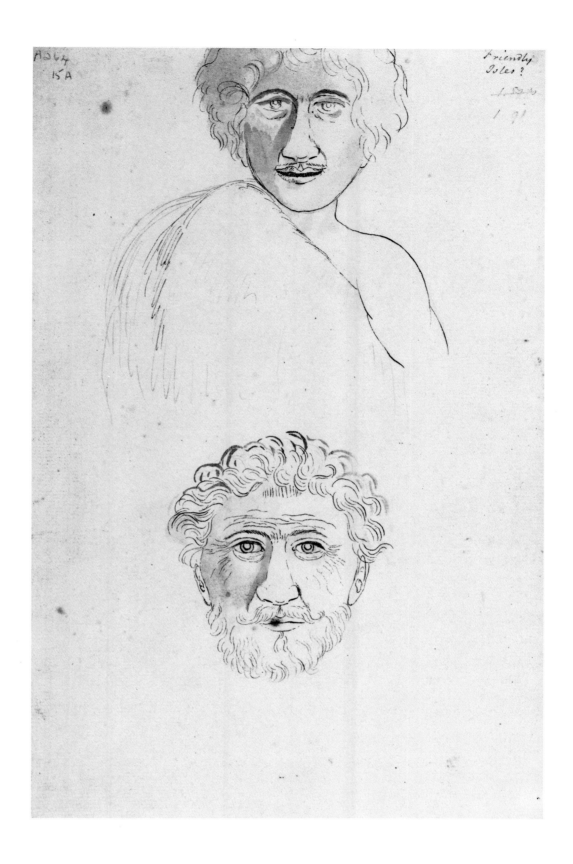

WILLIAM ELLIS

3.77   [Portraits of Two Men]   [c. May-Jul 1777]
pen and wash, 11½ × 7⁵⁄₁₆ : 291 × 186, unsigned;
w/m: 'GR' under a crown, surrounded by wreaths, in
a circle.

Inscribed 'Friendly Isles?' in black ink in corner (u.r.), beneath
it in pencil '1.59.70' crossed out and corrected to '1.91', referring
to Ellis (1782). On verso inscribed in ink '20'. On verso several
studies of different heads and faces of girls and a child, also the
study of an arm and a hand, see 3.424.

(a) Head and shoulders of a young man with a light moustache
and curly hair wearing a cloak over the right shoulder; (b) head
of an old man; both full-face.

'The people of both sexes are tall, well made, and exactly pro-
portioned. We did not see one instance of deformity amongst
them. The men are in general above the middle size, but now
and then you meet with one below that standard.' Ellis, (1782)
I, 91.

These and the following three drawings (3.78-3.80) are listed at
the end of this section since from the somewhat doubtful inscriptions, it is uncertain whether the sitters are Tongan.

ref: Murray-Oliver (1977) 32.

Alexander Turnbull Library, Wellington. A264.15A.

WILLIAM ELLIS

3.78 [Portraits of Two Men] [May, Jul 1777]
ink, wash and pencil, 11½ × 6⅞ : 292 × 175,
unsigned.

Inscribed 'Friendly Isles?' in black ink in corner (u.r.), and numbered '1.91' in pencil referring to Ellis (1782). On verso numbered '25' in brown ink (l.l.).

For two other portrait studies of a man on verso see 3.79.

(a) Full-face with short, wavy hair, small moustache and beard, (b) in profile with matted, wispy hair, a fuller beard and a moustache.

ref: Murray-Oliver (1977) 32.

Alexander Turnbull Library, Wellington. A264.16A.

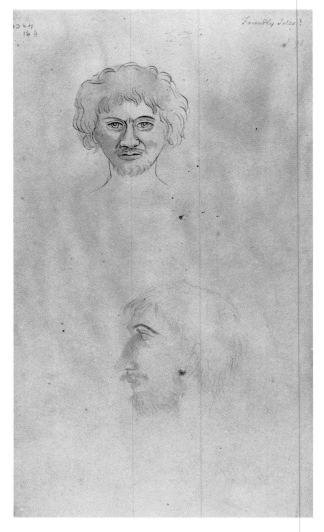

WILLIAM ELLIS

3.79 [Two studies of a Man's Head] [May-Jul 1777]
pencil and wash, 11⅜ × 6¹⁵⁄₁₆ : 290 × 176,
unsigned.

Inscribed 'Friendly Isles?' in black ink in corner (u.r.) and numbered in pencil '1.59.70' crossed out and '1.91' substituted, referring to Ellis (1782). Inscribed '25' in brown ink (l.l.). On verso is the drawing of portraits of natives, see 3.78.

The upper head is in three-quarter view facing left, wearing a light moustache and beard; the lower, in profile, with a heavier beard. Apparently different positions of the same head. Another head in faint but partly erased pencil lines is visible above the upper portrait.

ref: Murray-Oliver (1977) 32; Ellis (1782) 91.

Alexander Turnbull Library, Wellington. A264.16B.

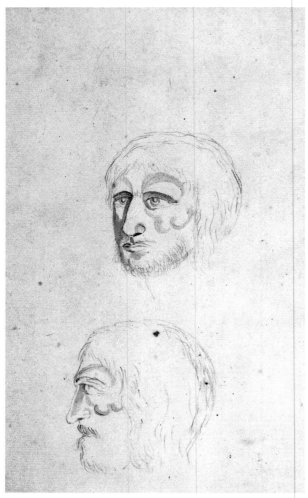

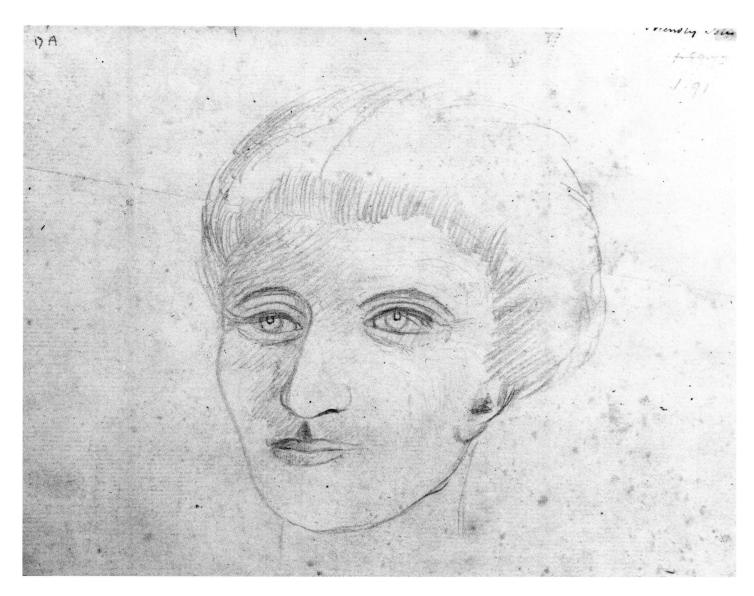

WILLIAM ELLIS

3.80   **[Portrait of a Woman]**   **[May-Jul 1777]**
pencil, 6⁷⁄₁₆ × 7⁹⁄₁₆ : 164 × 192, unsigned;
w/m: 'GR' under a crown surrounded by wreaths, in a
circle.

Inscribed 'Friendly Isles?' in black ink (u.r.) and numbered in
pencil '1.59.70', crossed out and '1.91' substituted, referring to
Ellis (1782). On verso the drawing of a canoe manned by two
natives, see 3.75. On verso numbered '21' in brown ink (l.l.).

A sketch portrait, with some hatched shading over forehead and
left cheek. Looking slightly towards the left, with hair brushed
up from face and neck.

'The women are tall in proportion, and rather masculine. Their
complexion is dark olive, but in those who are exposed to the
effects of the weather it is much darker, while those whose superior
station in life entitles them to a greater degree of indulgence, are
considerably lighter.' Ellis (1782) 91.

ref: Murray-Oliver (1977) 32.

Alexander Turnbull Library, Wellington. A264.17A.

VAITEPIHA BAY, TAHITI

12 to 23 August 1777   3.81–3.95A

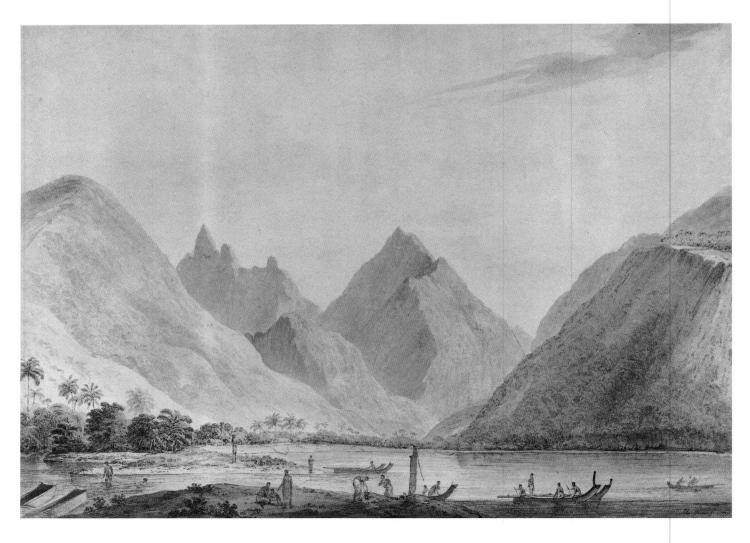

JOHN WEBBER

3.81   **A View in Vaitepiha Bay [plate 50]   [Aug 1777–]**
wash and water-colour, $17\frac{3}{4} \times 25 : 450 \times 635$, signed
and dated 'John Webber 1777' (l.r.).

The drawing may be tentatively identified as no. 53 'A Ditto'
['A View of Oaite Pehu Bay'] in Webber's Catalogue. The colours
have paled due to exposure to light.

A view looking up the Tautira Valley from the bay. In the
foreground boats and Tahitians, swimming, rowing, conversing.
In the background a peaked mountain flanked by mountain ranges
on either side. In the left central mid-distance a wooden post in
the form of a figure. In the extreme left foreground the end of
a double canoe.

ver: Compare with similar views in 3.82, 3.83 and 3.84.

ref: Brewington (1968) no. 1744, 455.

Peabody Museum, Salem. Gift of Stephen W. Phillips, 1947.
M. 12464.

342

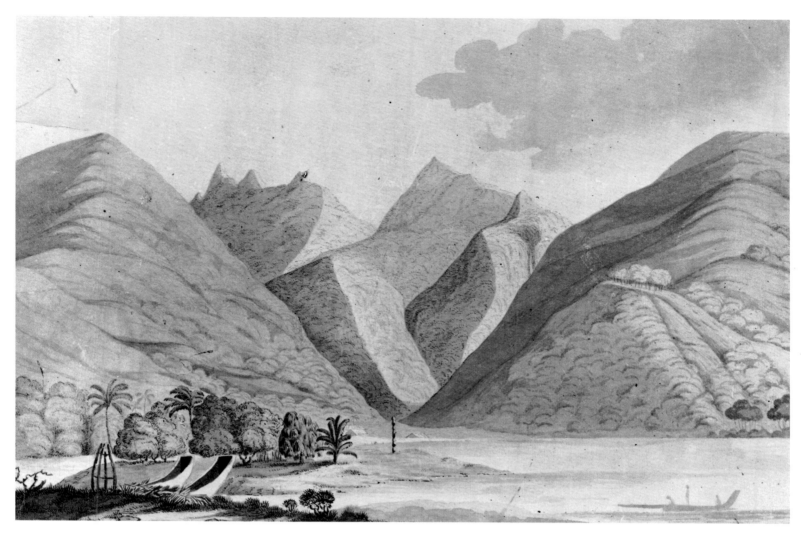

WILLIAM ELLIS (?)

3.82   **[A View in Vaitepiha Bay]**   **[Aug 1777–]**
pen, wash and water-colour, 12¼ × 17¹⁵⁄₁₆ : 311
× 455, unsigned.

The colour has faded and the paper has browned, some abrasions
and ink splashed on the surface. Mounted on a sheet, and separated from volume PXD 59⁻¹ where it was fol. 124.

A double canoe partly obscured by the slope of the left foreground;
another canoe in silhouette with three figures in the right foreground; a carved post in the central mid-distance; a group of trees
to the left and across the bay in the distance two native houses;
a mountainous background.

About Vaitepiha Bay Ellis says: 'The face of the country here
exhibits a very different appearance from that of the Friendly
Isles. Mountains and vallies, hills and dales, and in short everything, conspire to form the most romantic views imaginable
. . . At a little distance from the ships was a remarkably pleasant
valley, which ran winding between the mountains to a great
distance; in the midst of it is a fine stream of water, which at the
head of the valley takes its rise from a beautiful cascade that
appears to burst out of the rocks.

'On each side of the stream are placed the houses of the natives,
interspersed with plantations of bananas, coco nuts, breadfruit
and a kind of apple-tree; the lofty hills on each side, whose tops
reach beyond the clouds, the variety of birds, which are contin-
ually flying from place to place, and the noise of the falling water,
re-echoed by the surrounding hills, afford a scene striking beyond
description.' Ellis (1782) 128-9.

The passage echoes George Forster's lyrical description of the
landscape around Vaitepiha Bay in his *Voyage round the world*,
(London, 1777) I, 268-9.

Inscribed on the mount in ink 'Original Water-Colour sketch by
J. Webber. Made on Cook's third Voyage' and later crossed out.
To the right in a more recent hand in pencil 'View in Vaitepiha
Bay, Tahiti. Has been ascribed to Webber but shows same view,
except for minor variations as the signed and dated water-colour
by W. Ellis in the Bernice P. Bishop Museum (Beaglehole, vol.
3, pl. 21).' See 3.83.

Mitchell Library, State Library of New South Wales, Sydney.
PXD 59⁻² f.7.

WILLIAM ELLIS

3.83   **A View in Vaitepiha Bay**   [Aug 1777–]
wash and water-colour, $12^{3}/_{16} \times 19^{5}/_{16}$: 310
× 490, signed and dated 'W. Ellis fec^t 1777' in brown
ink (l.r.); w/m: (partial) 'VDL' = Van der Ley.

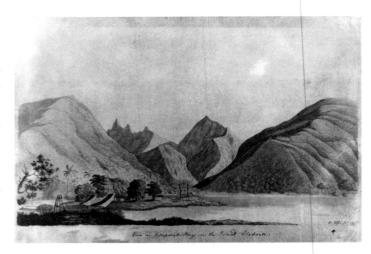

Inscribed 'View in Oitapeeah Bay, in the Island Otaheite' in ink
below the drawing, also 'no 6' (l.l.).

A double canoe in the left foreground; a carved post in the central
mid-distance, and beyond it Tahitian habitations. The post has
been identified as a *potua-ruu*, which was set up when a *rahui* or
food raising tabu was declared. Henry (1928) 209.

ver: For the same view see 3.81 by Webber and 3.82 by Ellis.

ref: Cook, *Journals* III, 1, pl. 21; Kaeppler (1978a) fig. 47 (col).

Museum Book Store, London, *Cat.* 94 (1924) 562/2 and again
in *Cat.* 107 (1928) 44/2, purch. by Governor George R. Carter.
Carter originally bought no. 9, titled 'View of part of the Beach
in Kealakeakua Bay'. When this title was found to be erroneous,
Carter returned the drawing in exchange for this one.

Bernice P. Bishop Museum, Honolulu. Acc. no. 1928.167 (Gift
of Gov. G. R. Carter).

WILLIAM ELLIS

3.84   **A View in Vaitepiha Bay**   [Aug 1777–]
pen, wash and water-colour, $12^{5}/_{8} \times 18^{1}/_{2}$: 326 × 470,
signed and dated 'W.W. Ellis pinx^{t}et delin^t 1777' in
brown ink (l.r.). Endorsed in brown ink: 'An Island
View in Oitapeeah Bay, in the Island Otaheite'. A
trace of an indecipherable number (u.l.); w/m: lily in
shield under crown, with the initials 'GR' below.

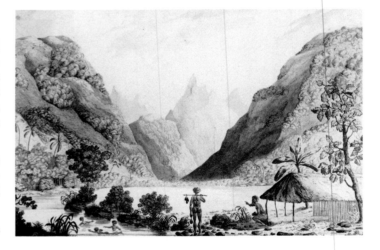

A deep valley with pointed peaks in the background. Three
natives swimming at left; another one standing by the river holding a stick across his shoulder with suspended fruit; a fifth seated
near a hut at right.

ver: For a study of the hut and a Tahitian with a pole on his
shoulder see 3.85.

ref: Rienits (1968) 119.

National Library of Australia, Canberra. Rex Nan Kivell Collection. NK 6577.

344

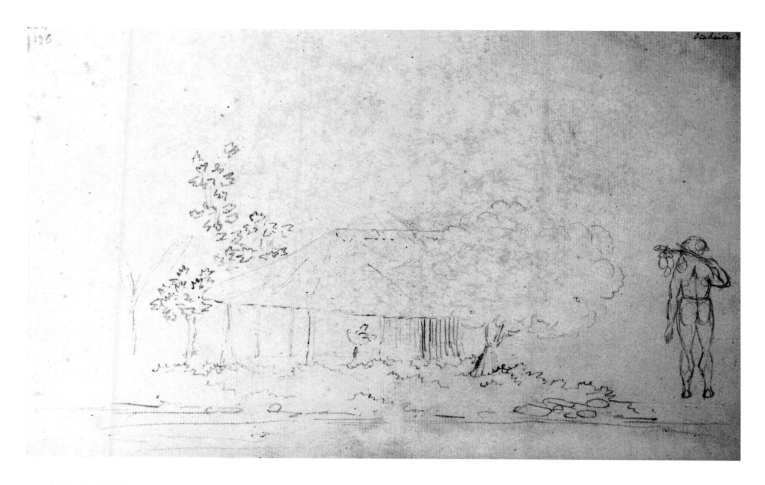

WILLIAM ELLIS

3.85   [A Tahitian and a Hut]   [Aug 1777]
        pencil, 7⁹⁄₁₆ × 12¼ : 192 × 311, unsigned; w/m:
        'Pro Patria' with Britannia.

Inscribed 'Otaheite?' in black ink in corner (u.r.), numbered '5'
in ink (l.r.) and 'e' (l.l.). On verso is a drawing of the Chief
Mourner of Tahiti (see 3.112).

A lightly drawn field-sketch. A small house among trees with at
right a back view of a man carrying fruit over his shoulder on a
stick.

ver: A study for the water-colour at 3.84.

ref: Murray-Oliver (1977) 33.

Alexander Turnbull Library, Wellington. A264.19B.

JOHN WEBBER

3.86 **A View in Vaitepiha Valley** [plate 51] [Aug 1777]
pen, wash and water-colour, 17⅝ × 25 : 447 × 635,
signed 'View of Hothiheite Peha drawn from nature by
John Webber del ['del' crossed out and replaced by 'in']
1777'.

Inscribed 'A View of Otaheite Peha' in pencil on lower mount,
and numbered '52' (u.r.), thus corresponding to the drawing of
'A view of Oaite Pehu Bay' no. 52 in Webber's Catalogue.

A view looking up the Vaitepiha river with two Tahitians in a
canoe in the foreground, and two more on the bank. Tahitian
houses to the right.

ver: For other and related versions of this view see 3.87-3.92.

ref: Cook, *Journals* III, 1, pl. 20; Starzecka (1979) pl. 32.

British Library, London. Add MS 15513, f.13.

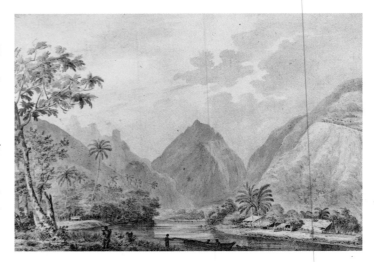

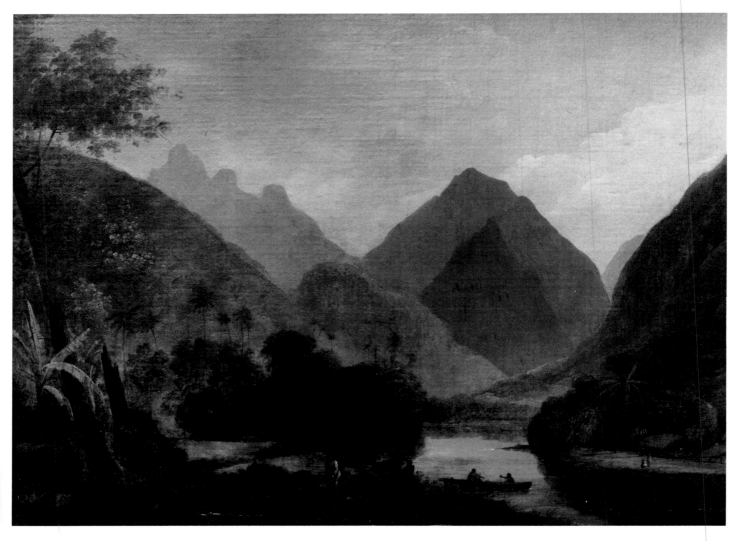

JOHN WEBBER

3.87 **A View of Otahaite Peha** [1783]
oil on canvas, 18⅛ × 25 : 460 × 635, signed and dated
'J. Webber pinx^t. 1783'. On verso is the following
inscription: 'A View of Otahaite Peha one of the Society
Isles JOHN WEBBER PINX^T . 1783. — Copied from the
back of the picture. Relined S. Holden Oct. 1936'.

This may be the painting exhibited at the RA 1786 (149) as
'View in Ohaite Pecka [sic.] Bay in Otaheite'.

Webber's signature was discovered by the Art Gallery of New

South Wales; its curator Ms Renée Free wrote to us: 'We have
looked at the signature under ultra violet light and the signature
and date both fluoresce and are above the varnish.' (*In litt.* 31
May 1985.)

ver: The composition of this picture is similar in 3.86-3.92.

P. D. Warren Esq. Sydney; 1960-74 shown on loan in the Art
Gallery of New South Wales, Sydney; Christie's Melbourne, 13
March 1975 (355) (col.), purchased by the Gallery in 1976.

Art Gallery of New South Wales, Sydney. Acc. no. 4. 1976.

346

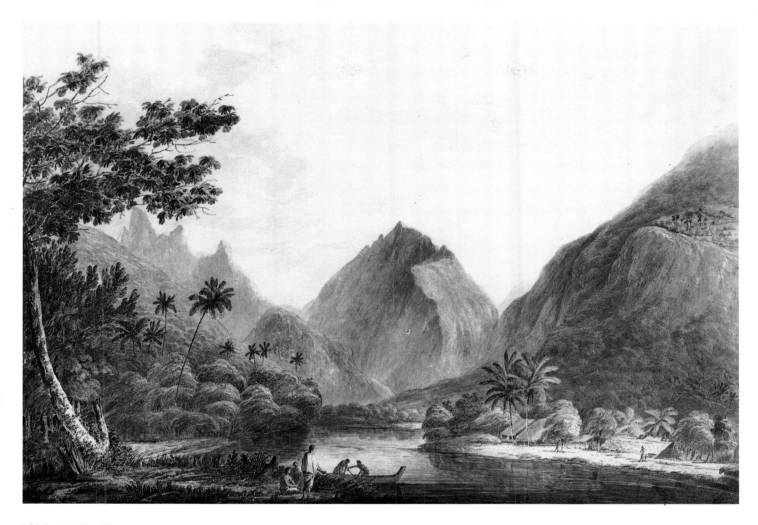

JOHN WEBBER

3.88   **A View in Vaitepiha Valley**   **[1784]**
water-colour, 14¾ × 21¼ : 375 × 540, signed and
dated in ink 'J. Webber del 1784' (l.r.).

ver: For similar compositions see 3.86-3.92.

Dixson Galleries, State Library of New South Wales, Sydney.
DG 189.

JOHN WEBBER

3.89   **A View in Vaitepiha Valley**   **[1786]**
water-colour, 16⅜ × 23⅝ : 411 × 600, signed and
dated in white colour 'J. Webber 1786' (l.l.).

ver: A later and slightly larger version than 3.88. Some minor
changes have been made in the figurative staffage of the
foreground.

ref: *Exh. Cat.* Auckland (1964) pl. 39; *Exh. Cat.* Auckland,
(1977) cat. no 44.

Maggs Bros., London (1927) cat. no. 491, 107 (146).

Dixson Galleries, State Library of New South Wales, Sydney.
DG27.

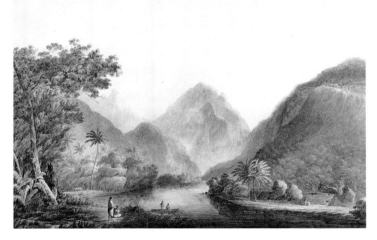

JOHN WEBBER

3.90   A View in Vaitepiha Valley   [1787]
oil on canvas, 23 × 31¹¹⁄₁₆ : 584 × 804, signed
and dated 'J. Webber p. 1787'.

On back inscribed in ink 'Otapia Bay in Otaheite'.

Looking up the Tautira Valley. Two figures, a woman standing
and a man sitting who points towards the river. There is no
canoe. Across the river a village beneath a steep cliff.

ver: For other versions of the same view see 3.86-3.92.

Gift of Richard A. Cooke and Theodore A. Cooke, 1935, who
bought it from P. and D. Colnaghi, London.

Honolulu Academy of Arts, Honolulu. Acc. no. 4268.

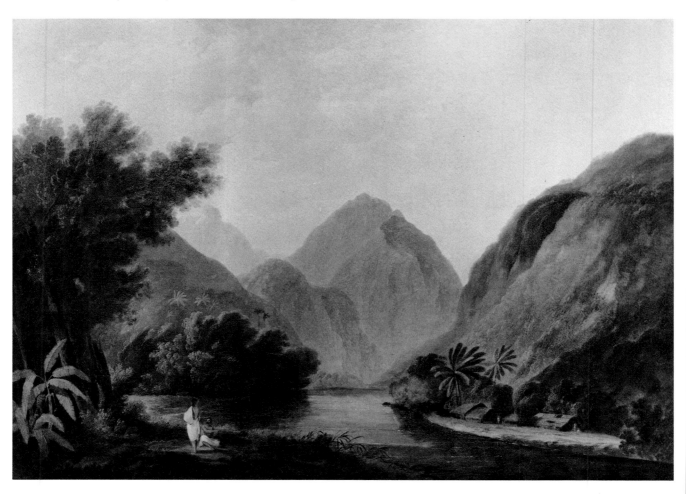

JOHN WEBBER

3.91   A View in Otaheipeha (Vaitepiha) Bay   [1791]
oil on canvas, 30¼ × 40¾ : 768 × 1035.

An inscription on the back of the original canvas (recorded before
lining) reads 'A View in Otaheipeha Bay in the Island of Otahaite
drawn in Capt. Cook's last Voyage by J. Webber'.

This was the painting which Webber submitted as his Diploma
work when admitted to membership of the Royal Academy in
1791.

ver: The picture derives from earlier compositions, see 3.86-
3.90.

ref: *Exh. Cat.* London (1951/52) no. 134; *Exh. Cat.* London
(1961/62) no. 39; *Exh. Cat.* London (1968/69) no. 64;
Apollo, January 1969, 38.

Royal Academy of Arts, Diploma Gallery, London.

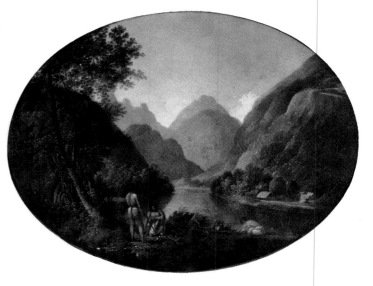

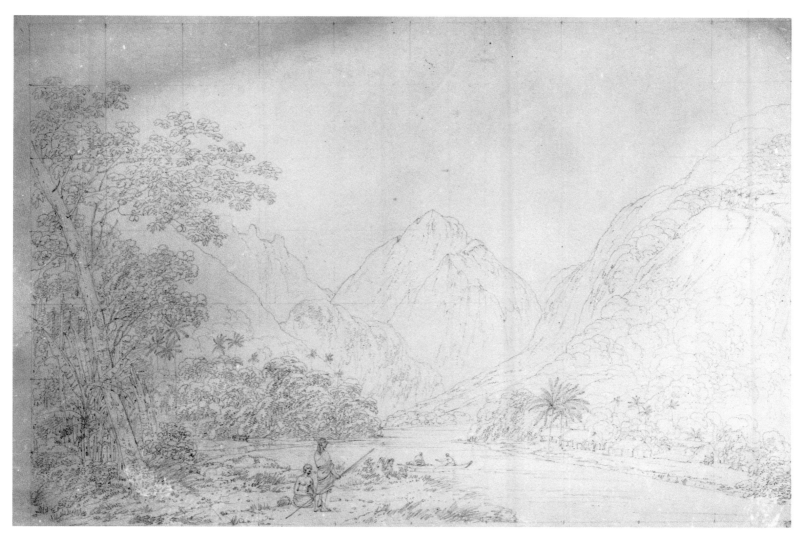

JOHN WEBBER

3.92 **A View in Oheitepeha Bay, in the Island of Otaheite**
[c. 1791]
pencil, 11³⁄₁₆ × 16⁷⁄₁₆ : 285 × 418; w/m: PORTAL
& BRIDGES.

The drawing is squared for transfer and is a preparatory study for
Webber's softground etching of the title above published 1 August
1791 (3.92A).

Comparison between the drawing and the print reveals a number
of small but significant differences: for example, there is a different
arrangement of trees growing between and behind the four native
huts on the right hand side; most notably the first hut on the far
right of the drawing shelters a long native canoe which is omitted
from the print. On the other side the print includes some long
stemmed coconut trees on the left hand side which do not appear
in the drawing. It may be concluded that the drawing is an original
work by Webber rather than a copy after the print.

Alexander Turnbull Library, Wellington. B 91/4.

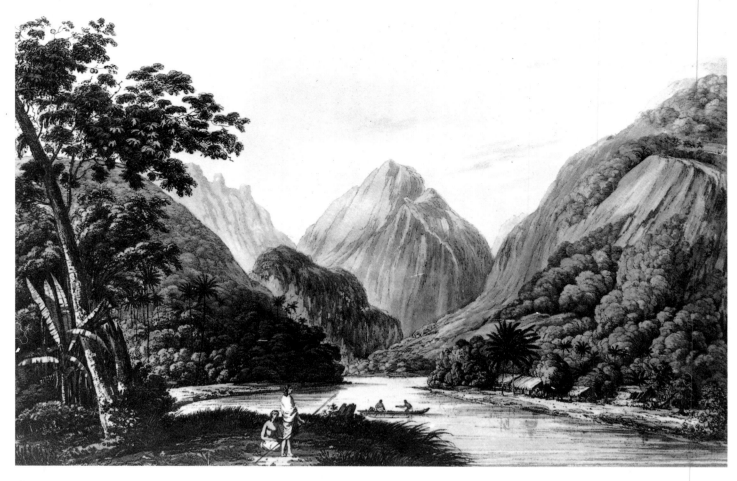

JOHN WEBBER

3.92A **a. 'A View in Oheitepeha Bay, in the Island of Otaheite'**
softground etching, tinted in brown and grey wash, or hand-coloured, 12⅞ × 17⅝ : 327 × 447 (11⅜ × 16¼ : 288 × 412). 'J. Webber, R.A. fecit'. 'London Pub.ᵈ Aug.ᵗ 1 1791 by J. Webber N.º 312 Oxford Street'. 'Vide Cooks last Voyage Vol. 2. Chap. 1'.

ref: Kaeppler (1978a), fig. 46 (103) reproduces a brown and grey coloured copy in the Fuller Collection, Bernice P. Bishop Museum.

British Museum, Department of Prints and Drawings, London, 246˙ a.2. and C. 6˙, as well as in the Bernice P. Bishop Museum, Fuller Collection.

b. 'A View in Oheitepeha Bay, in the Island of Otaheite'
coloured aquatint. 'J. Webber R.A. fecit'. 'London. Pub.ᵈ April 1 1809 by Boydell, & Comp.ʸ N.º 90 Cheapside'. 'Vide Cooks Last Voyage Vol. 2, Chap. 1'.

Issued by J. Boydell, *Views in the South Seas*, London, 1808, pl. V. National Maritime Museum, London; Bernice P. Bishop Museum, Honolulu.

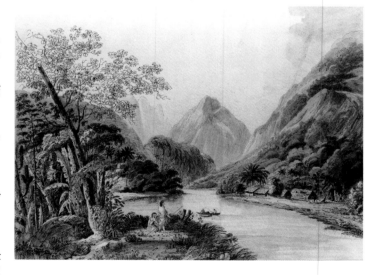

c.

A copy of this view by an unknown eighteenth-century copyist in pen, wash and water-colour measuring 14⅝ × 19⅜ : 372 × 492, inscribed in ink lower margin 'A View in Oheitepeha Bay, in the Island of Otaheiti. Vide Cook's last Voyage, Vol. 2, Chapt. 1' is in the National Maritime Museum, London. The drawing varies from Webber's print particularly on the left side, where a number of plants, including a cactus, have been added.

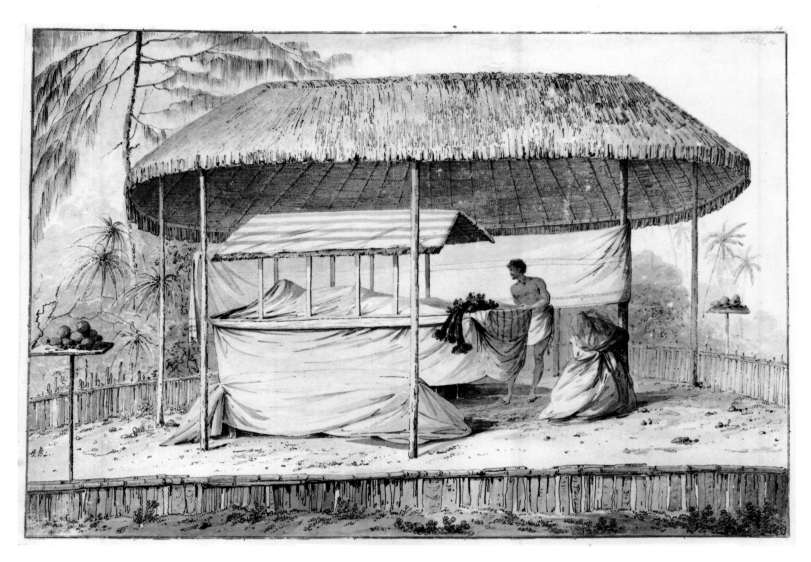

JOHN WEBBER

3.93   **Waheiadooa, Chief of Oheitepeha, lying in state**
[plate 56]   **[Aug 1777–]**
pen, wash and water-colour, 14¾ × 21⅜ : 375 × 543.

This drawing is listed in Webber's Catalogue as no. 40 'The Body of a Chief lying in State at Oparree'; 'Oparree' crossed out and replaced by 'Otahaite Peha'.

A funerary stage supporting a shrouded corpse with an attendant, sheltered by a grass-roofed awning and surrounded by a low palisade. At the extreme left and right, two stands for offerings (*whatta*) contain fruits, etc.

Cook recorded on 19 August 1777: 'Some of our gentlemen in their walks found what they were pleased to call a Roman C[at]holic Chappel, indeed from their account it was not to be doubted; for they discribed the alter and every other necessary article . . . I thought they might be misstaken and I had the curiosity to go and see it; it proved to be a Tupapow in which the remains of the late Waheatua laid as it were in state. It was a pretty large neat house which was inclosed with a low pallisade. The Tupapow was uncommonly neat and resembled, or perhaps had been one of those little houses or Awnings belonging to their traveling Canoes, it was covered and hung round with different Coloured cloth and Mats so as to have a pretty effect; there was one piece of scarlet broad Cloth of 4 or 5 Yards in length which had been given by the Spaniards. This cloth and a few Tassels of feathers which our gentlemen took for silk, made them believe it was a Chappel . . . Small offerings of fruit &c seemed to be daily made,

as some pieces were quite fresh; these lay on a whatta, or alter which stood without the pallisades, within which we were not allowed to go.' Cook, *Journals* III, 1, 190-1. Also see Samwell's description in ibid. 2, 1057.

ver: For a later version see 3.94.

ref: Cook, *Journals* III, 1, pl.22.

British Library, London. Add. MS 15513, f.14.

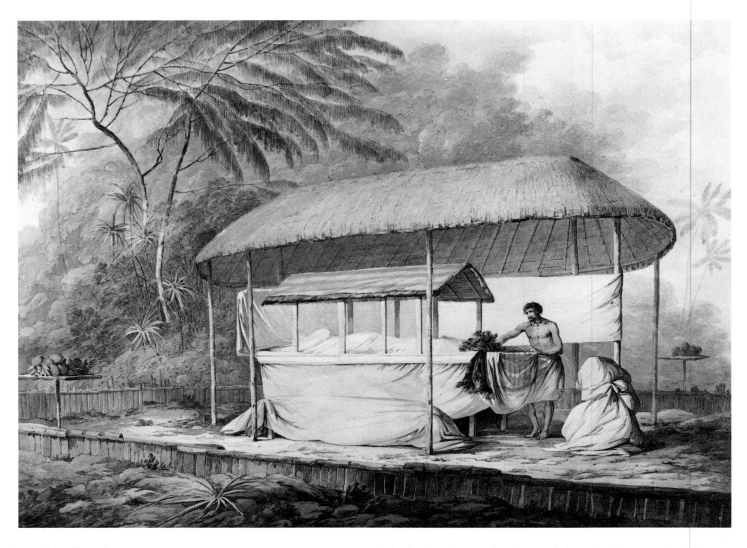

JOHN WEBBER

3.94 **Waheiadooa, chief of Oheitepeha, lying in state**
[c. 1777/89]

water-colour over pencil, 16¹¹⁄₁₆ × 22⁷⁄₈ : 424 × 581, pasted down on mount, signed in ink 'J. Webber del' in corner (l.r.).

Inscribed on verso 'A Chief Lying in State, Matavi Otaheite' in ink in an eighteenth century hand (by Webber?), also 'Waheiadooa, Chief of Oheitepeha, lying in State. Plate 6 in Webber's Views in the South Seas' in pencil. Mounted on cardboard (now badly damaged), and surrounded by fine framing lines.

ver: Similar to 3.93 but of a less frontal position and with more attention to the surroundings. For Webber's print of this composition see 3.95A from which the above title has been taken.

ref: *Exh. Cat.* Auckland (1977) cat. no. 46.

Maggs Bros. London (1927) cat. no. 491, 107.

Dixson Galleries, Library of New South Wales, Sydney. DG 28.

JOHN WEBBER

3.95 **Waheiadooa, chief of Oheitepeha, lying in state**
[c. 1789]

pencil, 10¹³⁄₁₆ × 16⁵⁄₁₆ : 276 × 414; w/m: lily in shield under crown, with 'GR' below.

Inscribed in ink (l.r.) 'J. Webber 1808' by a later hand.

The drawing is squared for transfer and is a preparatory study for

Webber's softground etching of the title above, published 1 July 1789.

Comparing the drawing with the print there are a number of small but significant differences: for example, the branches of the tree on the left, which in the drawing reach down almost to the roof of the open hut. There are also differences between drawing and print in the coconut tree in the right background, behind the platform of offering. It may therefore be concluded that the drawing is an original work by Webber rather than a copy after the print.

Alexander Turnbull Library, Wellington. B 91/5.

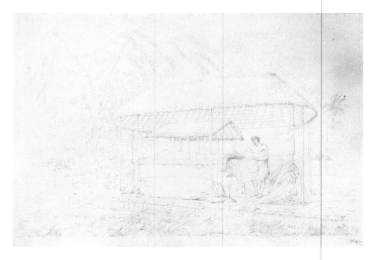

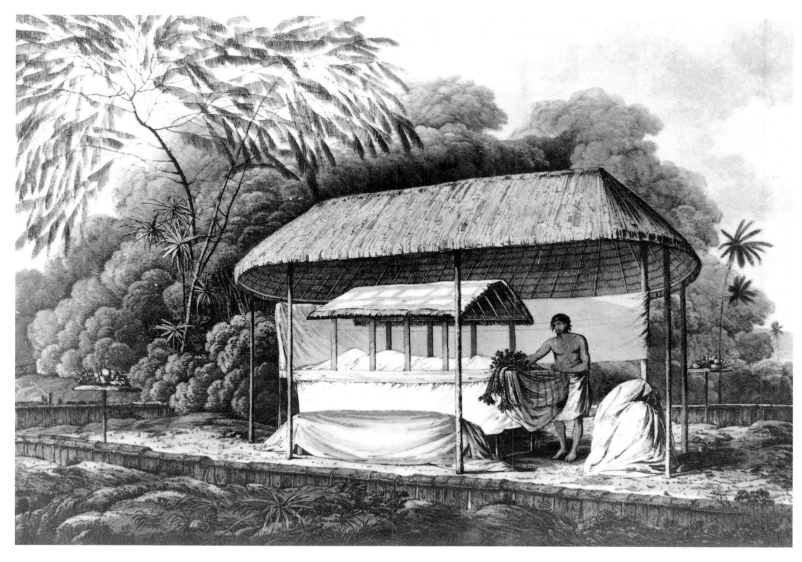

JOHN WEBBER

3.95A   **a. 'Waheiadooa, Chief of Oheitepeha, lying in State'**
softground etching, tinted in brown and grey wash, or
hand-coloured, 12¾ × 17⅝ : 323 × 447 (11⅛ ×
16¼ : 283 × 412). 'J. Webber fecit'. 'London Publish'd July 1 1789 by J. Webber N.º 312 Oxford Street'.
'Vide Cooks last Voyage Vol II. Chap. 1. page 17'.

ver: For Webber's original composition see 3.93.

British Museum, Department of Prints and Drawings, London,
246* a.2. and C. 6*.

       b. 'Waheiadooa, Chief of Oheitepeha, lying in State'
coloured aquatint. 'J. Webber fecit'. 'London. Pub.ᵈ
April 1, 1809 by Boydell & Comp.ʸ N.º 90 Cheapside'
'Vide Cooks last Voyage Vol II, Chap. 1 page 17'.

Issued by J. Boydell, *Views in the South Seas,* London, 1808, pl.
VI.

National Maritime Museum, London; Bernice P. Bishop
Museum, Honolulu.

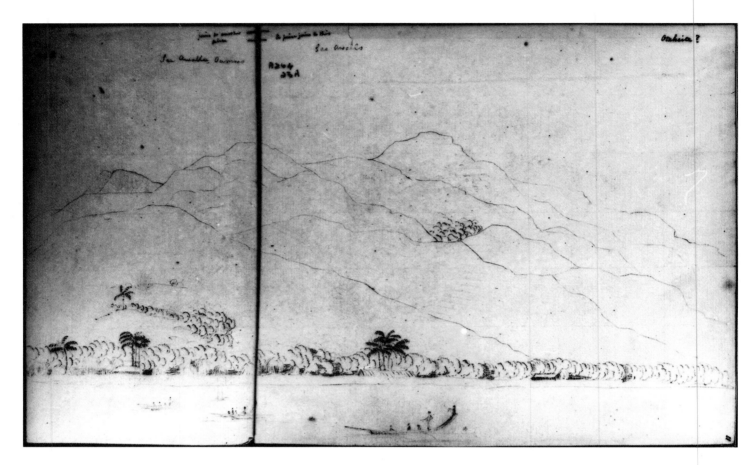

WILLIAM ELLIS

3.96   A View of the coast of Otaheite   [Aug 1777–]
pencil, on two sheets (A and B) fitting together, $7\frac{3}{8}$ × $3^{15}/16$: 188 × 100 and $7\frac{1}{2}$ × $8^{5}/16$: 190 × 211; both unsigned; w/m: 'Pro Patria' with Britannia.

Extending over both sheets. In (u.r.) corner of 23A inscribed 'Otaheite?' in black ink. On the left sheet is inscribed in pencil 'see Awallo' with 'Awallo' crossed out and 'Oammo' substituted; on the right sheet 'see Awallo' inscribed in pencil (u.l.). Numbered '33' in ink in corner (u.l.) of 22A and '32' in corner (l.r.) of 23A. On both drawings there are annotations, such as 'joins to another piece' (22A) and 'A piece joins to this' (23A) in black ink as to indicate that both drawings form a panorama. The handwriting seems to be that of the inscription 'Otaheite?'. On verso of 22A is the portrait of Awallo (3.162) and on verso of 23A is the portrait of Oammo (3.118).

Native craft in foreground, houses and palms along the foreshore; a mountainous background.

ref: Murray-Oliver (1977) 33-4.

Alexander Turnbull Library, Wellington. A264.22A-23A.

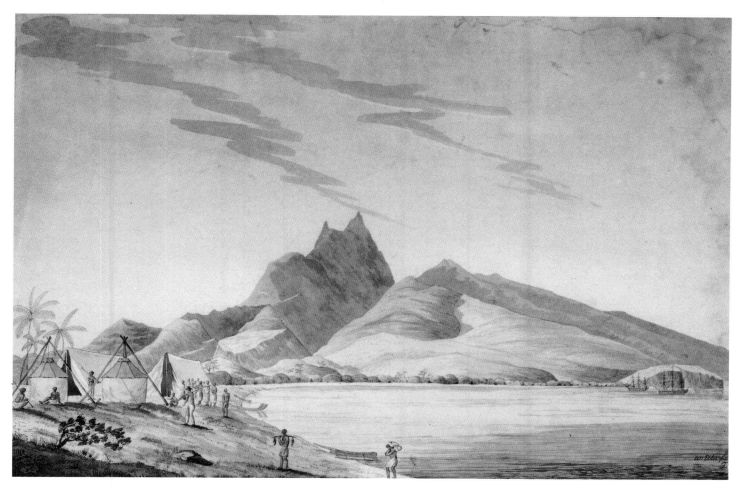

WILLIAM ELLIS

3.97   **View of Matavai-Bay, in the Island [of] Otaheite**
        [plate 53]   **[1777]**
        pen and brown ink and water-colour over pencil, 13⅞
        × 20⅜ : 353 × 520. Signed and dated (l.r.) 'W. Ellis
        fect./1777'; w/m: ' J. WHATMAN'.

The title in ink as above along lower margin. The drawing is
pasted to a mount.

'As Captain Cook intended to reside here some time, the astronomers tents, instruments, and other apparatus, were got on
shore, and erected upon point Venus. The ships tents were also
pitched, and the marines, with the coopers, and all the empty
casks with various other affairs, were sent on shore.' Ellis, (1782)
I, 133.

'As I intended to make some stay here, we set up the two observatorys on Matavai point, erected two tents for the reception
of a guard and such people as was necessary to have a Shore, and
Mr. King was intrusted with the Command, who at the same
time attended the observations for assertaining the going of the
Time Keeper and other purposes.' Cook, *Journals* III, 1, 194-5.
For a similar description see Samwell, ibid., 2, 1058 and King
in ibid., 2, 1374.

ver: For another version see 3.98.

ref: Sotheby's *Cat.* 26 January 1984, lot 95 (col.).

Rhona Townley Searle Collection.

Private collection, Australia.

WILLIAM ELLIS (after)

3.98   **A View of Matavai-Bay**   **[1777]**
water-colour, 12¼ × 19⅝ : 311 × 497, signed 'W.
Ellis fect. 1777' (l.r.). The title as above inscribed in
ink centred along the lower edge of the drawing followed by 'in the Island of Otaheite'.

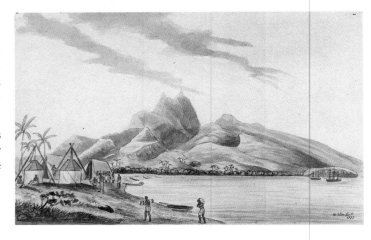

Tents, including the two astronomers' tents, and some of Cook's
men at left; two Tahitians bringing food in the centre; the bay
with the two ships at right. For the point of view, compare
Spöring's drawing 'A View from the Point at Otaheite' (1.21).

ver: For Ellis's drawing of the same scene, see 3.97.

ref: Cook, *Journals* III, 1, pl. 23; Rienits (1968) 137 (col.).

Collection of Captain A.W.F. Fuller.

National Maritime Museum, London.

JOHN WEBBER

3.99   **A Human Sacrifice at Otaheite**
[plate 54]   **[Sep 1777–]**
pen, wash and water-colour, 16⅝ × 23⁵⁄₁₆ : 422
× 625, signed and dated 'John Webber del. 1777'.

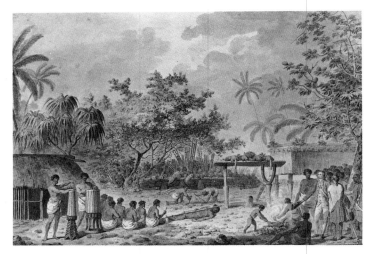

The title as above in pencil on the mount below the drawing.
The drawing is listed under the same title as no. 56 in Webber's
Catalogue.

A bound and prostrate figure in centre foreground; two men
beating drums at left; Cook and officers at right. Webber's drawing
incorporates most of the events which concluded the ceremony:
the chief priest seated near the feet of the victim, entoning and
gesturing, with other priests seated around him: the two drummers, the men digging a hole for the body, the broiling and
degutting of the dog and the *Whatta* containing two dogs and
three pigs sacrificed previously. For the whole ceremony of the
sacrifice which took place on 1 September 1777, see Cook, *Journals* III, 1, 198-205 as well as Anderson in Cook, *Journals* III, 2,
978-84. According to Beaglehole the place of action, which Cook
identified as the 'great Morai at Attahouroo', is Utuaimahurau,
ibid., 1, 198-9. Cook mentions a number of witnesses of the
ceremony, including Omai, Anderson and Webber. The ceremony was performed in the presence of Otoo [Tu], who is probably
represented next to Cook. The European to Cook's left, with
back turned, is possibly Anderson, and the figure at far right,
Omai.

ver: For a smaller version which served as the drawing for Woollett's engraving see 3.100.

ref: Smith (1950), 25d (1960) pl. 152; Cook, *Journals* III, 1,
pl. 24; Beaglehole (1974) pl 35; Kaeppler (1978a) fig. 303;
Joppien (1978) fig. 2, opp. 64; Starzecka (1979) pl. 29.

British Library, London. Add MS 15513, f.16.

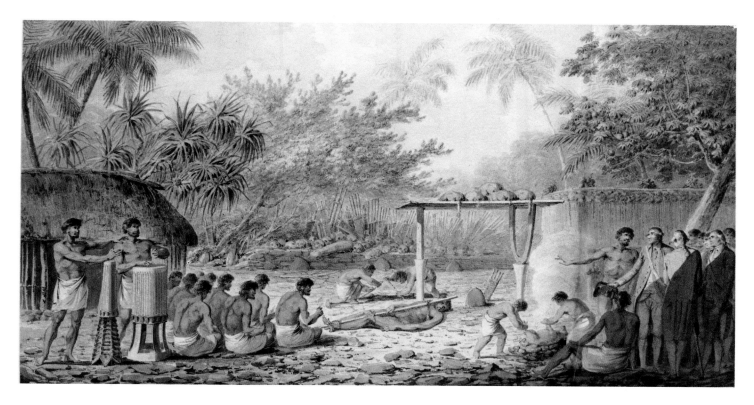

JOHN WEBBER

JOHN WEBBER (after)

3.100   **A Human Sacrifice at Otaheite**   [c. 1781-3]
pen, wash and water-colour, 9¾ × 18⅜ : 247 × 467,
unsigned.

3.100A   **'A HUMAN SACRIFICE, in a MORAI, in OTAHEITE'**
Engraving. 'J. Webber del.' — 'W. Woollett sc.'

Inscribed 'A Human Sacrifice, in a Morai, in Otaheite' in pencil
by a later hand on the folio beneath the drawing.

Published in Cook/King (1784) pl. 25, II, 32-6.

It differs from 3.99 in several respects. Cook and the figure at
far right (Omai?) are shown as older men. Cook's companion
(Tu?) now raises his right arm and points to the ceremony. The
number of squatting priests has been increased and the two grave
diggers moved slightly to the right. The *marae* has been extended
and more skulls and posts added. The height of the scene has
been reduced, the coconut trees now reaching beyond the top
of the picture.

A proof-state inscribed in pencil 'A Human Sacrifice. Otaheite'
in Webber's hand is kept in the National Library of Australia,
Canberra, in a folio of plates from the Skottowe Hall Library.

A singular print of this engraving, hand-coloured and measuring
11 × 19 : 279 × 483, inscribed partly in pencil: 'J. Webber del
& tinted', 'W. Woollett aquafortis fecit', also 'A Human Sacrifice
in Otaheite — Etched by Woollett & tinted by Webber', possibly
in Webber's hand, is kept in the British Museum, Department
of Prints and Drawings (C 17*). It is one of four successive proof-
states, which are also kept in the Department of Prints and Drawings under Woollett engravings, vol. 6, 31-4. All four states are
referred to by Fagan (1885), 37.

ver: A smaller version of 3.99, apparently the one on which
Woollett based 3.100A.

ref: Joppien (1978) fig. 3, 66.

Dixson Library, State Library of New South Wales, Sydney.
PXX 2, 10.

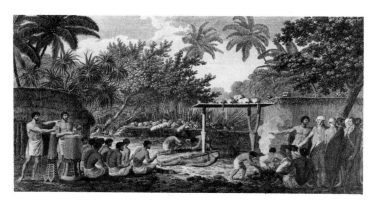

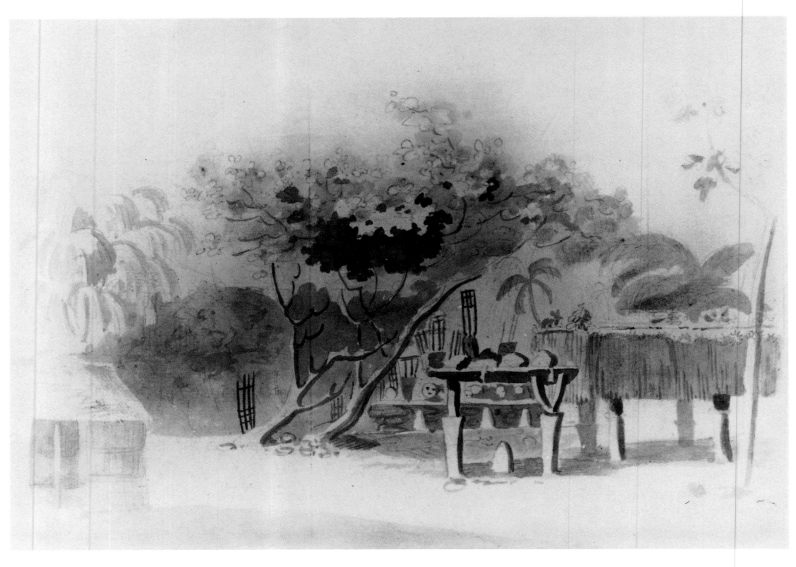

JOHN WEBBER

3.101   **A *Marae* in Tahiti**   [1 Sep 1777–]
pencil and wash, 9½ × 13 : 241 × 330, unsigned;
w/m: part of shield with fleur-de-lis and initials 'LVG'
= Lubertus van Gerrevink.

Inscribed in brown ink 'Sandwich Isles' (u.r.).

ver: Similar scene to 3.99 and 3.100 but without figures and
with some minor differences which suggests that this may
be a preparatory study by Webber.

Tipped into a copy of Captain George Dixon, *A Voyage Round
the World* (London, 1789) fp. 128.

National Library of Australia, Canberra. Rex Nan Kivell Collection. NK 7402.

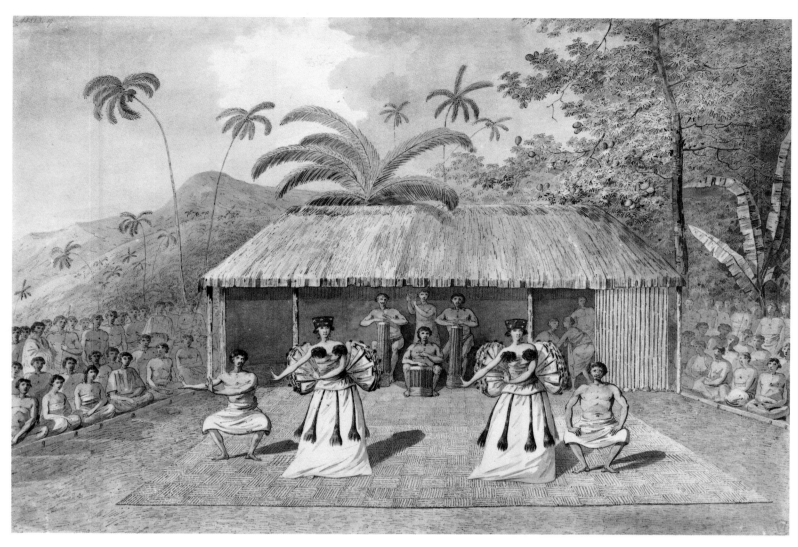

JOHN WEBBER

3.102   A Dance at Otaheite [plate 63]   [Sep 1777–]
pen, wash and water-colour, 17 × 21½ : 432 × 546,
signed and dated 'John Webber del 1777' (l.r.).

The title as above in pencil on the mount below drawing. This
drawing is listed as no. 57 'A Heiva or Dance' in Webber's
Catalogue.

Two men and two women dancing before a hut, spectators on
either side. Three drummers at the back.

The scene is similar to a description which Anderson gives of a
heiva on 2 September 1777, but does not fully correspond: 'We
landed in the evening and walk'd through a great part of Parre,
a pleasant fertile district near Mattavy, meeting in our road with
a kind of private Heeva or amusement, which consisted of about
a hundred of the inhabitants of the neighbourhood who wer[e]
sitting in a house and in the midst of them two women with an
old man behind, each beating very gently upon a drum, and the
women at intervals singing in a softer manner than I ever heard
at their other diversions. The assembly listened with great attention and were seemingly almost absorbed in the pleasure the
music gave them, as few took any notice of us and the performers
never once stop'd.' Anderson in Cook, *Journals* III, 2, 985.

When later at night Cook arrived at Otoo's house, he was entertained by another heiva 'at which his [Otoo's] three sisters were
the principal performers'. 'Their dress on this occasion was truly
picturesque and elegant . . .' (ibid., 985-6). A similar performance was held on 10 September, when Cook noted: 'The next
Morning a party of us went down to Oparre, where Otoo treated

us with a Play, his three Sisters were the actresses and appeared
in a new and elegant dress' (ibid., 1, 208).

Webber's drawing could have been done on either of these occasions. It could also give a general idea of a heiva. The dress
of the actresses closely corresponds to the ones witnessed in Raiatea during Cook's first voyage in August 1769 (1.83-1.85). Con-
sequently, Langdon suggested that Webber actually witnessed this
scene in Raiatea (1975, pl. 10 caption). However, not only is
the drawing inscribed 'Dance in Otaheite', the pencil annotations
in Webber's Catalogue (no. 46 and 57) also refer to Otaheite as
the place of location.

Webber (*pace* Langdon) certainly did distinguish between Ulaietea (Raiatea) and Tahiti (see Joppien, (1978) 53 entries under
Society Islands 32, 36, 56, 57).

ver: See 3.103 for a smaller and probably later version, upon
which Sherwin's engraving was based.
ref: Cook, *Journals* III, 1, pl. 26 (erroneously located as Add
MS 17277 no. 19); Langdon (1975) pl. 10, fp. 145; Kaeppler
(1978a) fig. 224; Cobbe (1979) pl. V (col.).

British Library, London. Add MS 15513, f.19.

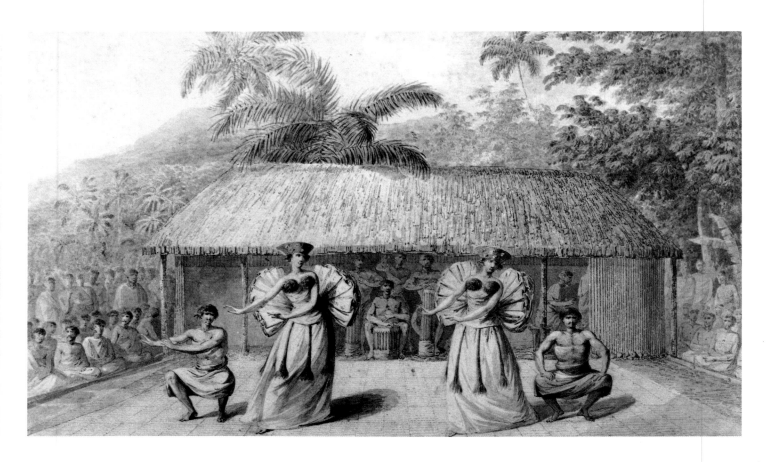

JOHN WEBBER

3.103   **A Dance in Otaheite**   [c. 1781-3]
         pen and water-colour, $8^{15}/_{16} \times 14^{7}/_{8} : 227 \times 378$,
         unsigned.

The title as above on the folio by a later hand beneath the
drawing.

ver: Similar to but smaller than 3.102. For the engraving from
        3.103 see 3.103A.

Dixson Library, State Library of New South Wales, Sydney.
PXX 2, 13.

JOHN WEBBER (after)

3.103A **'A DANCE in OTAHEITE'**
        Engraving. 'J. Webber del.' — 'J.K. Sherwin sc.'

Published in Cook/King (1784) pl. 28, II, 48.

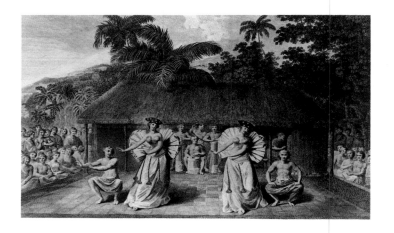

JOHN WEBBER

3.104   A Dancing Girl of Otaheite
[plate 66]   **[Sep 1777–]**
pencil, pen and wash with tints of water-colour, 17 ×
12½ : 432 × 317, unsigned.

Inscribed 'Otaheite Dancing Girl' in pencil above the drawing;
endorsed in ink 'Lot No 12' '12' crossed out and substituted by
'8', and in pencil 'Cap^n Campbell'. The original sheet has been
varnished and cut and laid down on board, probably for framing.

This is the drawing listed as no. 46 'A Heiva Girl in her Theatrical
Dress' in Webber's Catalogue.

ver: The girl wears a similar costume to the female dancers in
          3.102 and 3.103. This is probably the drawing for the
          engraving 3.104A.
ref: *Exh. Cat.* Auckland (1964) pl. 42.

Dixson Library, State Library of New South Wales, Sydney.
Pe 216.

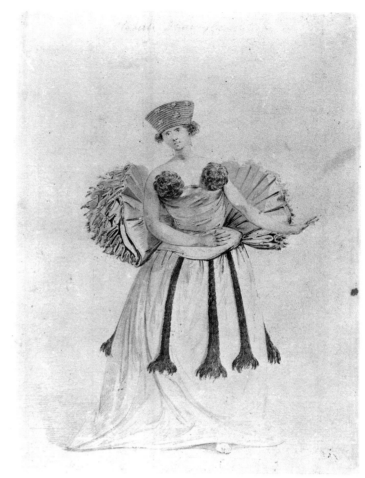

JOHN WEBBER (after)

3.104A   'A YOUNG WOMAN of OTAHEITE, DANCING'
Engraving. 'J. Webber del.' — 'J.K. Sherwin sc.'

Published in Cook/King (1784) pl. 29, II, 48.

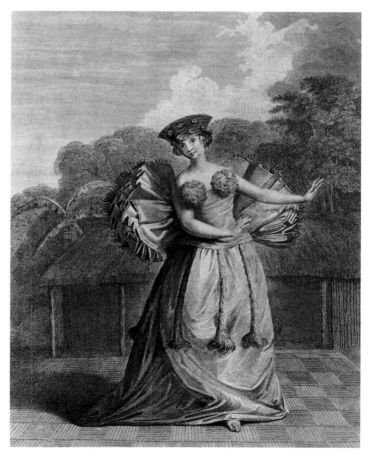

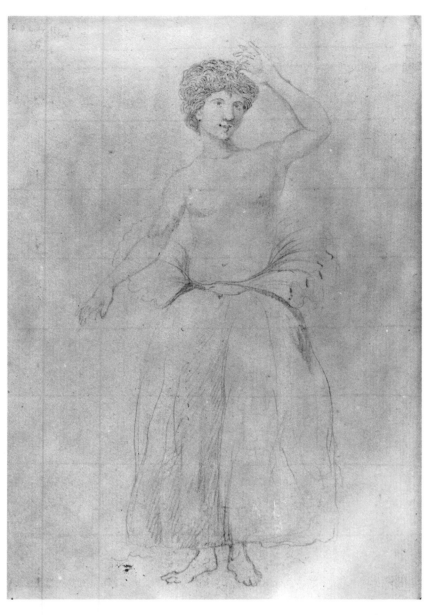

JOHN WEBBER

3.106 **A Young Woman of Otaheite, bringing a Present**
[plate 67] [Sep 1777–]
pen, wash and water-colour, 16¹/₁₆ × 12¼ : 404
× 311, signed and dated 'Jnº Webber del 1777' (l.l.).

Inscribed '37' (u.r.), corresponding to that number in Webber's
Catalogue, 'The Manner of a Chief sending a present to Captain
Cook. Cloth & other Articles'.

Cook recorded on 8 September 1777: 'I . . . went with him
[Otoo] to his Fathers where they were dressing two girls in a
prodigious quantity of fine cloth [tapa] in a manner rather curious;
the one end of each piece, of which there were a good many, was
held up over the girls heads while the remainder was wraped
round them under the armpits, then the upper ends were let fall
and hung down in foulds to the ground over the other and looked
some thing like a circular hooped petticoat. After ward round
the out side of all, were wraped several pieces of different Coloured
cloth, which considerably increased the Size so that the whole
was not less than five or six yards in circuit and was as much as
the poor girls could support. To each was hung two *Taame's*, or
breast plates by way of inriching the whole. Thus equiped they
were conducted on board the Ship together with Several Hogs
and a quantity of fruit as a present from Otoos Father to me.
Either men or women dress'd in this Manner they call Atee, but
I believe it is never done but when they want to make large
presents of cloth, at least I never saw it at any other time, nor
indeed did I ever see it before now, but both Captain Clerke and
I had Cloth given us in this manner after wards.' Cook, *Journals*
III, 1, 207-8.

ver: For a smaller version of this composition see 3.107, which
served as a model for an engraving by F. Bartolozzi, from
which the title above has been taken.
ref: Cook, *Journals* III, 1, pl. 25a; Starzecka (1979) pl. 43;
Joppien (1983) 70.

British Library, London. Add MS 15513, f.17.

WILLIAM ELLIS

3.105 **A Dancing Girl**
pencil, 8⅞ × 6⅛ : 225 × 156, unsigned.

Numbered '2' in ink (l.l) and 'b' (l.r.).

A young girl with the left arm raised to the head, wearing a skirt
frilled at the waist.

ver: Almost certainly copied from Hawkesworth's engraving (see
1.87B) to which it is very close in stance and detail. It is
therefore unlikely to be a field-drawing. It is placed here
for convenience.
ref: Murray-Oliver (1977) 34, pl. I; *Exh. Cat.* Auckland (1977),
cat. no. 41.

Alexander Turnbull Library, Wellington. A264.25.

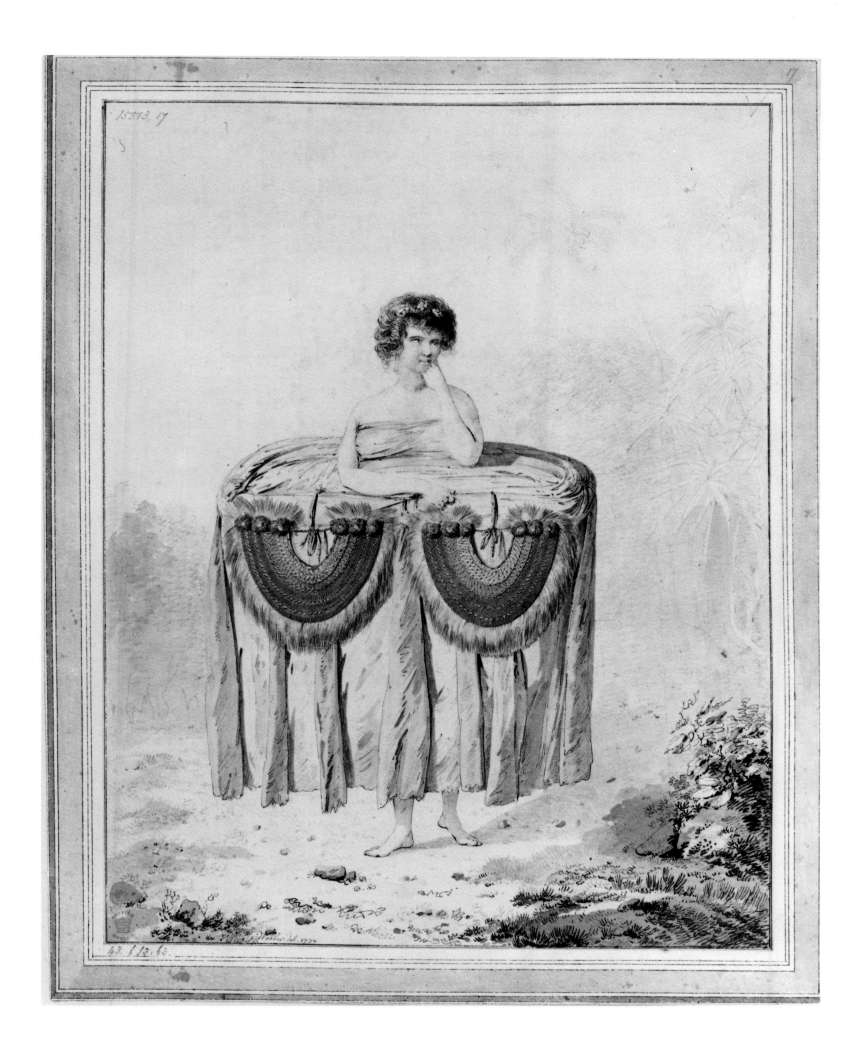

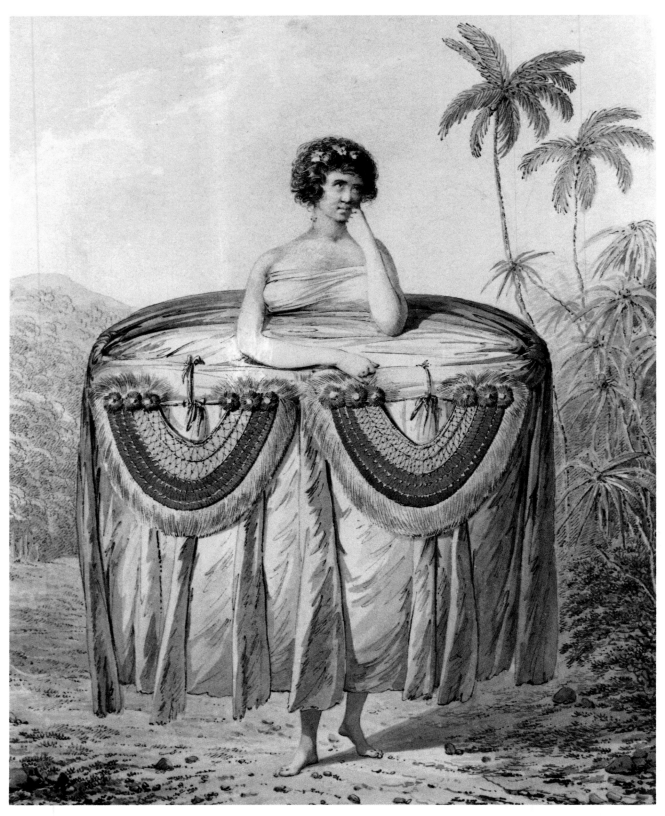

JOHN WEBBER

3.107 **A Young Woman of Otaheite, bringing a Present**
[c. 1781]
pen, wash and water-colour, 8⅞ × 7¼ : 225 × 184,
unsigned.

The title as above in pencil by a later hand on the folio beneath
the drawing.

ver: Similar to 3.106 but smaller and almost identical in size
with 3.107A for which it was probably drawn.

Dixson Library, State Library of New South Wales, Sydney.
PXX 2, 12.

JOHN WEBBER (after)

3.107A **'A YOUNG WOMAN of OTAHEITE, bringing a PRESENT'**
Engraving. 'J. Webber del.' — 'F. Bartolozzi sc.'

Published in Cook/King (1784) pl. 27, II, 50-1.

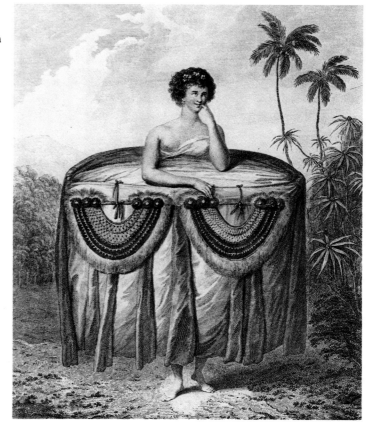

WILLIAM ELLIS

3.108 **A Girl of Otaheite bringing Presents** **[c. 1777]**
pencil, 9⁷⁄₁₆ × 7⅛ : 240 × 180, unsigned; w/m: lower section of a fleur-de-lis

The title is derived from an inscription in ink [u.r.] 'Girl of Otaheite bringing presents' in ink. Also inscribed '6' in ink on verso (l.l.) and 'f' (l.r.).

ver: Apparently a copy of Webber's drawing 3.106, with the presents (i.e. breast-plates suspended on the hoop) only faintly sketched in.

ref: Murray-Oliver (1977) 34; Joppien (1983) 69.

Alexander Turnbull Library, Wellington. A264.24.

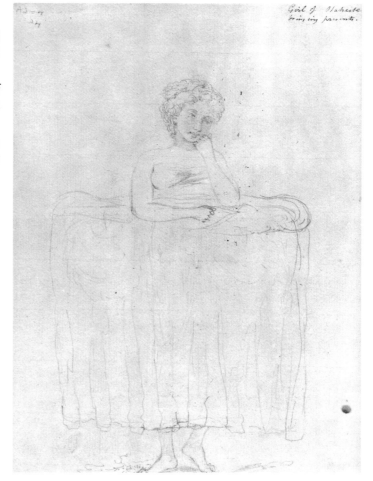

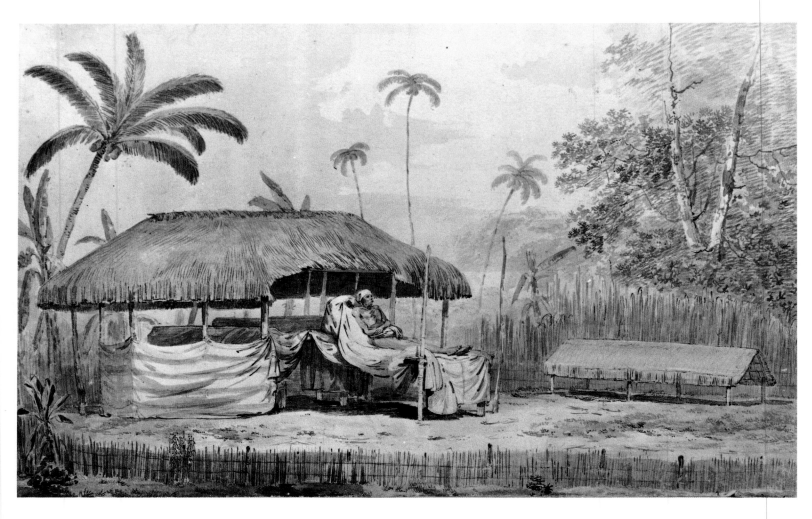

JOHN WEBBER

3.109 **The Body of Tee, a Chief, as Preserved after Death in Otaheite [plate 57]** [Sep 1777–]
pen, wash and water-colour, 12¼ × 19½ : 311 × 495, trace of signature (?) in ink (l.r.).

The title, as above, endorsed and inscribed 'reproduced in Atlas'. The enframing lines have been cut from the drawing; the drawing has been irregularly cut and laid down on cardboard. This is most probably the drawing to which Webber referred to in his Catalogue as no. 34 'The Body of a Chief lying in State at Oparree'.

The body is seated on a platform under a hut.

Cook recorded on 10 September 1777: 'The chief thing that carried me to Oparre was to see an Embalmed corse, which some of our gentlemen had met with at that place. It prooved to be the remains of Tee or [   ], a Chief well known to me when I was here last Voyage, it was lying in a Tupapow, in all respects such a one as that at Oaitipeha in which the remains of the late Waheatua lies, embalmed as this was. When we first went the body was under cover and wraped up in cloth in the Tupapow, but at my desire the Man who had the care of it, brought it out and laid it up on a kind of beir or bed place, in such a manner that we had as full a view of it as we could wish, but we were not allowed to go within the railing that enclosed the Tupapow. After he had placed the Corse, he hung the place with Mats and cloth in such order as to have a very good effect. This man had been dead above four months, and the body was so effectually preserved from putrefaction that there was not the least disagreeable smell about it. How this was performed I could not learn any more than what Omai told me, he said they mad[e] use of the juice of a plant which grows in the Mountains, Cocoanut Oile and frequent washing in the Sea. I was told that they preserve the bodies of all the great men who die a natural death in this manner, and expose them to a public view for a very considerable time after.' Cook, *Journals* III, 1, 208-9.

Samwell identifies the dead man lying in state as one of Tu's brothers. Ibid., 2, 1060-1.

ver: Similar to 3.110 but lacking the attendant.

ref: *Exh. Cat.* Portland (1974) no. 145.

Dixson Library, State Library of New South Wales, Sydney. Pf 50.

366

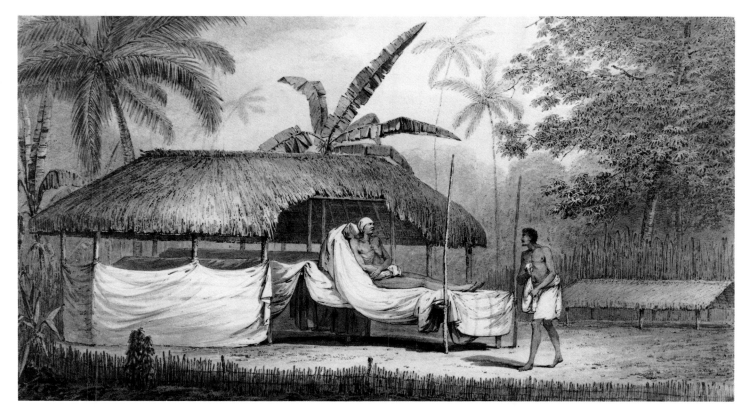

JOHN WEBBER

3.110   **The Body of Tee, a Chief, as Preserved after Death
        in Otaheite [plate 58]**   **[c. 1781-3]**
        pen and water-colour, 8½ × 14¾ : 215 × 375,
        unsigned.

The title as above on the folio by a later hand beneath the
drawing.

ver: A more finished version of 3.109, with the added figure
        of an attendant. Engraved in reverse but otherwise faithfully
        for 3.110A.

Dixson Library, State Library of New South Wales, Sydney.
PXX 2, 11.

JOHN WEBBER (after)

3.110A **'The BODY of TEE, a CHIEF, as preserved after
        DEATH, in OTAHEITE'**
        Engraving. 'J. Webber del.' — 'W. Byrne sculp.'

Published in Cook/King (1784) pl. 26, II, 51-3.

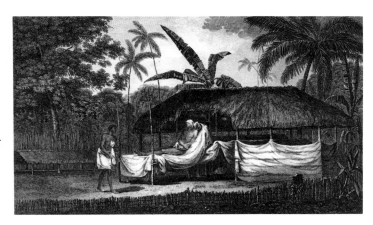

A proof-state inscribed in pencil 'Body of a Chief laying in State.
Otahaite' in Webber's hand is kept in the National Library of
Australia, Canberra, in a folio of plates from the Skottowe Hall
Library.

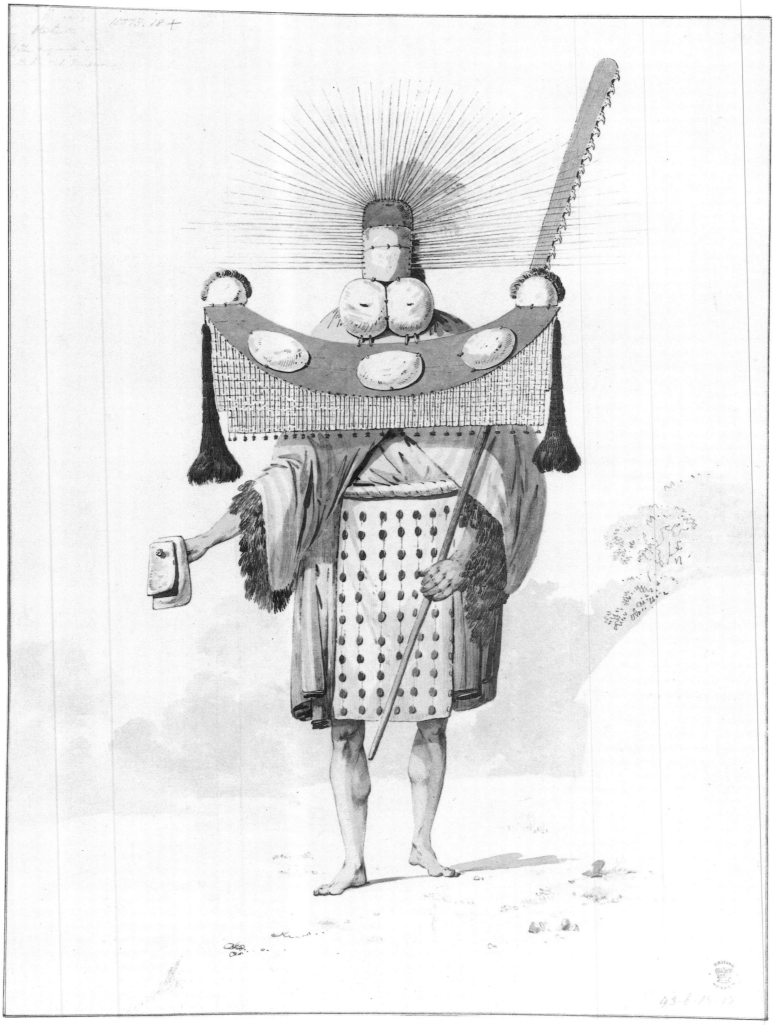

JOHN WEBBER

3.111   **A Chief Mourner**   **[c. 1777]**
pen, wash and water-colour, 14⅝₁₆ × 19⁷⁄₁₆ :
363 × 493, unsigned.

Inscribed 'No 43' (u.r.) thus identifying it with the drawing so
listed and titled in Webber's Catalogue (with reference to Otaheite), in a later hand (u.l.) in pencil 'ii early Otaheite. The
original is in the British Museum'.

Man in a ceremonial dress carrying a clapper in his right hand
and a shark toothed club in the left. For an account of mourning
dresses collected on Cook's voyages see Kaeppler (1978a) 121-8.

No person of this kind is recorded during the ships' stay at Otaheite. The precise date of Webber's drawing therefore remains
unresolved.

ref: Kaeppler (1978a) fig. 212.

British Library, London. Add MS 15513, f.18.

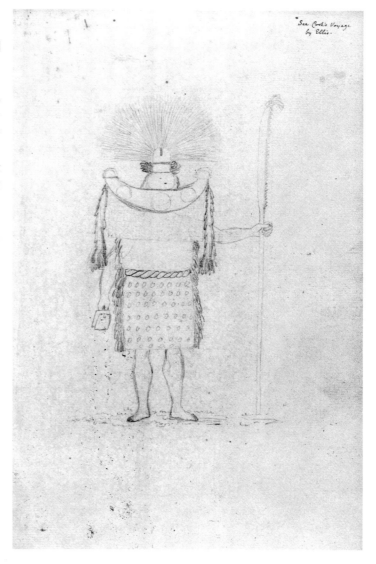

WILLIAM ELLIS

3.112   **A Chief Mourner**
pencil, 12¼ × 7½ : 311 × 191, unsigned; w/m: 'Pro
patria' with Britannia.

Inscribed in black ink 'See Cook's Voyage by Ellis' (u.r.). On
verso is the drawing of a native and a hut (3.85).

ver: The drawing bears considerable resemblance to Webber's
representation at 3.111. For an engraving by J. Collyer in
Ellis (1782) see 3.112A.

ref: Murray-Oliver (1977), 32-3.

Alexander Turnbull Library, Wellington. A.264.19A.

WILLIAM ELLIS (after)

3.112A   **'A Man of Otaheitee in a Mourning Dress'**
Engraving. 'W. Ellis del.' — 'J. Collyer sculp.'. 'Published Dec.ʳ 14ᵗʰ 1781, by G. Robinson'.

Published in Ellis (1782) I, fp. 130.

In Ellis's *Narrative* there is no specific description of the Chief
Mourner and his dress.

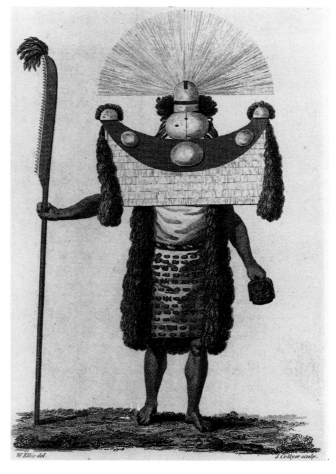

JOHN WEBBER

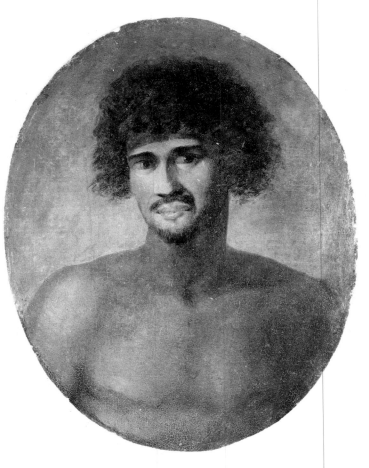

3.113 Portrait of Tu [plate 69] [Sep 1777]
oil on canvas cut of oval size and laid down on modern
board, 14½ × 11 : 362 × 279, unsigned.

It is possible that this is the picture which Webber mentions in
the section of 'Portraits in Oyl Colours' as 'Otoo King of Otaheite',
no. 3 in his Catalogue.

Bust portrait of Tu, Ariki of Pare; from 1791 Pomare I of Tahiti
who died in 1803. His bust bared and head turning slightly to
the left, looking right. Wearing blackish half-long hair and a
moustache. On his left breast two small crosses. During his third
voyage Cook met Tu first on 24 August 1777 (*Journals* III, 1,
192) in Matavai Bay. The portrait was probably executed some
time later during the stay.

'[The] portrait, as Mr Webber assures us, was obtained in the
following manner. O'too, by the Captain's particular desire, sat
to Mr. Webber, in order to furnish him such a memorial of his
features, as might serve for the subject of a complete whole length
picture, on the return of the ship to England. When the portrait
was finished, and O'too was informed that no more sittings would
be necessary, he anxiously enquired of Captain Cook, and Captain
Clerke, what might be the particular meaning and purpose of the
painting. He was informed, that it would be kept by Captain
Cook, as a perpetual memorial of his person, his friendship, and
the many favours received from him. He seemed pleased with the
idea, and instantly replied, that, for the very same reason, a
picture of Captain Cook would be highly acceptable to him. This
answer so unexpected, and expressed with strong tokens of real
attachment, made both Captain Clerke and Mr Webber his ad-
vocates, and Captain Cook, charmed with the natural sincerity
of his manner, complied with his request much more readily than
on any other occasion he would have gained such a favour.' *The
Voyage of Governor Phillip to Botany Bay* (1789) 293. Webber was
a subscriber to the book.

'Otoo is a tall stout man, of a very dark complexion, short curly
or rather frizled hair, heavy & want of animation, but this in a
great measure may be owing to the Frequent use of ye yava.'
Williamson in Cook, *Journals* III, 2, 1343.

ref: Murray-Oliver (1978) 112-14.

On the death of Cook the portrait came into the possession of
Captain James King, and by descent to King's elder brother Ed-
ward, then to his son Edward Bolton King; from thence to his
daughter Isabella Francis, to her son E.T.D. Francis, and to his
son R.A.D. Francis. Sold by Mrs R.A.D. Francis, London at
Christie's 14 October 1977. Purchased by Aquarius Gallery,
Hamilton, New Zealand, 1977, and acquired by the Alexander
Turnbull Gallery in 1978.

Alexander Turnbull Library, Wellington.

JOHN WEBBER

3.114 [A young Man of Tahiti] [1777?]
oil on canvas, 18⅛ × 14¼ : 460 × 362, unsigned.

Head and shoulder portrait of a young man of dark complexion
with curly but short hair, looking left. Wearing a light-coloured
cloak around his shoulders. From the likeness to the engraving
by Caldwall after Hodges (2.65A) the sitter could possibly be
Omai.

ref: Earp, (1902) 95, where the picture is erroneously catalogued
as being by the portrait painter, Charles Howard Hodges
(1764-1837). Cat. of Paintings, British School, Fitzwilliam
Museum, Cambridge, no. 454. The painting was originally
attributed to William Hodges in the manuscript 'Catalogue
of the Pictures and Drawings etc' bequeathed to the University of Cambridge by Daniel Mesman.

Bequeathed to the Fitzwilliam Museum by Daniel Mesman in
1834.

Fitzwilliam Museum, Cambridge. Inv. no. 454.

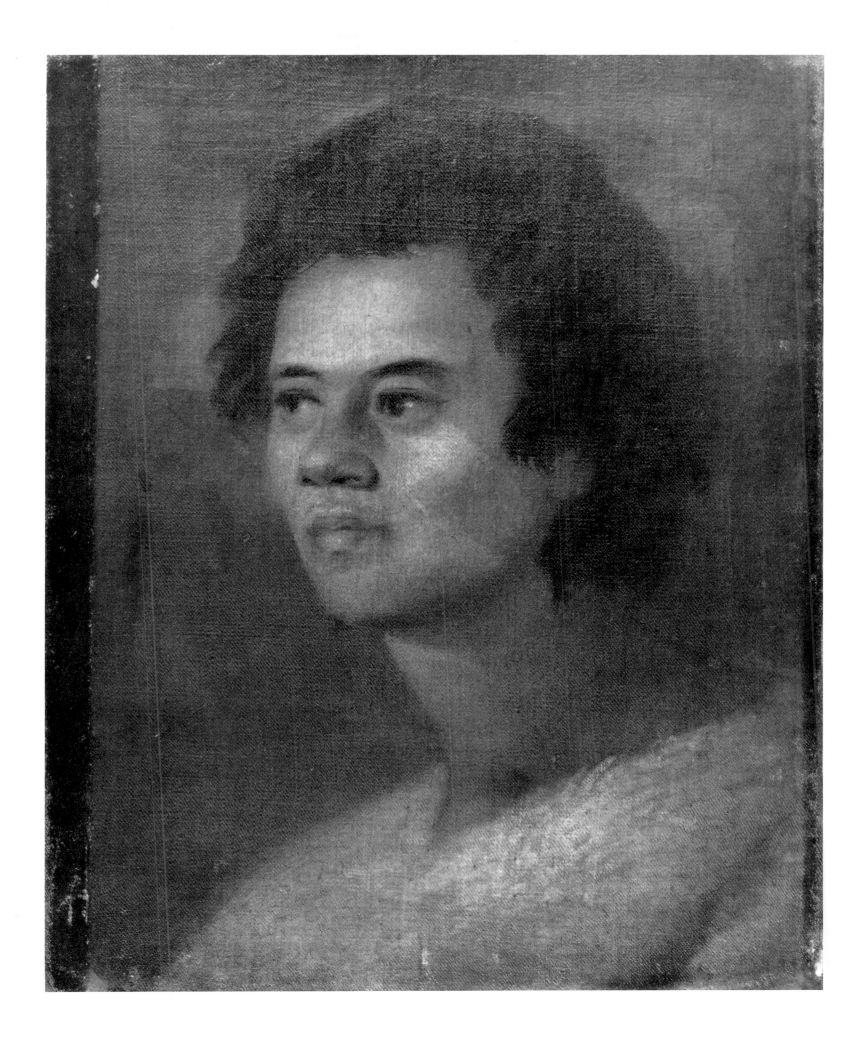

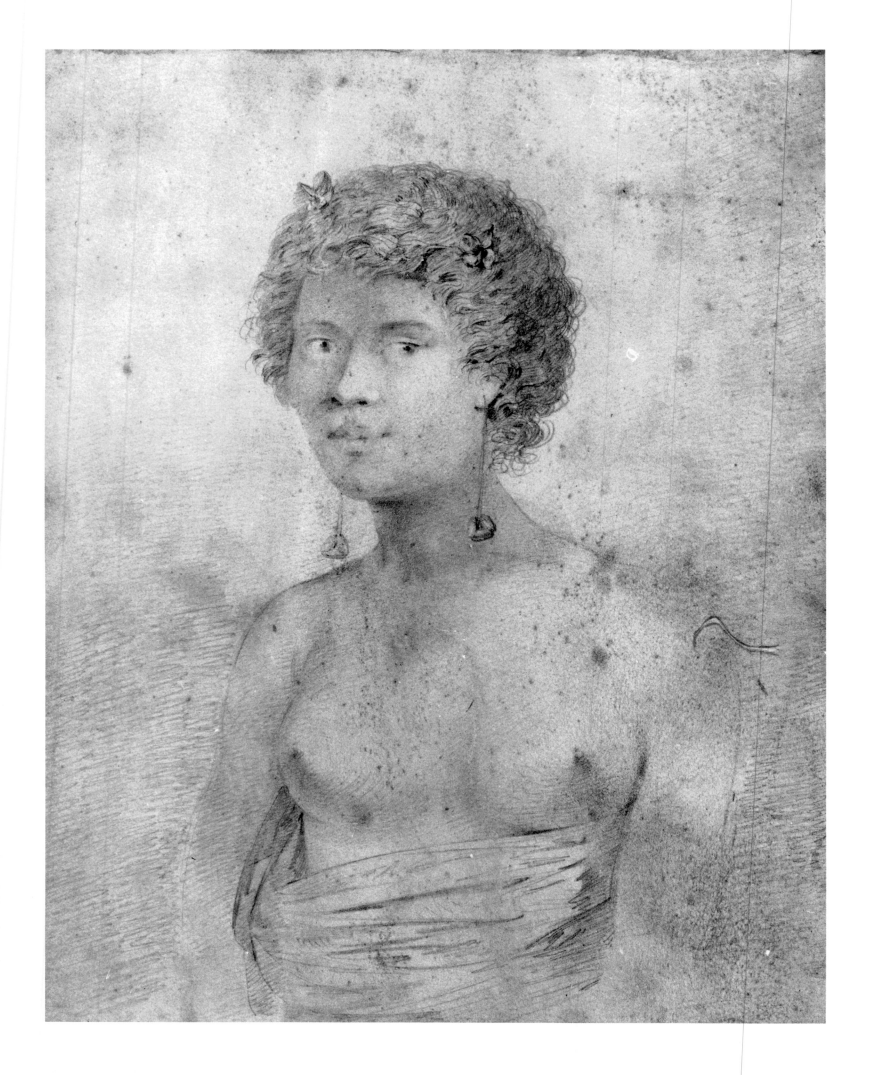

372

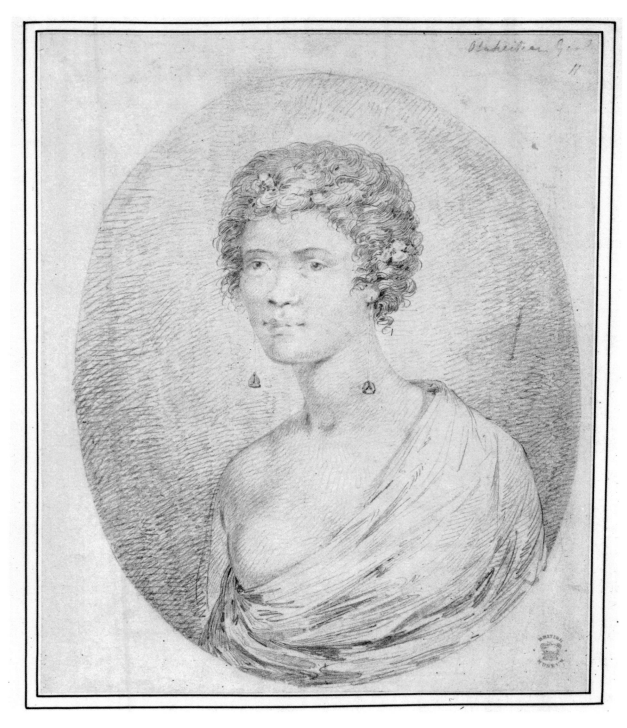

JOHN WEBBER

3.115   **A Girl of Otaheite**   [1777]
pencil, 10¾ × 8⁹⁄₁₆ : 273 × 217, unsigned.

The title taken from the back with 'Not published' added in pencil
in Sir William Dixson's hand. Also in an eighteenth century
hand in pencil 'Capⁿ Campbell', as well as 'Lot No 11' and '19'
in ink.

The original sheet mounted on another sheet of laid paper. Perhaps the drawing to which Webber refers to as no. 49 'A Portrait
of a Girl' in the section for the Society Islands in Webber's
Catalogue.

Draped beneath the breast, and wearing pendant ear ornaments
and two flowers in curly hair.

ver: For an earlier version see 3.116.

Dixson Library, State Library of New South Wales, Sydney.
Pe 213.

JOHN WEBBER

3.116   **A Girl of Otaheite**   [1777]
pencil, 11¹⁄₁₆ × 8¹⁵⁄₁₆ : 281 × 227 (oval
shaped) unsigned.

Inscribed 'Otaheitan Girl' in pencil (u.r.).

A girl with short curly hair, wearing pendant ear ornaments, the
right breast undraped.

ver: Possibly a field drawing from which 3.115 was developed.
ref: Kaeppler (1978a) fig. 226.

British Library, London. Add MS 17277, no 11.

373

WILLIAM ELLIS

3.117   **Tohaw [Teto'ofa]**   [1777]
         pencil, 10¹¹⁄₁₆ × 7⁵⁄₁₆ : 271 × 186, unsigned,
         w/m: 'Pro Patria' with Britannia.

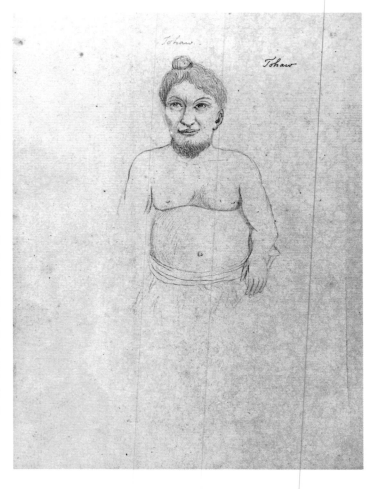

The title inscribed as above in ink and also in pencil above and
beside the figure. Numbered in pencil 'I.137' (u.r.) referring to
Ellis (1782). On verso inscribed '30' in brown ink (u.l.). On
verso is a drawing of Tahitians in canoes (see 3.164).

A heavily-built, middle-aged man seated, wearing a top-knot and
bare to the waist.

Teto'ofa (Tohaw, Towha, Tettowah) whom Cook had taken
during the second voyage to be the Admiral of the Tahitian fleet,
was the 'chief of Faaa or Tefana, and the most important chief
of the Oropaa division' of Tahiti (Beaglehole's note, Cook, *Journals*
III, 1, 198 5n). He was responsible for the ritual slaughter of the
man whose sacrifice was witnessed 'at the great Morai at Atta-
hourou' (see Cook *Journals* III, 1, 198, 205-6) and was visited
both before and after the event on 1 and 2 September, and on
later occasions. The precise date of this drawing is therefore
uncertain. Burney described him as 'the most gentlemanlike character of any of the Otaheite chiefs'. Cook, *Journals* III, 1, 219
n. Ellis called called him 'a man of a fine generous spirit . . .'
Ellis (1782) I, 137, 'We were now constantly visited by many of
the principal arees, among whom were Oammo (husband to the
late queen Oberea), Potatow, and Tohaw'. Ibid., 137.

ref: Murray-Oliver (1977) 33.

Alexander Turnbull Library, Wellington. A264.20A.

WILLIAM ELLIS

3.118   **A Portrait of Oammo [Amo]**   [1777]
         pencil, 8⁵⁄₁₆ × 7½ : 211 × 190, unsigned, w/m:
         'Pro Patria' with Britannia.

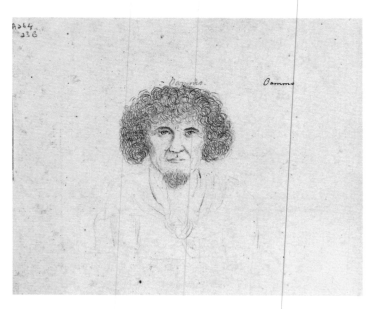

Inscribed 'Oammo' in ink and pencil near the head. Numbered
in pencil '1.145', referring to Ellis (1782). On recto a great
section of a view of the Tahitian coast (A 246.23 A) (see 3.96).

In full face with curly hair and small beard.

Amo, the *arii nui* of Papara, Tahiti, is mentioned in Banks's Journal (1962) 1, 293 as husband to Oberea. Both Cook and Ellis
mention his death after the ships had arrived at Moorea. Cook,
Journals III, 1, 226 and Ellis (1782) I, 145. This however seems
doubtful, see Beaglehole's note in Cook, *Journals* III, 1, 226 3n.

ref: Murray-Oliver (1977) 34.

Alexander Turnbull Library, Wellington. A264.23B.

JOHN WEBBER

3.119   **A View in the Valley of Matavai Bay [Tuauru Valley]**
         [plate 70]   **[1777]**
         pen, wash and water-colour, 12¼ × 19⅜ : 317 ×
         492.

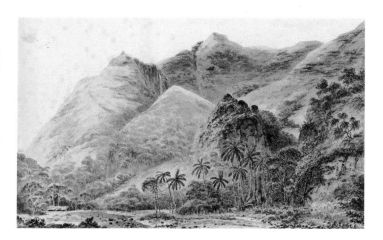

Formerly entitled 'Huaheine?' in pencil on the mount below the
drawing. Inscribed 'No 30' (u.l.) which corresponds to no. 30
'A View in the Valley of Matavy Bay' in Webber's Catalogue
from which the title above has been taken.

The valley of Matavai Bay is not commented upon by members
of the third voyage.

According to Bengt Danielsson of Tahiti, the view is 'from a
point about three kilometers up the Tuauru Valley behind Point
Venus'. *In litt.*, 29 May 1982.

ver: For two similar views by Webber and Ellis see 3.120 and
        3.121.

British Library, London. Add MS 15513, f. 15.

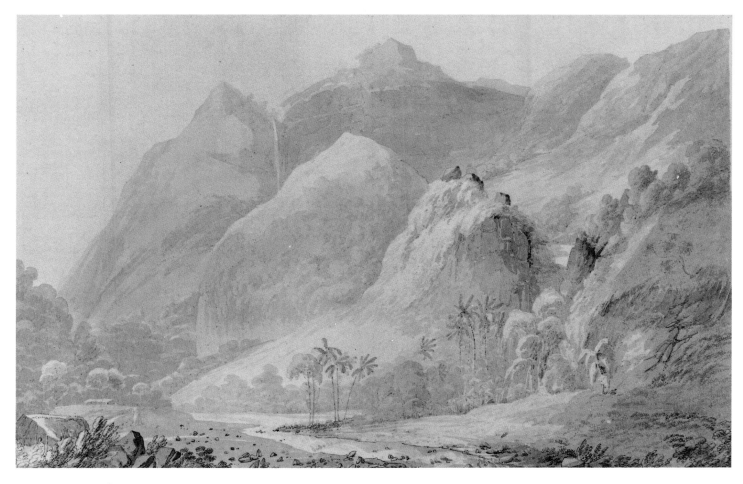

JOHN WEBBER

3.120   **A View in the Valley of Matavai Bay [Tuauru Valley]**
                                                  [c. 1786]
         pencil, pen, grey wash and water-colour, 12³⁄₁₆ ×
         17⅝ : 310 × 448 (including surrounding frame). Un-
         signed, w/m: lily in shield under crown and 'GR'
         underneath.

The drawing is very lightly washed with subtle shades of colouring
among areas of dominating grey wash. However, it does not have
the immediacy and spontaneity which Webber's earlier version
in the British Library (3.119) possesses.

ver: The drawing may have been prepared for Webber's etching
        'A View in O'Taheite' (3.120A). For an earlier version see
        3.119.

Collection of F. W. Hope, presented to the Bodleian Library in
1850 (together with portraits, topographical and caricature drawings), transferred to the Ashmolean Museum in 1924 together
with the Hope collection of prints.

Ashmolean Museum, Department of Prints and Drawings, Oxford.

375

JOHN WEBBER

3.120A a. 'A View in O'Taheite'
etching, 11⁷⁄₁₆ × 16⁷⁄₈ : 290 × 428. 'Drawn &
Etch'd by J. Webber'. 'Publish'd as the Act directs
Nov.ʳ 1st 1786 by J. Webber N.º 312 Oxford Street,
London'.

ver: For Webber's original composition see 3.119.
Hartnoll and Eyre, London (1978).

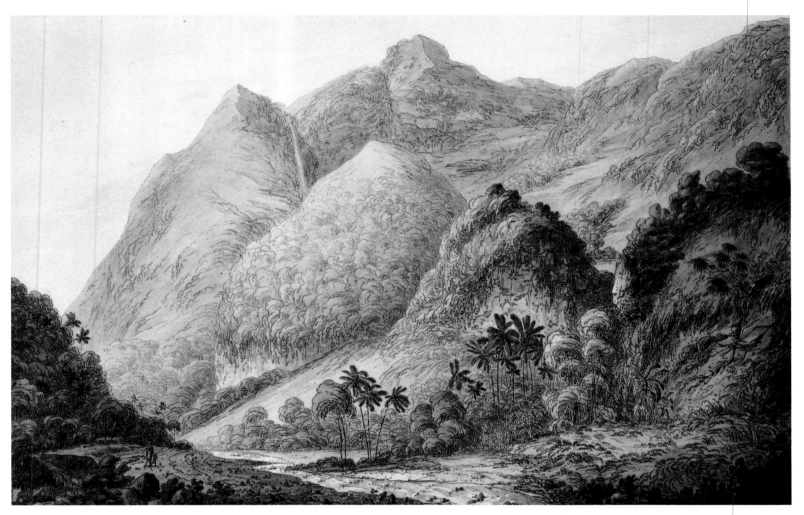

b. 'View in Otahaite'
the title in pencil along lower edge. Coloured etching,
mounted on cardboard, 13¼ × 18⁷⁄₁₆ : 337 × 468
(9¾ × 15¹⁄₁₆ : 248 × 382). 'J. Webber fecᵗ' in
pencil at l.l.

British Museum, Department of Prints and Drawings, London.
C. 6*.

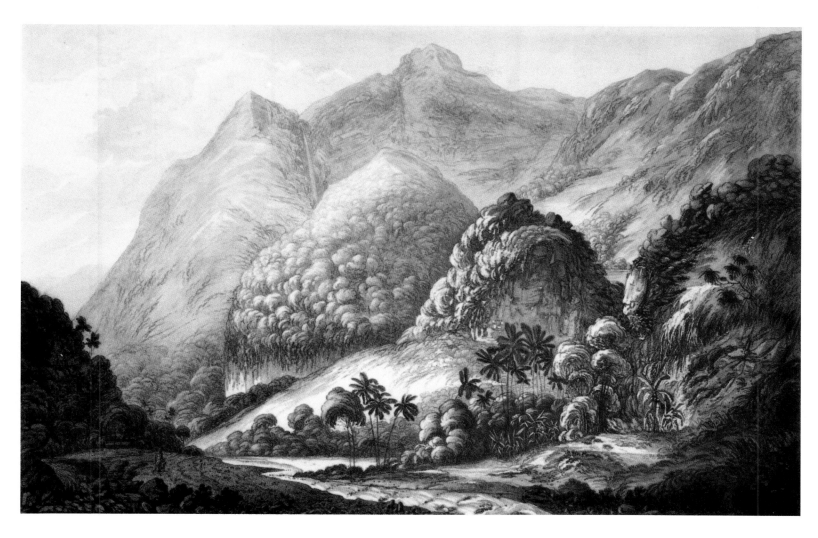

c. 'A View in Matavai, Otaheite'

monochrome aquatint, 11⁹⁄₁₆ × 17 : 294 × 432 (9⅞ × 15³⁄₁₆ : 250 × 385). 'Drawn & Etch'd by J. Webber'. 'Aqua Tinta by M.C. Prestel'. 'London Pub.ᵈ Feb.ʸ 1 1787 by I. Webber, N.º 312 Oxford Street'. 'Vide Cook's last Voy. Vol II. Chap. II'.

ref: Murray-Oliver (1969b), pl. 2 for the version in the Alexander Turnbull Library.

British Museum, Department of Prints and Drawings, London. 246* a.2. and C. 6*; Hartnoll and Eyre, London (1978); Alexander Turnbull Library, Wellington; National Library of Australia, Canberra.

This subject was not included in the series of Webber's *Views.* These are the only versions known to exist.

377

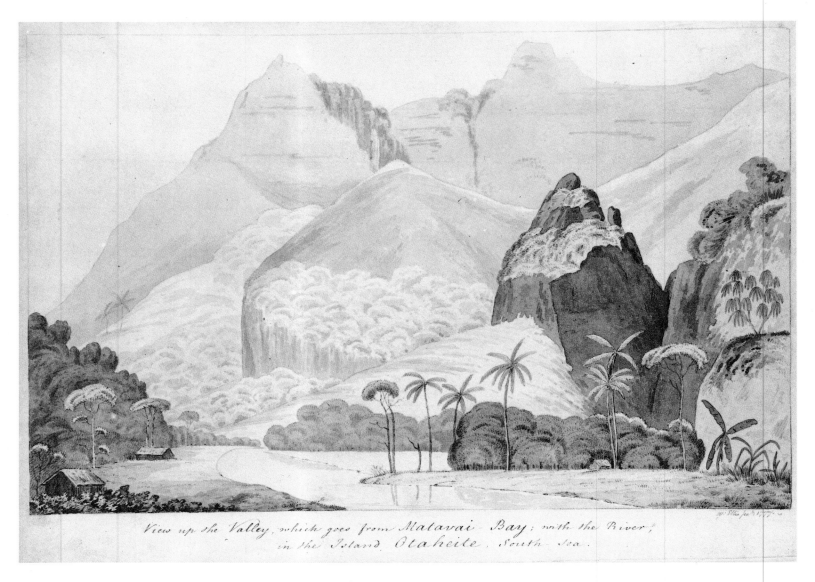

View up the Valley, which goes from Matavai-Bay; with the River, in the Island Otaheite, South Sea.

WILLIAM ELLIS

3.121   **A View up the Valley, which goes from Matavai-Bay [Tuauru Valley] [plate 71]   [Aug-Sep 1777]** water-colour over pencil, 9⅞ × 14⅞ : 252 × 378, signed and dated 'W. Ellis fec.ᵗ 1777' (l.r.) in black ink; w/m: lily in a shield under crown, with a 'W' underneath = J. WHATMAN.

The title as above in brown ink across the lower edge of the drawing, followed by 'with the River, in the Island Otaheite, South Sea'. Inscribed '18' in brown ink (u.l.).

Steep mountains with waterfalls and gently winding river; along the banks three huts and at right some dispersed coconut palms.

ver: See 3.119 and 3.120 for similar views by Webber, upon which this may be based.

ref: Rienits (1968) 119; Murray-Oliver (1969a) pl. 109 (col.).

Museum Book Store, London 1941, *Cat.* 125 (453) with the title as above.

National Library of Australia, Canberra. Rex Nan Kivell Collection. NK 53/0.

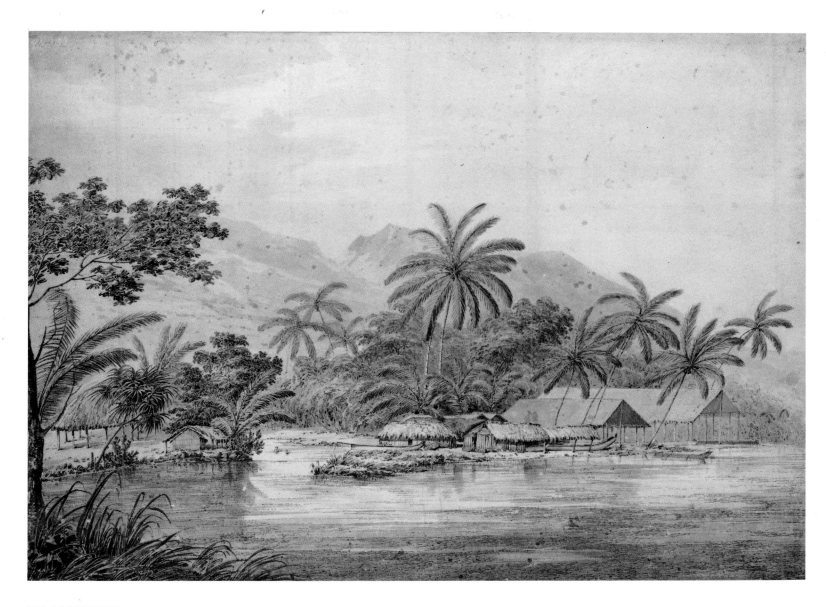

JOHN WEBBER

3.122   A View of Oparree [Pare]   [1777]
pen, wash and water-colour, 19 × 25¹³⁄₁₆ : 483 × 656, unsigned.

'No 46' (crossed out) (u.l.), substituted by 'no 50' (u.r.), corresponding to the drawing of that number in Webber's Catalogue, from which the title above has been taken.

A native village beside a bay. Native craft drawn up on the beach; two under boat sheds. Tall coconut palms and mountainous background.

While at Matavai Bay Cook visited Pare a number of times, the first being on 24 August 1777: 'About 9 oclock, Otoo the King, attended by a great many Canoes full of people came from Oparre and landed on Matavai point and sent word on board that he should be glad to see me there. Accordingly I went, accompanied by Omai and some of the Officers. . . . as soon as we had dined, a party of us accompanied Otoo to Oparre . . .' Cook, *Journals* III, 1, 192-3.

Bengt Danielsson suggests that the shore line is that of the northwest coast of Tahiti, 'perhaps in Pare or in Tataha', 'because the mountains slope down to the right and are approximately the same height as in those districts'. *In litt.* 29 May 1982.

British Library, London. Add MS 15513, f. 23.

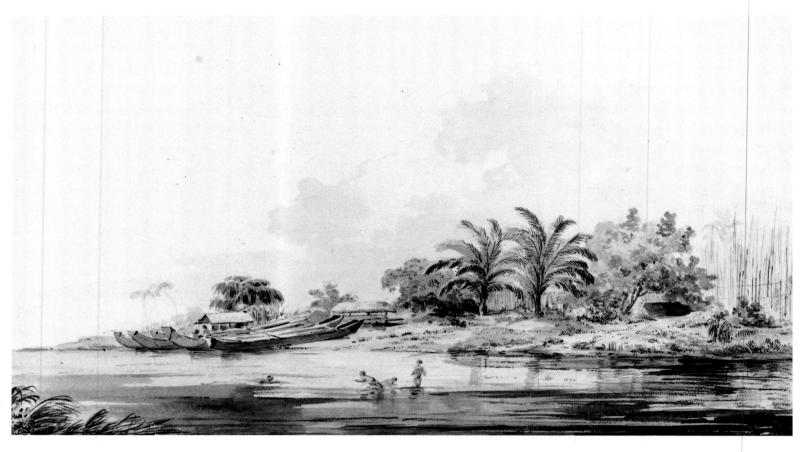

JOHN WEBBER

3.123   View in Otaheite [plate 72]   [Aug-Sep 1777]
wash and water-colour, 10¹⁄₁₆ × 18¹⁄₁₆ : 255 × 459, unsigned.

The title as above followed by 'Sketch from nature' in pencil on the mount below drawing.

Boats lying on the shore in the foreground, bathers in the water. This sketch was obviously taken from nature and represents a singular view among Webber's South Sea *oeuvre*.

ver: The palm trees bear some resemblance to Webber's study 3.430.

British Library, London. Add MS 17277, no. 14.

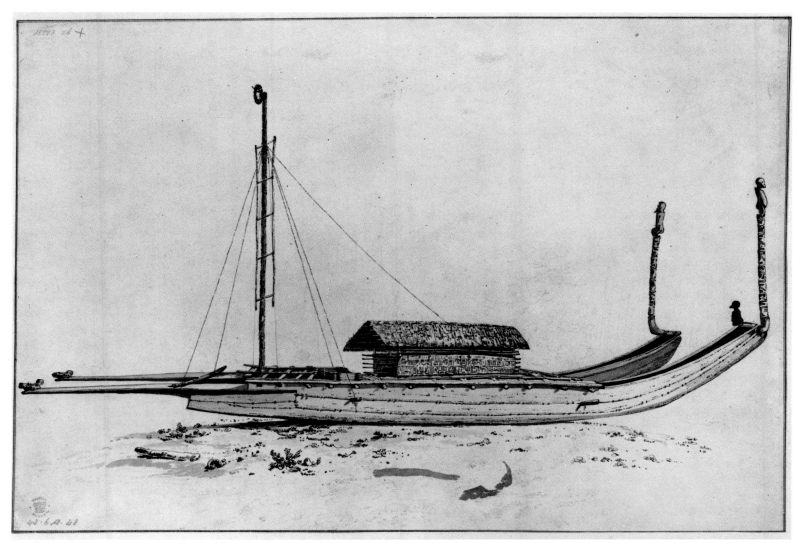

JOHN WEBBER

3.124   A Canoe of a Chief of Otaheite   [1777]
pen, wash and water-colour, $14^{5}/_{16}$ × $20^{3}/_{4}$:
364 × 527, unsigned.

Inscribed '41' (u.l.), which corresponds to 41 in Webber's Catalogue, from which the title above is taken.

It is possible, that this is the canoe which Tu wished to present
to Cook to take to England, but which Cook declined because
of its enormous size. Cook described it as follows: 'At first I
thought this Canoe had been a Model of one of their Vessels of
war, but I found it was a small Ivahah about sixteen feet long;
it was double and seemed to have been built for the purpose, and
was decorated with all those pieces of Carved work they usually
fix upon their Canoes.' Cook, *Journals* III, 1, 220.

For a discussion of a *tipairua*, or double traveling canoe, see Haddon and Hornell (1936) I, 129-32 where Webber's drawing is
described as 'the most careful drawing of this kind of craft known'
(131).

ver: For an almost identical but slightly smaller, less finished
          version, see 3.125. The same type of canoe appears in
          3.135, 3.138, 3.140 and 3.141.

ref: Haddon and Hornell (1936) I, fig. 87, (1938) III, fig. 29;
          Kaeppler (1978a) fig. 294; Durrans (1979) pl. 78.

British Library, London. Add MS 15513, f.26.

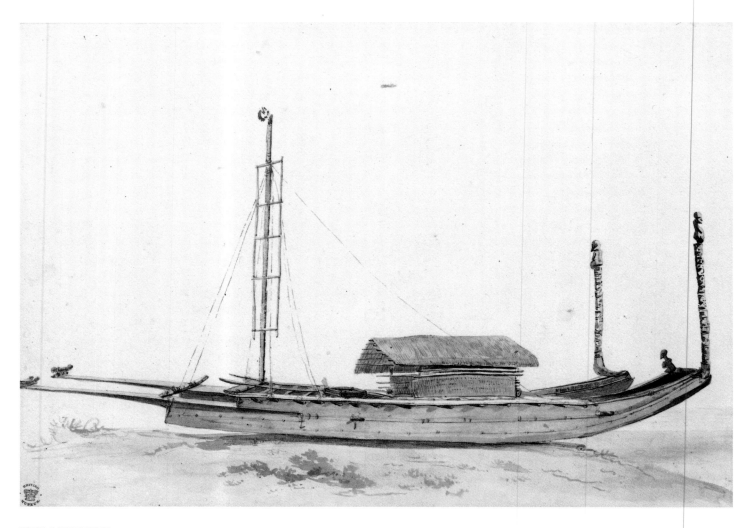

JOHN WEBBER

3.125   A Double Canoe of Otaheite   [Aug, Sep 1777]
water-colour, 12¼ × 17½ : 311 × 444, unsigned.

Inscribed 'Double Canoe Otaheite' in pencil on the mount below
drawing.

Apparently a field drawing.

ver: For a later and more developed version see 3.124.

ref: Cook, *Journals* III, 1, pl.25b.

British Library, London. Add MS 17277, no.13.

WILLIAM ELLIS

3.126   A Double Canoe of Otaheite   [1777]
pen, 7¼ × 9¾ : 185 × 250, unsigned; w/m: 'Pro
Patria' with Britannia.

Inscribed as above in ink across the lower edge of the drawing,
and 'Otaheite' [u.r.] also in ink. Numbered '35' [l.r.] On verso
is a drawing of a girl of Huaheine (3.147).

An outline drawing of a double canoe (*tipairua*) with a tall figure-
head mounted on the stern but without a thatched cabin and a
mast as in 3.124. It holds six Tahitians; two standing, one paddling.

ref: Murray-Oliver (1977) 34-5.

Alexander Turnbull Library, Wellington. A264.27B.

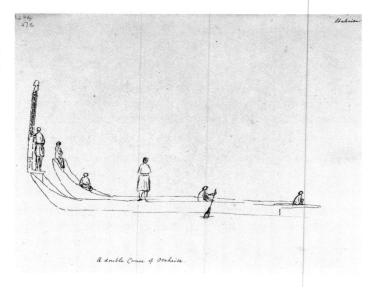

A double Canoe of Otaheite.

382

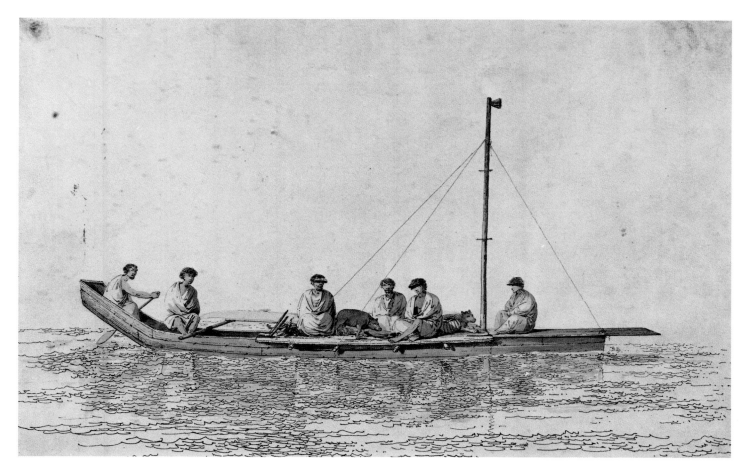

JOHN WEBBER

3.127   A Canoe of Otaheite   [1777]
pencil, pen and wash, 12$\frac{7}{16}$ × 19$\frac{5}{8}$: 317 × 498, unsigned; w/m: lower section of shield, with initials 'VDL' underneath = Van der Ley.

On verso 'Lot No 10' changed to '18' then crossed out, '17' substituted. Also endorsed in pencil in a later hand 'Canoe & Men of Tahiti unpublished'.

An outrigger island canoe (*va'a motu*) with a mast and three stay ropes. It contains six people, one rowing, and a pig, dog, basket and fruit. Three of the natives are wearing sun shades. On the type of canoe see Haddon and Hornell (1936) I, 112-20.

ver: The canoe is of the same kind as that depicted in 3.128. Another version (3.129) differs only in minor details, for example the absence of the dog and the basket at the mast.

Dixson Library, State Library of New South Wales, Sydney. Pf. 51.

JOHN WEBBER

3.128   A Canoe of Otaheite   [Aug-Sep 1777]
pen and wash, 5$\frac{13}{16}$ × 8$\frac{1}{16}$: 147 × 205, unsigned.

Inscribed 'Otaheitan Canoe — Sketch from Nature' in pencil on the mount below the drawing.

Probably a field-sketch and, as such, an earlier version of 3.127.

British Library, London. Add MS 17277, no. 12.

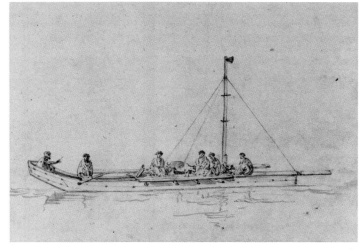

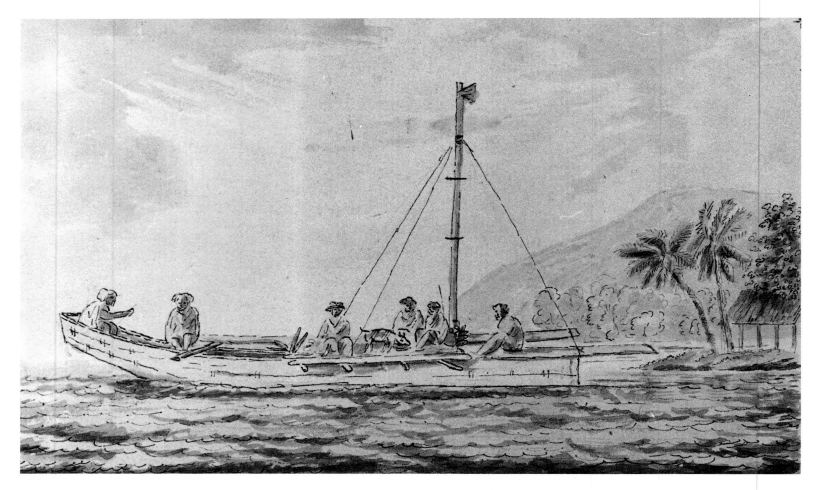

UNKNOWN ARTIST

3.129   A Canoe of Otaheite   [Aug–Sep 1777]
pen and water-colour, 4¹³⁄₁₆ × 8¼ : 122 × 210, within a lined frame on a sheet 7⁷⁄₁₆ × 10¾ : 188 × 275, unsigned; w/m: crown.

Inscribed 'A Boat of the Island Otahiete' in ink beneath a lined and sepia-bordered frame.

A canoe of the *va'a motu* type; at right a Tahitian house near two palm trees; a mountain rises in the distance.

ver: The drawing is another version of 3.127 and 3.128, but not by the same hand. The drawing has been attributed to Webber; Ellis has also been suggested. But the drawing is like neither in style. Henry Roberts is a possibility as is James Burney. Compare the treatment of foliage in 3.129, 3.142 and 3.319.

ref: *Exh. Cat.* Portland (1974) no. 146, where attributed to Ellis.

Purchased by H. O. Skinner, Hocken Librarian from Massey, London, June 1936.

Hocken Library Picture Collection, University of Otago, Dunedin. PaA 372 (6585).

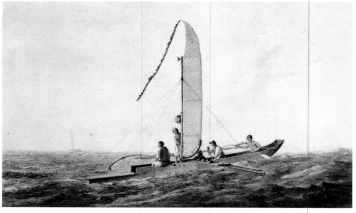

JOHN WEBBER

3.130   A Sailing Canoe of Otaheite   [1777–]
pen, wash and water-colour, 12¼ × 19¾ : 311 × 502, signed 'J. Webber del' [l.l.].

An outrigger canoe (*va'a motu*) with a balance platform under sail in the open sea, with one sail up, manned by four Tahitians. For the canoe see Haddon and Hornell (1936) I, 114-19.

ver: This drawing is a more accomplished version of 3.131 and 3.132, with minor differences in the figures and in the boat.

Smith gift, 1872, after having been exhibited at the Burlington Fine Arts Club, 1871.

National Gallery of Ireland, Dublin. Inv. no. 2303.

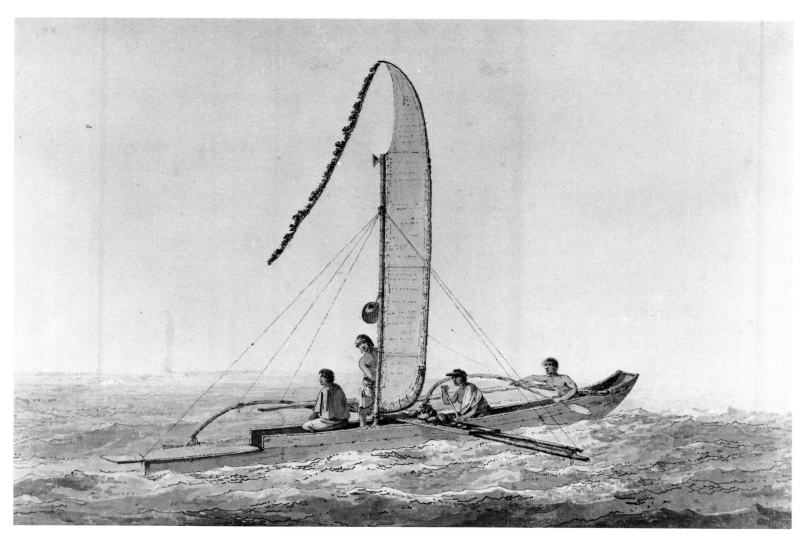

JOHN WEBBER

3.131   A Sailing Canoe of Otaheite   [1777–]
pen, wash and water-colour, 11⅞ × 18¾ : 301
× 476, unsigned.

Inscribed 'Canoe of Otaheite' faintly in pencil on the mount.
Mounted on board, and surrounded by enframing lines in sepia.
On verso inscribed in pencil 'Webber the Draftsman who went
with/Capt. Cook/ Vancouver probably instead of Capt. Cook'
and 'Roberts who went with Vancouver brought this to England'.

A canoe with a mast, manned by four natives, two rowing. The
first rower wearing an eye-shade.

ver: The drawing is similar to 3.130.

National Library of Australia, Canberra. Rex Nan Kivell Collection. NK 52/N.

JOHN WEBBER

3.132   A Sailing Canoe of Otaheite   [Aug-Sep 1777]
pen, pencil and sepia wash, 6⅝ × 9 : 168 × 229,
unsigned.

Inscribed 'Canoe Otaheite' in pencil (u.l.).

ver: A study for the sailing-boat (*va'a motu*) in 3.130 and 3.131.

National Maritime Museum, London. (In volume of plates to
Cook's Voyages.)

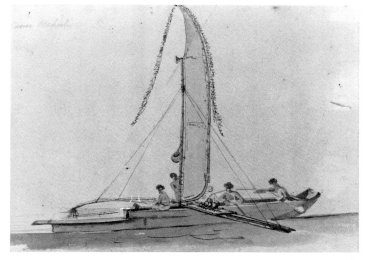

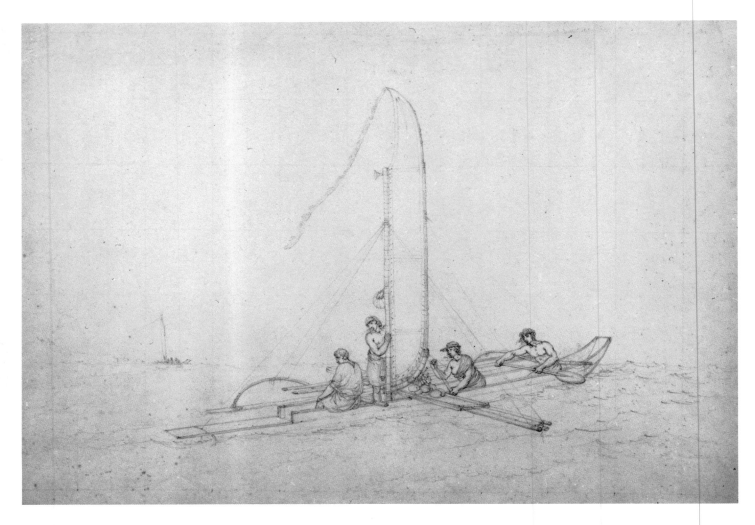

JOHN WEBBER

3.133   **A Sailing Canoe of Otaheite**   [c. 1792]
pencil, $11^{15}/_{16}$ × $17^{1}/_{8}$: 303 × 435 (sheet-size);
$11^{3}/_{16}$ ×17 : 284 × 432 (image-size); w/m:
'. . . MAN' (cut, probably Whatman).

The drawing is squared for transfer and is likely to be a preparatory
study for Webber's softground etching of the above title, published
1 August 1792 (3.133A). The softground etching is in reverse.

Close comparison between this drawing and Webber's print reveals a number of small but significant differences: The boat with
figures on the horizon is bigger than in the print. The woman
leaning against the mast shows tattoo marks on the back of her
hand, while the rower in the front of the boat has long hair in
comparison with his turban in the print. Such variations suggest
that the drawing is an original work by Webber and not a copy
after the print.

Eyre and Hobhouse, London (1984).

Private collection, England.

JOHN WEBBER

3.133A a. 'A Sailing Canoe of Otahaite'
softground etching, tinted in brown and grey wash, or hand-coloured, 15⁵⁄₁₆ × 17¹¹⁄₁₆ : 389 × 449 (11½ × 16½ : 292 × 419), 'I. Webber R.A. fecit'. 'London, Pub.ᵈ Aug.ᵗ [1] 1792 by I. Webber N.º 312 Oxford Street'. 'Vol. I' [sic. for II].

ver: For Webber's original composition see 3.130.

British Museum, Department of Prints and Drawings, London, 246* a.2. and C.6*.

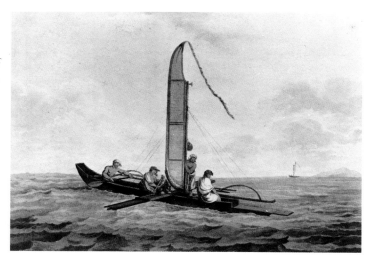

b. 'A Sailing Canoe of Otaheite'
coloured aquatint. 'I. Webber R.A. fecit'. 'London, Pub.ᵈ April 1. 1809 by Boydell & Comp.ʸ N.º 90 Cheapside'. 'Vol. I' [sic. for II].

Issued by J. Boydell, *Views in the South Seas* (London, 1808) pl. III.

National Maritime Museum, London; Bernice P. Bishop Museum, Honolulu.

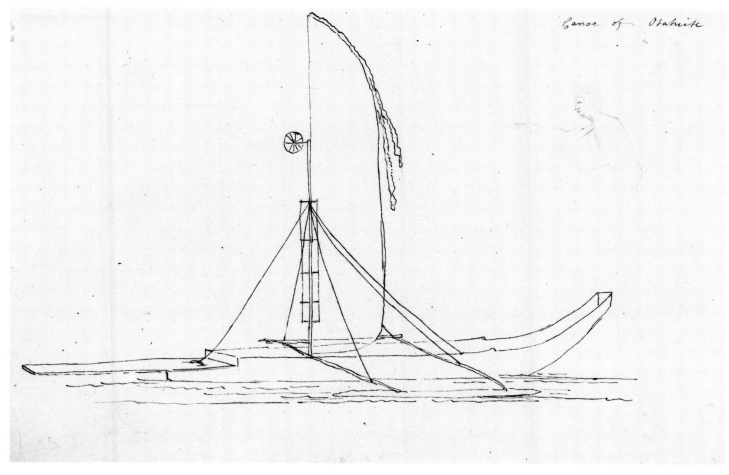

WILLIAM ELLIS

3.134 A Sailing Canoe of Otaheite [1777]
pen and pencil, 7¼ × 11¾ : 185 × 295, w/m: 'Pro Patria' with Britannia.

Inscribed 'Canoe of Otaheite' in ink (u.r.) and numbered 'n. 178' in pencil. On verso is a drawing of two natives of Hawaii (3.324).

A profile drawing of an unmanned outrigger canoe of the same kind as 3.130 and 3.133. At right, in pencil, a male figure with right arm outstretched and fingers extended. The canoe is a *va'a motu*. See Haddon and Hornell (1936) I, 112-22.

ref: Murray-Oliver (1977) 35.

Alexander Turnbull Library, Wellington. A264.29A.

MOOREA [AIMEO]

30 September to 11 October 1777   3.135–3.139

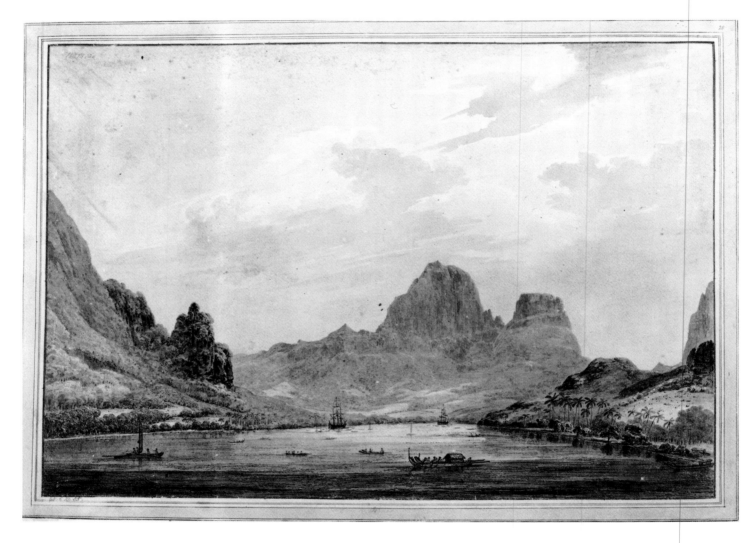

JOHN WEBBER

3.135   A View of Aimeo Harbour [Papetoai Bay]
         [plate 74]   [Oct 1777–]
pen, wash and water-colour, 17⅜ × 24⅞ : 441 × 632,
unsigned.

Titled 'A View in Aimeo' in pencil on the mount below the
drawing. The drawing is listed as no. 54 'A View of Aimeo
Harbour' in Webber's Catalogue.

The *Resolution* and *Discovery* and many kinds of native craft in
Papetoai Bay (or Baie d'Opunohu). The old name for the harbour
was Talough or Taloo. Two mountainous peaks in the background.

For Cook's description of the geographical situation of the bay
see Cook, *Journals* III, 1, 225.

ver: For another version see 3.136. The two canoes in the left
        and centre foreground can be related to studies of canoes
        by Webber in 3.124 and 3.125 and 3.132.

ref: Kaeppler (1978a) fig. 295; Cobbe (1979) pl. III (col.).

British Library, London. Add MS 15513, f. 20.

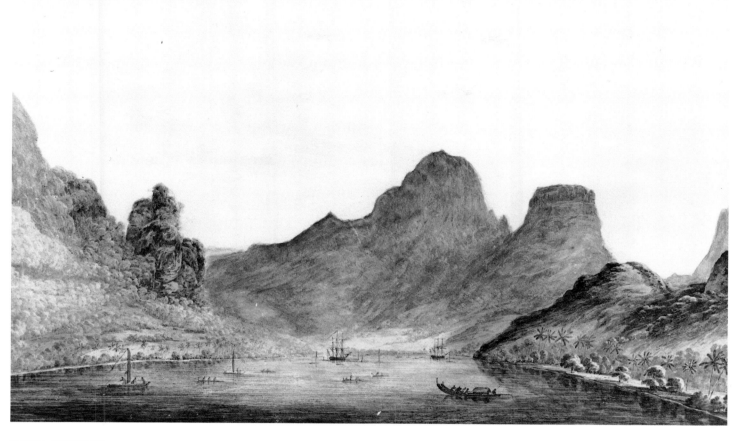

JOHN WEBBER

JOHN WEBBER

3.136   A View of Aimeo Harbour [Papetoai Bay]
[Oct 1777–]
water-colour, 16⅝ × 25⁷⁄₁₆ : 422 × 646, signed
and dated in ink 'J. Webber del. 1786' (l.l.).

Mounted on cardboard and surrounded by fine framing lines.
Titled 'A View of the Harbour of Toloo' in ink on the back of
the mount, possibly in Webber's hand. Also in pencil probably
in Sir William Dixson's hand 'View of the Harbour of Taloo,
Eimeo J. Webber 1786'.

ver: A later version of 3.135.

Maggs Bros., London (1927) no. 491, 107, acquired by Sir William
Dixson, 1929. 3.136 is the drawing 'never reproduced
. . . secured by Maggs and . . . sold to Australia', about which
Captain A. W. F. Fuller speaks (see 3.156).

Dixson Galleries, State Library of New South Wales, Sydney.
DG 24.

3.137   A View of Aimeo Harbour [Papetoai Bay]   [1777]
water-colour, 17 × 24 : 431 × 610, signed and dated
John Webber 'feᵗ 1777' (l.r.).

The drawing may be tentatively identified as no. 55 'A Ditto'
['A View of Aimeo Harbour'] in Webber's Catalogue.

A view looking south into the bay with the *Resolution* and *Discovery*
at anchor; a native hut at left by the shore and in the left
foreground a canoe by the shore with two natives nearby.

ver: The drawing gives a different view of the harbour from
3.135 and 3.136, moving further to the right and showing
additional mountain peaks, the ones to the right being Mt
Matotea and Mt Tautuapae.

ref: Brewington (1968) 455, no. 1745.

Gift of Stephen W. Phillips, 1947.
Peabody Museum, Salem. M 12,465.

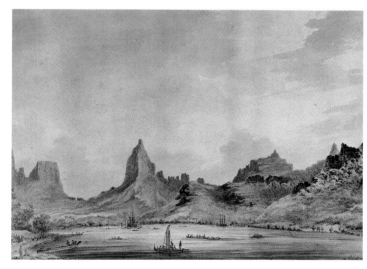

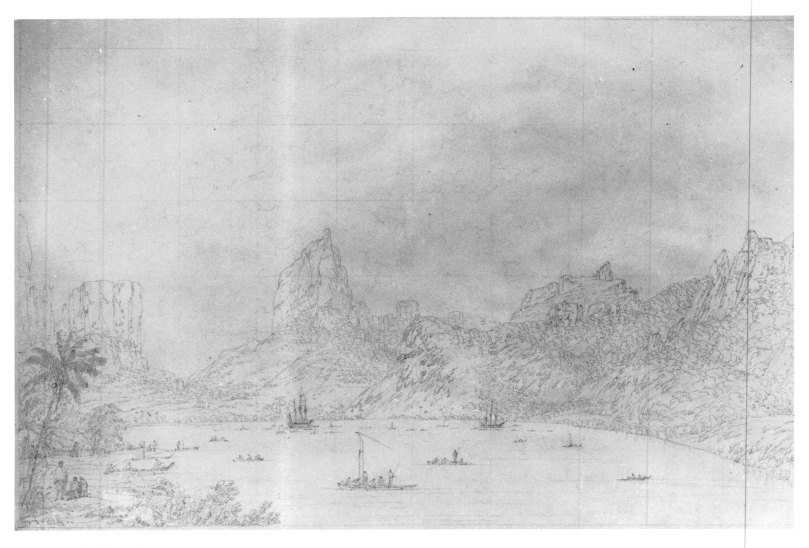

JOHN WEBBER

3.138   **A View of the Harbour of Taloo, in the Island of Eimeo**
[c. 1789]

pencil, 10¾ × 16⅛ : 274 × 410; w/m: PORTAL & BRIDGES.

On verso a squeeze of a drawing or of a print of 'A Toopapaoo for a Chief, with a Priest making his Offering to the Morai'. The drawing is squared for transfer and is likely to be a preparatory study for Webber's softground etching of the title above, published 1 July 1789 (3.138A).

Comparing the drawing with the print there are a number of small but significant differences: among the most noticeable of these are the figures standing next to the hut and in the opening of the hut at the left, which do not appear in the print. A canoe in the centre of the drawing is shown containing four natives, three rowing and one standing up; in the print the figures are reduced to three, with only two rowing. These and other minor variations suggest that the drawing is an original work by Webber rather than a copy after the print.

Alexander Turnbull Library, Wellington. B 91/6.

3.138A **a. 'View of the Harbour of Taloo, in the Island of Eimeo'**

softground etching, tinted in brown and grey wash, or hand-coloured, 12¾ × 17¹¹⁄₁₆ : 323 × 449 (11⅛ × 16⅜ : 282 × 416). 'J. Webber fecit'. 'London Pub.ᵈ July 1. 1789 by J. Webber N.º 312 Oxford Street'. 'Vide Cooks last Voyage Vol II. Chap. V'.

ver: For Webber's original composition see 3.137.

British Museum, Department of Prints and Drawings, London, 246˙ a.2. and C. 6˙.

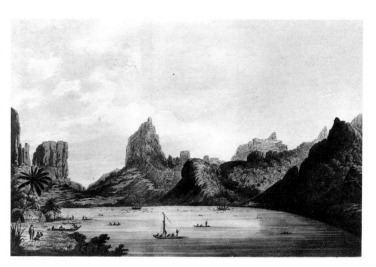

b. 'View of the Harbour of Taloo, in the Island of Eimeo'

coloured aquatint. 'J. Webber fecit'. 'London Pub.ᵈ April 1 1809 by Boydell & Comp.ʸ N.º 90 Cheapside'. 'Vide Cooks last Voyage vol II. Chap. V'.

Issued as J. Boydell, *Views in the South Seas* (London, 1808) pl. VII.

National Maritime Museum, London; Bernice P. Bishop Museum, Honolulu.

3.138 **c. A copy by an unknown copyist**

pen, wash and water-colour, measuring 14⅝ × 19½ : 373 × 495.

Inscribed in ink lower margin 'View of the Harbour of Taloo, in the Island of Eimeo. Vol II, Chap. V' by an eighteenth century copyist. Kept in the National Maritime Museum, London. The drawing makes some additions to the margins of the original composition.

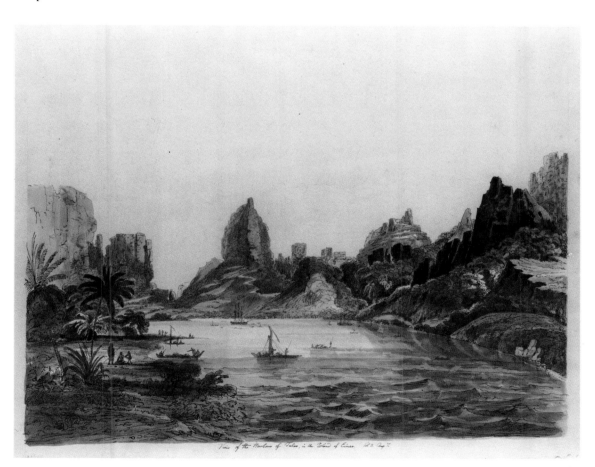

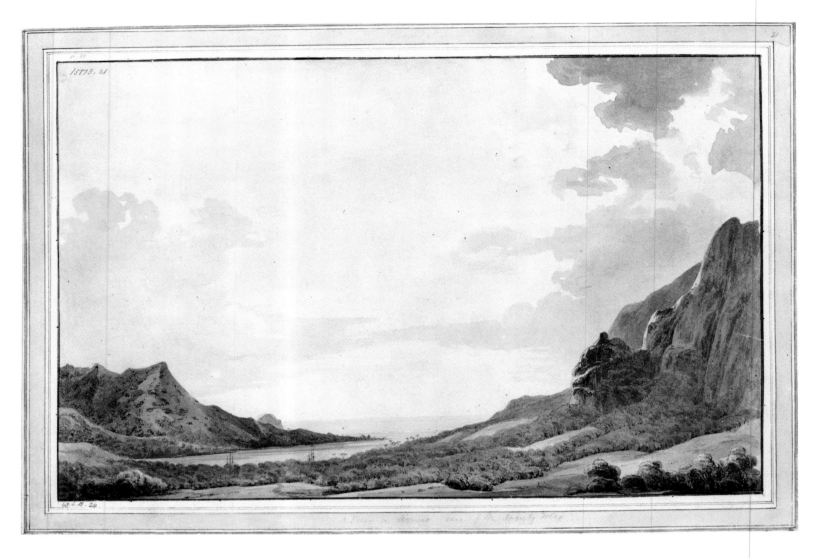

JOHN WEBBER

3.139   **A View of Aimeo Harbour [Papetoai Bay]**
         [plate 75]   **[Oct 1777]**
         wash and water-colour, 12½ × 19½ : 317 × 495,
         signed 'Drawn from Nature by John Webber'.

Inscribed 'A View in Aimeo, one of the Society Isles' in pencil
on the mount below the drawing. Inscribed '31' (u.l.) corresponding to the drawing no. 31 'A View of the Harbour of Aimeo
from the Hills' in Webber's Catalogue.

The drawing shows Papetoai Bay (or Baie d'Opunohu) towards
the sea and from an opposite viewpoint to that of 3.135 and
3.137. The masts of the two ships are seen in the bay.

One of Webber's most lyrical landscapes. Perhaps he was as sus-
ceptible to the beauty of the spot as Ellis, who wrote: 'Imaio is,
without exception, the most pleasant of all the Society Isles. Its
appearance is truly romantic, and it abounds with variety of landscapes that are delightful beyond description: it is divided nearly
in the centre by a range of mountains, that rise in a variety of
forms appearing like old ruined castles or churches. At the bottom
of them is a large tract of moderately high land, interspersed with
groves of various trees; on one side of this, the land makes a
sudden break, and forms a most delightful valley, beyond which
the scene is beautifully contrasted, and the view closed by several
irregular mountains.' Ellis (1782) I, 146-7.

ref: Cook, *Journals* III, 1, pl. 28.

British Library, London. Add MS 15513, f. 21.

HUAHINE [FARE]

12 October to 2 November 1777   3.140–3.148

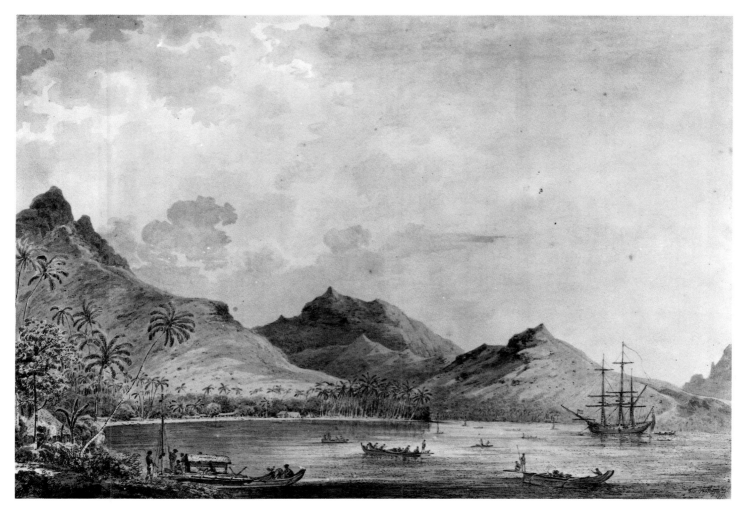

JOHN WEBBER

3.140   **A View of the Harbour of Huaheine [Fare]**
            [plate 78]   [12 Oct-2 Nov 1777]
            pen, wash and water-colour, 17½ × 25 : 445 × 633,
            signed and dated 'John Webber 1777 (l.r.).

Inscribed 'Huaheine Harbour' in pencil on the mount below drawing. This is probably the view entitled 'A View of the Harbour
of Huaheine' in Webber's Catalogue, no. 59.

A sweeping view of Fare Harbour with peaked mountains in the
back. In the bay at right the *Resolution* and many native craft;
palm trees at centre and left. By the shore a group of natives
tending a double canoe with a deck-house. In the background
and along the shore native huts and English tents. On the far
left a mountain, which may be identified as Mt Turi.

The view gives the location of Omai's settlement if only at a
distance in the depth of the bay. Cook had agreed with the chiefs
for a place for Omai to settle and describes it thus: 'The extent
along the shore of the harbour was about two hundred yards and
its depth to the foot of the hill something more, but a proportional

part of the hill was included in the grant. This point being settled
to the satisfaction of all parties, I set up a tent a shore, established
a post, there Set up the observatorys to make the necessary Observations and the Carpenters of both Ships were set to work to
build a small house for Omai to secure his property in; in the
mean time some hands were employed making a Garden, Planting
Shaddocks, Vines, Pine apples, Millons and several other articles,
all of which were in a flourishing state before we left the Island.'
Cook, *Journals* III, 1, 235. Samwell supplements the account:
'. . . this Business took us up about a fortnight' and gives a
description of Omai's house. Cook, *Journals* III, 2, 1070.

ver: Similar to 3.141.
ref: *Exh. Cat.* Auckland (1964), pl. 38; Cook, *Journals* III, 1,
        pl. 29.

British Library, London. Add MS 15513, f. 22.

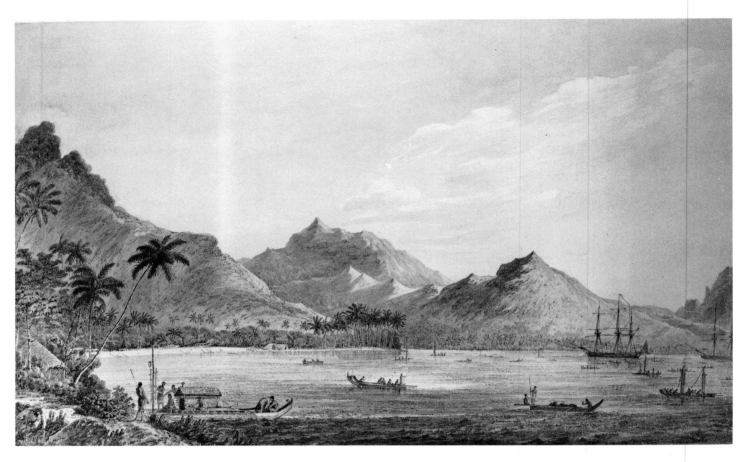

JOHN WEBBER

3.141   A View of the Harbour in Huaheine   [c. 1781-3]
pen and water-colour, 15½ × 25¼ : 394 × 641, signed
and dated 'J. Webber del 1778' (l.r.).

Inscribed 'A View of Huaheine slightly varying from the engraved'
in pencil by a later hand on the folio.

Almost the same view as 3.140, but slightly extended on the
right and also showing the *Discovery.* Many native craft plying
about the harbour. It is noteworthy that the drawing is dated
1778, and it seems that Webber, who executed it several years
after the voyage, was mistaken about the date of the visit to
Huaheine.

ver: Engraved by W. Byrne (3.141A) who altered the disposition and gestures of the group at left, and introduced a
sailing canoe in the central foreground, while removing one
at the right, and extending the mountain range at the back.

Dixson Library, State Library of New South Wales, Sydney.
PXX 2, 16.

JOHN WEBBER (after)

3.141A   'A VIEW of HUAHEINE'
Engraving. 'J. Webber del.' — 'W. Byrne sculp.'

Published in Cook/King (1784) pl. 31, II, 91.

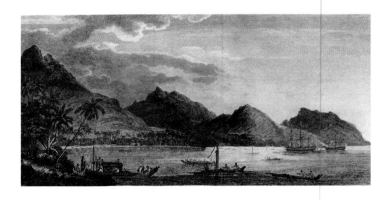

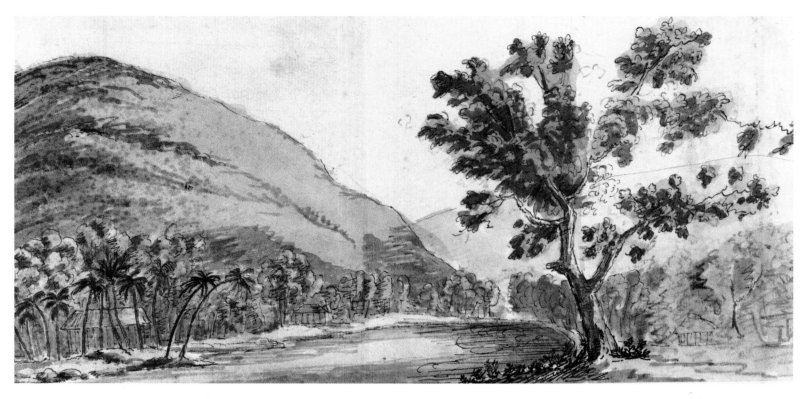

UNKNOWN ARTIST

3.142   **A View in Huaheine (?)**
pencil, pen and water-colour, $6\frac{1}{16} \times 12\frac{5}{8}$: 154 $\times$ 321, unsigned; w/m: lily.

The drawing is stuck on to f. 91 of James Burney's log.

A view of a bay or an inlet, surrounded by trees, including palm trees and native huts. Mountains in the background. The identification of the scene is tentative and is based upon the position of the drawing within the journal. On f. 93 Burney describes the carpenters of the ships going on shore and beginning to build Omai's house. Thus the place drawn here was apparently supposed to give an idea of the spot.

The drawing is characterized by a strong use of the pen, especially in the trees. The foliage of the trees is schematically blotted in yellow, brown and green water-colour. The draughtsmanship is quick and generous and seems to be modelled upon Webber's style but does not reach its precision, neither does it achieve Webber's sense of spatial shading. The particular style of the drawing seems to reappear in a few other drawings executed during the voyage, but the artist has not been identified. It is possible that it may be James Burney himself, on the other hand, the drawing has been stuck on to the page and thus could well have been acquired by Burney from another draughtsman.

Mitchell Library, State Library of New South Wales, Sydney. Log of James Burney, vol. II. f. 91 (Safe 1/64).

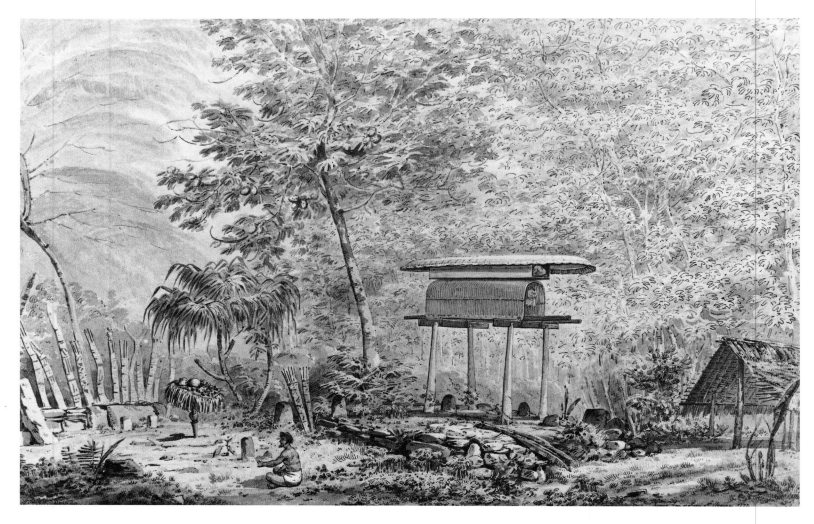

JOHN WEBBER

3.143   **A Toopapaoo [*tupapau*] for a Chief, with a Priest Making his Offering to the Morai**
[plate 60]   **[Oct 1777]**
pencil, pen, wash and water-colour, 12⁷⁄16 × 19½ :
316 × 495.

Inscribed in Webber's hand (l.r.) 'drawn from nature at Huaina 1777'. The original sheet surrounded by frame lines in ink and pasted on cardboard. The title as above in Sir William Dixson's hand in pencil on verso, followed by 'Huaheine. Reproduced in Views in the S. Seas'. Also on verso in ink 'Lot No 5' deleted, '3' substituted; in pencil endorsed 'glass 3'. This is probably the drawing referred to in Webber's Catalogue as no. 45 'A Toupapow or Burying Place at Huaheine'.

A bearded native squatting in the central foreground in an enclosure surrounded by masonry walls, an 'offering table' to his left and a large *fata tupapau* to his right; an open roofed enclosure at extreme right. This scene is not referred to in Cook's Journals.

The picture has faded considerably because of exposure to light. There are deeper shades of blue along the upper edge, where it has been protected.

ver: For other versions see 3.144, 3.145.

Dixson Library, State Library of New South Wales, Sydney. Pf 56.

JOHN WEBBER

3.144 **A Toopapaoo [*tupapau*] of a Chief, with a Priest Making his Offering to the Morai** [1786]
pen, wash and water-colour, 16½ × 22⁹⁄₁₆ : 419 × 573, signed 'J. Webber del' (l.l.) and on the frame 'J. Webber del 1786'.

ver: Another version of 3.143 and 3.145, except for minor alterations in the foliage and the figure.

Collection of Captain A. W. F. Fuller. This is the drawing of a 'Toopapaoo of a Chief in Huaheine' about which Captain Fuller speaks in connection with Webber's 'View in Ulietea'. Fuller bought the drawing at Sotheby's in the 1920s (see 3.156).

National Maritime Museum, London.

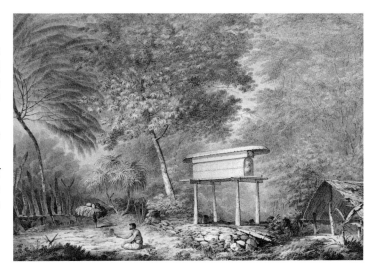

JOHN WEBBER

3.145 **A Toopapow [*tupapau*] of a Chief, with a Priest making his Offering to the Morai** [1788]
pen, wash and water-colour, 7 × 9¼ : 176 × 235, signed and dated 'J. Weber del 1788' in grey ink at l.l. on the frame.

Inscribed on verso in ink in Webber's hand 'Place d'Enterrement at Otahaiti'. Also later inscription 'Begräbnisplatz auf einer Südsee Insel. Gezeichnet von Wäber, Beitrag von Herrn von Mülinen 1852', also 'Künstlerbuch'. Pasted on cardboard and surrounded by frame lines.

The date of 1788 and the Germanized spelling of Webber's name suggest that the drawing was made as a presentation copy and given away by Webber during his stay in Bern in 1787.

ver: Another version of 3.143 and 3.144. The drawing served as a model for a handcoloured engraving by F. Hegi (5⁵⁄₁₆ × 6¹¹⁄₁₆ : 135 × 170) published as a frontispiece to the siebenzehntes *Neujahrsstück*, see Wagner (1821).

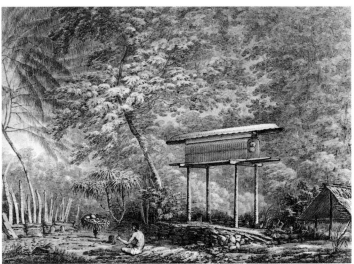

Collection Schultheiss Nikolaus Friedrich von Mülinen (1760-1833), Bern, included in the Künstleralbum (1852) vol. 2, 20. (Mülinen, who later became burgermeister of Bern, spent his early years as a student of the anthropologist J. F. Blumenbach in Göttingen and as such certainly had an interest in ethnology and travel literature. In 1811 he was instrumental in founding the historical society in Bern. He performed functions as a diplomat and politician. Possibly he received Webber's drawing in 1787, when Webber visited Bern.

Kunstmuseum, Bern. Inv. no. A6436.

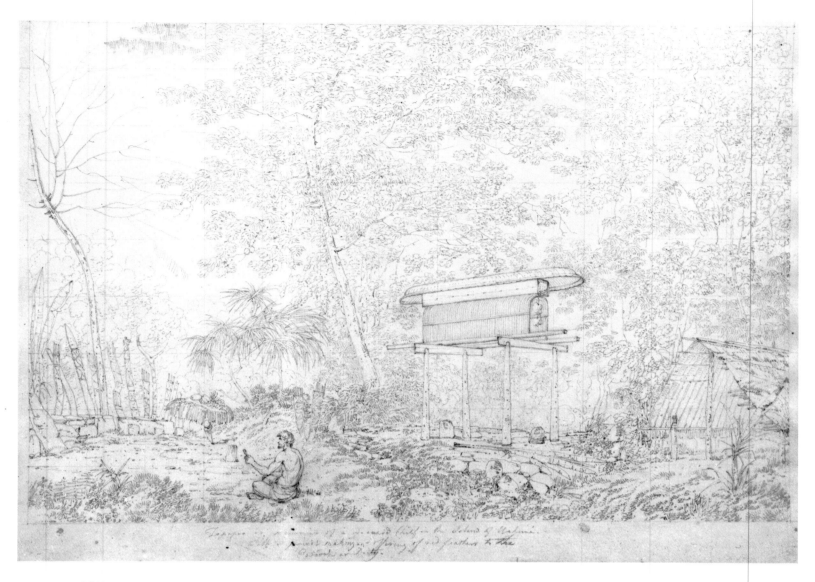

JOHN WEBBER

3.146 **A Toopapaoo of a Chief, with a Priest making an Offering to the Morai, in Huaheine** [1789]
pencil, 12⅜ × 17⅝ : 315 × 447 (sheet-size); 10⅞ × 16⅜ : 276 × 416 (image-size); w/m: lily in shield under crown, with 'GR' below.

Inscribed in pencil along lower edge in Webber's hand: 'Topapao or monument of a Deceased Chief in the Island of Uaheine with a priest making an offering of red feathers to the Eatooah or Deity'.

The drawing is squared for transfer and thus a preparatory study for Webber's softground etching of the title above, published 1 October 1789 (3.146A). The softground etching is in reverse.

Close comparison between this drawing and Webber's print reveals a number of small but significant differences: the drawing shows a slab of stone between the priest and the offering platform, which in the print has been pushed back and made considerably smaller. Also the tree on the left of the drawing is only outlined. In the drawing there are only two slabs of stone below the structure as opposed to three in the print. Also there are no boulders overgrown by lichens in the drawing. Finally there is a notable difference between the height: 276 in the drawing, 285 in the print. Such details and the inscription in Webber's hand indicate that this drawing is an original work by Webber.

Eyre and Hobhouse, London (1984).

Private collection, England.

398

JOHN WEBBER

3.146A   **a. 'A Toopapaoo of a Chief, with a Priest making his offering to the Morai, in Huoheine'**
softground etching, tinted in brown and grey wash, or hand-coloured, $12\frac{7}{8} \times 17\frac{5}{8}$: 326 × 447 ($11\frac{1}{4} \times 16\frac{3}{8}$: 285 × 416).'J. Webber fecit'. 'London Pub. Oct. 1 1789 by I. Webber N.° 312 Oxford Street'. 'Vide Cook's last Voy. Vol II. Ch. VI.'

ver: For Webber's original composition see 3.143.

British Museum, Department of Prints and Drawings, London, 246* a.2. and C. 6*. (The copy in 246* a.2. is signed 'J. Webber fecit R.A.'.)

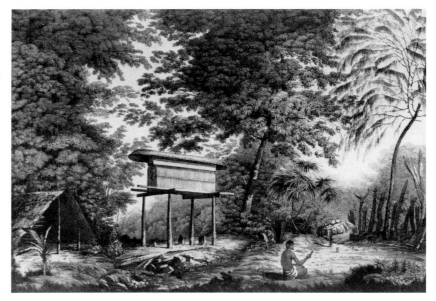

b. 'A Toopapaoo of a Chief, with a Priest making his offering to the Morai, in Huoheine'
coloured aquatint. 'J. Webber fecit R.A.'. 'London Pub.ᵈ April 1 1809 by Boydell & Comp.Y N.° Cheapside'.'Vide Cook's last Voy. Vol II. Ch. VI'.

Issued as J. Boydell, *Views in the South Seas* (London, 1808) pl. VIII.

National Maritime Museum, London; Bernice P. Bishop Museum, Honolulu.

3.146   **c. A copy of 3.146A**
pen, wash and water-colour, measuring $15\frac{9}{16} \times 19\frac{11}{16}$: 396 × 500, inscribed in ink along lower margin 'A Toopapaoo of a Chief, with a Priest making his offering to the Morai in Huoheine, London 1789 par Webber' by an eighteenth century copyist.

Kept in the Yale Center for British Art, New Haven (Paul Mellon Collection). The drawing adds some foliage around the margins of the original composition.

We are indebted to M. Patrick Noon of the Yale Center for British Art for the following observation: 'The copy after Plate VIII is noticeably larger than the other compositions. In fact $1\frac{1}{2}$ in. have been added to the composition along the top, bottom, and left edges. The right side has been extended only $\frac{1}{2}$ inch. These additional areas have been filled with rather unusual foliage, including numerous cacti, none of which appears in the published etching.' *In litt.* 3 January 1978.

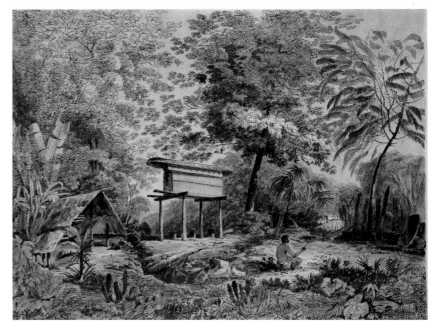

The inscription suggests a French source and the use of drawings of cactus plants in the foreground of many of the copies suggests that deception was not the intent but some form of illustrative purpose for which Webber was a useful source. It is possible that the copies were made for a French edition of Cook's voyages, or were drawn for a publication directed at a different audience, for example a geographical text providing a wide coverage of exotic lands and peoples.

399

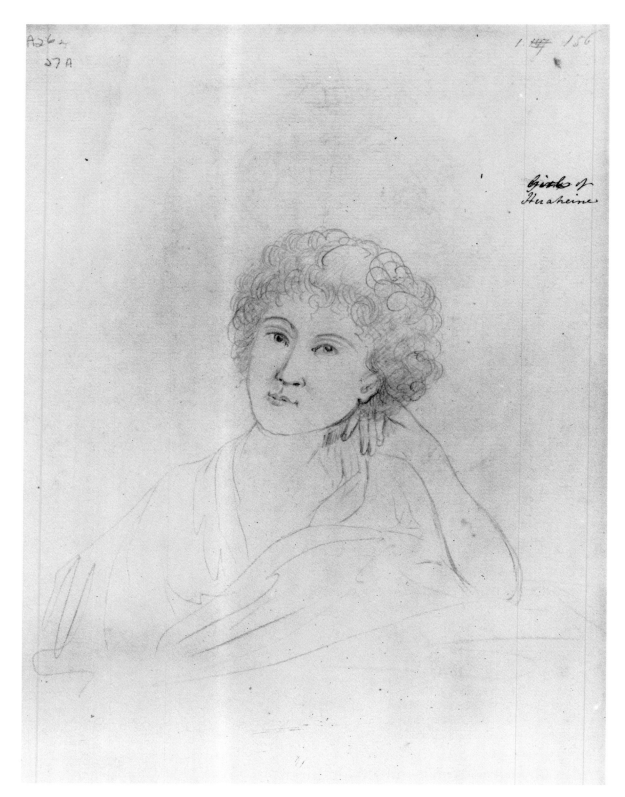

WILLIAM ELLIS

3.147   A Portrait of a Girl of Huaheine   [Oct 1777]
pencil, 9¾ × 7¼ : 250 × 185, unsigned; w/m: 'Pro Patria' with Britannia.

Inscribed 'Girl of Huaheine' (u.r.). Numbered in pencil '1.197' crossed out and '156' substituted (u.r.) referring to Ellis (1782). On verso is a drawing of a double canoe of Tahiti see 3.126.

Head and shoulders of a young woman, almost full-face, leaning on her left hand. Judging by the page reference she is the woman who on Raiatea warned Captains Cook and Clerke against a plot of being taken prisoners. According to Cook she had accompanied one of the officers from Huaheine (Cook, *Journals* III, 1, 250).

'In the evening, several of the chiefs had formed a design of seizing captains Cook and Clerke, as they took their evening walk, and would certainly have put it in execution, had he not received timely intelligence from a girl who came with us from Huaheine. She had been on shore almost the whole day, and towards evening came on board in a great fright, telling us that Tootee and Taatee (the names the captains went by) would be killed.' Ellis (1782) I, 156. Since it is not known to which island the young woman belonged she is here assumed to be, as the inscription implies, from Huaheine.

ref: Murray-Oliver (1977) 34.

Alexander Turnbull Library, Wellington. A264.27A

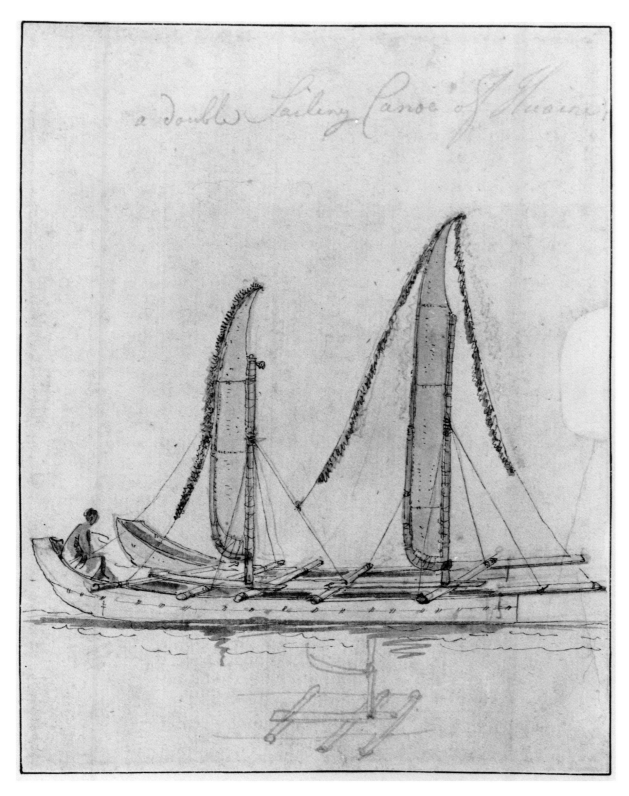

JOHN WEBBER

3.148   A Double Sailing Canoe of Huaine   [Oct 1777]
pencil, pen, wash and traces of water-colour, 7½ ×
5¾ : 190 × 146, unsigned.

Inscribed as above across top centre in Webber's hand. The
drawing may correspond to one listed in Webber's Catalogue, no.
44.

The drawing is similar to the representation of a canoe at the far
right of 3.141 and is probably a field study. The canoe is a variant
of the *va'a motu*.

National Maritime Museum, London. (In volume of plates to
Cook's Voyages.)

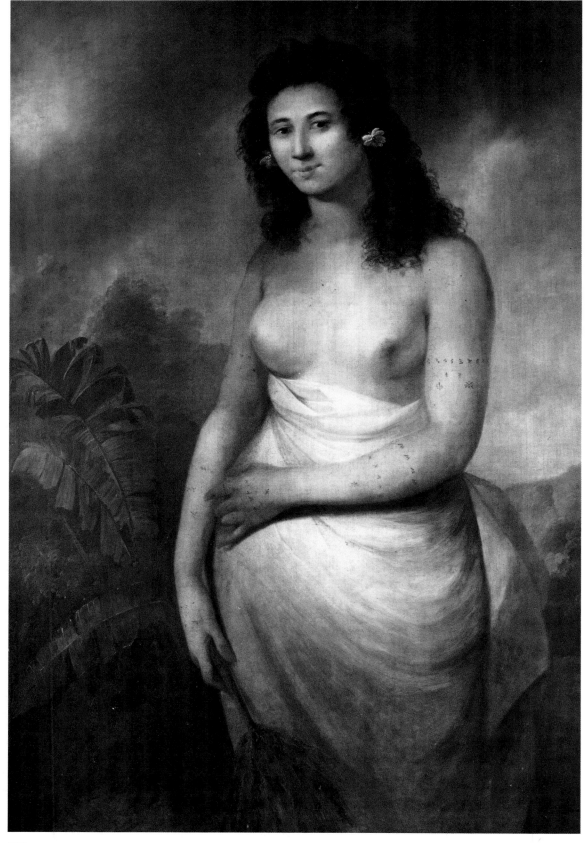

JOHN WEBBER

3.149   **A Portrait of Poedua (Poetua, Poedooa)**
        [plate 79]   [Nov 1777]
        oil on canvas, 56 × 37 : 1422 × 940, unsigned.

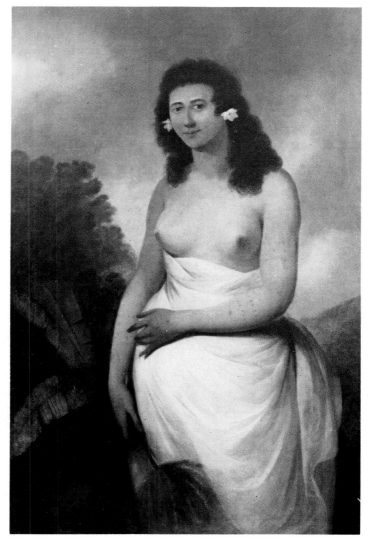

Possibly the painting referred to in Webber's Catalogue under
'Portraits in Oyl Colours', no. 7 'Poedua, the Kings Daughter of
Ulaietea' and the one exhibited at the Royal Academy in 1785
(392) as 'Poedua, daughter of Oree, chief of Ulaietea, one of the
Society isles'.

Three-quarter length figure of a young woman, draped beneath
the breast, holding a fan, and wearing two flowers at her ears,
with long black hair falling over her shoulders. Her arms and
hands are covered with small 'calligraphic' tattooing. A plantain
tree at left. Poedua was the daughter of Orio (Oree), a chief of
the district of Haamanino in Raiatea. Edgar judged her to be
about fifteen years of age (Cook, *Journals* III, 1, 248, fn.3). On
24 November 1777 two men of the *Discovery* deserted at Raiatea.
In order to ensure their return Captain Cook enticed Orio's son
Ta-eura, his daughter Poedua, and her husband Moetua on board
the *Discovery* and held them hostage in his cabin until the return
of the deserters. This occurrence is related by Cook, *Journals* III,
1, 248; by Samwell, ibid., 2, 1076 and Ellis (1782) I, 154. See
also Beaglehole's extensive note in Cook, *Journals* III, 1, 248,
3n. It was probably during this occasion that Webber painted
Poedua's portrait. The thinly applied colour and coarse cloth
suggest that it was this painting which was executed during the
voyage.

ver: For other versions see 3.150 and 3.151.
ref: Smith (1960) 93, pl. 70; Cook, *Journals* III, 1, pl. 30;
        Murray-Oliver (1969a) pl. 112 (col.); Beaglehole (1974)
        pl. 36; Langdon (1975) 136-40.

National Maritime Museum, London. L. 36-6.

JOHN WEBBER

3.150   **A Portrait of Poedua**
        oil on canvas, 57 × 37 : 1448 × 940, unsigned.

ver: Same representation as in 3.149 with minor variations.

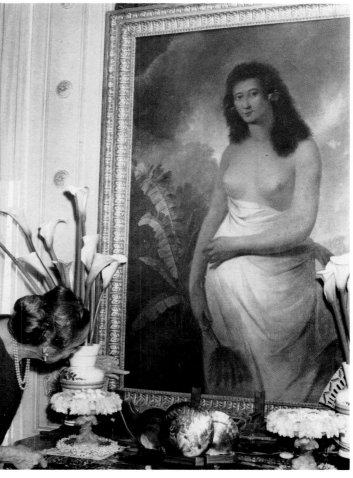

A portrait of Poedua of a similar size 56¾ × 36½ : 1442 × 928
was offered for sale at Sotheby's on 12 December 1956, lot 57
and purchased by Maggs Bros., London.

ref: Smith (1985) pl.13 (col.).

National Library of Australia, Canberra. Rex Nan Kivell Collection. NK 5192.

JOHN WEBBER

3.151   **A Portrait of Poedua**
        oil on canvas, measurements unknown.

ref: Langdon (1975) pl.9.

Formerly in the possession of Takau Pomare (1887-1976), Nice.
Information kindly supplied by Patrick O'Reilly (B. Smith, *in.
litt.* 8 October 1979).

Private collection, France.

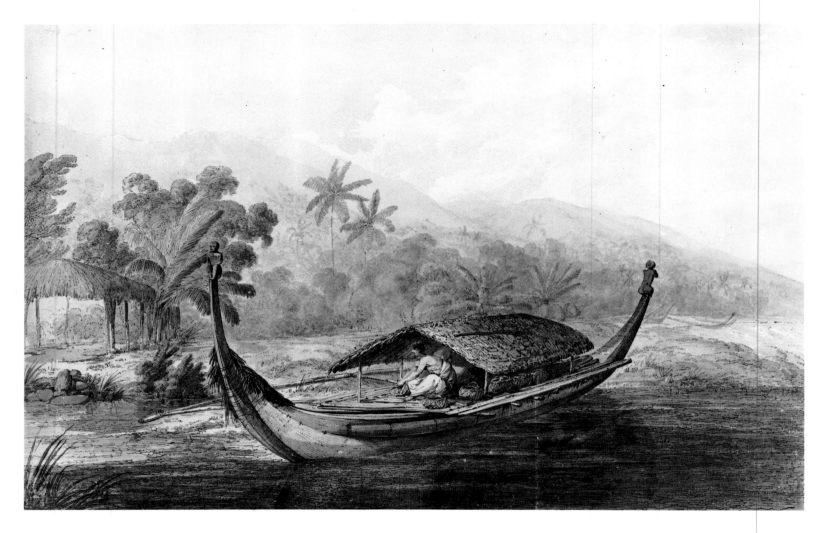

JOHN WEBBER

3.152   **A Canoe of Ulietea [plate 80]**   [Nov 1777–]
pen, wash and water-colour, 13½ × 20⅞ : 343 × 530,
unsigned.

Traces of '33' (u.l.) identifies this drawing as '33 A Ditto' (i.e.
'Sailing canoe of Ulaietea') in Webber's Catalogue.

A man holding a native basket sitting on the planks of an outrigger
pahi which has a thatched roof, head and stern are surmounted
by a carved, seated *ti'i* figure. An empty shed at left. In the right
background canoes are beached on the shore.

This drawing is discussed in Haddon and Hornell (1936) I, 122-
4, where it is suggested that it is a canoe of the Austral Islands.
The authors were not aware of the provenance of the drawing
from Raiatea.

ver: The drawing is similar to the compositions of 3.154-3.157,
but differs in the outrigger extending to the right as well
as in the distribution of figures. A study for this drawing
is at 3.153.

ref: Haddon and Hornell (1936) I, fig. 82; Starzecka (1979)
pl. 33, titled 'A Tahitian Canoe with a portable house on
the platform'.

British Library, London. Add MS 15513, f.25.

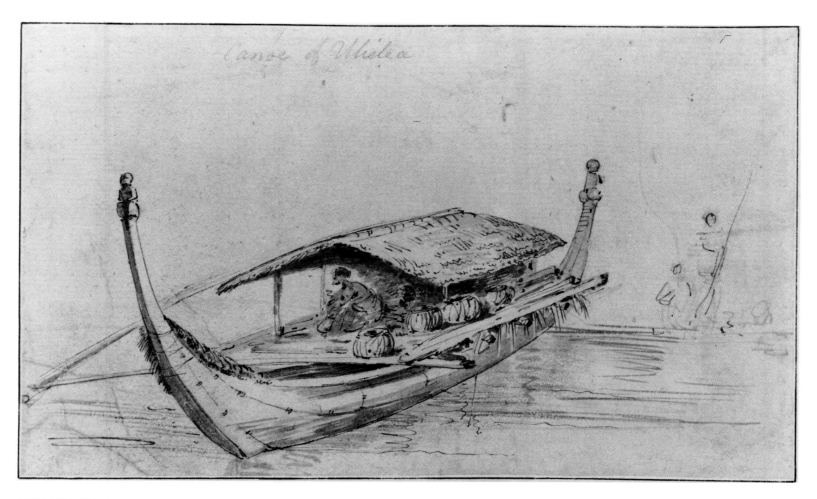

JOHN WEBBER

3.153   **A Canoe of Ulietea**   [Nov-Dec 1777]
      pencil, pen and sepia wash, 4¾ × 8 : 121 × 203,
      unsigned. The title in pencil across upper centre.

This drawing is a study for the drawing at 3.152.

National Maritime Museum, London. (In volume of plates to
Cook's Voyages.)

JOHN WEBBER

3.154   **A View in Ulietea [plate 81]**   [1786]
      oil on canvas, 17⅛ × 24 : 433 × 610, signed and
      dated 'J. Webber pinx. 1786' (l.l.).

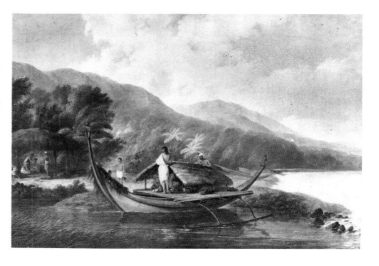

Several natives aboard a large canoe of the *pahi* type. The drawing
is basically the same as 3.152 but with an extended platform and
an outrigger to the left. Other figures on shore, some in a thatched
hut at extreme left.

Of the many versions of 'A View in Ulietea' this is the only one
known in oil. It was probably this one which Webber exhibited
at the Royal Academy in 1787 (143), see Fuller's note in 3.156.

ver: For similar versions of this composition see 3.155-3.157.

National Library of Australia, Canberra. Rex Nan Kivell Collection. NK 5929.

JOHN WEBBER

3.155   A View in Ulietea   [1787]
pen, pencil and water-colour, 13½ × 19½ : 343 ×
495, signed and dated 'J. Webber del 1787'.

Inscribed in ink on verso in an old hand 'A View in Ulaietea one
of the Society Islands by J. Webber 1787' and underneath in
pencil in modern hand 'Royal Academy 1787 no. 143'.

ver: A variant version of 3.154, 3.156 and 3.157 with differences in detail: in the number of figures in the shed at left
and in the placement of rocks and plants in the lower left
of the picture. In the background to the right two canoes
are beached on the shore and attended by figures; on the
extreme right another canoe in the bay (which is lacking
from the painting). Unlike most other versions there is no
waterfall at the right.

ref: *Exh. Cat.* Portland (1974) no 152.

Fuller Collection, compare the notes in 3.156.

National Maritime Museum, London.

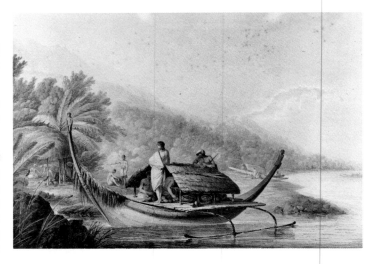

JOHN WEBBER

3.156   A Canoe of Ulietea   [c. 1787]
water-colour, 13¾ × 22⁷⁄₁₆ : 350 × 570 inside
mount, signed 'John Webber del' (l.r.).

Inscribed 'A view in Ulietea' on the mount within framing lines
on the mounting card.

ver: For other versions of the subject see 3.152 and 3.154-3.157.
This version as well as those at 3.154 and 3.157 is distinguished by rapids over rocks at the lower right. For a study
of the canoe see 3.153.

Maggs Bros., London (1927) cat. no. 491, 107. This drawing
is the one upon which Captain A. W. F. Fuller commented in
a note on Webber's aquatinted *Views,* tipped into the atlas of the
Third Voyage in the Bernice P. Bishop Museum, Honolulu (DU
12 C. 77. C. 5). Apropos the aquatint of a 'View in Ulietea'
by M. C. Prestel, Fuller says: 'The original water-colour of this
was purchased by Maggs at Sotheby's 192(7?) at the same time
as I bought the water-colour of pl. 8 [Toopapaoo of a chief in
Huaheine (3.144)] herein. I was the underbidder for this one as
I was also for the other 3 which came up at the same time [6.
Waheidooa, Chief of Oheitepeha (3.94), 5. A View in Vaitepiha
Bay (3.89) and one never reproduced] also secured by Maggs and
all sold to Australia. The water-colour of the above [View in
Ulietea] was a replica by Webber of the one I possess (except for
the little waterfall) and on which he has inscribed a note in ink
that it was exhibited at the R.A. 1787. No 143.'

Dixson Galleries, State Library of New South Wales, Sydney.
DG 23.

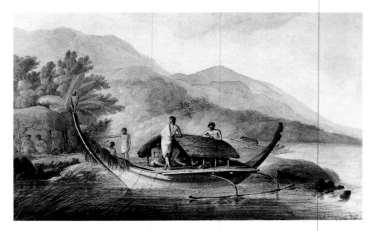

JOHN WEBBER

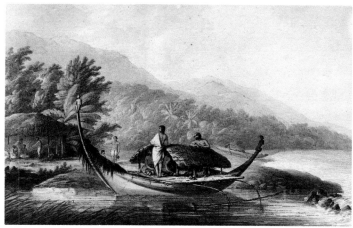

3.157   A View in Ulietea   **[c. 1787]**
pen, wash and water-colour over pencil on paper laid
down on cardboard, 10⁵⁄₁₆ × 15¾ : 262 × 400,
unsigned.

In the corner (l.r.) a collector's mark: a monogram under a crown.
Inscribed in pencil on verso in an eighteenth century hand 'Canoe
Ulietea, Friendly Isles' and 'Canoe Ulietea Society Islands'; the
same repeated in a modern hand.

ver: The drawing is of the same subject and composition as
3.154-3.156. Judging from the details it was this version
which served as the drawing for Webber's etching of a 'View
in Ulietea' and M. C. Prestel's aquatint of the same title
(3.157A).

John Sheepshank Gift in 1857 to the South Kensington Museum.

Victoria and Albert Museum, Print Room, London. F.A. 482.

JOHN WEBBER

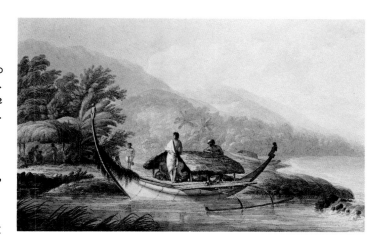

3.157A   a. 'View in Ulietea'
hand-coloured etching, 11½ × 16⅞ : 291 × 429 (10
× 15¾ : 254 × 400). 'Drawn & Etch'd by J. Webber'.
'London, Publish'd Feb.ʸ 1 1787 by I. Webber N.° 312
Oxford Street'. 'Vide Cook's last Voy. Vol. II, Chap.
VII'.

ver: For Webber's original composition see 3.157.

British Museum, Department of Prints and Drawings, London,
C. 6*.

b. 'View in Ulietea'
hand-coloured or monochrome aquatint, 11⁹⁄₁₆ ×
17 : 294 × 431 (10⅛ × 15¹³⁄₁₆ : 257 × 402).
'Drawn & Etch'd by J. Webber'. 'Aqua tinta by M.C.
Prestel'. 'London Publish'd Feb.ʸ 1 1787 by J. Webber
N.° 312 Oxford Street'. 'Vide Cook's last Voy. Vol
II, Chap. VII'.

ref: Murray-Oliver (1969b), pl. 3 showing the version in the
Alexander Turnbull Library.

Hartnoll and Eyre, London (1978); British Museum, Department
of Prints and Drawings, London (C. 6*); Alexander Turnbull
Library, Wellington.

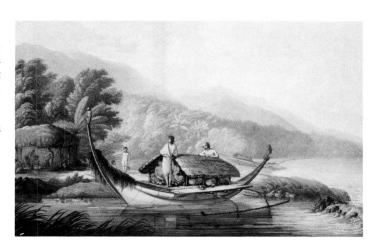

c. [Other copies]
aquatint copies with a differing publication line 'London,
Publish^d Feb.ʸ 1 1788 By I. Webber N.° 312 Oxford
Street' are kept in the British Museum, Department
of Prints and Drawings, London, 246* a.2, and C. 6*,
and in the National Library of Australia, Canberra.

This subject was not included in the later series of Webber's
Views, thus no further version exists.

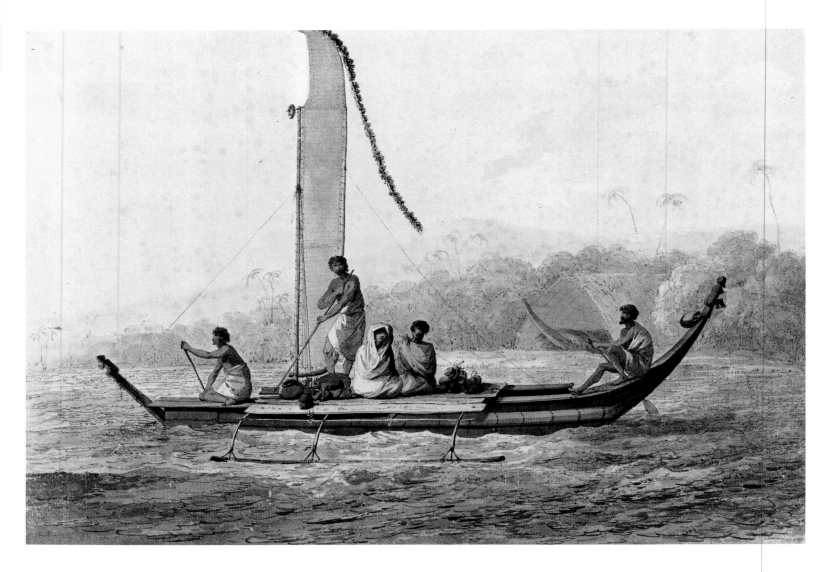

JOHN WEBBER

3.158   A Sailing Canoe of Ulietea   [1778]
pen, wash and water-colour, 12¼ × 17¹⁵⁄₁₆ : 311
× 457, signed and dated 'Jnº Webber del. 1778' in
ink (l.r.).

Endorsed in ink with 'Lot no 7' crossed out '2', also in pencil in
an eighteenth century hand 'glass 2'. Further below titled by a
later hand 'Sailing canoe of Otaheite' and 'unpublished' in the
same hand. Mounted on cardboard, the drawing surrounded with
frame lines of black ink.

A canoe with an outrigger and a tall, flat sail containing five
people: two rowing, one standing, a man and a woman seated.
There are carved figures at both ends of the canoe. On the
platform of the canoe is a live pig, pot and coconuts. Behind,
a tree-covered shore with a boat-house. The canoe possesses
features of a *va'a motu*, whereas the stern has the character of a
pahi, see Haddon and Hornell (1936) I, 112-24.

ver: For a preliminary sketch of this drawing see 3.159.

Dixson Library, State Library of New South Wales, Sydney.
Pe 215.

408

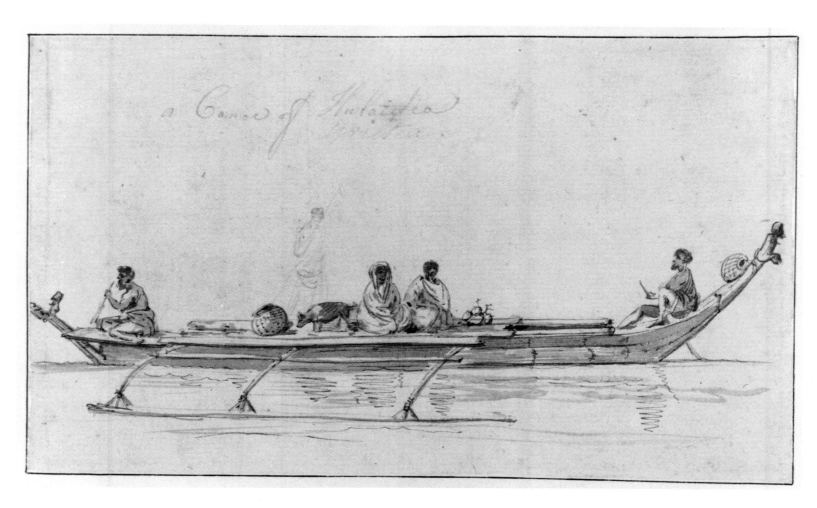

JOHN WEBBER

3.159   **A Canoe of Ulietea**   [1777]
         pencil, pen and sepia wash, 4¾ × 8 : 120 × 203,
         unsigned.

Inscribed 'A Canoe of Hulaietea/Urietea' in pencil in top centre
in Webber's hand.

A canoe with an outrigger containing a number of people, sitting
on a decking platform, with fruit and a hog.

ver: For a developed version with a sail, see 3.158.

National Maritime Museum, London. (In volume of plates to
Cook's Voyages.)

BORABORA [BOLABOLA]

8 to 9 December 1777

JOHN WEBBER

3.160 A Portrait of a Chief of Oparapora [Borabora]
[plate 83] [Dec 1777-]
pencil and wash, 12⅜ × 19⅛ : 314 × 486, signed
and dated 'Jn Webber del 1777' in pencil (l.r.).

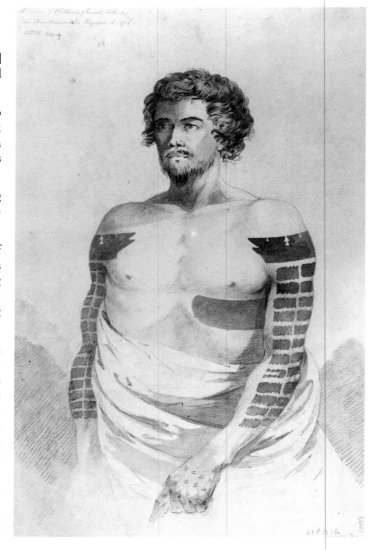

Traces of an old pencil inscription 'Nu-na . . .' (?) (u.r.), also
numbered 'No 35' (u.r.), corresponding to the drawing no 35
titled as above in Webber's Catalogue. Also inscribed (u.l.) in
pencil 'A Man of Oheteroa Society Islands. See Hawkesworth's
Voyages II, 276'.

A half-length portrait of a bearded man with curly hair facing
three-quarter left with the arms heavily tattooed with flat rectangular patches and a large patch beneath the left breast.

Kaeppler (1978a) fig. 292, believes that the man is a native of
Oheteroa (Rurutu) on the ground of his peculiar tattooing. Banks
described the tattooing of the natives of Rurutu when during
Cook's first voyage that island was visited (Banks, *Journal* (1962)
330); compare the reference to Hawkesworth on the drawing
cited above.

Contrary to this opinion, we believe that the sitter is a native
of Borabora,, both on account of the reference in Webber's Catalogue, and the fact that the sketch for this portrait (3.161) is
inscribed as representing a native from Borabora. Cook did not
visit Rurutu on the third voyage. Our opinion seems to be supported by a passage from Ellis (1782) I, 159: 'The society of the
areeois is esteemed the most polite establishment in these islands;
the members of which are always people of rank and fortune; and
are distinguished by being tattowed in a peculiar manner, particularly those who are natives of Borabora.' It is conceivable,
though unproven, that the man is Puni (Opoony) who was instrumental in returning the two deserters at Raitea and from whom
Cook purchased an anchor which Bougainville had lost at Tahiti
in April 1768. Cook, *Journals* III, 1, 252.

ver: For a sketch for this portrait see 3.161.

British Library, London. Add MS 15513, f. 24.

JOHN WEBBER

3.161 A Portrait of a Chief of Bora Bora [Dec 1777]
pencil and wash, 14⅞ × 10 : 378 × 254, unsigned.

Inscribed 'Native of Bola Bola, Society Islands' (u.r.).

ver: A sketch for 3.160; but here the native holds a lance in
his left arm.

British Library, London. Add MS 17277, no. 10.

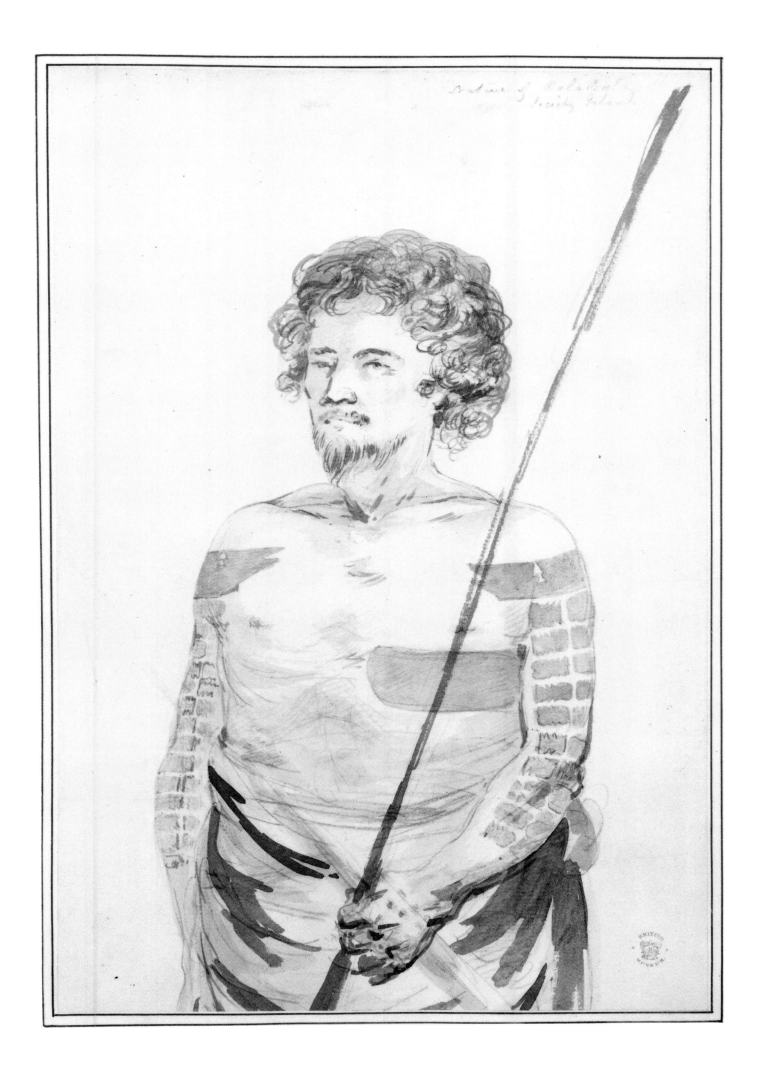

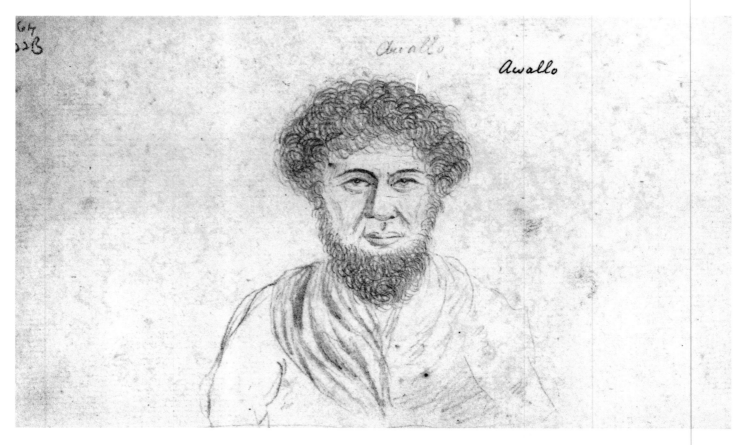

WILLIAM ELLIS

3.162   **A Portrait of Awallo**
         pencil, 4 × 7⅜ : 100 × 188, unsigned; w/m: 'Pro
         Patria'.

Inscribed 'Awallo' in pencil and ink above and to the right of the
head. On verso is a part of a panoramic view of the Tahitian
coast (3.96).

A bearded man, full-face, head and shoulders. His identity is not
known.

ref: Murray-Oliver (1977) 34.

Alexander Turnbull Library, Wellington. A 264.22B.

WILLIAM ELLIS

3.163   **[Head of a young man and a seated figure]**   **[1777]**
pencil, 12¼ × 7⅞ : 310 × 200, unsigned; w/m: 'Pro
Patria' with Britannia.

Numbered in ink '9' (l.l.) and 'i' (l.r.). On verso is a drawing
of an old man seated reading and a study of a hand (3.423).

(a) A full-face drawing of the head and shoulders of a young
    man.
(b) A bearded male figure seated in a Windsor chair, bare to the
    waist, and bare legs, looking three-quarter right. He holds
    a bundle of tapa.

ref: Murray-Oliver (1977) 34.

Alexander Turnbull Library, Wellington. A 264.26A.

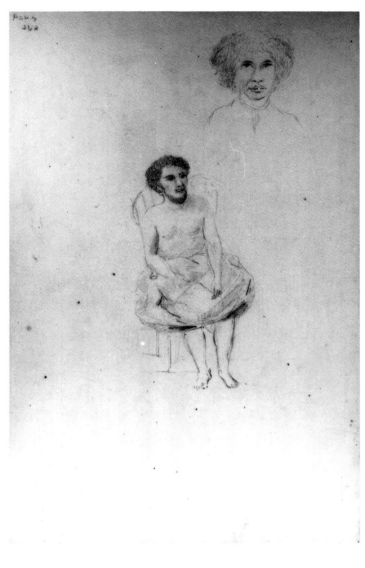

WILLIAM ELLIS

3.164   **Studies of Tahitians in Their Canoes**
                                   [Aug-Dec 1777]
    pencil, 10¹¹⁄₁₆ × 7⁵⁄₁₆ : 271 × 186, unsigned;
    w/m: 'Pro Patria' with Britannia.

Inscribed 'Otaheite?' in ink (u.r.), also numbered in ink '30'
(u.l.).

(a) an outrigger canoe holding three Tahitians. The boat appears
    to be a paddling canoe of Raiatean design. See Haddon and
    Hornell (1936) I, 112.
(b) a double canoe with five Tahitians, some fishing, three adults
    and two children. The boat appears to be a *tira*, a double
    fishing canoe, see Haddon and Hornell (1936) I, 127-9, fig.
    85.
(c) head of a Tahitian wearing a sunshade. Tahitian sunshades
    were collected on Cook's voyages. See 2.60 and Kaeppler
    (1978a) 131.

ref: Murray-Oliver (1977) 33.

Alexander Turnbull Library, Wellington. A 264.20B.

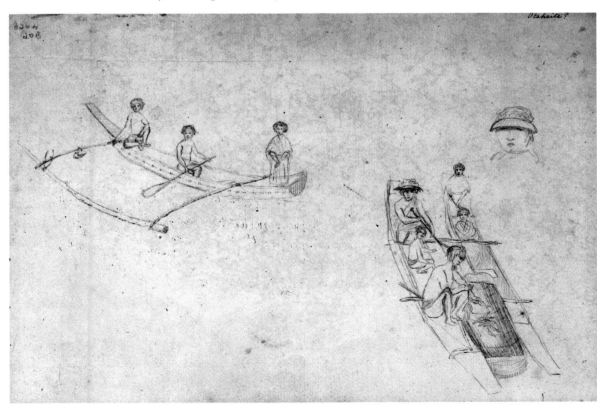

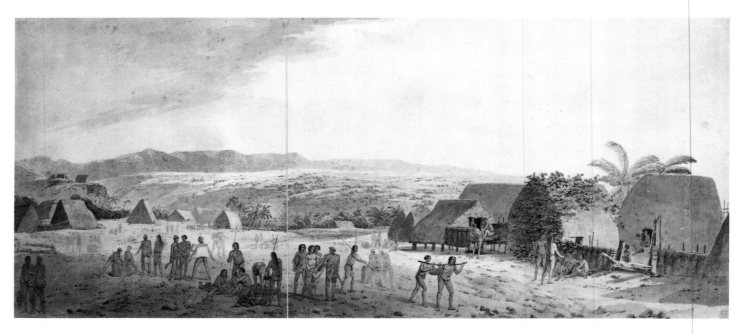

JOHN WEBBER

3.165   **An Inland View at Waimea, Atooi [Kauai]**
         [plate 84]   **[Jan 1778–]**
         pen, wash and water-colour, 17 × 38½ : 432 × 978,
         unsigned.

This drawing is most likely the one referred to in Webber's Catalogue under the title of 'An Inland View at Atooi', no. 103.

The drawing depicts Cook's visit to the village of Waimea; some men rolling barrels; others bartering with Hawaiians; at right, two natives carrying a pig strung to a pole. Behind them many native habitations, and a panoramic view of the interior.

'We no sooner landed, that a trade was set on foot for hogs and potatoes, which the people gave us in exchange for nails and pieces of iron formed into some thing like chisels. We met with no obstruction in watering on the contrary the Natives assisted our people to roll the Casks to and from the pond.' Cook, *Journals* III, 1, 269.

'At sun set I brought every body on board, having got during the day Nine tons of water, and by exchanges chiefly for nails and pieces of iron, about sixty or eighty Pigs, a few Fowls, a quantity of potatoes and a few plantains and Tara roots.' Ibid., 272.

ver: A field study for the left side of this view is at 3.170, and for the right side at 3.169. For two other versions see 3.166 and 3.167.

A copy of this drawing of the late nineteenth century is in the Bernice P. Bishop Museum, Honolulu (Kaeppler (1978a) fig. 19 (col.)).

ref: Cook, *Journals* III, 1, pl. 32; Rienits (1968) 121; Starzecka (1979) pl. 98.

British Library, London. Add MS 15513, f. 29.

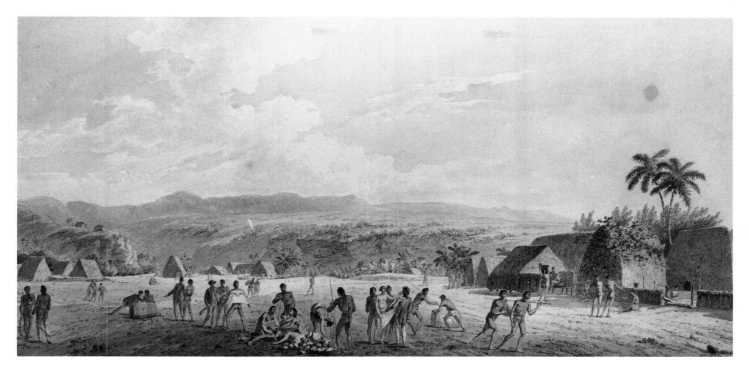

JOHN WEBBER

3.166   An Inland View in Atooi   [Jan 1778–]
pen and water-colour, 12¾ × 25⅞ : 323 × 657, signed
'J. Webber del' (l.r.).

Inscribed 'An Inland View in Atooi' in pencil on the folio by a
later hand beneath the drawing.

The drawing is larger than most of the drawings in PXX2. It is
sketched with sensitivity and is light in colour.

ver: See other versions at 3.165 and at 3.167 with slight
variations.

Dixson Library, State Library of New South Wales, Sydney.
PXX 2,20.

JOHN WEBBER

3.167   An Island View, in Atooi   [c. 1781-3]
pen and water-colour, 8¾ × 18½ : 223 × 469, signed
'J. Webber del' (l.r.)

Inscribed 'An Island View, in Atooi' in pencil on the folio by
a later hand beneath the drawing.

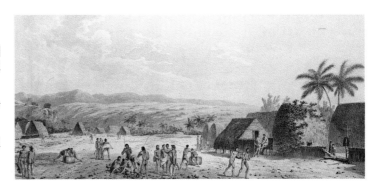

ver: The drawing is a smaller version of 3.165 and 3.166, and
was engraved (3.167A).
ref: Murray-Oliver (1975) pl. 20 (col.).

Dixson Library, State Library of New South Wales, Sydney.
PXX2, 19.

JOHN WEBBER (after)

3.167A   'An ISLAND VIEW in ATOOI'
engraving. 'J. Webber del.' — 'S. Middiman sc.'

Published in Cook/King (1784) pl. 35, II, 199.

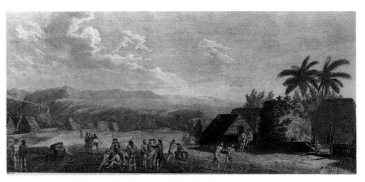

JOHN WEBBER

3.168   [Habitations of the Natives at Waimea]
         [plate 86]   [Jan 1778–]
         pen and wash, 19 × 26 : 483 × 660, unsigned.

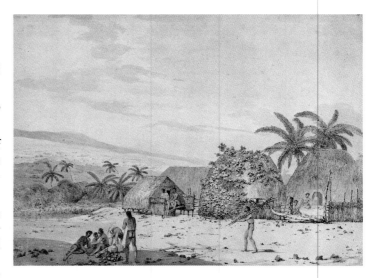

A group of natives at left. Man carrying sugar-cane at right. Two figures before a hut in the centre.

This is a smaller and modified version of the right hand side of 3.165. There are differences in the groups of people outside the fence; the main group has been made up from various configurations of 3.165.

3.168 is interesting for the hair-piece which the native in the front, seen from the rear, is wearing. It is made of human hair and falls down his back. Samwell singled it out for comment, and at least one hair-piece was traded. Kaeppler (1978a), fig.155. In terms of visual representations Webber's drawing is the only one to show this feature.

ref: Kaeppler (1978a), fig. 154.

British Library, London. Add. MS 15513, f.30.

JOHN WEBBER

3.169   **Native Habitations at Waimea [plate 85] [Jan 1778]**
         pen, wash and water-colour, 12½ × 21 : 317 × 533, unsigned.

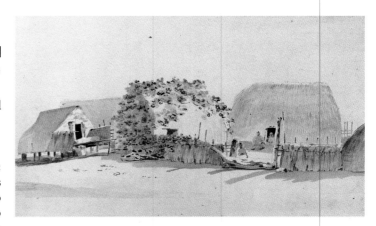

Inscribed 'Natives Habitations — Sandwich Island' in pencil (u.r.).

Two huts flanking a central hut which is covered with foliage.

Concerning the houses in the village of Waimea, Cook reported: 'Their houses are not unlike oblong corn stacks, they are of various sizes from forty or fifty feet long and twenty or thirty broad to little huts: they have low walls and a high roof consi[s]ting of two flat sides inclining to each other, and terminating in a ridge like the thatched houses in England. The framing is of wood, and both walls and roof consi[s]ts of Course dry grass which is very closely put together so that they appear to afford too warm a retreat for the climate. The door is so low that a man can hardly get in without going upon his hands and knees . . . ' Cook *Journals* III, 1, 283.

Another extensive description of houses on Hawaii (similar to those on Kauai) is provided by Samwell, ibid., 2, 1176.

ver: This is a study for the right side of 3.165, 3.166, 3.167 and 3.168. A copy of this drawing of the late nineteenth century is in the Bernice P. Bishop Museum, Honolulu, titled 'Native habitations in Sandwich Islands'.

British Library, London. Add MS 17277, no. 18 (recto).

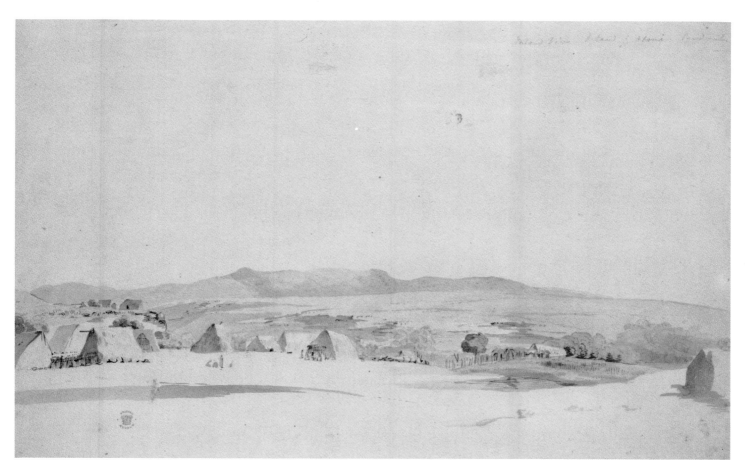

JOHN WEBBER

3.170   **An Inland View at Waimea [plate 87]**   **[Jan 1778]**
pen, wash and water-colour, 13⅜ × 21⅛ : 340 × 536,
unsigned.

Inscribed 'Inland View — Island of Atooi Sandwich Is.' in pencil
(u.r.).

ver: This is a study for the left side of 3.165.

A copy of this drawing from the late nineteenth century is in the
Bernice P. Bishop Museum, Honolulu, titled 'Island View, Island
of Atooi. Sandwich Islands'.

British Library, London. Add. MS 17277, no. 15.

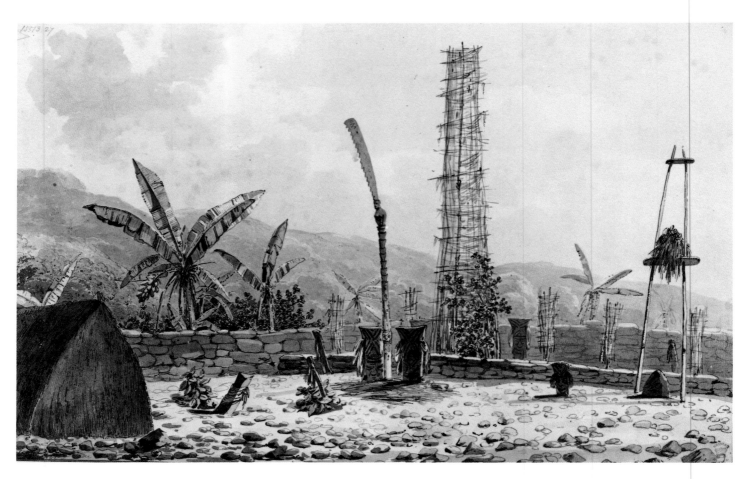

JOHN WEBBER

3.171   A 'Morai' at Atooi [A *heiau* at Waimea]
[plate 88]   [Jan 1778–]
pen, wash and water-colour, 12¼ × 19½ : 311 × 495,
signed and dated 'Jn Webber 1778' (l.l.).

This drawing may be identified with that listed as 94 in Webber's
Catalogue 'A Marrai or Burying Place at Attooi'.

Within the walled enclosure or *heiau* is to be seen the tall, open-
work oracle tower, or *lananu'u*, and at the extreme left the long
house, or *mana*.

On 21 January 1778 Cook reported: 'The *Pyramid* which they call
[Henananoo] was erected at one end, it was 4 feet square at the
base and about [20] feet high, the four sides was built of small
sticks and branches, in an open manner and the inside of the
pyramid was hollow or open from bottom to top. Some part of
it was, or had been covered with a very thin light grey cloth,
which seemed to be consecrated to Religious and ceremonious
purposes, as a good deal of it was about this Morai and I had some
of it forced upon me on my first landing. On each side and near
the Pyrimid, stood erect some rude carved boards, exactly like
those in the Morais at Otahiete. At the foot of these were square
places, a little sunk below the common level and inclosed with
stone, these we understood were graves. About the middle of the
Morai were three of these places in a line, where we were told
three chiefs had been buried; before them was another that was
oblong, this they called Tanga[ta] taboo and gave us clearly to
understand that three human sacrifices had been buried there,
that is one at the burial of each chief. The next thing that fixed
our attention, was a house or close shed on one side of the Morai,
it was 40 feet long, 10 broad in the middle, each end being
narrower, and about 10 feet high.' Cook, *Journals* III, 1, 270.
'This Morai was inclosed by a wall of stone about 4 feet high like
many of those at Otaheite . . .' Ibid., 271.

ver: For a study for this view see 3.173, where the objects are
depicted from a closer viewpoint. Another version is at
3.172. A copy of this drawing from the late nineteenth
century is in the Bernice P. Bishop Museum, Honolulu,
titled 'A Morai in Atooi (Webber 1793)'.

ref: Cook, *Journals* III, 1, pl. 31; Starzecka (1979) pl. 96.

British Library, London. Add MS 15513, f.27.

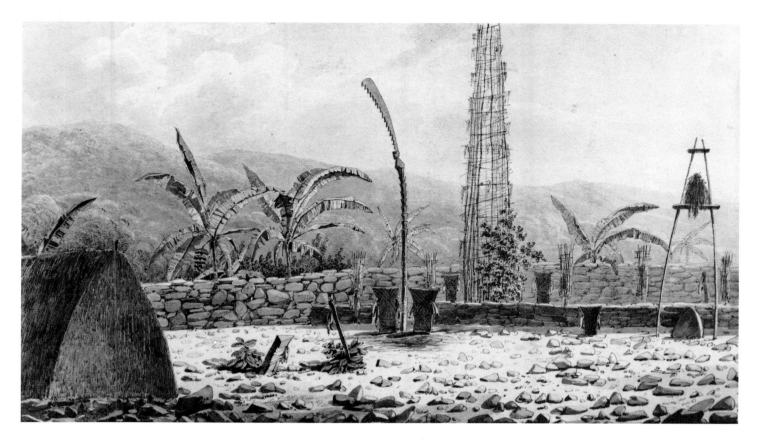

JOHN WEBBER

3.172   **A 'Morai' at Atooi [A *heiau* at Waimea]** [c. 1781-3]
pen, wash and water-colour, 8¾ × 14⁹⁄₁₆ : 223
× 376, unsigned.

Inscribed 'A Morai in Atooi' in pencil on the folio by a later hand
beneath the drawing.

ver: A smaller version of 3.171, and used for the engraving
3.172A.

ref: Murray-Oliver (1975) pl. 21 (col.).

Dixson Library, State Library of New South Wales, Sydney.
PXX 2, 17.

JOHN WEBBER (after)

3.172A   **'A MORAI, in ATOOI'**
Engraving. 'J. Webber del.' — 'Lerpernere sc.'

Published in Cook/King, (1784) pl. 33, II, 200-1.

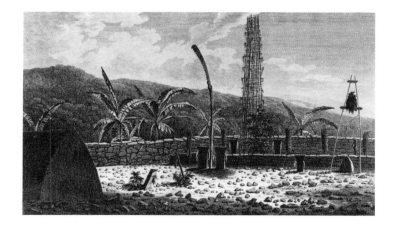

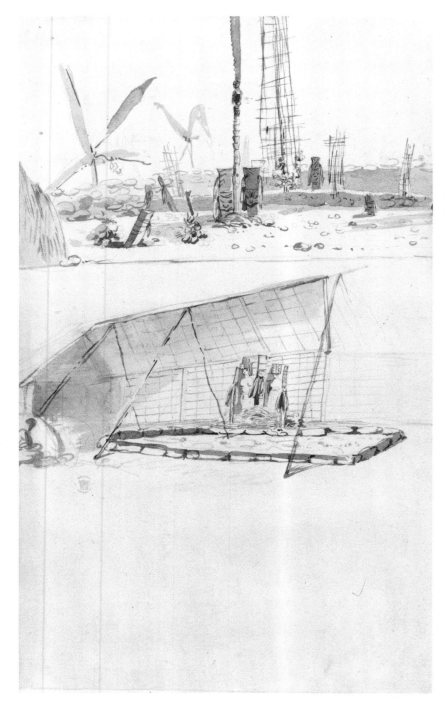

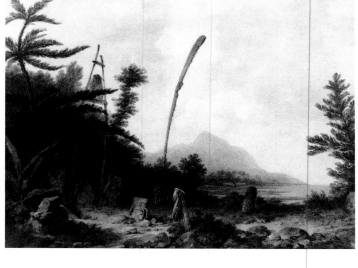

JOHN WEBBER

3.174 **[Coastal landscape, Sandwich Islands]** **[c. 1785]**
oil on paper on panel, 9⅝ × 12¼ : 245 × 311.

Inscribed on back on old label 'Hamilton Bay with Mitre Hill in the background. New Zealand. Said to be by John Webber, who was with Captain Cook on his last Voyage'.

The painting is freely modelled on Webber's own drawing of the *heiau* at Waimea and represents a scene for 'Omai, or, a Trip round the World' staged by P. J. de Loutherbourg and J. Webber in Covent Garden on 20 December 1785. Another drawing of this scene, possibly a copy, has been attributed to Henry Hodgins, the stage painter who collaborated in the production of 'Omai', see Joppien (1979) pl. 57 and 58. Though the painting can not be considered authentic in a topographical sense it has been included for the reason that Webber himself painted it from his general knowledge of Hawaiian scenery and rituals.

Collection of Sir Bruce Ingram, sold Sotheby's 18 March 1964 (lot 161).

Yale Center for British Art, Paul Mellon Collection, New Haven.

JOHN WEBBER

3.173 **[Studies of the *heiau* at Waimea]** **[Jan 1778]**
pencil and wash, 12½ × 21 : 317 × 522, unsigned.

(a) Study of a *heiau*, see 3.171 and 3.172.
(b) Study of the interior of the house in the *heiau*, see 3.175 and 3.176.

Cook commented on 21 January 1778: 'After having seen everything that was to be seen about this Morai and Mr Webber had taken a drawing of it, we returned.' Cook, *Journals* III, 1, 271.

British Library, London, Add MS 17277, no. 18 (verso).

JOHN WEBBER

3.175   **An Inside of a House showing their Idols**
       [plate 89]   **[Jan 1778–]**
       wash and water-colour, 12¼ × 19 : 311 × 483,
       unsigned.

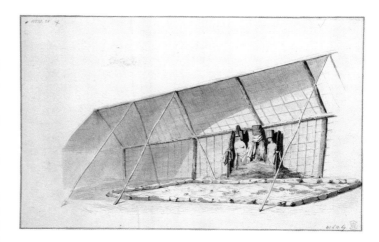

Inscribed '97' (u.l.) which corresponds to the drawing with the above title in Webber's Catalogue.

Showing the interior of the long house or *mana* in the *heiau* at Waimea, Kauai with carved representations of the gods.

Cook reported on 21 January 1778: 'The entrance was at the middle of the side which was in the Morai, fronting it on the other side was a kind of Altar, composed of a piece of carved wood set ere[c]t and on each side the figure of a Woman carved in wood, neither very ill designed nor executed; on the head of one was carved a cap like a helmet worn by the ancient warriors and on the other a round cap, like the head dress at Otaheite called Tomou. These two images, which were about three feet high, they called Eatua no Veheina, Godess's, but that they worship them may be doubted, as they had no objections to our going to and examining them; be this as it may, they here make some kind of offerings, as several strips of the cloth before mentioned hung to and about them, and between them before the other piece of carving, lay a heap of a plant called [. . .] and by them [. . .]. It was obvious it had been laid there piece by piece and at different times, as there was of it in all states, from quite decayed to fresh and green. Before this place, and in the middle of the house, was an oblong space, inclosed by a low edging of stone and covered over with the thin cloth; this they told us was the grave of seven chiefs.' Cook, *Journals* III, 1, 270-1.

ver: For a smaller and more developed drawing see 3.176. For a study of 3.175 see 3.173(b), and a late nineteenth century copy of it titled 'Inside of the house in the Morai in Atooi' is in the Bernice P. Bishop Museum, Honolulu.

British Library, London. Add MS 15513, f. 28.

JOHN WEBBER

3.176   **The Inside of The House in the Morai [*heiau*] in Atooi**
                             [c. 1781-3]
       pen, wash and water-colour, 7 × 9 : 178 × 229,
       unsigned.

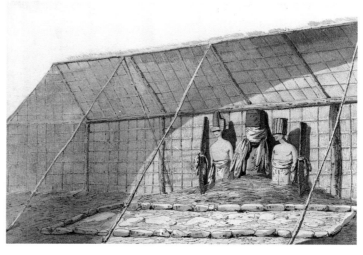

The title inscribed as above in pencil by a later hand on the folio beneath the drawing.

ver: A smaller version of 3.175; used for the engraving 3.176A.

ref: Murray-Oliver (1975) pl. 22 (col.).

Dixson Library, State Library of New South Wales, Sydney. PXX 2, 18.

JOHN WEBBER (after)

3.176A   **'The INSIDE of the HOUSE in the MORAI, in ATOOI'**
       Engraving. 'J. Webber del.' — 'Scott sculp.'

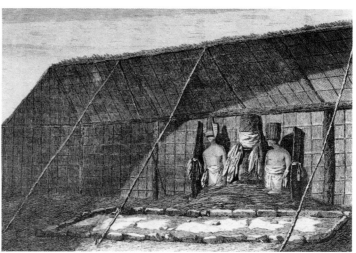

Published in Cook/King (1784) pl. 34, II, 202-3.

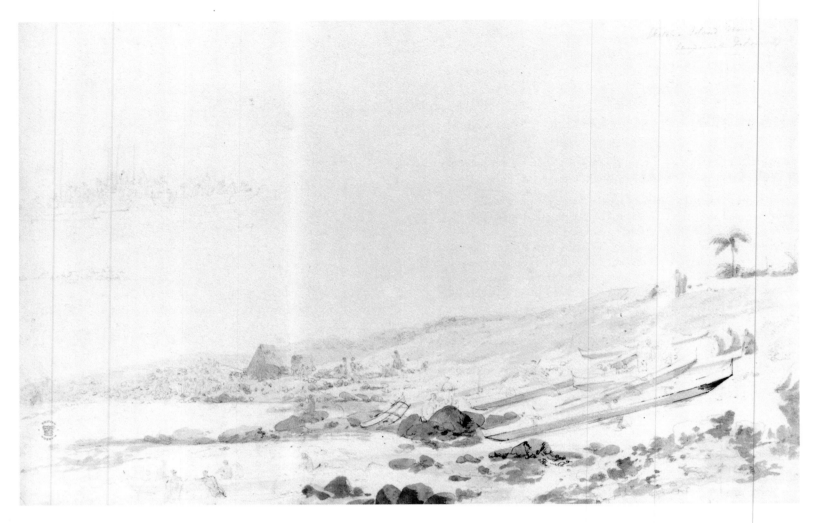

JOHN WEBBER

3.177   **[A View in Atooi]**   [Jan 1778]
pencil and wash (unfinished), 13⅝ × 21¼ : 346 × 540, unsigned.

Inscribed 'Sketch — Island Atooi Sandwich Islands' in pencil (u.r.).

Natives gathered round several canoes beached at right. At left, in the bay, canoes crowded with natives. In the left foreground natives launching a canoe. Behind the land slopes up to the right. A faint pencil sketch (u.l.) of a number of canoes thronged by natives. The location cannot be identified.

ver: A late nineteenth century copy of this drawing is in the Bernice P. Bishop Museum, Honolulu, titled 'Island of Atoui, Sandwich Islands'.

British Library, London. Add MS 17277, no. 16.

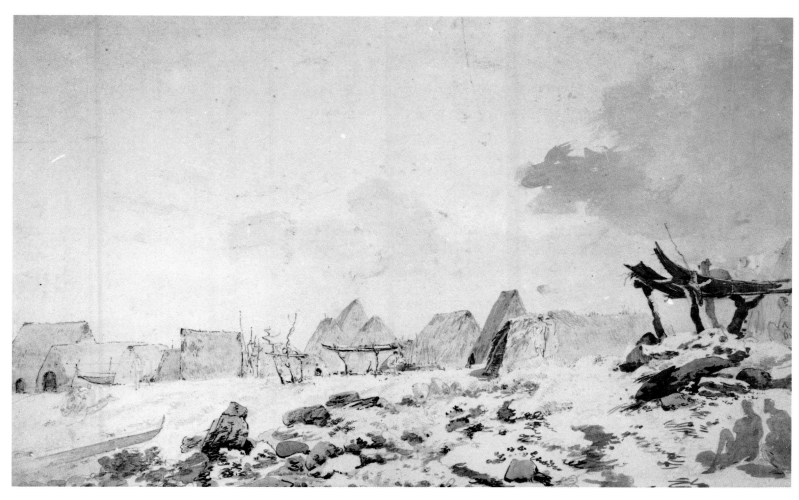

JOHN WEBBER

3.178   **View in Atooi**   [Jan 1778]
         pen and ink wash over pencil, 13¼ × 21¼ : 337 ×
         540, unsigned.

Inscribed 'View in the Island of Atoui, Sandwich Islands.' in
pencil in an eighteenth century hand beneath framing lines, also
in pencil 'Webber R.A.' at right. Mounted on cardboard and
surrounded by sepia framing lines.

An unfinished drawing of huts and natives on the shore. Rocks
in the foreground, two figures in the extreme right foreground,
and two lightly sketched in pencil behind and above them, beside
a stage of tree trunks or posts serving as a rack for canoes. There
are also two similar racks in the central mid-distance and groups
of lightly pencilled figures. A canoe in the extreme left foreground.

National Library of Australia, Canberra. Rex Nan Kivell Collection. NK 52/J.

JOHN WEBBER

3.179   Portrait of a Man of Atooi [plate 92] [Jan 1778–]
pen and ink wash, 15¾ × 12½ : 400 × 317, unsigned.

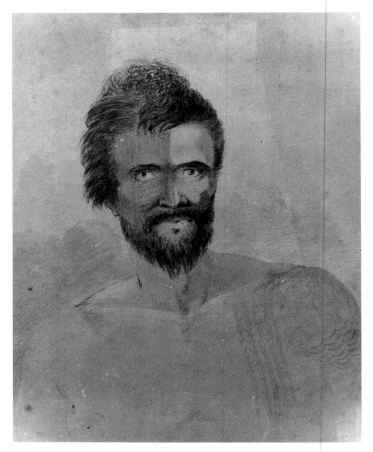

Mounted on old carboard; traces of pencil no '90' (u.r.) identifying the drawing as from Webber's Catalogue '[The Portrait] of a Man of Attooi'. On the back in old ink '13' and 'No 25'.

'The men often had it [their hair] cut, or shaved, on each side, in such a manner, that the remaining part, in some measure, resembles the crest of their caps or helmets . . .' Cook/King (1784) II, 231. This observation echoes Samwell's: 'They have their Hair cut close on each side of the Head with a ridge abᵗ a hand's breadth left to grow long on the top of the head, which reaches from the forehead to the Occiput.' Samwell in Cook, *Journals* III, 2, 1179.

'The men are frequently punctured . . . Sometimes there are a few marks upon their hands, or arms, and near the groin . . . a few individuals had more of this sort of ornament, than we had usually seen at other places, and ingeniously executed in a good variety of lines and figures, on the arms and fore-part of the body.' Cook/King (1784) II, 232-3. Samwell's remarks are the most specific: 'They are tattawed or marked in various parts: Some have an arm entirely tattawed, others more frequently the Thighs and Legs . . . their bodies are marked with figures of Men and other Animals; Some few among them had one side of their faces tattawed, & we saw 2 or 3 who had the whole of the face marked, differing sometimes from the New Zealanders in being done in strait not in spiral Lines.' Samwell in Cook, *Journals* III, 2, 1178. Samwell's description was written during the second stay at Hawaii, in 1779.

ver: The sitter resembles the man in J. Grignion's engraving of 'A Man of the Sandwich Islands, dancing' published in Cook/King (1784), pl. 62. For a field-sketch of the man taken from life, 3.180; and another probably later version, 3.181.

ref: Cook, *Journals* III, 1, pl. 59a; Rienits (1968) 123; Kaeppler (1978a) fig. 130 (col.); Smith (1979a) pl. 33.

Francis Edwards, London, *Cat.* 416 (July 1921) under no. 769 as 'Portrait of a Sandwich Islander, in sepia (15½ × 12 in), unpublished'. Purchased by Spencer Bickerton, Honolulu, from whom it was acquired in September 1922.

Bernice P. Bishop Museum, Honolulu. Acc. no. 1922. 129.

JOHN WEBBER

3.180   [A Native of Atooi] [plate 91]   [Jan 1778]
pencil and sepia wash, 8½ × 6³⁄₁₆ : 216 × 157, laid on a sheet of paper on which the oval impress of a w/m is visible near the neck and the shoulders of the native.

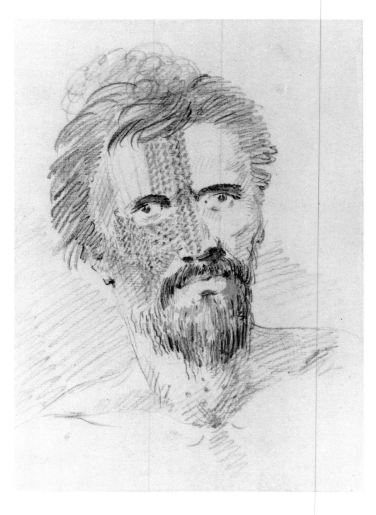

Mounted and framed with three framing bands in sepia. Inscribed in pencil 'A Native of the Island of Mangea' in an eighteenth century hand beneath the frame. Inscribed on back of mount 'No 8'.

A full face study of a bearded man with a central ridge of hair back from the top of the forehead, and with tattoo marks from the forehead to the point of the nose and across his right cheek. Apparently a field-sketch for 3.179.

Francis Edwards, London, *Cat.* 551 (1932) no 13. 'Native of the Island of Mangea 9 × 6 in'.

Francis P. Farquhar Collection, Berkeley, California.

JOHN WEBBER

3.181   A Native of Atooi   [Jan 1778–]
sepia wash over pencil, $13^{13}/_{16} \times 11^{1}/_{8}$: 351 ×
283.

The title as above and the location 'Sandwich Isles' inscribed in
pencil in Webber's hand, and numbered '3' (u.l.). Inscription
on the back in a recent hand 'by Webber, see Cook's *Atlas* to the
first [sic] Voyage "A Man of Sandwich Islands, dancing".'

ver: For another, probably earlier, version see 3.179.

ref: Joppien (1976a), 36-7.

Hartnoll and Eyre, London (1976).

Private collection, England.

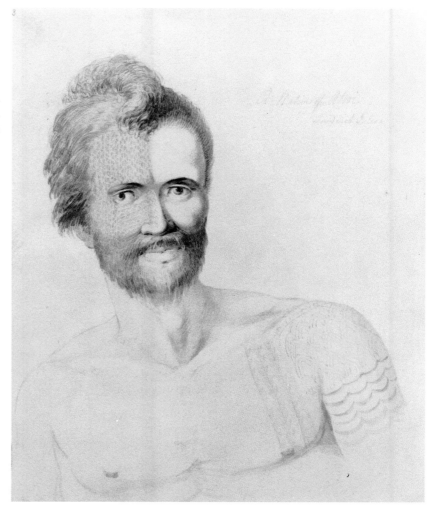

JOHN WEBBER (after)

3.181a   A Native of Atooi   [c. 1790]
grey wash and traces of water-colour, $12^{5}/_{8} \times 9^{3}/_{16}$:
320 × 234, unsigned, numbered '3a' (u.l.).

The portrait framed by a double line in black ink.

The drawing is a copy after 3.181 and may have been executed
by a German artist, after it was acquired by George Forster from
John Webber in 1790. The position of the head is shifted to the
vertical, and is less lively than the original.

ref: Joppien (1976a), 39, repr. 38.

Hartnoll and Eyre, London (1976).

Private collection, England.

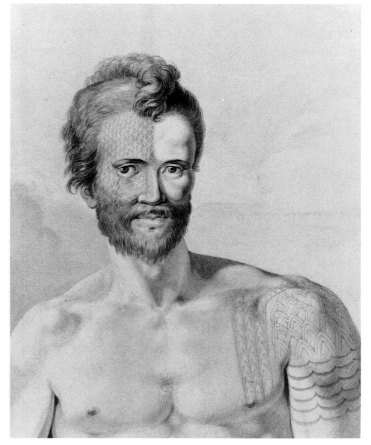

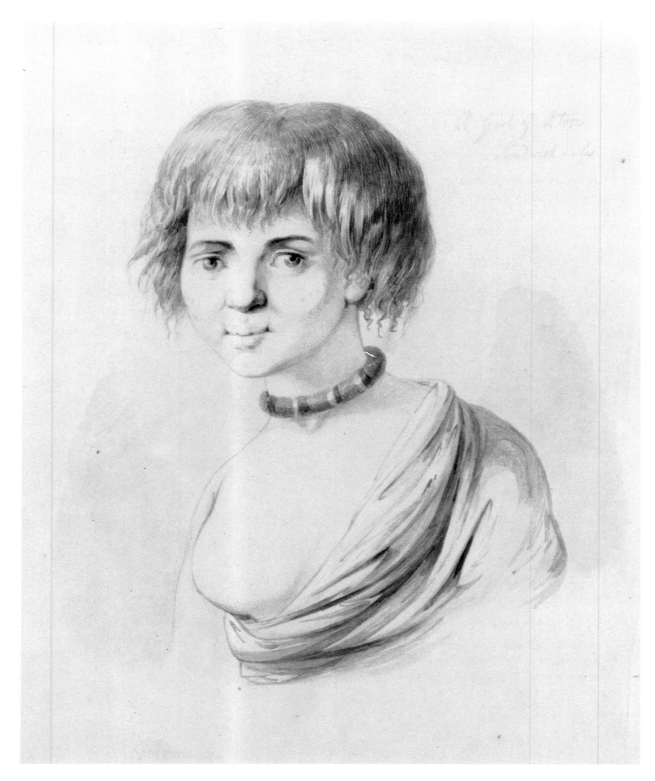

JOHN WEBBER

3.182   **A Girl of Atooi**   [Jan 1778–]
sepia wash over pencil, 14 × 11⅜ : 355 × 289,
unsigned.

The title as above and the location 'Sandwich Isles' inscribed in
Webber's hand in pencil and numbered '4' (u.l.).

Bust portrait of a girl with loose hair falling over her forehead
and ears in ringlets. She is draped over the left shoulder leaving
the right breast bare and wears a necklace of feathers. There are
small star-shaped tattoos on both cheeks.

'The better sort [of women] have large Pieces of Cloth brought
several times round their middle, which comes as low as the Knee
& makes them very bulky but does not cover the Breasts . . .
Their Ornaments are the Ereis or feathered ruffs which they wear
on their Heads & round their Necks; they are very proud of these
& wear sometimes 4 or 5 on their Heads & one or two about
their necks & they have a very beautiful appearance, being made
of red and yellow feathers, black, white and green variously disposed, they are about an inch in thickness & long enough to go
round their Necks, these are worn only by the young women.'
Samwell in Cook, *Journals* III, 2, 1180. For a similar description
see also King in ibid., 1391 and the published account in Cook/
King (1784) vol. III, 138-9.

ref: Joppien (1976a) 40-1.

Hartnoll and Eyre, London, (1976).

Private collection, England.

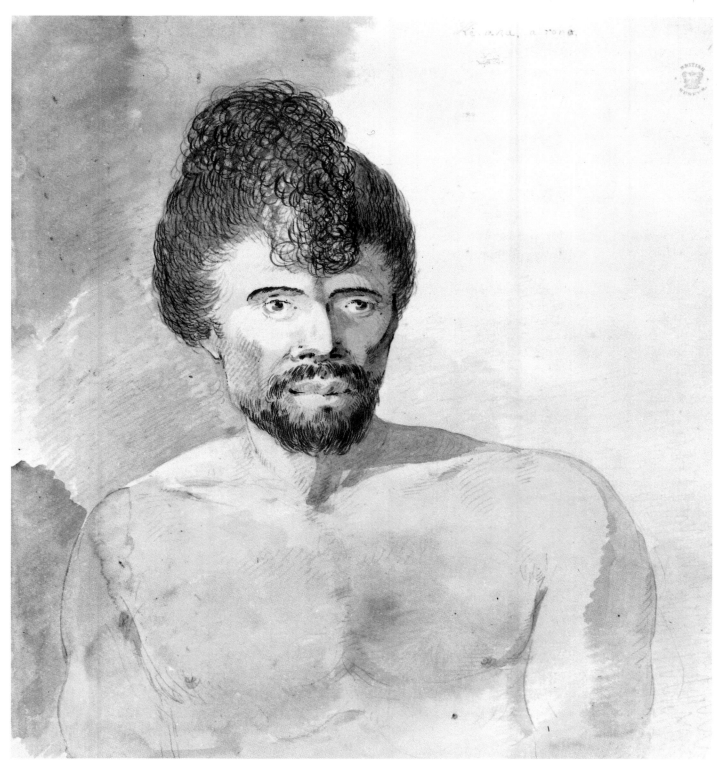

JOHN WEBBER

3.183   [A Portrait of a Man of Atooi (?)]
         [plate 94]   [Jan 1778]
         pencil and wash, 13 × 11⅞ : 330 × 302, unsigned.

Inscribed with the name 'Ke-a ka a rona' in pencil [u.r.] but the
remainder illegible.

Portrait study of head and shoulders, with a crest of hair on the
crown of the head.

ver: He is about the same age as the man depicted in 3.179 and
        3.181, but lacks tattooing. The position of the head and
        the features are similar to the native wearing a helmet with
        a feather ring in 3.184. It is possible that both were drawn
        from the same sitter.

British Library, London. Add MS 17277, no.47.

3.184   [A Warrior of Atooi or of Niihau]
          [plate 95]   [Jan 1778–]
          pen, sepia and water-colour, $17\frac{1}{2} \times 12\frac{1}{2} : 445 \times 317$,
          unsigned.

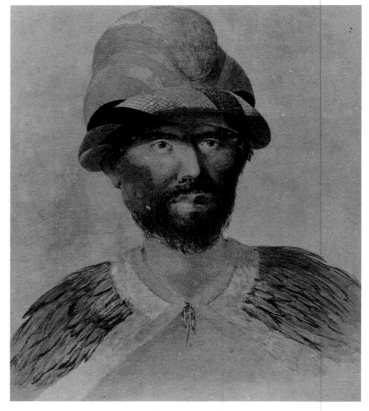

The paper is mounted on linen on a redwood stretcher. The surface has been varnished and has yellowed.

On verso: three notations in different hands: 'Lot no 10' in faded ink; '5- Dark maple No 7 in Frame the same size'; 'Captn Campbell'.

Perhaps the drawing is the one listed as no. 101 'A Portrait of a Warrior of Atooi' in Webber's Catalogue.

He wears a feather cloak (*ahu-ula*) and feather helmet (*mahiole*), round the lower edge of which is a cylindrical band or roll of feather work.

'They have also neat Tippets made of red and yellow feathers, and Caps and Cloakes covered with the same or some other feathers; the cloakes reach to about the middle of the back, and are like the short cloakes worn by the women in England, or like the riding cloaks worn in Spain. The Caps are made so as to fit very close to the head with a semicircular protuberance on the crown exactly like the helmets of old. These and also the cloaks they set so high a value upon that I could not procure one, some were however got.' Cook, *Journals* III, 1, 280.

Interesting is Samwell's reference to natives of Atooi and Niihau, when he says: 'These people wear thick feathered rolls called Ehooretooa round their feathered Caps which gives the whole Head dress the appearance of a rich and elegant Turband, none of thes[e] Rolls at Ouwhaiee.' Ibid. 2, 1231, also Beaglehole's note, ibid. Samwell made this remark on 14 March 1779 during the second stay of the ships at Niihau, but, since Webber might have depicted the sitter during the first stay, the portrait is included here in the first group of drawings relating to Hawaii.

Two similar bands were given to Major Behm by the 'Capt[ns] & Officers of both Ships' in return for his many kindnesses bestowed upon them in Kamchatka. Of the 'several articles from the different Islands we had visited in the South Sea' Samwell says: 'with the latter he was much pleased & intended to present them to the Empress'. Ibid., 2, 1248. The two bands are now in the Museum of Anthropology and Ethnography, Leningrad. See Kaeppler (1978a), 75.

ref: *The Conch Shell* (Bernice P. Bishop Museum, Honolulu)
         vol. 1, no. 4 (1963) 48; Kaeppler (1978a) Fig. 90 (col.).

Collection of James Edge Partington (Edwards, 1934, 169, item 2538, with the following inscription: 'A cock's feather cloak is over his shoulders and he is wearing a feather helmet, round the lower edge of which is a cylindrical band of feather work, resembling the "Collar" in the British Museum. (See Partington and Heape's "Ethnographical Album" first series, pl. 52, fig. 1)'; Captain A. W. F. Fuller; presented to the Museum by Mrs A. W. F. Fuller in 1963.

Bernice P. Bishop Museum, Honolulu. Acc. no. 1963.254 (Fuller Collection).

JOHN WEBBER

3.185   **A Native of Atooi [Kauai]**   [c. 1778–]
pen and wash, 17½ × 12¼ : 445 × 311, signed 'J.
Webber del 1779' (l.r.).

Faint traces of 'no 96' (u.r.) which would identify the drawing
as 'A Portrait of a Native of Morowee' (Maui), no. 96 in Webber's
Catalogue.

Full face, the hair falling to the shoulders. The head in 3.186
is obviously the same head as in 3.185, and the latter is a preliminary sketch for the former. Webber's inscription on 3.186
is therefore to be preferred to his description of the same man in
his Catalogue, which was not completed until the end of the
voyage.

Cook arrived at Maui on 26 November 1778 but made no landing.
Canoes came out to the ships and King wrote of the encounter:
'We could only observe that the Canoes, which had three Men
in Each resembled in every respect the Smaller ones we had seen
at Atou-i.' Cook, *Journals* III, 1, 496. Although some men came
aboard it is doubtful whether Webber had time for a portrait.
Perhaps he used the study (3.186) of a man of Kauai to represent
a man of Maui. Or, on the other hand 3.186 may be a quick
sketch of the man who came on board off Maui who claimed that
he had been on board the ship at Kauai. See Clerke in Cook,
ibid., 474, 3n.

ver: For a study see 3.186. A late nineteenth century copy of
3.185 is in the Bernice P. Bishop Museum, Honolulu,
entitled 'Man of the Sandwich Islands (Webber 1793)'.

ref: Cook, *Journals* III, 1, pl 58a, where titled 'Hawaiian Man',
Murray-Oliver (1975), pl 40.

British Library. Add. MS 15514, f.24.

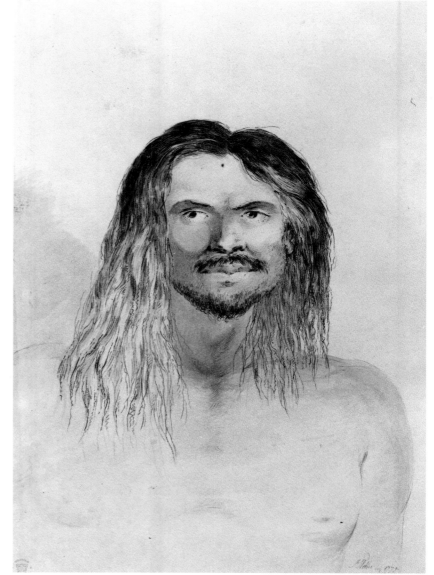

JOHN WEBBER

3.186   **A Native of Atooi [plate 93]**   [Jan 1778]
crayon, pencil and sepia, 11½ × 10 : 292 × 254,
signed and dated 'J. Webber 1778' (l.r.).

Inscribed 'A Native of Atowi' and 'Sandwich Islands' in Webber's
hand across upper edge.

ver: A preliminary sketch for 3.185.

Francis Edwards, London, *Cat.* 551 (1932) no. 14 'Native of
Utowi, Sandwich Islands, signed 'J. Webber 1778' 11½ in × 10
in'.

Francis P. Farquhar Collection, Berkeley, California.

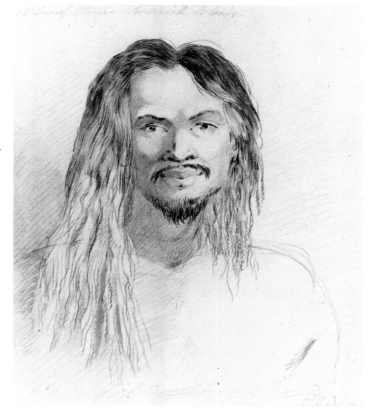

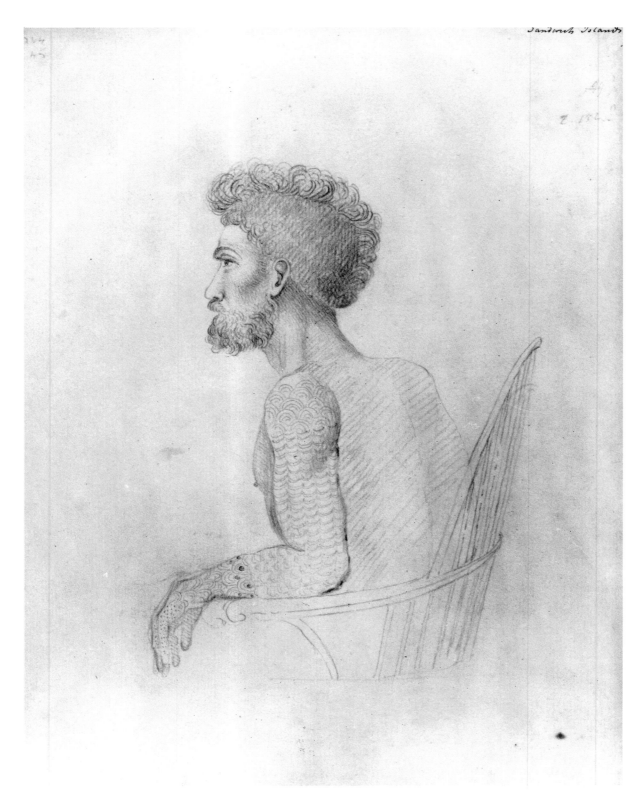

WILLIAM ELLIS

3.187 **[A Man of Atooi (?)]**
pencil, $11^{13}/_{16} \times 8^7/_8$: 300 × 225, unsigned.

Inscribed 'Sandwich Isles?' in ink [u.r.] Annotated in
pencil '99' (u.r.) crossed out '2.152' substituted, referring to Ellis (1782). Inscribed on verso '71' in ink
[l.l.].

Bearded and heavily tattooed on the left arm, seated in Windsor
chair, in profile facing left. His hair dressed in a central roll across
the top of the head.

'The custom of tattowing prevails greatly among these people,
but the men have a much larger share of it than the women;
many (particularly some of the natives of Mow'whee) have one

half of their body, from head to foot, marked in this manner,
which gives them a most striking appearance. It is done with
great regularity, and looks remarkably neat: some have only an
arm marked in this manner, others a leg; some again have both
arm and leg, and others only the hand.' Ellis (1782) II, 151-2.

ver: This may be the same man whom Webber depicted in 3.179
despite the slightly different treatment of the beard, which
in Ellis's drawing is much fuller. Cf. the tattoo design on
the shoulder with that of the man depicted in 3.179.
ref: Davidson (1977) 21, pl. VI; Murray-Oliver (1977) 36-7.

Alexander Turnbull Library, Wellington. A264.45.

430

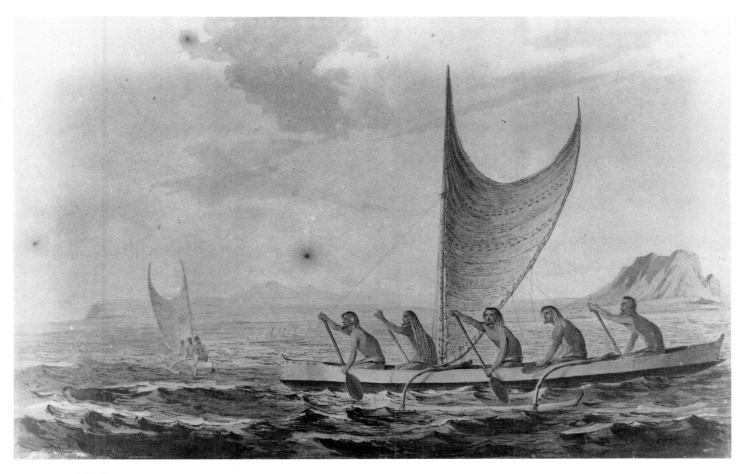

JOHN WEBBER

3.188   Sailing Canoes off Niihau   [1778]
pen, and wash, mounted on cardboard, 12³⁄₁₆ ×
19⅛ : 309 × 481, signed 'J. Webber, del. 1778'
(l.r.) partly erased.

A pencil number like '91' (u.l.) which would identify this drawing
as no. 91 in Webber's Catalogue 'A canoe of Attooi'.

The drawing might well be the one which is listed in the note
about 'Drawings omitted in the list selected for Publication referred to by Capt. Cook' (National Library of Australia, Department of Manuscripts, MS 9/29) under 'Febr. 1778' as 'Drawing
of the Canoes at Sandwich Island'.

On verso in ink inscribed in eighteenth century hand 'No. 28'
and 'Lot No 2', as well as in pencil, in a late eighteenth century
hand 'glas 3' and 'No. 8 Maple largest frame of guilt edge'.

Five men paddling an outrigger canoe (wa'a kaukahi) with a sail
set, another canoe to the left, foreshortened, and two in the
distance closer to the shore. On the type of canoe see Haddon
and Hornell (1936) I, 20-6.

Cook's remarks, during his stay on Kauai, on the local canoes
correspond closely to Webber's drawing: 'Although we saw very

few trees except the Cocoanut tree, they must have some of a
good size on which they make their Canoes; as they are in general
about twenty four feet long and the bottom for the most part
formed of one piece, hollowed out to about an inch, or an inch
and a half thick, and brought to a point at each end: the sides
consi[s]ts of three boards, each about an inch thick and neatly
fited and lashed to the bottom part. The extremeties of both
head and stern is a little raised, and both are made sharp, something like a wedge but flatenes more abruptly, so that the two
side boards join each other side by side for more than a foot; but
the drawing will explain this better than words. As they are not
more than fifteen or eighteen inches broad, those that go single
have out riggers, which are shaped and fited with more judgement
than any I had before seen. They are rowed by paddles and some
have a light triangler sail, like those of the Friendly islands,
extended to a mast and boom.' Cook, *Journals* III, 1, 282-3.

A similar description is found in Samwell's Journal: 'Of Canoes
they have two sorts, the single and the double; they are made
exactly alike, but those that form the double Canoe are much
larger than any single one, which in general are from five to 7
or 8 yards long & will hold from 4 to ten people; the bottom of
the Canoe is made out of one piece of wood hollowed which they

often dye black, on this they rise the sides with thin white boards which they bring together about two feet from the head & stern, where they end in a point turned up a little; they have outriggers on the larboard side, they are made of three pieces of wood, one large which serves to balance the Canoe & two bent & fastened to the Canoe. The paddles are broad and made of light Wood in the shape of a Spade.' Ibid., 2, 1183.

The title given to this drawing is that of the Bernice P. Bishop Museum. It is based upon the topography of the island in the background.

ref: Kaeppler (1978a) fig. 194 (col.).

Francis Edwards, London, *Cat.* 416 (July 1921) under no. 769 'A Sailing Canoe of the Sandwich Islands, sepia and colour, 19 by 12½ in, unpublished', purchased by Spencer Bickerton, Honolulu and acquired from him in September 1922.

Bernice P. Bishop Museum, Honolulu, Acc. no. 1922.129.

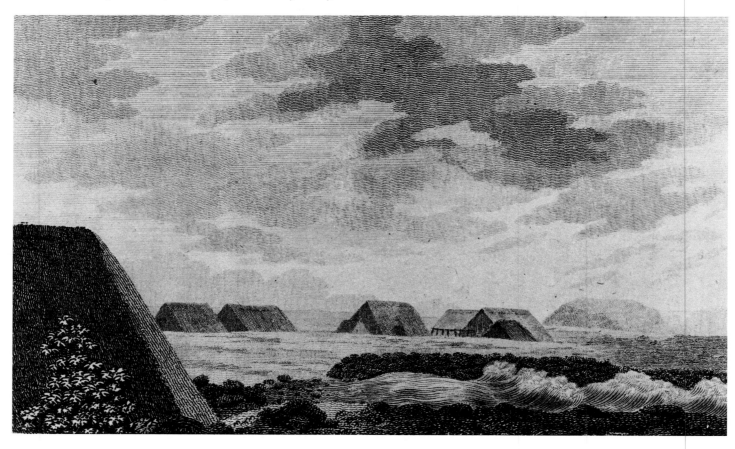

WILLIAM ELLIS (after)

3.188A 'A View in the Island of O'neehow'.
Engraving. 'W. Ellis del.' — 'W. Ellis direx!' 'Published 1 Jan! 1782, by G. Robinson.'

Published in Ellis (1782) I, fp. 175.

No drawing for this engraving is known.

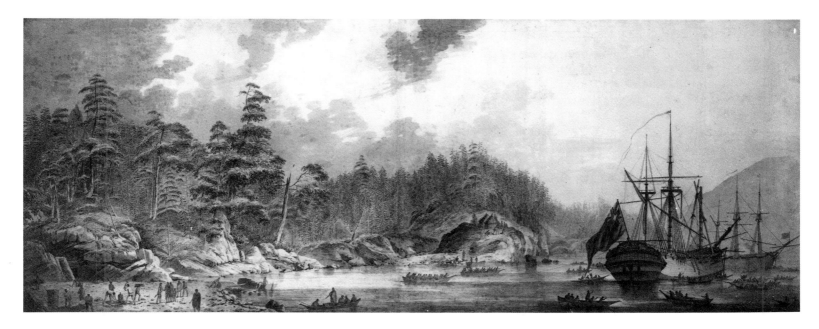

JOHN WEBBER

3.189 The *Resolution* and *Discovery* in Ship Cove
[plate 96]   [Apr 1778]
pen, wash and water-colour, 23½ × 58½ : 598 ×
1486, unsigned.

The drawing may be tentatively identified as no. 71 'A view at
our first anchoring place' in the roll section of King George's
Sound America of Webber's Catalogue.

In the left foreground, seamen splitting and sawing logs; many
native craft in the bay and about the two ships. In the central
mid-distance the astronomers' encampment upon a high rock and
men taking observations; beyond, a heavily-forested foreshore.
On the beach smiths are forging mast fittings, two sailors are
rolling casks of water to a landing stage. At right the *Resolution*
and *Discovery* surrounded by Indians in canoes. A shear-legs for
raising and lowering the masts has been set up on the deck of the
Resolution.

Cook described the station on 1 April 1778: 'As soon as the Ships
were securely Moored, other business was taken in ha[n]d; the
observatorys and Instruments for making observations were set
up on a elevated rock on one side of the Cove close to the
Resolution; a party of men with an officer was sent ashore to cut
wood and clear a place and make conveniences for watering and
the Forge was set up to make the iron work wanting about the
foremast, for bisides one of the bibs being defective the larboard
Trestle-tree and one of the cross-trees was sprung.' Cook, *Journals*
III, 1, 298. See also King, ibid. 2, 1396-7. The action depicted
taking place on the *Resolution* suggests a later day than 1 April.
King describes work on 6 April: 'We set about unrigging the
foremast & also the Mainmast, & in the Afternoon had them
unrigged & sheers erect'd for getting out the foremast.' Ibid. 2,
1399.

ver: For a study for the right half of this drawing see 3.194a.
For related but less panoramic views see 3.190 and 3.191.
A water-colour copy of 3.189 by Mabel B. Messer (active
in London c.1925) is in The Public Archives of Canada,
Ottawa.

ref: Cook, *Journals* III, 1, pl. 33; Murray-Oliver (1969a) pl.
117 (col.); Tippett/Cole (1977) 19 (col.); Fisher (1979)
fig. 1.

National Maritime Museum, London. On loan from the
Admiralty.

JOHN WEBBER

3.190   A View in Ship Cove [plate 98]   [Apr 1778–]
pen, wash and water-colour, 19¹¹/₁₆ × 26¼ : 500 × 667, unsigned.

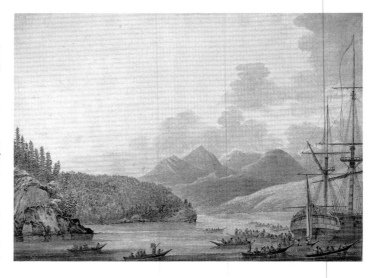

This drawing may be tentatively identified as no. 73 or no. 74 'A View in Ship Cove' in Webber's Catalogue.

The *Resolution* lying at right, stern forward, surrounded by native craft. In the mid-foreground two canoes; in one of which a chief stands wearing an imposing headdress. Wooded shores and mountains in the background.

'A considerable number of the Natives visited us daily and we every now and then saw new faces. On their first coming they generally went through a singular ceremony; they would paddle with all thier strength quite round both Ships, A Chief or other principal person standing up with a Spear, or some other Weapon in his hand and speaking, or rather holloaing all the time, sometimes this person would have his face cover[ed] with a mask, either that of the human face or some animal, and some times in stead of a weapon would hold in his hand a rattle. After making the Circuit of the ships they would come along side and begin to trade without further ceremony. Very often indeed they would first give us a song in which all joined with a very agreable harmony.' Entry for 1 April 1778, Cook, *Journals* III, 1, 298-9.

For the days between 1 - 4 April, King has the following entry: 'The Natives were not so numerous: but we had every day new Visitors, who generally came in large boats, & apparently from some distance. On their arrival they always perform'd what seemed a necessary ceremony, which was pulling & making a circuit round both Ships with great swiftness, & their Paddles kept in exact time; one man would stand up in the middle with a Spear or rattle in his hand, & a mask on which was sometimes the figure of a human face, at others that of an Animal, & kept repeating something in a loud tone; At other times they would all join in a Song, that was frequently very Agreeable to the Ear, after this they always came alongside & began to trade without Ceremony.' Ibid., 2, 1397.

ver: For another version of this drawing, which differs in the number and placement of the native craft on the water, see 3.191.

ref: Beaglehole (1974) pl. 37; Rienits (1968) 122; King (1979) pl. 73; Henry (1984) 76.

British Library, London. Add MS 15514, f.10.

JOHN WEBBER

3.191   A View in Ship Cove   [Apr 1778–]
pen and wash, with some touches of water-colour, probably faded. 16⅛ × 24¾ : 410 × 629, signed and dated 'John Webber del 1778'.

ver: For another version of this view see 3.190.

Sir John Soane's Museum, London.

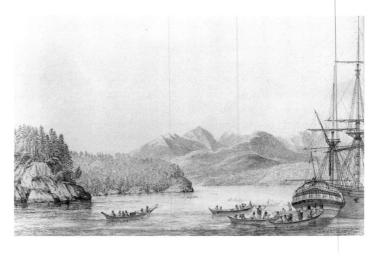

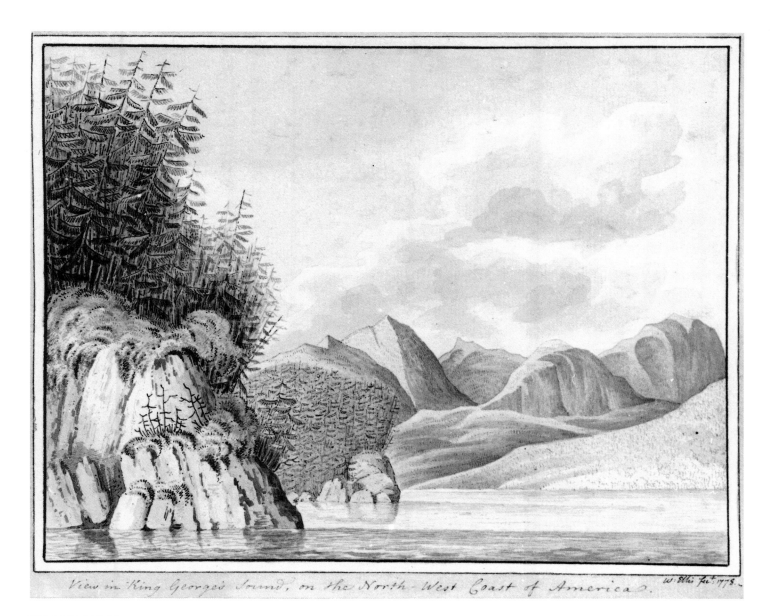

View in King George's Sound, on the North-West Coast of America.   *W: Ellis fect. 1778.*

WILLIAM ELLIS

3.192   A View in King George's Sound   [1778]
pen, ink and water-colour, 9 × 10¹¹/₁₆ : 228 ×
271, signed and dated in black ink 'W: Ellis fec! 1778'
(l.r.); w/m: part of the fleur-de-lis in a shield, with
'W' underneath = J. Whatman.

Titled 'View in King George's Sound' followed by 'on the North-
West Coast of America' in brown ink beneath the drawing within
a grey band between four enframing lines.

In the left foreground rocks rising sharply from the water, clad
with tall fir trees; in the distance at right high mountains rising
from the Sound.

ver: The viewpoint similar to that in Webber's drawing 3.190
and 3.191 but closer. The same background scenery appears
in Ellis's drawing 3.193, which no doubt was a preliminary
study.

Museum Book Store, London, *Cat.* 94 (1924) 562/5, *Cat.* 107
(1928) 41/5, *Cat.* 125 (1941) 453: 'This appears to be a view
near Ship Cove, with the forest of spruce-pine reaching to cliffs
at the water's edge'.

National Library of Australia, Canberra. Rex Nan Kivell Collection. NK 53/B.

WILLIAM ELLIS

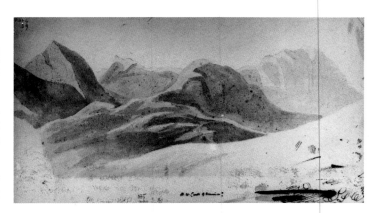

3.193 **[Mountainous landscape, Ship Cove]** **[Apr 1778]**
grey and faint blue wash over pencil, $7\frac{1}{4} \times 12\frac{7}{8}$: 181 × 327, unsigned.

Inscribed in brown ink across lower edge 'N.W. Coast of America?', as well as in pencil (l.) 'Ellis Voyage Vol 1 p. 369, 235?' (the last two numbers crossed out and substituted by '269'). On verso inscribed in ink '56'.

Mountainous landscape, with a spit of land at left, overgrown by shrub and fir trees. Paint squiggles (l.r.). The scenery is similar to that depicted in 3.192 and may well be a study for it.

ref: Murray-Oliver (1977), 35-6.

Alexander Turnbull Library, Wellington. A. 264.39.

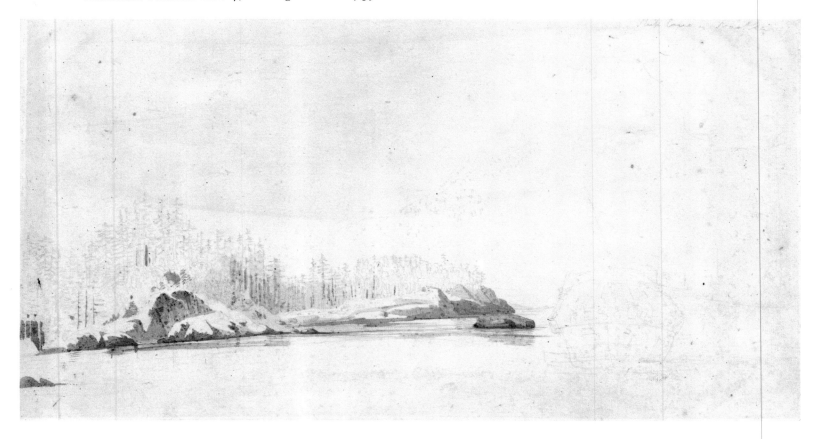

JOHN WEBBER

3.194a **Ship Cove, Nootka** **[Apr 1778]**
pencil and wash (unfinished), $10\frac{1}{4} \times 19\frac{7}{16}$: 261 × 493, unsigned.

Inscribed as above in pencil (u.r.) and numbered '21' (u.r.).

The drawing is a field-sketch showing one side of Ship Cove with Astronomer's Rock. It continues on verso, where the bow of the *Resolution* is depicted on the left (see 3.194b). The position of the *Resolution* at right reappears in Webber's drawings of 3.189-3.191.

British Library, London. Add MS 17277, no. 21 (recto).

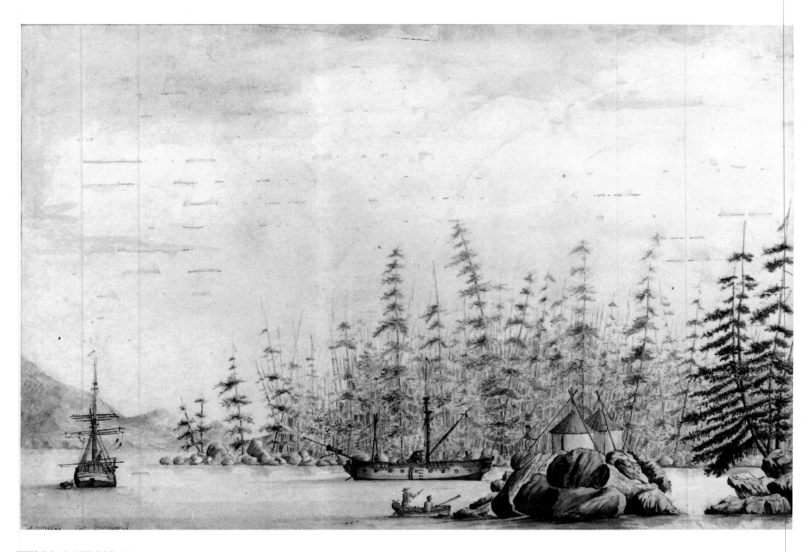

WILLIAM ELLIS (?)

3.196 A View in Ship Cove [Apr 1778]
pen and water-colour, 14¹⁄16 × 20¹¹⁄16 : 357 × 525, unsigned; w/m: PVL = Pieter van der Ley.

Inscribed 'Americaa [sic] — Col Morrison's[?]' in brown ink (l.l.). 'Discovery' inscribed on stern of the ship at left.

The *Resolution* is shown with only the main mast in position and a shear-legs erected for placing the foremast in position. The foremast was removed on 7 April, the mizen on 11 April. The new foremast was in position on 16 and the new mizen on 21 April. The drawing therefore appears to have been executed between 11 and 16 April 1778.

Ellis writes: 'The Resolution's fore-mast, upon examination proved so bad, that Captain Cook thought it necessary to get it out to repair [6 April].' 'The best part of the day was employed in getting out the Resolution's mast, which, with the assistance of most of the Discovery's hands, and a great deal of trouble, was at last effected [7 April].' 'In the course of the squalls last night the Resolution sprung her mizen-mast, which therefore was obliged to be got out, and a new one placed in its room [9 April].' 'The Resolution's people were busily employed in getting out the mizen-mast, forming the new one, and getting the fore-mast alongside [16 April].' 'On Tuesday the 21st, the Resolution's new mizen-mast was got in . . .' Ellis (1782) I, 201-4.

Ellis describes the ship's mooring place, 'it was agreed that the vessels should next day be removed to a cove, not far from the spot where they then lay; and as the shore was steep-to, and no danger could happen in consequence of rocks or shoal-water, they were to be secured to the trees on shore by hawsers' (193); the latter observation is also apparent from the drawing, which shows ropes at the prow and the stern of the *Resolution.*

ver: From a very similar viewpoint as drawing 3.195 with only slight differences in the trees and the addition of the boat. A sentry stands on a rock at left guarding the astronomers' tents.

ref: Henry (1984) 72.

Purchased from Aquarius Fine Arts, Hamilton, New Zealand, 1976.

National Library of Australia, Canberra. R 7595.

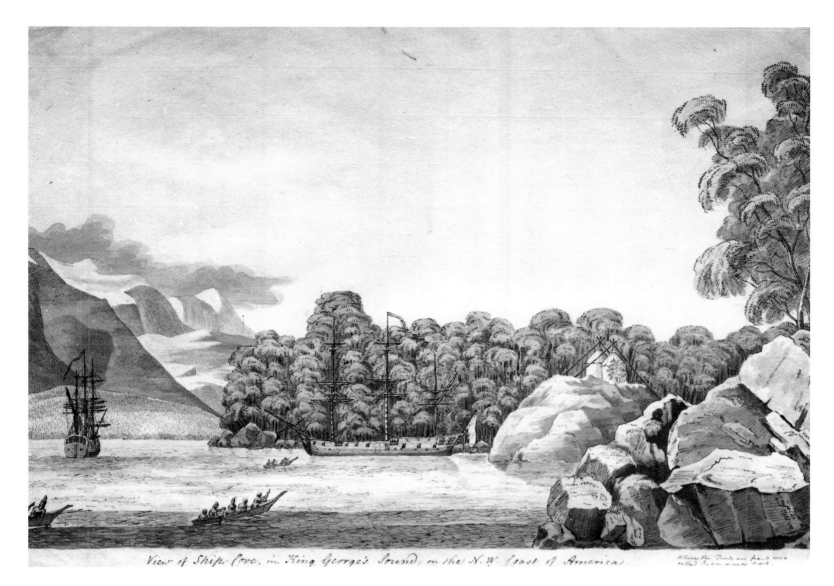

View of Ship-Cove, in King George's Sound, on the N.W. Coast of America

WILLIAM ELLIS

3.197   View of Ship Cove   [Apr 1778–]
pen, ink and water-colour, 12 × 17½ : 305 × 444, signed in ink 'W. Ellis fec! 1778' (l.r.), underneath the second '7' there is some erasion, as if the number had been changed or corrected; w/m: lily in a shield under crown with 'W' = J. Whatman, underneath.

Inscribed 'View of Ship-Cove, in King George's Sound, on the N.W. Coast of America' in brown ink beneath the drawing, and inscribed at right also in brown ink 'Where the Tents are fixed was called Astronomer's Rock', which is written over faint pencil apparently of the same text. Inscribed in pencil '14' (l.l.).

Showing *Resolution* and *Discovery* at anchor, with Nootkan canoes nearby; snow-covered mountains in the distance at left; a wooded foreshore of cedar trees in the mid-distance, and at right some high rocks upon which the two astronomers' tents are fixed.

ver: The drawing possesses curious features. The terrain of Nootka Sound opposite Ship Cove does not possess a mountainous background as high as that depicted at left. The point of view is similar to that of 3.195 and 3.196: but Astronomer's Rock is shown higher and larger. Also all other drawings of this scene (except 3.189 which depicts mixed vegetation) depict coniferous trees only about the Cove. The *Resolution* itself is shown as if refitted and ready for departure. The drawing, therefore appears to be a retrospective composition made from available field studies at least after 21 April 1778 and into which an imaginative element, perhaps unintentionally, has crept.

ref: Cook, *Journals* III, 1, pl. 34b; Rienits (1968) 124; Tippett/ Cole (1977) 19 (col.); *Exh. Cat.* Portland (1982) 188 (col.); Henry (1984) 70.

Museum Book Store, London, *Cat.* 94 (1924) 562/3 and *Cat.* 107 (1928) 41/3, *Cat.* 125 (1941) 453: 'The view shows the *Resolution* and *Discovery* at anchor in the Sound . . . a very fine drawing'.

National Library of Australia, Canberra. Rex Nan Kivell Collection. NK 53/J.

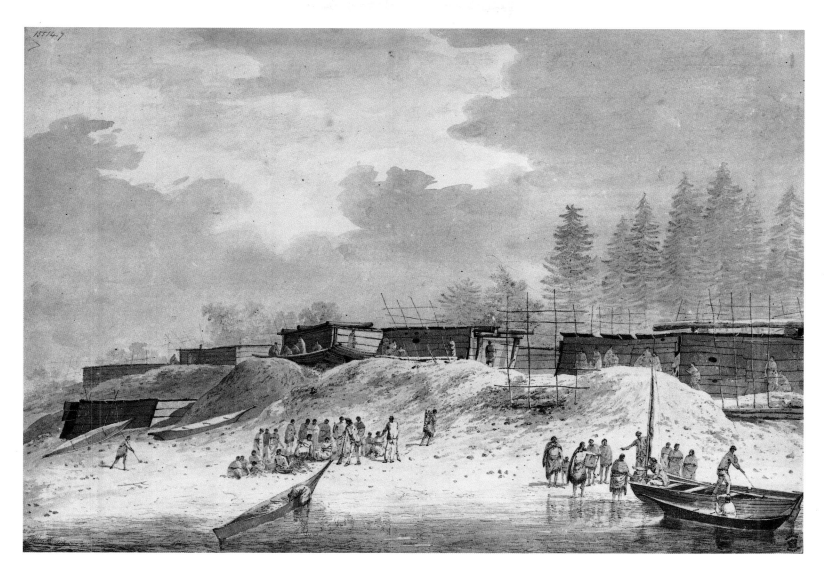

JOHN WEBBER

3.198   **Habitations in Nootka Sound**
[plate 102]   **[Apr 1778–]**
pen, wash and water-colour, 17⁵⁄₁₆ × 25 : 440 × 635, signed and dated 'J. Webber del 1778'.

Inscribed in full 'Habitations of the Natives outside of a House in King George's Sound in America' in pencil below the drawing. Number inscribed (u.r.) indecipherable, but the drawing is probably no. 72, 'A View of the Natives Habitations' in the King George's Sound section of Webber's Catalogue.

Groups of people clad in skins standing on beach, two boats at extreme right, one at centre left, flat-roofed houses in the background, the right one with a trunk on the roof. Before and around the houses are racks for drying fish.

It is possible that the houses depicted belong to the village of Yuquot, which Cook visited together with Webber and Clerke on 22 April 1778. Cook, *Journals* III, 1, 306. See also Clerke, ibid., 2, 1327-8.

Cook gives the following account of the natives' houses and their situation along the shore: 'their houses or dwellings are situated close to the shore. They consist in a long range of buildings, some of which are one hundred and fifty feet in length, twenty four or thirty broad and seven or eight high from the floor to the roof, which in them all is flat and covered with loose boards. The Walls, or sides and ends, are also built up of boards and the framing consi[s]ts of large trees or logs. They first fix firm in the ground three rows of large posts, on these are fixed longitudanally,

large trees the whole length of the building, a cross these they lay the boards that serve for the covering, and those of the sides are fastened to the posts. Many of these boards are thirty feet in length and from three to five broad, and are all procured by spliting large trees. Some of these buildings are raised on the side of a bank, these have a flooring consisting of logs supported by post[s] fixed in the ground; before these houses they make a platform about four feet broad, and on a level with the floor, or rather the floor is continued four feet without the fro[n]t wall of the house and so allows of a passage along the front of the building: They assend to this passage by steps, not unlike some at our landing places in the River Thames.' Ibid., 1, 317.

The drawing contains a large trunk of a tree resting on the house on the right, which is a peculiar feature. It was noticed by King who talks about it in his journal: 'Upon one of the buildings in the West town was a tree supported by two posts of an uncommon size, capable of making a Mast for a first rate. It must have requir'd no small force to have placed it, Although they cou'd perceive no use or end that it could Answer.' King in Cook, *Journals* III, 2,1409. See also Beaglehole's footnote.

ver: A larger and earlier version of 3.199. For a study see 3.200.

ref: Cook, *Journals* III, 1, pl. 35; Sendey (1977) 14-15; King (1979) pl. 74 where titled 'The Village of Yuquot in Nootka Sound'; Fisher (1979) fig. 3; Henry (1984) 77.

British Library, London. Add MS 15514, f. 7.

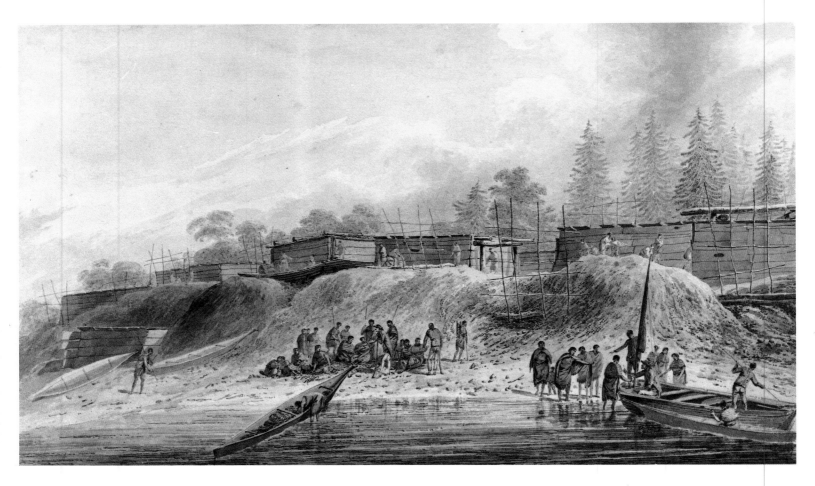

JOHN WEBBER

3.199   A View of the Habitations in Nootka Sound

[c. 1781-3]

pen, wash and water-colour, 8¾ × 14¾ : 221 × 375.

Inscribed 'A View of the Habitations in Nootka Sound' in pencil by a later hand on the folio, beneath the drawing.

ver: A smaller version of 3.198, almost identical in size to the engraving 3.199A.

ref: *Exh. Cat.* Portland (1974) no. 164; *Exh. Cat.* Portland (1982) 184.

Dixson Library, State Library of New South Wales, Sydney. PXX 2, 23.

JOHN WEBBER (after)

3.199A   'A VIEW of the HABITATIONS in NOOTKA SOUND'

Engraving. 'J. Webber del' — 'S. Smith sculp.'

Published in Cook/King (1784) pl. 41, II, 313-14.

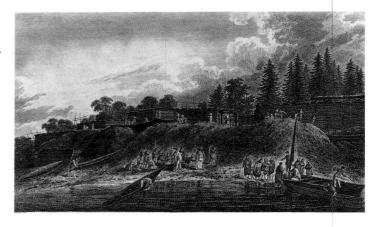

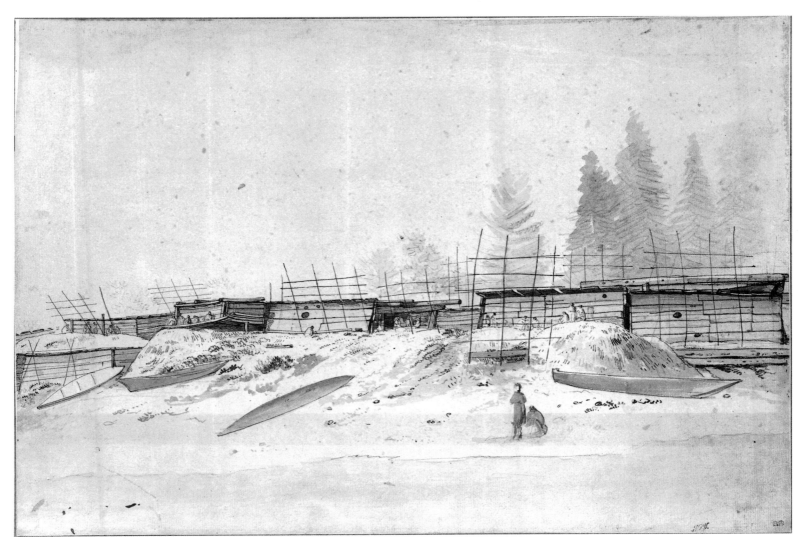

JOHN WEBBER

3.200   Habitations of the Natives in Nootka Sound
[22 Apr 1778]
pencil, pen and wash, 14½ × 20⅜ : 363 × 517.

On the back of the old mount is written: 'Captn Cook's 3rd
Voyage No. 41. A drawing by J. Webber of a view of the habitations in Nootka Sound has been engraved by J. Smith'.

Showing same scenery as 3.198 and 3.199 for which it is a study
most probably taken on the spot. The beach is considerably less
steep than in the finished drawings, suggesting Webber's idea of
a grander composition. The 'sky-line' of the houses is not so
graduated as in 3.198 and 3.199. The former is much more
consciously composed.

National Gallery of Scotland, Department of Prints and Drawings,
Edinburgh. D.1452.

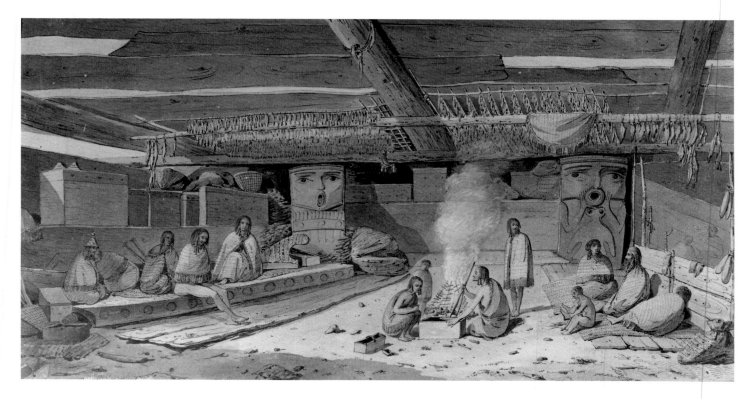

JOHN WEBBER

3.201   **An Inside View of the Natives' Habitations**
[plate 103]   [Apr 1778–]
pen, ink and water-colour, 10 × 19 : 254 × 483, signed
and dated 'J. Webber. del. 1778' (l.l.).

This is probably the drawing referred to in Webber's Catalogue
no. 67 in the King George's Sound section and entitled 'An
Inside View of the Natives Habitations'. Preserved on the back
of the present frame is a strip of former backing on which is
inscribed in pencil 'glass 3' and 'Inside a Kamschatka House (sic)'.

Five figures seated on a platform at left; in the centre, four figures,
including a child, around an open fire in a kerfed cedar box. At
right, four more figures seated, including another child. Beyond
them, in another section of the house two more figures sketched
in. Fish hang from poles near the roof, and at the back two large
carved images.

The drawing probably originated from Cook's excursion to the
village of Yuquot on 22 April 1778, when he was accompanied
by Webber and Clerke: 'During the time I was at this village M.r
Webber who was with me, made drawings of everything that was
curious both within and without doors.' Cook, *Journals* III, 1,
306.

Already on his first visit to Yuquot on 20 April, Cook had been
inside the natives' houses: 'there [the Indians] spread a mat for
me to sit down upon and shewed me every other mark of civility'
(ibid., 303). It was on this occasion that Cook remarked on the
women weaving and the Indians' method of smoking herrings.
Both Cook and Clerke give an illuminating account of Indian
cooking (ibid., 1, 318 and 2, 1328). Referring to cooking and
boiling the water in a wooden trough, the published account
makes a special reference to Webber's drawing: 'This operation
is represented by Mr. Webber, in his drawing of the inside of a
Nootka house.' Cook/King (1784) II, 321.

From King's account one can surmise that the house that Webber
drew was 'the largest of the buildings' that Cook and his party
visited. It 'was ab.t 140 feet long, between 30 & 40 broad, & 8
in height, but this had many separate divisions'. King in Cook,

Journals III, 2, 1409. This becomes apparent from his second remark: 'for in the largest house in the west Village, on the top of
which we have observed was suspended a prodigious tree, in the
inside at the middle & at the N end were two large trees, the
upper parts of which had the figures of human faces; every feature
of which was strangely distorted, out of proportion & of a vast
size'. Ibid., 1414.

Concerning the wooden figures, which are prominent features in
Webber's drawings, Cook says: 'At the upper end of many of the
appartments, were two large images, or statues placed abreast of
each other and 3 or 4 feet usunder, they bore some resemblance
to the human figure, but monstrous large; the best idea will be
had of them in a drawing which Mr Webber made of the inside
of one of thir appartments wherein two of them stood. They call
them Acweeks, which signifies supreme, or chief . . .' Cook,
Journals III, 1, 319; also 322, where Cook states that the idols
were also called Kulmina [Klumma].

The sculpture next to the left 'idol' appears to represent the tail
of a whale. A similar structure, which otherwise is extremely rare,
was excavated at the Makah site of Ozette in the State of Washington (information supplied by J. King, London and W. Stur-
tevant, Washington).

For Webber's personal account of the execution of this drawing
see Cook, ibid., 1,319, fn.

ver: For another version see 3.202; for a study 3.203.

ref: Bushnell Jr (1928) pl. 3; Cook, *Journals* III, 1, pl. 36; Rienits
(1968) 125; Sendey (1977) 16-17; King (1979) pl. 86 where
titled 'Interior of a house at Yuquot, Nootka Sound'; *Exh.
Cat.* Portland (1982) 185.

Campbell Collection. Listed in Francis Edwards, *Cat.* 416 (London
July 1921) under no. 769 as 'Another Similar View [of the Inside
of a House, Nootka Sound] (19½ × 10 in), in colours'. Purchased
by David I. Bushnell, Jr in 1925 and presented to the Peabody
Museum.

Peabody Museum of Archaeology and Ethnology, Harvard University, Cambridge, Massachusetts. Inv. no. 41-72-10/499.

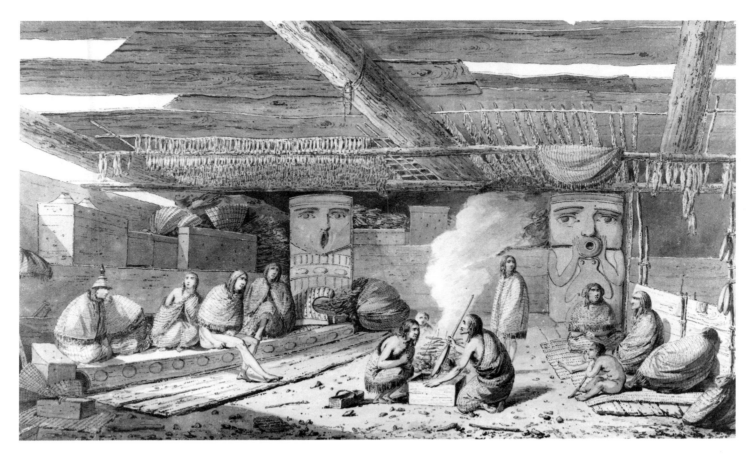

JOHN WEBBER

3.202   **The Inside of a House in Nootka Sound**   [c. 1781-3]
         pen, wash and water-colour, 8⅞ × 14¾ : 225 × 375.

Inscribed 'The Inside of a House in Nootka Sound' in pencil by
a later hand on the folio beneath the drawing.

ver: Similar to 3.201 but redrawn at reduced size for the en-
          graving 3.202A.

ref: *Exh. Cat.* Portland (1974), no. 165; Smith (1984) pl. 44
          (but with incorrect location).

Dixson Library, State Library of New South Wales, Sydney.
PXX2, 24.

JOHN WEBBER (after)

3.202A   **'The INSIDE of a HOUSE in NOOTKA SOUND'**
          Engraving. 'J. Webber del.' — 'W. Sharp sculp.'

Published in Cook/King (1784) pl. 42, II, 315-18, 321.

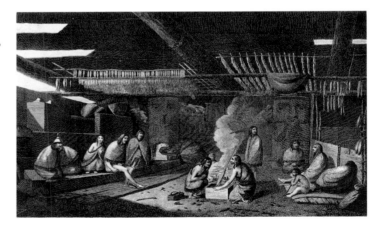

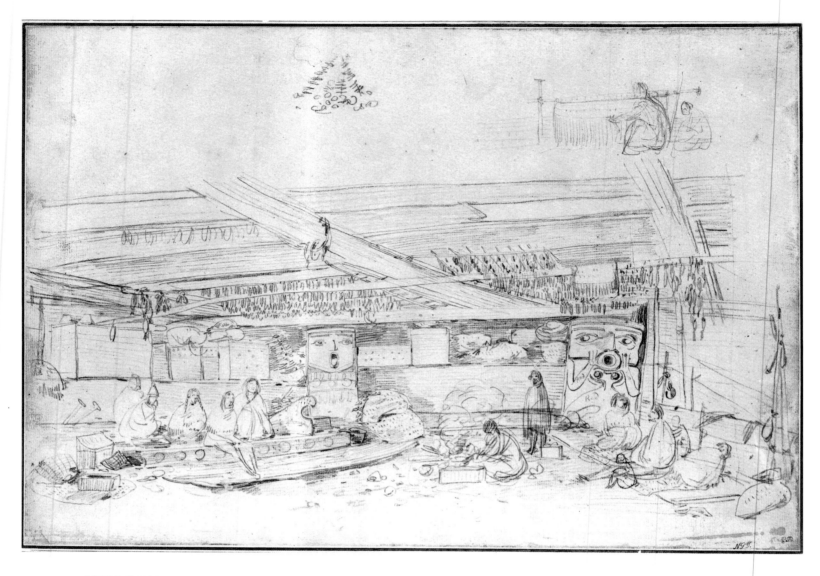

JOHN WEBBER

3.203 **The Inside of a House in Nootka Sound**
[plate 104] [Apr 1778]
pencil, 14½ × 20¼ : 363 × 511, unsigned.

On the back of the old mount is written: 'Cook's 3rd Voyage, No. 42. The Inside of a house in Nootka Sound. J. Webber del. It has been engraved'. A pencil sketch of two figures seated weaving (u.r.).

A field study for 3.201 and 3.202, as indicated by colour annotation.

ref: Smith (1979a) pl. 35.

National Gallery of Scotland, Department of Prints and Drawings, Edinburgh. D.1453.

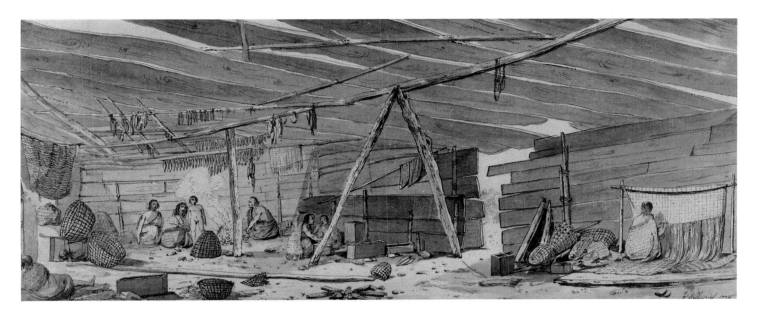

JOHN WEBBER

3.204   An Inside view of the Natives Habitations
[Apr 1778–]
pen, ink and grey wash, 7 × 17 : 176 × 430, signed
and dated 'J. Webber del 1778' (l.r.).

This drawing may be tentatively identified as no. 68 'A Ditto'
[An Inside view of the Natives Habitations] in Webber's Catalogue.

The interior of a long-house. At the left are three women seated
and a naked child, standing. Nearby, at centre, two more seated
women. At extreme right a woman weaving. Fish hang from the
rafters drying; a net is suspended from the ceiling, at the extreme
left, many fishing baskets lie strewn about the room.

Commenting on the natives and the houses of Yuquot, Cook says:
'. . . there were Women at work making dresses of the bark or
plant before mentioned which they performed in every respect
in the same manner as the New Zealanders.' (To which Beaglehole explains: 'That is, the material was woven, not beaten out
from the bark as in the islands. The women of the Nootka Indians
were famous for their weaving in this fashion and for their basketry.') 'Others were at work opening and Smoke drying Sardins
. . . they hang them on small rods at first about a foot from the
fire, afterwards they remove them higher and higher to make
room for others till they get to the roof of the house.' Cook, *Journals*
III, 1, 303. After a first visit to the village on 20 April, Cook
returned on 22 April, this time accompanied by Webber who
made 'drawings of every thing that was curious both within and
without doors'. Ibid., 1, 306. For Cook's description of the interior of the houses at Nootka see also ibid., 1, 317-18.

ver: This long-house is somewhat different from that depicted
in 3.201-3.203. The woman weaving is similar to the one
represented in 3.205.

ref: Bushnell Jr (1928) pl. 2; Sendey (1977) 18-19; *Exh. Cat.*
Portland (1982) 186.

Listed in Francis Edwards, *Cat.* 416 (London, July 1921), as 'View
of the Inside of a House, Nootka Sound (17 by 7 in) in sepia'.

Peabody Museum of Archaeology and Ethnology, Harvard University, Cambridge, Massachusetts. Inv. no. 41-72-10/500.

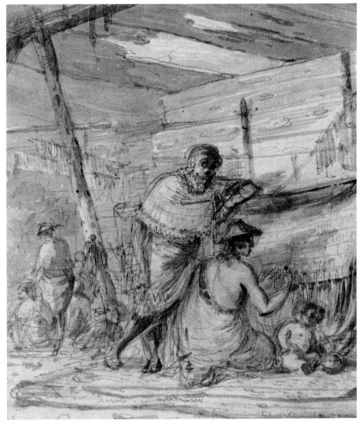

JOHN WEBBER

**3.205   [A Family Group in a Communal House at Nootka
Sound] [plate 110]**   [Apr 1778]
grey wash on pencil, 7½ × 5¹³⁄₁₆ : 191 × 148,
unsigned. On verso '1-12 L-98 WED 1888-1986'.

A field drawing made in a Nootka house. A figure stands leaning
against an upright loom, at which a kneeling woman weaves, a
baby by her side; at far left a group of figures seated around a
fireplace. For a woman weaving see also 3.204.

ref: Cook, *Journals* III, 1, pl. 38.

The Public Archives of Canada, Ottawa. I-12 (C 2821).

447

WILLIAM ELLIS

3.206 **A Rock and a distant View in King George's Sound**
[plate 100]   **[Apr 1778]**
pen, wash and water-colour, 11 × 9⅜ : 279 × 238,
signed and dated 'W. Ellis fec^t/1778' in black ink on
rock at lower centre. The second '7' erased, as if corrected or changed; w/m: shield with initials underneath,
of which only 'V' can be read = perhaps Van der Ley.

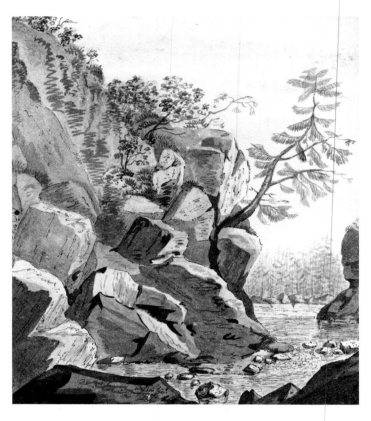

Inscribed in brown ink 'A Rock, and a distant View, in King
George's Sound, N.W. Coast of America' on verso, also on verso
(u.l.) in brown ink '70'.

A steep, rocky cliff with a fir tree and some shrubs growing on
it; to the right a view of the sound, and part of a rocky island
(Astronomer's Rock?).

ref: Tippett/Cole (1977) 21.

Museum Book Store, London, *Cat.* 107 (1928) 41/13, and *Cat.*
125 (1941) 453: 'A fine drawing, showing the scenery of the
Sound and displaying great artistic genius.'

National Library of Australia, Canberra. Rex Nan Kivell Collection. NK 53/G.

WILLIAM ELLIS

3.207 **View in King George's Sound [plate 101] [Apr 1778]**
pen, wash and water-colour over pencil, 11¾ × 17⅞ :
296 × 495 (the sheet slightly irregularly cut), signed
and dated in black ink 'W. Ellis fec^t 1778' (l.r.);
w/m: 'J. WHATMAN'.

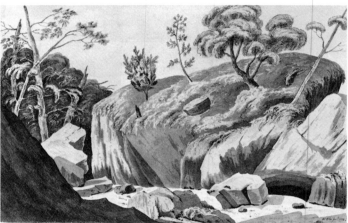

Inscribed 'View in King George's Sound, N.W. Coast of America'
in brown ink across the lower edge, beneath the drawing. Number
'15' written in brown ink (u.l.).

A cleft between rocks possibly of a creek or rivulet, with some
dispersed trees clinging to the rocks. Irregular slabs of rock in the
fore- and middleground.

Probably referred to in *Cat.* 107 of the Museum Book Store,
London, 1928, as 41/4 'View in King George's Sound. N.W.
Coast of America', signed 'W. Ellis, fecit 1778', 'Size 10 × 15
ins'.

National Library of Australia, Canberra. Rex Nan Kivell Collection. NK 53/A.

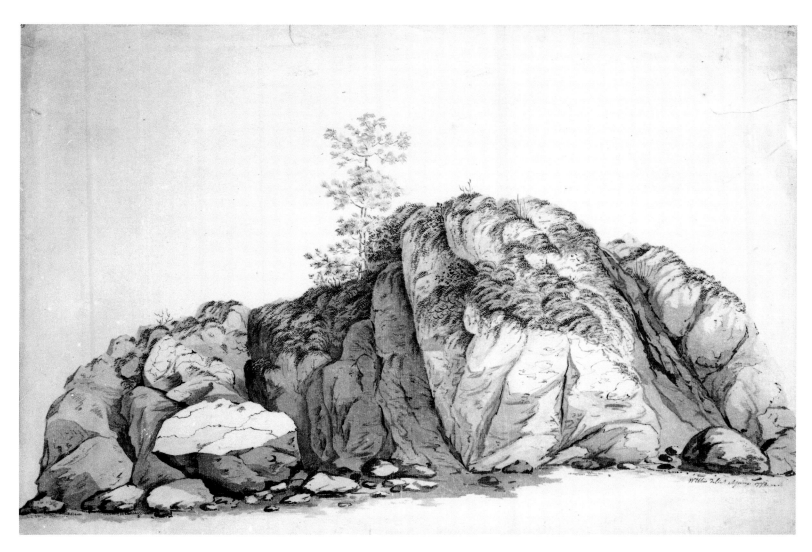

WILLIAM ELLIS

3.208   A View of Astronomer's Rock, Ship Cove   [1778]
pen, wash and water-colour, 12¾ × 18⅜ : 325 × 467,
signed and dated in brown ink 'W Ellis delin^t et pinx
1778' (l.r.); w/m: 'IHS I. VILLEDARY'.

Inscribed 'Another View of the Astronomer's Rock, in Ship Cove,
King George's Sound, on the North-West Coast of America' in
brown ink on verso. Also no. '13' in brown ink on recto (u.l.).
The drawing is surrounded by two enframing lines in ink. The
sheet is damaged along the edges and the two lower corners.

A cliff with two trees and some shrubs growing on it, placed
against the whitish background of the paper.

ref: Exh. Cat. Portland (1982) 189.

Perhaps the drawing referred to in *Cat.* 107 of the Museum Book
Store, London 1928, 41/15 as 'The Entrance into Ship Cove,
King George's Sound, N.W. Coast of America' with the size
given as '8½ by 12 in' (misprint for 18½ × 12?). There is no
other drawing in the list of the Museum Book Store to which the
title as inscribed and given above fits. In a later catalogue of the
Museum Book Store, *Cat.* 125 (1941) 453, the title has been
changed to 'View of the Astronomers' Rock in Ship Cove, King
George's Sound, on the North-West Coast of America, 18½ by
13 in., signed W. Ellis, fect. 1778'.

National Library of Australia, Canberra, Rex Nan Kivell Collection. NK 53/H.

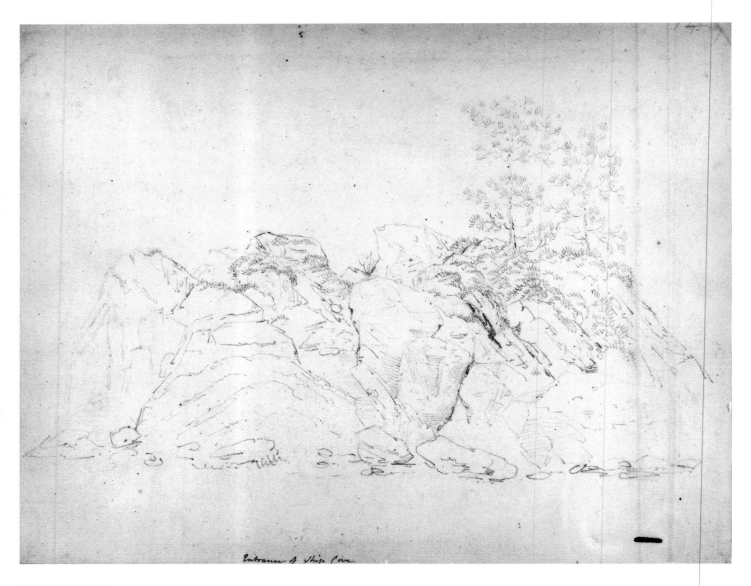

Entrance of Ship Cove

JOHN WEBBER

3.209 **Entrance of Ship Cove** [1778]
pencil, 9⁵⁄₁₆ × 11⁵⁄₈ : 237 × 295; w/m: lower
end of shield and VDL.

The title as above in brown ink along the lower margin of the
sheet. Inscribed in pencil '1.193' (u.r.) but crossed out and '209'
substituted. Inscribed on verso in brown ink '44' (l.l.).

Perhaps another drawing of the same rock formation as in 3.208.

Private collection, England.

JOHN WEBBER

3.210 **[Rocks at Nootka Sound]** [1778]
pencil, with a few touches of pen and ink, 11¹¹⁄₁₆
× 9½ : 297 × 241, unsigned. W/m: part of a shield
with fleur-de-lis and crown (cut-off). Inscribed in pencil '1.193' (u.r.), crossed out, substituted by '1.209'.
Inscribed on verso in brown ink '45' (l.l.).

Study of rocks, most probably at Nootka Sound.

ver: The rock boulder in the lower left foreground is introduced
into Ellis's drawing of Ship Cove (3.197) and there placed
at l.r. as well as into 3.207.

Private collection, England.

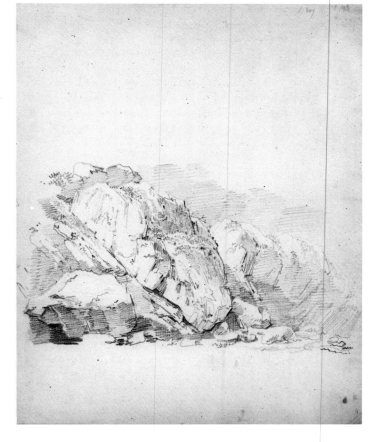

450

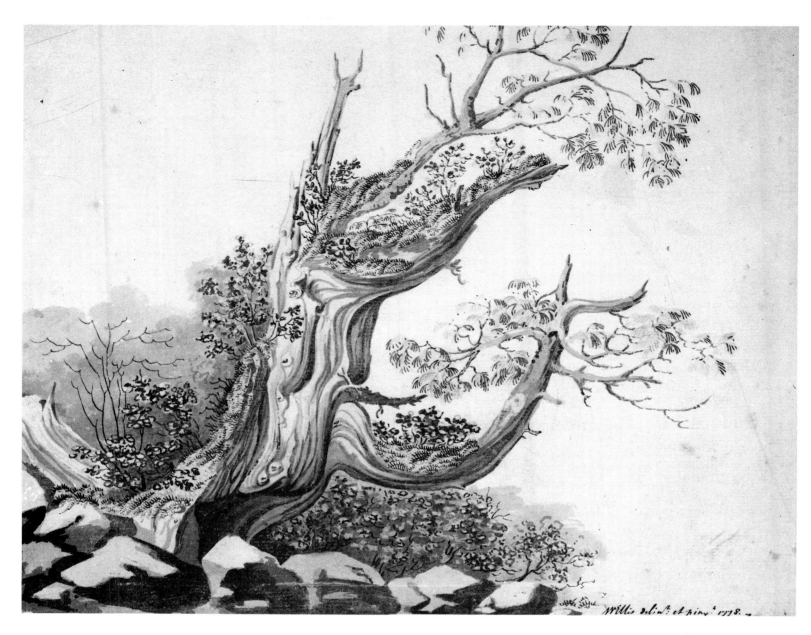

WILLIAM ELLIS

3.211   **A View of a Singular Tree in King George's Sound**
[1778]

pen, wash and water-colour, $9\frac{5}{8} \times 11\frac{15}{16}$: 243
× 303 (the sheet irregularly cut), signed and dated in
brown ink 'W Ellis delin^t et pinx^t 1778' (l.r.).

Inscribed 'View of a singular Tree, in King George's Sound, N.W.
Coast of America' in brown ink on verso, and '16' in brown ink
(u.l.) on recto, just outside two black enframing lines.

The leafy stump of an old tree with moss and other plants growing
from the trunk. In the left foreground lumps of rocks.

Commenting upon the trees of Nootka Sound, Ellis writes: 'The
most prevailing ones are fir of several species, yew, and *arbor vitae*.
The others are birch, maple, poplar, willow, and elder.' Ellis
(1782) I, 209-10.

Museum Book Store, London, *Cat.* 107 (1928) 41/16, *Cat.* 125
(1941) 453 under the title as inscribed.

National Library of Australia, Canberra. Rex Nan Kivell Collection. NK 53/E.

JOHN WEBBER

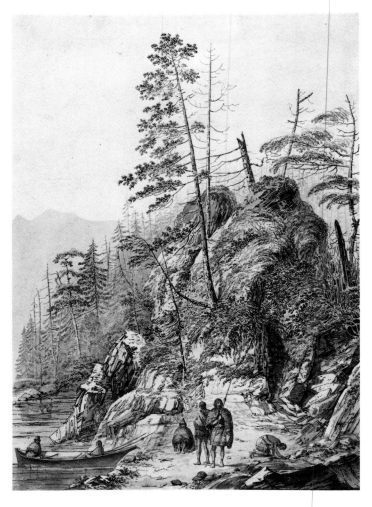

3.212   A View in King George's Sound
            [plate 99]   **[Apr 1778]**
            pen, wash and water-colour, 20½ × 14½ : 572 × 368,
            signed and dated 'J. Webber del 1778' (l.r.). The
            vestige (indecipherable) of a numerical notation re-
            mains in the u.r. corner.

Two standing figures; one sitting, one filling a cup at a stream,
in the central foreground. Two figures in a boat at left. Steep
rocks and conifers behind.

The central figure holding a spear offers an interesting detail of
costume which Webber seems to have depicted nowhere else.
According to Cook: 'Two pieces makes a compleat dress, that is
a cloak and a petticoat; the cloak is circular at the bottom, five
feet broad, three or three and a half long and longer behind then
before the petticoat is nearly of the same shape; the one is tied
over the Shoulders and the other is wrapped round the waist and
reaches to the middle of the leg. The lower garment is mostly
worn by the women, the men seldom wearing any thing about
their Middles nor are they ashamed to appear naked.' Cook,
Journals III, 1, 313. It would appear that because of the spear the
figure is a man. Webber may have thus erred in the costume,
making the figure appear more decent.

ver: For a water-colour drawing of the same composition see
         3.214, and the painting in the Yale University Art Gallery
         (3.213) but with a number of small variations both in the
         figures and the landscape.
ref: Described incorrectly by Lawrence Binyon as a 'View on
         the coast of one of the South Sea Islands' (1907) 316;
         Rienits (1968) 140 (col.); Tippett/Cole (1977) 20.

Purchased for the British Museum in 1859, together with other
drawings by Webber showing scenery of Great Britain.

British Museum, Department of Prints and Drawings, London.
1859-7-9-102.

JOHN WEBBER

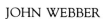

3.213   A View in Nootka Sound   **[1783]**
            oil on canvas, 50⅛ × 38 : 1273 × 967, signed and
            dated 'J. Webber pinx. 1783'.

The painting has been folded horizontally, slightly below the base
of the two pines at centre.

Four Indians of Nootka on a rocky shore, one scooping water
from a stream; to the left two natives sitting in a canoe drawn
up to the shore. A massive rock with fir and pine trees behind.

This is possibly the painting Webber exhibited at the Royal Academy in 1785.

ver: This painting differs only in details from 3.212 and 3.214.

ref: Eberstadt (1948) 50, repr. 46; *Cat. Western Americana* (1952)
         301.

William Robertson Coe Collection.

Yale University Art Gallery. Inv. No. 1946.323. Yale University
Library, The William Robertson Coe Collection of Western
Americana, New Haven.

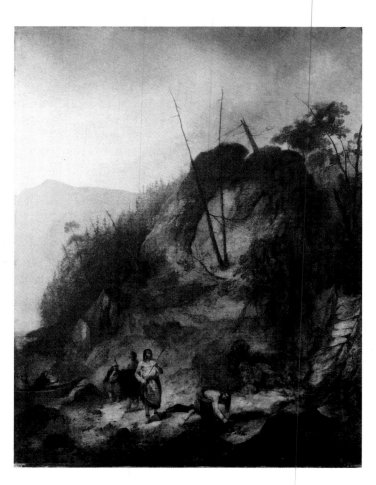

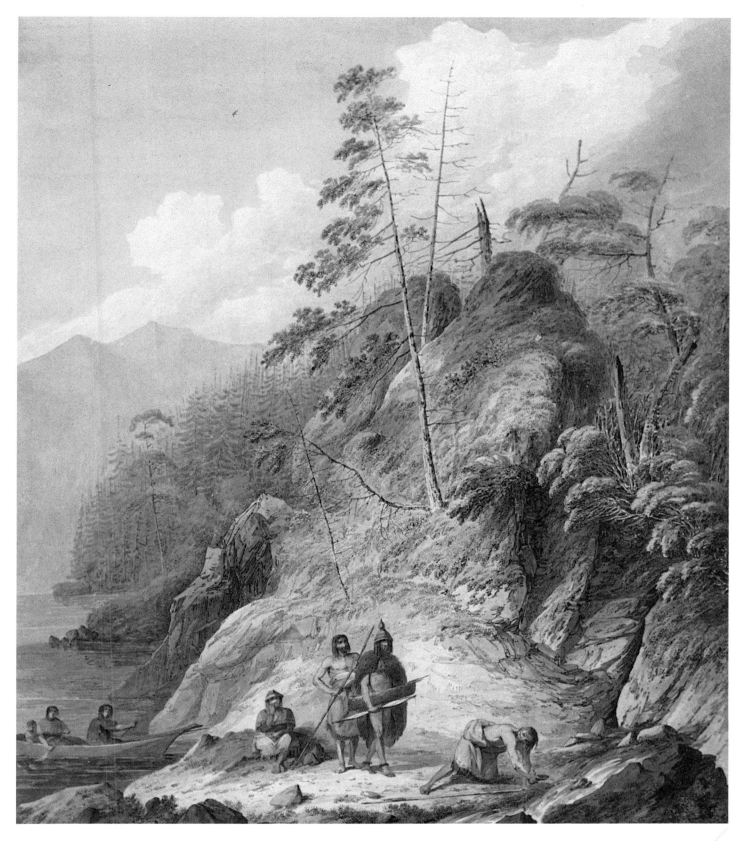

JOHN WEBBER

3.214   [A View in Nootka Sound]   [1784]
water-colour, 22½ × 18¼ : 571 × 464, signed and
dated 'J. Webber del. 1784'.

A rugged pine-covered coast with seven figures; three including
a child in a canoe; four ashore, the two central ones standing
with implements in their hands, the one at right kneeling and
scooping at the ground.

ver: For similar compositions see 3.212 (which is less developed)
and 3.213. With both 3.214 shares some variations in the
figures. The figure of the hunter with a bow in the foreground appears in other Webber drawings, such as 3.215-
3.217.

The drawing, once believed to represent Indians of Kamchatka
is listed in an unnumbered catalogue by Francis Edwards (1929)
no. 6 ('A fine spirited picture of a view on the Coast of Kamschatka, showing natives in a canoe, others by the side of a
stream, with hills and mountains raising up in the rear') and in
Partington (1934) 169 (2539); in 1962 still recorded in the collection of Sir Bruce Ingram.

Mrs Carl Schaefer Dentzel, Northridge, California.

3.215 **A Native prepared for Hunting**
[plate 111] [Apr 1778–]
pen, ink and water-colour on yellowed paper, 17 ×
12 : 432 × 305, signed 'J. Webber del.' (l.r.).

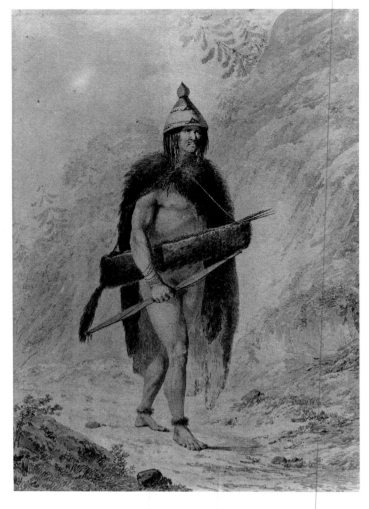

Inscribed faintly in pencil '65' (u.l.), which identifies it with '65'
'A Native prepared for Hunting' under 'King George's Sound
America' in Webber's Catalogue.

A full-length figure of an Indian in a heavy fur cloak fastened
over his shoulders, carrying a bow in his right hand and a quiver
slung over his right shoulder. He wears a copper nose ring, decorated strands of hair on either side of his face, a small moustache,
and a basketry hat with a bulbous top, showing a whaling scene.
'Their Cloaths are made of the Skins of land and Sea animals,
in the making of which there is very little of either art or trouble,
besides that of dressing the Skins and Sewing them together for
they do no more than form them into a kind of Cloak which is
tied over the shoulders with a string and reaches as low as the
knees.' [They] 'are chiefly worn by the men . . .' Cook, *Journals*
III, 1, 312.

'On their Arms they wore Bracelets of Copper or a string of white
Beads several times round, which they also wore ab.ᵗ their Legs
. . . Small ropes made of Hair tyed round their Legs.' Samwell
in Cook, *Journals* III, 2, 1100.

Concerning the quiver, D. I. Bushnell Jr remarked: 'The quiver,
in which are resting several arrows, opened lengthwise, not at
one end, this was not described in the narrative and thus tends
to prove the value of Webber's drawings.' Bushnell Jr (1928) 6.

'They keep their Arrows in wooden Cases in general tho' when
they travel they carry them in quivers made of the skins of wild
Beasts.' Samwell in Cook, *Journals* III, 2, 1102.

ver: The same figure as depicted in this drawing appears in 3.216
and 3.217.

ref: Cook, *Journals* III, 1, pl. 37; Bushnell Jr (1928) pl. 1; *Exh.
Cat.* Montreal (1967) pl. 68; Murray-Oliver (1969a) pl. 116
(col.); Honour (1975) no. 178; Sendey (1977) 39; *Exh.
Cat.* Portland (1982) 183.

Possibly the drawing listed in Francis Edwards's *Cat.* 416 (London,
July 1921), under no. 769 'A Man of Nootka Sound (17 by 12
in), a fine full-length figure in sepia and colour, on strainer and
varnished (unpublished)'.

Peabody Museum of Archaeology and Ethnology, Harvard University, Cambridge, Massachusetts. 41-72-10/496.

JOHN WEBBER

3.216   [Natives outside a Communal House]   [Apr 1778]
pencil, pen and grey wash, 7 × 5¼ : 177 × 133.

A group of four Nootka Indians near a log house; two standing,
two seated. The central figure wears a conical cap; a quiver, with
a mantle and fur around the shoulders. He holds a bow and carries
a quiver slung across his right shoulder. Though the log house
is reversed and there are a number of other differences, the whole
composition suggests a strong relationship to drawing 3.217. The
central figure is also repeated in 3.215.

The Public Archives of Canada, Ottawa. I-13 (C. 2822).

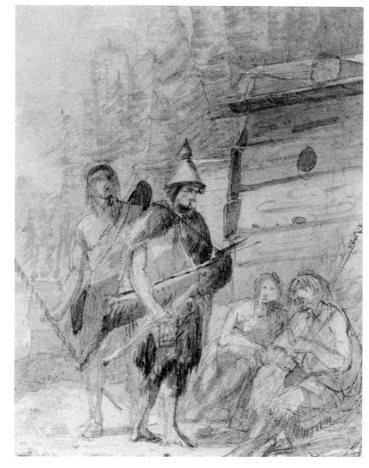

JOHN WEBBER

3.217   Indians of Nootka Sound   [Apr 1778]
wash, 7⅜ × 5⅜ : 187 × 136, unsigned.

The sheet is laid down on mount with sepia enframing lines.

Three Nootka Indians in front of a log house, two standing, one
sitting. The man in the centre wears a fur coat fastened at the
collar and carries a quiver and bow. The same figure is depicted
in 3.215 and 3.216.

This drawing was formerly attributed to Thomas Daniell (1749-
1840).

National Library of Australia, Canberra. Petherick Collection.
Acc. no. R. 6879.

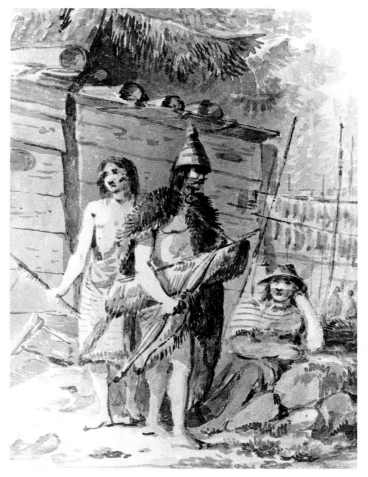

455

3.218   **A Man of Nootka Sound** [plate 114]   [c. 1781-3]
pencil, pen and wash and some water-colour, 9⅛ ×
6⅞ : 232 × 175, unsigned.

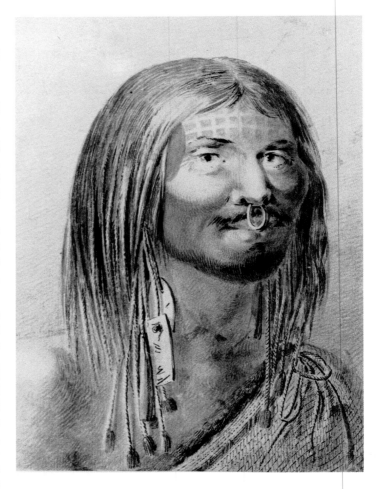

The title as above in pencil on the folio in an unknown hand
beneath the enframing lines.

The head of a native facing three quarters left with a squared
pattern on his forehead and a copper ring through his nose,
wearing ornaments suspended from the right ear. His face is
painted with a red oval patch at the right temple and the face
below the cheekbones is also painted red.

'Their hair is black or dark brown, straight, strong and long, in
general they wear it flowing, but some tie it up in a bunch on
the crown and others twist it into large locks and add to it false
hair, so that thier heads looks like a swab.' Cook, *Journals* III,
1, 311.

'Both sexes bore their ears, to which they hang various ornaments
cheifly made of Copper . . . Besides these some have suspended
to the ears long straps either of leather or plating that reach as
low as the breast . . .' 'Both Men and Women paint their faces,
their colours are black read and white and seemed to be a kind
of ochre mixed with oil, which . . . they lay on with a liberal
hand: in this plaster they make various scrawls on the face and
particularly on the fore head. Besides this daubing they have
another ornament to the Face, which is a small circular plate,
or flat ring in the shape of a horse shoe, but not more in circum-
ference than a shilling; the upper part is cut asunder, so as the
two points may gently pinch the Bridle of the Nose, to which
it hangs over the upper lip. These ornaments were made of either
iron or copper and the rims of some of our buttons were appropriated to this use.' Ibid., 314.

'When they have a mind to be particular, they make use of a
kind of stamp, composed of the small twigs of trees, and formed
according to fancy: this they dip into the prepared mixture of
black, red or brown earth, and oil, and then press it upon their
face, which leaves the impression behind.' Ellis (1782) I, 212-
13.

ver: Apparently drawn for the engraving 218A. For a related
study in the field see 3.219.

ref: *Exh. Cat.* Portland (1974), no. 166.

Dixson Library, State Library of New South Wales, Sydney.
PXX2, 21.

JOHN WEBBER (after)

3.218A   'A MAN of NOOTKA SOUND'
Engraving. 'J. Webber del.' — 'W. Sharp sculp.'

Published in Cook/King (1784) pl. 38, II, 304-6.

A proof-state inscribed in pencil 'A Man of Nootka Sound' in
Webber's hand is kept in the National Library of Australia, Canberra, in a folio of plates from the Skottowe Hall Library.

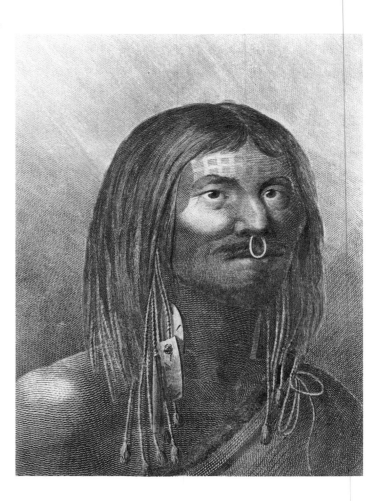

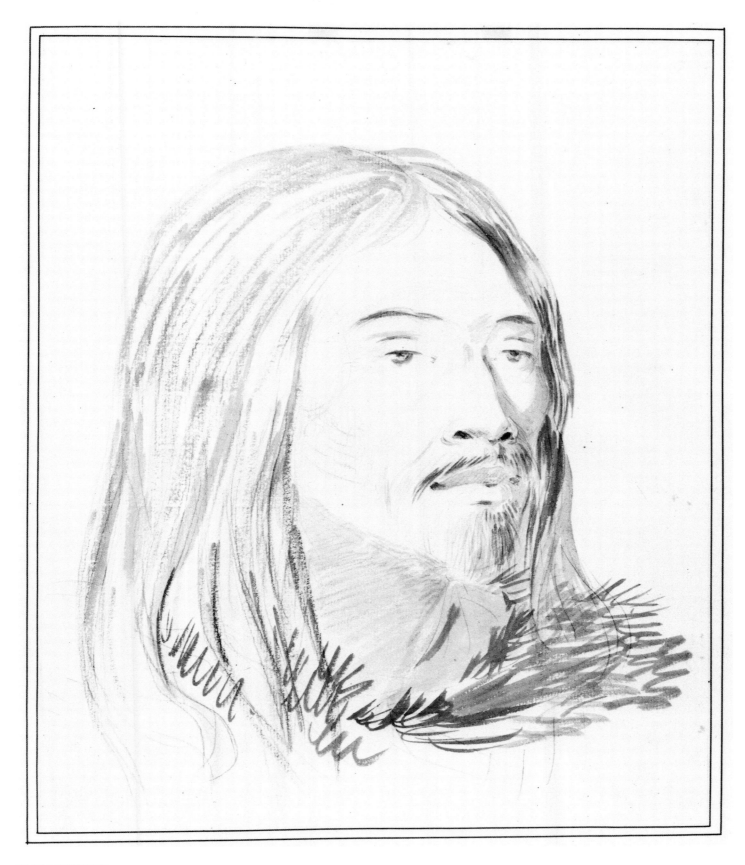

JOHN WEBBER

3.219   [A Man of Nootka Sound]   [Apr 1778]
        pencil and wash, 15⅛ × 12⅜ : 384 × 314, unsigned.

A study of head and shoulders.

ver: A copy of this drawing of the late nineteenth century is in
        the Bernice P. Bishop Museum, Honolulu, titled erro-
        neously 'Man of the Sandwich Islands'.

British Library, London. Add MS 17277, no. 17.

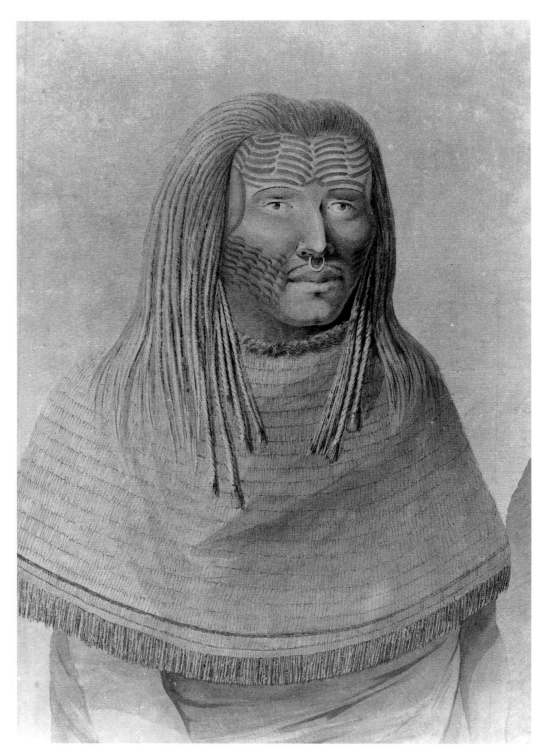

JOHN WEBBER

3.220   A Man of Nootka Sound   [Apr 1778–]
pen, ink and water-colour on apparently sepia-washed
paper, 17 × 12 : 432 × 305, unsigned.

On verso (u.l.) in brown-black ink 'Lot no. 9' and upper centre
in pencil 'Man of King George's Sound' and 'Capt. Campbell'.
At centre bottom edge of strainer 'Portrait of a Native of Nootka
Sound unpublished' in ink on white label in pen (u.l.) 'No. 37'.
Varnish removed February 1977. The drawing may be tentatively
identified as 'A Portrait of a Man', no. 69 in the 'King George's
Sound' section of Webber's Catalogue.

Head and shoulders, wearing a fur-trimmed cap of woven cedar,
the hair falling in long straight, plaited strands; ornamentation
on forehead and cheeks, a ring through the nose. There are red
crescents at his temples and below the nose the face is coloured
red.

'They have also another cloak, which in shape resembles a round
dish cover, it is close all round with a hole in the middle just big
enough to admit the head through. To most of these dresses they
work borders of differen[t] Colours, the collar or part that goes
round the neck is edged or lined with beaver skin and the skirts
are fringed.' Cook, *Journals* III, 1, 313.

ver: For a drawing of the same man see 3.221 and 3.222.

ref: Bushnell Jr (1928) pl. 4; Sendey (1977) 6; *Exh. Cat.* Portland (1982) 193.

Francis Edwards, *Cat.* 416 (London, July 1921), under no. 769
as 'Portrait of a Native of Nootka Sound (17 by 12 in), in sepia
and colour, on strainer and varnished (unpublished)'.

Peabody Museum of Archaeology and Ethnology, Harvard University, Cambridge, Massachusetts. Inv. no. 41-72-10/497.

458

JOHN WEBBER

3.221   **A Man of Nootka Sound**   [Apr 1778–]
          black and red chalk, wash and ink over pencil,
          17¹⁵⁄₁₆ × 12⅛ : 456 × 308, unsigned; w/m:
          'IHS/I. VILLEDARY'.

Inscribed faintly along u.l. of sheet 'A Native of . . . ' indecipherable, but probably 'King George's Sound'. On verso 'Shelf
IB vol 3-Cook'.

ver: For another version and for a study for this drawing see
        3.220 and 3.222. The pattern on the forehead differs slightly
        from that on the man depicted in 3.220. The parallel strokes
        are longer here and the sea-otter fur collar thicker.

ref: Cook, *Journals* III, 1, pl. 39a.

The Public Archives of Canada, Ottawa. I-1 (C. 13415).

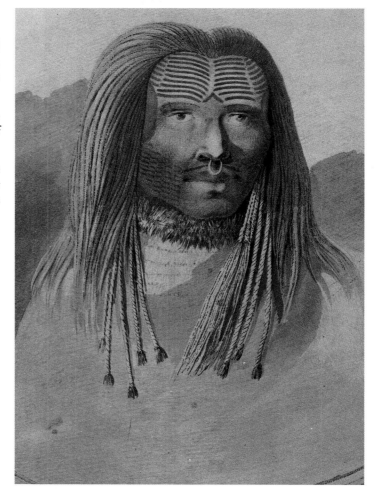

JOHN WEBBER

3.222   **A Man of Nootka Sound [plate 115]**   [Apr 1778]
          pencil, red and blackish chalk, 13½ × 11½ : 343 ×
          292, unsigned.

The head of a man facing slightly towards the right. The man
wears dark wavy chevron marks of paint radiating from the centre
of the forehead, oval patches of red ochre at the temples, and
the face below the cheek bones is pointed with traverse lines in
red ochre. A copper nose ornament is worn, and braids with
ornaments attached hang from the ears or the hair.

ver: For drawings developed from this one see 3.220 and 3.221.

ref: Folan/Dewhirst (1970) 276-86; Sendey (1977), cover.

Francis Edwards, *Cat.* 551 (London 1932) entry 10, as a 'Native
of Nootka 13½ in × 11½ in'.

Francis P. Farquhar Collection, Berkeley, California.

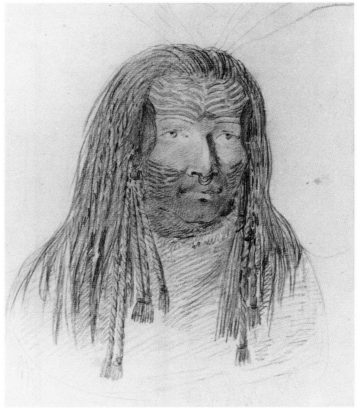

JOHN WEBBER

3.223   **A Woman of Nootka Sound**   [Apr 1778–]
        pen, ink and grey wash, 15 × 12 : 381 × 305, unsigned.

There may be traces of 'no 70' (u.l.), thus identifying this drawing as no. 70 'A Ditto [Portrait of a Woman]' in the King George's Sound Section in Webber's Catalogue.

Wearing a cedar bark rain cape with a sea otter fur collar and a basketry rain hat with a bulbous top decorated with scenes of whale-hunting.

'Their Hats or Caps are made of a kind of basket work, in a conical form, these they fasten under the Chin to keep them firm upon the Head; they are so compact, and by their Shape so well contrived for the purpose, that they will shelve off a vast deal of Rain, which seems their principal intent, as they seldom wear them at any other time than in wet Weather.' Clerke in Cook, *Journals* III, 2, 1325-6.

Samwell comments on an example similar to the one in 3.223: '. . . the others were more curious, having a Knob at the top of them which came to a point, these were white & into them are worked in black a description of their Whale Fishery, a man standing up in a Canoe in the action of striking a Whale.' Ibid., 2, 1099.

Similar hats, on which whale hunts can be seen, are preserved in the National Museum of Ireland, Dublin, in the Royal Scottish Museum, Edinburgh and in the Cook/Banks Collection of the Museum of Mankind (British Museum), London. See the examples in Kaeppler (1978a) 254 and King (1981) 82-3, pl. 67 and 68.

ver: For a smaller version of this drawing see 3.224. The cape is similar to the one described in 3.220. The woman appears to be the same as in the sketch of 3.225, though the latter wears a different hat. The two different hats present a problem, in so far as Nootka women were unlikely to wear whaling hats. Jonathan King makes the point, that 'although the members of Cook's expedition understood that the hats showed scenes of "whale fishery" they did not understand that whale hunting was an occupation for chiefs, and that only chiefs wore these hats'. King (1981) 82. Webber's field-sketch (3.225) of the same woman shows her wearing a painted hat, which was probably what she wore. Wishing however to introduce a more interesting artefact, Webber — instead of showing it on the head of the man (3.220) — transferred it to a woman. King thinks that Webber may have done so in order not to obscure the painted face decoration on the male portrait (3.220). Webber thus strictly speaking falsified his original sketch.

King also draws attention to the fact that the bulb-top hat of the woman is of a generalized decoration. 'The drawing . . . shows the hat without the precise details one would expect — the hats are not all the same and in particular have varied and specific geometric details below the bulb which Webber does not indicate.' *In litt.* 17 January 1984.

What one might have expected in the design of Webber's hat is a standing man ready to strike a whale with a harpoon, as James King had observed in his journal. King in Cook, *Journals* III, 2, 1411.

ref: Bushnell Jr (1928) pl. 5; Cook, *Journals* III, 1, pl. 39b; Rienits (1968) 124; Sendey (1977) 2; King (1981) pl. 67; *Exh. Cat.* Portland (1982) 187.

Francis Edwards, *Cat.* 416 (London, July 1921) under no. 769 as 'A Woman of Nootka Sound (16 × 12 in) in sepia'.

Peabody Museum of Archaeology and Ethnology, Harvard University, Cambridge, Massachusetts. Inv. no. 41-72-10/498.

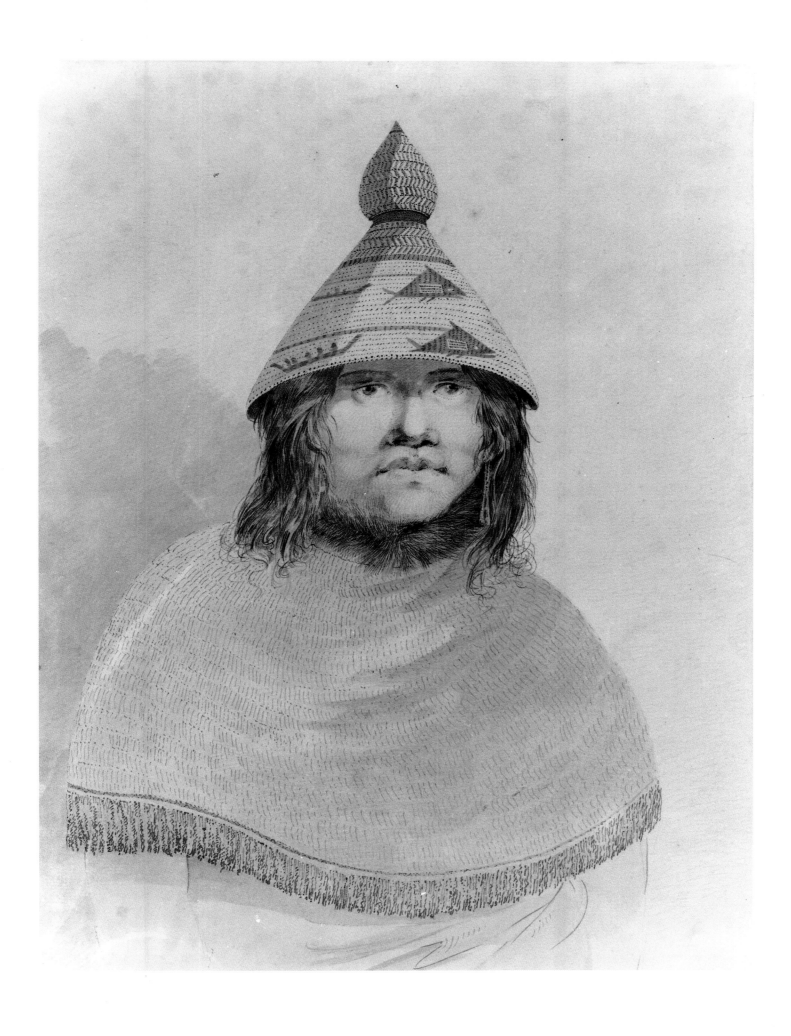

461

JOHN WEBBER

3.224   **A Woman of Nootka Sound [plate 112]   [c. 1781-3]**
        pencil, pen and wash, 9 × 7 : 228 × 178, unsigned.

The title as above in pencil by a later hand on the folio beneath
the drawing.

ver: A smaller and slightly modified version of 3.223, drawn for
        the engraving 3.224A with which it is virtually identical
        in size.

ref: *Exh. Cat.* Portland (1974) no. 166.

Dixson Library, State Library of New South Wales, Sydney.
PXX2, 22.

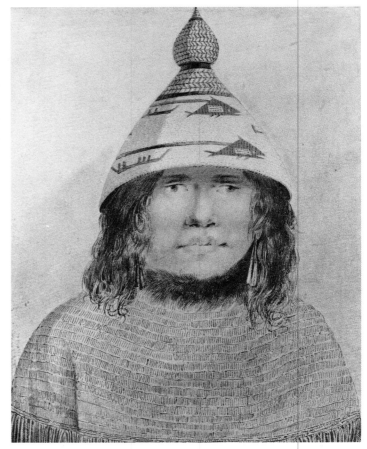

JOHN WEBBER (after)

3.224A   'A WOMAN of NOOTKA SOUND'
        Engraving. 'J. Webber del.' — 'W. Sharp sculp.'

Published in Cook/King (1784) pl. 39, II, 303-4.

A proof-state inscribed in pencil 'A Woman — Nootka Sound'
in Webber's hand is kept in the National Library of Australia,
Canberra, in a folio of plates from the Skottowe Hall Library.

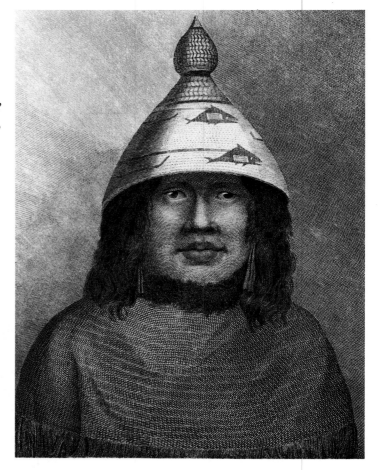

JOHN WEBBER

3.225   A Woman of Nootka Sound [plate 113] [Apr 1778]
pencil and chalk, 8¾ × 7 : 227 × 177, unsigned.

Bust portrait of a woman in a yellow cedar bark cape with fur trim. The flat-topped basketry hat painted, with tassels.

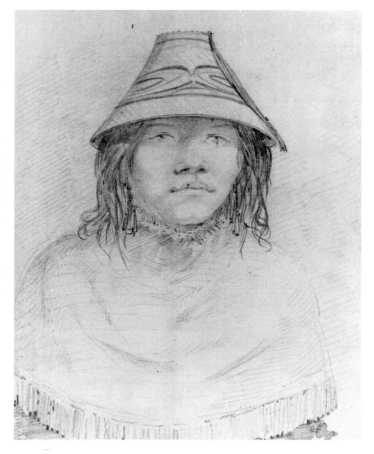

The hat answers Cook's description, who says that their straw hats were 'shaped like a flower-pot'. Cook *Journals* III,1, 313-14.

Samwell's comments are more detailed: 'They wear a kind of straw Hat or Cap much like those of the Chinese, they are something in the shape of a Sugar Loaf flattened at the top, from which hung tossels with which they took them off, they tye them under the Chin with a String; they have two sorts of them, the above were the most common.' Samwell in ibid. 2, 1099.

'Flat-topped hats are often confused with those from Prince William Sound since both are made of roots, painted and of similar form.' King (1981) 82, and pl. 94, showing a Nootkan hat in the Museum of Mankind, London which might have served as prototype to Webber's drawing.

ver: The drawing seems to be a study for the more developed version 3.223, except for the hat, which represents a different type.

ref: Sendey (1977) 3; King (1981) pl. 66.

Probably identical with the drawing listed in Francis Edwards, *Cat.* 551 (London 1932), entry no. 12 'Woman of Nootka Sound' with dimensions given as '11 in × 9 in'.

Francis P. Farquhar Collection, Berkeley, California.

WILLIAM ELLIS

3.226   Nootka men and a Polynesian [?] head. [c. 1777-8]
pencil, 11¹⁵⁄₁₆ × 7¼ : 304 × 180, unsigned;
w/m: 'Pro Patria' with Britannia.

Inscribed 'King George's Sound' in ink (u.l.) and in pencil 'Bonnet described Ellis, Voyage, vol I, page 214' (u.r.). On verso inscribed in ink '55'. On verso three drawings of unidentified coastal profiles in pencil and wash (A 264. 37B).
(a) figure with long hair and conical bonnet, and a cloak over right shoulder, holding a paddle.
(b) a long canoe with a figure at either end.
(c) head and shoulders of a bearded man (inverted on the page). Not of Nootka Sound, possibly Polynesian.

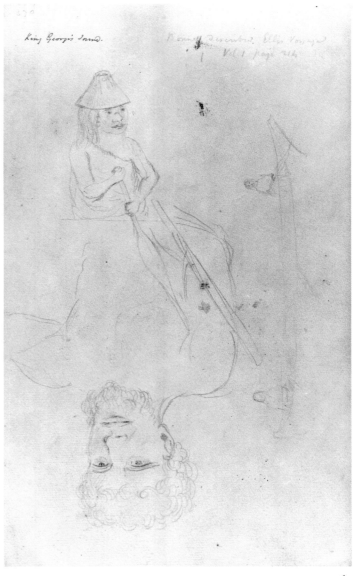

'Upon their heads they wear a kind of bonnet of a very compact texture, from the top of which hangs a tassel made of leather; these bonnets are sometimes made with a round globular top, but in general flat. They are frequently painted or stained, in a rude though ingenious manner, with the form of some large fish resembling a whale, pursued by several canoes, and a man in one of them in the act of striking him.

'Round their shoulders they wear a kind of cloak, made of the interior bark of the fir-tree, and formed or wove in the same manner as some of the New Zealand hahoos: the bottom is generally fringed, and the neck part trimmed with the fur of the sea-beaver.' Ellis (1782) I, 214.

About their paddles Ellis remarks: 'Their paddles were about five feet long, rather broad in the middle and terminating in a long narrow point.' Ibid., 191.

ref: Murray-Oliver (1977) 35.
Alexander Turnbull Library, Wellington. A264. 37A

WILLIAM ELLIS (after)

3.226A **'Native of King Georges Sound'**
Engraving. 'W. Ellis del.' — 'J. Heath sculp.' 'Publish'd Dec.ʳ 14 1782 by G. Robinson'.

Published in Ellis (1782) I, opp. 191 (191).

No drawing for this engraving is known; the engraving may however have been developed from Ellis's drawing of a native in his canoe (3.226).

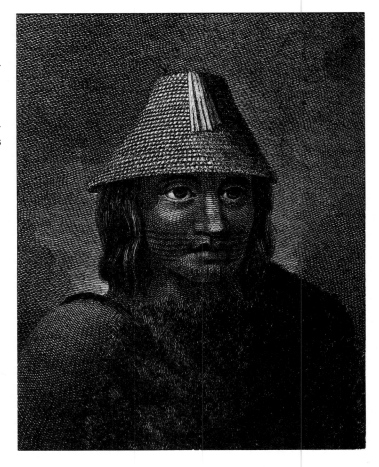

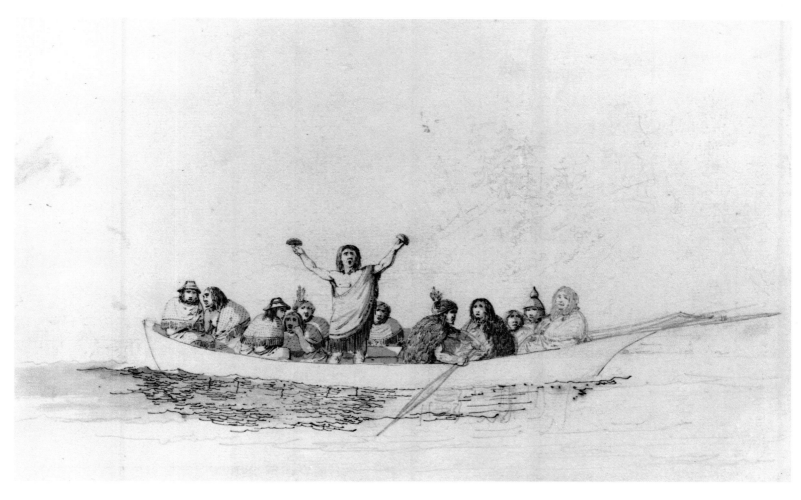

JOHN WEBBER

3.227   A Canoe of Nootka Indians   [Apr 1778]
pencil, pen and wash, 11 × 16 : 280 × 406, unsigned.

The boat is crowded with 12 Nootka Indians, one standing with
arms outstretched, holding a rattle in each hand and apparently
singing, as observed from the deck of one of the ships. In the
background faint pencil drawing of a coastline and fir trees.

'On their first coming they generally went through a singular
ceremony; they would paddle with all their strength quite round
both ships, A Chief or other principal person standing up with
a Spear or some other Weapon in his hand and speaking, or rather
halloaing all the time . . . Sometimes instead of a weapon [he]
would hold in his hand a rattle.' Cook, *Journals* III, 1, 298-9.
This description is echoed in King's journal, who speaks of a man
in a canoe who 'worked himself into the highest frenzy, uttering
something between a howl & a song, holding a rattle in each
hand, which at intervals he laid down . . . '. Ibid., 2, 1394.

The scene that Webber depicted must have occurred a number
of times, thus no fixed date can be attached to the drawing.

Compare also Cook's description of the natives' canoes: 'Thier
Canoes are 40 feet long, 7 broad and about 3 deep, some greater
some less; they are made out of one tree hollowed out to an inch
and half in the sides, and in shape very much resemble a Norway
yawl only longer in proportion to their breadth and the head and
Stern is higher. In the upper part of the former, or prow, is a
groove or hollow for the conveniency of laying thier spears, darts,
harpoons &c. They are generally without carving or any other
ornament except paint and but few have it. The paddles are small
and light the shape in some measure resembling a large leaf,
pointed at the bottom, broadest in the middle, and gradually
losing it self in the shaft, the whole being about five feet long.'
Ibid., 1, 316-17.

ver: Similar demonstrations by the Nootka in canoes are shown
in the foreground of 3.190 and 3.191.

ref: Cook, *Journals* III, 1, pl. 34a; Sendey (1977) frontispiece.

Listed in Francis Edwards, *Cat.* 551 (1932) entry no. 11 'Canoe
of Nootka and Natives on their first approach to the ship, (16
by 11 in)'.

Francis P. Farquhar Collection, Berkeley, California.

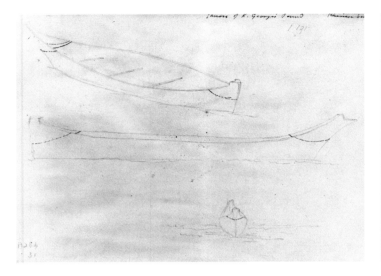

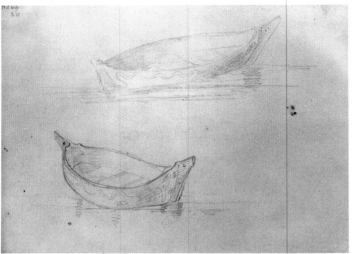

WILLIAM ELLIS

3.228   Canoes of King George's Sound
pencil and ink, 5½ × 7⁹⁄₁₆ : 140 × 192, unsigned;
w/m; 'Pro Patria' with Britannia.

The title is from the inscription in brown ink (u.r.) also. 'Chinese boat?' in brown ink crossed out (u.r.) and in pencil '1.191'; referring to Ellis's *Narrative* (1782). Inscribed in ink on verso '39'.

Three outline drawings in pencil of canoes (a) from above, showing the seats and breadth; (b) in profile; (c) end-on. The additions to the hull, stern and prow, are indicated in ink.

'Their canoes were different from any we had seen before; they were wide, without an out-rigger, and rather pointed at both ends, when they paddle they sit in the bottom. Their paddles were about five feet long, rather broad in the middle, and terminating in a long, narrow point.' Ellis (1782) I, 191.

'Their canoes are of various sizes; the largest being capacious enough to contain fifty people, the smallest three. The principal ones are ornamented at the head and stern with human teeth placed in various forms, and their sides with the figures of beasts and large fish, rudely painted in white. They are apparently made out of one tree, but the upper part of the head and stern are separate pieces, and tied on by cords, made of the twisted bark of the fir-tree.' Ibid., 219-20.

ref: Murray-Oliver (1977) 35.

Alexander Turnbull Library, Wellington. A264.31.

WILLIAM ELLIS [?]

3.229   Boats at King George's Sound   [Apr 1778]
pencil, 7¼ × 9¼ : 183 × 235, unsigned; w/m: 'GR', under a crown, surrounded by wreaths, in a circle.

The title as above in ink centred along the lower edge; in pencil '1.191' (u.r.) referring to Ellis's *Narrative* (1782). Inscribed on verso in ink '38'.

Two boats broad in beam and decorated along the side with sinuous markings.

The competent fore-shortening of the boats and the firm handling of the pencil puts some doubt on the attribution to Ellis. Moreover, it is to be wondered whether the boats really represent examples of boats from Nootka. Both the boats' prow and stern differ from the standard form of Nootkan boats, the prow of the upper boat being too straight in comparison. Different also from boats drawn by Webber and Ellis are the holes in the stern and the prow.

Jonathan King has suggested the boats could represent Kwakiutl canoes such as would have come from further north rowed by strangers to Nootka Sound.

The boats do have some similarity to the type which Franz Boas identified as Kwakiutl (*The Jesup North Pacific Expedition, Memoir of the American Museum of National History*, vol. V, II, 'The Kwakiutl of Vancouver Island', Leiden, New York, 1909, 444-5. Jonathan King, to whom we owe this reference, also draws our attention to a north-west coast boat of similar form in the British Museum (Museum of Mankind, London, VAN 149) collected by Captain George Vancouver in 1791-95. A second model, collected by Admiral Sir Edward Belcher during the expedition of HMS *Sulphur* in the 1830s has a similar painted design on its side, showing the lightning serpent or *haietlik*, 'the mythological helper of thunderbirds'. King, *in litt.* 17 January 1984. It would therefore appear that the boats are Nootkan in ornament and perhaps Kwakiutl in general design, thus providing some evidence of cultural contact.

ref: Murray-Oliver (1977) 35.

Alexander Turnbull Library, Wellington. A264.30.

3.230   Representations of Animals used as Decoys
[plate 116]   [Apr 1778–]
wash and water-colour, 21 × 15 : 533 × 381, unsigned.

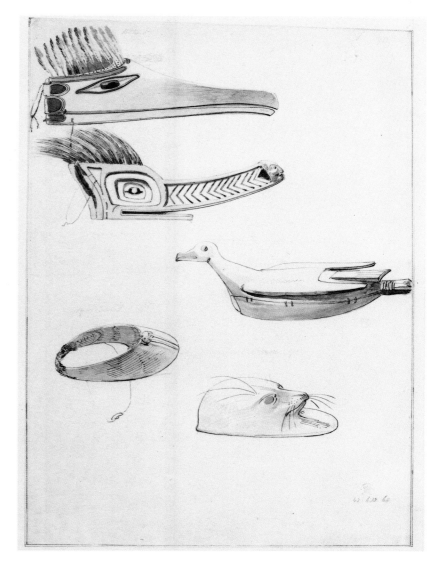

The full title 'Representations of Animals used as Decoys by the Americans of K.G. Sound — A Rattle — Tschutzki bonnet — American cap' in pencil in Webber's hand on the drawing, and '70' in corner (u.r.), which corresponds to no. '70˙ different ornaments' [in pencil] in Webber's Catalogue.

The drawing includes two Nootkan wood bird masks, a bird rattle, an Alaskan or Siberian bentwood visor and an Alaskan seal decoy helmet, on the one sheet.

Of the Nootkan masks Cook wrote: 'The men on some occasions wore Masks of which they have many and of various sorts such as the human face, the head of birds and other Animals, the most of them both well designed and executed. Whether these masks are worn as an Ornament in their public entertainments, or as some thought, to guard the face against the arrows of the enimy, or as decoys in hunting, I shall not pretend to say; probably on all these occasions. The only times however we saw them was by some of the chiefs when they made us a ceremonious visit and in some of their Songs.' Cook, *Journals* III, 1, 314-15. See also Samwell and Beaglehole's note, ibid., 2, 1091.

Of the rattle Cook comments: 'The rattles are for the most part made in the shape of a bird, with a few pebble stones in the belly and the tail is the handle, they have however others that bear rather more resemblance to a childs rattle.' Ibid., 1, 316. An actual bird-form rattle which might have served Webber for his drawing is preserved in the Cook Collection, Hunterian Museum, University of Glasgow (cf Kaeppler (1978a), fig 571).

For the description of the visor see Cook, *Journals* III, 1, 459-60 and Samwell, ibid., 2, 1142. Both sources agree the visors observed were ornamented with whiskers and beads, a feature missing from that drawn here. Possibly it was a traded and incomplete one. This possibly was the reason for leaving the visor out of the subsequent engraving (3.231; 3.231A). Cook mentions seal decoy helmets from Prince William Sound only in passing: 'The Men . . . [had] high-crowned conical straw caps; also others made of wood resembling a seals head.' Ibid., 1, 349-50. A specimen similar to the one depicted is in the British Museum (Museum of Mankind, Cook-Banks Collection NWC 11).

ver: Similar to 3.231 but objects differently arranged.

ref: Cook, *Journals* III, 1, pl. 40; Honour (1975) no. 180; King (1981) pl.3; Kaeppler (1978a), 260, figs 571, 572.

British Library, London. Add MS 15514, f.5.

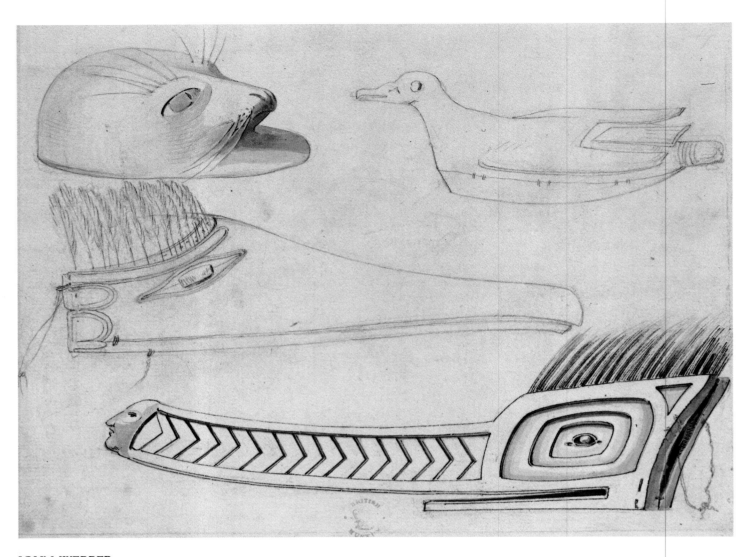

JOHN WEBBER

3.231   **Forms of Animals used as Decoys**   [c. 1781-3]
pencil, pen and wash, $7^{11}/_{16} \times 10^{1}/_{4}$: 195 × 260,
unsigned.

The title as above in pencil on the mount, followed by 'see atlas
pl. 40' in an eighteenth century hand.

ver: The same objects, a bird rattle and three masks, as depicted
in 3.230, enclosed in a frame arranged in the form in which
they were engraved, but without the bentwood visor.

Engraved by J. Record, 3.231A.

ref: Kaeppler (1978a) fig. 567; King (1981) pl. 4.

After it was engraved, the drawing was not returned to the Admiralty or to Sir Joseph Banks, as was most of the other drawings
now in the Dixson Library PXX 2. It must have been retained
by Webber among his other sketches.

British Library, London. Add MS 17277, no. 19.

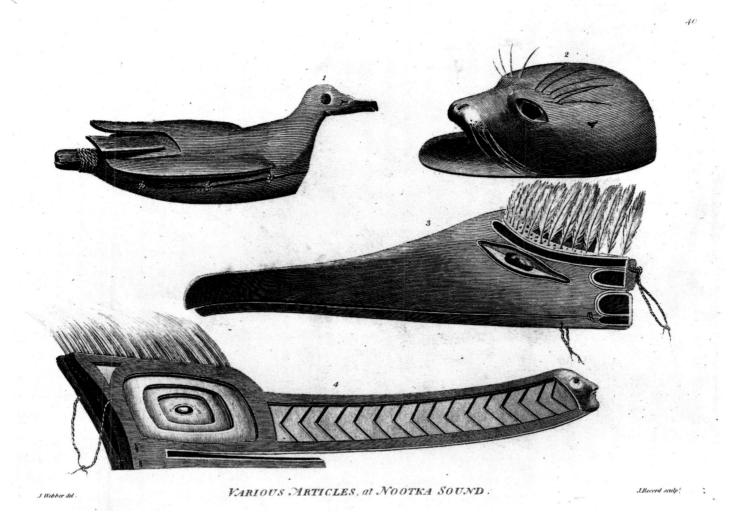

VARIOUS ARTICLES, at NOOTKA SOUND.

J. Webber del.   J. Record sculp.

JOHN WEBBER (after)

3.231A 'VARIOUS ARTICLES, at NOOTKA SOUND'

Engraving. 'J. Webber del.' — 'J. Record sculp.'

Published in Cook/King (1784) pl. 40, II, 306-7 for the bird masks, 311 for the rattle and 369 for the seal decoy from Prince William Sound.

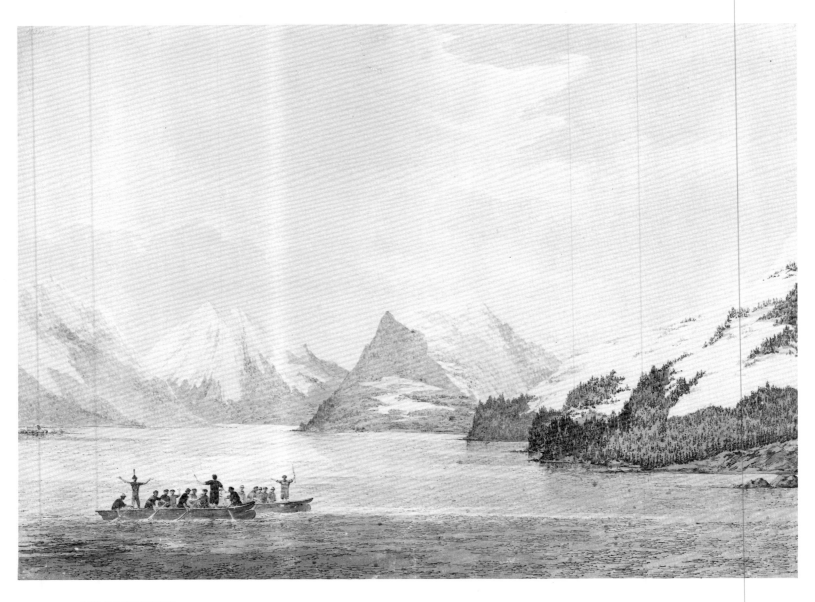

JOHN WEBBER

**3.232   A View in Prince William Sound
[plate 117]**   **[May 1778–]**
pen, wash and pale tints of water-colour, 19⅜ × 26⅛ :
492 × 664, unsigned.

The drawing may be tentatively identified as no. 80 'A view with the first appearance of the Natives' in the 'Sandwich Sound' section of Webber's Catalogue.

Two canoes manned by Indians close together in the left foreground, steep fir-clad and icy hills in the background. They appear to be addressing men in Cook's ships.

3.232 corresponds to a drawing in the British Library (Add MS 15514, f.4j) which is inscribed in pencil in Webber's hand 'View of the Continent taken from the first day place to the North of Cape Hinchingbrooke'.

This provides a clue as to the spot depicted. After having passed Cape Hinchinbrook Cook noted in his journal on 12 May 1778: 'With this View [i.e. awaiting clearer weather] I hauled close under Cape Hinchinbrook and anchored before a small Cove a little within the Cape, in 8 fathom water a clayey bottom and about ¼ of a Mile from the shore.' Cook, *Journals* III, 1, 343. Beaglehole identifies the place as English Bay (ibid. 4n). The further circumstances of the stay which Cook relates correspond with the drawing, notably the appearance of two canoes manned by about twenty Indians. 'They would not venture along side but kept talking to us at a distance, not one word of which we understood; they were cloathed in skins made into a dress like a shirt, or rather more like a wagonners frock, it reached nearly as low as the knee and their was no slit either behind or before. The Canoes were not built of wood like those of King Georges Sound; the frame only was of wood or slender laths and the out side seals skin, or the skin of some suchlike animal. When these people first came to the Ships, they displayed a white dress and unfolded their arms to the utmost extent, this we understood to be a sign of friendship and answered them in the same manner.' Ibid., 1, 344. A good account of the behaviour of the Indians is given by Samwell. Ibid., 2, 1106.

ver: For similar views which could have been made in preparation of this drawing, see 3.233 and 3.234. The depiction of the boat in the front of 3.232 is similar to Webber's study of a boat in 3.242.

ref: Honour (1975) no. 165.

British Library, London. Add MS 15514, f.9.

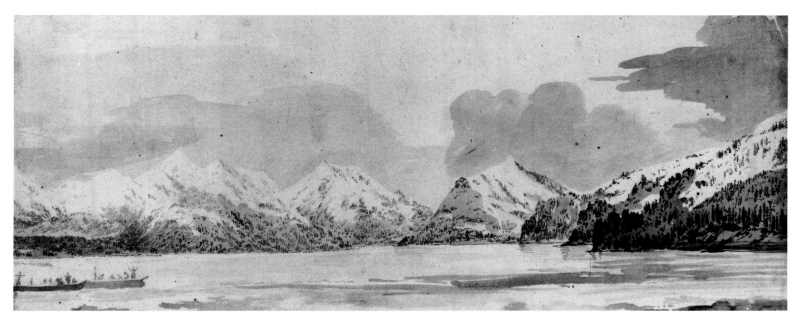

JOHN WEBBER

3.233   A View in Prince William Sound   [May 1778]
grey wash, 8 × 18¹⁵⁄₁₆ : 203 × 481, unsigned.

Inscribed on back evidently by a later hand 'Prince William Sound — Webber'.

A panoramic view of a mountainous shoreline; in the foreground figures in two open boats.

ver: The drawing is a preparatory sketch, perhaps a field-sketch for 3.232. The mountain range was again drawn by Webber in 3.234 and in a small sketch in the British Library, Add MS 15514, f.4j.

ref: Cook, *Journal* III, 1, 356-7; Allodi (1974) II, 1631.

Purchased in 1957 from the Old Print Shop, New York.

Royal Ontario Museum, Toronto. 957.261.

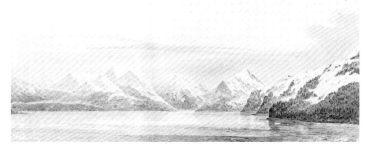

JOHN WEBBER

3.234   A View in Prince William Sound   [May 1778]
pen and wash, 9½ × 21¹⁄₁₆ : 241 × 535, unsigned.

Inscribed 'ii. 258 Prince William Sound' in pencil at centre left. Also numbered '3'.

As in 3.232 and 3.233 the drawing represents the coastline around Cape Hinchinbrook, as witnessed on 12 May 1778. Though the drawing is a coastal view, it has been catalogued here because of its fine representation of the Alaskan landscape. It is engraved in Cook/King (1784) II, pl.86, fp. 410.

British Library, London. Add. MS 15514, f.2b.

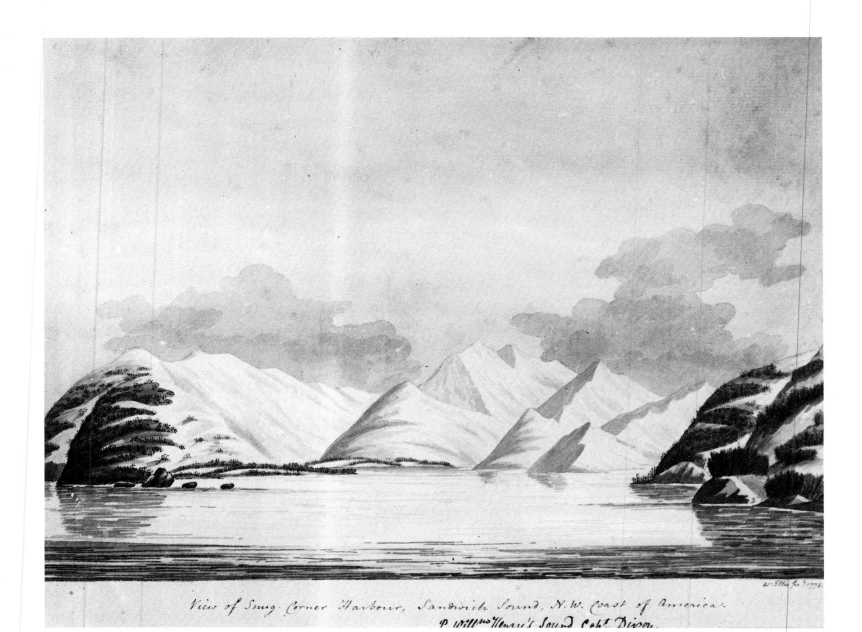

View of Snug-Corner Harbour, Sandwich Sound, N.W. Coast of America.
P Will^ms Henry's Sound Cap.t Dixon

WILLIAM ELLIS

3.235   A View in Prince William Sound   [May 1778]
pen, wash and water-colour, 8⁹/₁₆ × 12 : 218 ×
305, signed and dated 'W: Ellis fec^t 1778' in black ink
[l.r.].

Titled 'View of Snug-Corner Harbour, Sandwich Sound, N.W.
Coast of America' in brown ink across the lower edge of the
drawing; beneath in a different hand 'P Willm. Henry's Sound.
Capt Dixon' also in brown ink. Numbered '4' in brown ink [u.l.].

A distant view from across the Sound; snow-covered slopes and
sparse vegetation along the foreshores.

'The harbour in which we lay, appeared to be surrounded in every
direction by land, which was much higher than at King George's
Sound, and more covered with snow. The shore was composed
almost entirely of rocks, nearly perpendicular, but of no very great
height, with here and there a small sandy beach. The trees were
of the same kind as at the last place, but not so large or numerous,
nor did they grow up to the tops of the mountains.' Ellis (1782)
I, 235.

The drawing does not represent Snug Corner Harbour as inscribed
on the drawing, but the area of Cape Hinchinbrook. During the
time of preparing the official account for publication the name
was changed to Prince William's Sound, after Prince William

Henry (1765-1837), third son of King George III and the name
was only generally made known through the publication of Cook's
third voyage (1784). Calling it 'P. Willm. Henry's Sound', the
information supplied by Captain Dixon, is thus even more 'precise'
than 'Prince William's Sound', which was used on the maps.

ver: In a rather general way the view recalls Webber's *A View
of Prince William Sound* (3.232).

Museum Book Store, *Cat.* 94 (1924) 562/7, *Cat.* 107 (1928)
41/7, and *Cat* 125 (1941) 453.

National Library of Australia, Canberra. Rex Nan Kivell Collection. NK 53/K.

JOHN WEBBER

3.236   **A Man of Prince William Sound**
         [plate 123]   [May 1778–]
         pen and ink, grey and red wash, 15 × 12 : 381 × 305,
         unsigned.

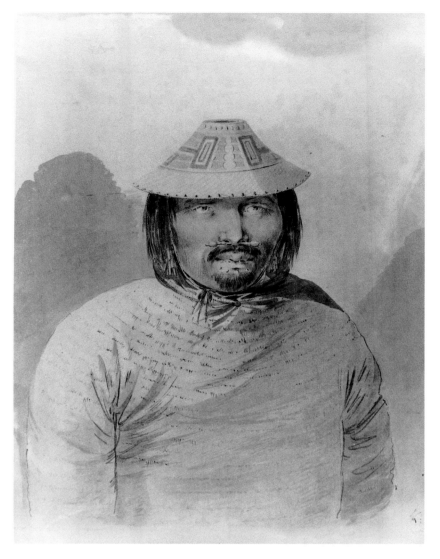

The sheet was formerly laid down on card and backed by linen.
When the backing was removed an inscription in brown ink 'no
10' was found on the verso of the former mount. Discoloured
varnish on the drawing was removed by the Conservation Department of the Fogg Art Museum, Harvard University in February
1977.

The drawing may be tentatively identified as no. 77 'A Ditto
[Portrait] of a Man' in the 'Sandwich Sound' section of Webber's
Catalogue.

The man is almost full-face but looking slightly towards the right.
He wears a conical shaped basketry hat (with a chin-strap) which
is decorated with geometrical designs near the top and glass beads
on the crest around the rim. Plaided braid pendants are attached
to his hair about his ears. He wears a moustache, a short beard,
and a nose-ornament beaded at either end.

The sitter may possibly be the man who came aboard the *Resolution*
on 14 May 1778. Cook called him 'a good looking middle aged
man . . . he was cloathed in a dress made of the Sea beaver skin
and on his head such a Cap as is worn by the people of King
Georges Sound, Ornamented with sky blue glass beads about the
size of a large pea.' Cook, *Journals* III, 1, 346.

Describing the inhabitants of Sandwich Sound in general terms,
Cook says: 'Men, Women and Children were all Cloathed alike,
in a kind of frocks made of the Skins of different animals . . .
most of the men wore what Crantz calls a leather pelt, or rather
a shirt made of the skin of large guts, probably those of the whale,
they are made to draw tight round the neck, the sleeves reach
as low as the wrist round which they are tied with a string
. . .' Ibid., 349. 'The men had beards though not large to which
they hang beads or pieces of bone . . . Some both men and
women have the underlip slit quite through horizontally, and so
large as to admit the tongue which I have seen them thrust
through . . .' Ibid., 350.

ver: For another and smaller version see 3.237. A study for this
          portrait is at 3.238.

ref: Bushnell, Jr (1928) pl. 6; *Exh. Cat.* Portland (1982) 191.

Listed in Francis Edwards, *Cat.* 416 (London, July 1921) as 'A
Man of Prince William's Sound (16 by 12 in) in sepia and colour'.

Peabody Museum of Archaeology and Ethnology, Harvard University, Cambridge, Massachusetts. 41-72-10/502.

JOHN WEBBER

3.237 **A Man of Prince William's Sound** [c. 1781-3]
pen, pencil, wash and water-colour, 9 × 7⅛ : 228 ×
181, unsigned.

The title as above by a later hand on the folio beneath the
drawing.

ver: The drawing is a more developed version of 3.236 and
served for the engraving 3.237A. For a study for this drawing
see 3.238.

ref: *Exh. Cat.* Portland (1974) no. 169; *Exh. Cat.* Anchorage
(1978) pl. 2.

Dixson Library, State Library of New South Wales, Sydney.
PXX 2, 26.

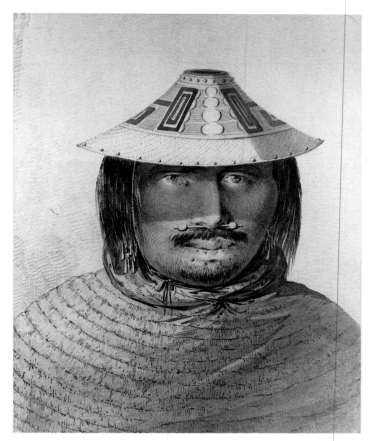

JOHN WEBBER (after)

3.237A **'A MAN of PRINCE WILLIAM'S SOUND'**
Engraving. 'J. Webber del.' — 'J. Basire sculp!'

Published in Cook/King (1784) pl. 46, II, 367-70.

A proof-state inscribed in pencil 'Man of Sandwich Sound' in
Webber's hand and crossed out again, is kept in the National
Library of Australia, Canberra, in a folio of plates from the Skot-
towe Hall Library.

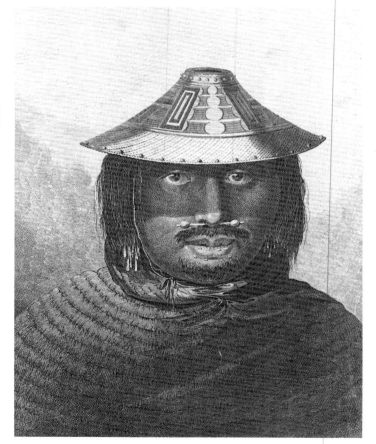

JOHN WEBBER

3.238   **A Man of Prince William Sound**   [May 1778]
pencil, chalk and reddish wash, 8 × 6 : 203 × 152,
unsigned.

ver: A field-sketch of the man depicted in 3.236 probably drawn
on 14 May. The hat is similarly shaped, but without detail
of pattern.

ref: Cook, *Journals* III, 1, pl. 45a; where called, Man of 'Cook's
River'.

Listed in Francis Edwards, *Cat.* 551 (London 1932) entry no. 7
as 'Native of Cook's River . . . 8 in × 6 in'.

Francis P. Farquhar Collection, Berkeley, California.

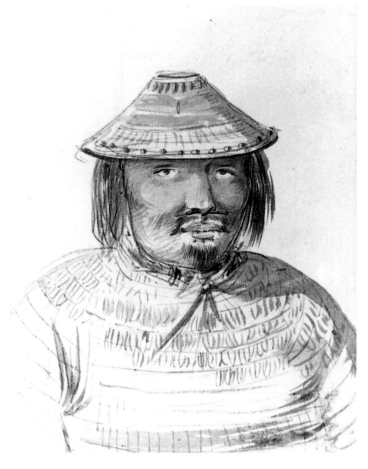

WILLIAM ELLIS

3.239   **A Man of Prince William Sound**   [May 1778]
pencil, 10⅝⁄16 × 7⅝ : 262 × 193, unsigned; w/m:
'GR' under crown surrounded by wreaths in a circle.

Inscribed 'N.W. Coast of America' (u.r.) in brown ink and 'Lat
60.50' in black ink as well as in pencil 'Lat 60:50:13' (l.l.) and
'Snug Corner Cove' (l.r.).

Portrait of a man wearing a fur-trimmed jacket and a conical
basketry hat, decorated with geometrical motives. He wears an
ornament through the septum of his nose, some strings of beads
are attached to his chin below his underlip.

'These people vary in some things from those we saw the day
before yesterday. Their dress was made of the guts of fish sewed
together, with sleeves down to their wrists; under this they had
jackets made of the skins of beasts. They had caps on their heads
like the last Indians, and their under lip was cut through lengthwise; through this opening they frequently put their tongue. Some
of them had blue beads, and other ornaments fixed in this slit,
and also through the gristle of the nose.' Ellis (1782) I, 240. 'The
inhabitants of this place seem to form the line of connexion
between those of King George's Sound and the natives of Unalaschka, and the other western parts of America. Like the former
they daub their faces . . . and some of them are clothed in the
skin of beasts.' Ibid., 248.

Tipped into a copy of *A Voyage Round the World* by Captain George
Dixon (London, 1789) fp. 154.

National Library of Australia, Canberra. Rex Nan Kivell Collection. NK 7402.

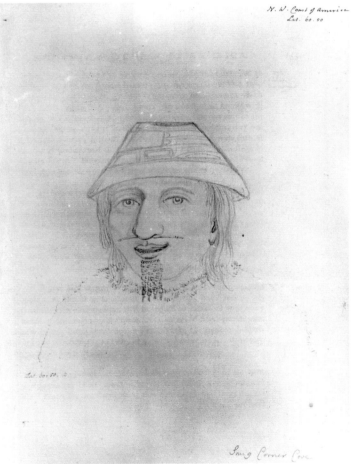

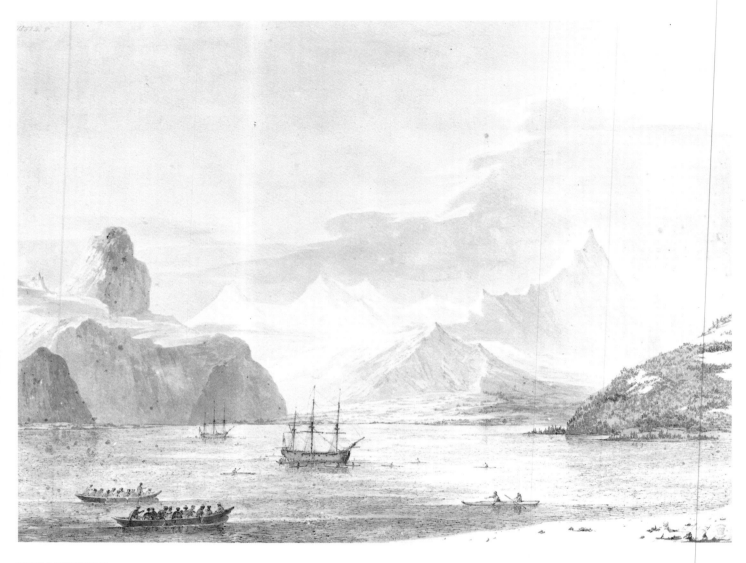

JOHN WEBBER

3.240 **A View of Snug Corner Cove**
[plate 118] [May 1778–]
pen, wash and water-colour, 19¹³⁄₁₆ × 26¼ : 563 × 667, unsigned.

The drawing is probably the one which is listed in Webber's Catalogue as no. 81 in the roll section 'A Ditto [i.e. View] in Snug Corner Harbour, our second Station'.

The *Resolution* and *Discovery* shown in the Sound, towering ice-covered cliffs on either side; two large canoes crowded with natives approaching the two ships from the left; at right a kayak holding two, and in the distance, closer to the ships, others, with single oarsmen. Prabably drawn on 16 May 1778.

Cook described Snug Corner Cove on 16 May: 'The land near the shoar is low, part clear and part wooded; the clear ground was covered two or three feet thick with Snow, but very little lay in the woods. The trees were all of the spruce or fir kind and some were tolerably large. The very summits of the neighbouring hills were covered with wood, but those farther inland seemed to be naked rocks buried in snow.' Cook, *Journals* III, 1, 351. King gives a further description for 17 May: 'The bad Weather by the Afternoon was followed by light Airs, clear & fair W! The transition was made striking by its giving us a prospect of snowy Mountains & deep bays to the NW that had hitherto been hid from our sight.' Ibid., 2, 1417.

ver: For a smaller version see 3.241. For a similar view of the *Resolution* for this drawing see 3.447. For studies for the canoes see 3.242.

ref: Cook, *Journals* III, 1, 351, pl. 43; Rienits (1968) 128; Skelton (1969) pl. XIII; Cobbe (1979) pl. 23; Henry (1984) f/piece.

British Library, London. Add MS 15514, f. 8.

JOHN WEBBER

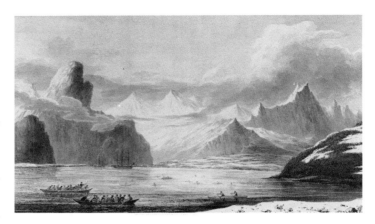

3.241   **A View of Snug Corner Cove**
       [plate 119]   [c. 1781-3]
       pen, wash and water-colour, 8¾ × 14⅞ : 222 × 378,
       unsigned.

Inscribed 'A View of Snug Corner Cove, in Prince William's
Sound' in pencil by a later hand on the folio beneath the drawing.

Resolution and *Discovery* at left in the distance, before a mountainous and snowy landscape; two long boats in left foreground
filled with people; many canoes dispersed about the sound.

ver: Similar, but reduced in scale, to 3.240 and probably drawn
      for the engraving 3.241A with minor differences, such as
      the position of the ships.
ref: Murray-Oliver (1969a) pl. 120 (col.); *Exh. Cat.* Anchorage
      (1978) pl. 3; *Ext. Cat.* Portland (1982) 190.

Dixson Library, State Library of New South Wales, Sydney.
PXX 2, 25.

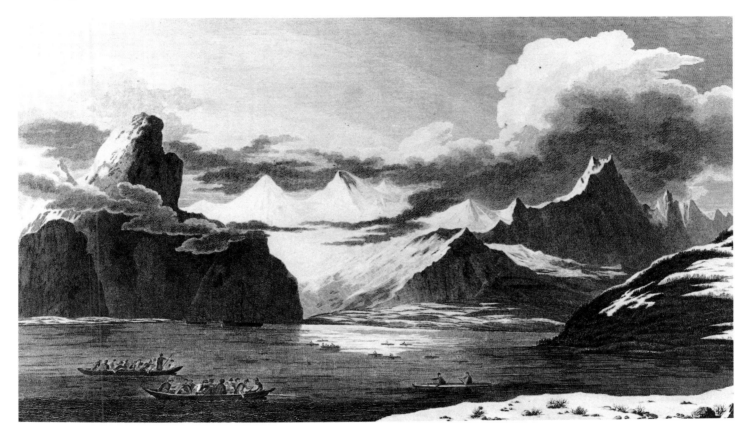

JOHN WEBBER (after)

3.241A   'A VIEW of SNUG CORNER COVE, in PRINCE
        WILLIAM'S SOUND'
        Engraving. 'J. Webber del.' — 'W. Ellis sculp.'

Published in Cook/King (1784) pl. 45, II, 361-2.

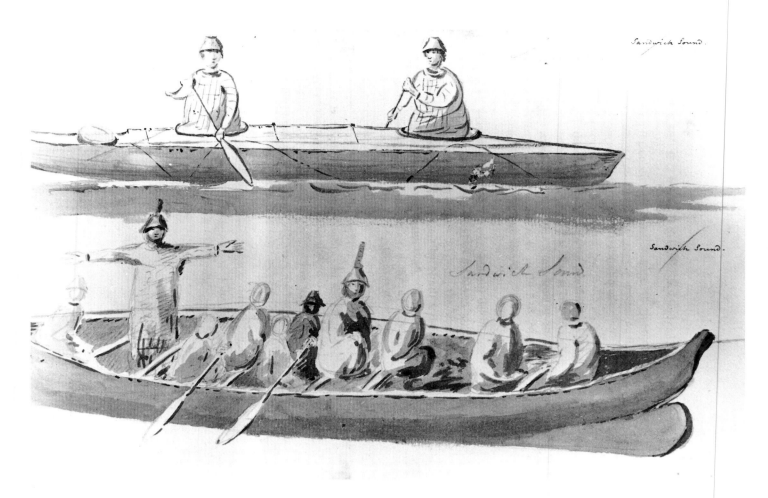

JOHN WEBBER

3.242 [People of Prince William Sound in their Canoes]
[May 1778]

pencil and wash, 7¹⁄₁₆ × 10⅝ : 179 × 270, unsigned; w/m: 'GR' under crown, surrounded by wreath,
in a circle.

Inscribed twice in pencil 'Sandwich Sound' and twice in black
ink but the latter crossed out in both cases. In pencil (l.r.) 'P.W.
Henry's Sound Capt. D.'.

Two studies of boats one above the other; the upper is a kayak
manned by two oarsmen; the lower is manned by ten figures one
at left standing with outstretched arms.

'Their canoes are of two sorts, one large & open capable of holding
30 or 40 people, the other small & covered & never carrying
above one or two Persons. The large & open Canoes are made
of a slight frame of wood something in the shape of a London
Wherry & covered with Seal Skin closely sewed together, they
are from 20 to 40 feet long, their Sides are something higher in
the Middle than at the head & stern; being very light and buoyant
they will carry great Weights and they hardly make any Water,
being much superior in both these respects to wooden Canoes,
which generally admit so much water as to keep one person almost
constantly bailing.

'The small Canoes consist like the others of slight wooden frames,
which are entirely covered with Seal skins except a round Hole
or Hatchway which is left open for one Man to sit in; this Hatchway is surrounded by a Hoop or Combing, round the lower edge
of which the Indians bladder frock is gathered with a string &
so effectually prevents any water getting into the Canoe; we saw
a few with two Hatchways but those with one were the most
common, the latter were something shorter than the others which
in general were about 12 or 14 feet long and about two wide. In

the middle where the Canoe is broadest & whence it gradually
tapers towards the head and stern, the upper part on the Deck
has a ridge running for[e] & aft, on each side of which is a gentle
declivity so much as that nothing will conveniently lie upon it,
& therefore there are straps fastened at each side of the Canoe,
& running across under which they thrust their Spears, Bows
& arrows & such things as they carry with them & are wanted
at hand.' Samwell in Cook, *Journals* III, 2, 1112-13. Compare
also King in ibid., 2, 1415.

ver: Both types of boats are depicted in the foreground of 3.240.
The upper boat is a study for 3.249. The lower boat is
related to the boat in the foreground of 3.232.

Tipped into a copy of Captain George Dixon, *A Voyage Round
the World* (London, 1789) fp. 68 to illustrate the facing text.

National Library of Australia, Canberra. Rex Nan Kivell Collection. NK 7402.

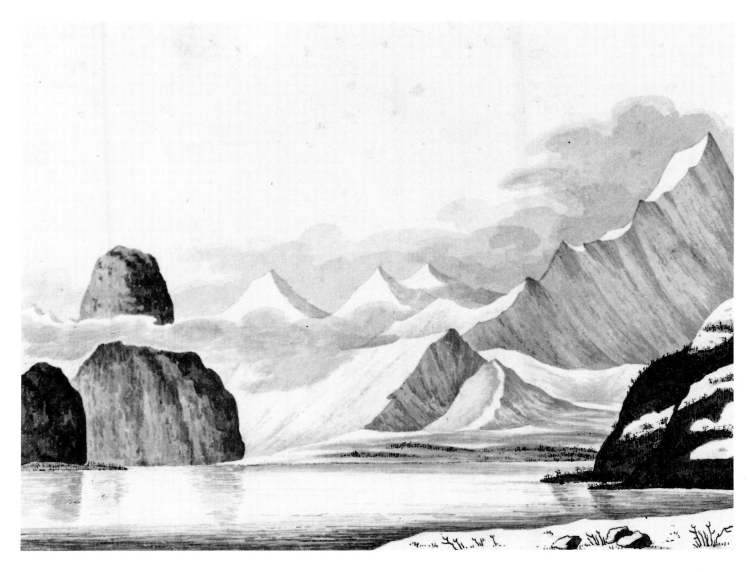

WILLIAM ELLIS

3.243   A View of Snug Corner Cove
[plate 122]   [May 1778–]
pen, wash and water-colour, 8¹³/₁₆ × 10¾ : 223
× 272, signed and dated in black ink 'W: Ellis fec!
1778' in l.r. Part of w/m: fleur-de-lis in shield under
crown.

Titled 'Prince William's Sound, in Sandwich Sound, on the
N.W. Coast of America' in brown ink beneath the drawing
within the grey band of the lined frame; also inscribed beneath
the frame in brown ink 'Snug Corner P W Henry's Sound. Capt.
G.D.'. No. '84' inscribed in brown ink (u.l.). The drawing is
surrounded by the same kind of enframing lines as 3.192.

Beyond the sound, steep, snow-covered slopes; in the right foreground a snow-covered shoreline and rocky cliff with sparse
vegetation.

'At eleven [16 May 1778], we shoaled from ten to five fathom,
and soon after the winds became very light, and the weather had
an unpromising appearance, in consequence of which Captain
Cook gave orders to bring the ships to an anchor, as soon as they
could be got to a convenient spot. At noon, our latitude was 60
deg. 51 min. N and at half past two we came to in nineteen
fathom, a muddy bottom.' [Snug Corner Cove.] Ellis (1782) I,
244.

The title seems to suggest some confusion on part of the inscriber,
calling the view 'Prince William's Sound, in Sandwich Sound'.
When Ellis's Narrative was published in 1782, there was as yet

no indication that the place-name of Sandwich Sound was to be
given up in favour of Prince William Sound. 'Prince William's
Sound' is not mentioned in the Narrative. The inscription thus
could only have been written after the publication of Cook/King
Voyage (1784) though it is still confusing. The information 'Snug
Corner' supplied by Captain Dixon is correct and represents a
later date of inscription.

ver: Similar view to Webber's water-colour at 3.240 and 3.241
      depicting the same location, omitting the ships and canoes
      in the Sound.

Museum Book Store, London, Cat. 94 (1924) 562/6, Cat. 107
(1928) 41/6, and Cat. 125 (1941) 453.

National Library of Australia, Canberra. Rex Nan Kivell Collection. NK 53/C.

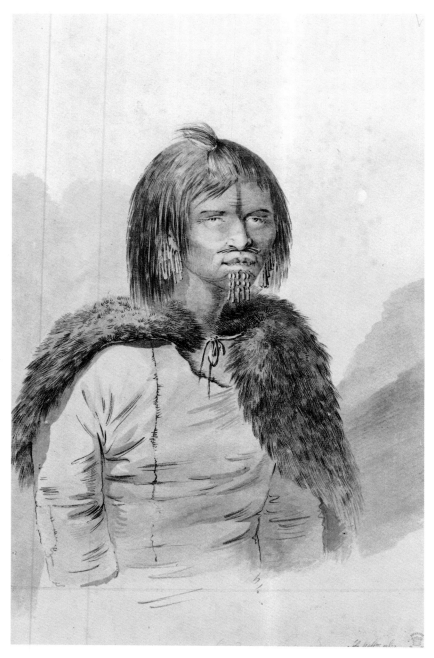

3.244   **A Woman of Prince William Sound**
       [plate 124]   **[May 1778–]**
       pencil, wash and water-colour, 19⅜ × 12¼ : 492 ×
       311, signed 'John Webber. del' (l.r.).

Inscribed 'Woman of Sandwich Sound' in pencil on the sheet
below drawing and traces of number '76' (u.r.). This is probably
no. '76 A Portrait of a Woman' in the 'Sandwich Sound' section
in Webber's Catalogue.

A half-length portrait facing three-quarters towards the right.
She wears a close-fitting skin jacket and a fur slung over the
shoulders; two bone ornaments through the septum; beads attached
in strings to the lower lip and from the ears.

'I saw not a woman with a head dress of any kind, they had all
long black hair a part of which was tied up in a bunch over the
forehead . . . though the lips of all were not slit, yet all were
bored, especially the women and even the young girls; to these
holes and slits they fix pieces of bone of this size and shape, placed
side by side in the inside of the lip; a thread is run through them
to keep them together, and some goes quite through the lip and
fastens, or fore-locks on the out side to which they hang other
pieces of bones or beads. This Ornament is a very great impe-
diment to the Speach and makes them look as if they had a double
row of teeth in the under jaw. Besides these lip-jewels which they
seemed to value above all others, they wear a bone, or some bugle
beads strung on a stif string or Cord 3 or 4 inch long, run through
the cartilage that divides the nostril from each other. Their ears
are bored all round to which they hang beads or pieces of bone.'
Cook, *Journals* III, 1, 350.

ver: For a modified and smaller version see 3.245. A field-sketch
        of the woman is at 3.246.

ref: Cook, *Journals* III, 1, pl. 44 b; King (1979) pl. 95.

British Library, London. Add MS 15514, f.11.

JOHN WEBBER

3.245 **A Woman of Prince William's Sound** [c. 1781-3]
pencil, pen, wash and water-colour, $8^{15}/_{16} \times 7$:
227×178, unsigned.

The title as above in pencil by a later hand on the folio beneath
the drawing.

ver: Portrait of. the same woman as represented in 3.244, this
version was drawn in preparation for 3.245A.

Dixson Library, State Library of New South Wales, Sydney.
PXX 2. 27.

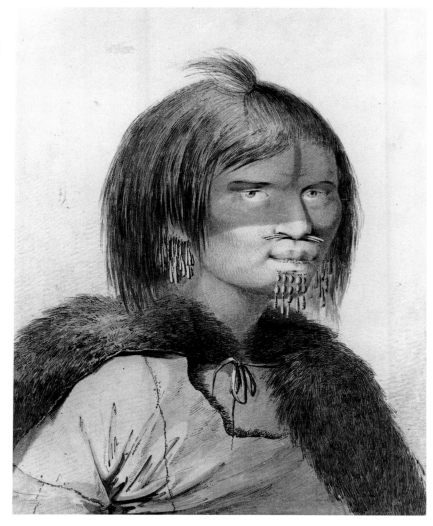

JOHN WEBBER (after)

3.245A **'A WOMAN of PRINCE WILLIAM'S SOUND'**
Engraving. 'J. Webber del.' — 'J. Basire sculp.'

Published in Cook/King (1784) pl. 47, II, 369-70.

A proof-state inscribed in pencil 'A Woman Sandwich Sound.
America' in Webber's hand and crossed out again and numbered
in pencil 'N° 46' (u.r.) is kept in the National Library of Australia,
Canberra, in a folio of plates from the Skottowe Hall Library.

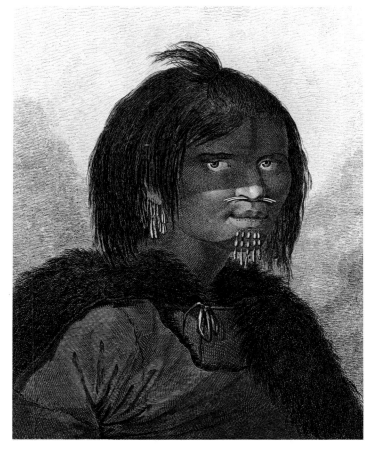

481

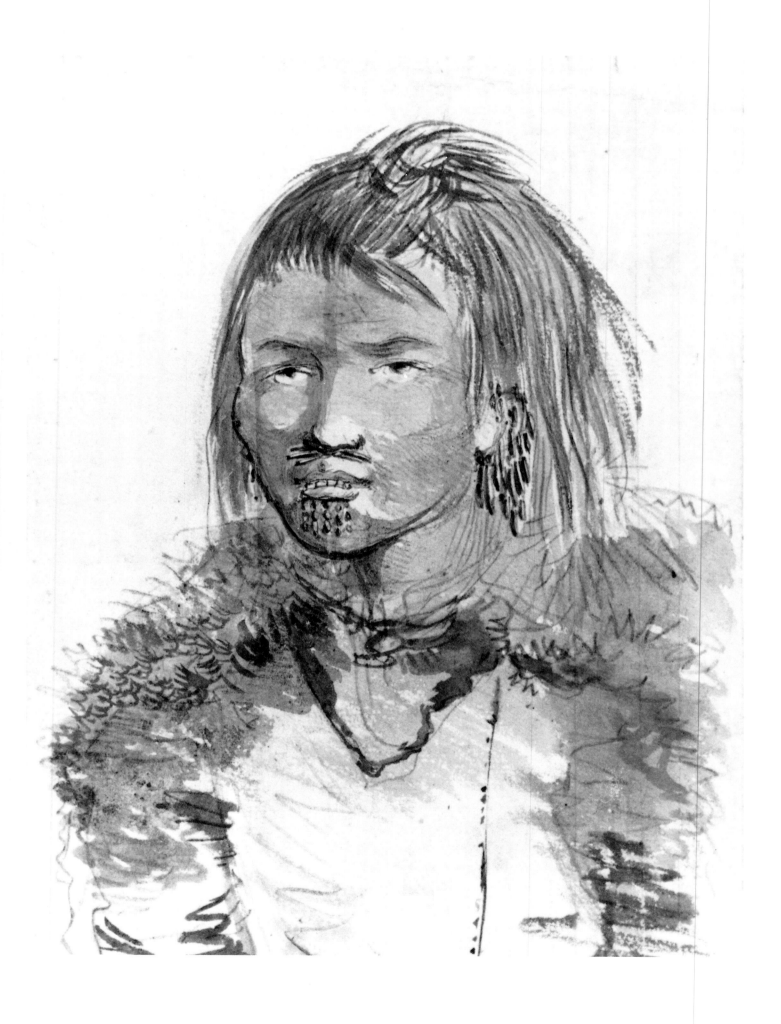

482

JOHN WEBBER

3.246   A Woman of Prince William Sound   [May 1778]
pencil, chalk and sepia, 11 × 9 : 279 × 229, unsigned.

Enclosed within a lined frame of two narrow side bands and one central broad band.

A freely drawn field-sketch which served as the preparatory study for 3.244.

ref: Cook, *Journals* III, pl. 45 b under the title 'Woman of Cook's River'.

Listed in Francis Edwards, *Cat.* 551 (London 1932), as no.8 'Woman of Cook's River 11in × 9 in'.

Francis P. Farquhar Collection, Berkeley, California.

WILLIAM ELLIS (after)

3.246A   'A Native [Woman] of Sandwich Sound'

Engraving. 'W. Ellis del.' — 'J. Heath sculp.' 'Publish'd Dec.ʳ 14 1781 by G. Robinson'.

Published in Ellis (1782) I, fp 236, 248.

No drawing by Ellis of this sitter is known. The drawing however, was probably copied from a study by Webber (3.246) with some alterations, particularly in the daubing of the face.

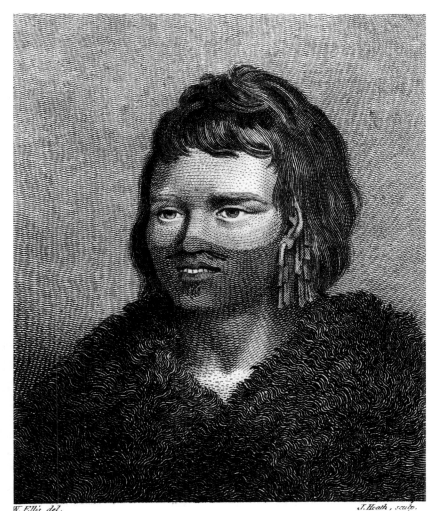

W. Ellis del.   J. Heath, sculp.

A Native

of Sandwich Sound.

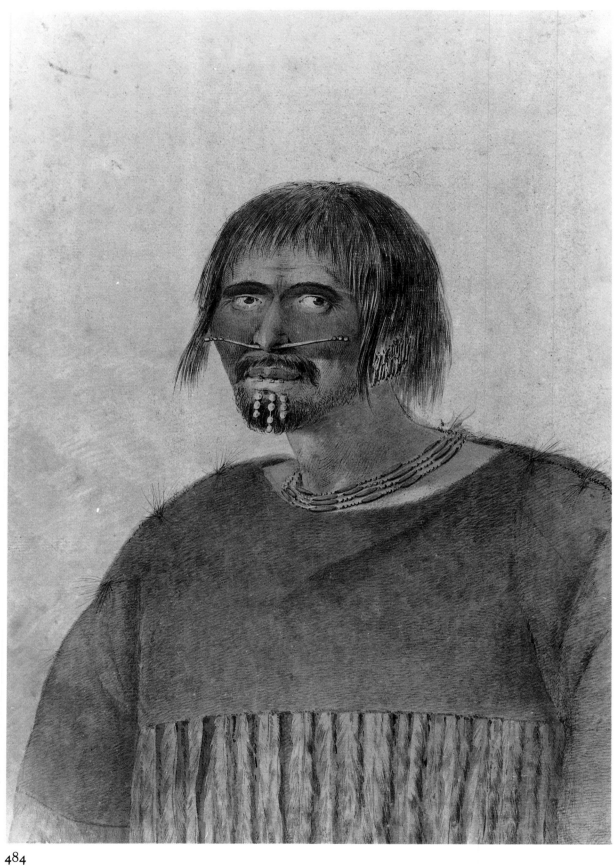

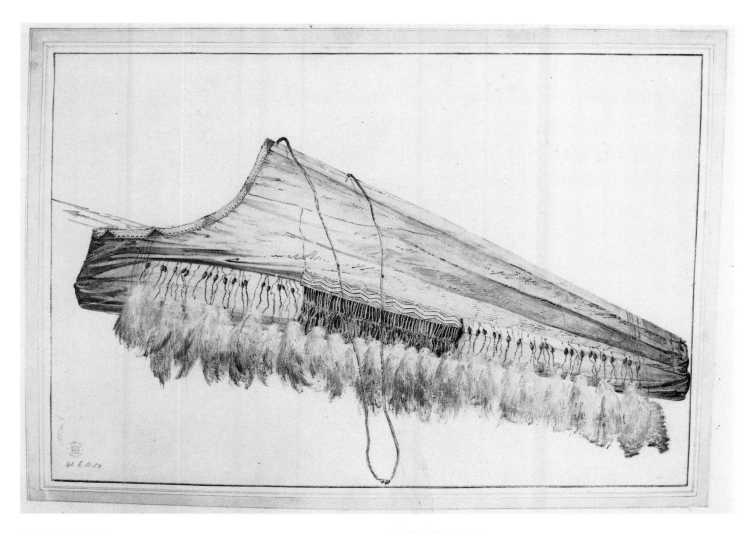

JOHN WEBBER

JOHN WEBBER

3.247   **A Man of Turnagain River**   [May-Jun 1778]
pen, wash and water-colour, 17 × 12 : 432 × 305,
unsigned.

Inscribed on verso in ink 'lot. no 12'. The drawing was cleaned
of discoloured varnish by the Conservation Department of the
Fogg Art Museum, Harvard University, in February 1977. The
drawing can be tentatively identified as no. 82 'A Portrait of a
Native' in the 'River Turnagain' section of Webber's Catalogue.

A portrait of head and shoulders. A half-length portrait of a man
with straight hair looking slightly towards the left. He wears an
elaborate coat of skins with pendant feathers beneath the chest.
His forehead is painted red, there is a long slightly-curved bone
ornament through his nose, and strands of plaited braids are
fastened to his hair. A necklace is strung four times around his
neck. The lower lip has been perforated and holds three beaded
pendants.

ref: Bushnell, Jr (1928) pl. 7; Cook, *Journals* III, 1, pl. 44 a,
referred to as 'Man of Sandwich Sound'; Rienits (1968)
127; *Exh. Cat.* Portland (1982) 194.

Listed in Francis Edwards, *Cat.* 416 (London, July 1921) as 'Native
of Prince William's Sound (17 by 12 in), sepia and colour, on
strainer and varnished (unpublished)'.

Peabody Museum of Archaeology and Ethnology, Harvard University, Cambridge, Massachusetts. Inv. no. 41-72-10/501.

3.248   **A Quiver and Arrows from Turnagain Arm**
[plate 125]   [May 1778–]
pen, water-colour and gouache, 14½ × 21 : 368 ×
533.

Traces of inscription (l.r.) in pencil. In lower left '83' in pencil
which corresponds to no. 83 'A Quiver' in section 'River Turnagain' in Webber's Catalogue.

A quiver adorned with coloured pattern and white feathers.
Quiver and arrows of a similar kind were also found at Prince
William Sound.

Samwell noted on 2 May 1778: 'We were visited every Day by
many Canoes full of Indians who sold us fine Sea Beaver & other
Skins for Iron, and they also sold us some excellent Salmon &
Hallybut fresh & dried, *curious Quivers* for Nails & other trifles
[our italics].' Cook, *Journals* III, 2, 1117.

ref: Kaeppler (1978a) fig. 590.

British Library, London. Add MS 15514, f.6

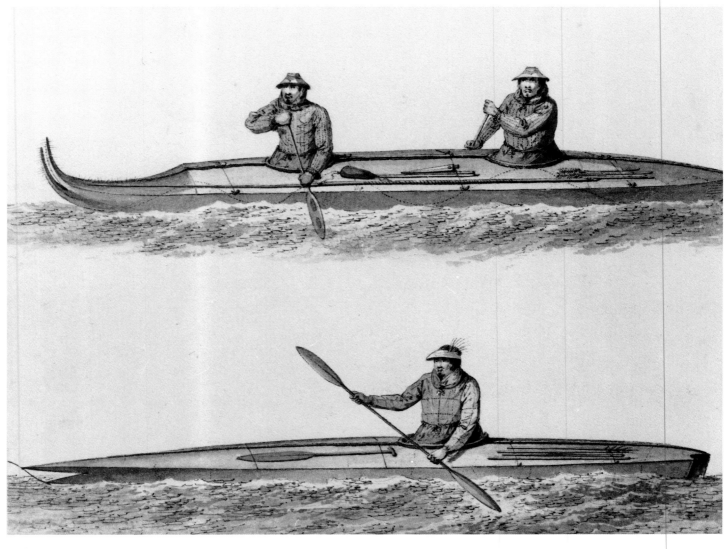

JOHN WEBBER

3.249   Kayaks of Prince William Sound and Unalaska
         [plate 126]   **[c. 1781-3]**
         pen, wash and water-colour, 7 × 8⅞ : 177 × 225,
         unsigned.

Inscribed 'Canoes of Oonalashka' in pencil by a later hand on
the folio beneath the drawing, and 'Prince William's Sound' in
Webber's hand inscribed faintly in pencil along top of the drawing.

Two figures in the top canoe, and one in that below. The two
figures in the top canoe come from Prince William Sound. The
canoeist below is a native of Unalaska.

Of the canoe from Prince William Sound Cook says: 'The small
Canoes were . . . made nearly of the same form and of the same
materials as those used by the Greenlanders and Esquemaux's, at
least the difference is not material; some of these as I have before
observed carry two men; they are considerably broader in pro-

portion to their length than those used by the Esquimauxs, and
the head or fore part curves up some thing like the head of a
fiddle.' Cook, *Journals* III, 1, 349.

The lower drawing could represent a native who was seen on 21
June 1778 and about whom Samwell gives the following account:
'While we were busy fishing, a small Canoe came off the Shore
with one Man in her . . . His Dress was like that of the Indians
we had seen in the River, & his underlip had a Hole in it. He
wore a kind of Cap made of the Birch Bark different from any
we had seen before, his Canoe was longer & narrower than those
we saw in the river & the Darts he had were not feathered like
those of Sandwich Sound.' Ibid., 2, 1119.

ver: For a more sketchy version of this drawing see 3.242. For
        two related versions of the lower drawing see 3.250 and
        3.268. 3.249 was drawn for the engraving 3.249A.

Dixson Library, State Library of New South Wales, Sydney.
PXX 2, 30.

486

JOHN WEBBER (after)

3.249A 'CANOES of OONALASHKA'

Engraving. 'J. Webber del.' — 'W. Angus sc.'

Published in Cook/King (1784) pl. 50, II, 371 for the
upper canoe, and 391 and 515-16 for the one below.

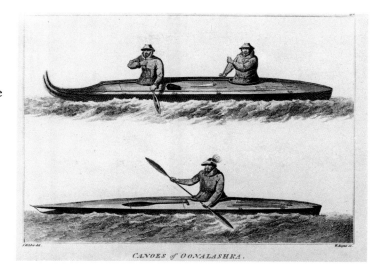

CANOES of OONALASHKA.

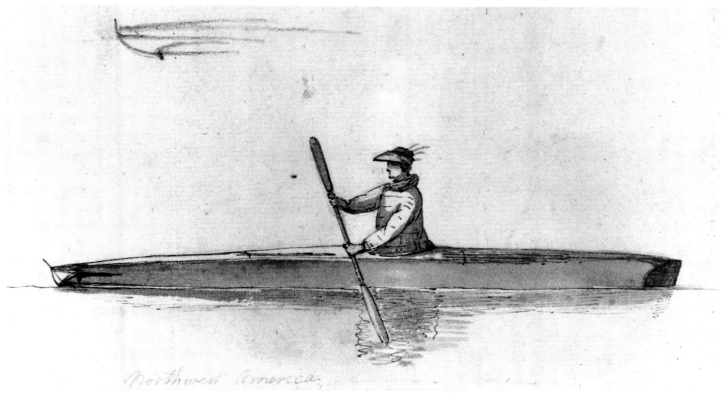

JOHN WEBBER

3.250   A Kayak of Unalaska   [Jun 1778]

pencil and sepia, 4½ × 8 : 144 × 203, unsigned.

Inscribed 'North-West America' in pencil across lower centre by
another hand.

A Unalaskan in his kayak, similar to 3.249 (bottom) and related
to 3.268.

National Maritime Museum, London. (In volume of plates to
Cook's Voyages.)

SAMGOONOODHA [ENGLISH BAY], UNALASKA: FIRST VISIT

28 June to 2 July 1778   3.251–3.267

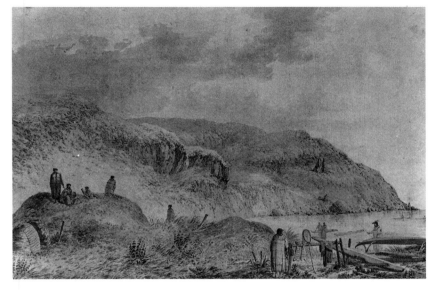

JOHN WEBBER

3.251   **Natives of Unalaska and their habitations**
      [plate 127]   **[Jul 1778–]**
      pen and ink on sepia-washed paper, 16½ × 24½ : 419 × 622. Signed and dated 'J. Webber del. 1778' (l.l.); w/m: 'J. WHATMAN'.

Inscribed on card of a former backing preserved in the present frame 'Lot No. 15' in brownish ink, and in pencil 'Captain Campbell'. Also a strip of canvas of a former backing inscribed 'Natives of Oonalaska and their habitations'. Cleaned by Department of Conservation, Fogg Art Museum, Harvard University, in February 1977.

The drawing can be tentatively identified as no. 88/9 'A View with Habitations' in the 'Aoonalaska' section of Webber's Catalogue.

Several figures, two standing, two seated on the roof of a house from which another is emerging by a ladder. Towards the right near the shore other figures and some upturned kayaks; nets and fishing gear drying in the sun.

It would appear that the scene depicted was observed on 1 July 1778 around Samgoonoodha Harbour (English Bay) in the Island of Unalaska. In the afternoon, Lieutenant Gore 'accompanied by three more Gentlemen', so Samwell informs us, 'visited an Indian Town which lies at the distance of about 2 Miles from the Ship. . . . having followed a well frequented Path, which on our first leaving the sea Shore ascended a very steep Hill for about a mile and a half, we came in sight of the Indian Town lying in a low Valley close to the Water Side which there forms a deep Bay . . . the Houses were not to be seen till we came close upon them, & then we were much surprized at finding small Hillocks of earth & dirt scattered about here & there with a hole in the top of them, through which we descended down a Ladder made of a thick piece of wood with steps cut in it . . .' Samwell in Cook, *Journals* III, 2, 1122-3; 'in fine Weather they generally sit on the top of their Houses.' Ibid., 2, 1124.

ver: For a smaller version see 3.252. Two field-sketches are at 3.253 and 3.254.

ref: Bushnell, Jr (1928) pl. 10; Cook, *Journals* III, 1, pl. 51; Rienits (1968) 127.

Listed in Francis Edwards, *Cat.* 416 (London, July 1921) under no. 769 as 'Natives of Oonalashka and their Habitations (24 by 17 in) in sepia and colour, on strainer and varnished'.

Peabody Museum of Archaeology and Ethnology, Harvard University, Cambridge, Massachusetts. 41-72-10/507.

JOHN WEBBER

3.252 **Natives of Oonalaska and their habitations**
[c. 1781-3]
pen, ink and water-colour, 8½ × 14½ : 216 × 368, unsigned.

ver: The figures are disposed as in 3.251 with minor variations in detail. The drawing is a smaller version of 3.251 and was drawn for the engraving 3.252A.

ref: Not reproduced in Bushnell (1928) though from his collection; *Exh. Cat.* Portland (1928) 196 (col.).

Peabody Museum of Archaeology and Ethnology, Harvard University, Cambridge, Massachusetts. 41-72-10/506.

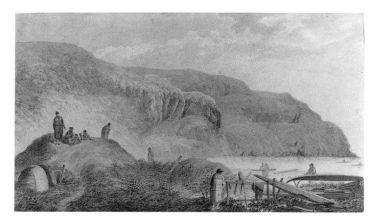

JOHN WEBBER (after)

3.252A **'Natives of Oonalashka, and their habitations'**
Engraving. 'J. Webber del.' — 'J. Hall & S. Middiman sc.'

Published in Cook/King (1784) pl. 57, II, 512.

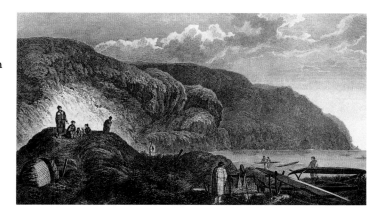

JOHN WEBBER

3.253 **[Natives of Oonalaska and their habitations]**
[plate 128] [Jul 1778]
wash and water-colour over pencil, 14¹⁄₁₆ × 20⅞ : 357 × 530, laid down on cardboard within double brown framing bands.

Inscribed 'View in the Island Oonalaska' in pencil in an eighteenth century hand centred beneath the framing bands, also 'Webber R.A.' probably by a later hand.

A hilly foreshore with two figures at left on top of a house another figure lightly sketched in the centre, some drying racks at extreme right. Probably drawn on 1 July 1778 (see 3.251).

ver: This is a preparatory drawing for 3.251 and 3.252.

National Library of Australia, Canberra. Rex Nan Kivell Collection. NK 52/B.

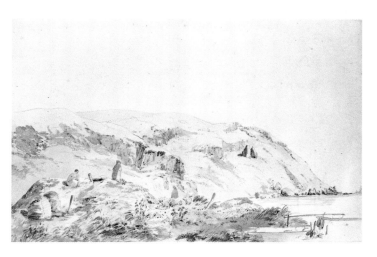

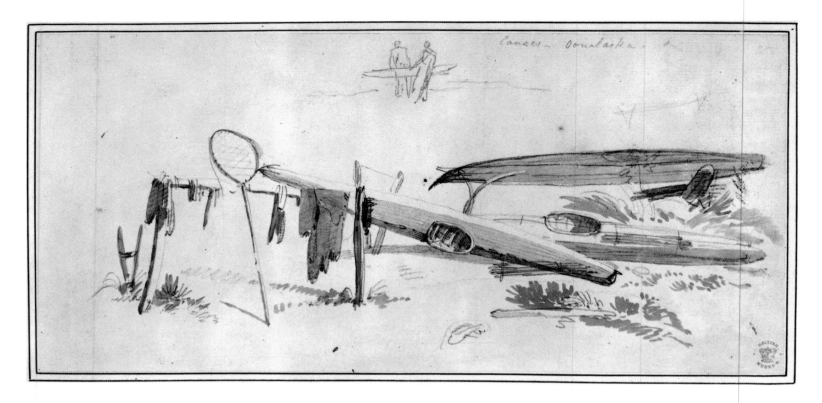

JOHN WEBBER

3.254 Canoes of Oonalaska [Jul 1778]
pencil and wash, 6¾ × 14½ : 171 × 368, unsigned.

Inscribed 'Canoes — Oonalaska' in pencil (u.r.).

Upturned kayaks with nets and fishing gear drying in the sun. Two figures in pencil in background carrying a canoe.

The drawing is a study for l.r. part of 3.251 and 3.252.

British Library, London. Add MS 17277, no 25.

WILLIAM ELLIS

3.255 Huts at Unalaska [Jul 1778–]
water-colour, 9¾ × 13¼ : 248 × 336, signed and dated 'W. Ellis fec. 1778' in black ink (l.r.); part of w/m: fleur-de-lis in a shield with 'W' underneath = J. Whatman.

Fully titled 'Outside of the Huts at Unalaschka, N.W. Coast of America' in brown ink across the lower edge of the sheet. Inscribed '5' in brown ink in corner (u.l.).

In the centre foreground a winter house with entrance in the roof and a ladder for entrance, with two figures walking behind it. To the right, other houses with side entrances. At the extreme left a third figure standing and a rack from which mats and gourds hang.

It would seem that this drawing was not done on the spot; it bears some notable similarity to Webber's drawing 3.251, from which it might have been developed. In his *Narrative* Ellis talks about a party of gentlemen who 'were permitted to go on shore and gather herbs, or amuse themselves in any other manner they thought proper; and some of the gentlemen having been informed that there was a small Indian village near the entrance of the harbour, on the eastern shore, took this opportunity of walking there . . . Upon their arrival at the village, they were civilly received by the inhabitants, who pulled off their bonnets, and made very low bows: there were not more than eighteen or twenty, including women and children. The town consisted of eight or ten houses, one of which was large, the others much smaller; the largest was about thirty feet in length and eighteen feet wide, raised nearly six feet above the surface, and hollowed the same depth below it: there were two openings on the top, one, which was in the middle, for the admission of light, the other as an entrance to the house, which was effected by means of a long post, with notches cut in it for the reception of the feet in descending: the bottom was lined with dry grass, and the roof supported by stakes set upright, across which were placed balks, and over the whole was thrown dry grass and earth, which gave it the appearance at the distance of a large hillock . . . At some distance from the houses, were erected stages for the purpose of

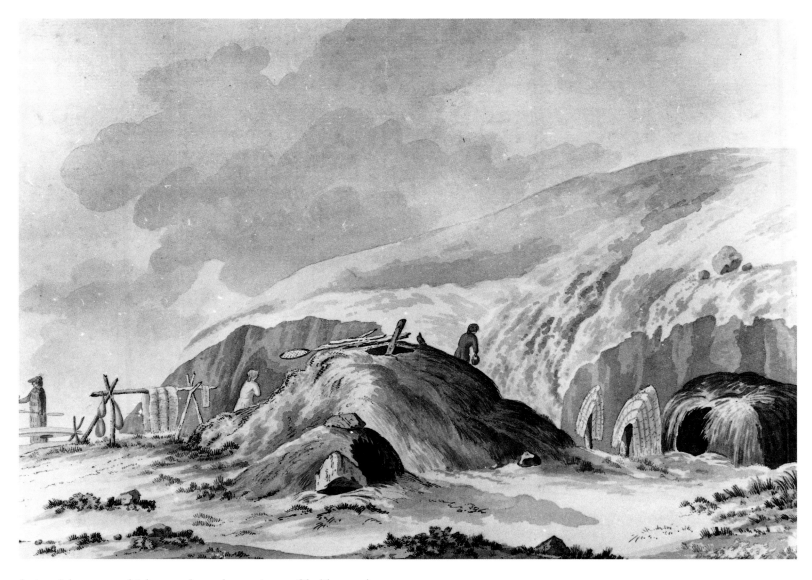

drying fish, upon which were hung large pieces of halibut and whale's flesh . . . After having looked about as much as they thought necessary, the gentlemen returned, the natives bowing very respectfully at their departure . . .' Ellis (1782) I, 287-9.

It would seem from this report that Ellis did not belong to the party who saw the village but has his information from hearsay. Concerning the canoes of Unalaska, on the other hand, Ellis says: 'They are very careful of them, and as soon as they return from fishing, or any other expedition, they are conveyed from the beach to their huts, and, after being cleared of the water . . . they are placed, with the hole downwards, upon four stakes placed crosswise for that purpose, about two feet from the ground.' Ibid., II, 50-1. And so he portrays them in his drawing probably from the result of his own observation, for Webber in 3.251 portrays the canoe supports differently.

ref: Rienits (1968) 131; *Exh. Cat.* Portland (1982) 192; Henry (1984) 69.

Museum Book Store, London, *Cat.* 107 (1928) no. 41/12, and *Cat.* 125 (1941) 453 under the title as inscribed 'size 8½ by 11¾ in, signed W. Ellis, fect. 1779. A view of a native settlement in early spring, the tents are apparently built with turf, outside, on posts, pelts are drying'.

National Library of Australia, Canberra. Rex Nan Kivell Collection. NK 53/M.

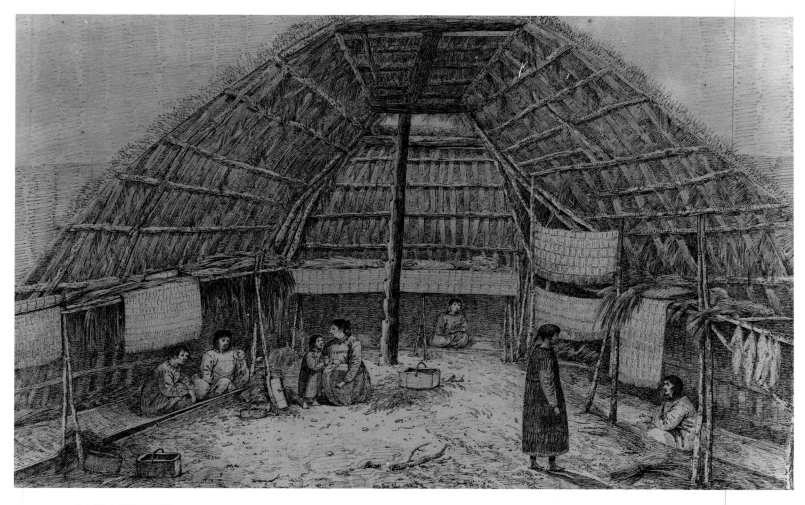

JOHN WEBBER

3.256 Inside of a House in Unalaska
[plate 129]   [Jul 1778–]
pen and ink, 12 × 19 : 305 × 482, signed and dated
'J. Webber del. 1778'.

Inscribed on verso of original backing 'Inside of an Oonalashka house' (u.r.), 'glass 3'. This is probably the drawing '88/1 An inside view of the Natives Habitations' in the 'Aoonalaska' section of Webber's Catalogue. Cleaned by the Conservation Department of Fogg Art Museum, Harvard University, October 1978.

Five figures seated; next to the woman at centre is a child standing, and another standing figure at right; around the walls are shelves, with baskets, mats, fish and other provisions.

The drawing corresponds closely to a description of the interior of the houses which Samwell gives for 1 July 1778. 'Descending the Ladder we were brought into a Passage about four foot wide which intersects the House from one end to the other . . . at one end of this Passage close to the foot of the Ladder is the fire place. On each side and at each end of this passage are the Apartments where they sit & work in the day time and sleep at Night: these are something wider than the passage & sunk in the ground about half a foot lower and are covered with matts. Over these Apartments is a kind of a Loft where they keep their Seal Skins, dryed gutt of the Whale and various other Articles; before them they have Matts which they let down occasionally like Curtains to skreen them from the view of the Common Passage. . . . Tho' these Huts are seemingly under ground & the entrance is from the top, yet in general they are only sunk in the ground about half a Yard, they are built of a rude wooden frame of an oval oblong square form, irregularly & clumsily put together, over which they first put straw & then over all heap a great quantity

of earth & all kind of rubbish to a considerable thickness. The highest part within side is about 4 yards. They are rather dark, having no light but what comes by the Door or Hatchway. They are in general about 10 yards long & 5 or 6 in breadth & each House is occupied by three or four different Families . . .' Cook, *Journals* III, 2, 1123.

'After having staid here about 2 Hours during which time M.r Webber our Draughtsman made a Sketch of their Houses and other curious Objects which presented themselves, we took our leave of these Indians . . .' Ibid., 2, 1124. For Cook's observations see *Journals* III, 1, 460-1.

ver: For a smaller version see 3.257.

ref: Bushnell, Jr (1928) pl. 11; Cook, *Journals* III, pl. 53; Rienits (1968) 126; *Exh. Cat.* Portland (1982) 197.

Listed in Francis Edwards, *Cat.* 416 (London, July 1921) under no 769 as 'Inside of a House in Oonalashka (19½ by 12 in) in sepia.'

Peabody Museum of Archaeology and Ethnology, Harvard University, Cambridge, Massachusetts. 41-72-10/505.

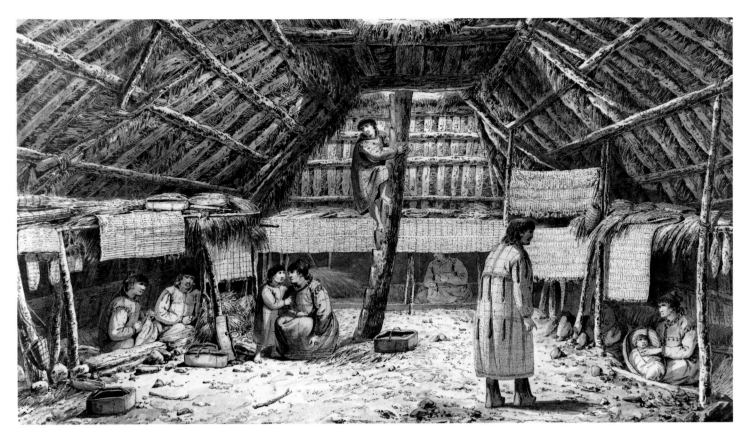

JOHN WEBBER

3.257 Inside of a House in Oonalaska   [c. 1781-3]
pen, wash and water-colour, 8⅝ × 14¹³⁄₁₆ : 218
× 376, unsigned.

Titled 'The Inside of a House in Oonalashka' in pencil by a later
hand on the folio beneath the drawing.

ver: A smaller version of 3.256, to which is added a man descending the ladder in the centre mid-distance, with var-
iation of two figures, at right a seated woman holding a
child in a basket, as well as a native in a frock. The composition was thus redrawn for the engraving 3.257A.

Dixson Library, State Library of New South Wales, Sydney.
PXX 2,34.

JOHN WEBBER (after)

3.257A 'The INSIDE of a HOUSE, in OONALASHKA'
Engraving. 'J. Webber del.' — 'W. Sharp sculp.'

Published in Cook/King (1784) pl. 58, II, 512-13.

A proof-state inscribed in pencil 'Inside of an House Oonalaska
America' in Webber's hand and numbered in pencil 'N°. 49'
(u.r.) is kept in the National Library of Australia, Canberra, in
a folio of plates from the Skottowe Hall Library.

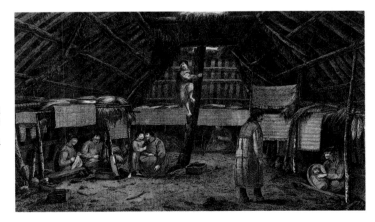

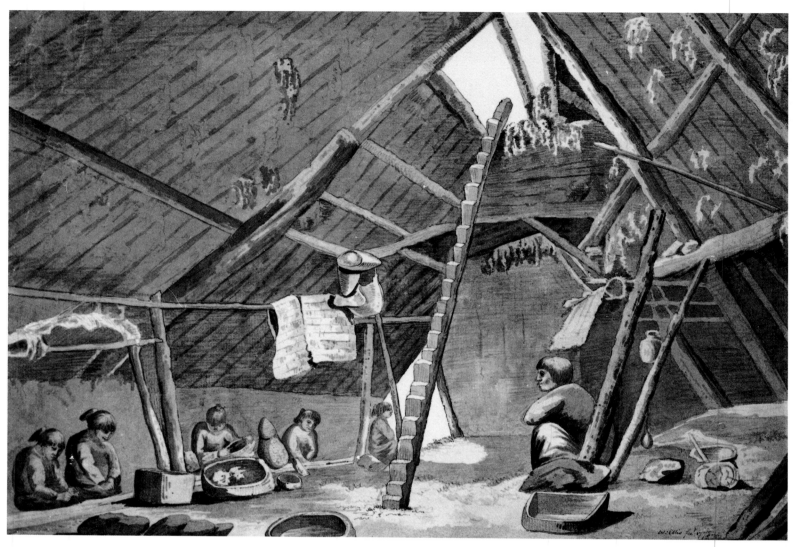

WILLIAM ELLIS

3.258   **Inside of a Hut at Unalaska**   [1 Jul 1778]
         pen and wash over pencil, 11⅛ × 15⅝ : 282 × 397,
         signed and dated in black ink 'W: Ellis fecᵗ 1778' (l.r.).

Inscribed 'Inside of a hut at Unalaschka on the N.W. Coast of
America' in brown ink along the lower edge of the sheet. Inscribed
'6' in brown ink corner (u.l.). On verso 'View of the Inside of
a Hut at the Island Unalaschka, on the North-West Coast of
America Lat. 53 N', again in brown ink.

Five figures seated at left beside the wall of the hut; a larger figure
squatting at right faces them; in the centre a ladder leads to a
hole in the roof.

A description of the construction of this type of hut is given by
Ellis. Of the interior and utensils he writes: 'The space behind
the wooden posts which support the ridge poles, is destined for
their bed places, &c, which they cover with mats . . . They are
not very expensive in their house hold-furniture, which consists
chiefly of wooden bowls, troughs, and platters, of various sizes
and for various uses, and a copper kettle for the purpose of boiling
fish.' Ellis (1782) II, 48-50.

ref: Henry (1984) 68.

Museum Book Store, London, *Cat.* 125 (1941) 453, with the
title as inscribed.

National Library of Australia, Canberra. Rex Nan Kivell Collection. NK 53/N.

494

JOHN WEBBER

3.259   **A Native of Unalaska** [plate 134]   [1778]
pen, wash and water-colour, 21½ × 14½ : 546 × 369,
unsigned.

Titled 'Native of Oonalashka' in pencil (u.l.), preceded by 'ii
509'.

Probably the drawing referred to as '88/6 A man in their Usual
Dress' in the 'Aoonalaska' section of Webber's Catalogue.

A full-figure drawing unfinished of a Unalaskan man in a bird-
skin cloak reaching below the knee. He holds an 'eye-shade' cap
in his right hand and two fish in his left (the fish in pencil only).
A companion drawing to 'Woman of Oonalaska', see 3.263.

It is possible that the sitter represents the young Aleut native
Yermusk, whom Samwell identifies by name. Cook, *Journals* III,
2, 1121. On 28 June he was taken on board the *Resolution*, and,
because his canoe had capsized, he was newly clothed in Captain
Cook's cabin: 'His dress was an upper Garment like a Shirt, made
of the large gut of some sea animal, probably the Whale, and an
under garment of the same shape, made of birds skins dressed
with the feathers on and neatly sewed together; the feathered side
he wore next to his skin.' Cook, *Journals* III, 1, 391-2. Samwell
adds: 'Yermusk staid with us most part of the Day & then went
ashore enriched with Presents of Tobacco & other things which
Capt. Cook gave him.' Ibid., 2, 1121.

Webber thus would have had ample opportunity to draw him.
Concerning the appearance and dress of the Unalaskans Cook
says: 'These people are rather low of Stature, but plump and well
shaped, with rather short necks, swarthy chubby faces, black eyes,
small beards, and streight long black hair, which the Men wear
loose behind and cut before . . . Thier dress . . . both, Men
and Womens are made alike, the only difference is in the Materials,
the Womans frock is made of Seal skin and the Mens of birds
skin and both reach below the knee . . . some of them wear
boots and all of them a kind of oval snouted Cap made of wood
with a rim to admet the head: these are dyed with green and other
Colours and round the upper part of the rim, are stuck the long
bristles of some sea animal on which are strung glass beads
. . . both men and Women bore the underlip to which they fix
pieces of bone, but it is as uncommon at Onalaska to see a man
with this ornament as a women without it.' Ibid., 1, 459-60.
Neither Clerke nor Samwell however make such a comment. It
may not have been so uncommon for men to wear an ornament
through the underlip as Cook suggests.

ver: For two related drawings, probably field-sketches, see 3.260
and 3.261.

British Library, London. Add MS 15514, f.21.

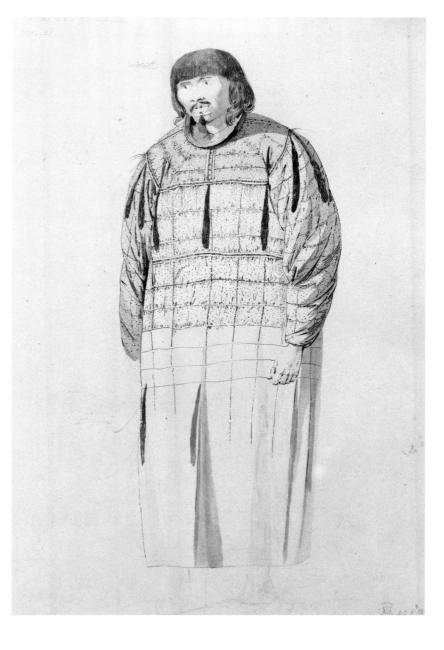

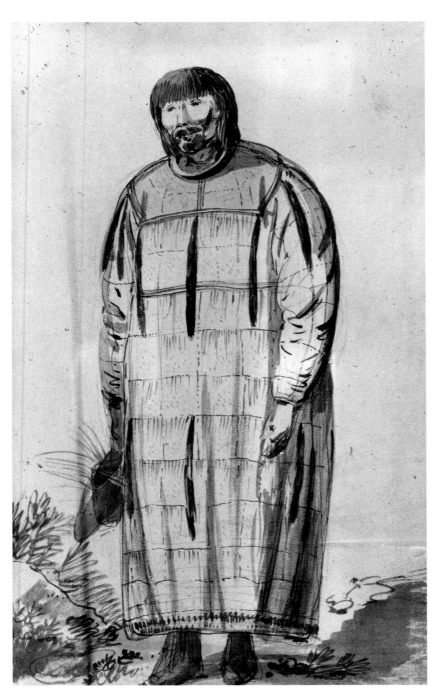

JOHN WEBBER

3.260   **A Man of Unalaska [plate 133]**   **[Jul 1778]**
pencil, sepia wash, red chalk and water-colour, 21⅛
× 12¾ : 537 × 324, unsigned.

A full-length study of a man in a long gown holding an eye-shade in his right hand and a fish in his left, (faintly sketched in). The feet and eye-shade have been worked over with red chalk.

ver: A study for 3.259.

National Maritime Museum, London. (In volume of plates to Cook's Voyages.)

JOHN WEBBER

3.261   A Man of Unalaska   [1778]
pencil, wash and water-colour, 14⁵/₁₆ × 8¼ : 355 × 209, unsigned.

Unfinished sketch. The figure has a similar posture and dress as 3.259. The breast-plate is coloured in light red.

British Library, London. Add MS 17277. no.29.

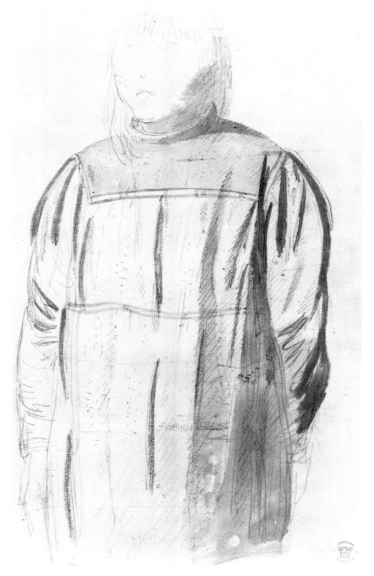

JOHN WEBBER

**3.262   A Portrait of a Native of Unalaska
          [plate 135]   [1778–]**
wash, and water-colour, 8⅜ × 9⅜ : 213 × 238, unsigned.

Titled 'A Portrait of a Native of Oonalashka, America' in pencil (u.r.) in Webber's hand; 'ii 509' inscribed on mount (u.l.), relating to Cook/King (1784). The drawing is probably one of the two portraits of a man listed as no. 88/3 and 88/4 in the 'Aoonalaska' section of Webber's Catalogue.

ver: The sitter bears some resemblance to the man depicted in 3.259 and may be the same man.

British Library, London. Add MS 15514, f.22.

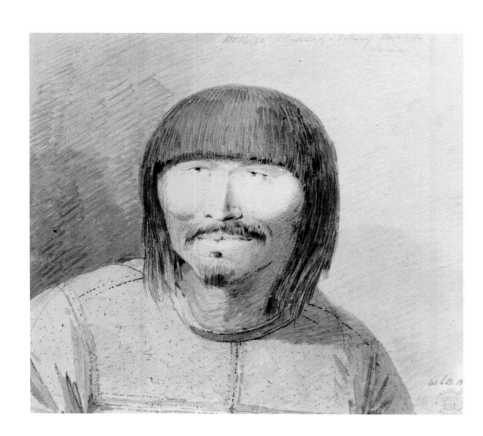

JOHN WEBBER

3.263   A Woman of Unalaska [plate 132]   [Jul 1778–]
water-colour, 20¹³⁄₁₆ × 14½ : 529 × 368, signed
'J. Webber del'.

This drawing is probably the one referred to as '88/7 A Woman
in Ditto [ie. in their Usual Dress]' in the 'Aoonalaska' section
of Webber's Catalogue.

A full-length figure of a Unalaskan woman, clad in a tubular
cloak, standing on the top of a house. A bay at right; mountains
in the background.

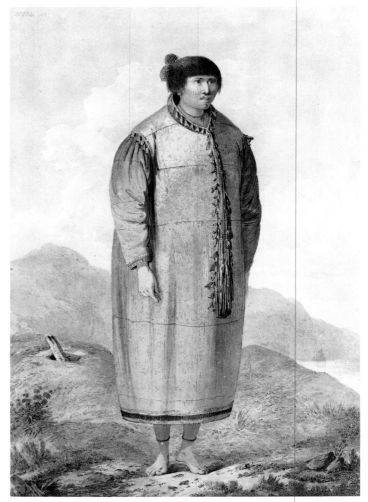

The woman can be identified with the one about whom Samwell
speaks, after his excursion to some native houses in the harbour
of Samgoonoodha: 'We met several Indians in our Way back,
& having arrived at the Brow of the Hill which overlooks the
Harbour where the Ships lie, we met with a very beautiful young
Woman accompanied by her Husband who having some Ornaments about her we had not noticed before, & being altogether
very prettily dressed M.ʳ Webber was willing to have a sketch of
her, and as we had time enough on our Hands we sat down
together and he made a drawing of her; we were all charmed with
the good nature & affability with which she complyed with our
Wishes in staying to have her picture drawn, & with what readiness she stood up or sat down according as she was desired, seeming
very much pleased in having an opportunity to oblige us. She
was withal very communicative & intelligent & it was from her
I learnt that the Name of the Harbour where the Ships lie is
Samgoonoodha.' Cook, *Journals* III, 2, 1124.

Samwell provides a much longer description of the Aleut women
than Cook: 'They are of a copper complexion with a strong red
in their Cheeks, their hair is black and coarse which they tye
behind in a large Club; they have their Cheeks & chins tattawed
or marked and likewise their Arms, their cheek bones are high
like a Scotchman's with this difference that they are well covered
with Flesh, which makes their Faces broad & plump; their Eyes
are black & small and not at right angles with the Nose but
slanting obliquely upwards. They are all cloathed in a seal skin
Frock which reaches from their Necks down to their Feet & the
Sleeves reach to the Hand, so that they are entirely covered
except their Faces & Hands, they wear nothing on their Heads.
They sometimes wear boots & have always a piece of Seal Skin
tyed round the small of their Legs.' Ibid., 2, 1143.

For Samwell's description of the face ornaments see 3.265.

ver: For another drawing of the same woman see 3.264, as for
two related portrait drawings, 3.265 and 3.266. Cf. 3.251
and 3.252 where this or a similar woman is shown on the
house.

British Library, London. Add MS 15514, f.15.

JOHN WEBBER

3.264   A Woman of Unalaska [plate 131]   [Jul 1778]
pencil and grey wash, 20⅜ × 12⅞ : 517 × 328, signed
'J.W. del'.

A full-length figure study for 3.263.

National Maritime Museum, London. (In volume of plates to
Cook's Voyages.)

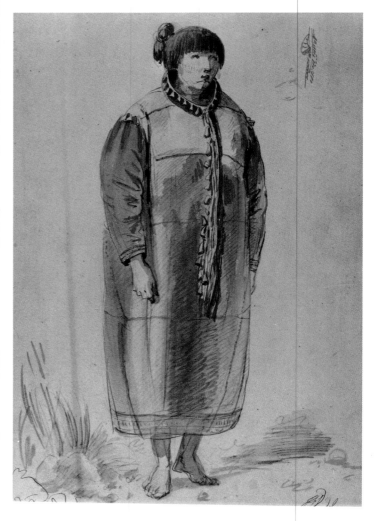

JOHN WEBBER

3.265   A Woman of Oonalaska   [Jul 1778–]
         pen, ink and wash, 17 × 12 : 432 × 299, unsigned.

The drawing can be tentatively identified as no. 88/2 'A portrait
of a Woman' in the 'Aoonalaska' section of Webber's Catalogue.

A half-length figure wearing a close-fitting necklace and a tubular-
shaped seal-skin coat from the seams of which hang pendant
beads; the hair is tied in a knot at the back of the head, and
worn as a fringe across the forehead. There are tattoo lines across
both cheeks, and nose and chin ornaments. The lower lip is
perforated.

'They [the women of Unalaska] have two holes in their under-lip
in which they wear a kind of ornament made of white stone,
which turn up & appear something like whiskers, they have
likewise a string of beads which is made fast to the gristle of the
nose & hangs down to their Chins, by these & the Tattawing
of their Faces they are distinguished from the men as well as by
their dress, the Seal Skin Frock being worn by them only & the
Bird skin Frock & Fish Gut by the Men.' Samwell in Cook,
Journals III, 2, 1143.

It is just possible that the sitter is the same one represented in
3.263 and 3.264. Against that however, are the slight differences
in the ornamentation of the nose (here with a string of beads),
and the different necklaces. Also this sitter has a fringe band
across her breast which is missing from 3.263. Samwell's observations support the facial similarity between 3.263 and 3.265.
'There is a remarkable Similarity, or uniformity in the Countenances of all the Women, much more than we ever saw among
any other People, & same may be said of the Men'. Ibid., 2,
1143.

ver: For a field study of 3.265 see 3.267, and, for a smaller
         version see 3.266, drawn for the engraving, 3.266A.

ref: Bushnell, Jr (1928) pl. 12; Cook, *Journals* III, 1, pl. 52b;
         Exh. Cat. Montreal (1967) no. 67; Honour (1975) no. 179;
         Exh. Cat. Portland (1982) 198.

Listed in Francis Edwards, *Cat.* 416 (London, July 1921) under
no. 769 as 'A Woman of Oonalashka (17 by 12 in), in sepia'.

Peabody Museum of Archaeology and Ethnology, Harvard University, Cambridge, Massachusetts. 41-72-10/504.

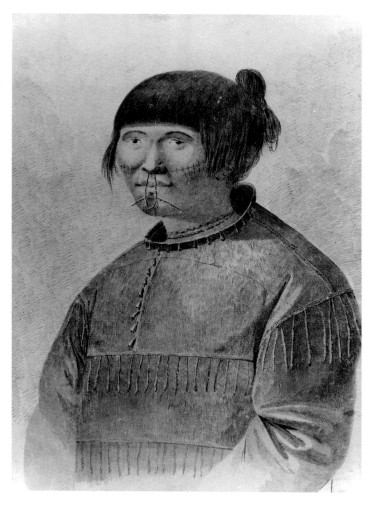

JOHN WEBBER

3.266   A Portrait of a Woman of Oonalaska   [c. 1781-3]
         pencil, pen and light grey washes, 9 × 7 : 228 × 178,
         unsigned.

Inscribed 'A Woman of Oonalashka' in pencil by a later hand
on the folio beneath the drawing.

ver: The same sitter as for 3.265 and 3.267. It has been de-
         veloped from 3.265, but shows minor differences, for ex-
         ample, the fringes of the dress and the necklace. Such
         differences may be based on other studies, or on artefacts
         Webber had at his disposal. This drawing served for the
         engraving 3.266A.

Dixson Library, State Library of New South Wales, Sydney.
PXX 2, 29.

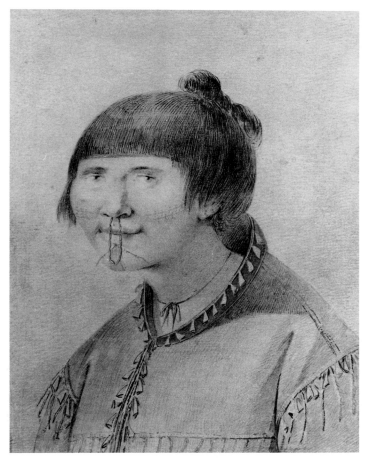

JOHN WEBBER (after)

3.266A 'A WOMAN of OONALASHKA'
Engraving. 'J. Webber del.' — 'Delattre sc.'

Published in Cook/King (1784) pl. 49, II, 510.

A proof-state inscribed in pencil 'A Woman of Oonalaska' in Webber's hand is kept in the National Library of Australia, Canberra, in a folio of plates from Skottowe Hall.

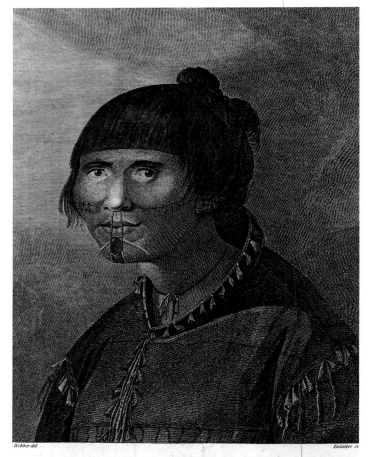

A WOMAN of OONALASHKA.

JOHN WEBBER

3.267 A Portrait of a Woman of Unalaska   [Jul 1778]
charcoal, 8 × 6 : 203 × 152, unsigned.

Half-length portrait of a woman looking right.

A preparatory sketch for 3.265 and 3.266 probably drawn on the spot.

This drawing could be the one listed in Francis Edwards, *Cat.* 551 (London 1932), no. 9 'Native of Cook's River, (8 by 6 in)'.

Francis P. Farquhar Collection, Berkeley, California.

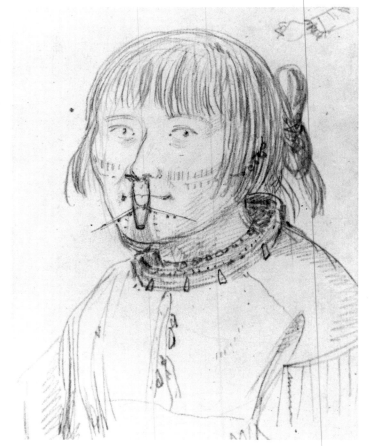

JOHN WEBBER

3.268   **Natives of Unalaska in their kayaks**   [Jul 1778]
pen and water-colour, 12 × 19 : 305 × 483, signed
and dated 'Jn Webber del 1778' (l.r.).

Inscribed in pencil above the lower canoe 'Cape Newenham
America'. The drawing may be tentatively identified as no. 88/8
'Canoes' in the 'Aoonalaska' section of Webber's Catalogue.

Showing two Aleuts in their kayaks on one drawing. For the man
above see 3.249. The lower one is a native from Cape Newenham
and the drawing is therefore placed in this section.

Canoeists of Cape Newenham who approached the ships on 21
July 1778, 'ventured near enough to receive some trifles . . .'
and 'seemed to be the same sort of people as we had lately met
with . . . but were far more dirty and not so well cloathed
. . . For a covering for the head they wore a hood of skin, and
a bonnet which appeared to be of wood . . . The canoes were
made of skins in the same manner as those before mentioned;
they differed a little in their construction from those we saw at
the last place, these were broader and the hole in which the man
sits was wider than any I had before seen.' Cook, *Journals* III, 1,
403. Samwell makes the interesting comment. 'Their Canoes are
exactly the same in shape & make but rather larger & higher out
of the Water; these Indians have double Paddles, but they make
more use of single ones whereas the Natives of Nawanalaska make
use of none but double paddles for their Canoes.' Ibid., 2, 1129.

ver: The drawing at the top is another version of 3.249 (bottom)
and resembles Webber's drawing, 3.250. The top drawing
was engraved (3.249A).

ref: *Exh. Cat.* Portland (1974) 172; *Exh. Cat.* Anchorage (1978)
where the upper drawing (pl. 5) is entitled 'Native of the
Aleutian Islands', and the lower (pl. 6) 'Native of Cape
Newenham'.

Presented by Edward W. Allen 1968. It is not known, whether
the drawing was purchased from Francis Edwards in 1921 when
'Three Drawings of Canoes of Oonalashka (12 by 5in.) in colours'
were listed in *Cat.* 416. under no. 759. Allen bought the drawing
of 'Sea Horses' also listed under 769, (3.278), and we might
assume he bought 3.268 at the same time, were there not a
discrepancy both in the number of canoes and the size of the
drawing, as described by Edwards.

University of Washington, Seattle, Suzzallo Library, Edward W.
Allen Collection.

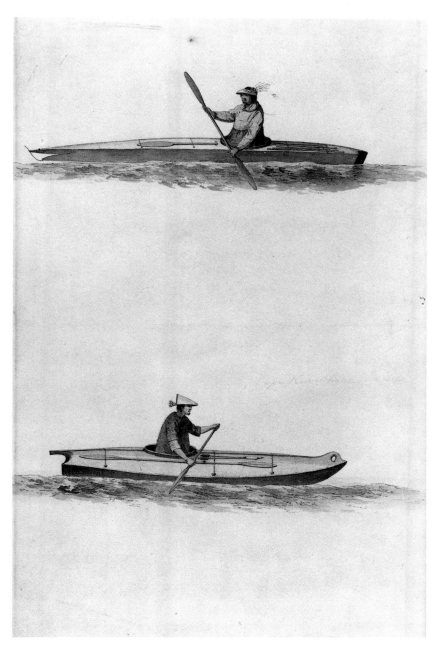

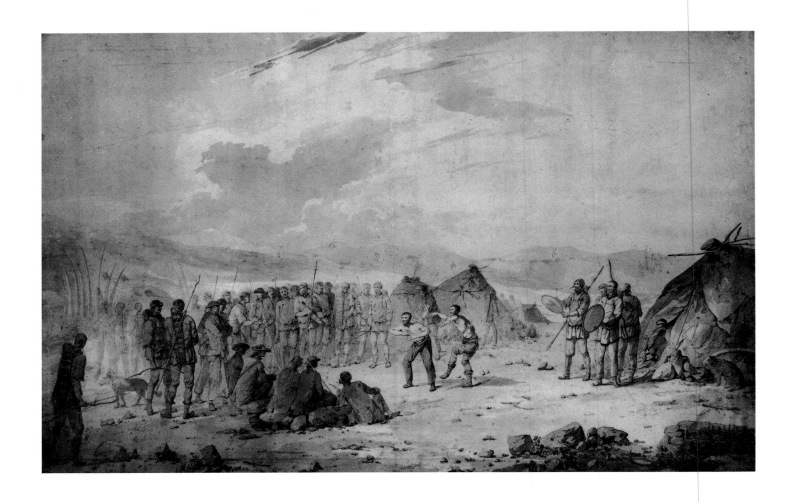

JOHN WEBBER

3.269   **Captain Cook's meeting with the Chukchi at St Law-
         rence Bay [plate 136]**   [Aug 1778–]
         pencil, pen, wash and traces of water-colour, 25½ ×
         39 : 648 × 991, unsigned.

The drawing is listed in the roll section of Webber's Catalogue
as no. 130 'A Tchuski Dance before Capt.ⁿ Cook and his Officers,
with a View of their Habitations'.

Two men dancing, surrounded by armed Chukchi standing nearby;
to the left men of Cook's party mostly seated.

On 10 August 1778 Cook wrote: '. . . nothing we had to offer
them would induce them to part with a Spear or a Bow, which
they held in constant readiness never once quitting them, excepting one time, four or five laid them down while they gave
us a Song and a Dance . . . All the Americans we had seen
before were rather low of Stature with round chubby faces and
high cheek bones, whereas these are long visaged Stout made
men and appeared to be a quite different Nation. . . . The
Country appeared to be exceeding barren, yeilding neither Tree
nor shrub that we could see, some distance in land to the westward

was seen a ridge of Mountains covered with snow that had lately
fell.' Cook, *Journals* III, 1, 411-14.

Samwell also mentions Cook's meeting with the Chukchi and the
scene depicted: 'To entertain us they performed what we supposed
to be their warlike Exercise which consisted of dancing to the
beat of the Drum.' Samwell in ibid., 2, 1133.

ref: Cook, *Journals* III, 1, pl. 46; Skelton (1969) pl. XIV;
         Beaglehole (1974) pl. 40; Smith (1984), pl. 22 (with in-
         correct title and location).

         National Maritime Museum, London. On loan from the
         Admiralty.

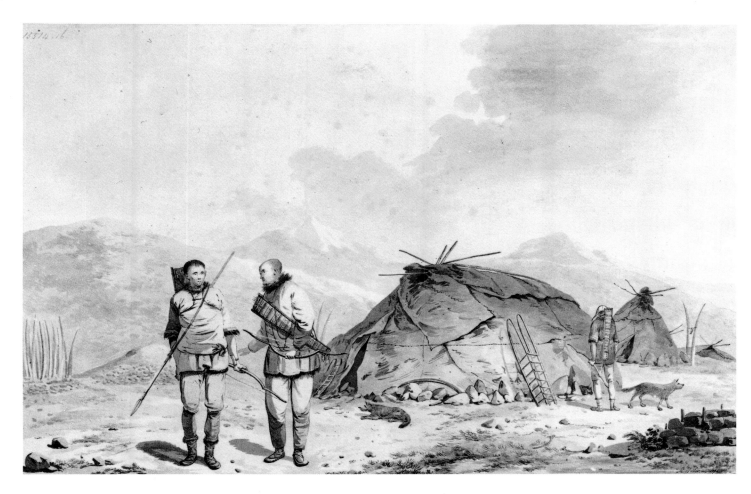

JOHN WEBBER

3.270   Two Chukchi   [Aug 1778–]
pen and wash, 12½ × 19½ : 317 × 495, signed and
dated 'Jn Webber del 1778'.

Titled 'Two Natives of Schutsche' in pencil on lower mount.
The drawing can be tentatively identified as no. 131 'Two of the
Natives with a view of Ditto [their habitation]' in the 'Tchutschi'
section of Webber's Catalogue.

Two Chukchi men armed with bows and arrows at left, a third
figure and a dog at right. Three summer huts (*yarangas*) at right.
In the background behind the figures a hillock (*semidugout*) serving
as another habitation underground.

The tents are summer huts of the Chukchi, which Cook describes
as 'pretty large, and circular and brought to a point at the top;
the framing was of slight poles and bones, covered with the skins
of Sea animals . . . About the habitations were erected several
stages ten or twelve feet high, such as we had observed on some
part of the American coast, they were built wholly of bones and
seemed to be intended to dry skins, fish &ca upon, out of the
reach of their dogs . . .' Cook, *Journals* III, 1, 413. About the
'yarangas' Antropova and Kuznetsova write that the cover was
made of sewn walrus skins 'To prevent its being blown over by
the violent winds . . . the yaranga was tied round with straps,
to which large stones were attached' (1964) 816.

The hillock on the far left appears to be a winter house of the
natives, of which Cook observed that the floor 'is sunk a little
below the surface of the earth'. It was of an oval form, with a
framing of wood and whale bones. 'Over this framing is laid a
covering of strong coarse grass and over it a covering of earth;
so that on the out side it looks like a little hillock, supported by
a wall of stone, about 3 or 4 feet high which is built round the
two sides and one end, at the other end the earth is raised sloaping

to walk up to the entrance which is by a hole in the top of the
roof over that end.' Ibid., 1, 412-13. This last feature is better
shown in 3.271.

A similar description is given by Samwell (ibid., 2. 1133).

The 'semidugouts' had two entrances: a corridor in winter 'and
a round opening on the top, closed with a whale's shoulder blade
and used only in summer' (Antropova/Kuznetsova (1964) 816).

ver: For a smaller version see 3.271. Preparatory studies are at
          3.272 and 3.273.

ref: Kaeppler (1978a) fig. 600; Antropova/Kuznetsova (1964)
          816.

British Library, London. Add MS 15514, f.16.

JOHN WEBBER

3.271 **The Chukchi and Their Habitations**
[plate 138] [c. 1781-3]
pen, wash and water-colour, 8⅞ × 15⅛ : 225 × 384,
unsigned.

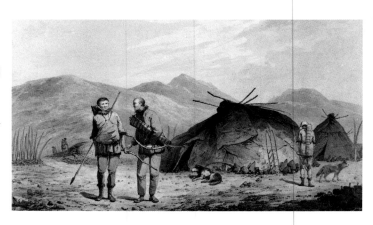

Inscribed 'The Tschuktschi and Their Habitations' in pencil by
a later hand on the folio beneath the drawing.

ver: A small version of 3.270 with variations and drawn for the
engraving 3.271A.

Dixson Library, State Library of New South Wales, Sydney.
PXX 2, 31.

JOHN WEBBER (after)

3.271A **'The TSCHUKTSCHI and their HABITATIONS'**
Engraving. 'J. Webber del.' — 'Lerpiniere sc.'

Published in Cook/King (1784) pl. 51, II, 450-1.

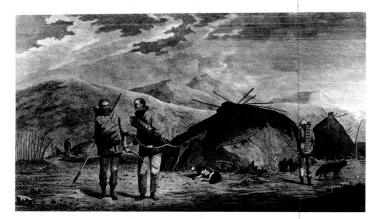

JOHN WEBBER

3.272 **Two Chukchi armed [plate 137]** [Aug 1778–]
pencil, pen, wash and water-colour, 10 × 14⅞ : 254
× 378, unsigned.

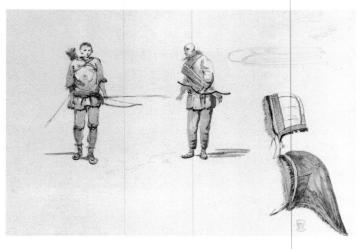

Fully titled 'Natives of Tschutski armed — Sketch from nature'
in pencil on lower mount below the drawing and the enframing
sepia lines.

A study of two Chukchi warriors, used for the warriors in 3.270
and two studies of a cap and a hood. A pencil sketch of a Chukchi
sledge (u.r.).

Cook made extensive notes about the natives' clothes and weapons: 'Thier cloathing consisted of a Cap, a Frock a pair of Breeches,
a pair of Boots and a pair of gloves, all made of leather of the
Skins of Dear, Dogs, Seals &ca all extremely well dress'd some
with the fur or hair on and other with it off. The caps were made
to fit the head very close, and besides these caps which most of
them had on, we got from them some hoods made of dog skins
that were large enough to cover both head and Shoulders. Their
hair seemed to be black, but their heads were either shaved or
the hair cut close off and none wore any beard.' Cook, *Journals*
III, 1, 412.

'The Bow[s] were such as we had seen on the America Coast and
like those used by the Esquimaux's; the Spears or Spontoons were
of Iron or steel and of European or Asiatic workmanship in which
no little pains had been taken to ornament them with carving
and inlayings of brass and a white Metal. Those who stood ready
with Bow and arrows in hand had the Spear slung over their
Shoulder by a leather strap. The Arrows they carried in a lather
quiver slung over the left Shoulder; some of the quivers were
extremely beautifull, being made of red leather on which was very
neat embroidery and other ornaments.' Ibid., 1, 411-12.

British Library, London. Add MS 17277, no. 27.

JOHN WEBBER

3.273 **Summer Huts of the Chukchi** [Aug 1778]
pencil, pen and wash, 10 × 19.¼ : 254 × 489, unsigned. Inscribed 'Tschutski' in pencil on mount (l.r.).

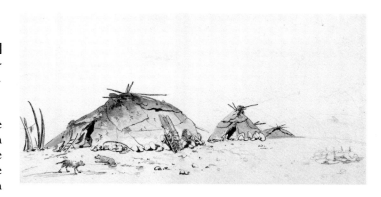

Three huts with two dogs at left.

Writing of the many dogs of the Chukchi, Cook observed: 'These
Dogs are probably of no other use than to draw their sledges in
Winter, for sledges they have as I saw a good many laid up in one
of the Winter-huts; It is also not improbable but dogs may make
a part of their food; several laid dead among them that had been
killed that Morning.' Cook, *Journals* III, 1, 413.

ver: A preparatory study for 3.270.

British Library, London. Add MS 17277, no. 26.

WILLIAM ELLIS

3.274 **Tents of the Chukchi** [Aug 1778]
pen, wash and water-colour, 10 × 13½ : 254 × 343,
signed and dated 'W: Ellis fecᵗ 1778' in black ink (l.r.).
W/m: fleur-de-lis in shield under a crown.

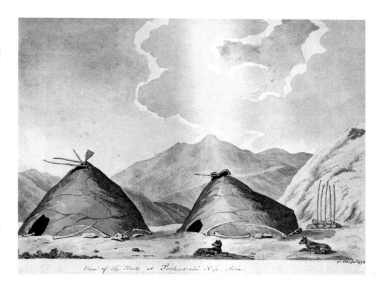

Inscribed in brown ink 'View of the Huts at Tschutschi Noss,
Asia' beneath drawing, and '19' in brown ink (u.l.).

Two tents with mountains behind and two dogs in the foreground.

'Those [huts] which were supposed to be their summer habitations,
were nearly of a cylindrical form, covered with the skins of the
morse, or sea-horse, and propped up or supported by the bones
of whales, as were likewise the roofs of their winter huts.' Ellis
(1782) I, 329.

'There were numbers of dogs, which they keep for the purpose
of drawing their sledges; they were much like those of Kamtschatka, and quite as large . . . In various spots, at some little
distance from their houses, were piles of stones, in which were
placed upright the ribs or jaw-bones of whales.' Ibid., 332.

It seems that Ellis was not speaking from personal observation but
based his story on evidence brought back to the ships. For he
writes: 'Soon after we had anchored, the Resolution's pinnace,
in which was Captain Cook, attended by the large cutters of both
ships, all well manned and armed, proceeded to that part of the
shore where the village was situated.' Ibid., 327. He continues
to relate what 'they' saw, without including himself in the story.
It seems therefore reasonable to conclude that Ellis never saw the
tents of the Chukchi but based his drawing on drawings Webber
had made.

ver: For a study of the dog on the right see Webber's pencil
drawing, inscribed 'Dogs at Kamtschatzka' (3.365).

Museum Book Store, *Cat.* 107 (1928) 41/14 and *Cat.* 125 (1941)
453, with the title as inscribed and 'size 8½ by 11¾ in., signed
W. Ellis, fect. 1778'.

National Library of Australia, Canberra. Rex Nan Kivell Collection. NK 53/L.

505

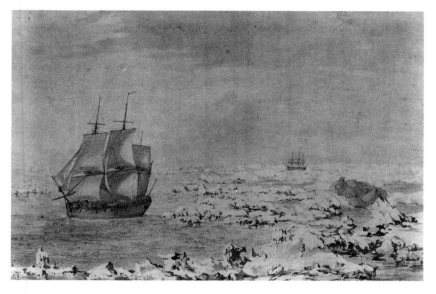

JOHN WEBBER

3.275   The *Resolution* and *Discovery* among the Ice
         [plate 139]   [Aug 1778–]
         pen and wash on sepia-washed paper, 16½ × 24½ :
         419 × 623, signed 'J. Webber del.'.

Inscribed on verso 'Lot 16' in ink and 'Capt. Campbell's' in pencil
on a piece of card preserved in the back of the existing frame.
This may be the drawing described as no. 87 'The Discovery
blocked up' followed by 'in the Ice' in pencil, in Webber's Catalogue. The title is also suggested by the size of the drawing which
is of 'roll' format as opposed to the 'portefeuille' section.

The *Resolution* at left, the *Discovery* apparently blocked in the ice
at right in the distance. A group of sea-elephants in mid-distance
at right.

Cook comments upon the ships' struggle with the ice near Icy
Cape on 18 August 1778 in Lat. 70° 44' 'Our situation was now
more and more critical, we were in shoald water upon a lee shore
and the main body of ice in sight to windward driving down upon
us.' Cook, *Journals* III, 1, 418.

Webber's drawing might also have been prompted by the danger
of the *Discovery* on 23 July 1779, of which Lieutenant James
Burney gives a hair-raising account: 'At 4 in the morning were
obliged to shorten sail on account of the Ice being so thick about
us that we could not avoid running against many large Clumps
which tore off much of our Sheathing . . . At 11 when almost
clear out, got entangled amongst some large pieces which stopped
the Ships way so much that she fell bodily to leeward . . . our
run was so shortened on each tack by the Ice closing that instead
of gaining ground, we fell broadside foremost on the edge of a
small field; having almost an open Sea to windward, the Surf
made the Ship strike violently. The field at length breaking, we
set all our sails for another trial: but before the ship gathered way

enough to be under command, we again fell to leeward on some
more. As the swell made it very dangerous and unsafe to lay
windward of all, and as there was no chance of getting clear, we
pushed for a small opening into the Ice . . . The Resolution bore
SEbE distant 3 miles, under sail and seemingly clear of the ice.
Half an hour after Noon lost sight of her. Found the Ship drift
with the body of the ice towards the NW at above half a Knot.

'At 4 in the Afternoon the Ice was close all round and as far as
could be seen except between the South and ESE, where at the
distance of 3/4 of a mile from us it was still loose and open. At
5 the wind veered round to the NE, and at 6 to the North, which
made the Ice begin to seperate. Took up our Ice hooks and made
Sail towards the SE, the Ice slowly giving way as the Ship pressed
against it. Heard a Gun from the Resolution which we answered.'
Burney in Cook, *Journals* III, 1, 697-8.

Though the description by Burney makes it possible (if unlikely)
that the moment represented in Webber's drawing was experienced on 23 July 1779, when the two ships were commanded by
Captain Clerke, the drawing has been catalogued in the section
here for August 1778. It is possible that both engagements with
the ice were fused by Webber into the one picture.

ver: For Webber's pencil drawing in the preparation of his soft-
         ground etching, see 3.276.

ref: Bushnell, Jr (1928), pl. 8; *Exh. Cat.* Montreal (1967), no.
         18; *Exh. Cat.* Portland (1982), 195, there erroneously cat-
         alogued as from the Peabody Museum, Salem.

Listed in Francis Edwards, *Cat.* 416 (London, July 1921) under
no. 769, as 'The Resolution Beating through the Ice with the
Discovery in Danger in the Distance (24½ by 17 in), in sepia'.

Peabody Museum of Archaeology and Ethnology, Harvard University, Cambridge, Massachusetts. 41-72-10/508.

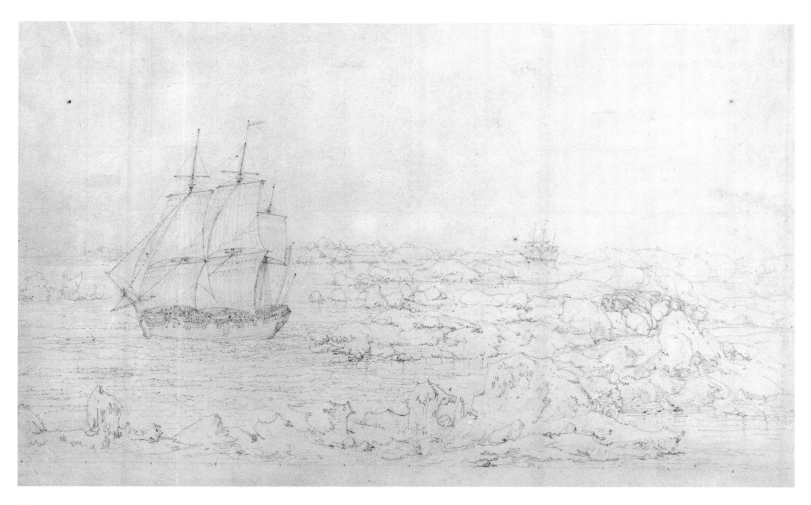

JOHN WEBBER

3.276   **The *Resolution* beating through the Ice with the *Discovery* in the most eminent danger in the distance** [c. 1792]
pencil, 10⅛ × 16¾ : 260 × 426; w/m: 'J. WHATMAN'

On verso inscribed 'Dessein d' Apres la Nature Voyez' (followed by indecipherable words).

The drawing is squared for transfer and is likely to be a preparatory study for Webber's softground etching of the title above, published 1 August 1792 (3.276A).

In comparing the drawing with the print one notices a few small differences: for example the drawing does not show the lookout man on the foremast, it also lacks the ice floats in the front of the *Resolution* at the extreme left which are clearly visible in the print. There are further minor differences concerning the sea elephants. These differences suggest that the drawing is an original work by Webber prepared for the softground etching rather than a copy after the print.

ref: White (1977) 42, no. 65.

Purchased by Mr Mellon from the American book dealer Eberstadt.

Yale Center for British Art, Paul Mellon Collection, New Haven.

3.276A   **a. 'The *Resolution* beating through the Ice, with the *Discovery* in the most eminent danger in the distance'** softground etching, tinted in brown and grey wash, or hand-coloured, $12^{11}/_{16}$ × $17^5/_8$: 322 × 448 ($11^5/_{16}$ × $16^7/_{16}$: 287 × 417). 'J. Webber R.A. fecit'. 'London Publish^d Aug! 1 1792 by J. Webber N°. 312 Oxford Street'. 'Vide Cooks last Voyage vol. III page 257'.

ver: For Webber's original drawing see 3.276.

British Museum, Department of Prints and Drawings, London. 246˙ a.2 and C. 6˙.

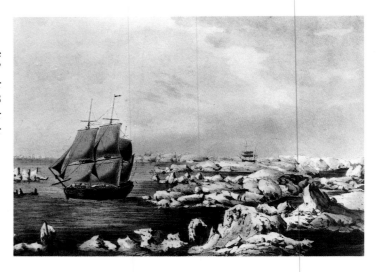

  b. 'The *Resolution* beating through the Ice, with the *Discovery* in the most eminent danger in the distance' Coloured aquatint. 'I. Webber R.A. fecit'. 'London Pub^d April 1. 1809 by Boydell & Comp.^{y} N°. 90 Cheapside'. 'Vide Capt. Cooks last Voyage Vol. III page 257'.

Issued as J. Boydell, *Views in the South Seas* (London, 1808) pl. IX.

National Maritime Museum, London; Bernice P. Bishop Museum, Honolulu.

3.276   **c.**

A copy of 3.276A by an unknown eighteenth century copyist in pen, wash and water-colour, measuring $14^7/_8$ × $19^1/_2$: 378 × 496 inscribed in ink lower margin 'The Resolution beating through the Ice with the Discovery in the most eminent danger in the distance V. III, p. 257'. The drawing has been considerably enlarged in the foreground. It also has errors in the ships' rigging. *In litt.* B. T. Carter, 6 November 1969.

Mistakenly attributed to Webber by Beaglehole in Cook, *Journals* III, 1, pl. 47; Rienits (1968) 130; Skelton (1969) pl. XVI.

National Maritime Museum, London.

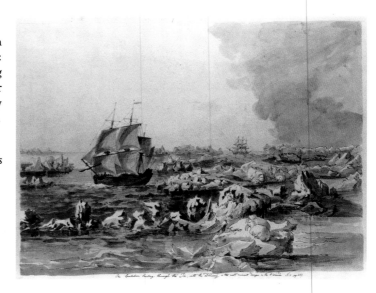

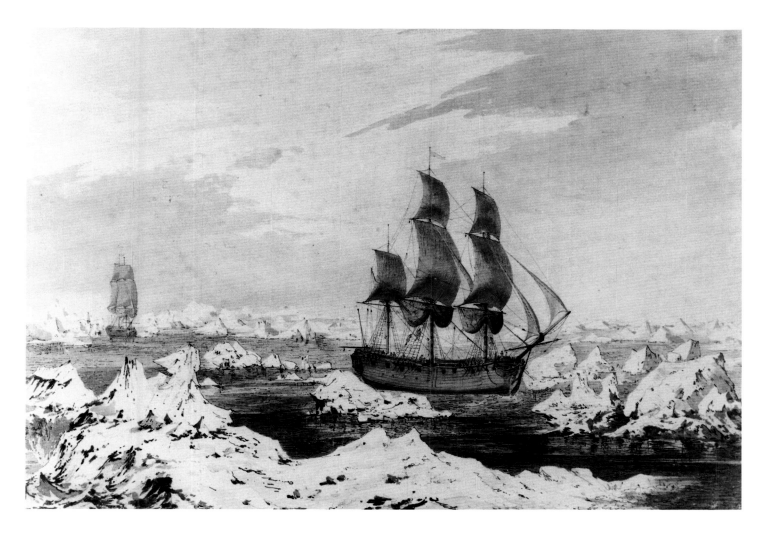

JOHN WEBBER

3.277   The *Resolution* and *Discovery* Among the Ice
[Aug 1778–]
pen, wash and water-colour, 12 × 19 : 305 × 482,
unsigned.

For inscriptions on the back see below. The drawing may .be tentatively identified as no. 86 'A View of the Resolution and Discovery among the Ice' in Webber's Catalogue.

The *Resolution* in the front and to the right sailing from left to right, but largely surrounded by ice. The *Discovery* in the distance on the left.

ver: The composition, though reversed, is somewhat similar to the drawing of 3.275.

ref: Brewington (1968) 455, no. 1746.

Laid down on the backing of the present frame is a piece of card from a former backing, bearing the inscription in ink 'Hawaian Collection 379 of Stephen W. Phillips. Bt. in London 1921 of Francis Edwards TX 24, Cook's ships in the Ice an unpublished sketch by James Webber. The artist who accompanied Cook on the Third Voyage'. On another card below in pencil:'. . . these original sketches by Webber were sold in London 1920-1, for very large prices. I was able to get this one but couldn't get the Hawaiian ones as they were sold together.' S.W. Phillips, Salem 1921.

Peabody Museum, Salem. Gift of Stephen W. Phillips, 1947. M. 12463.

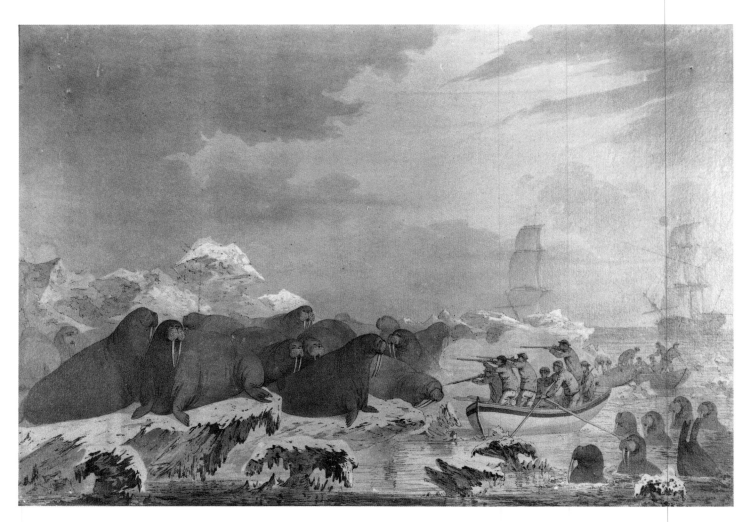

JOHN WEBBER

3.278   **Shooting Sea Horses [plate 141]**   [Aug 1778–]
pen and water-colour, 17¼ × 24¾ : 438 × 629, signed and dated 'J. Webber del. 1778'.

The drawing can be tentatively identified as no. 88 'Our Method of Killing the Sea Horse or Morse' in Webber's Catalogue.

A party of men from the ships firing at walrus. In the background one shot is loaded on to a boat; towards the horizon are the two ships.

The first shooting of walrus occurred on 19 August, a second and third on 27 and 28 August 1778: 'On the ice lay a prodigious number of Sea horses and as we were in want of fresh provisions the boats from each ship were sent to get some. (19 August)' Cook, *Journals* III, 1, 419. 'They lay in herds of many hundred upon the ice, huddling one over the other like swine, and roar or bray very loud, so that in the night or foggy weather they gave us notice of the ice long before we could see it. We never found the Whole herd a sleep, some were always upon the watch, these, on the approach of the boat, would wake those next to them and these the others, so that the whole herd would be awake presently. But they were seldom in a hurry to get away till after they had been once fire[d] at, then they would tumble one over the other into the sea in the utmost confusion, and if we did not at the first discharge kill those we fired at out right we generally lost them tho' mortally wounded. They did not appear to us to be that dangerous animal some Authors have discribed, not even when attacked, they are rather more so to appearance than reality.'

Ibid., 420. 'Pennant in his *Syn. Quadr.* p.335, has given a very good discription of this Animal under the Name of Arctick Walrus, but I have no were seen a good drawing of one. Why they should be called Sea horses, is hard to say unless it be a corruption of the Russian name Morse, for it has not the least similitude to a Horse . . ..' Ibid., 420-1.

Walrus were again shot during the ships' second stay in the ice, on 11 July 1779 (cf. Clerke in ibid., 1, 692).

ver: A similar but smaller drawing at 3.279. There exist two similar drawings of a walrus by William Ellis, which bear a close resemblance to Webber's walrus in the centre of the picture, lying on the edge of the ice. Ellis's drawings are preserved in the British Museum (Natural History), London among his '115 original water-colour sketches of animals . . .', see 3.432, and in the Alexander Turnbull Library, Wellington, see 3.433.

ref: *Exh. Cat.* Portland (1974) no. 174; *Exh. Cat.* Anchorage (1978) pl. 7; Henry (1984) 79.

The drawing has the same dimensions as the one listed in Francis Edwards's *Cat* 416 (London, July 1921) under no. 769 as 'Sea horses (24½ by 17 in), in sepia) and is no doubt identical. Presented by Edward W. Allen 1968.

University of Washington, Seattle. Suzzallo Library, Edward W. Allen Collection.

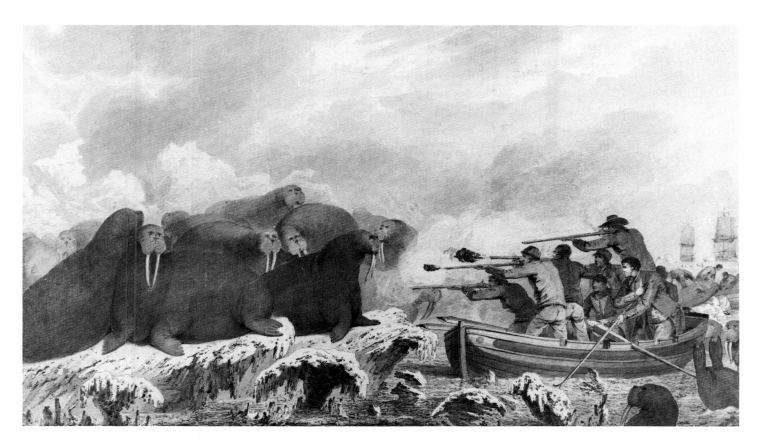

JOHN WEBBER

3.279 Sea Horses [c. 1781-3]
pen, wash and water-colour, 8⅝ × 14⅞ : 220 × 378, unsigned.

Titled 'Sea Horses' in pencil by a later hand on the folio beneath the drawing.

The drawing for the engraving 3.279A.

Dixson Library, State Library of New South Wales, Sydney. PXX 2, 32.

JOHN WEBBER (after)

3.279A 'SEA HORSES'
Engraving. 'Drawn by J. Webber' — 'Engraved by E. Scott' — 'The Figures by J. Heath'.

Published in Cook/King (1784) pl. 52, II, 457-8, 464.

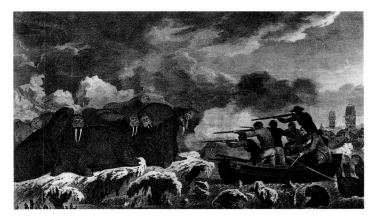

A proof-state inscribed in pencil 'Shooting Sea Horses Lat. 71 N.' in Webber's hand is kept in the National Library of Australia, Canberra, in a folio of plates from the Skottowe Hall Library.

JOHN WEBBER

3.280 **A Party from His Majesty's ship *Resolution*, shooting Sea Horses [plate 142]** [1784]
oil on canvas, 49 × 61½ : 1245 × 1562, unsigned.

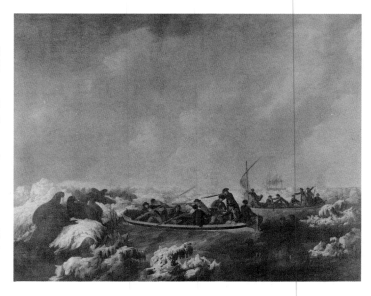

Group of walrus at left being fired at by men in a boat. Several in the water, right foreground; further off a second boat. *Resolution* and *Discovery* in the distance among the ice.

Exhibited at the R.A. in 1784 (140) under the title 'A Party from his Majesty's ship Resolution, on Captain Cook's last voyage, shooting sea horses, Latitude 71° north in the year 1778'.

ver: Similar to the engraving 3.279A.

ref: Listed as 'A Party from H.M. Ships "Resolution" and "Discovery" shooting Sea Horses, Lat. 71° N' in the Admiralty *Cat.* (1911), no. 48; *Exh. Cat.* London (1951/52) 35 (54); Smith (1960) pl. 61; (1985) pl. 72.

Admiralty House, London.

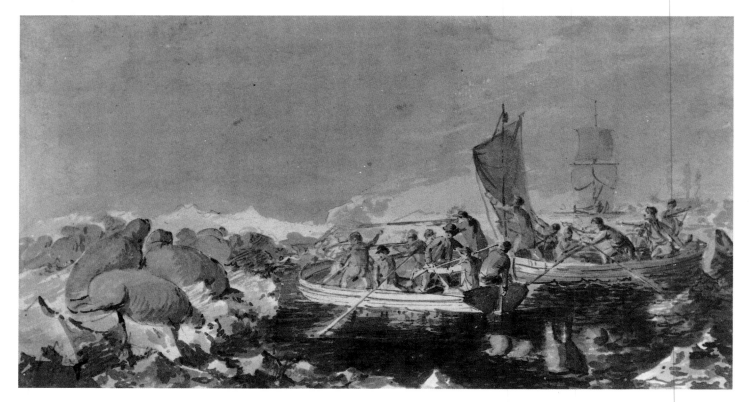

JOHN WEBBER

3.281 **Shooting Sea Horses on an Ice flow**
[plate 143] [Aug 1778–]
charcoal and grey wash, 5⅜ × 10⅛ : 137 × 258, unsigned. On verso random ink jottings.

At left a herd of walrus on an ice-floe; in the central foreground a ship's boat, and behind it to the right another, both filled with men preparing to hunt the walrus; in the first boat one man stands aiming a musket at the herd. One of the ships in the distance.

ver: A version developed from 3.282. Both 3.281 and 3.282 resemble 3.278 to 3.280 and probably depict the same incident.

ref: Smith (1960) pl. 59; Cook, *Journals* III, 1, pl. 48; Henry (1984) 78; Smith (1985) pl. 70.

The Public Archives of Canada, Ottawa. I-10 (c. 2620).

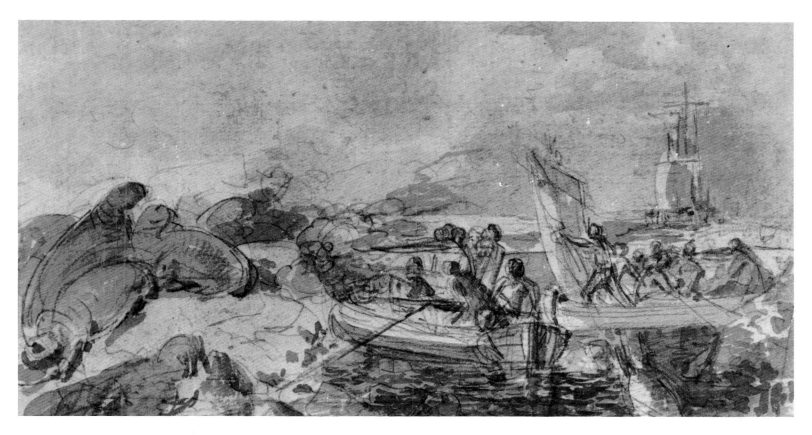

JOHN WEBBER

3.282 **Shooting Sea Horses on an Ice flow** **[Aug 1778]**
pencil, pen, charcoal and wash, 6⅜ × 11¹³⁄₁₆ :
162 × 300, unsigned, laid down on card; w/m:
'[PO]RTAL'.

A study for 3.281, possibly made on location.

ref: Smith (1960) pl.60, (1985) pl.71; Rienits (1968) 116.

The Public Archives of Canada, Ottawa. I-11 (c 2621).

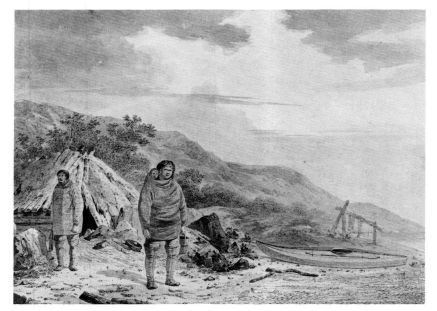

JOHN WEBBER

3.283   **Inhabitants of Norton Sound and their Habitations**
         [plate 145]   **[Sep 1778]**
         pen, wash and water-colour, 12½ × 16¾ : 317 × 426,
         signed and dated 'J. Webber 1778'.

Inscribed 'Norton Sound' in pencil on mount below drawing. This drawing is probably the one referred to as '84 A View of the Natives and their Habitations' in the Norton Sound section of Webber's Catalogue.

In the central foreground a woman with a child on her right shoulder, both covered by a cloak, and carrying a wooden bucket; at left behind her a man and a log hut. A kayak drawn up on the shore at right, behind a rack for hanging nets and drying fish.

Descriptions of the inhabitants of Norton Sound, who were only encountered briefly, are sparse. The family whom Webber has drawn may be the one which Cook met on the afternoon of 13 September ' . . . a family of the Natives came near to the place where we were taking off wood . . . I saw no more than a Man, his wife and child . . .' Cook, *Journals* III, 1, 438.

The description that King gives in part reflects Webber's representation: 'Some of their Jackets were made with a good deal of Taste & instead of resembling a close shirt or farmers frock, as amongst the other Indians, those had an opening at the hips & hung down before & behind in circular flap; they wore leather breeches, or rather trousers, that came half way down the leg, some had boots. All their Jackets had hoods to them, & we did not observe that they had any covering to their head. . . . The good woman had a child upon her back cover'd with the hood of her Jacket; I thought it some bundle till it began to whimper, but on the womans saying some words in a Soothing tone, it remain'd very quiet.' Ibid., 2, 1439.

Samwell described the houses: 'This part of the Coast is but thinly inhabited, the Houses are built together in small Villages on the Sea Shore but we saw a lonely hut here & there on the flat land at a great distance from any others; they are built of different Shapes but mostly square, they are but small, will not contain above 6 or 7 people conveniently; some of them have flat roofs others slanting, they are ab.! six feet high in the middle & 5 or six yards long & as many broad; the sides of them are made by laying one Timber on another horizontally, others are constructed with Timbers fixed in the Ground & slanting obliquely upwards, with the interstices filled up with Grass; the Tops are covered with Grass & stones.' Ibid., 2, 1136.

ref: Cook, *Journals* III, 1, pl.50.

British Library, London. Add MS 15514, f.18.

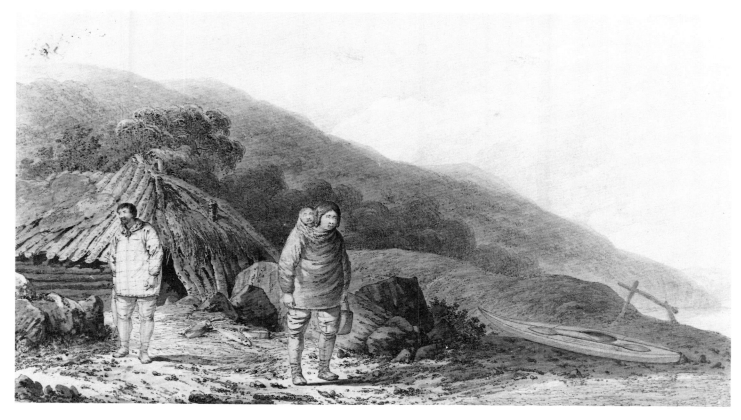

JOHN WEBBER

3.284   Inhabitants of Norton Sound and their Habitations
                                                [c. 1781-3]
pen, wash and water-colour, 8¾ × 15 : 222 × 381,
unsigned.

The title as above in pencil by a later hand on the folio beneath
the drawing.

ver: A small version of 3.283 drawn for the engraving 3.284A.

Dixson Library, State Library of New South Wales, Sydney.
PXX 2, 33.

JOHN WEBBER (after)

**3.284A   'INHABITANTS of NORTON SOUND, and their
HABITATIONS'**
Engraving. 'J. Webber del.' — 'B.T. Pouncy sc.'

Published in Cook/King (1784) pl. 54, II, 480-1.

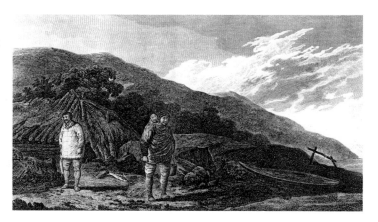

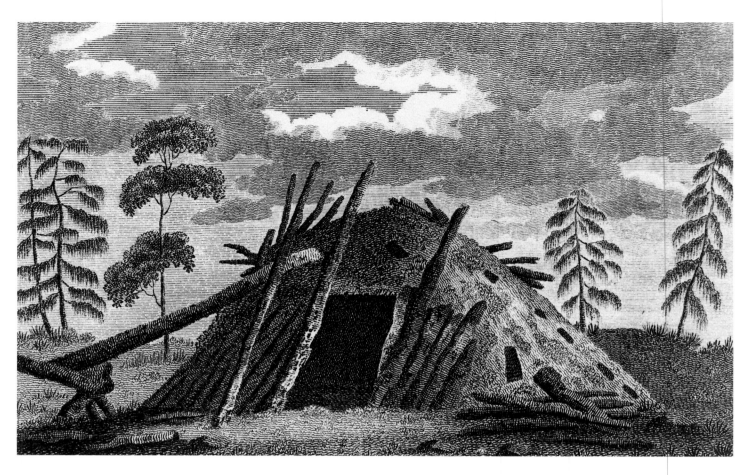

WILLIAM ELLIS (after)

3.284B **'A Hut in the West Coast of America, Lat. 65° 30′ N.'**
Engraving. 'W. Ellis del.' — 'W. Ellis direx!' 'Published Dec! 14th 1781 by G. Robinson'.

Published in Ellis, (1782) II, fp. 11.

The place of this hut cannot be properly identified. Judging from the placement of the engraving within Ellis's account, it could be one of the huts which were observed near Cape Denbigh (1 September 1778).

'Upon different parts of the beach, under the hills were several huts, but in a very ruinous condition, from their appearance, we supposed them to be erected merely for the temporary employment of fishing: they were built of drift-wood, the roofs, which were almost flat, with a hole in the middle for the evacuation of smoke, were supported by four stout posts.' Ellis (1782) II, 11.

The hut also corresponds to a type of habitation found near Norton Sound. King described them: 'their houses differd widely, for we saw none underground [like those at Samgoonoodha]; these here are form'd of stout upright posts about 6 feet high, & extending 8 or 10 feet on each side; upon the top of these were laid cross posts of the same thickness, a little slanting, cover'd with Sod, the sides were all chinced with Moss; in the front on the inside was the fire Place, & on the two sides & back were smaller logs covered with dried hay, on which they slept.' Cook, *Journals* III, 2, 1440.

No drawing for this engraving is known.

SAMGOONOODHA, [ENGLISH BAY], UNALASKA: SECOND VISIT

3 to 26 October 1778   3.285–3.292A

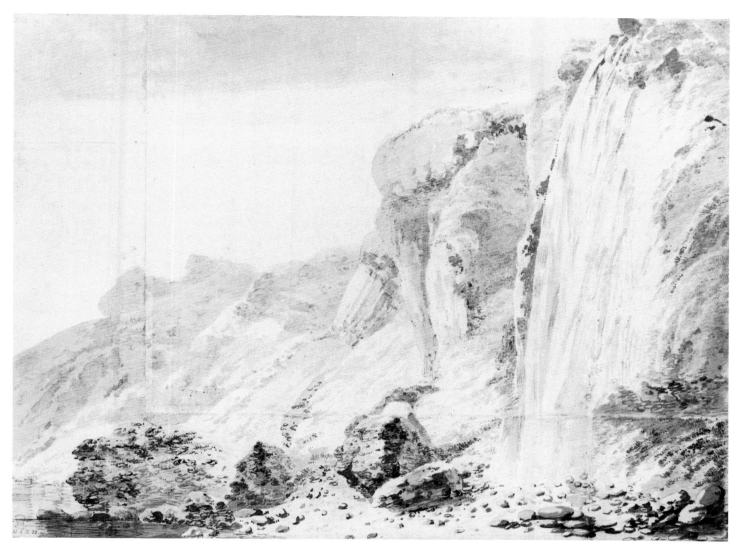

JOHN WEBBER

3.285   [A Waterfall in Unalaska]   [1778]
pencil and wash, 19½ × 26 : 495 × 660. There are
traces of a signature (l.l.), where dated 1778.

This is probably the drawing referred to in Webber's Catalogue
88/10 'Aoonalaska — America 10. A Water Fall'.

Rugged and rocky scenery with a waterfall on the right. The
slopes grown over by moss and shrubs. In the foreground lumps
of stone, partly overgrown. The place depicted has not been
identified.

British Library, London. Add MS 15514, f. 19.

3.286   **A Man of Oonalaska**   [Oct 1778]
pen and ink on browned paper, 17 × 12 : 432 × 300, unsigned.

On the verso of a former piece of card backing now preserved in the new frame, is inscribed 'Lot No. 9' and in pencil 'Men at King George's Sound. Capt. Campbell.' Cleaned by the Department of Conservation, Fogg Art Museum, Harvard University in February 1977. This drawing is likely to be one of the two portraits of a man listed as no. 88/3 and 88/4 in the 'Aoonalaska' section of Webber's Catalogue.

A half-length portrait of an Aleut man looking three-quarter left. He wears an eye-shade or visor, with whiskers to which beads are attached. A small figure carved of walrus ivory is fastened to the crest. He wears an ornament through the nose and another one button-shaped beneath the lower lip, and a frock with a hood drawn around the neck.

Compare Cook's description of Unalaskan dress: '. . . Over this frock the Men wear a nother made of Gut which resists water and has a hood to it to draw over the head. . . . all of them [wear] a kind of oval snouted Cap made of wood, with a rim to admet the head: these are dyed with green and other Colours, and round the upper part of the rim, are stuck the long bristles of some sea animal on which are strung glass beads, and on the front is a small image or two made out of bone.' Cook, *Journals* III, 1, 459-60.

A good description of the caps or visors is provided by Samwell (ibid., 2, 1142); Ellis specifies that the caps 'are generally painted blue and green' and decorated 'with the beards of whales, upon which they place beads and some of them fix two or three small carved pieces of bone (in the form of an image) upon the upper part, and on one side'. Ellis (1782) II, 47.

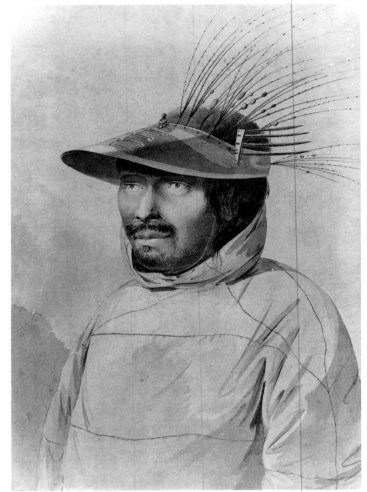

It is interesting that in this and the other portrait drawing (3.287) Webber represents two different chin ornaments, echoing an observation by King: '. . . what the men have thrust thro the hole in the underlip has the resemblance of 2 Boars tusks, and are 2 pieces of bone about 1½ Inch long joining in the middle of the lip, & seperating, by means of the tongue they can move these bones, & make them point up and down. Others have a single polished bone the shape and size of a large Stud.' Cook, *Journals* III, 2, 1427.

ver: For a smaller version see 3.287. For a field study, 3.288.

ref: Bushnell Jr (1928) pl. 9; Cook, *Journals* III, 1, pl. 52a; Rienits (1968) 141; King (1981) pl. 11; *Exh. Cat.* Portland (1982) 199.

Listed in Francis Edwards, *Cat.* 416 (London, July 1921) under no. 769 as 'A Man of Oonalashka (17 by 12 in) in sepia, on strainer and varnished'.

Peabody Museum of Archaeology and Ethnology, Harvard University, Cambridge, Massachusetts. 41-72-10/503.

JOHN WEBBER

3.287   **A Portrait of a Man of Oonalaska**   [c. 1781-3]
pencil, pen, wash and water-colour, 8⅞ × 6⅞ : 226 × 175, unsigned.

Inscribed 'A Man of Oonalashka' in pencil by a later hand on the folio beneath the drawing.

ver: A smaller version of 3.286 prepared for the engraving 3.287A.

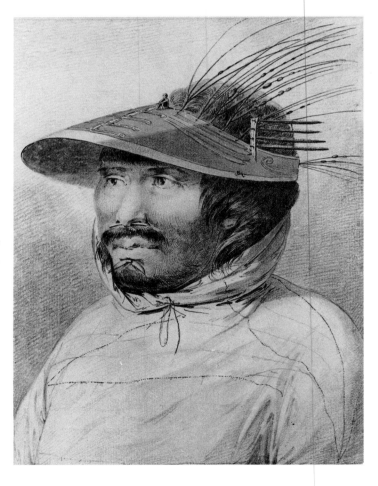

Dixson Library, State Library of New South Wales, Sydney. PXX 2, 28.

JOHN WEBBER (after)

3.287A 'A MAN of OONALASHKA'
Engraving. 'J. Webber del.' — 'W. Sharp sc.'

Published in Cook/King (1784) pl. 48, II, 510.

A proof-state inscribed in pencil 'A Man of Oonalaska' in Webber's hand and numbered in pencil 'N°. 50' in upper right is kept in the National Library of Australia, Canberra, in a folio of plates from the Skottowe Hall Library.

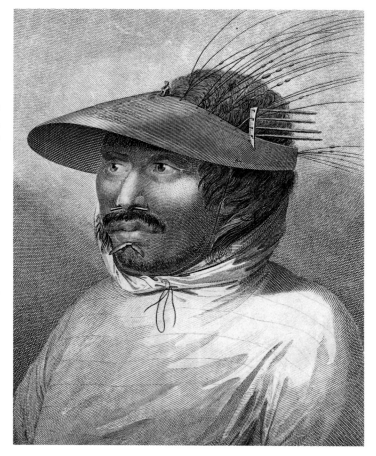

JOHN WEBBER

3.288 A Man of Oonalaska [Oct 1778]
charcoal and wash, 9 × 6¹⁵⁄₁₆ : 228 × 176, unsigned.

Inscribed 'Oonalashka' in pencil (u.r.).

Field study of the head of a man wearing a visor with thin whiskers and beads attached to the rim.

ver: For more developed drawings of a man wearing a similar cap see 3.286 and 3.287.

British Library, London. Add MS 17277, no. 24.

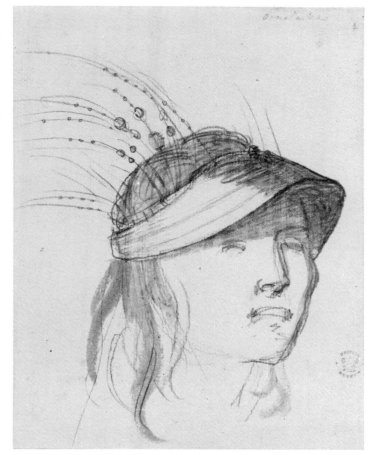

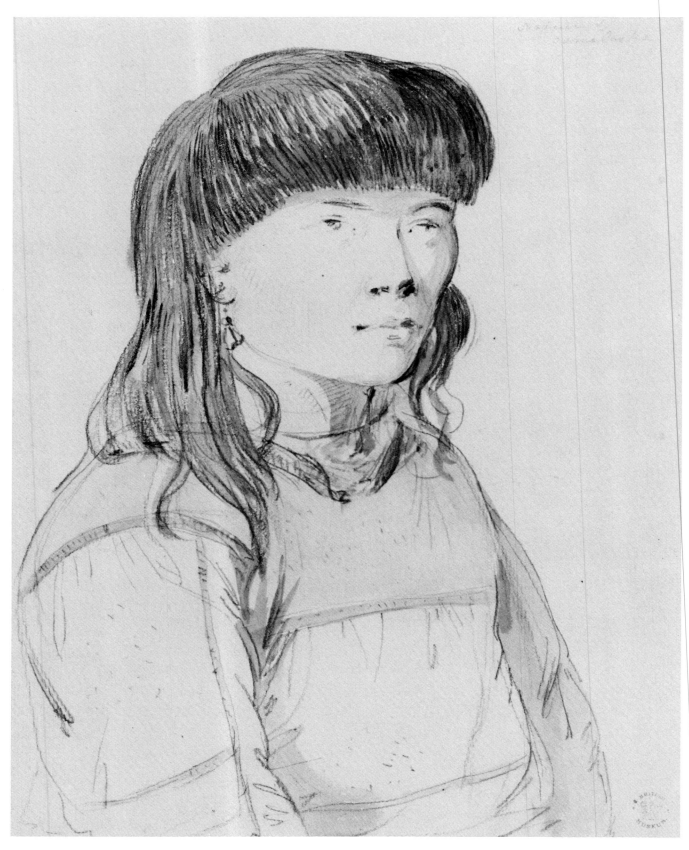

JOHN WEBBER

3.289   **A Woman of Oonalaska**   [Oct 1778]
        charcoal, wash and water-colour, 12¹¹⁄₁₆ × 10¹⁄₁₆:
        322 × 255, unsigned.

Inscribed in pencil' Native of Oonalaska' (u.r.).

The head of a woman wearing ear-ornaments, which are lacking
from Webber's other known portraits of women of Unalaska. It
may be noted that the sitter wears neither nose nor chin ornaments.

British Library, London. Add MS 17277, no. 28.

520

WILLIAM ELLIS

3.290   A Man of Unalaska   **[1779]**
pencil, wash and water-colour, 7¼ × 6¾ : 181 ×
175, signed and dated in pencil 'W. Ellis fect 1779' (l.r.);
w/m: 'VG' (cut off, but probably LVG = Lubertus van
Gerrevink).

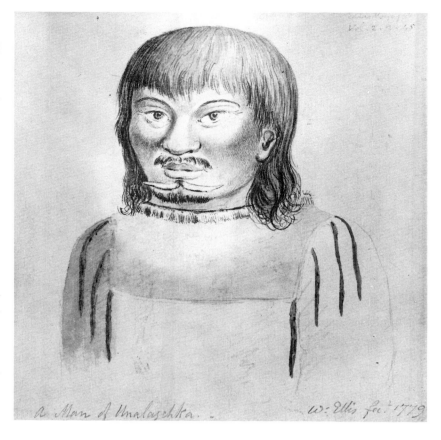

A Man of Unalaschka.   W: Ellis fect 1779

Inscribed by Ellis (?) 'A Man of Unalaschka' in pencil (l.l.);
annotated in a different hand in pencil 'Ellis Voyage Vol 2 p.
45' (u.r.). Inscribed in ink on verso '65'.

The head and shoulders of a man facing slightly to the left, with
moustache and small beard beneath the chin, and wearing an
ornament beneath the lower lip; the jacket fur-trimmed at the
neck, with stripes of fur around the shoulders.

The head is apparently a study for the engraving 3.290A. 'Their
face is broad, their eyes rather small, their nose in general flat,
their mouth wide, and lips thick . . . Their hair is black, and
rather long behind, but cut before, so as to reach nearly to their
eye-lids . . . The common dress of the men is a jacket, made of
the skins of birds, the feathered side worn inwards; but their best
jackets are painted red on the fore and hind part, as low as the
shoulders and breast, and at the insertion of the sleeves along
the seam, and on the body of the jacket, are fastened strips of
fur, in rows, one row about eight inches above the other.' Ellis
(1782) II, 45.

ver: The sitter is vaguely similiar to Webber's drawing of 3.259.
          However, the shape and position of the ornament differs.

ref: Murray-Oliver (1977) 36.

Alexander Turnbull Library, Wellington. A 264.41.

WILLIAM ELLIS (after)

3.290A   'A Man of the Island of Unalaschka'
Engraving. 'W. Ellis del.' — 'J. Collyer sculp!'. 'Publish'd Dec! 14th 1781.by G. Robinson'.

Published in Ellis (1782) II, fp. 45 (45 as well as I, 289).

No exact drawing for this engraving is known. There is some
similarity between this figure and Ellis's portrait (3.290) as well
as Webber's representations (3.259 and 3.260) though with differences: Ellis's is bare-footed and holds a basket.

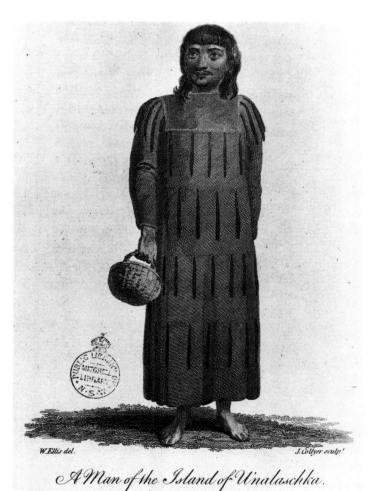

W. Ellis del.   J. Collyer sculp!

A Man of the Island of Unalaschka.

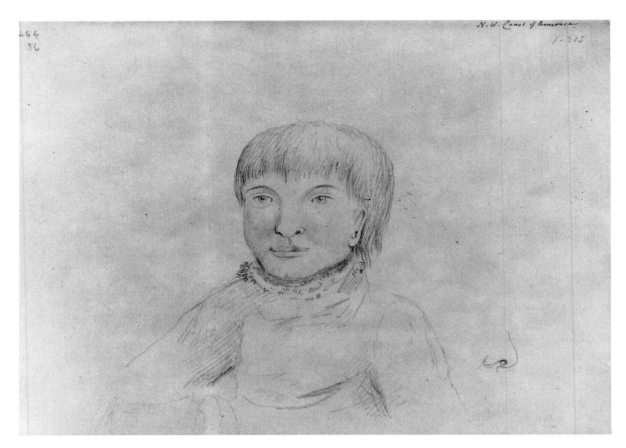

WILLIAM ELLIS

3.291   A Woman of Unalaska   [1778]
pencil, 7⅜ × 10⁷⁄₁₆ : 187 × 265, unsigned.

Inscribed in ink 'N.W. Coast of America' (u.r.). Numbered in pencil (u.r.) '1.213' referring to Ellis (1782). On verso inscribed in ink '54'.

A full-face portrait of the head and shoulders, wearing a jacket with a fur-trimmed neck; at right, the detail of a nose with the septum perforated for holding an ornament.

The inscription '1.213' is misleading for it refers to the Indians of Nootka and in particular to the men. It seems however more likely that the sitter was depicted on the Alaskan coast, judging from the jacket worn and the short hair. The piercing of the septum of the nose and the bored ears are also characteristic of people of this area.

ref: Murray-Oliver (1977) 35 where A264.36 is described as a man.

Alexander Turnbull Library, Wellington. A 264.36.

WILLIAM ELLIS (after)

3.291A   'A Woman of Unalaschka'
Engraving. 'W. Ellis del.' — 'J. Heath sc.'. 'Publish'd Dec.ʳ 14ᵗʰ 1781 by G. Robinson'.

Published in Ellis (1782) II, fp. 46 (46-7 as well as I, 289).

'There were only two women, one very old and grey-headed, the other who appeared to be about twenty, had a child in her arms; she was dressed in a seal-skin jacket, and her cheeks were marked or tatowed in a particular manner; she had an ornament in her under-lip made of bone, and was to all appearance, tolerably neat and clean.' Ellis (1782) I, 289.

No drawing for this engraving is known.

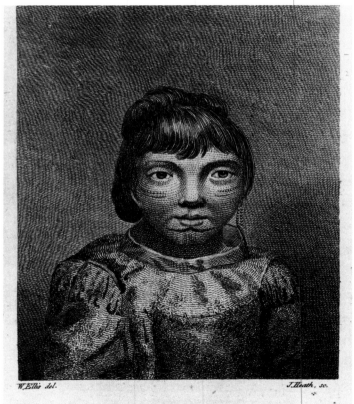

A Woman
of Unalaschka.

Publish'd Dec.ʳ 14ᵗʰ 1781, by G.Robinson.

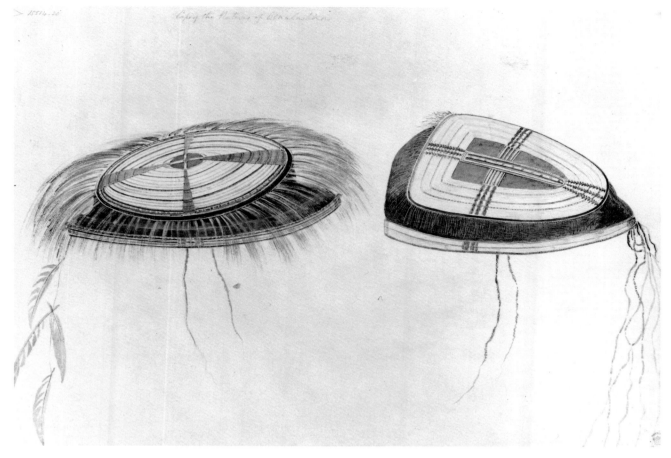

JOHN WEBBER

3.292 Caps of the Natives of Oonalaska [Oct 1778–]
water-colour, wash and gouache, 14⅝ × 21¹⁄₁₆ :
371 × 535, unsigned.

The title as above in pencil. (u.c.). This drawing may probably
be identified with '88/5 Caps wore at particular Ceremonies' in
the 'Aoonalaska' section in Webber's Catalogue.

Two caps of triangular and oval shape. They do not appear to
have been described in the journals.

Samwell probably comes nearest when talking about the women's
dexterity with the needle: 'The Women make very curious Baskets
of different Kinds variously ornamented & beautiful Matts, some
of their Baskets are worked so close with Straw that they will hold
Water; they have Tobacco pouches & other little articles such
as small Bags &c made of Skins which they ornament very pretty
with their Needles. *curious Caps.* [our italics].' Cook, *Journals*
III, 2, 1146.

Ellis provides the interesting addition that because of the women's
love for embroidery: ' . . . our needles being so far superior to
their own, proved a good article of trade'. Ellis (1782) II, 55.

ver: Engraved by J. Record for Cook/King (1784) pl. 56.

British Library, London. Add MS 15514, f. 20.

JOHN WEBBER (after)

3.292A 'CAPS of the NATIVES of OONALASHKA'
Engraving. 'J. Webber del.' — 'J. Record sculp!'

Published in Cook/King (1784) pl. 56. There is no proper description of the natives' caps, however, they may correspond to
the passage of the women's art in embroidery. Cook/King (1784)
II, 513.

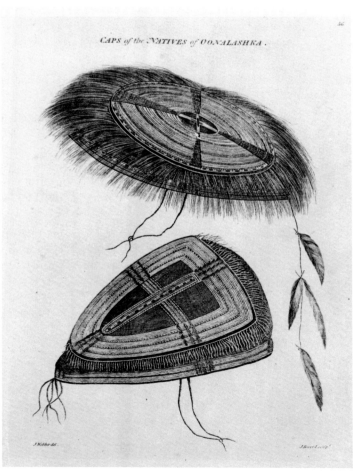

CAPS of the NATIVES of OONALASHKA.

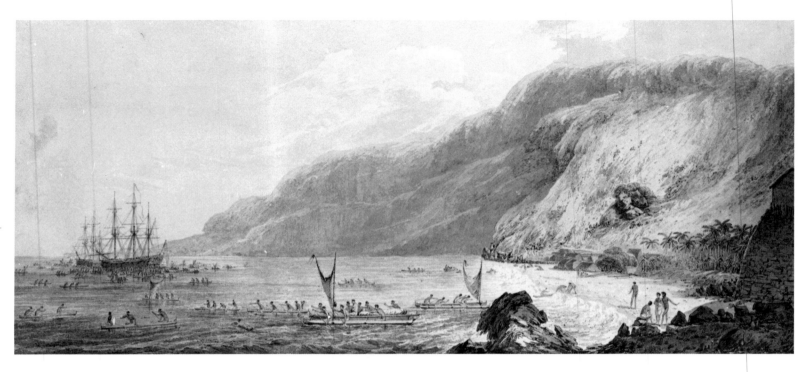

JOHN WEBBER

3.293   **A View of Kealakekua Bay** [plate 146] [c. 1781-3]
pen, wash and water-colour, $8^{15}/_{16}$ × $20^1/_{16}$:
228 × 508, unsigned.

Inscribed 'A View of Karakakooa, in Owyhee' in pencil by a later
hand on the folio beneath the drawing.

A view taken from the shore. The two ships at anchor to the left
with native craft about them. Native habitations to be seen along
the shore are part of the town of Kealakekua. Near the houses
sailors rolling barrels indicating the situation of the pond (see
chart in Cook, *Journals* III, 2, 1175). In the central foreground
canoes which are putting off towards the ships, and a man riding
a surfboard.

'At 11 AM anchored in the bay (which is called by the Natives
[Karakakooa]) in 13 fathom water over a Sandy bottom and a
quarter of a mile from the NE shore. In this situation the South
point of the bay bore S 1/4 W and the North point W 1/4 S.
Moored with the Stream Anchor and Cable to the Northward.
Unbent the sails and struck yards and topmasts. The Ships very
much crouded with Indians and surrounded by a multitude of
Canoes. I have no where in this Sea seen such a number of people
assembled at one place, besides those in the Canoes all the Shore
of the bay was covered with people and hundreds were swimming
about the Ships like shoals of fish.' Cook, *Journals* III, 1, 490-1.
The same situation is described by King (ibid., 502-3) and by
Samwell (ibid., 2. 1158). King reckoned that in the afternoon
'there could not be less than 15 hundred [canoes] about both
Ships, which at 6 persons in each make 9000; besides these when

we came near to the bay, at least 300 Women & Young boys
swam (who I supposed could get no canoes) from the Shore to
the Ships, & a number of men upon pieces of Plank. There were
not many regarding us from the shore, however we should not
exaggerate, in saying we saw at this time 10000 of the inhabitants.'
King in ibid., 1, 503.

ver: The drawing for 3.293A. A copy, from the engraving, of
       the late nineteenth century is in the Bernice P. Bishop
       Museum, Honolulu, titled 'A View of Korakakooa — in
       Owyhee' from an engraving after Webber 1793.
ref: Murray-Oliver (1975) pl. 24 (col.).

Dixson Library, State Library of New South Wales, Sydney.
PXX 2, 39.

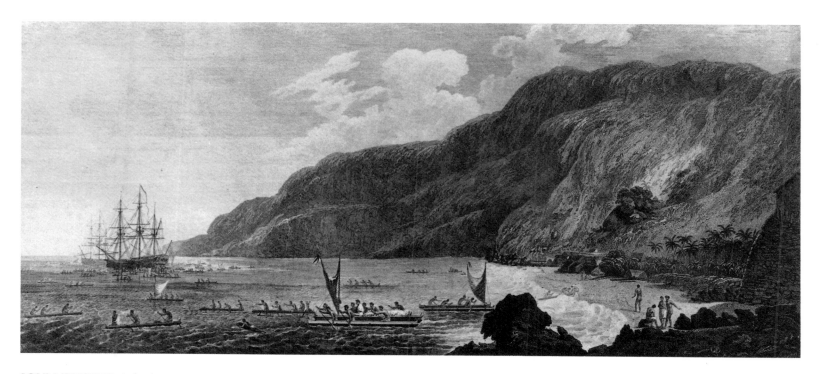

JOHN WEBBER (after)

3.293A **'A VIEW of KARAKAKOOA, in OWYHEE'**
Engraving. 'J. Webber del.' — 'W. Byrne sculp.'

Published in Cook/King (1784) pl. 68, III, 1-2, 54.

A proof-state inscribed in pencil 'View of Karracacooah — Owhyhee' in Webber's hand is kept in the National Library of Australia, Canberra, in a folio of plates from the Skottowe Hall Library.

WILLIAM ELLIS (after)

3.293B **'A View of Karaka-cooah Bay, in the Island of Owhyhee'**
Engraving. 'W. Ellis del.' — 'W. Ellis direx!' 'Published 1 Jan! 1782 by G. Robinson'.

Published in Ellis (1782) II, fp. 140.

No drawing for this engraving is known.

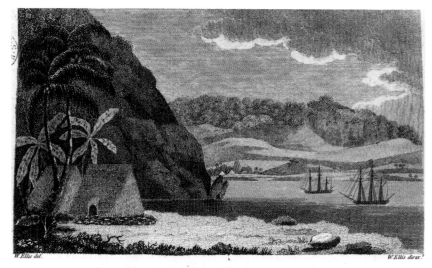

A View of Karaka-cooah Bay, in the Island of Owhyhee.

WILLIAM ELLIS (after)

3.293C 'A View of the Huts and a Boat House, at Owhyhee'
Engraving. 'W. Ellis del.' — 'W. Walker sculp!', 'Published Dec! 14 1781, by G. Robinson'.

Published in Ellis (1782) II, fp.165 (165 as well as I, 178).

No drawing for this engraving is known. The composition however shows some features, such as the houses and the racks for the canoes which makes it vaguely comparable to Webber's drawing of a view in Atooi (3.178).

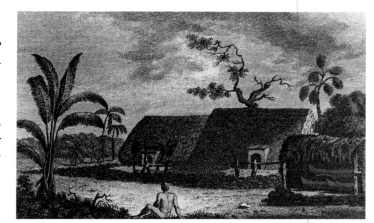

JOHN WEBBER

3.294 **An Offering before Captain Cook**
[plate 150]   [Jan 1779–]
pen and wash with slight touches of water-colour. On old mount, 17¼ × 24¾ : 435 × 629, unsigned.

The drawing has been varnished. Verso in old handwriting 'Lot N° F 1 (?)', crossed out and 'Lot No. 1' substituted. The drawing is listed as no. 107 'A ceremonious offering before Capt!. Cook and some of his Officers on their landing at Owhyhee' in Webber's Catalogue.

The grand ceremony of acknowledging Cook as an incarnation of the God Lono. In the centre a thatched house surrounded by a palisade; before it Cook seated between three of his officers is receiving a pig from a native. Behind Cook and his men two tall wooden images covered with cloth around the lower portions; and in front fifteen men seated, with one kneeling, somewhat apart near a pile of gourds. A fire is burning at left before a dry masonry wall.

Cook was ceremoniously received twice, first on 17 January 1779 when Koa'a, the priest, conducted the ceremony in a *heiau* 'called Hikiau'. See King's report, Cook, *Journals* III, 1, 505-6 and Samwell's ibid., 2, 1159, and again on 19 January when ' . . . he [Cook] was placed at the foot of a wooden image at the Entrance of a hut, to which from the remnants of Cloth round the trunk, & the remains of Offerings on the Whatta, they seem to pay more than ordinary devotion; I was here again made to support the Captains Arms, & after dressing him, a young pig was brought by Koah, (when they went thro' a deal of ceremony in presenting it to him, he & about a dozen standing in a line;) & One of them stifled the Pig, & instantly a fire was kindled, the Pig not quite dead was thrown upon the embers & cleard of its hair when it was again present'd, but with a greater variety of tones or recitation in the sentences & responces, than on the first day at the Morai, the dead pig was held up, sometimes under the Captains nose, & at last laid with a Coco nut at his feet; afterwards the Performers sat down, Kava was made & presented, a fat hog cut up & we were fed as before.' King in ibid, 1,509-10; also Samwell in ibid, 2, 1161-2.

Webber's drawing relates to both ceremonies. It was however, the second which Webber depicted. In the third volume of the official account King refers to the second reception of Captain Cook when he says: '. . . as he [Cook] expected to be received in the same manner as before, he brought Mr. Webber with him to make a drawing of the ceremony.' Cook/King, (1784) III, 13. King refers to pl. LXI, which no doubt is a misprint for pl. LX.

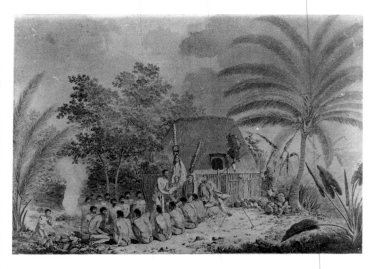

ver: For a water-colour of the same scenery but without figures see 3.296 and for the engraving 3.294A.

ref: Cook, *Journals* III, 1, pl. 55; Rienits (1968) 142; Kaeppler (1978a) fig. 54 (col.); Joppien (1983) 75.

Francis Edwards, *Cat.* 416 (London, July 1921) under no. 769 'An Offering before Capt. Cook in the Sandwich Islands, showing Capt. Cook, in sepia and colour, on strainer and varnished'. Purchased by Spencer Bickerton and acquired from him in September 1922.

Bernice P. Bishop Museum, Honolulu, Acc. no. 1922.129.

JOHN WEBBER (after)

3.294A 'An OFFERING before CAP.T COOK, in the SAND-WICH ISLANDS'

Engraving. 'Drawn by J. Webber' — 'The Figures by Hall. The Landscape Eng.d by Middiman'.

Published in Cook/King (1784) pl. 60, III, 13-14.

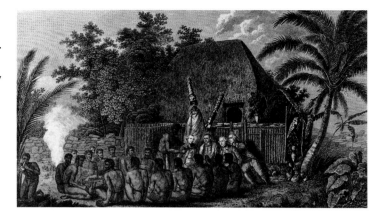

JOHN WEBBER

3.295 A Taro Plant [Jan-Feb 1779]

pen, wash and water-colour, 7³⁄₁₆ × 8³⁄₈ : 183 × 213, unsigned.

The paper is unlined, unlike most of the paper used during the voyage. The drawing seems to have been cut down. Inscribed in black ink 'Taro plant, grows in Water, at Otaheite' and '1. 169' in pencil (u.l.) referring to Ellis's *Narrative* (1782). On verso inscribed in brown ink '37'.

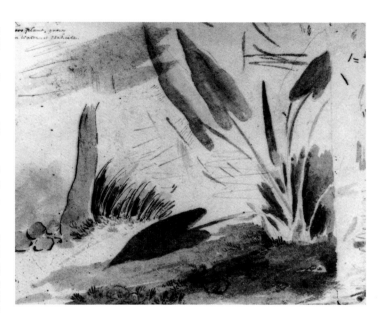

'The natives came off as yesterday, and we bought a few hogs, tarrow, sweet potatoes, and sugar cane, of all which they appeared to have plenty . . .' Ellis (1782) 1, 169.

Cook notes on 21 January 1778: 'the Plantations, which were chiefly of Tara, [were] a little sunk below the common level so as to contain the water necessary to nourish the roots.' Cook, *Journals* III, 1, 269.

Taro is also common on Tahiti, and the inscription reads like a recollection of it. However, the drawing seems to have served as a study for the plants growing on the right of Webber's drawing (3.294), and the drawing is in his style. Had Ellis made the drawing, as has been generally assumed, he would have handled the sketch less freely. The Ellis drawing 3.296 is probably copied from Webber (3.294).

ref: Murray-Oliver (1977) 35; Joppien (1983) 75.

Alexander Turnbull Library, Wellington. A 264.28.

WILLIAM ELLIS

3.296 The Friendly Priest's House [1779]

water-colour, 11½ × 16½ : 292 × 419.

The title according to an old inscription, which continues '(Na-poopoo, Hawaii 1779)'. For the title see provenance.

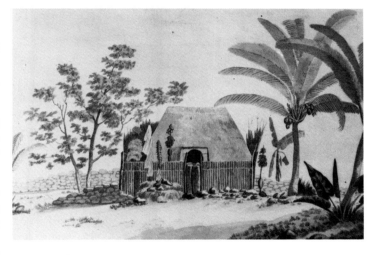

ver: The drawing depicts the same view as Webber's *An Offering before Captain Cook* (3.294) but omits the figures. There are minor differences in the vegetation. It is quite likely that Ellis copied Webber's drawing.

Museum Book Store, London, *Cat.* 94 (1924), 562/8, there explained as: 'The house, according to a note at the foot, was that of the friendly priest; this priest was probably the man who brought Captain Cook's remains back to the ship'; Museum Book Store, *Cat.* 107 (1928), 41/8; bought by Governor George R. Carter of Hawaii, in 1928. At that time the drawing was photographed by Dr Kenneth Emory. 'Sometime later it was established that it had been "lost".' (Mrs Cynthia Timberlake, Bernice P. Bishop Museum, *in litt.* 19 July 1984).

Unknown location. Photograph in the Bernice P. Bishop Museum, Honolulu. Neg. 935.

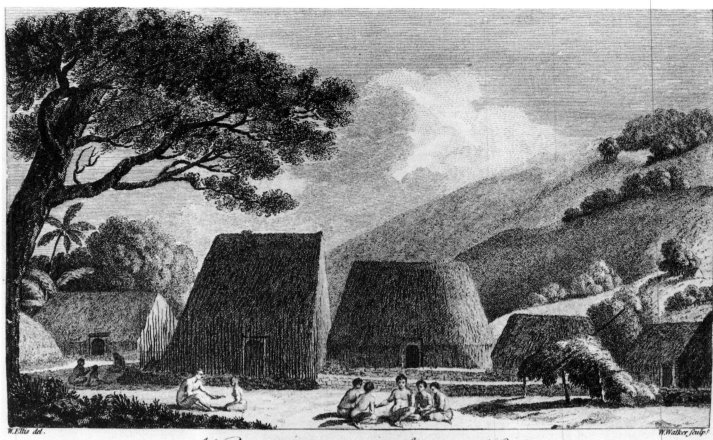

A View in O'whyhee, with one of the Priest's *Houses.*
Published Jan.ʳ 1 1782 by G. Robinson.

WILLIAM ELLIS (after)

3.296A   'A View in Owhyhee, with one of the Priests' Houses'
Engraving. 'W. Ellis del.' — 'W. Walker sculp.ᵗ' 'Published Jan.ʸ 1, 1782, by G. Robinson'.

Published in Ellis (1782) II, fp. 182.

No drawing for this engraving is known.

WILLIAM ELLIS (after)

3.296B   'A View of a Morai at Owhyhee' [plate 151]
Engraving. 'W. Ellis del.' — 'W. Walker sculp.' 'Published Dec.ᵗ 14. 1781 by G. Robinson'.

Published in Ellis (1782) II, fp. 180.

No drawing for this engraving is known, neither is there a drawing
of the *morai* or *heiau* at Hawaii by Webber. Ellis's representation
is thus of great importance. It corresponds with several comments
about the Hawaiian *hikiau* and the display of carved images and
skulls. 'we were led to the end of the Area where the Scaffold
was; At the foot of this were 12 Images ranged in a semicircular
form.' 'There was a stout Railing all round, on which were stuck
20 Skulls, the most of which they gave us to understand were
those of Mowee men, whom they had killd on the death of some
Chief.' King in Cook, *Journals* III, 1,505. For other references
see Samwell, ibid., 2, 1159, 1177.

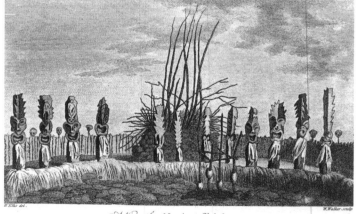

A View of a Morai *at* O'whyhee.
Published Dec.ᵗ 14.1781. by G. Robinson.

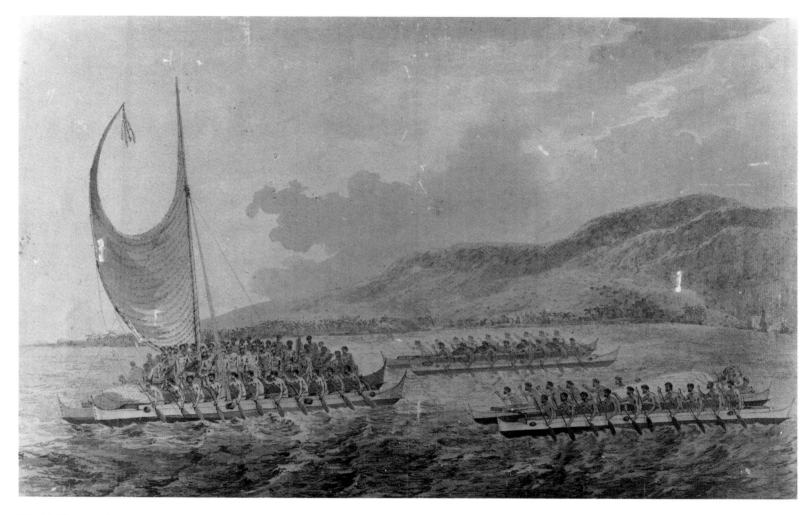

JOHN WEBBER

3.297   **Tereoboo [Kalani'opu'u], King of Owyhee bringing presents to Capt. Cook [plate 148]   [Jan 1779–]**
pen and wash with touches of red water-colour, varnished, 15¾ × 24¾ : 400 × 629, unsigned.

The title, as above, was inscribed on an original stretcher, now removed. On the back in pencil 'The King and Chiefs visit Captain Cook, Owyhee'.

This drawing is probably the one referred to as '108 The King with a Number of Chiefs — bringing presents for the reception of Capt? Cook at Owyhee' in Webber's Catalogue.

Three large double canoes manned by natives, coming from the shore; the leading canoe with a large upright lateen sail; the second canoe at right carries large images in basket work and cloth. Behind, the shoreline of Kealakekua Bay. For the type of canoes see Haddon and Hornell (1936) I, 6-19, figs 1 and 2, where 3.298A and 3.309A are reproduced. For 3.309A see also ibid (1938) III, fig.33.

'At Noon (26 January 1779) Terreeoboo in a large Canoe attended by two others set out from the Village, & paddled towards the Ships in great state. In the first Canoe was Terreeoboo, In the Second Kao with 4 Images, the third was fill'd with hogs & Vegetables, as they went along those in the Center Canoe kept Singing with much Solemnity; from which we concluded that this procession had some of their religious ceremonys mixt with it; but instead of going on board they came to our side, their appearance was very grand, the Chiefs standing up drest in their Cloaks & Caps, & in the Center Canoe were the busts of·what we suppose their Gods made of basket work, variously covered with red, black, white, & Yellow feathers, the Eyes represent'd

by a bit of Pearl Oyster Shell with a black button, & the teeth were those of dogs, the mouths of all were strangely distorted, as well as other features.' King in Cook, *Journals* III, 1, 512. Samwell also records Terreoboo's visit (ibid., 2, 1168). King estimated that Terreeboo's canoe was '70 feet long. 3 1/2 deep & each in breadth 3 feet' (ibid., 1, 626). The same canoe was probably described by Cerke: 'Their Canoes are exceedingly well built and some very large; we saw among them a vessel seventy feet long, something more than three feet deep and about the same measurements in breadth, and there were many among them nearly of the same dimensions; the bottom of this was formed out of one tree, with a plank about a foot broad firmly secured by lashing on the Top to compleat the side and form the Gunwale.' Ibid., 1, 598.

ver: For a smaller version see 3.298. For a study of the canoes see 3.299.

ref: Cook, *Journals* III, 1, pl. 56; Kaeppler (1978a) fig. 64 (col.).

Listed in Francis Edwards, *Cat.* 416 (London , July 1921) under 769 'Tereboo, King of Owyhee, bringing presents to Capt. Cook (24½ by 16 in) sepia and colour, on strainer and varnished'. Purchased by Spencer Bickerton, Honolulu, from whom it was acquired in September 1922.

Bernice P. Bishop Museum, Honolulu. Acc. no. 1922. 129.

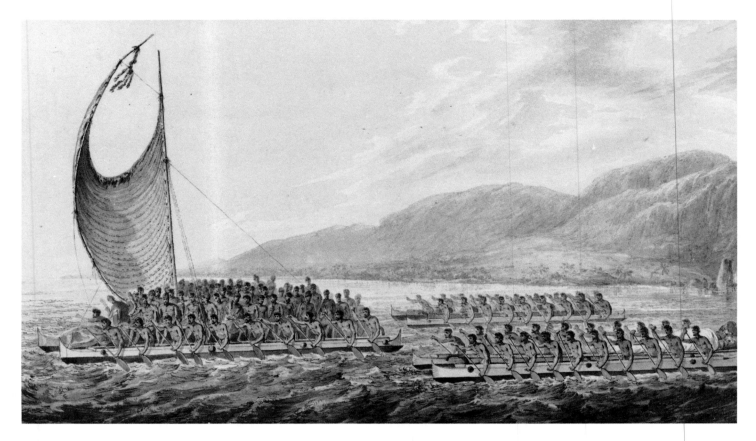

JOHN WEBBER

3.298   **Tereoboo [Kalani'opu'u], King of Owyhee, bringing
presents to Capt. Cook**   [c. 1781-3]
pen, wash and water-colour, 8¾ × 14⅞ : 225 ×
378, unsigned. The title as above in pencil by a later
hand on the folio beneath the drawing.

ver: A smaller version of 3.297 drawn to be engraved (3.298A).
A late nineteenth century copy of 3.298A is in the Bernice
P. Bishop Museum, titled: 'Tereoboo, King of Owyhee
bringing presents to Capt. Cook (from engraving after
Webber 1793)'.

ref: Murray-Oliver (1969a) pl. 125 (col.); Murray-Oliver (1975)
pl. 26 (col.)

Dixson Library, State Library of New South Wales, Sydney.
PXX 2, 35.

JOHN WEBBER (after)

3.298A   **'TEREOBOO, KING of OWYHEE, bringing PRE-
SENTS to CAPT. COOK'**
Engraving. 'J. Webber del.' — 'B. T. Pouncy sc.'

Published in Cook/King (1784) pl. 61, III, 16-17.

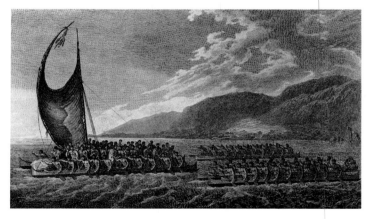

ver: A proof-state inscribed in pencil 'King bringing presents to
Cap! Cook Sandwich Isles' in Webber's hand and numbered
in pencil 'N°. 60' in u.r. is kept in the National Library
of Australia, in a folio of plates from the Skottowe Hall
Library.

On 8 January 1784 Captain James King wrote to Dr Douglas,
the editor: 'On examining the prints I find that N°. 61
"Terreoboo bringing presents to Capt. Cook" has not quite
its right title. It is intended to represent the ceremony of
Terreoboo's rowing round the ships the day after his arrival,
to prevent mistakes therefore would it not be proper to add
the following note at the foot of the Page where the account
of this ceremony ends. "This curious ceremony is represented in the annexed engraving. The presents mentioned
in the title were made to Capt. Cook after he came on
shore".' British Library, Egerton MS 2180, f.115. King's
suggestion was complied with; the additional sentence is
printed in Cook/King (1784), III, 17.

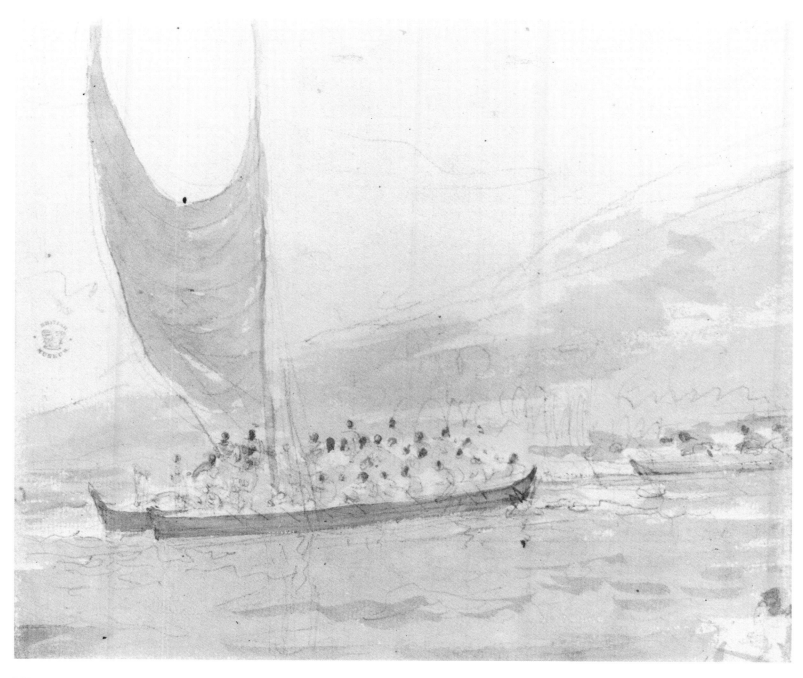

JOHN WEBBER

3.299 Canoes of Hawaii [Jan-Feb 1779]
pencil and wash, 11½ × 10 1/16 : 292 × 255,
unsigned.

At centre a large double-canoe with an upright sail, crowded with
Hawaiians.

ver: A preparatory drawing for 'Tereoboo, King of Owhyhee
bringing presents to Capt. Cook' (3.297 and 3.298).

British Library, London. Add MS 17277, no. 32v.

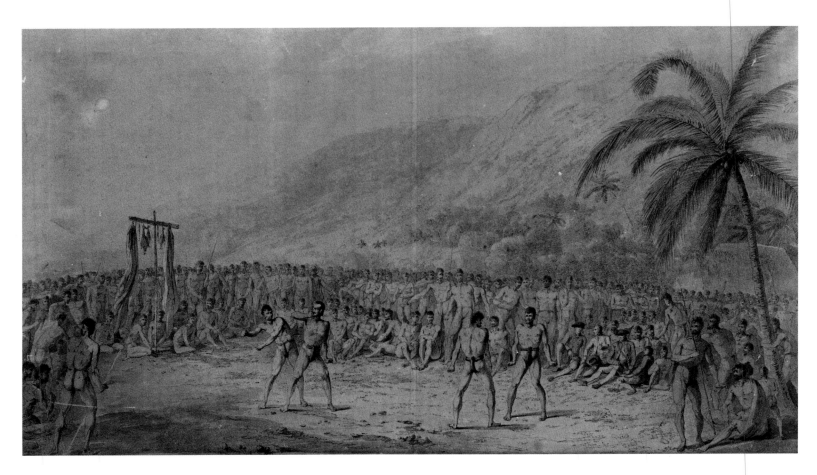

JOHN WEBBER

3.300   **A Boxing Match before Captain Cook**
        [plate 152]   **[Jan-Feb 1779—]**
        pen, wash and water-colour, 22 × 38⅞ : 560 ×
        987, unsigned.

Two sheets joined together in the centre; tack holes along sides
and top where originally attached to a stretcher. '2' in pencil
(u.r.) (rest of 102). The drawing is listed as no. 102 'Boxing
Matches for the entertainment of Captⁿ. Cook and his Officers
at Owhyee' in Webber's Catalogue.

A large assembly of Hawaiians seated, with Cook and other members of his party at right. Before them two pairs boxing. At left,
poles representing the *akua pa'ani* or god of sports; at far right a
large coconut palm.

Cook's men witnessed wrestling and boxing matches of the natives
on 31 January and on successive days from 1 to 3 February. (King
in Cook, *Journals* III, 1, 516, 518.) Samwell gives a detailed
account of the match of 1 February: 'In the afternoon the Indians
exhibited some boxing matches on a level piece of Ground a little
way from the Tents. An oblong square was formed by the People,
at the bottom of which were displayed three Ensigns or whatever
else they may be called, they are made of a long pole with a stick
about a Yard & a half long made fast at the upper end of it so
as to form a Cross, to this stick are hung pieces of Cloth of various
Colours with a few red Feathers, two or three Geese & other
birds.' Ibid., 2, 1173. He continues to give an extended account
of the action of the boxers (ibid., 2, 1173-4). On 2 February a
boxing match was repeated 'on the sandy beach' (ibid., 2, 1174).
For King's account of two boxing matches in the passage referring
to the natives' ceremonies see ibid. 1, 627. Differing from the
(authentic) dates in the *Journals*, the official account of Cook's
voyage gives the date of the boxing match as taking place on 28
January 1779. Cook/King (1784) III, 22-4.

ver: In 1919, the bookseller Francis Edwards of London pub-
        lished a photogravure based on this drawing entitled 'A
        Boxing Match before Captain Cook, at Owhyee (Hawaii)
        Sandwich Islands, Thursday, Jan 28th, 1779, a reproduction
        in the finest photo-gravure of an unpublished drawing by
        James [sic] Webber, draughtsman to the Expedition. Pub-
        lished by Francis Edwards London'. Of this 50 copies were
        printed on India paper, 100 copies on art paper.

ref: Kaeppler (1978a) fig. 30 (col.); for the photogravure: Mur-
        ray-Oliver (1969a) pl. 128; *idem* (1975) pl. 63 (col.); Smith
        (1979a) pl. 32.

Francis Edwards, *Cat.* 416 (London, July 1921) under no. 769
'A Boxing Match between Men of the Sandwich Islands before
Capt. Cook, a Large and Fine Drawing (38 × 22 in) in sepia
and colour, showing Capt. Cook and his Officers, on strainer and
varnished (unpublished)'. It was purchased by Spencer Bickerton,
Honolulu, from whom it was acquired in September 1922.

Bernice P. Bishop Museum, Honolulu. Acc. no. 1922.129.

JOHN WEBBER

3.301   A Man of Hawaii dancing   [c. 1781-3]
water-colour and wash, $9\frac{1}{2} \times 7 : 241 \times 178$, unsigned.

Inscribed 'A Man of the Sandwich Islands Dancing' in pencil by
a later hand on the folio beneath the drawing.

Full-length drawing of a man dancing, wearing a necklace of
seaweed, a *maro* and ornaments beset with dog's teeth around the
legs. In his right hand he is holding a rattle. An Hawaiian house
and a stone enclosure in the background.

Webber saw an Hawaiian dancing in early February 1779. There
is no account of it in the *Journals* but King described the scene
in the official publication: 'We were this day much diverted, at
the beach, by the buffooneries of one of the natives. He held in
his hand an instrument, of the sort described in the last volume
[a rattle]; some bits of sea-weed were tied round his neck; and
round each leg, a piece of strong netting, about nine inches deep,
on which a great number of dogs' teeth were loosely fastened, in
rows. His style of dancing was entirely burlesque, and accompanied with strange grimaces, and pantomimical distortions of
the face; which though at times inexpressible ridiculous, yet, on
the whole, was without much meaning, or expression. Mr. Webber thought it worth his while to make a drawing of this person,
as exhibiting a tolerable specimen of the natives; the manner in
which the *maro* is tied; the figure of the instrument before
mentioned, and of the ornaments round the legs, which, at other
times, we also saw used by their dancers.' Cook/King (1784)
III, 27.

ver: The drawing was probably developed from the central figure
       in 3.302. Identical in size with the engraving 3.301A for
       which it was prepared. A copy of the engraving is in the
       Bernice P. Bishop Museum, Honolulu, titled 'A man of the
       Sandwich Islands dancing'.

ref: Murray-Oliver (1969a) pl.127 (col.); *idem* (1975) pl. 62
       (col.).

Dixson Library, State Library of New South Wales, Sydney.
PXX 2, 36.

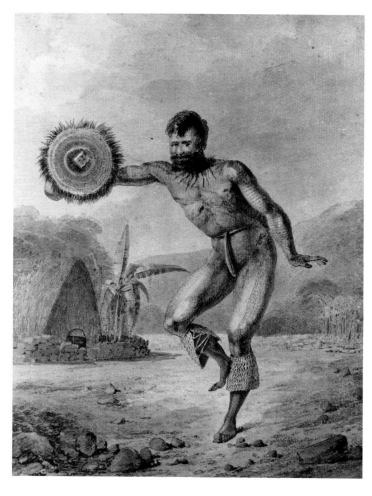

JOHN WEBBER (after)

**3.301A   'A MAN of the SANDWICH ISLANDS,
DANCING'**
Engraving. 'J. Webber del.' — 'C. Grignion sc.'

Published in Cook/King (1784) pl. 62, III, 27.

ver: A proof-state inscribed in pencil 'A Man dancing. Owhyhe'
       in Webber's hand, also 'Webber' and 'Grignion' in a dif-
       ferent hand, is kept in the National Library of Australia,
       Canberra, in a folio of plates from the Skottowe Hall Library.

       Neither Cook nor any other reporter provided an account
       of the Hawaiians' dance. Captain King, observing the dis-
       crepancy between text and print, wrote to Dr Douglas, the
       editor, on 8 January 1784: 'As the plate N. 62 has no place
       in the work to which it can be referred, I send you a
       description of a "man of the Sandwich Islands dancing"
       which is to come in, in the 2nd chapter.' British Library,
       Egerton MS 2180, f.115.

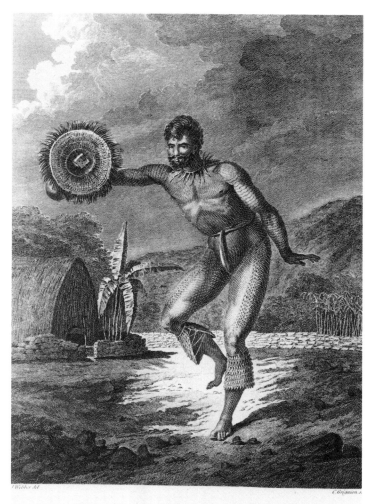

A MAN of the SANDWICH ISLANDS, DANCING.

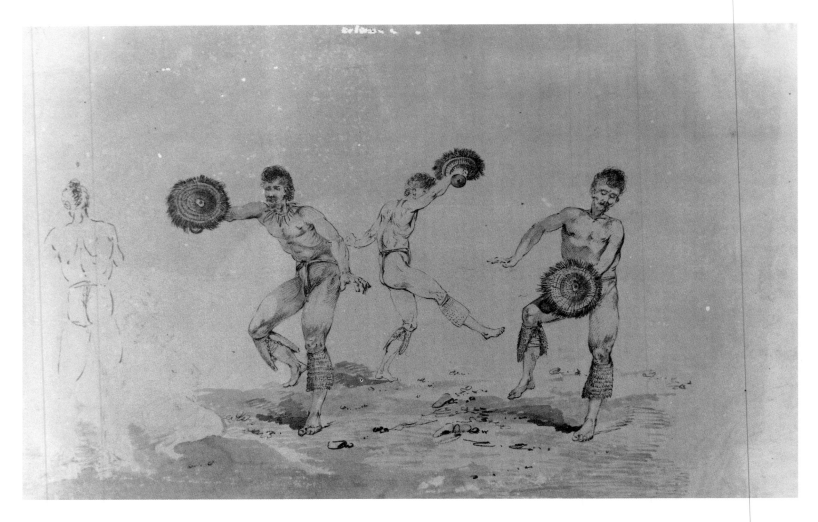

JOHN WEBBER

3.302   **Dancers of Owhyhee**   [Feb 1779]
         pen and wash with tints of water-colour, the unfinished
         sections in pencil, 12 × 18⅞ : 305 × 480, unsigned.

This drawing is probably the one referred to, under the title above,
in Webber's Catalogue, no. 93.

Four dancers in different positions, stamping the ground and
shaking gourd rattles. The dancer on the left is only drawn in
outline, next to him another figure sitting on the ground. Despite
the title of the drawing it would also seem conceivable that in
reality one dancer was drawn in different movements of his dance.

ver: For a developed drawing of the central figure see 3.301.

ref: Cook, *Journals* III, pl. 60a; Rienits (1968) 142; Kaeppler
          (1978a) fig. 164 (col.); Smith (1979a) pl. 34.

Listed in Francis Edwards, *Cat.* 416 (London, July 1921) under
no. 769 'Men of the Sandwich Islands Dancing (19 by 12 in),
sepia and colour'; purchased by Spencer Bickerton, Honolulu and
acquired from him in September 1922.

Bernice P. Bishop Museum, Honolulu. Acc. no. 1922.129.

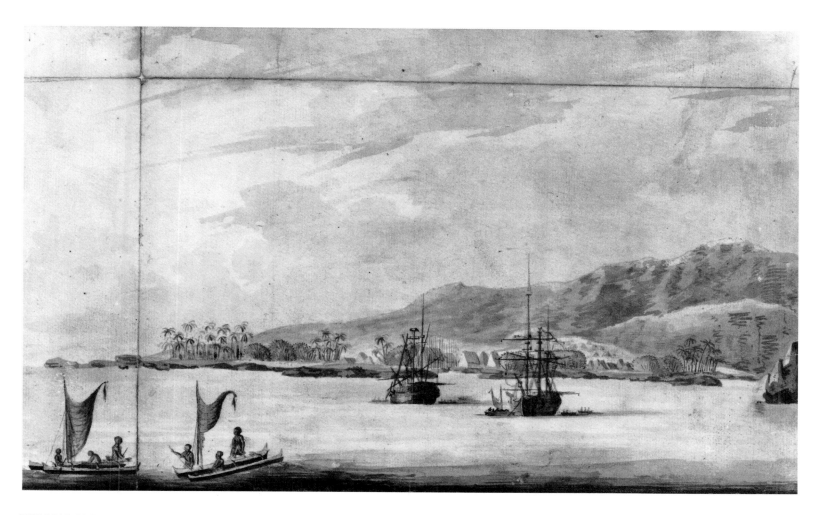

WILLIAM ELLIS (attributed)

3.303   **Kealakekua Bay with the Ships at anchor**
                                        [Feb 1779]
         wash and some tints of water-colour, 9¼ × 14¾ : 235
         × 375, unsigned; w/m 'IV'.

Two Hawaiian craft with figures in the left foreground. The
Resolution and *Discovery* with some canoes around them; in the
distance the shore of Kealakekua Bay with huts of the village of
Kowrooa [Kaawaloa] indicated by the letter 'K' in ink, coconut
palms and hills beyond.

The ships appear disproportionally small in relation to the huts
on the shore. The drawing reflects a time after 11 February, when
Cook's ships returned to Kealakekua Bay due to the repairs on
the *Resolution's* foremast, which is here missing in the drawing.

ver: Taken from almost the same viewpoint as 3.307. The two
         Hawaiian canoes in the front are copied from 3.320 and
         3.321.

ref: Cook, *Journals* III, 1, pl.57; Beaglehole (1974) pl. 42; Begg
         (1969) pl. 176 (partly cut at left); Murray-Oliver (1975)
         pl. 49.

Originally in Thomas Edgar's log (ADM 55/24), but has since been
detached and is now preserved in the museum of the Public Record
Office.

Public Record Office, Maps and Plans, London. MPM 44.

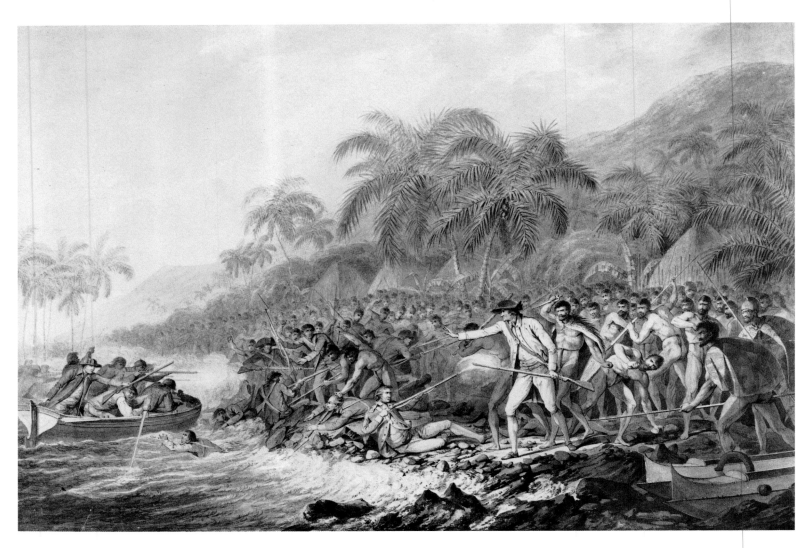

JOHN WEBBER

3.304   **The Death of Captain Cook [plate 153] [c. 1781-3]**
pen, wash and water-colour, 14¹⁄₁₆ × 21¹⁄₁₆ :
357 × 535, unsigned.

Inscribed in ink on mount 'Death of Capt. J. Cook (Original
water-colour by J. Webber)'. The drawing is mounted on a sheet
which derives from the bound volume of Cook material PXD 59⁻².

The circumstances of Cook's death are described in the *Journals*
III, 1, 531-8 (Clerke) and 549-58 (King), as well as in an abridged
form in Cook/King (1784) III, 45-6. See also J.C. Beaglehole,
The Death of Captain Cook (Alexander Turnbull Library, Wellington, 1979).

Like Webber's oil of the same subject (3.305) the picture is full
of figures and is Webber's most ambitious effort at history painting.
It is however, not an eye-witness report, for Webber was not on
the spot when Cook's murder took place. It is likely however,
that he collected verbal and visual information about the event.
Cook is dressed totally in white clothes. This is probably symbolic.
For the coat of the English seamen and the feather capes of the
natives Webber uses an unusual amount of red. The bodies of
the natives are depicted in yellow ochre, the palm trees in varying
degrees of light and dark green, the mountains in the back greyish-
blue. The sky on the left is coloured in shades of blue and white;
the light coming from the left. Large sections of the picture
however, are washed rather darkly, particularly the right foreground. Webber obviously sought powerful contrasts.

Mitchell Library, State Library of New South Wales, Sydney.
PXD 59⁻², f.1.

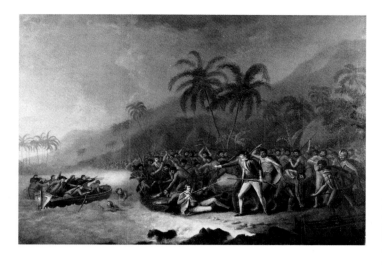

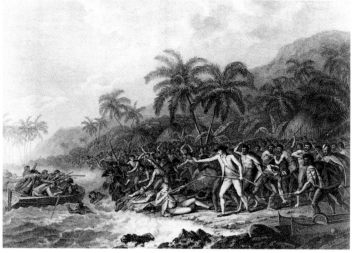

JOHN WEBBER

JOHN WEBBER (after)

3.305   The Death of Captain Cook   [c. 1781-3]
oil on canvas, 34 × 48 : 865 × 1220, unsigned.

While Cook raises his right hand to stop the men in the *Resolution's* pinnace and launch from firing at the enraged Hawaiians a tall warrior stabs him in the back. Molesworth Phillips, Lieutenant of Marines, seated on the shore, fires his musket into the mob while other marines, two of whom are in the water, are attacked.

ver: For a water-colour version see 3.304. There are significant differences between 3.305 and 3.304: in the treatment of the helmet on the warrior at the far right; the omission of a third head in the water near the prow of the near boat, and the differing disposition of the coconut palms in the background on the extreme left. In these and other details the engraving follows 3.305 from which it was probably executed. Cf. the engraving of 2.134A from Hodges's oil painting 2.134.

ref: Murray-Oliver (1975), pl. 5 (col.).

Francis Edwards, London, unnumbered *Cat.* (1929) 2-4, offered as 'The Original Oil Painting . . . Murder of Cook by the Natives of Hawaii On Sunday, the 14th of February, 1799 [sic]. A remarkably Fine and Spirited Canvas in an excellent state of preservation . . . Price £1000'.

Dixson Gallery, State Library of New South Wales, Sydney. DG 26.

3.305A   The Death of Captain Cook
Engraving.

Inscribed: 'Drawn by J. Webber. The Figures Engraved by F. Bartolozzi, R.A. Engraver to His Majesty. The Landscape by W. Byrne. Published as the Act directs 1 Jan? 1784, by J. Webber, N? 312 Oxford Street, and W. Byrne, N? 79 Titchfield Street, London'. Dedication line: 'To the Right Honourable the Lords Commissioners for executing the Office of Lord High Admiral of Great Britain, &c This Plate representing the DEATH OF CAPTAIN COOK is humbly inscribed. By their LORDSHIPS most obedient and devoted Servant, JOHN WEBBER'.

ver: This well known print is kept in many collections specializing in South Sea and Cook material, including British Museum, the Department of Prints and Drawings, London (C. 17*), the National Library of Australia, Canberra, Rex Nan Kivell Collection (NK 553-J) and the Bernice P. Bishop Museum, Honolulu, Fuller Collection.

The Public Archives of Canada, Ottawa, own another impression which is dated 1 January 1783. (Schoenherr 1977, 30), and so does the Mitchell Library, dated 1 January, 1782 (Cook-Bibliography 1970, no. 2610 — p478). Other versions dated 1 July 1785 and 4 January 1787 also exist.

The British Museum has a proof before letters, and an engraving of oval size (15½ × 10⅝ : 395 × 270), inscribed: 'The Death of Captain Cook. In February 1779 by the murdering Dagger of a Barbarian at Carakakooa, in one of the Sandwich Isles. He having there become a Victim to his own Humanity. This Distressing Scene is Part of the Original Plate after Webber by Mess?; Bartolozzi & Byrne. London Sold in Spur Street, Leicester Square'. Another version is in the National Library of Australia, Canberra. A French publication of this print titled 'Mort Tragique du Capitaine Cook', engraved by Fessard, is inscribed 'se vend à Paris rue de Gèvre chez Isabey'.

ref: Mitchell (1944) 58; Smith (1979b), fig. 7.

British Museum, Department of Prints and Drawings, London. C17*.

JOHN WEBBER

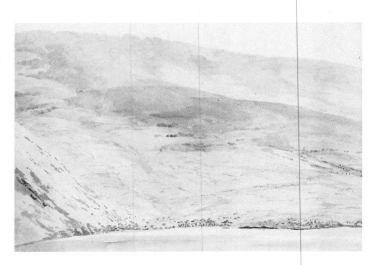

3.306   A Section of Kealakekua Bay   [1779]
pencil, wash and water-colour, 14¼ × 20¹³⁄₁₆ :
362 × 529, unsigned.

Inscribed 'Part of Karakakooa Bay-Owehye' in pencil (u.r.).

This drawing probably represents a part of a wider panorama, and
may represent the Hawaiian coast between Kealakekua and
Kalama.

British Library. London. Add MS 17277, no. 31.

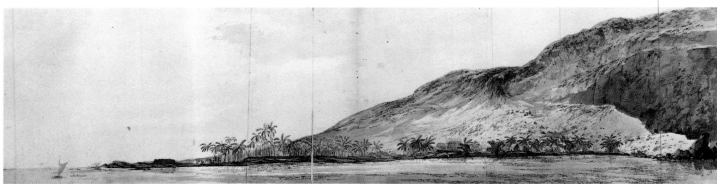

JOHN WEBBER

3.307   A View of Kealakekua Bay [plate 147]   [Jan 1799]
pencil, pen, wash and water-colour, 12½ × 47 : 318
× 1194, unsigned.

Inscribed on verso in pencil in Webber's hand: 'A View of the
North Point of Karakakooa Bay, Owhye taken from the Anchoring Place'. Two sections of paper are joined together to make
up the extensive format of the view; two folds.

A view of the shore apparently taken from the deck of the *Resolution*. At left a rocky point at the head of the bay followed to
the right by clusters of palms and the habitations of the village
of Kowrooa [Kaawaloa]. At the extreme right a group of rocks
and a deep cleft in the hill.

'At the Town of Kavaroa are large groves of cocoa nut Trees
inclosed in with high walls . . .' Samwell in Cook, *Journals* III,
2, 1176.

ver: The shore and promontory provide the background also for
the drawings, 3.297, 3.298 and 3.309, see also 3.298A,
3.303 and 3.309A.

ref: Cook, *Journals* III, 1, pl. 54; Rienits (1968) 143; Murray-
Oliver (1975) pl. 64 (col.).

British Library, London. Add MS 17277, no. 30.

JOHN WEBBER

3.308   A Canoe of Hawaii, the Rowers Masked
         [plate 149]   [Jan-Feb 1779]
         pen, pencil, wash, tints of water-colour, 11⅞ ×
         17⅞ : 302 × 454, unsigned and unfinished. The
         paper slightly yellowed.

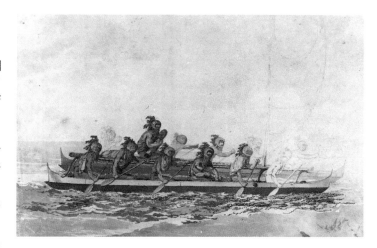

Inscribed in pencil on verso 'Lot no 6(?)' and 'Capn. Campbell'.
This drawing is probably the one listed as no. 98 'A Ceremony
at Owhyhee where the Natives came on board masked' in Webber's
Catalogue.

A double canoe with an upright lateen sail holding ten rowers
wearing gourd helmets, two holding small images, a third one,
blowing a conch, in the back on the left sketched in by pencil.
It is curious that the scene, so visually striking, is not mentioned
in the journals. For the type of canoes see Haddon and Hornell
(1936) I, 6-19, fig.1, and (1938) III, fig. 33.

ver: For a more developed drawing see 3.309. A copy (probably
       of the engraving) of the late nineteenth century, is in the
       Bernice P. Bishop Museum, Honolulu, titled 'A canoe of
       the Sandwich Islands the Rowers Masked'.

ref: Cook, *Journals* III, 1, pl. 60b; Rienits (1968) 121; Kaeppler
       (1978a) fig. 89.

Listed in Francis Edwards, *Cat.* 416 (London, July 1921) under
no. 769 'Canoe of the Sandwich Islands, the Rowers Masked
(18 by 12 in) in sepia and colours', purchased by Spencer Bickerton, Honolulu, from whom it was acquired in September 1922.

Bernice P. Bishop Museum, Honolulu. Acc. no. 1922.129.

JOHN WEBBER

3.309   A Canoe of Hawaii, the Rowers Masked
                                        [c. 1781-3]
         pen, wash and water-colour, 8¹¹⁄₁₆ × 15 : 220 ×
         380, signed 'Jn. Webber del'.

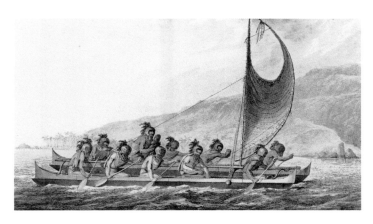

Titled 'A Canoe of the Sandwich Islands. The Rowers Masked'
in pencil on the folio beneath the drawing.

ver: A developed version of 3.308. The shoreline in the back-
       ground represents the north-west side of Kealakekua Bay
       (see 3.307) and is also introduced into Webber's drawing
       Tereoboo, King of Owhyhee, bringing presents to Capt. Cook,
       see 3.297 and 3.298. Redrawn on a smaller scale than
       3.308 it served for the engraving 3.309A.

Dixson Library, State Library of New South Wales, Sydney.
PXX 2, 37.

JOHN WEBBER (after)

3.309A   'A CANOE of the SANDWICH ISLANDS, the
         ROWERS MASKED'
         Engraving. 'J. Webber del.' — 'C. Grignion sc.'

Published in Cook/King (1784) pl. 65, III, 139.

ver: A proof-state inscribed in pencil 'A Ceremony of Mask'd
       figures — Owhyhee Sandwich Isles. A mask' in Webber's
       hand and numbered in pencil 'N⁰ 63' (u.r.) is kept in the
       National Library of Australia, in a folio of plates from the
       Skottowe Hall Library.

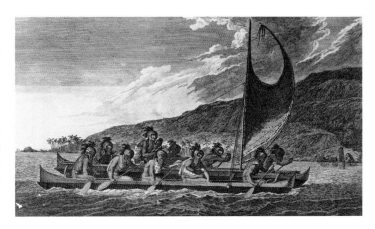

JOHN WEBBER

3.310   **A Man of the Sandwich Islands in a Mask**   [1779]
wash and water-colour, 20½ × 14½ : 508 × 368,
unsigned.

Titled 'A Man of the Sandwich Islands in a Mask' in pencil across
the lower margin of the sheet. Traces of '100' (u.r.), referring
to 'no 100' in Webber's Catalogue entitled 'A Portrait of a Mask'
in the section of the Sandwich Islands.

The mask of the native is a gourd helmet. It is surmounted by
fern fronds (*pala*).

The mask does not seem to be referred to in the various journals,
it is however mentioned by King in the official account: 'There
remains to be mentioned another ornament . . . The figure of
which may be better conceived from the annexed print, than any
written description. It is a kind of mask, made of a large gourd,
with holes cut in it for the eyes and nose. The top was stuck full
of small green twigs, which, at a distance, had the appearance
of an elegant waving plume; and from the lower part hung narrow
stripes of cloth, resembling a beard. We never saw these masks
worn but twice, and both times by a number of people together
in a canoe, who came to the side of the ships laughing and drolling
with an air of masquerading. Whether they may not likewise be
used as a defence for the head against stones, for which they seem
best designed, or in some of their public games, or be merely
intended for the purpose of mummery, we could never inform
ourselves.' Cook/King (1784) III, 139-40.

ver: For a smaller version see 3.311. A field study is at 3.312.

British Library, London. Add MS 15514, f. 26.

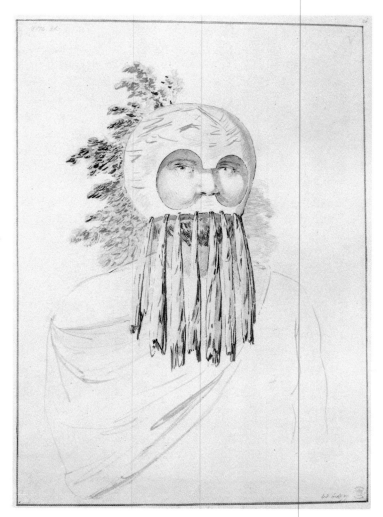

JOHN WEBBER

3.311   **A Man of the Sandwich Islands in a Mask**
[c. 1781-3]
pencil, pen and wash, 9¼ × 6⅞ : 235 × 175, unsigned.

The title 'A man of the Sandwich Islands in a Mask' inscribed
in pencil by a later hand on the folio beneath the drawing.

ver: A smaller version of 3.310 drawn for the engraving 3.311A.

ref: Murray-Oliver (1975) pl. 29 (col.).

Dixson Library, State Library of New South Wales, Sydney.
PXX 2, 38.

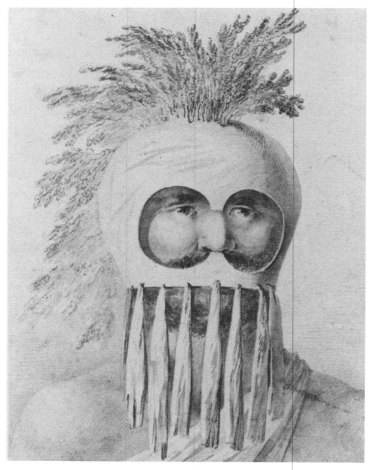

540

JOHN WEBBER (after)

3.311A 'A MAN of the SANDWICH ISLANDS, in a MASK'
Engraving. 'J. Webber del.' — 'T. Cook sculp!'.

Published in Cook/King (1784) pl. 66, III, 139.

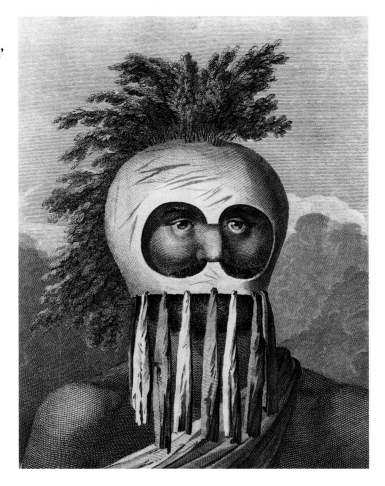

JOHN WEBBER

3.312   A Man of the Sandwich Islands in a Mask [1779]
pencil and wash, 11½ × 10⅟₁₆ : 292 × 256,
unsigned.

Inscribed 'Sandwich Islands' in pencil (u.r.) and 'see atlas pl. 66'
on lower mount.

A study of head and shoulders.

ver: A preparatory drawing for 3.310 and 3.311. A late nineteenth century copy of this drawing is in the Bernice P.
Bishop Museum, Honolulu, titled 'Man of Sandwich Islands
in a mask (Webber)'.

British Library, London. Add MS 17277, no. 32r.

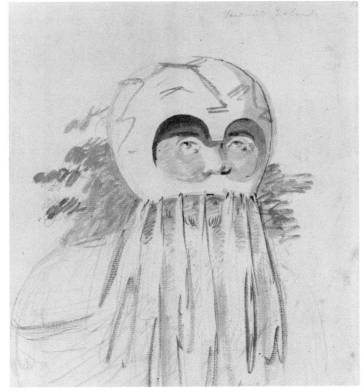

3.313 **A Chief of the Sandwich Islands leading his party to battle** [plate 154]   [1787]
oil on canvas, 58 × 45 : 1470 × 1143, signed and dated 'J. Webber 1787'.

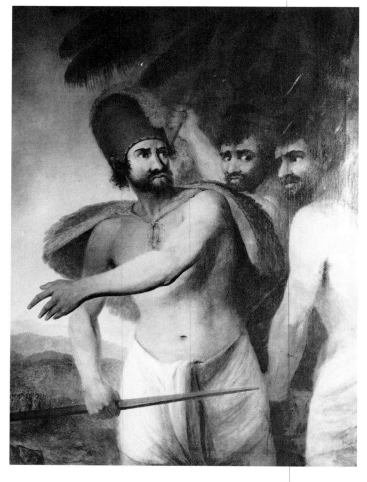

A chief wearing a large red helmet, a feather cloak and a fanciful *maro*. His left hand points to the left towards a battle in the background. He holds a spear. Two other men at his right-hand side. This is most probably the painting exhibited at the R.A. in 1787 (no. 32), with the above title.

Clerke writes about the natives' garments: 'The feathered Caps and Cloaks which I described in the account of our last years transactions among them are I find the Apparel of the Chiefs in Battle and exceedingly well calculated they are for the purpose . . . the Basket work of the Cap is so strong and compact as to render the head perfectly secure from any assault of this sort, and the Cloak being loose about the body in a great measure destroys the force of any stone that may take place there. . . . Besides their Spears many of the Arees have now . . . large Iron Spikes (what they call Pah' hoo' ahs) indeed they had this weapon before, made of hard black wood, and the time we were first off of Mow'wee an Aree visited me with many of his attendants, one of whom had two of these Iron Spikes . . ., these of black wood we found an universal weapon among their Chiefs, but the Iron utensil must very far exceed all their wooden materials in the work of destruction, which they seem truely sensible of and value them accordingly.' Cook, *Journals* III, 1, 594-5. On Hawaiian daggers (observed at Kauai) see Cook's comments, ibid., 1, 282, and Beaglehole's note (595 1n).

King's comments on Webber's work are particularly relevant here: 'Some Portraits which our Painter has drawn, will I think equal, in Nobleness of Countenance & manliness of figure any Islanders we have seen; what takes much from their general good appearance, is the paucity of their Cloathing, which in all is no more than a narrow Marrow, pass'd between the legs & round the loins & which, however beautiful, leaves them too Naked.' Ibid., 1, 612.

Judging from Webber's representation of the *maro* which is exaggerated (perhaps to make it 'more noble'), King's point was well taken.

ref: Murray-Oliver (1975) pl. 36 (col.).

National Library of Australia, Canberra. Rex Nan Kivell Collection. NK 1.

JOHN WEBBER (after)

3.313A 'A MAN of the SANDWICH ISLANDS, with his HELMET'
Engraving. 'J. Webber del.' — 'J.K. Sherwin sc.'

Published in Cook/King (1784) pl. 64, III, 4,125.

No drawing by Webber has survived. The sitter, wearing a feather cloak and helmet made of feathers, can be identified as the Hawaiian chief Kana'ina (Kanina, Kaneina, Kaneena) of whom King speaks: 'Kaneena especially, whose portrait Mr. Webber has drawn, was one of the finest men I ever saw.' Cook/King (1784) III, 4. 'The annexed print of A MAN OF SANDWICH IS-LANDS, was taken from a portrait of our friend Kaneena' (ibid., 125). Kana'ina was killed in the fighting ensuing from the death of Cook.

Of Kana'ina's vestments King says: '. . . they [the natives of Hawaii] have another [dress], appropriated to their Chiefs, and used on ceremonious occasions, consisting of a feathered cloak and helmet, which, in point of beauty and magnificence, is per-haps nearly equal to that of any nation in the world.' Ibid., 136. 'The helmet has a strong lining of wicker-work, capable of break-ing the blow of any warlike instrument, and seems evidently designed for that purpose.' Ibid., 137.

A copy of this print in the Bernice P. Bishop Museum, Honolulu has the following inscription: 'J.F.G. Stokes, after a thorough study of Captain King's account, decides that the references leave no doubt that the name of the chief pictured was Kanina, or possibly Kanaina.'

A proof-state inscribed in pencil 'A Man in his helmet, Sandwich Isles' in Webber's hand is kept in the National Library of Australia, in a folio of plates from the Skottowe Hall Library.

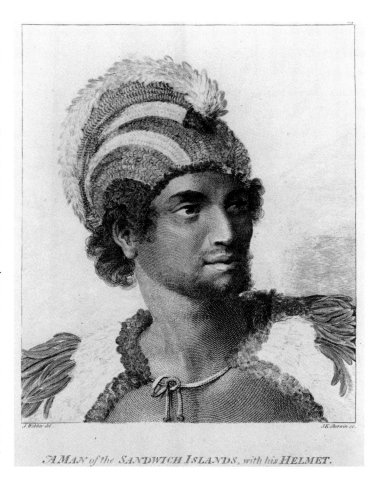

A MAN of the SANDWICH ISLANDS, with his HELMET.

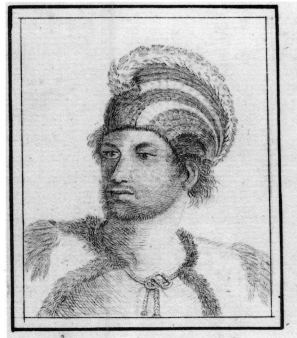

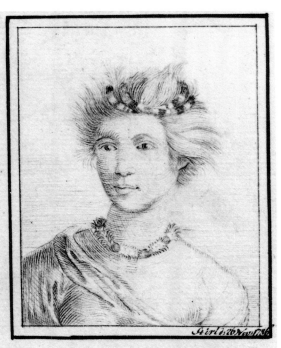

A Man and Woman of Sandwich Islands.

3.313b
A pencil copy apparently after the print, accompanied by the pendant of a young woman of the Sandwich Islands, signed and dated 'Stirl d 26 Nov: 1786' passed through the sale rooms of Christie's, South Kensington in Autumn 1982 (see 3.317B).

JOHN WEBBER

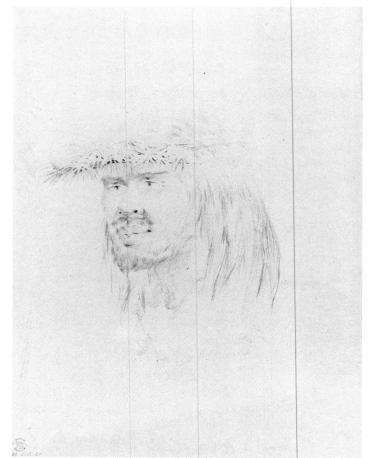

3.314 **A Man of the Sandwich Islands**   [1779]
pencil, 18⅞ × 14⅜ : 480 × 365, unsigned.

Three-quarter portrait of a man with long loose hair wearing a
necklace and a garland of leaves round his head as a sun-shade.

ver: Possibly the same man as in 3.185. A late nineteenth
century copy of 3.314 is in the Bernice P. Bishop Museum,
Honolulu, titled 'Man of Sandwich Islands (1793)'.

British Library, London. Add MS 15514, f 23.

WILLIAM ELLIS

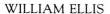

3.315 **[A Portrait of an Hawaiian]**
pencil and wash, 11⅛ × 10⅜ : 283 × 263, signed
and dated in pencil (l.r.) 'W.W. Ellis ad viv. delin
1779'; w/m: 'ALCV'.

Annotated in pencil (u.r.) '2.88?', referring to Ellis's *Narrative*
(1782); the title inscribed in ink: 'Sandw. Isle . . .' (u.r.), partly
cut off. Inscribed in ink on verso '66'. On verso four water-colour
sketches of rock, trees, water, a study of a leafy branch (see
3.425).

A young man facing three-quarter left, with moustache, a small
beard on the chin, and a ridge of curly hair over the crown of
the head. Possibly a portrait of Palea, a sub-chief under Ka-
lani'opu'u (Terriaboo).

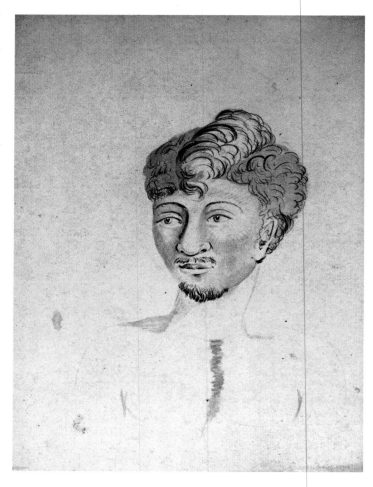

'We had several other visitors of consequence, amongst which
was a young man whose name was Purráah [Palea, Parea] . . .
a principal attendant of Terriaboò, who was the King of the
island: he was about five feet eight in height, his person was
pleasing, and he appeared to be possessed of great good nature.'
Ellis (1782) II, 88.

'Parea is generally on board the Discovery & keeps the ship clear,
& as the great number of Women that lye on board every night
would rather be in the Way in the day time Parea comes on board
early every morning & sends them ashore, telling them that there
will be no Occasion for them till Night.' Samwell in Cook, *Journals*
III, ii, 1161.

Of the general physical appearance of Hawaiian men Ellis writes:
'The hair both of the head and beard is black; that of the head
the men wear in the form of a helmet, that is, a long frizzled ridge
from the forehead to the neck, the sides being much shorter.
This fashion seems to prevail only among the principal people,
that of the inferior sort being of an equal length in every part.'
Ellis (1782), II, 150.

ref: Murray-Oliver (1977) 36.

Alexander Turnbull Library, Wellington. A 264.44 A.

WILLIAM ELLIS (after)

3.315A   'A Man of Sandwich Islands'
Engraving. 'W. Ellis del.' — 'J. Collyer sculp.'. 'Published Dec.ʳ 14ᵗʰ 1781 by G. Robinson'.

Published in Ellis (1782) II, fp. 150.

The position of the head follows 3.315, but 3.315A seems an older man, and the beard differs. The long head and full beard may reflect the influence of Webber, for example 3.183.

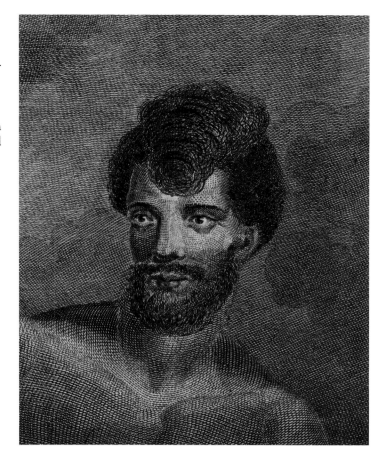

JOHN WEBBER

3.316   The Portrait of a Girl of Owhyhee   [1779]
pencil, 19⅛ × 12⁵⁄₁₆ : 486 × 313, signed and dated 'Jn Webber del 1779'.

Inscribed 'Head of a Young Woman of the Sandwich Islands' in pencil on the mount below the drawing and 'No 89' (u.r.) which identifies it as the drawing with the title above in Webber's Catalogue. Also inscribed 'Atlas 63'.

A head and shoulder portrait. The girl wears two feathered rings on the top of her head, and one around her neck.

'Another beautiful ornament, called *eraie* (*lei*), which is generally put about the neck, but is sometimes tied like a garland round the hair . . . It is a ruff of the thickness of a finger, made, in a curious manner, of exceedingly small feathers, woven so close together as to form a surface as smooth as that of the richest velvet.' King in Cook/King (1784) III, 138-9. For a similar description see Samwell, Cook, *Journals* III, 2, 1180.

ver: For another version see 3.317. A late nineteenth century copy of 3.316 is in the Bernice P. Bishop Museum, Honolulu, titled 'Young Woman of the Sandwich Islands (Webber 1793)'.

ref: Cook, *Journals* III, 1, pl. 58b; Murray-Oliver (1975) pl. 39; Starzecka (1979) pl. 102.

British Library, London. Add MS 15514, f. 25.

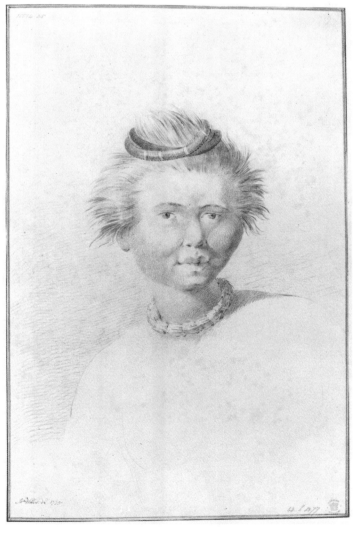

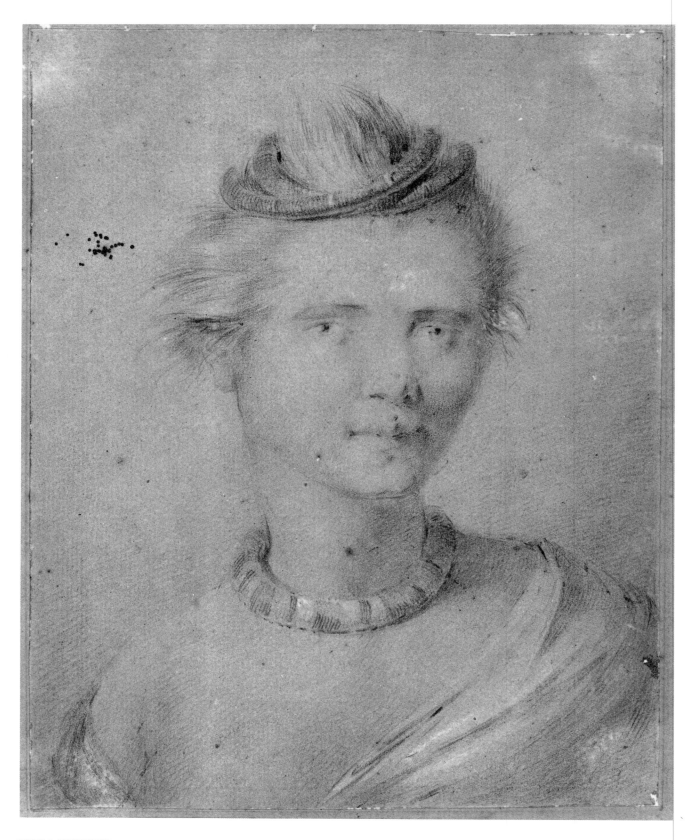

JOHN WEBBER

3.317   **Portrait of a Girl of Owhyhee**   [c. 1781-3]
pencil with some ink and faint water-colour, 9 × 7 :
228 × 178, unsigned.

Inscribed 'A Girl of the Sandwich Islands' in pencil on verso.

Head and shoulder portrait of an Hawaiian girl with feathered
rings (*lei*) on the top of her head and round her neck. Her breast
covered in cloth.

ver: For a portrait probably of the same sitter, see 3.316. The
drawing was prepared for 3.317A.

ref: Kaeppler (1978a) fig. 98 (col.).

Listed in Francis Edwards, *Cat.* 416 (London, July 1921) under
no. 769 'A Young Woman of the Sandwich Islands (9 by 7 in)
sepia and little colour'; purchased by Spencer Bickerton and
acquired from him in 1922.

Bernice P. Bishop Museum, Honolulu. Acc. no. 1922.129.

546

JOHN WEBBER (after)

3.317A 'A YOUNG WOMAN of the SANDWICH ISLANDS'

Engraving. 'J. Webber del.' — 'J.K. Sherwin sc.'.

Published in Cook/King (1784) pl. 63, III, 125, 138.

ver: A proof-state incribed in pencil 'A Girl, Owhyhe Sandwich Isles' in Webber's hand and numbered in pencil 'N⁰. 62' (u.r.) is kept in the National Library of Australia, Canberra in a folio of plates from the Skottowe Hall Library.

3.317b

A pencil copy apparently after the print, signed and dated 'Stirl d 26 Nov: 1786', accompanied by a pencil drawing of the 'Man of the Sandwich Islands, with his helmet', passed through the sale rooms of Christie's, South Kensington, in Autumn 1982. (See 3.313b.)

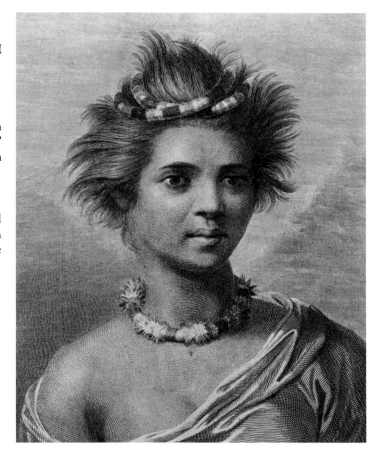

WILLIAM ELLIS (after)

3.317B 'A Woman of Sandwich Islands'

Engraving. 'W. Ellis del.' — 'J. Heath sc.'.
'Publish'd 14ᵗʰ Decʳ 1781 by G. Robinson'.

Published in Ellis (1782) II, fp. 151, 150, 156-7.

No drawing for this engraving is known, but the sitter bears some similarity to the one depicted by Webber (3.316).

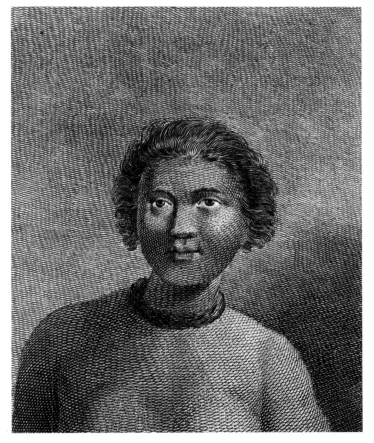

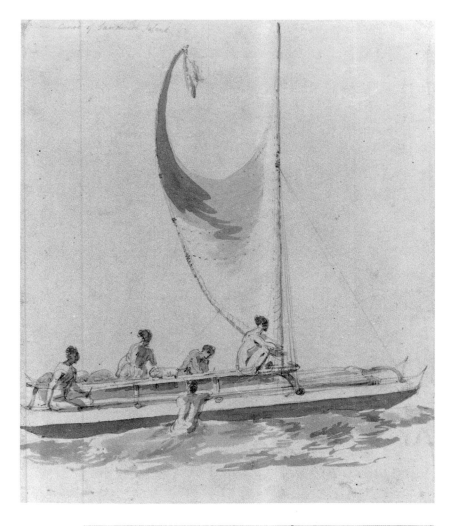

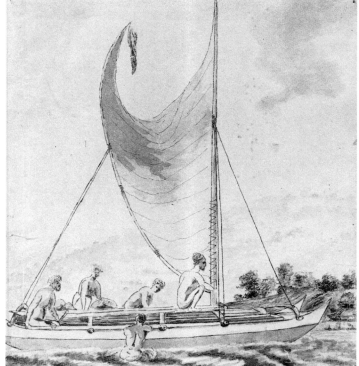

JOHN WEBBER

3.318   **A Sailing Canoe**   [1779]
pencil and sepia, 12¼ × 10⅛ : 311 × 256, unsigned;
w/m: (partly cut) lily in shield below 'VDL' = Van der
Ley.

Inscribed 'Canoe of Sandwich Island' in pencil (u.l.) in another
hand.

Four naked figures seated in a double canoe (*wa'a kaulua*), one
in the water holding to the side of the canoe. For the type of
canoe see Haddon and Hornell (1936) I, 6-19.

After an extensive explanation about the construction of the
Hawaiian canoe, both single and double, Samwell gives some
more information on the striking appearance of the double ones:
'The double Canoe consists of two large ones joined together by
cross pieces of wood, forming an arch between them, on which
a platform is erected where the Chiefs generally sit & where they
carry their Hogs and other Articles of Trade. On one of these
cross pieces near the middle of the Canoe the Mast rests and is
secured by shrouds and stays. One end of the Yard rests against
the foot of the Mast and taking a sweep forms an Arch of a Circle,
the upper end of which is as high as the mast head; the Sail is
made of strong Matting sewed together and is joined to the Mast
and the Yard, & at the upper end forms a half Moon which gives
their Canoes when under sail a very singular appearance; they
generally have a bunch of black feathers at the mast head and
at the end of the yard a kind of pendant flying made of Cloth.
. . . Some of the double Canoes are twenty yards long, are
strongly put together, and will answer the purpose very well of
going from one Island to the other which probably is the Extent
of the Navigation of these people. Some of the largest Canoes
will hold about sixty or seventy Men.' Cook, *Journals* III, 2,
1183-4.

ver: The subject of the drawing is similar to 3.319.

National Maritime Museum, London. (In volume of plates to
Cook's Voyages.)

UNKNOWN ARTIST

3.319   **A Sailing Canoe of the Sandwich Islands**   [1779]
pen, wash and water-colour, 11⅝ × 10¾ : 295 × 273,
unsigned; w/m: (half cut off) 'I.H.S. = Villedary.

The sheet has been cut down close to the pen frame line containing the drawing.

Inscribed in full 'Sailing Canoe of the Sandwich Islands or Owyhe'
on the back, probably in a later hand and in pencil 'taken on
board Capt. Cook's vessel at the front of'.

Compare Webber's drawing 3.318, but at right also a small house
on a wooded shore. For reasons of style this drawing can be
attributed neither to Webber nor Ellis. It is stylistically similar
to some other drawings by an unknown draughtsman (cf. 3.129
and 3.142).

ref: Exh. Cat. Portland (1974) no. 157; Murray-Oliver (1975)
pl. 35 (col.), where attributed to Webber.

Purchased by H. D. Skinner, Hocken Librarian, from Massey,
London, June 1936.

Hocken Library, University of Otago, Dunedin. Picture Collection. PaB 372 (6584).

WILLIAM ELLIS

3.320   Double Canoe of Sandwich Isles   [1779]
pencil and wash, 10⅛ × 7¼ : 256 × 180, unsigned;
w/m: 'Pro Patria' with Britannia.

The title as above in ink centred along lower edge of drawing
and annotated in ink after inscription 'See Ellis's Voyage Vol. 2.
p. 177' by the same hand. On verso are two studies of natives
and canoes and of a feather cloak, see 3.323.

Five people seated in a double canoe (*wa'a kaulua*) with a trilateral
sail (misconception of a crab-claw sprit-sail?). Three natives paddling, two and a dog resting on the platform. Above, in pencil
outline, the back view of a squatting figure.

'their canoes . . . are as well made, and highly finished as any
in the world. As their tools (like these of Otaheitee) are very
few; constructing one of them, must of course be a work of time.
The bottom is composed of a trunk of one entire tree hollowed
out, the colour of which is something like mahogony. The sides
are formed of a different wood, of a light yellowish colour, they
are well secured to the bottom part, by strong cords, which are
passed through holes made with a kind of augur. The head and
stern are both alike with respect to form, so that they may be
paddled either way without any inconvenience. The single canoes
are furnished with an out-rigger, which is placed on the left side.
The double ones are of the same form as the single, and are joined
together in the same manner as at the Society Isles: both vary
greatly in size, from twelve to sixty feet, and sometimes more;
the largest we saw belonged to Terriaboo and measured seventy-
two feet. All the double and many of the single ones carry a sail,
the form of which is something like those of the Friendly Isles;
none have more than one mast.' Ellis (1782) II, 177-8.

ver: Compare with the second canoe from left in 3.303. The
         drawing is also similar to the canoe in 3.320A.
ref: Murray-Oliver (1977) 37.

Alexander Turnbull Library, Wellington. A. 264.47 A.

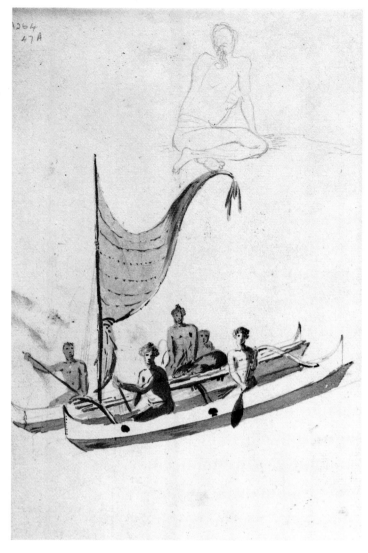

WILLIAM ELLIS (after)

3.320A   'A Double Canoe of Sandwich Islands'
Engraving. 'W. Ellis del.' — 'W. Walker sculp.'.
'Published Dec.ʳ 14 1781, by G. Robinson'.

Published in Ellis (1782) II, fp. 175, 177-8.

Probably developed from 3.320.

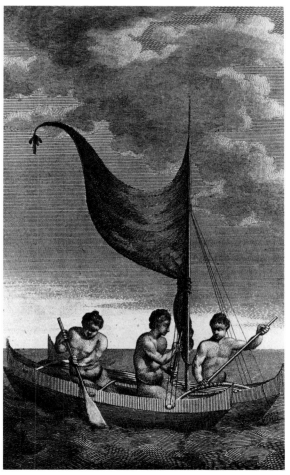

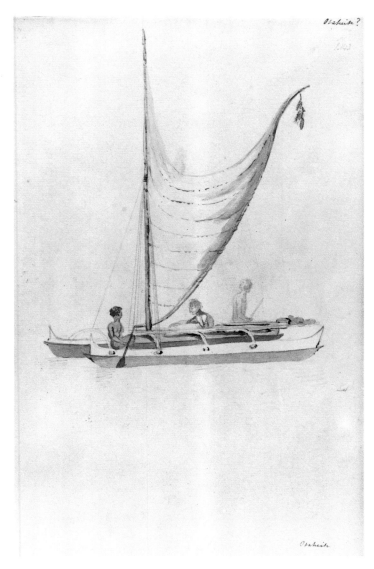

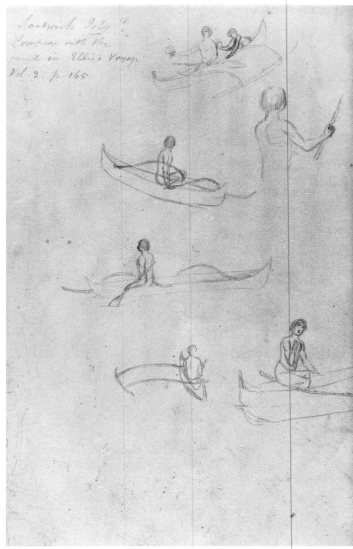

WILLIAM ELLIS

WILLIAM ELLIS

3.321   **A Double Canoe of the Sandwich Islands**   [1779]
pencil and grey wash, 12¹/₁₆ × 7⁵/₁₆ : 306 × 185, unsigned; w/m: 'Pro Patria' with Britannia.

Inscribed 'Otaheite?' in brown ink (u.r.), repeated without query (l.r.). Numbered in pencil 'I.143', referring to Ellis's *Narrative* (1782). On verso are two coastal profiles of (possibly) Tahiti (A 264.21 B).

Three figures in a large double canoe with a triangular sail. The reference above in Ellis's *Narrative* refers to 'Omai in a large canoe, which he had purchased here' [i.e. Tahiti]; but there appears to be a confusion, since the canoe is not Tahitian. It would follow that the inscription is not by Ellis himself but by a later hand.

ver: For similar canoes see 3.303 and 3.320.

ref: Murray-Oliver (1977) 33.

Alexander Turnbull Library, Wellington. A 264.21 A.

3.322   **[Studies of outrigger Canoes paddled by Hawaiians]**
[1779]
pencil, 10⁷/₈ × 7¹/₄ : 275 × 185, unsigned; w/m: 'Pro Patria' with Britannia.

Inscribed in pencil 'Sandwich Isles?' (u.l.) followed by 'Compare with the print in Ellis's Voyage Vol 2 p 165'. Inscribed in ink '3' (l.l.) and 'c' (l.r.). On verso a coastal profile of unknown location (A 264.46 B).

Six studies of figures in various postures and points of view in an outrigger-canoe (*wa'a kaukahi*); along the left side of the drawing, vertically, are the faint outlines of a coastal profile. For the type of canoes represented see Haddon and Hornell (1936) I, 20-3.

'They have outriggers on the larboard side, they are made of three pieces of wood, one large which serves to balance the Canoe & two bent & fastened to the Canoe. The paddles are broad and made of light Wood in the shape of a spade.' Samwell in Cook, *Journals* III, 2, 1183.

ref: Murray-Oliver (1977) 37.

Alexander Turnbull Library, Wellington. A 264.46 A.

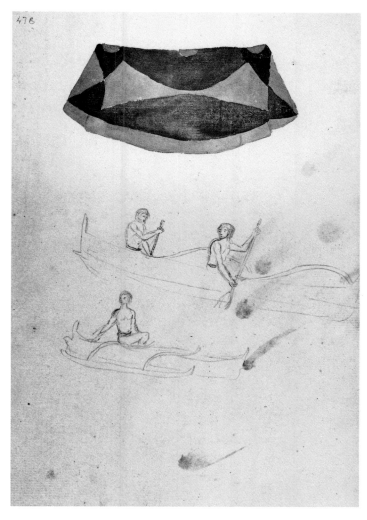

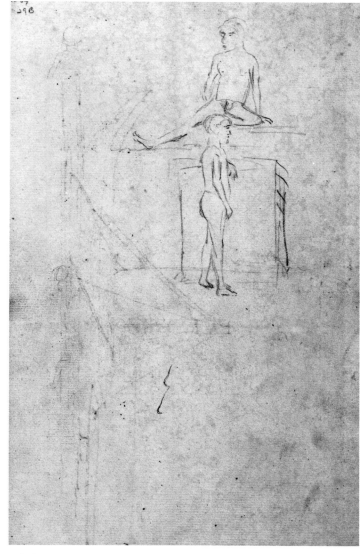

WILLIAM ELLIS

WILLIAM ELLIS

3.323   [An Hawaiian cloak and two canoes]   [1779]
pencil and water-colour, 10¹⁄₁₆ × 7¼ : 256 × 180, unsigned; w/m: 'Pro Patria'.

Numbered '72' (l.l.). On recto is a drawing of a double canoe and a squatting figure (3.320).

(a) A chief's cloak (*ahu-ula*) of red and yellow feathers (in water-colour).

(b) Two figures paddling an outrigger canoe (in pencil).

(c) A figure seated in an outrigger canoe (in pencil).

Of the cloak Ellis writes: 'The principal ornaments of the men are the feather-caps and cloaks; some of the latter reach down to their heels, and have a most magnificent appearance. They are made for the most part of red and yellow feathers, which are tied upon fine net work . . . Both caps and cloaks are made of various patterns and sizes. The cloaks are not all composed of the same kind of feathers, but are sometimes varied with the long tail feathers of the cock, with a border of yellow or red, and sometimes with those of the tropick bird. Both caps and cloaks, however, are only seen in the possession of the principal people.' Ellis (1782) II, 155.

ref: Murray-Oliver (1977) 37.

Alexander Turnbull Library, Wellington. A 264.47 B.

3.324   [Two men of Hawaii]   [1779]
pencil, 11⅝ × 7¼ : 295 × 185, unsigned; w/m: 'Pro Patria' with Britannia.

On recto is a drawing of a canoe of Otaheite, see 3.134.

One man seated with legs splayed, the other standing. Both wear the *maro*. A drawing in pencil of a canoe has been rubbed out. The drawing is uninscribed, but if the *maro* is any indication, was drawn, probably on board ship, at Hawaii.

'Their clothing consists of cloth of different kinds, that worn by the men, which is called marro, is about half a yard wide, and four yards long; that of the women, three quarters of a yard wide, and of the same length as the men's; this they call pah-ouwa, they both wear it round the middle, but the men pass it between their legs.' Ellis (1782) II, 153-4.

ref: Murray-Oliver (1977) 35.

Alexander Turnbull Library, Wellington. A 264.29 B.

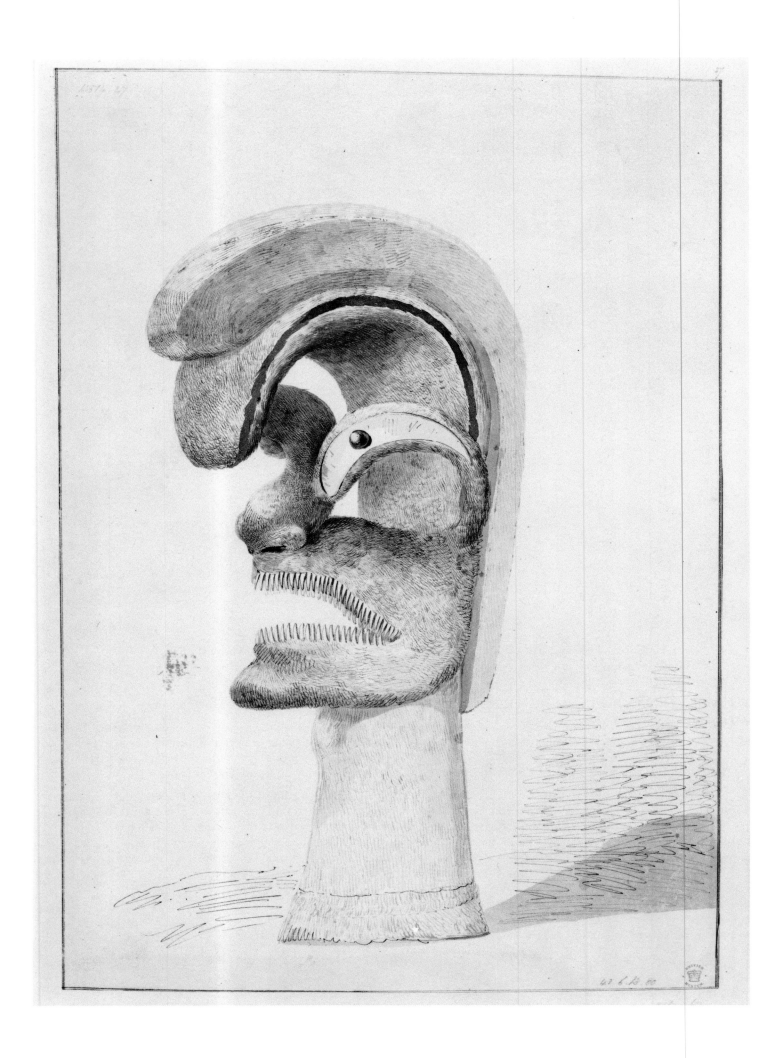

3.325   **An Idol made of Wicker, and covered with red Feathers** [1779–]
pen and wash, 20½ × 14¼ : 521 × 368, unsigned.

Inscribed 'no 99' (u.r.) which identifies it with no. 99 bearing the title above, in Webber's Catalogue. Also inscribed 'Atlas 67' in pencil on the mount below drawing.

'. . . in the Center Canoe were the busts of what we supposd their Gods made of basket work, variously covered with red, black, white, & Yellow feathers, the Eyes represent'd by a bit of Pearl Oyster Shell with a black button, & the teeth were those of dogs, the mouths of all were strangely distorted, as well as other features.' King in Cook, *Journals* III, 1, 512.

For another account see Samwell (ibid., 2, 1185). 3.325 is a drawing of a feather image collected on the voyage and now in the British Museum ((Museum of Mankind) VAN 231) cf. Kaeppler (1978a) 53.

ver: Drawn for the engraving at 3.327A. A late nineteenth century copy of the drawing is in the Bernice P. Bishop Museum, Honolulu, titled 'Article of the Sandwich Islands (Webber 1793)'.

ref: Cook, *Journals* III, 1, pl. 59 b; Rienits (1968) 141; Murray-Oliver (1975) pl. 48.

British Library, London. Add MS 15514, f. 27.

3.326   **[Hawaiian rattles]** [1779–]
pen, wash and water-colour, 13 × 18¼ : 330 × 464, unsigned.

'No 95' (l.l.) identifies this drawing with the one listed and titled 'Instruments of Music' in Webber's Catalogue; and traces of an inscription of which 'and when dancing' is faintly legible. Also inscribed 'Atlas 67' in pencil on mount below drawing.

Cook observed and first mentioned these rattles (*uli' uli*) during his stay in Kauai in February 1778: 'Another instrument was seen among them, but it can scarcely be called an instrument of music, this was a small gourd with some pebblestones in it, which they shake in the hand like a childs rattle and are used, as they told us, at their dances.' Cook, *Journals* III, 1, 284-5.

Beaglehole explains that these gourd rattles contained seed and that their handle 'ended in a circular fringe of cock's feathers' (ibid., 285 1n).

ver: A Hawaiian rattle is depicted in 3.327A. A late nineteenth century copy of 3.326 is in the Bernice P. Bishop Museum, Honolulu.

ref: Kaeppler (1978a) fig. 163; *idem* (1979) pl. 125.

British Library, London. Add MS 15514, f. 28.

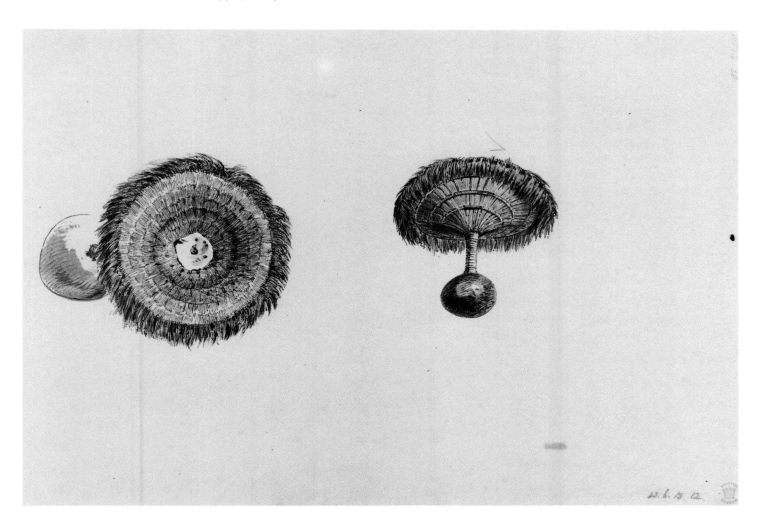

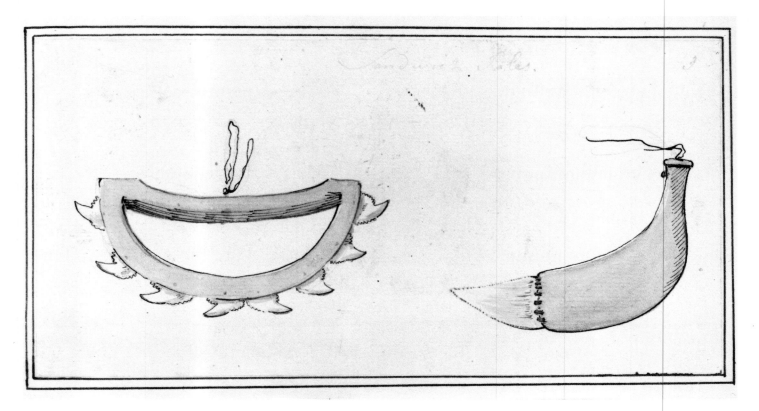

JOHN WEBBER

3.327   [Weapons or tools of Hawaii]   [1779–]
pen, wash and water-colour, 5⅛ × 10⅛ : 130 × 257, unsigned.

Inscribed 'Sandwich Isles' in pencil at top.

'They have also little instruments made of a single shark's tooth, some of which are fixed to the fore-part of a dog's jaw-bone . . . These serve as Knives occasionally, and are, perhaps, used in carving.' Cook/King (1784) II, 239. Also: 'The Knife or saw, formerly mentioned, with which they dissect the dead bodies, may also be ranked amongst their weapons, as they both strike and cut with it, when closely engaged. It is a small flat wooden instrument, of an oblong shape, about a foot long, rounded at the corners, with a handle, almost like one sort of the *patoos* of New Zealand; but its edges are entirely surrounded with sharks' teeth strongly fixed to it, and pointing outward; having commonly a hole in the handle, through which passes a long string, which is wrapped several times round the wrist.' Ibid., 247-8.

ver: The knife on the right appears in the engraving 3.327A. A late nineteenth century copy is in the Bernice P. Bishop Museum, Honolulu, titled 'Articles of the Sandwich Islands'.

British Library, London. Add MS 17277, no. 33.

JOHN WEBBER (after)

3.327A   'VARIOUS ARTICLES at the SANDWICH ISLANDS'
Engraving. 'J. Webber del.' — 'J. Record sculp.'.

Published in Cook/King (1784) pl. 67; II, 239 and 247-8 for the shark tooth implements; for the boar tusk bracelet and the rattle II, 232 and 236; for the dagger II, 247 and III, 152; and for the idol III, 17, 159-60.

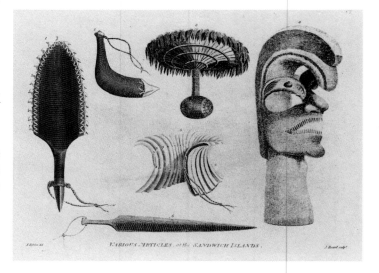

AVACHA BAY, KAMCHATKA: FIRST VISIT

29 April to 16 June 1779   3.328–3.353

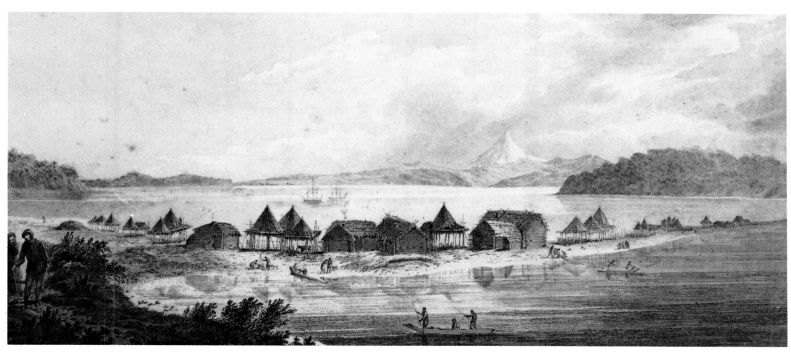

JOHN WEBBER

3.328   **A View of the Town and Harbour of St Peter and St Paul [Petropavlovsk] [plate 155]   [c. 1781-3]**
pen, wash and water-colour, 8⅞ × 20⅛ : 225 × 511, unsigned.

The title, as above, followed by 'in Kamtschatka' in pencil by a later hand on the folio beneath the drawing.

The view is towards the entrance of Avacha Bay. The village is shown on the sandy peninsula with Kamchatkan summer huts and Russian log huts. A man and woman at left; a canoe containing three men in the central foreground, other groups of figures along the shore; the *Resolution* and *Discovery* in the Bay in the distance, further off a volcano.

'The Town or Ostrog of S.t Peter & Paul stands upon a long narrow spit of Sand, which forms & seperates the Harbour from the Bay of Awatschka except at a narrow entrance about a Stones throw across. It consists of 5 or six Russian log Houses and about 15 Kamtschadale Houses called Balagans & 3 or 4 Joorta's.' Samwell in Cook, *Journals* III, 2, 1258.

An interesting but minor point is the animal standing below one of the balagans. This could be the bull which Samwell refers to on 15 May, saying that 'the Butchers were sent on shore to kill a Bullock which was procured for the Use of the Ships from the Serjeant'. Ibid., 1244. The bull may have been the only item of livestock in the ostrog, since milk which Clerke drank during his last period of illness, was brought from Paratunka.

The time depicted by the drawing is not clear. The preparatory drawings which Webber made of the houses (3.329-3.331) were taken during the snowy period, but 3.328 represented a time more advanced in the season, perhaps the end of May. The two ships are shown in the bay further to the sea, whereas during the second stay, when the bay had become more navigable, the ships were positioned nearer the head of the bay. The drawing itself however was most probably developed in London for the engraving 3.328A, from an original drawn on the voyage but now lost.

An earlier topographical rendering of the bay and the harbour of St Peter and St Paul was provided by Krasheninnikov (1764) fp. 14.

ver: For the engraving see 3.328A.

Dixson Library, State Library of New South Wales, Sydney. PXX 2, 41.

JOHN WEBBER (after)

3.328A 'A VIEW of the TOWN and HARBOUR of
ST PETER and ST PAUL, in KAMTSCHATKA'
Engraving. 'J. Webber del.' — 'B.T. Pouncy sc.'.

Published in Cook/King (1784) pl. 74, III, 184-5.

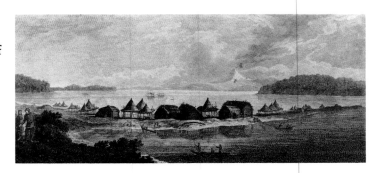

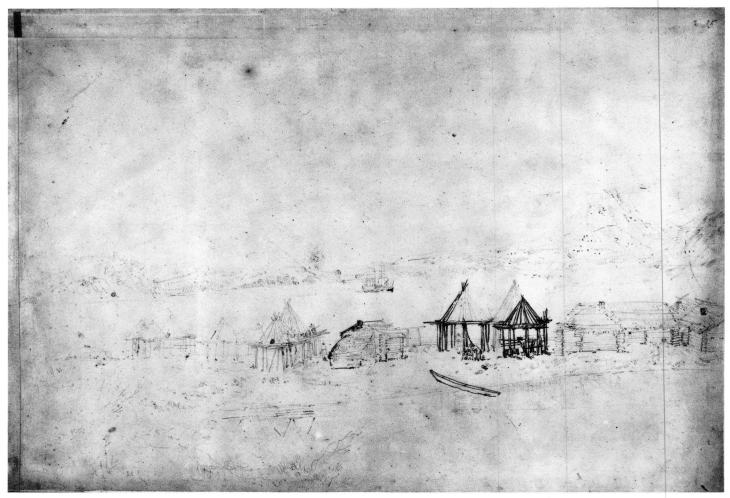

JOHN WEBBER

3.329a A View of the Town and Harbour of St Peter and
St Paul (Petropavlovsk) [May 1779]
pen and pencil, 14½ × 20⅞ : 368 × 530, unsigned.

A view across the bay with a spit of land in the middle distance
with several log houses and conical structures (balagans, or summer habitations of the Kamchadals). A volcano in the background. Two ships in the bay. The bushes in the foreground are
without leaves, indicating that the drawing was made early during
the first visit to Kamchatka. The drawing forms a panorama with
3.329b.

ver: A preparatory study for the left side of 3.328.

British Library, London. Add MS 17277, no. 35.

JOHN WEBBER

**3.329b   A View of the Town and Harbour of St Peter and
             St Paul (Petropavlovsk)   [May 1779]**
        pen and pencil, 13¼ × 19¾ : 337 × 502, unsigned.

The spit of land continued, densely covered with log houses and
conical summer houses. In the background the bay is terminated
by a mountain range. The drawing forms a panorama with 3.329a.

ver: Preparatory study for the right side of 3.328.

British Library, London. Add MS 17277, no. 36.

JOHN WEBBER

**3.330   A View in Kamchatka with balagans and a log house
                                               [May 1779]**
        pen and wash, 14½ × 21 : 366 × 533, unsigned.

This drawing may be one of the two listed as no. 115 and no.
116 'Several Ballagans Summer habitations' and 'Several Ditto'
in the 'Kamschatka' section of Webber's Catalogue.

Petropavlovsk. Four huts, including two balagans, upon piles,
and a log house. In the left foreground, a boat landing with three
figures, bringing in fish, also two dogs. Judging from the snowy
ground and sparse vegetation it was drawn in early May.

ver: The huts in the background are repeated in the etching
         3.340A. For a study of the dog in profile but laterally
         inverted see 3.366.

British Library, London. Add MS 15514, f. 31.

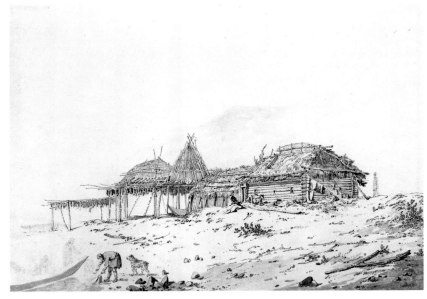

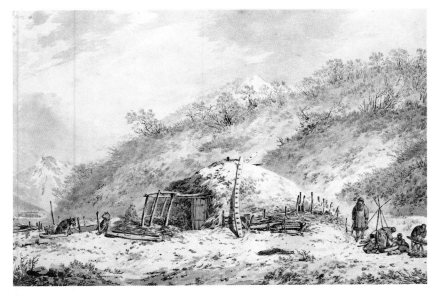

JOHN WEBBER

3.331 **A Jourte [Yurt] or Kamchadale Winter Habitation**
[plate 157] **[May 1779]**
pen, wash and water-colour, 14¹¹/₁₆ × 21³/₁₆ :
373 × 538, signed and dated 'Jn Webber del 1779'.

This drawing is probably the one referred to as 114 with the title as above in Webber's Catalogue.

The dwelling in the central foreground with a ladder to provide entrance from the roof resting against it. A side door with some posts and rack in front of it; to the left, a man seated and two dogs; at the extreme right four figures, one standing, near a bench, fireplace and cooking pot. The standing man holds a fish. At left background a river or bay with a boat near a block-house.

'We were no less struck with the strange Appearance of the Houses, both Russian and Kamtschadale; of the latter were two sorts, one under ground the other mounted on stilts in the Air . . .' Samwell in Cook, *Journals* III, 2, 1241. The same author makes an observation which is much to the point of this drawing: 'The Joorta is built partly under ground & the roof covered with Earth. The entrance to these was formerly at the Top, but since the Russians have been here they make the Door at the Side.' Ibid., 1258. To judge from the snowy countryside, the view was taken in early May, probably before 7 May when Webber left for Bolsheretsk.

ver: For a study of the standing man holding a fish see 3.348.

British Library, London. Add MS 15514, f. 38.

JOHN WEBBER

3.332 **The Inside of a Winter Habitation**
[plate 159] **[May 1779]**
pencil, pen, wash and water-colour, 13⅛ × 19⅝ :
333 × 498, unsigned.

The drawing is surrounded by three thin black framing lines but has been sharply cut at the edges. On verso 'Lot No 5' in brown ink.

At left, a figure crouching over a pot by a fire, nearby a dog licking from a trough; at centre, a standing figure looking right; at the right a woman with a child seated on a low bunk, holding a small child in her lap. Two large posts at either side of the drawing in the foreground.

King supplies the following information: 'The *jourt* consists of one apartment, of the form of an oblong square. Along the sides are extended broad platforms made of boards, and raised about six inches from the ground, which they use as seats, and on which they go to rest, after strewing them with mats and skins. On one side is the fire-place, and the side opposite is entirely set apart for the stowage of provisions and kitchen utensils. At their feasts, and ceremonious entertainments, the hotter the *jourts* are made for the reception of the guests, the greater the compliment.' Cook/King (1784) III, 374-5.

Samwell remarks that formerly the entrance to the yurts was from the top, in Cook, *Journals* III, 2, 1258. This observation compares well with an engraving from Krasheninnikov's *History of Kamtschatka* (1764), opp. 181 'The Inside of a Winter Hut', which shows the wooden beam with carved steps leaning inside the entrance hole.

ver: For another, smaller and more finished drawing see 3.333.

National Library of Australia, Canberra. Rex Nan Kivell Collection. NK 52/G.

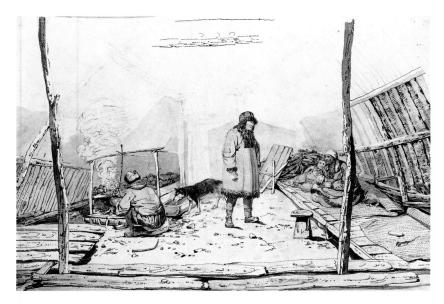

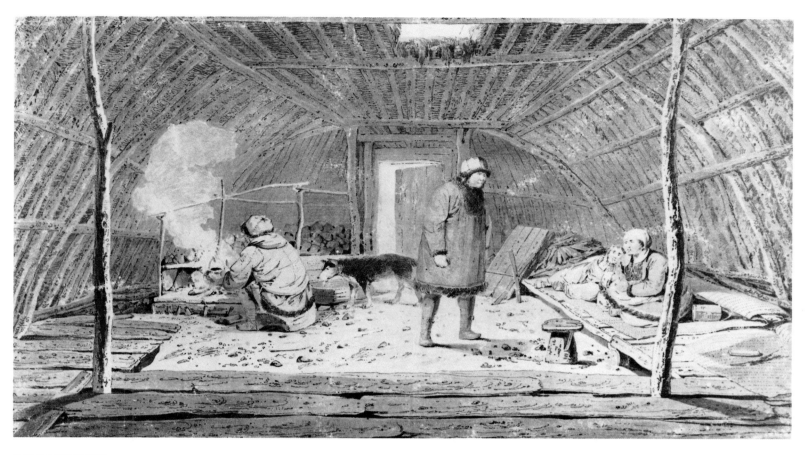

JOHN WEBBER

3.333   The Inside of a Winter Habitation   [c. 1781-3]
pen, wash and water-colour, 8¾ × 15⅜ : 222 × 391,
unsigned.

Laid down on cardboard; on verso 'Kamschatka Winter Habitation' in pencil in an eighteenth century hand, partly erased; 'glass'
in pencil (u.r.); 'No 8 Flat Maple Frame' along right edge, no.
'5' (u.r.) and no. '10' (l.r.). Surface discoloured probably due
to exposure to light. The drawing may be identified as no. 111
'The Inside of a Winter Habitation called a Jourte' in Webber's
Catalogue.

At left a person cooking. On the ground, next to him, a dog.
In the centre a man standing. At right a woman and child seated
on a bench, the woman holding a small baby in her arm.

ver: Another version of 3.332; which served for the engraving
3.333A. The woman bears a resemblance to the one portrayed in 3.350. The man standing near the centre may
be compared with the man portrayed in 3.343 and 3.347.

Listed in Francis Edwards, *Cat.* 416 (London, July 1921) under
no. 769 as 'The Inside of a Winter Habitation in Kamtschatka
(15½ by 9 in), in sepia and colour'.

National Library of Australia, Canberra. Rex Nan Kivell Collection. NK 52/H.

JOHN WEBBER (after)

**3.333A   'The INSIDE of a WINTER HABITATION in
KAMTSCHATKA'**
Engraving. 'J. Webber del.' — 'W. Sharp sculp.'.

Published in Cook/King (1784) pl. 78, III, 374-5.

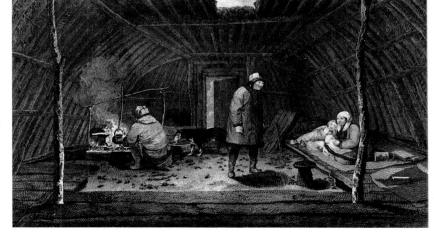

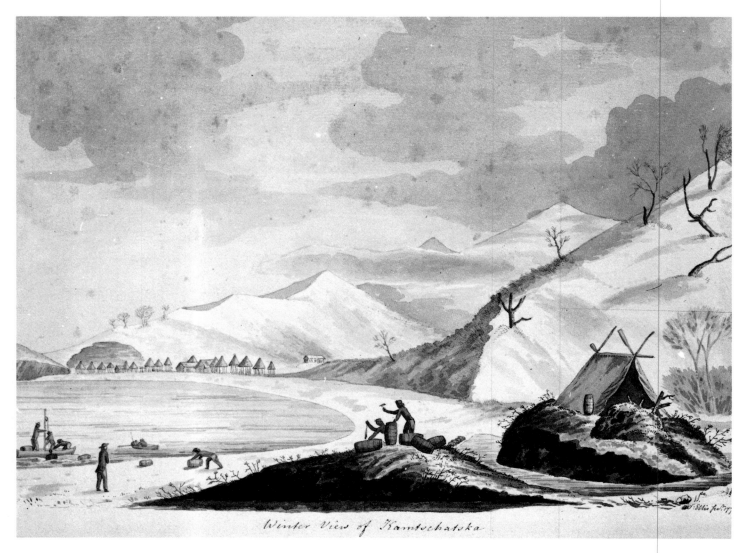

Winter View of Kamtschatska

WILLIAM ELLIS

3.334   **A Winter View near the harbour of St Peter and St Paul**   [May 1779–]
pen and wash drawing tinted with blue, $9^{15}/_{16}$ × $13^{5}/_{16}$: 250 × 338, signed and dated in black ink 'W: Ellis fec^t 1779' (l.r.); part of w/m: fleur-de-lis in a shield with 'W' underneath = J. Whatman.

The title 'Winter View of Kamtschatska' inscribed in brown ink below the drawing, and 'no 7' (u.l.).

A beach scene covered with snow, with huts in the distance belonging to the village of St Peter and St Paul. The view is directed towards the spit of land. In the foreground Europeans caulking barrels and others rolling them into a small boat in the foreground. At right, a tent pitched on a rock beside a stream. A background of high, snowy mountains.

'. . . on the 12th [May 1779] a party was sent to cut wood, and our empty casks were got on shore to repair.' Ellis, *Narrative* (1782) II, 219. Samwell communicates for 13 May: 'The Resolution erected a Tent on shore abreast of the Ship for the Use of the Waterers and sent all their Water Casks on shore.' Cook, *Journals* III, 2, 1244. The drawing thus appears to be one of the earliest drawn in Kamchatka.

ref: *Exh. Cat.* Portland (1982) 200.

Museum Book Store, London, *Cat.* 94 (1924) no. 562/10 and *Cat.* 107 (1928) no. 41/10; *Cat.* 125 (1941) 453.

National Library of Australia, Canberra. Rex Nan Kivell Collection. NK 53/F.

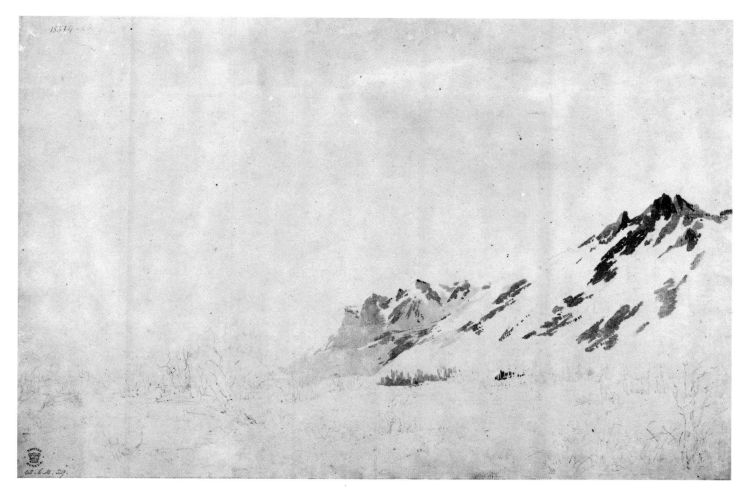

JOHN WEBBER

3.335   **A View in Kamchatka**   **[May 1779]**
pencil and wash (parts incomplete in pencil), 14 ×
20⅞ : 355 × 530, unsigned.

On the right mountains covered by snow, on the left a river
banked by barren trees. On the river a man in a boat punting.
In the centre a figure sitting on a cart.

The view was probably drawn during the journey by Gore, King
and Webber to Bolsheretsk, which was partly over water. That
the boats were moved by punting is attested in King's remark:
'The river was by the account of our guides very low, & which
was very favourable for pushing against the Stream . . .' King
in Cook, *Journals* III, 1, 660. Compare also Ellis, who, though
he did not participate in the journey, says that travelling to
Bolsheretsk was very tedious 'which was sometimes by water in
flat-bottomed boats, forced on by two men with poles'. (1782)
II, 219.

British Library, London. Add MS 15514, f. 61.

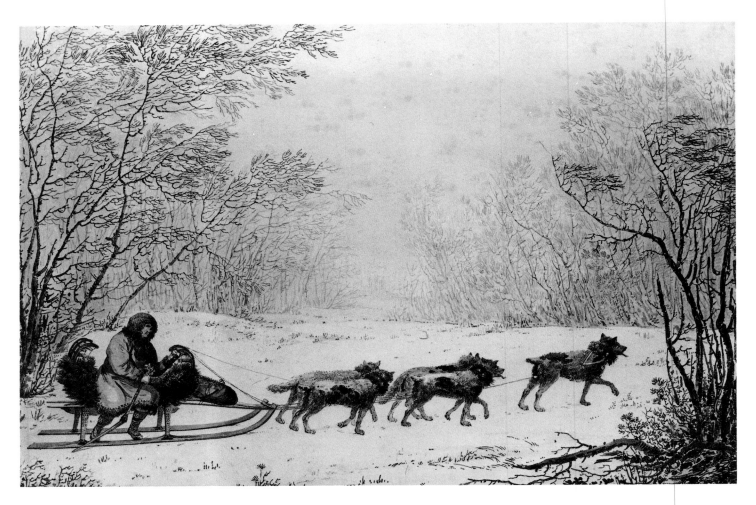

JOHN WEBBER

3.336 The manner the Kamchadals travel in Winter
[plate 161] **[May 1779–]**
pen and wash, 12½ × 18 : 317 × 457, signed and
dated 'Jn° Webber del 1779' in ink (l.l.).

Laid down on cardboard; on verso in pencil 'Manner of travelling
in Kamtschatka' in an eighteenth century hand, partly erased,
also 'glass 2' and along right edge 'Cedar frame'; in ink the Lot
'No 26'. Also in pencil 'Captain C[ampbell]' across the back.
The drawing may be identified as no. 119 'The manner the
Kamschadales travel in Winter' in Webber's Catalogue.

Bare trees surrounding a clearing where a man is seated on a high
sledge drawn by a team of five dogs.

The first sledges drawn by dogs were observed in early May in the
village of Petropavlovsk (King in Cook, *Journals* III, 1, 652). The
drawing most probably refers to the journey from Petropavlovsk
to Bolsheretsk or during the return in which Gore, King and
Webber took part (between 7-12 and 17-21 May 1779). King
gives an account of the mode of sledge travelling in the *Journals*,
663, but elaborates on this in the official account: 'They [the
sledges] are seldom used to carry more than one person at a time,
who sits aside, resting his feet on the lower part of the sledge,
and carrying his provisions and other necessaries, wrapped up in
a bundle, behind him. The dogs are usually five in number,
yoked, two and two with a leader. The reins not being fastened
to the head of the dogs, but to the collar, have little power over
them, and are generally hung upon the sledge, whilst the driver
depends entirely on their obedience to his voice for the direction
of them . . . The driver is also provided with a crooked stick,

which answers the purpose both of whip and reins; as by striking
it into the snow, he is enabled to moderate the speed of the dogs,
or even to stop them entirely.' Cook/King (1784) III, 263.

ver: For a study for 3.336 see 3.337 and for the engraving see
3.336A. Cf also 3.336B.

Listed in Francis Edwards, *Cat.* 416 (London, July 1921) under
no. 769 as 'A Man of Kamtschatka, Travelling in Winter (17¾
by 12½ in), in sepia and colour'.

National Library of Australia, Canberra. Rex Nan Kivell Collection. NK 52/C.

JOHN WEBBER (after)

3.336A   'A MAN of KAMTSCHATKA, TRAVELLING in WINTER'
Engraving. 'J. Webber del.' — 'S. Middiman sc.'.

Published in Cook/King (1784) pl. 70, III, 203.

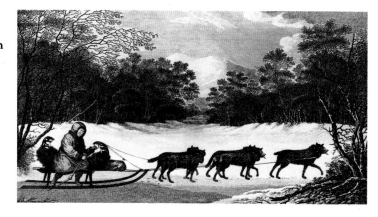

WILLIAM ELLIS (after)

3.336B   'A Kamtschadale travelling in Winter'
Engraving. 'W. Ellis del.' — 'W. Walker sculp.'.
'Published Jany 1, 1782 by G. Robinson'.

Published in Ellis (1782) II, fp. 207.

The drawing bears considerable similarity to Webber's drawing 3.336.

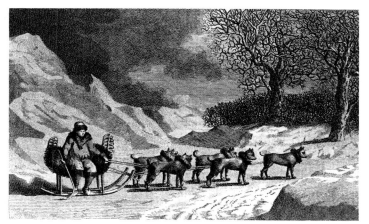

JOHN WEBBER

3.337   [Men of Kamchatka travelling in Winter]
                                        [May 1779]
pen, wash and pencil (unfinished), 13⅝ × 20⁵⁄₁₆ :
345 × 515, pasted on sheet, unsigned.

Inscribed in ink at left in Webber's hand 'This sledge, in the Russian Language is called [crossed out] named a Sandkey'.

Two men on a sledge carried by five dogs, with another on skis drawn in pencil; a background of trees lightly outlined in. The traveller on the sledge looks like Webber himself (cf. plate 202).

Contrast with 3.336 which gives a general representation. This one reflects the actual travelling to Bolsheretsk, as expressed by Webber. King points out: 'As we did not choose to trust to our own skill [in manoevering the sledges] we had each of us a man to drive and guide the sledge, which from the state the roads were now in, proved a very laborious business.' Cook/King (1784) III, 205.

Probably purchased by David Scott Mitchell from Bernard Quaritch, London.

Mitchell Library, State Library of New South Wales, Sydney. PXD 59⁻¹, f 115.

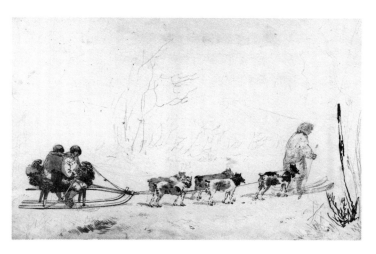

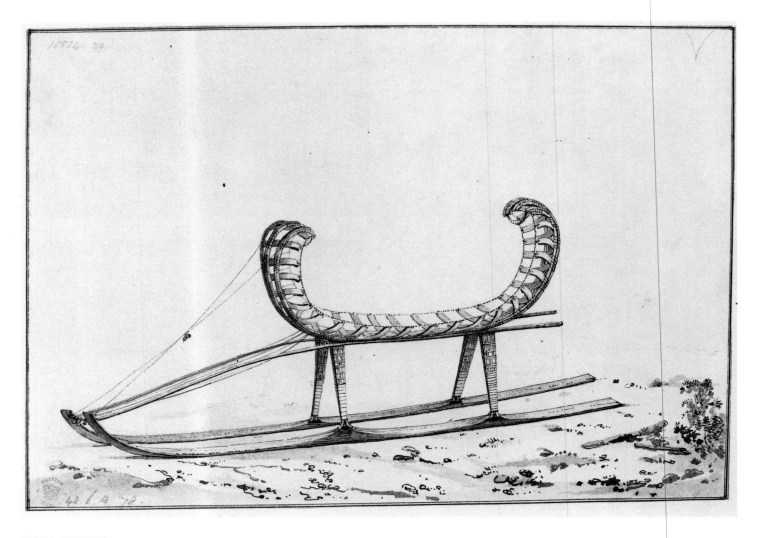

JOHN WEBBER

3.338   **A Sledge of Kamchatka**   [May 1779]
         pen, wash and water-colour, 9 × 12½ : 228 × 317,
         unsigned.

Inscribed 'A Sledge of Kamschatka' in pencil on the mount below
the drawing; 'no 123' (u.r.) which identifies it as '123 A Sledge'
in the 'Kamschatka' section of Webber's Catalogue. Also 'Atlas
71' in pencil on mount below drawing.

'The figure of the sledges will be best conceived by the annexed
engraving, which was taken from one I brought over with me,
that is now in the possession of Sir Ashton Lever.' Cook/King
(1784) III, 202. There follows a long description of the construction of the sledge. Ibid., 202-3. See also Samwell: 'we brought
a dozen or 14 dogs with us in the 2 Ships, and C[aptain] K[ing]
brought one of their Sledges away with him.' Samwell in Cook,
Journals III, 2, 1282.

ref: Cook, *Journals* III, 1, pl. 65 b.

British Library, London. Add MS 15514, f. 29.

JOHN WEBBER

3.339   **A Sledge of Kamchatka**   **[c. 1781-3]**
        pen, wash and water-colour, 7⅛ × 8¾ : 180 × 223,
        unsigned.

The title, as above, in pencil by a later hand on the folio beneath
the drawing.

ver: A smaller version of 3.338 with the addition of a conical
        hut (*balagan*) and snowy slopes. Drawn for the engraving
        3.339A. The motif of the balagan and the hilly background
        appear again in Webber's painting at 3.346.

Dixson Library, State Library of New South Wales, Sydney.
PXX 2, 40.

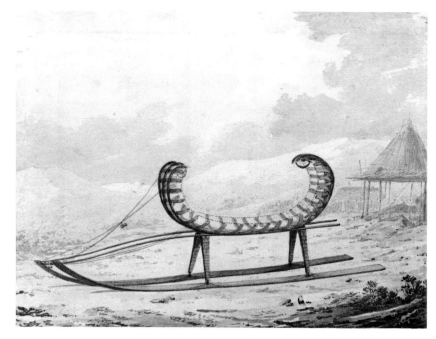

JOHN WEBBER (after)

3.339A   **'A SLEDGE of KAMTSCHATKA'**
          Engraving. 'J. Webber del.' — 'Woodyer sc.'.

Published in Cook/King (1784) pl. 71, III, 202-3.

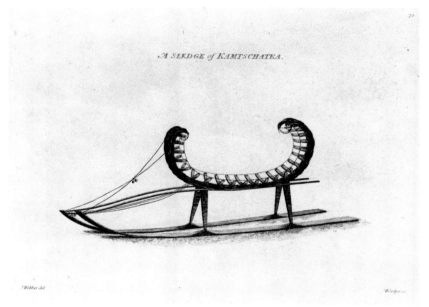

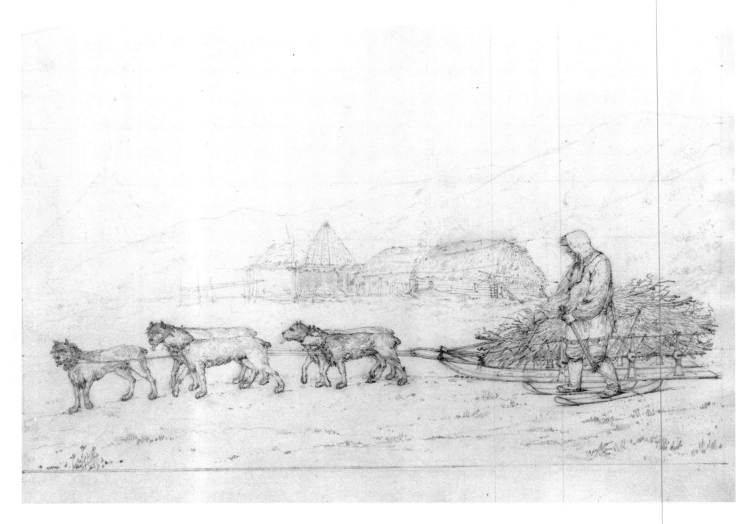

JOHN WEBBER

3.340   **The Narta, or Sledge for Burdens in Kamtchatka**
[1789]

pencil, 12$\frac{1}{16}$ × 17$\frac{7}{16}$: 306 × 443 (sheet-size);
10$\frac{11}{16}$ × 15$\frac{15}{16}$: 272 × 405 (image-size); w/m:
lily in shield under crown with 'GR' below.

The drawing is squared for transfer and is likely to be a preparatory
study for Webber's softground etching of the title above, published
1 July 1789 (3.340A).

Close comparison between the drawing and Webber's softground
etching reveals a number of small but significant differences: the
drawing lacks the rock on the slope in the right background, and
it omits figures underneath the balagans; it likewise has no foot
steps of the dogs as clearly marked in the print. The drawing is
about 1cm shorter in height, more sky has been added to the
etching. It is therefore reasonable to conclude that the drawing
is an original work by Webber and not a copy after the print.

ver: The houses in the background echo Webber's drawing at
3.330, from which they seem to be copied.

Eyre and Hobhouse, London (1984).

Private collection, England.

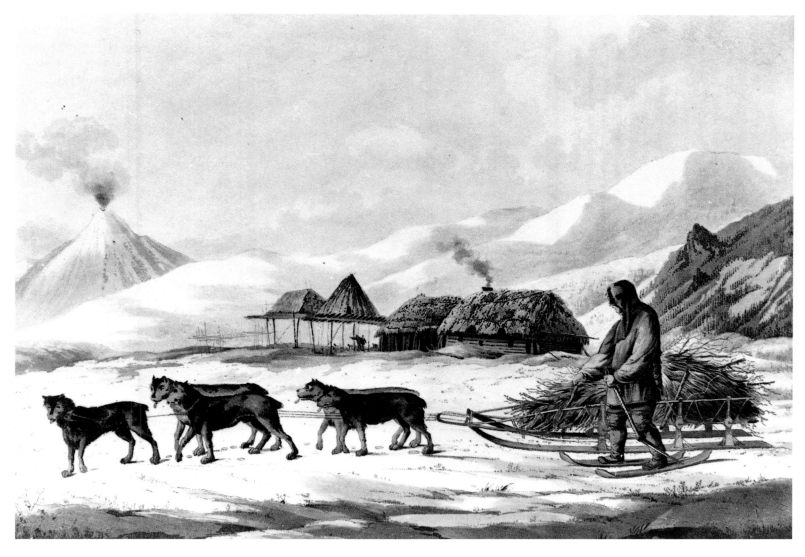

JOHN WEBBER

3.340A **a. 'The Narta, or Sledge for Burdens in Kamtchatka'**
softground etching, tinted in brown and grey wash, or
hand-coloured, 12⅞ × 17¹³⁄₁₆ : 327 × 452 (11⅛
× 16⁵⁄₁₆ : 282 × 415). 'J. Webber fecit'. 'London
Pub.ᵈ July 1. 1789 by J. Webber Nº. 312 Oxford Street'.
'NB not mention'd in Cooks last Voyage'.

ver: For Webber's drawing of a similar scene see 3.336 and
3.337. The volcano in the back is derived from Webber's
view in the British Library, Add MS 15514, 33 ab.

British Museum, Department of Prints and Drawings, London.
246˙ a.2 and C. 6˙.

b. 'The Narta, or Sledge for Burdens in Kamtchatka'
coloured aquatint. 'J. Webber fecit.'. 'London Pub.ᵈ
April 1 1809 by Boydell & Comp.ʸ Nº. 90 Cheapside'.
'NB not mention'd in Cooks last Voyage'.

Issued as J. Boydell, *Views in the South Seas* (London, 1808) pl. X.

National Maritime Museum, London; Bernice P. Bishop Museum, Honolulu.

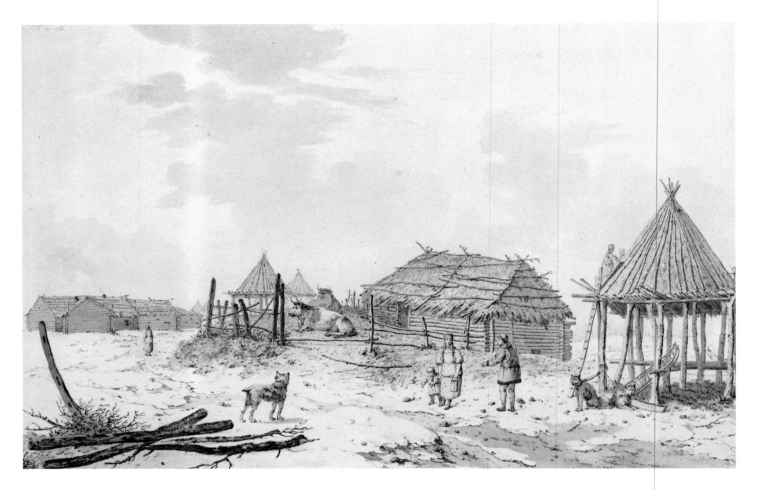

JOHN WEBBER

3.341   A View of part of Bolchoiercka (Bolsheretsk)
[May 1779]
pen, wash and water-colour, 15⅞ × 24¾ : 404 × 629,
signed and dated 'Jn Webber del 1779'.

The traces of '125' (u.r.) identifies this drawing as no. 125 in
Webber's Catalogue with the title as above.

Kamchatka houses with at right a man, woman and child; in the
left background, another figure; cattle and a dog. Webber's visit
to Bolsheretsk occurred between 12-16 May 1779.

King mentions the village at greater length on 13 May: 'we employ'd the afternoon in seeing the town & Country; the Country
for many miles about is a low swamp . . . The Earth was in most
parts cover'd with snow; . . . We saw I suppose 20 or 30 Milch
Cows, & the Major [Behm] had 6 stout horses, all of which were
in good Case; These & the dogs are the only domestic Animals
. . . The houses are all after one fashion, that is built of logs
& thatch'd . . . At one end of the town are a Number of Bal-
laggans.' King in Cook, *Journals* III, 1, 667-8.

ver: Engraved by P. Benezech for 3.341A. For a study of the
dog see 3.366.

British Library, London. Add MS 15514, f. 32.

JOHN WEBBER (after)

3.341A   'A VIEW at BOLCHERETZKOI, in
KAMTSCHATKA'
Engraving. 'J. Webber del.' — 'P. Benezech sc.'

Published in Cook/King (1784) pl. 72, III, 215-16.

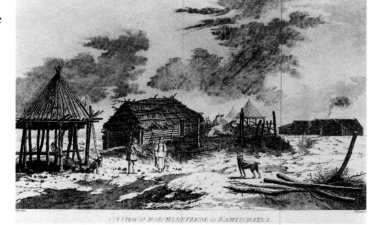

A View at BOLCHERETZKOI in KAMTSCHATKA.

JOHN WEBBER (or after?)

3.342 **Portrait of Magnus von Behm, governor of Kamchatka**
      [plate 164]   **[May 1779–]**
      gouache, 6⅞ × 5⅞ : 175 × 150, on a sheet tipped
      into a book (see below), the sheet inscribed in pencil,
      possibly in Webber's hand 'Major Behm'.

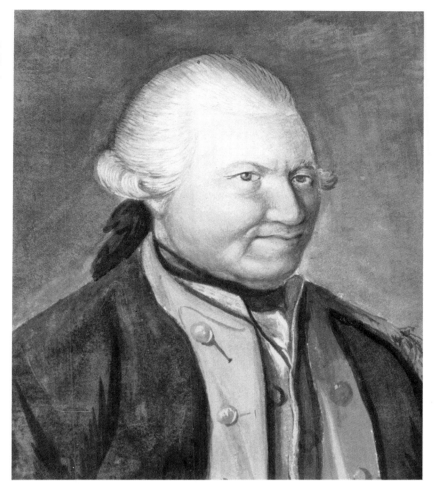

Breast portrait of the governor, looking to the right. His face is
of reddish colour, his hair is white and terminates in a pigtail with
a hair-ribbon. His coat is green, with red collar and buttons,
underneath an orange-coloured westlet. The background is
brownish. On verso are contours of Behm's portrait in pencil.

Behm is well remembered for providing ample provision for the
two ships. On 7 May Captain Gore, Lieutenant King and Webber
set out for Bolsheretsk to meet the governor at his house hoping
for beef and flour. They returned with him to St Peter and St
Paul on 21 May. The next day Behm was received by Captain
Clerke on board the *Resolution* and the day after by Captain Gore
on board the *Discovery*. Samwell informs us that, 'He sat for his
picture to Mʳ Webber who took a very good likeness of him.'
Cook, *Journals* III, 2, 1247.

'The Major whose name is Frederick Magnoos Behm or Boem is
about 50 years of age, was born in Livonia & had been Governor
here about six years; he is a stout, good looking Man and much
of a Gentleman both in his Behaviour and Appearance.' Ibid.,
1246.

Ellis gives another description of him in his official dress: 'He was
near six feet high, rather corpulent, and was very polite and
affable in his address. He wore his uniform, which was dark green,
with plain gold buttons, a scarlet waistcoat trimmed with broad
gold lace, and a gold laced hat with a white cockade.' Ellis (1782)
II, 225.

The portrait is here tentatively attributed to John Webber, showing a positioning of the head and a somewhat timid expression
of the face that seems characteristic of Webber's portraits, for
example his portrait of Cook. The technique of the picture in
gouache however is rare in Webber's *oeuvre* and there is no ab-
solute way of deciding whether the picture was actually drawn
in Kamchatka or copied later in England. A more finished portrait
of Governor Behm by Webber of the same composition may still
come to light. The portrait belonged to the Welsh naturalist
Thomas Pennant (1726-1798), author of *Arctic Zoology* (1784-87)
who had a strong interest in Cook drawings relating to the Arctic.

Previously owned by Thomas Pennant. Pennant may have received Behm's portrait through the agency of his friend, Peter
Simon Pallas, the German scientist attached to the Russian court
and Professor of Natural History in the Imperial Academy of
Sciences at St Petersburg. Pallas concludes a letter sent to Pennant
from St Petersburg (15-26 December 1779 — which provided a
detailed account of the circumstances leading to Cook's death)
by stating that 'As Major Behm is expected here this winter, and
carries with him the Resolution's log-book and a chart sent by
Capt. Cook you may expect some more account respecting America
and the streights, if I should be favoured with a sight of these'.
HRNSW (1893) I, pt i, 431.

Tipped into a copy of volume III of Cook/King, *Voyage*, 2nd edn,
Nicol and Cadell (London, 1785) fp. 226.

Dixson Library, State Library of New South Wales, Sydney.
Q 77/37.

JOHN WEBBER

3.343   A man of Kamchatka [plate 162]   [May 1779]
pencil, chalk and sepia wash, 11 × 8 : 279 × 203,
unsigned.

A full-length study of a man wearing a fur-trimmed coat and hat.
This man is repeated in a similar stance in 3.345.

King gives a description of the winter dress of the Kamchadal,
distinguishing between a skin frock, a pair of leather trousers, dog
or deer skin boots and a fur cap with flaps. During his visit to
Bolsheretsk King was given by Major Behm's son a magnificent
dress as worn by the principal Toions [or chiefs] of Kamchatka.
King's account of the dress corresponds to Webber's drawing in
a number of points, however Webber's drawing is too general for
close comparison. 'A border of six inches breadth, wrought with
threads of different-coloured leather, and producing a rich effect,
surrounds the bottom, to which is suspended a broad edging of
the sea-otter skin. The sleeves are turned up with the same
materials; and there is likewise an edging of it round the neck,
and down the opening at the breast. . . . A cap, a pair of gloves,
and boots, wrought with the utmost degree of neatness, and made
of the same materials constitute the remainder of this suit.' Cook/
King (1784) III, 377. King brought the dress back to England
but whether it still exists is not known.

ver: The figure was introduced into 3.331.
ref: Cook, *Journals* III, 1, pl. 66 a.

Francis Edwards, *Cat.* 551 (London 1932) entry 3 as 'A man of
Kamtschatka (11 by 8 in)'.

Francis P. Farquhar Collection, Berkeley, California.

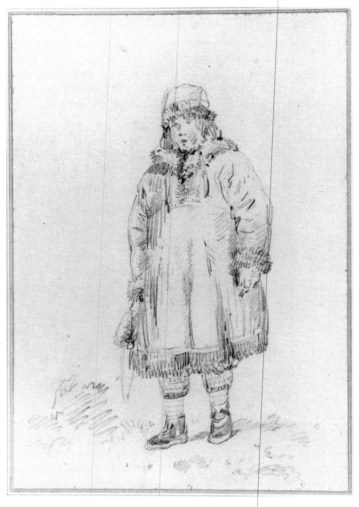

JOHN WEBBER

3.344   A Woman of Kamchatka   [May 1779]
pencil, 11⁷⁄₁₆ × 7¹³⁄₁₆ : 290 × 198, unsigned.

'Woman of Kamtshatka' inscribed on mount beneath the lined
frames. The sheet mounted on cardboard with enframing bands
in sepia. Some of the sepia of the inner band has spread on to
the edge of the sheet. There is some evidence of erasures at the
top of the drawing above the head.

A full-length study of a woman facing three-quarter right with
her hand tucked into an overgarment hung by straps over the
shoulders over a full-length dress; a bonnet or scarf worn on the
head.

This drawing could have been taken on 8 May in the ostrog of
Karatchin, where Gore, King and Webber 'were receiv'd by the
Kamskadales men & women . . . Every one was drest out in their
best, & the womens dress was very pretty & gay, compos'd of
diff. coloured Nankins, & some had part of their dresses made
of a slight silk; their shifts were also silk, & the Married women
had hansome Silk Handkerchiefs bound round their heads'. King
in Cook, *Journals* III, 1, 661.

'The Women follow the Russian Fashion & are dressed in Russian
& Chinese Manufactures.' Samwell in ibid., 2, 1259. For an
even more extensive description of the women's dress, see Cook/
King (1784) III, 200.

ver: A woman with a similar dress appears in 3.341.

Listed in Francis Edwards, *Cat.* 551 (London 1932) entry 4 as
'Woman of Kamtschatka (12 × 8 in)'.

Francis P. Farquhar Collection, Berkeley, California.

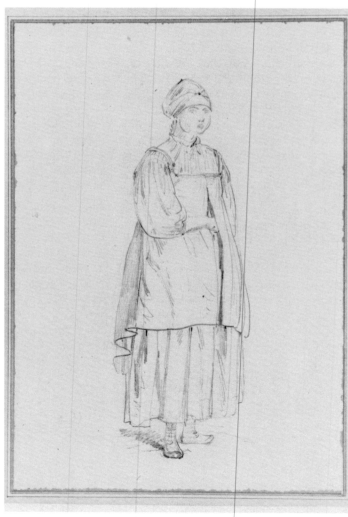

JOHN WEBBER

3.345 Native(s) of Kamchatka [plate 163]   [May 1779]
pencil and crayon, 14 × 10 : 407 × 254, unsigned.

Apparently a drawing of one male figure only seen full-face and in profile.

Because of the heavy winter outfit of the native one might assume that the drawing was taken during Webber's journey to Bolsheretsk. Judging from the staff, the man might have been a driver of the dog-sledges.

Described as 'Kamtskadales' in the Francis Edwards *Cat.* 551 (London 1932) no. 5, '14 × 10 in'.

Francis P. Farquhar Collection, Berkeley, California.

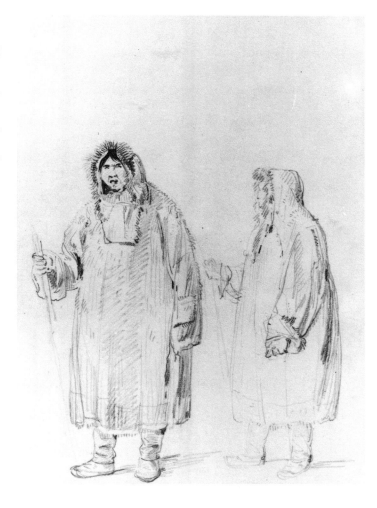

JOHN WEBBER

3.346 Natives of Kamchatka   [1786]
oil on panel, 17¾ × 14⁹⁄₁₆ : 450 × 370, signed and dated 'J. Webber pᵗ 1786' (l.l.).

Though the two adult figures seem to be dressed as men, the picture obviously represents a family. This is suggested by the eye contact between the central figure (who carries a bucket) and the child kneeling on the ground. The man to the right is holding a staff and possibly unfastening the dogs to set out in the sledges at the back. In the background, at left, a *jourte*; on the right, two *balagans* or summer habitations.

Webber exhibited a painting of 'Natives of Kamchatka' at the Royal Academy in 1786 (17) which seems to be the one represented.

ref: Sotheby's *British Paintings 1500-1850* (London, 21 November 1984) no.89 (col.).

The Harvey Family of Langley Park, Berskshire during the eighteenth and nineteenth centuries, then by descent.

Private collection, England.

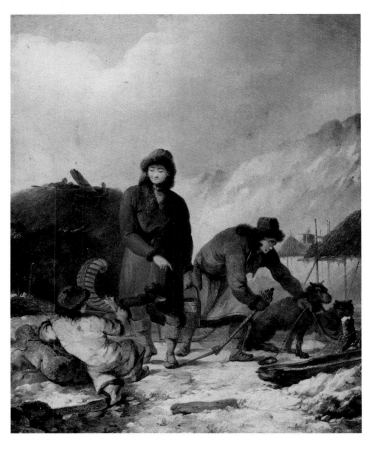

JOHN WEBBER

3.347   A Man of Kamchatka   [May 1779]
pencil and wash, 9⅛ × 7 : 232 × 178, unsigned.

Laid down on cardboard within sepia framing lines. 'No 10' inscribed on mount on lower margin. On verso in ink the Lot 'No
20' and 'A Man of Kamschatka' in pencil in an eighteenth century
hand.

Perhaps this is the drawing listed as no. 113 'A Portrait of a Man'
in the 'Kamschatka' section of Webber's Catalogue.

A three-quarter view, with long hair, a fur-trimmed coat, facing
right. This and the following portraits of the natives of Kamchatka
seem still to have been taken during the winter period.

ver: Engraved by W. Sharp for 3.347A.

Listed in Francis Edwards, *Cat.* 416 (London, July 1921), under
no. 769 as 'A Man of Kamtschatka (9 by 7 in) in sepia'.

National Library of Australia, Canberra. Rex Nan Kivell Collection. NK 52/E.

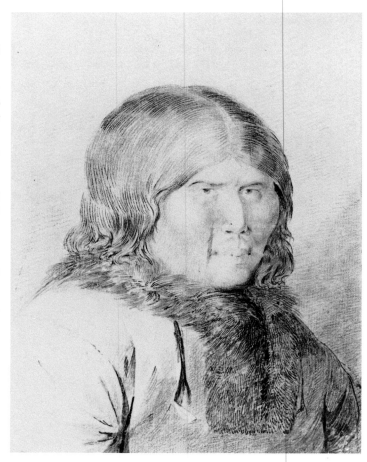

JOHN WEBBER (after)

3.347A   'A MAN of KAMTSCHATKA'
Engraving. 'J. Webber del.' — 'W. Sharp sc.'

Published in Cook/King (1784) pl. 75, III, 377.

A proof-state inscribed in pencil 'A Man of Kamtchatka' in
Webber's hand and numbered in pencil 'N°. 75' (u.r.) is kept
in the National Library of Australia, Canberra, in a folio of plates
from the Skottowe Hall Library.

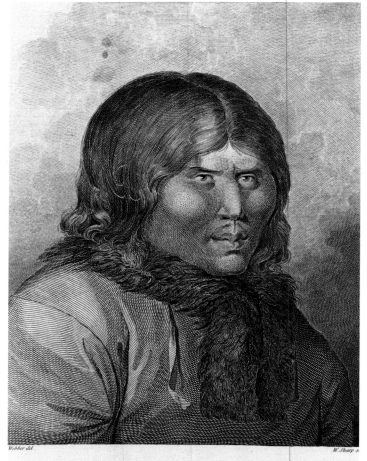

A MAN of KAMTSCHATKA.

JOHN WEBBER

3.348   A Man of Kamchatka   [May 1779]
pencil and wash, 17⅛ × 12³⁄₁₆ : 435 × 315,
unsigned.

A portrait of the head and shoulder of a Kamchadal; with protruding cheek bones and narrow eyes, looking right; wearing a
fur-trimmed coat.

'the Kamskadales . . . very round and flat fac'd, large heads, high
Cheek bones, & small Eyes, the Forehead very low, nose small,
& a great distance between that & the Chin, in proportion to
the rest of the face; they were redder in the Cheeks and much
more chubby in the face. Their dress was like that of the Russians,
A Jacket clos'd in the front . . .'. King in Cook, *Journals* III, 2,
1452, when describing the Kamchadals met in Alaska.

ver: For a study of the same man see 3.349.

ref: Cook, *Journals* III, 1, pl. 66b mistakenly as 'Woman of
         Kamchatka'.

British Library, London. Add MS 15514, f. 35.

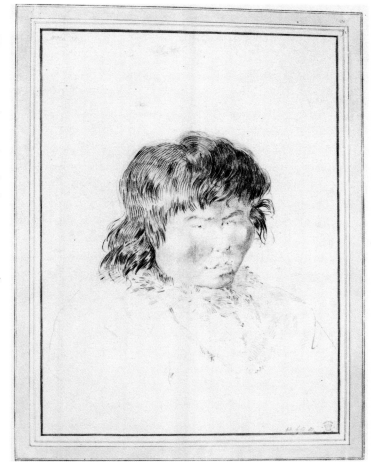

JOHN WEBBER

3.349   A Native of Kamchatka   [May 1779]
pencil, 13⅞ × 10 : 353 × 253, unsigned.

Inscribed 'Native of Kamtshatka' on the mount beneath the drawing. Inscribed 'no 4' on verso of the mount. Mounted on card
with enframing bands in sepia wash.

ver: For another version of the portrait see 3.348.

Listed in Francis Edwards, *Cat.* 551 (London 1932) entry no. 2
'Native of Kamtschatka (14 by 10 in)'.

Francis P. Farquhar Collection, Berkeley, California.

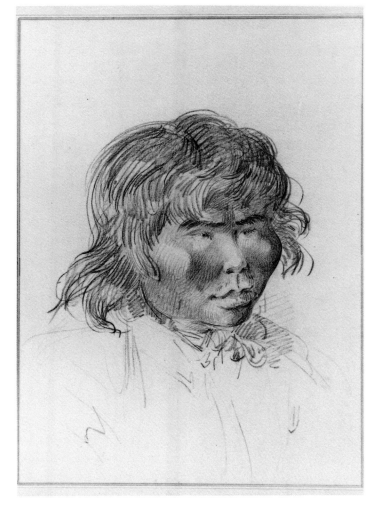

JOHN WEBBER

3.350   A Woman of Kamchatka   [May 1779–]
pencil, 16½ × 12⅜ : 420 × 313, unsigned.

Laid down on cardboard. On verso the title in pencil as above; in ink 'Lot No 9' (crossed out) and '13' substituted; also '6' in ink.

Perhaps this is the drawing listed as 112 'A Portrait of a Woman' in the 'Kamschatka' section of Webber's Catalogue.

Portrait of a woman in three-quarter view looking towards the left. Wearing a head-scarf with side-flaps over either shoulder.

ver: For a preparatory sketch see 3.351. Engraved by W. Sharp (3.350A). There is some similarity between this woman and the one depicted in Ellis (1782) (3.351A).

Listed in Francis Edwards, *Cat.* 416 (London, July 1921) under no. 769 as 'A Woman of Kamtschatka (17 by 12 in) in sepia'.

National Library of Australia, Canberra. Rex Nan Kivell Collection. NK52/F.

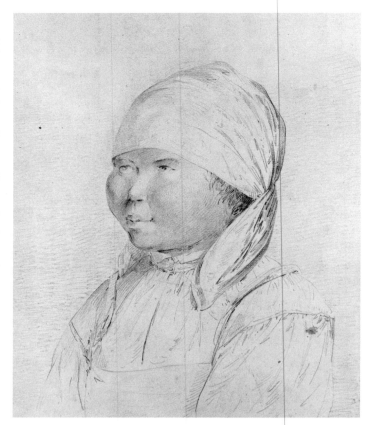

JOHN WEBBER (after)

3.350A   "A WOMAN of KAMTSCHATKA"
Engraving. 'J. Webber del.' — 'W. Sharp sc.'

Published in Cook/King (1784) pl. 76, III, 200.

A proof-state inscribed in pencil 'A Woman Kamtchatka' in Webber's hand and numbered in pencil 'N°. 76' (u.r.) is kept in the National Library of Australia, Canberra, in a folio of plates from the Skottowe Hall Library.

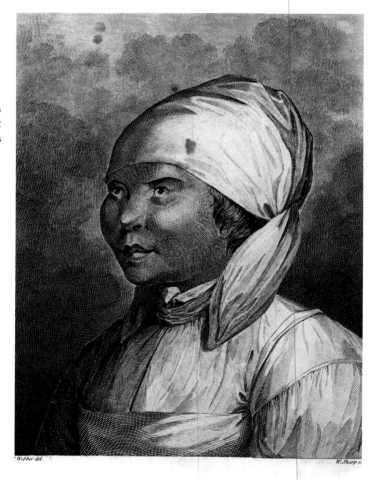

'Webber del.'   *W. Sharp sc.*

A WOMAN of KAMTSCHATKA.

JOHN WEBBER

3.351   A Woman of Kamchatka   [May 1779]
          pencil, 19¾ × 13⁵⁄₁₆ : 502 × 338, unsigned.

Mounted on card and enframed by three framing bands in sepia
wash. Inscribed on mount in pencil 'Woman of Kamtshatka'.
Inscribed '3' on verso of mount.

Listed in Francis Edwards, *Cat.* 551 (London 1932), entry 1 as
'Woman of Kamtschatka' with slightly differing dimensions given
as '16 by 12 in'. It is likely that this is the drawing referred to
as no. 1, since in an additional line the catalogue notes: 'With
the exception of No. 1, these drawings are unpublished . . ..'
The drawing was however 'published' as early as 1784 (see 3.350A).

Francis P. Farquhar Collection, Berkeley, California.

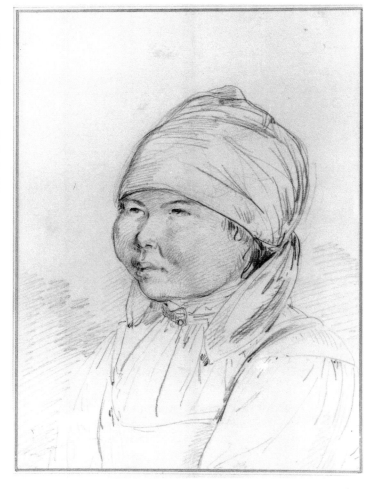

WILLIAM ELLIS (after)

3.351A   'A Woman of Kamtschatka'
          Engraving. 'W. Ellis del.' — 'J. Heath sc.' 'Publish'd
          Dec.ʳ 14ᵗʰ 1781 by G. Robinson'.

Published in Ellis (1782) II, fp. 238.

No drawing by Ellis for this engraving is known.

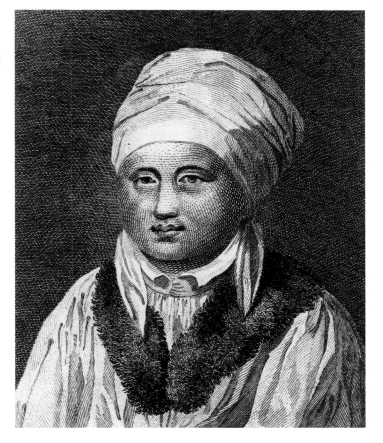

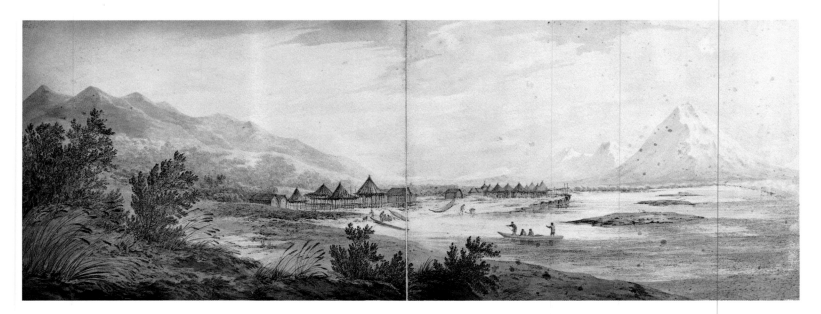

JOHN WEBBER

3.352   **A View of the Village of Paratounqua (Paratunka)**
        [plate 156]   **[May 1779–]**
        pen, wash and water-colour, 19⁵⁄₁₆ × 52 : 491 ×
        1321, unsigned.

The title, as above, inscribed in pencil in Webber's hand (u.l.).
'No 127' faintly discernible in pencil (u.r.), which would identify
this drawing as '127. A View of the Village Paratounka, with the
Mountains Awachinskoi' in Webber's Catalogue.

In the foreground at left the shoreline of the bay showing small
bushes and long grasses bearing grain; in the mid-distance the
village, with log huts and summer houses (*balagans*). In the bay
to the right, four figures in a canoe, and further canoes and figures
along the shore. In the background on the far right, the high
snow-covered peak of the volcano, Avachinskaya.

'Paratoonka is situated on the banks of a river of the same name
and is distant about 20 miles from the Harbour of S.ᵗ Peter and
Paul, contains a Church, six Russian Houses and 16 Balagans or
Kamtschadale Houses built upon high Pillars and a few Joortas
or Huts built partly underground. The Church was built by Bering,
is constructed like the Russian Houses of Timbers & has a kind
of Cupola upon it.' Samwell in Cook, *Journals* III, 2, 1251.

Webber visited Paratunka at least once on 26 May when he and
King accompanied Major Behm as far as this village. Additionally
there were frequent contacts between the ship's company and the
priest of Paratunka, Pope Romanoff Vereshagen, who supplied
the dying Clerke with fresh milk. Cf. King in ibid., 1, 673 and
Samwell in ibid., 2, 1243. The drawing cannot have been taken
before late May, after Webber's return from Bolsheretsk, when
the grounds were still partly covered by snow.

ver: For a more sketchy version of the right part of this drawing
          see 3.353.
ref: Cook, *Journals* III, 1, pl. 63 under a mistaken title and an
          incorrect folio no. 'The village of Petropavlovsk, Avacha
          Bay', 'Add. MS 17277.30'.

British Library, London, Add MS 15514, f.30.

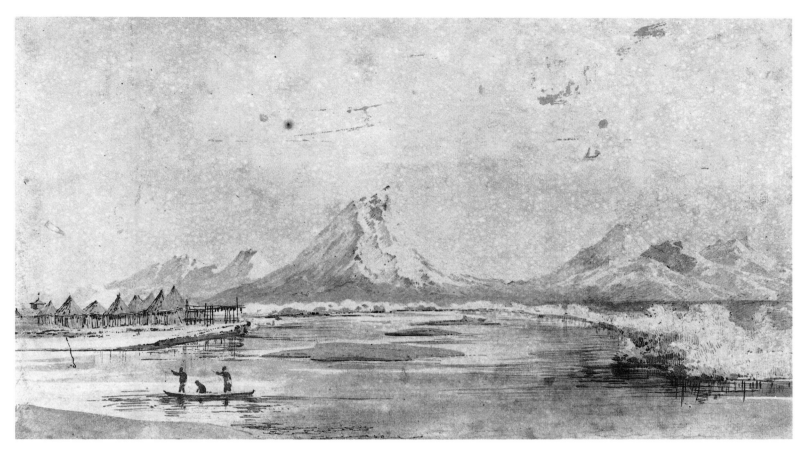

JOHN WEBBER

3·353   **A View of the Village of Paratunka**   [May 1779]
pen, pencil and wash, with some tints of water-colour,
12 × 20¾ : 305 × 527, pasted down on mount,
unsigned.

Inscribed in ink on the mount 'Original Water-Colour Sketch
by J. Webber (Made on Cook's Third Voyage)' and towards the
right in pencil 'View of the Village of St. Peter and St. Paul,
probably by Webber', then followed by a reference to Cook,
Journals III, 640. The drawing is mounted on a folio which orig-
inates from the volume PXD 59⁻¹, where it was kept as f. 123.

Three men in a boat near the shore, two standing and pointing
to the shore; the middle man seated; a cluster of houses in mid-
distance, with the church at extreme left. Nearby at the water's
edge some drying racks. Jagged snow-capped mountains in the
back.

ver: The drawing is a study for Webber's panorama composition
of 3.352, but taken somewhat to the right of that view.

ref: *Exh. Cat.* Portland (1974), 185, where mistakenly identified as the village of Petropavlovsk.

Probably purchased by David Scott Mitchell from Bernard Quaritch, London.

Mitchell Library, State Library of New South Wales, Sydney.
PXD 59⁻², f.6.

577

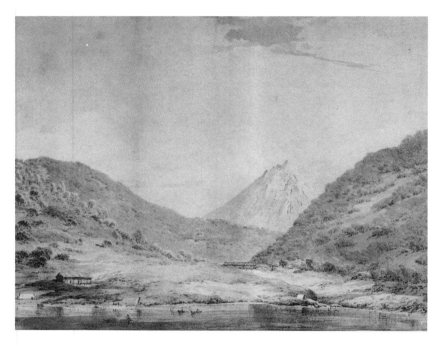

JOHN WEBBER

3.354   [View in Avacha Bay] [plate 165]   [Aug 1779–]
water-colour, 18 × 23 : 458 × 584, unsigned.

The drawing can be tentatively identified as no. 126 'A view of the North End of the Harbour Peter and Paul with the Mountain Awachinskoi' in Webber's Catalogue.

A Russian log hut near the shore at left, in the central mid-distance the store-house and hospital of St Peter and St Paul, behind which the volcano Avachinskaya (2741 m) rises. Three tents from left to right with boats and figures along the foreshore. Drawn in August or September 1779 after the return from the Arctic voyage to Avacha Bay.

'in the Afternoon Anchord and Moord in the harbour of St. Peter and Paul. The Country has now a most beautiful appearance; Kamtschatka in Summer and Kamtschatka in winter one would Scarcely call the same place'. J. Burney's remark on 24 Aug 1779 in Cook, *Journals* III, 1, 701.

Note also Samwell's entry for 25 August: 'The Astronomers' Observatories were erected on shore and a Tent for both Captains. Tents were likewise erected for the Use of the Waterers, Wooders, Brewers & Oil Boilers & Sailmakers . . . August 26 : Fine pleasant Weather. People employed in wooding, watering & brewing small Beer & the Carpenters repairing the Ship . . .' Ibid., 2, 1273.

Another passage from Samwell's journal is worth quoting for the impression which the country of Avacha Bay made upon the men after their return from the Arctic circle: 'What struck us most on our Arrival here now was the pleasant Appearance of the Country, which forms a perfect Contrast to what it was on our first arrival here in May, being then entirely covered with Snow; whereas now Hill and Dale is adorned with the most delightful and cherishing Verdure which has sprung up with a Luxuriancy which we never could have expected to see in this Country. The Hills about the Bay rising with a gentle ascent & covered with Trees afford many prospects equal and not unlike to Mount Edgecombe near Plymouth. There is one View here that excells any I ever met with, which is that of the Summit of a very high Mountain far inland that is covered with Snow, which rising behind some Hills of a moderate height covered with Verdure presents through a Vally a most delightful and grand Picture, exhibiting the Image of Summer and Winter at one View.' Ibid., 2, 1273.

ver: The drawing by Ellis (3.355) is from the same viewpoint.

ref: Brewington (1969), no. 1747, 455.

Peabody Museum, Salem. Gift of Stephen W. Phillips (1947). M. 12466.

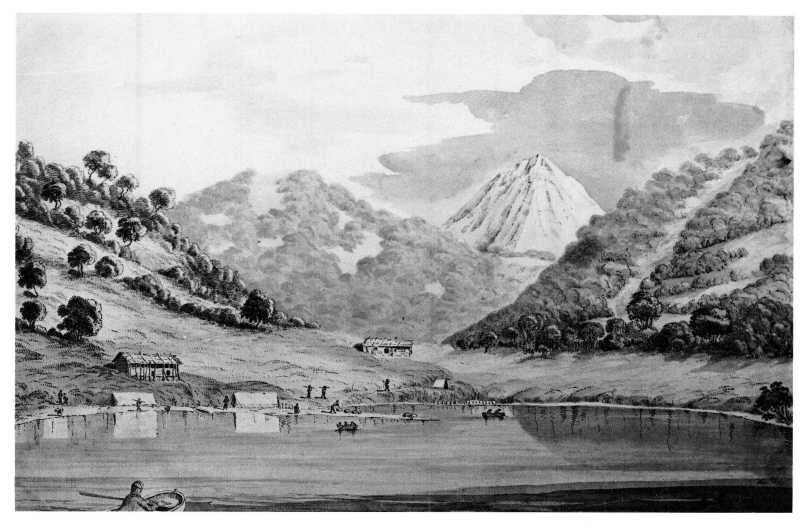

WILLIAM ELLIS

3.355   **View in Avacha Bay**   [Aug 1779–]
pen, wash and water-colour, 12⅝ × 18½ : 320
× 463, signed and dated in black ink 'W W Ellis fecᵗ
1779'; w/m: 'I.H.S. I. VILLEDARY'.

Number '8' written in ink (u.l.).

A shore scene, two Russian huts, three tents, figures on the beach
carrying beams, others rolling barrels. Wooded rising ground and
the volcano Avachinskaya in the background. A figure in a rowing
boat in the left foreground.

'All our hands were employed in erecting the tents and observatories on shore, and getting up the empty casks, and blubber to
boil down, and the coppers to brew spruce beer . . . ' 25 August,
Ellis (1782) II, 295.

'The caulkers, brewers, wooders, coopers, &c were all busied in
their respective departments . . .' 27 August, ibid., 296.

ver: The same viewpoint was chosen by Webber for his drawing
of Avacha Bay, see 3.354.

Museum Book Store, London, *Cat.* 94 (1924), no. 562/9 and
Cat. 107 (1928), 41/9, where mistakenly titled 'View of part of
the beach in Kealakeakua Bay, Hawaii' and *Cat.* 125 (1941) 453.
The earlier catalogues have the following caption: 'This is the
only drawing in the collection without title. It appears to be that
part of the Bay where the astronomers' tents were erected, behind
which are two roughly constructed huts, with the huge peak of
the Mauna Loa volcano in the background. This is the first
drawing of this famous volcano, and no other drawing executed
during this voyage appears to have survived which shows this

mountain.' In 1928 the drawing was bought by Governor George
R. Carter of Hawaii, but returned to the Museum Book Store
when it became apparant that the drawing did not in fact represent
Kealakakua Bay. The description was not repeated in the 1941
catalogue. It was purchased by Rex Nan Kivell for his collection.

National Library of Australia, Canberra. Rex Nan Kivell Collection. NK 53/I.

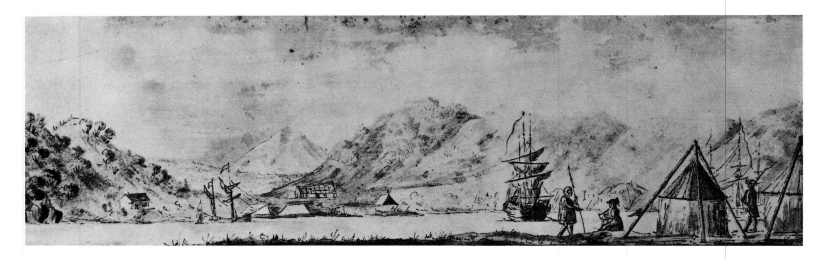

EDWARD RIOU

3.356   The Harbour of St Peter and St Paul   [Sep 1779–]
pen, wash and water-colour, 3¾ × 12 : 95 × 305.

Inscribed below drawing in ink: 'A Sketch of the Harbour of St Peter & St Paul, with Mount A'wantchka, as taken from the Spit'. The drawing forms the upper part of a rectangular chart titled: 'A Plan of the / Bay of Avatch'ka / by Edward Riou' in ink. The drawing somewhat faded.

At the right the astronomers' tents with a guard mounted. Near-by a seated man (Webber ?) drawing a Kamchadal holding a spear. Compare the costume worn by the man in 3.343. The Kamchadals used spears for hunting bears (cf. Cook, *Journals* III, 2, 1279). Behind this group the *Resolution* and *Discovery* at anchor. At left by the farther shore a low-hulled two-masted vessel, probably the Russian galliot from Okhotsk, which came into the harbour on 10 September 1779. See Edgar's journal in ibid., 1, 705.

Inside the big chart of Avacha Bay there is also a detail chart of the ships' harbour which explains the topography of Riou's drawing; this is titled: 'The Harbour of St Peter and St Paul'. The attribution of the drawing to E. Riou is made on the basis of the chart's signature. There are no figurative drawings known by him which confirm this suggestion.

ref: Skelton (1955), pl. LVII; Skelton (1969), pl. XV.

Hydrographic Department of the Admiralty, Taunton. HD 524/1.

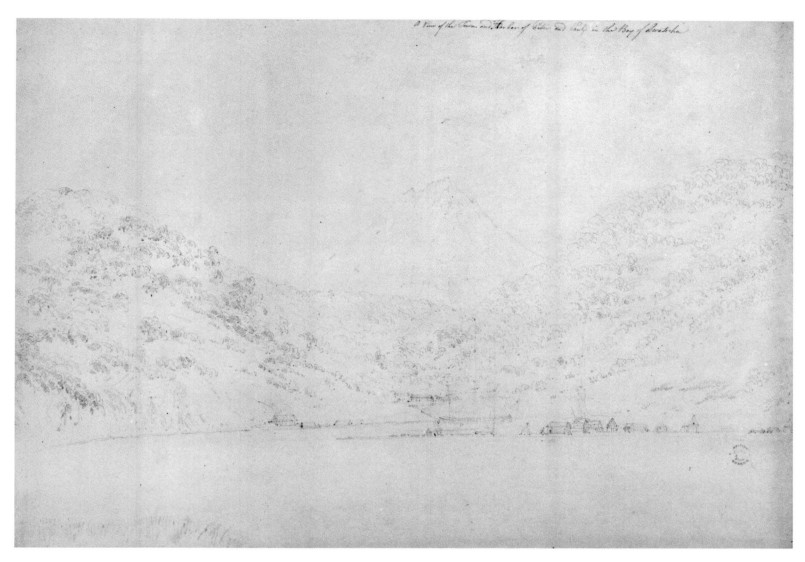

JOHN WEBBER

3.357   **A View of the Town and Harbour of St Peter and Paul (Petropavlovsk)**   **[Aug, Sep 1779]**
pencil, 14¾ × 20¹³/₁₆ : 375 × 529, unsigned.

The title as above, followed by 'in the Bay of Awatscha' in pen in Webber's hand (u.r.).

Looking into the bay, with a curving shoreline and conical mountain. In the middle distance behind the spit of land with native houses, the *Resolution* and *Discovery* at the bottom of the bay. The position of the ships thus differs from that of the first stay.

Drawn in late August or September 1779 on the second visit to Avacha Bay, as indicated by the green foliage.

ver: Cf. 3.354 and 3.355.

British Library, London. Add MS 17277, f. 37.

JOHN WEBBER

3.358   Village of St Peter and Paul (Petropavlovsk)
                                          [Aug-Sep 1779]
pencil, wash and water-colour, 13⅜ × 21³/₁₆ :
340 × 538, unsigned.

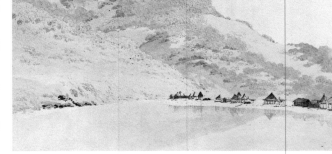

The title, as above, followed by the word 'Kamchatka' in pencil
(u.r.).

The peninsula and houses as seen from the bottom of the bay,
probably from the ship during the second visit.

ver: Apparently taken from the same viewpoint as Ellis's drawing
         (3.359).

British Library, London. Add MS 17277, no. 38.

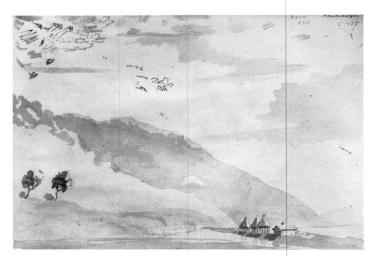

WILLIAM ELLIS

3.359   View of St Peter and St Paul (Petropavlovsk)
                                          [Aug-Sep 1779]
pen, wash and water-colour, 7½ × 10¹¹/₁₆ : 190
× 272, unsigned.

Inscribed 'Kamtschatzka' in ink (u.r.) and annotated in pencil
beneath the title '2.205', corrected to '2:237', referring to Ellis's
Narrative (1782). On verso inscribed in ink '76'. The verso has
a page of colour-test, brush strokes.

A field-sketch showing a log hut and three small conical houses
near the shore at right, high hills behind, some paint daubs and
squiggles (u.l.).

'The town of St. Peter and St. Paul which is situated upon a spit
of low land that extends nearly across the harbour, at present
consists of only twenty-one buildings including jourts (huts partly
under ground), ballagans (houses elevated upon poles) and houses;
the best of which are composed of wood, and the intermediate
chinks filled up with moss, &c. At the head of the harbour are
two other buildings, one of which serves for a storehouse, the
other is the kasarma or hospital.' Ellis (1782) II, 236-7.

ver: A similar viewpoint is adopted in Heath's engraving,
         3.359A. The print however, shows many more houses. A
         similar viewpoint to that in Webber's drawing 3.358.

ref: Murray-Oliver (1977) 37.

Alexander Turnbull Library, Wellington. A 264. 49A.

WILLIAM ELLIS (after)

**3.359A   'A View of the Town of S.ᵗ Peter & S.ᵗ Paul in the
           Bay of Awatchka'**
Engraving. 'W. Ellis del.' — 'J. Heath sc.' 'Pub.ᵈ Dec.ʳ
14 1781 by G. Robinson'.

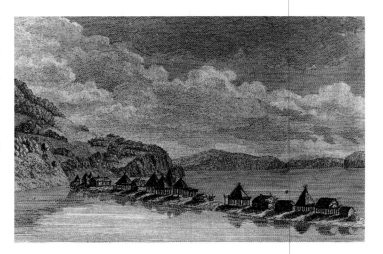

Published in Ellis (1782) II, fp. 237, 236-7.

The engraving seems to have been developed from Ellis's drawing
3.359, on the basis of Webber's drawing of the same view, 3.358.

JOHN WEBBER

3.360   Summer and Winter Habitations in Kamchatka
[Aug, Sep 1779–]
pen, wash and water-colour, 12½ × 19¼ : 317 × 489,
signed and dated 'J. Webber del 1779'.

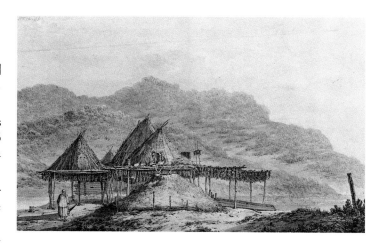

Inscribed 'Summer huts' in pencil on mount below drawing. This
drawing may be one of the two listed as no. 115 and no. 116
'Several Ballagans Summer Habitations' and 'Several Ditto' in
the 'Kamschatka' section of Webber's Catalogue.

Native houses on the peninsula of Petropavlovsk. Four summer
huts with conical roofs resting on poles. A winter house in the
centre foreground. In the left foreground a woman carrying a bag.
An upturned boat at right. Water on both sides. Two figures in
the centre seated on a raised platform.

'The Balagans are rudely built in the shape of a Cone with a broad
base, upon the Top of a Stage supported by pillars about 4 yards
high, upon which they ascend by a ladder or a thick piece of
Wood with steps cut in it. The Joorta is built partly underground
& the roof covered with Earth. The Entrance to these was formerly
at the Top, but since the Russians have been here they make the
Door at the Side. Those at this place are falling to decay, the
Balagan being the Chief residence of the Kamtschadales.

'Before these Houses they have Stages built on which great Quan-
tities of dried fish Hang for the Dogs & underneath the Balagans
they hang the fish for their own use.' Samwell in Cook, *Journals*
III, 2, 1258.

Another description of the balagans is given by King in Cook/
King, (1784) II, 375; King adds the interesting observation: 'The
proportion of *jourts* to *balagans*, is as one to six; so that six families
generally live together in one *jourt*'.

By contrast, balagans appear to have been reserved for the individual family, compare Antropova (1964). For an image with
similar motifs, the yurt, ballagans, fishracks etc. see the engraving
'Summer Huts' in Krasheninnikov (1764), opp. 182.

ver: For a smaller version see 3.361

British Library, London. Add MS 15514, f. 36.

JOHN WEBBER

3.361   Summer and Winter Habitations in Kamschatka
[c. 1781-3]
pen, wash and water-colour, 8⅜ × 14⅞ : 214
× 378, unsigned.

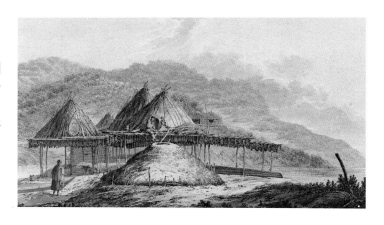

Inscribed as above in pencil by a later hand on the folio beneath
the drawing. Drawn for the engraving 3.361A.

ver: For an earlier version, see 3.360.

Dixson Library, State Library of New South Wales, Sydney.
PXX 2, 42.

JOHN WEBBER (after)

3.361A 'SUMMER and WINTER HABITATIONS in KAMSCHATKA'
Engraving. 'J. Webber del.' — 'S. Smith sc.'

Published in Cook/King (1784) pl. 77, III, 374-5.

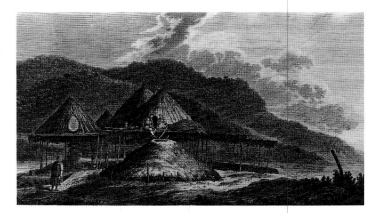

JOHN WEBBER

3.362 Summer Habitations in Kamchatka
[plate 158] [Aug, Sep 1779–]
pen, wash and water-colour, $14^{9/16}$ × $20^{15/16}$: 370 × 532, unsigned.

Traces of '117' (u.r.) identify this drawing with no. 117 'Several ditto. [i.e. Ballagans, Summer habitations]' in Webber's Catalogue. The catalogue lists three drawings with this title (115-117).

Huts with conical roofs. A man standing on a raised platform before the entrance to the hut at right. In the foreground a woman cooking at a kettle suspended from a tripod of poles.

ver: For Webber's softground etching of 3.362 see 3.362Aa.

ref: Cook, *Journals* III, 1, pl. 67.

British Library, London. Add MS 15514, f. 37.

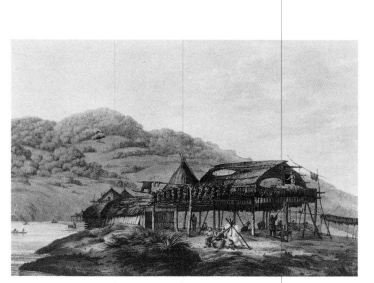

JOHN WEBBER

3.362A a. 'Balagans or Summer Habitations with the method of Drying Fish at S.ᵗ Peter & Paul. Kamtschatka'
softground etching, tinted in brown and grey wash, or hand-coloured, $12^{7/8}$ × $17^{11/16}$: 327 × 450 ($11^{5/16}$ × $16^{7/16}$: 288 x 418). 'I. Webber R.A. fecit'. 'London Pub.ᵈ Aug.ᵗ 1 1792 by In° Webber N°. 312 Oxford Street'. 'Vol. III. Book VI. page 375'.

ver: For Webber's original drawing see 3.362.

British Museum, Department of Prints and Drawings, London. 246˙ a.2 and C. 6˙.

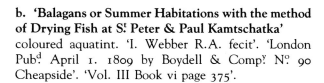

b. 'Balagans or Summer Habitations with the method of Drying Fish at S.ᵗ Peter & Paul Kamtschatka'
coloured aquatint. 'I. Webber R.A. fecit'. 'London Pub.ᵈ April 1. 1809 by Boydell & Comp.ʸ N°. 90 Cheapside'. 'Vol. III Book vi page 375'.

Issued by J. Boydell, *Views in the South Seas* (London, 1808), pl. XI.

National Maritime Museum, London; Bernice P. Bishop Museum, Honolulu.

3.362   **c.**

a copy of the above subject, in pen and water-colour, measuring 14⅜ × 19³⁄₁₆ : 362 × 488; w/m: 'LIMPID WATER' and inscribed on verso 'Balagans or Summer Habitations, with the Method of Drying Fish at St. Peter et Paul, Kamtschatka' by an eighteenth century copyist.

National Library of Australia, Canberra. Rex Nan Kivell Collection. 6788/C.

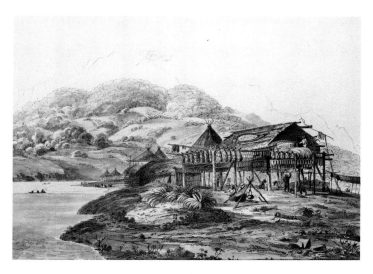

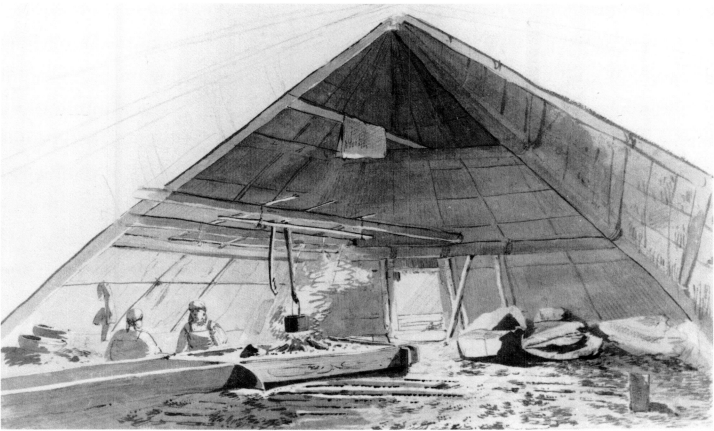

JOHN WEBBER

3.363   **[The Inside of a Summer Habitation]**
[plate 160]   **[Aug-Sep 1779]**
pencil, chalk and sepia wash, 17 × 11½ : 432 × 292, unsigned.

Two figures seated at left, near a pot suspended over a fire; bedding at right. The pointed, pyramidical shape of the hut would suggest this to be a summer habitation.

ref: Cook, *Journals* III, 1, pl. 65a, where incorrectly described as 'a winter dwelling'.

Francis Edwards, *Cat.* 551 (London 1932), entry no. 6, where mistakenly listed as 'Inside of a Winter Habitation, Kamtschatka (17 × 11 ½ in)'.

Francis P. Farquhar, Berkeley, California.

WILLIAM ELLIS

3.364 **A Russian Hut** [plate 166]   [1779]
pen, wash and water-colour, 8¾ × 12⅛ : 226 × 308,
signed and dated in black ink 'W: Ellis fec.ᵗ 1779' (l.r.)
rest of w/m: crown above shield.

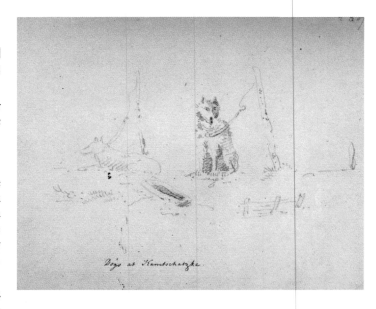

The title in full 'A Russian Hut, in the Harbour of S.ᵗ Peter and
S.ᵗ Paul, in Kamtschatska' in brown ink below the drawing. On
verso an outline sketch in pencil of a wood-pecking bird.

A log hut near the shore in the right foreground, to the left a
dog tethered to a post, and nearby, a trough. Hills in the distance
across the bay.

'The log houses (*isbas*) are raised with long timbers piled horizontally, the ends being let into one another, and the seams
caulked with moss. The roof is sloping like that of our common
cottage-houses, and thatched with coarse grass or rushes.' Cook/
King (1784) III, 375-6.

The location of this hut is unidentified. The rather damaged roof
suggests that it could be the hut which was visited by a party on
its way to Paratunka on 31 May 1779: 'about noon we landed in
a large Bay called South Bay or Behm's Harbour, after the Major,
on a Spot where formerly had stood a large Kamtschadale Town
but now only one small Hut remained . . . We unloaded the
Boat and took up our residence here for the Night. We endea-
voured to make the Hut as comfortable as such a place would
admit of by repairing the roof & covering it to windw.ᵈ with a
Marquee & the Boat's Sail; . . . after Supper we kindled a fire
in the middle of the Hut and retired to our Straw beds.' Samwell
in Cook, *Journals* III, 2,1249.

ver: A study of the dog held to the pole is at 3.365.

Museum Book Store, London, *Cat.* 107 (1928) 41/11; *Cat.* 125
(1941) 453.
National Library of Australia, Canberra. Rex Nan Kivell Collection. NK 53/D.

JOHN WEBBER

3.365 **Dogs at Kamchatka**   [1779]
pencil, 5¹¹⁄₁₆ × 6¹³⁄₁₆ : 145 × 173; unsigned;
w/m: indecipherable initials (cut off).

Inscribed 'Dogs at Kamtschatzka' in black ink on sheet at lower
centre. Also '2.307' in pencil (u.r.) referring to Ellis's *Narrative*
(1782). Inscribed on verso in brown ink '78' (l.l.).

Two dogs tied to a pole.

The Ellis reference is as follows: 'The dogs are always let loose
in the summer season, during which time they frequently run
wild in the woods, but return at the approach of winter, when
they are secured again; and upon the first appearance of a sledge,
they set up a general howl, as being concious of the labour they
have to undergo for the remaining part of the year.' (1782) II,
306-7.

ver: The dog on the left is introduced in Ellis's drawing 3.274
without collar and pole and is similar to Webber's representation in 3.271. It is interesting that Ellis used these
dogs, (here identified as 'Dogs at Kamtschatzka') both in
drawings of Kamchatkan and Chukchi subject matter. The
dog on the right is similar to that in Ellis's drawing 3.364,
the style of draughtmanship however clearly suggests Webber's hand.

Private collection, England.

586

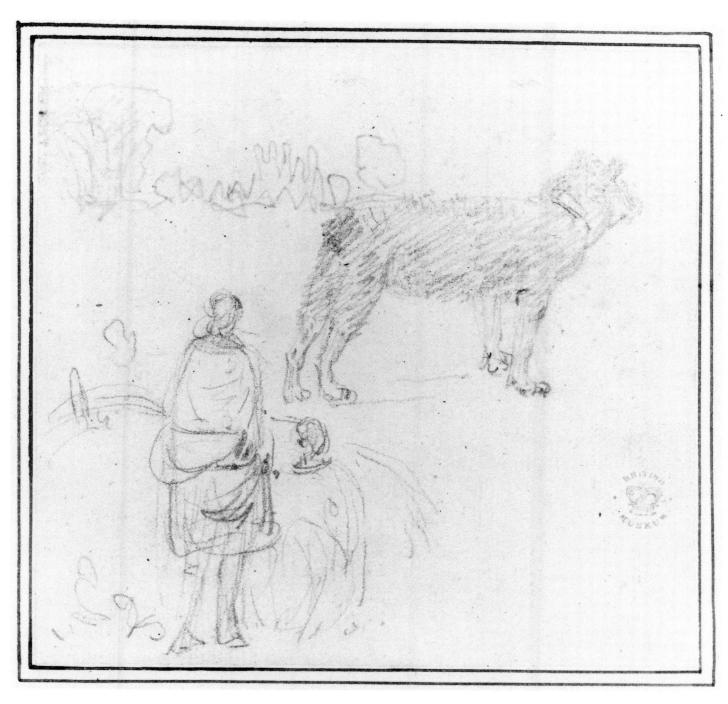

JOHN WEBBER

3.366 [Two Figures and a Dog] [1779]
pencil and red chalk, 5⅞ × 6¹⁄₁₆ : 149 × 154, unsigned.

Studies on a page, probably from a sketchbook. The dog appears a number of times in Webber's Kamchatka drawings, see for example, 3.330 or 3.341. The figures appear to be Alaskan.

British Library, London. Add MS 17277, no. 34.

JOHN WEBBER

3.367 A Water Mill or a Raft, Kamchatka [1779]
pen and sepia wash, 5¹⁄₁₆ × 8⅝ : 128 × 219, unsigned.

Inscribed 'Kamtschatka' in pencil on mount (l.r.).

A wooden hut, with a cross on top, towed to the land at right. The subject has not been identified but would appear to derive from Kamchatka.

British Library, London. Add MS 17277, no. 39.

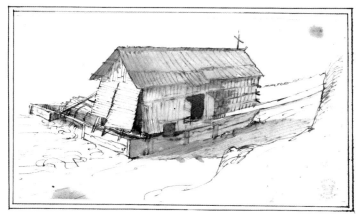

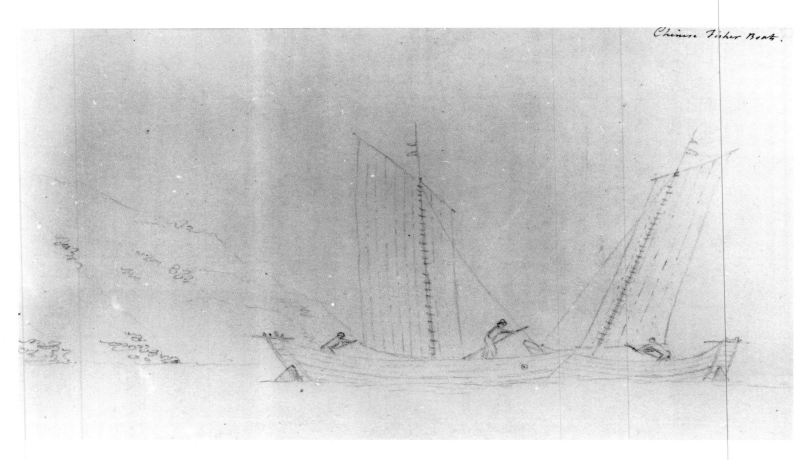

Chinese Fisher Boat

WILLIAM ELLIS

3.368   Chinese Fisher Boats   **[Nov 1779]**
pencil outline drawing, 5⅝ × 10 : 143 × 254, unsigned.

Inscribed 'Chinese Fisher Boats' in brown ink (u.r.).

Two Chinese junks side by side; that at left, containing two figures, the other, one. A hilly foreshore nearby at left.

'At six o'Clock this Morning [29 November 1779] we saw several Chinese Fishing Boats with one Mast, two of which we passed pretty near . . . At two o'Clock we passed close by four or 5 More of them & were struck with their singular Appearance so unlike that of any European Vessels, they had their Trawls out for fish.' Samwell in Cook, *Journals* III, 2, 1294-5.

Tipped into a copy of Captain George Dixon, *A Voyage Round the World* (London, 1789) fp. 308.

National Library of Australia, Canberra. Rex Nan Kivell Collection. NK 7402.

MACAO

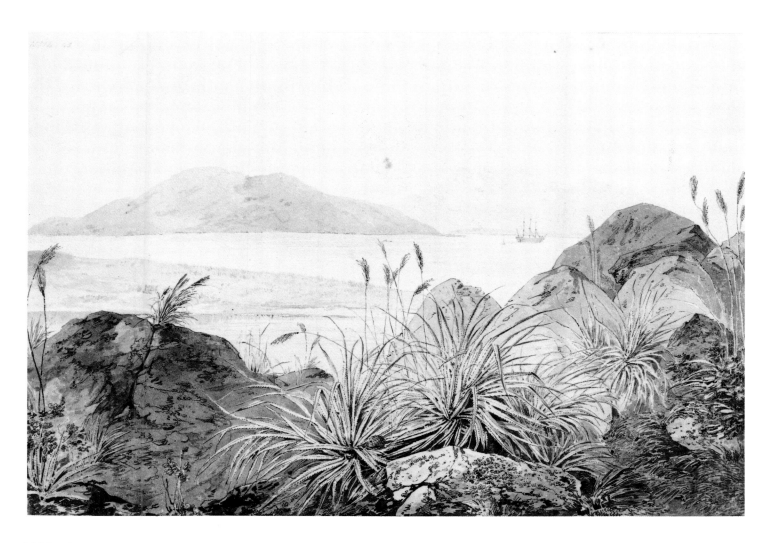

JOHN WEBBER

3.369   **A View in the Typa outside Macao**
          [plate 167]   **[Dec 1779-Jan 1780]**
          pen, wash and water-colour, $14^{11}/_{16}$ × $21^{1}/_{16}$:
          373 × 535, unsigned.

Inscribed 'Entrance to Canton River?' in pencil on the mount
below drawing and traces of no. '138' (u.l.) which identifies the
drawing as the one so numbered and titled, as above, in Webber's
Catalogue.

Large rock-plants with serrated sword-like leaves (order *Pandan-
aceae*) in centre foreground, growing between rocks. A three-
masted ship, probably the *Resolution* in the harbour at right.
Mountainous background.

Beaglehole identifies the anchoring place of the ships between
Tai Pa and Macarira in 3½ fathoms. Cook, *Journals* III, 1, 713n.

ref: Cook, *Journals* III, 1, pl. 68.

British Library, London. Add MS 15514, f. 43.

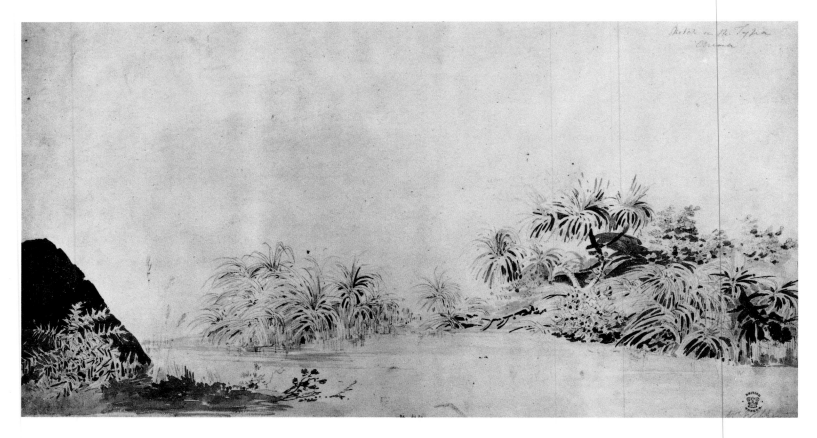

JOHN WEBBER

3.370   **Sketch in the Typa**   [Dec 1779–]
pencil and wash, 11 × 20¹³⁄₁₆ : 279 × 525.

The title as above in pencil (u.r.) and 'Mr Webber' also in pencil
(l.l.).

British Library, London. Add MS 17277, no. 40.

JOHN WEBBER

3.371   **Temple in the Inner Harbour of Macao**
      [plate 169]   [Dec 1779-Jan 1780]
pen, wash and water-colour, 14¼ × 21⅛ : 362
× 537, unsigned.

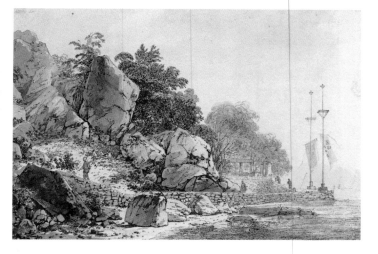

The title, as above, inscribed in pencil on the mount below. This
is possibly the drawing listed in Webber's Catalogue as 137 'A
View with a Temple of Worship', in his section on China.

Large rocks at left with an ascending causeway built by the foreshore. The temple at right with three standing figures nearby.
In front of the temple two flagstaffs fronting the sea. A mountainous background; a ship (or ships) with raking masts, far right.

ver: The composition is repeated in Webber's oil painting but
with additional figures and an oriental boat in the foreground (3.372). For Webber's print after this composition
see 3.372A.

British Library, London. Add MS 15514, f. 40.

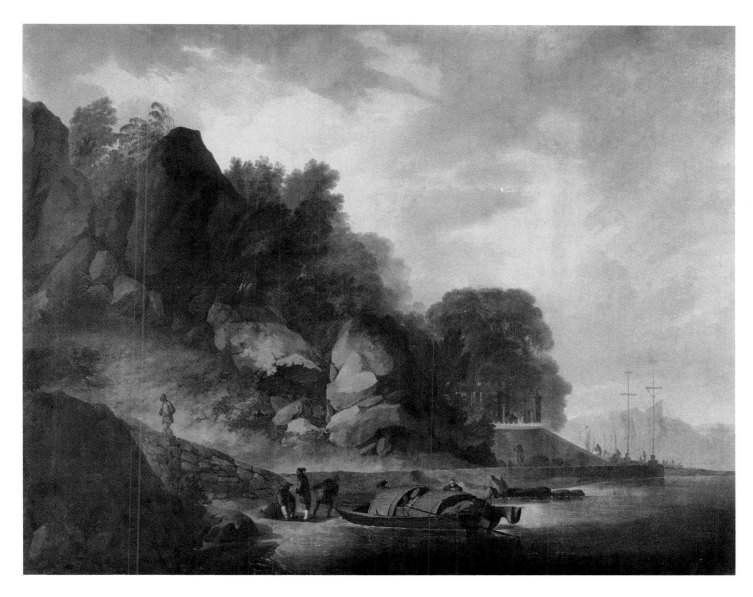

JOHN WEBBER

3.372   **A View at Macao [plate 170]**   [1784]
oil on canvas, 48 × 61¾ : 1219 × 1569, signed
and dated 'John Webber pinx 1784'.

Perhaps identical with Webber's 'View at Macao near the entrance
of the river Canton, China' exh. R.A. (1785) 231, upon which
the *Morning Post* of 30 April 1785 commented: 'The *rocks* and
the *water* in particular are executed with great boldness'.

ver: For an earlier version in water-colour see 3.371. Compare
also with Webber's print 'View in Macao' (3.372A) with
differences in the positioning of the boat in the foreground
and the rocky boulders along the shore in the front.
ref: Listed as 'View of Macao near the Canton River' in the
Admiralty *Cat.* (1911) no. 50; *Exh. Cat.* London 1951/52,
34 (51); Hermann (1973) pl. 120.

Admiralty House, London.

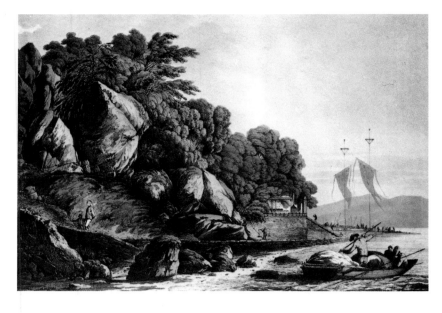

JOHN WEBBER

3.372A a. 'View in Macao'
softground etching, tinted in brown and grey wash, or hand-coloured, 12⅞ × 17⅝ : 327 × 448 (10⅞ × 15¹⁵⁄₁₆ : 277 × 405). 'J. Webber fecit 1788'. 'London, Pubᵈ Augᵗ 1 1788 by J. Webber Nᵒ 312 Oxford Street'. 'Vide Cooks last Voyage Vol. 3. Chap. 11'.

ver: For Webber's original drawing see 3.371.

British Museum, Department of Prints and Drawings, London. 246* a.2 and C.6*.

b. 'View in Macao'
coloured aquatint, 'J. Webber fecit 1788'. 'London Pubᵈ April 1. 1809 by Boydell & Compʸ Nᵒ 90 Cheapside'. 'Vide Cooks last Voyage Vol 3 Chap. 11'.

Issued by J. Boydell, *Views in the South Seas* (London, 1808) pl. XIII.

National Maritime Museum, London; Bernice P. Bishop Museum, Honolulu.

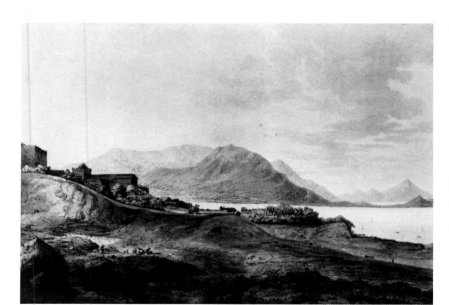

JOHN WEBBER

3.372B a. 'View in Macao, Including the residence of Camoens, when he wrote his Lusiad'
softground etching, tinted in brown and grey wash, or hand-coloured, 12¹³⁄₁₆ × 17½ : 325 × 445 (11 × 16¹⁄₁₆ : 280 × 407). 'J. Webber fecit 1788'. 'London Pubᵈ Augᵗ 1 1788 by J. Webber Nᵒ 312 Oxford Street'. 'Vide Cooks last Voyage Vol. 3. Chap. XI. [sic]'.

No original drawing of this scene by Webber is known.

British Museum, Department of Prints and Drawings, London. 246* a.2 and C. 6*.

b. 'View in Macao, including the residence of Camoens, when he wrote his Lusiad'
coloured aquatint. 'J. Webber fecit 1788'. 'London Pubᵈ April 1. 1809 by Boydell & Compʸ Nᵒ 90 Cheapside'. 'Vide Cook's last Voyage Vol. 3 Chap. XI [sic]'.

Issued as J. Boydell, *Views in the South Seas* (London, 1808) pl. XII.

Compare with King's remark: 'Whilst we lay in the Typa, I was shewn, in a garden belonging to an English gentleman at Macao, the rock, under which, as the tradition goes, the poet Camoens used to sit and compose his Lusiad. It is a lofty arch, of one solid stone, and forms the entrance of a grotto dug out of the rising ground behind it. The rock is overshadowed by large spreading trees, and commands an extensive and magnificent view of the sea, and the interspersed islands.' Cook/King (1784) III, 441.

National Maritime Museum, London; Bernice P. Bishop Museum, Honolulu.

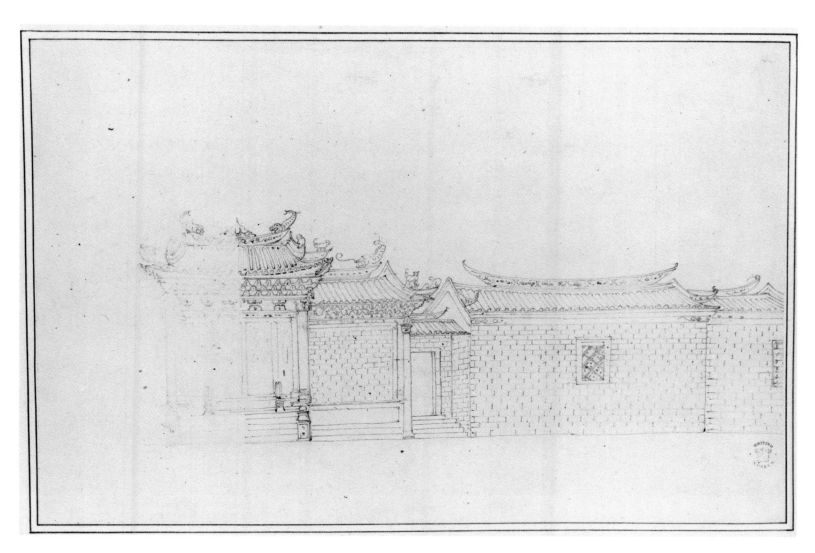

JOHN WEBBER (?)

3.373   **A Chinese Temple**
         pen and pencil, 10 × 15⅛ : 254 × 384, unsigned.

Possibly associated with the temple ground drawn in 3.371.
Feebleness in draughtmanship, both with regard to the pencil
work as well as to perspective, leaves some doubt whether the
drawing is actually by Webber. The attribution mainly rests on
the inclusion of the drawing in an album of Webber sketches.

British Library, London. Add MS 17277, no. 43.

JOHN WEBBER

3.374   **A View near Macao**
         [plate 171]   [Dec 1779-Jan 1780]
         pen, wash and water-colour, 14⅜ × 20⅞ : 365
         × 530, unsigned.

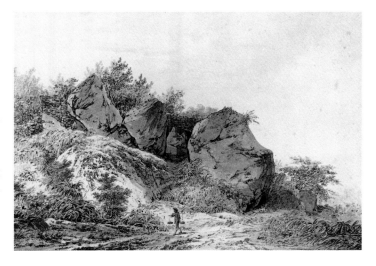

Inscribed 'Near Macao?' on the mount below the drawing. Traces
of a number '3.' (u.r.) corner suggest that this drawing may be
identified with '139 A View near Macao' in Webber's Catalogue.

A figure in the central foreground is carrying two baskets slung
from a stick across the shoulders. Large rocks filled with rough
masonry.

British Library, London. Add MS 15514, f. 41.

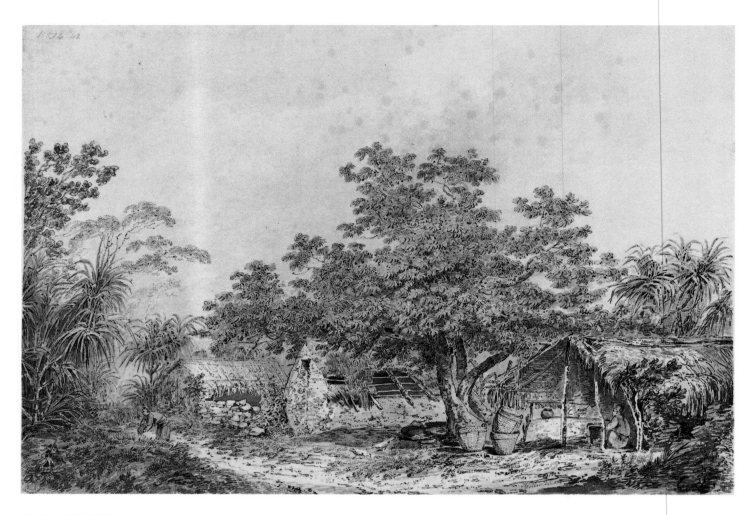

JOHN WEBBER

3.375   A View near Macao [?]   [1783]
pen, wash and water-colour, 14⅛ × 20¾ : 359 × 530, signed 'J. Webber del 1783'.

Inscribed '?near Macao' in pencil on the mount below drawing.

A figure in blue crouching in a hut in the right foreground. Three large baskets at the entrance. Another figure also in blue binding and gathering rushes in the left foreground.

This is the only drawing in this portfolio dated subsequent to the voyage.

ver: For two similar compositions see 3.376 and 3.377.

British Library, London. Add MS 15514, f. 42.

JOHN WEBBER

3.376   **A View near Macao [?]**   **[1786]**
water-colour on paper, laid down on cardboard, 13¼ × 18⅝ : 337 × 474, signed and dated (l.l.) on cardboard 'J. Webber, 1786'; w/m: lily in shield under crown, 'GR' below.

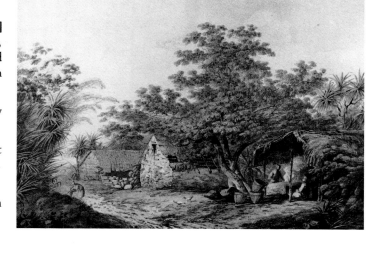

Inscribed in pencil on verso in an eighteenth century hand 'View in Cracatoa Island — near the Straits of Sunda'.

ver: Similar in composition to 3.375, except that on the right another Chinese figure has been added behind the store. Three more figures are added in 3.377.

ref: Warner (1952) 85 with the incorrect title 'View of Cracatoa Island in the China Seas'.

John Sheepshank Gift 1857 to the South Kensington Museum.

Victoria and Albert Museum, London. Print Room FA 481.

JOHN WEBBER

3.377   **A View near Macao [?]**   **[c. 1792]**
pencil, 10⅜ × 15¾ : 264 × 400, w/m: 'J. WHATMAN'.

The drawing is squared for transfer and is likely to be a preparatory study for a print which Webber might have intended for his series of *South Sea Views*. Webber's premature death could have frustrated that intention.

ver: Compare with the two other versions of the subject 3.375 and 3.376. This drawing adds three figures, including one seen from the rear with a stick on his shoulders and two suspended baskets.

Yale Center for British Art, Paul Mellon Collection, New Haven.

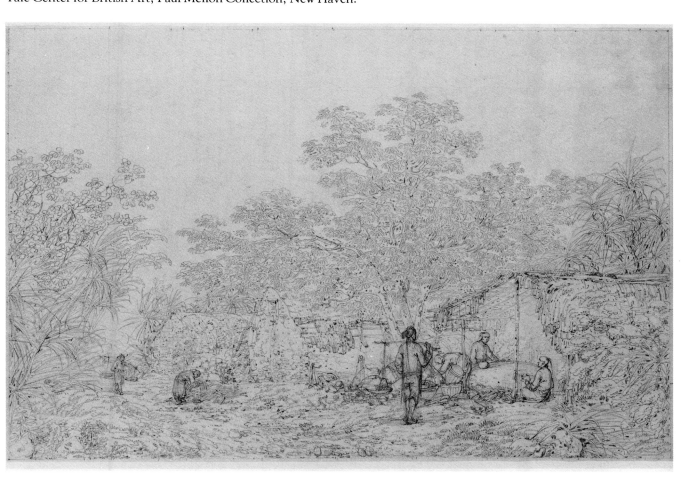

JOHN WEBBER

3.378   A Chinese Man   **[1780–]**
sepia wash over pencil on paper, 15³⁄₁₆ ×
11³⁄₈ : 386 × 289, unsigned.

Numbered '10' (u.l.).

The drawing is framed by a single line in ink, 14⁷⁄₁₆ ×
10⁵⁄₈ : 367 × 269 (inside frame). Impressions along the edge
of the drawing suggest that it has been subjected to a squeezing
process.

A full-length figure drawing of a Chinese man, wearing a middle-
buttoned, high-collared gown over an underskirt, a mandarin cap
and a pigtail. His right hand is hidden inside his gown.

ref: Joppien (1976a) 52-3 (repd).

Eyre and Hobhouse, London (1976).

Private collection, England.

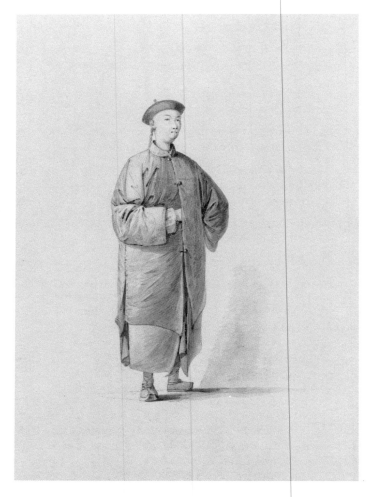

JOHN WEBBER

3.379   A Chinese Woman   **[1780–]**
sepia wash over pencil, 15³⁄₁₆ × 11³⁄₈ : 386
× 289, unsigned.

Numbered (u.l.) '11', and framed by a single line in black ink
(measurements inside frame 14⁵⁄₈ × 10⁵⁄₈ : 371 × 270).

Impressions along the edge of the drawing suggests that it has
been subjected to a squeezing process.

A full-length drawing of a Chinese woman, wearing a half-length
high-collared gown over two underskirts; her hair is knotted and
fastened with pins.

ref: Joppien (1976a) 54-5 (repd).

Eyre and Hobhouse, London (1976).

Private collection, England.

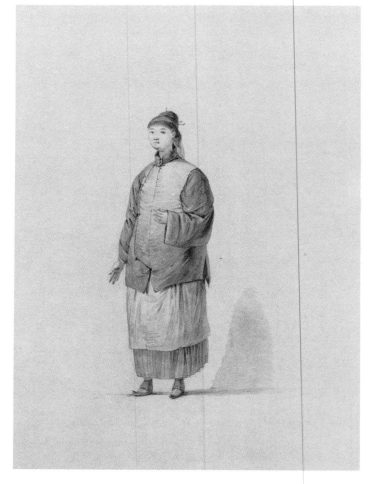

JOHN WEBBER

3.380   **Portrait of a Chinese** [plate 172]   [1780]
         pen and wash, 12¼ × 10⅜ : 311 × 263, unsigned.

'No 145' inscribed (u.r.), which identifies the drawing with '145
A Ditto [i.e. a Portrait] of a Chinese' in Webber's Catalogue.

A head and shoulder portrait of a man wearing a large straw hat,
moustache and beard about the chin. His gown is ornamented
by a furry collar.

British Library, London. Add MS 15514, f. 48.

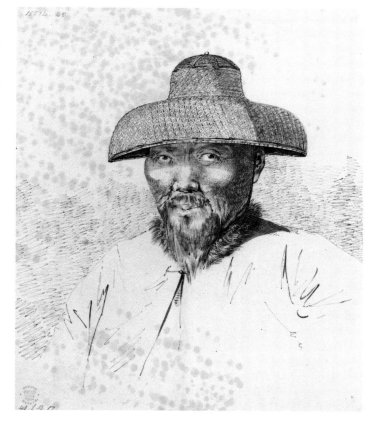

JOHN WEBBER

3.381   **A Portrait of a Chinese Girl**   [1780]
         pen and wash, 8⅜ × 6½ : 213 × 165, unsigned.

Numbered '144' (u.r.), which identifies this drawing with the
drawing listed 144 and titled as 'A Portrait of a Tartar Girl' in
Webber's Catalogue.

A portrait of the head and shoulders, wearing a gown buttoned
at the right. The girl's hair is combed straight back and built into
a crown fastened by pins.

British Library, London. Add MS 15514, f. 49.

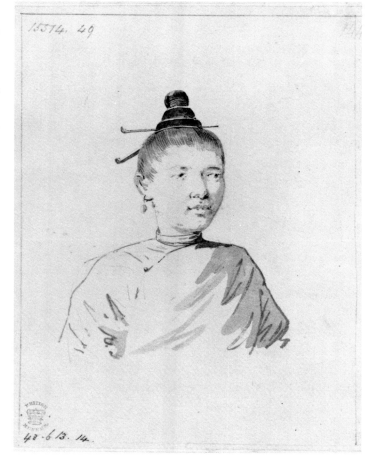

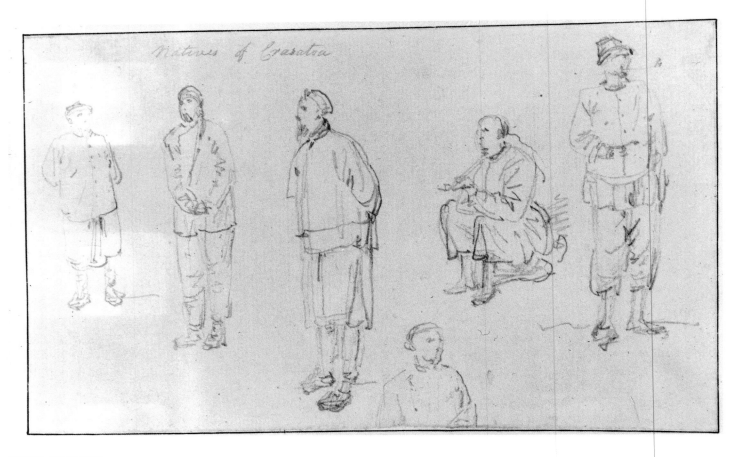

JOHN WEBBER

3.382   Natives of Macao (?)   [Dec 1779-Jan 1780]
        pencil, 5⅞ × 9⅝ : 149 × 244, unsigned.

Inscribed 'Natives of Cracatoa' in pencil at top centre by a later hand.

Six studies of natives who are apparently Chinese: four standing, one seated, one cut off by lower edge.

National Maritime Museum, London. (In volume of plates to Cook's Voyages.)

JOHN WEBBER

3.383   Chinese Boats [and a Chinese Man]   [1780]
        pencil, pen and wash, 9 × 9 : 228 × 228, unsigned.

The title above inscribed in pencil (u.r.). On verso a sketch of an Asian head in pencil (3.416).

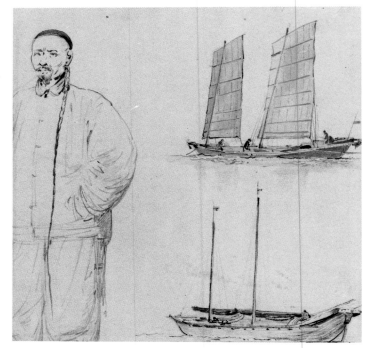

Two Chinese junks each with two masts, the upper one with two square bamboo batten sails. On the left a study of a Chinese man with a long pigtail.

British Library, London. Add MS 17277, no. 42r.

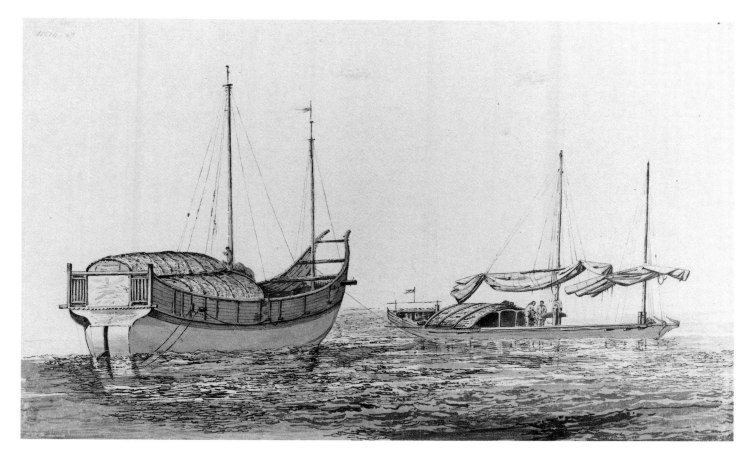

JOHN WEBBER

3.384 **Two Chinese Junks** [1780]
pen and wash, 12¾ × 20⅞ : 324 × 530, unsigned.

Inscribed in pencil 'iii 435' and '142' (u.l.) identifying it as the drawing thus numbered and titled in Webber's Catalogue.

For a study of the boat on the left see 3.385, for that on the right (in fact, a larger sampan) see 3.386.

British Library, London. Add MS 15514, f. 47.

JOHN WEBBER

3.385 **A Chinese Junk** [c. 1780]
pencil, pen and wash, 8 × 5⅜ : 203 × 136, unsigned; w/m: (half cut off) shield with diagonal lines, below 'GR'.

The title above inscribed in pencil across the lower centre in another hand. On verso a drawing of a leg and a boot (3.394).

This is a study for the boat on the left in 3.384.

National Maritime Museum, London. (In volume of plates to Cook's Voyages.)

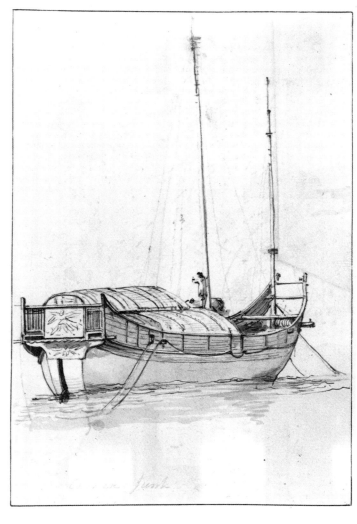

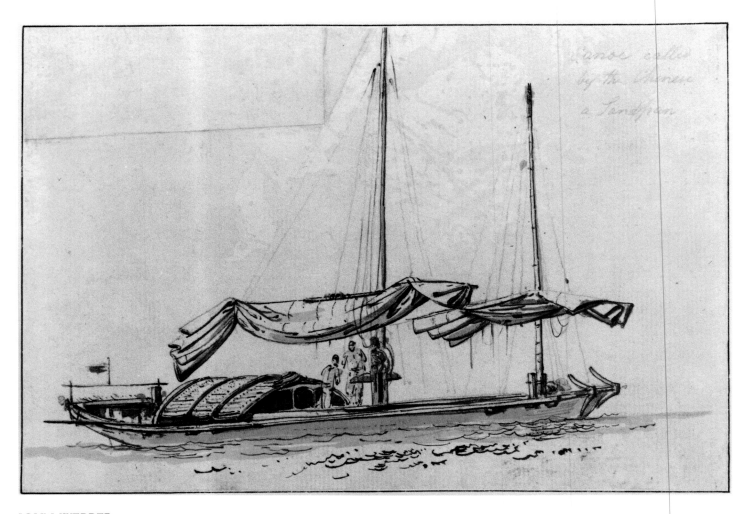

JOHN WEBBER

3.386   A Sampan   [1780]
        pencil, pen and wash, 5½ × 8 : 130 × 204, unsigned.

Inscribed 'Canoe called by the Chinese a Sandpan' in pencil
(u.r.) in another hand.

A boat with an arched house, two masts and sails furled. For a
more developed version see 3.384.

National Maritime Museum, London. (In volume of plates to
Cook's Voyages.)

JOHN WEBBER

3.387   Chinese Junks   [1780]
        pen and wash, 13⅛ × 21 1/16 : 333 × 535, signed
        'J. Webber del' (l.l.) in ink.

Inscribed 'iii 425' in pencil [u.l.], and '143' in pencil. This is the
drawing referred to as 143 in Webber's Catalogue.

The small boat in the right foreground is a sampan.

ver: For a study for this drawing see 3.388. The little boat (l.r.)
        is similar to the one introduced into 3.372 A.

British Library, London. Add MS 15514, f. 46.

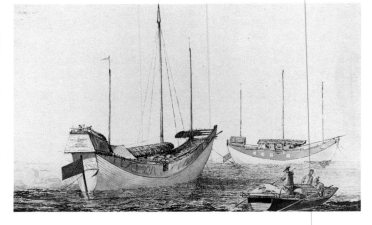

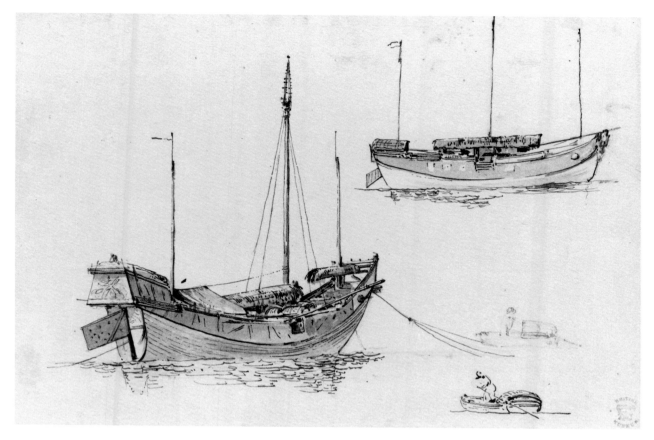

JOHN WEBBER

3.388   Chinese Vessels   [1780]
pencil, pen and wash, $7\frac{5}{8}$ × $11\frac{3}{16}$: 194 × 284, unsigned.

The title, as above, in pencil below the drawing on lower mount and sepia framing lines.

ver: The two big junks are studies for 3.387.

British Library, London. Add MS 17277, no. 41.

JOHN WEBBER

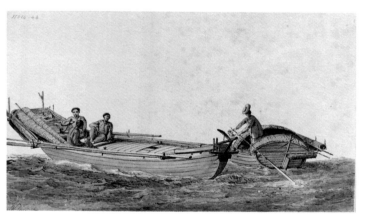

3.389   Sampan, Boats of China   [1780]
pen, wash and water-colour, $8\frac{1}{2}$ × $14\frac{1}{2}$: 211 × 368, signed 'J. Webber del'.

The title as above in pencil on mount below the drawing, also 'iii 425' in pencil on mount (u.l.).

Two small boats with three figures in one, two in the other.

For a study of the boat on the right hand side see 3.390.

British Library, London. Add MS 15514, f. 44.

JOHN WEBBER

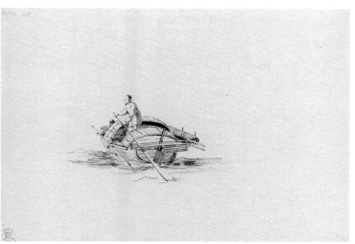

3.390   A Sampan   [1780]
pen and wash, $10\frac{1}{2}$ × $14\frac{1}{2}$: 267 × 368, unsigned.

Inscribed '140' (u.l.), thus identifying this drawing as the one so numbered and titled 'Tartar Boat' in Webber's Catalogue. Also inscribed 'iii 425' in pencil (u.l.).

A man standing rowing. A study for the boat on the right-hand side in 3.389.

British Library, London. Add MS 15514, f. 45.

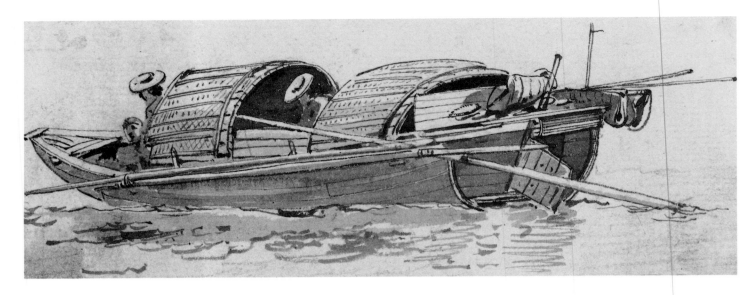

JOHN WEBBER

3.391   A Sampan   [1780]
      pen and wash, $2\frac{5}{8} \times 6\frac{3}{4} : 67 \times 172$, unsigned.

Boat of a similar type as the previous one (3.390), manned by
three figures, two with a broad-rimmed hat.

Collection A. G. B. Russell, Esq. by whom presented to the
British Museum.

British Museum, Department of Prints and Drawings, London.
1909-7-3-2.

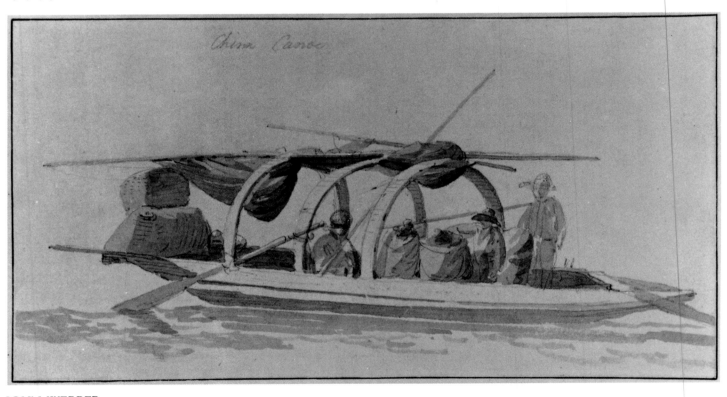

JOHN WEBBER

3.392   A Sampan   [1780]
      pencil and wash, $4\frac{1}{2} \times 8\frac{5}{8} : 115 \times 219$, unsigned.

Inscribed 'China Canoe' in pencil at top centre in another hand.

Boat with three arched roof structures, about five people inside,
paddles fastened alongside.

National Maritime Museum, London. (In volume of plates to
Cook's Voyages.)

JOHN WEBBER

3.393 [Figure drawings from the Chinese coast] [1780]
pencil, 8⅝ × 6⅜ : 219 × 162, unsigned.

On verso the drawing of a sailing boat of Pulau Condore (3.406).

Sketch of a Chinese woman sitting on the arched roof of a Chinese boat. A sketch of a Chinese man with a broad-rimmed hat (u.r.).

National Maritime Museum, London. (In volume of plates to Cook's Voyages.)

JOHN WEBBER

3.394 Study of a leg and boot [1780]
pen and pencil, 8 × 5⅜ : 203 × 136, unsigned.

On verso a drawing of a Chinese junk (3.385).

The boot with ornamented (embroidered) top, the front turning up. The leg at length cut off.

The geographical place to which this drawing belongs has not been identified for certain, but it may derive from China or the Asian coast. See similar boots worn by the Mandarin in 3.378; they are also vaguely reminiscent of the boots of Kamchatka.

Detail drawings of this kind are rare among the body of visual material from the third voyage.

National Maritime Museum, London. (In volume of plates to Cook's Voyages.)

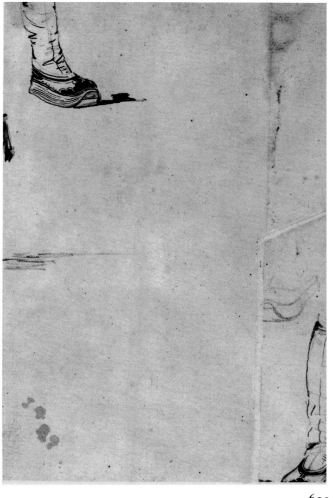

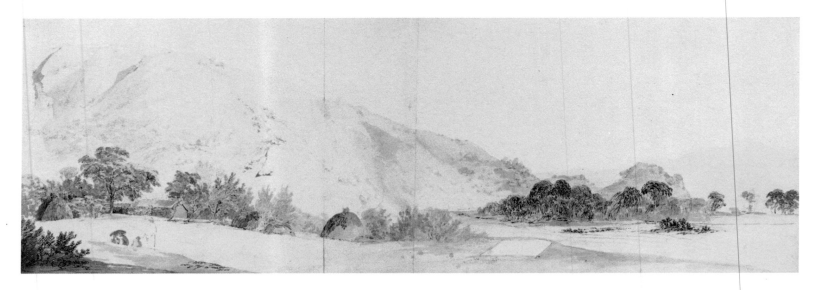

JOHN WEBBER

3.395   **A View in the Island of Pulo Condore [?], China Seas**   **[Jan 1780]**
pencil, pen, wash and water-colour, $14\frac{1}{2} \times 42\frac{1}{4}$: 368 × 1073, unsigned.

The title as above inscribed in pencil on verso in an eighteenth-century hand.

A panoramic view of the countryside with mountains in the back. Stone houses to the left. Groups of figures in the foreground.

The inclusion of this drawing in this section is tentative and based upon the endorsed inscription. Otherwise the scene does not seem to correspond to King's description of that island, and neither can we be convinced of the existence of houses, built of stone. King rather describes them as being constructed of reeds. Cook/King (1784) III, 453. Judging from the figures in the front, their wide brimmed hats and the character of landscape depicted the view could have been drawn on the Chinese mainland, somewhere around Macao.

British Library, London. Add MS 17277, no. 44.

JOHN WEBBER

3.396 **A View in the Island of Pulo Condore [Con Son]**
[plate 173] [Jan 1780]
pen, wash and water-colour, 14¾ × 21⁷⁄₁₆ : 375
× 545, unsigned.

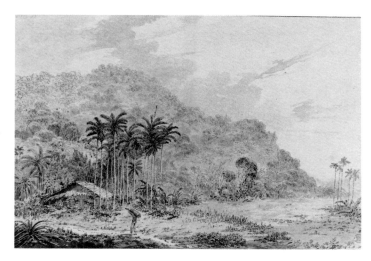

Inscribed 'Pulau Condore?' in pencil on the mount below drawing.
The drawing could be the one listed as 147 'A View with their
Natives Habitations' in Webber's Catalogue, in the 'Pulo Con-
dore' section.

At left, a hut among tropical foliage; behind, a clump of tall
coconut trees. A man carrying rushes on his shoulder.

ver: The location depicted in the drawing is repeated in 3.397
and 3.397A.

British Library, London. Add MS 15514, f. 53.

JOHN WEBBER

3.397 **A View in the Island of Pulo Condore** [1792]
pencil, 11¹⁄₁₆ × 16⅝ : 282 × 423, unsigned;
w/m: 'J. WHATMAN'.

Inscribed in pencil on verso ' J. Webber 1792'.

ver: The drawing is similar in composition to 3.396 except for
the background and the figure of the buffalo-leader. The
buffalo itself compares surprisingly closely with a drawing
of that animal by W. Ellis (see. 3.432).

The drawing is squared for transfer, and it would seem that
it is a preparatory study for Webber's etching of the title
above, published on 1 August 1792 (3.397A).

Yale Center for British Art, Paul Mellon Collection, New Haven.

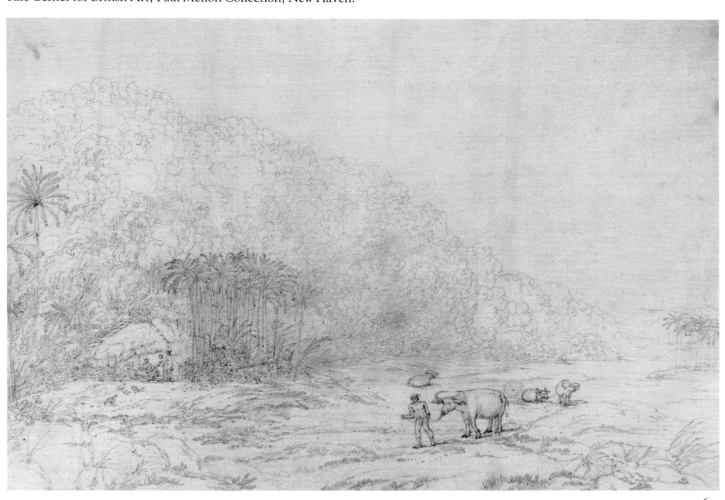

3.397A a. [A View in Pulo Condore]
uncoloured etching.

Proof before letters.

ver: For a similar drawing by Webber see 3.396.

Hartnoll and Eyre, London (1978).

b. 'A View in Pulo Condore'
hand-coloured etching, .11⅞ × 16⁵⁄₁₆ : 301
× 414 (10³⁄₁₆ × 15¾ : 259 × 400). The title
in pen along the lower edge. 'Drawn & etch'd by J.
Webber' in pen (l.l.). in Webber's hand 'Vide Cooks
last Voy, Vol III, Chap. X' in pen (l.r.). No date
given.

British Museum, Department of Prints and Drawings, London.
C. 6˙.

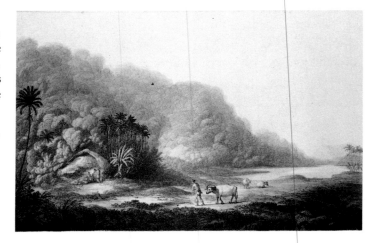

c. 'View in Pulo Condore'
uncoloured aquatint, 11¹⁵⁄₁₆ × 17¹⁄₁₆ : 303
× 433 (10¼ × 15¾ : 260 × 400). 'Drawn
& Etch'd by I. Webber'. 'Aqua tinta by M.C. Prestel'.
'London, Pub.ᵈ Feb.ʸ 1 1787 by I. Webber N.ᵒ 312
Oxford Street'. 'Vide Cook's last Voy. Vol III Chap.
X'.

ref: Murray-Oliver (1969b) pl. 4 for a print in the Alexander
Turnbull Library, Wellington.

Hartnoll and Eyre, London (1978); British Museum, Department
of Prints and Drawings, London. 246˙ a.2. and C. 6˙; Alexander
Turnbull Library, Wellington. A coloured version is also in the
Bernice P. Bishop Museum, Honolulu. Fuller Collection.

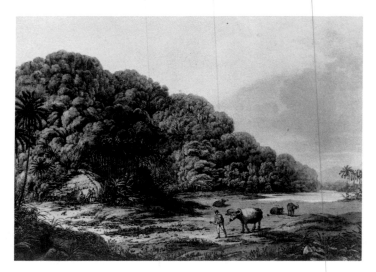

d. 'A View in the Island of Pulo Condore'
  [plate 174]

softground etching, tinted in brown and grey wash, or
hand-coloured, 12¾ × 17⅝ : 324 × 448
(11⁵⁄₁₆ × 16⁵⁄₁₆ : 287 × 415). 'I. Webber
R.A. fecit'. 'London Pub.ᵈ Aug.ᵗ 1 1792 by I. Webber
N.ᵒ 312 Oxford Street'. 'Vol III. Book VI p. 450'.

British Museum, Department of Prints and Drawings, London.
246˙ a. 2. and C. 6˙.

Version **a-c** and **d** are almost identical except for minor details.
It should be noted that in **a-c** the buffalo driver is walking sideways
turning his back on the viewer, while in **d** he is almost frontal.
The two cows which are shown standing and lying have been
reversed. There are also slight differences in the figures near the
hut in the back on the left.

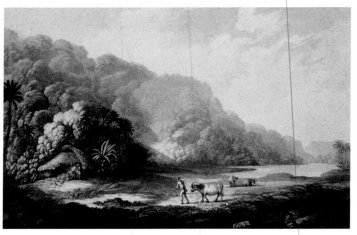

e. 'A View in the Island of Pulo Condore'
coloured aquatint. 'I. Webber R.A. fecit'. 'London
Pub.ᵈ April 1 1809 by Boydell & Comp.ʸ N.º 90 Cheapside'. 'Vol III Book VI p.450'.

Issued as J. Boydell, *Views in the South Seas* (London, 1808) pl.
XIV.

National Maritime Museum, London; Bernice P. Bishop Museum, Honolulu.

f. A copy of the View in the Island of Pulo Condore
pen, wash and water-colour, 14¼ × 19¼ : 361 ×
490.

By an unknown eighteenth century copyist, inscribed in ink on
verso as above.

National Library of Australia, Canberra. Rex Nan Kivell Collection 6788/A. The drawing shows some modification in the
figure of the buffalo-driver. The Rex Nan Kivell Picture File 788
in the National Library of Australia records that the drawing was
found with the fake signature of Richard Wilson. This however,
was removed by Rex Nan Kivell.

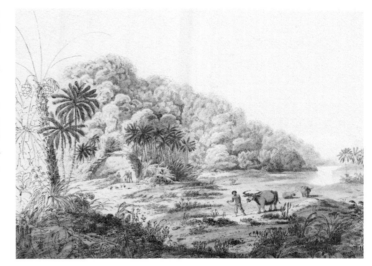

JOHN WEBBER (?)

3.398   **Coastal Landscape**   [1786]
oil on panel, 7¾ × 10¼ : 197 × 260, signed
and dated 'J. Webber pinxt 1786'.

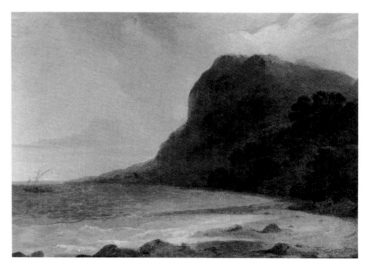

On the verso of the panel is a) an inscription in whitish paint
'A View in the Harbour of Pulo Condore. J. Webber pinxt.
1786', b) a clearly visible erasure at centre, c) a label with 'Gooden
and Fox Ltd 38 Bury Street St. James', London and d) a pink
label 'formerly in the National Gallery of Art — PM 2040 Cat.'.

The attribution of this picture to J. Webber must be regarded
with caution, since its style is not particularly like Webber's. The
sketchy, preparatory nature of the picture and the fact that it is
painted on panel, which is rare among Webber's *oeuvre*, could
suggest that the picture was possibly painted during the voyage
and constitutes an experiment rather than an accomplished
performance.

ver: For studies of the sailing boat see 3.405 and 3.406.

Gooden and Fox Ltd, London (see above).

Yale Center for British Art, Paul Mellon Collection, New Haven.

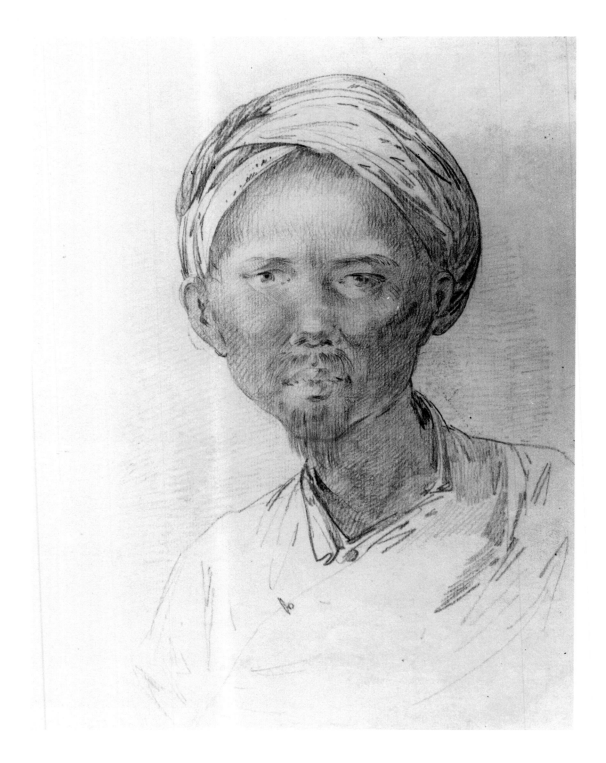

JOHN WEBBER

3.399   **A Man of Pulo Condore [plate 175]**   [Jan 1780]
red crayon, $14\frac{1}{8}$ × $10\frac{3}{16}$: 357 × 259 unsigned.

Inscribed in pencil '154' (u.r.), thus identifying it as the drawing of the same number 'A Portrait of a Cochin Chinese' in the 'Pulo Condore' section of Webber's Catalogue.

Bust portrait of a man with high cheek-bones, a moustache, small beard and pointed chin. He wears a white gown buttoned at right and a white turban.

ver: Similar to 3.400.

Probably the drawing listed in Francis Edwards, *Cat.* 416 (London, July 1921) under no. 769 as 'Native Man . . . in red crayon (14 by 10 in) unpublished'.

National Library of Australia, Canberra. Rex Nan Kivell Collection. NK 52/M.

JOHN WEBBER

3.400   **A Man of Pulo Condore**   [1780—]
             pencil, 17⅝ × 12¾ : 448 × 324, unsigned;
             w/m: 'J. WHATMAN'.

Numbered in corner (u.l.) '1'. There is a plate-mark impression
around the extreme edges of the drawing suggesting that it may
have been pressed to obtain a squeeze-off impression (3.401).

ver: For a laterally inverted but otherwise identical drawing of
        the subject see 3.401. For a smaller version see 3.399.

ref: Joppien (1976a) 32-3.

Eyre and Hobhouse, London (1976).

Private collection, England.

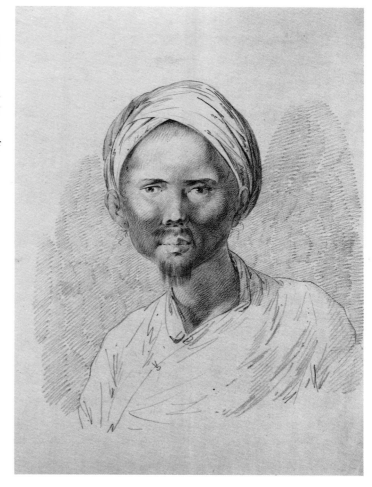

JOHN WEBBER

3.401   **A Native of Pulo Condore**
             pencil, 17½ × 12½ : 445 × 318, unsigned.

Inscribed, as above, followed by 'Chinese Seas' in pencil (u.r.).

ver: It would seem that this drawing is a squeeze or offset taken
        from 3.400 with which, apart from being laterally inverted,
        it is identical. For a smaller version in red crayon see 3.399.

British Library, London. Add MS 17277, no. 45.

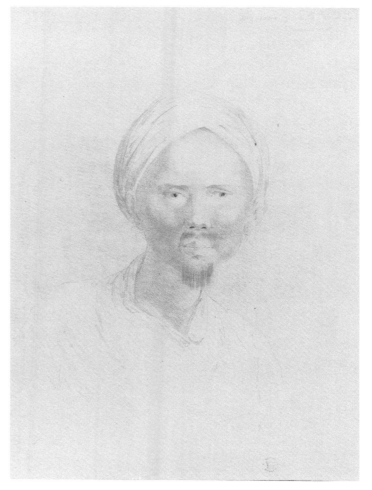

3.402   A Woman of Pulo Condore [plate 176] [Jan 1780]
red crayon, 14⅛ × 10⅛ : 359 × 257, unsigned.

Inscribed in pencil '155' (u.r.), thus identifying it as the drawing of the same number 'A Ditto of a Woman' [i.e. a portrait of a woman of Cochin China], in the 'Pulo Condore' section of Webber's Catalogue. On verso 'No 10' in ink and '15' in ink in a later hand (l.l.).

A bust portrait of a woman looking towards the right. Her hair is combed straight back fastened in a knot at the back of her head. She wears a gown which buttons on the right side.

ver: Same composition as 3.403 and 3.404.

Probably the drawing listed in Francis Edwards, *Cat.* 416 (London, July 1921) under no. 769 as 'Native . . . Woman . . . in red crayon (14 by 10 in) unpublished'.

National Library of Australia, Canberra. Rex Nan Kivell Collection. NK 52/L.

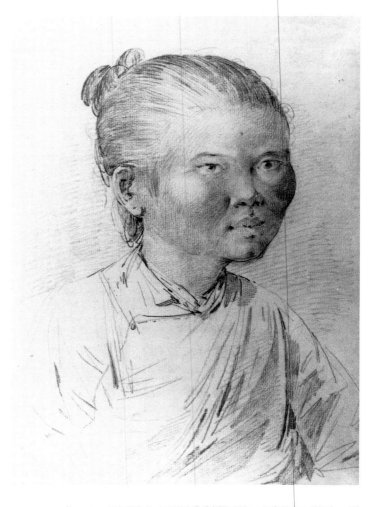

3.403   A Woman of Pulo Condore   [1780]
pencil, 17⅝ × 12¾ : 448 × 324, unsigned.

Numbered in pencil '2a' (u.l.). Traces of a squeezing process in the form of impressions around the edges.

ver: For a smaller version in red crayon see 3.402, and for what is probably a squeeze-off impression see 3.404.

ref: Joppien (1976a) 34-5.

Eyre and Hobhouse, London (1976).

Private collection, England.

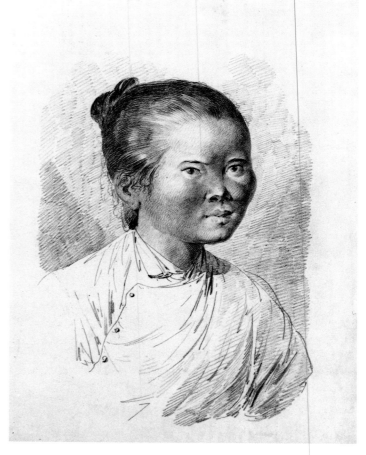

610

JOHN WEBBER

3.404   A Woman of Pulo Condore
pencil, 17⅝ × 12⁹⁄₁₆ : 448 × 319, unsigned.

Inscribed 'A Woman of Pulo Condore, China Seas' in pencil
(u.r.).

ver: This drawing is probably a squeeze or offset taken from
3.403, with which, apart from being laterally inverted, it
is identical. For a smaller version in red crayon see 3.402.

British Library, London. Add MS 17277, no. 46.

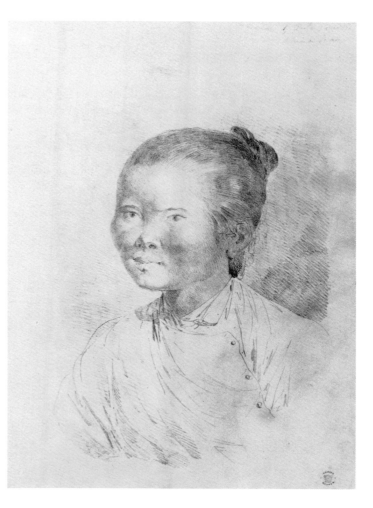

JOHN WEBBER

3.405   A Sailing Vessel, Pulo Condore   [1780]
pen, wash and water-colour, 13½ × 20⅞ : 344 ×
530, unsigned.

No. '148' in (u.l.) corner identifies this drawing with that so
numbered and titled 'A Sailing Vessel. Pulo Condore' in Webber's
Catalogue.

A native boat with three figures near a rocky shore. Mountainous
background.

For a study for the boat see 3.406.

British Library, London. Add MS 15514, f. 55.

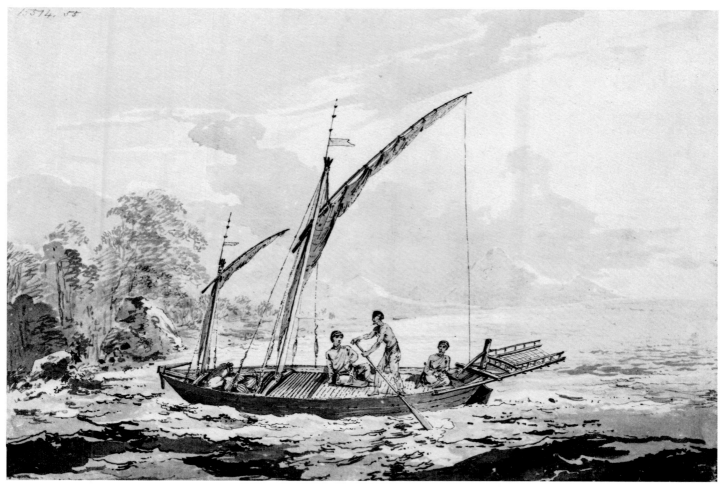

JOHN WEBBER

3.406   A Sailing Vessel, Pulo Condore   [1780]
pencil, pen and wash, 8⅝ × 6⅜ : 219 × 162, unsigned.

Inscribed 'Canoe Pulo Condore' in pencil across the lower centre.
On verso two small pencil studies of a Chinese girl on the roof
of a vessel and the head of a Chinese man (3.393).

A study for the canoe in 3.398 and 3.405.

National Maritime Museum, London. (In volume of plates to
Cook's Voyages.)

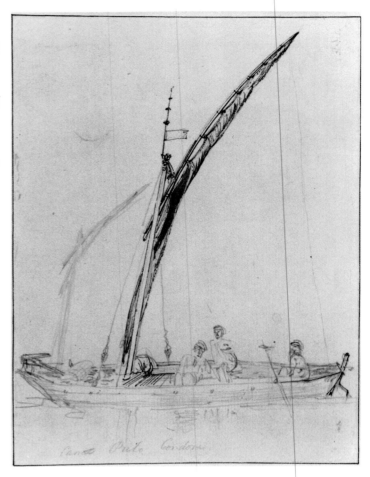

WILLIAM ELLIS

3.407   A boat of Pulo Condore [?]   [1780]
pencil drawing, 7⁵⁄₁₆ × 10 : 185 × 254, unsigned.

Inscribed 'Chinese boat' in brown ink (u.r.). On verso a faint
sketch of a Chinese boat, similar to Webber's drawing of a boat
in 3.390.

An outline drawing of a boat with a seated figure and a basket
laden with provisions.

The inscription may be incorrect. The open hull of the boat,
even without a mast, bears some resemblance to the sailing boats
of Pulau Condore. Note too that the seated figure does not wear
the typical broad-rimmed hat of the Chinese seamen depicted on
this voyage.

Tipped into a copy of Captain George Dixon, *A Voyage Round
the World* (London, 1789) fp.309.

National Library of Australia, Canberra. Rex Nan Kivell Collection. NK 7402.

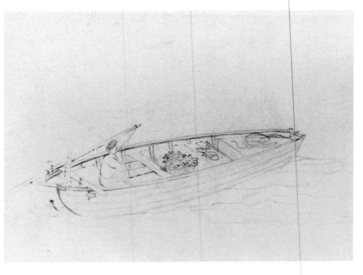

KRAKATAU, SUNDA STRAITS

9 to 14 February 1780   3.408–3.419

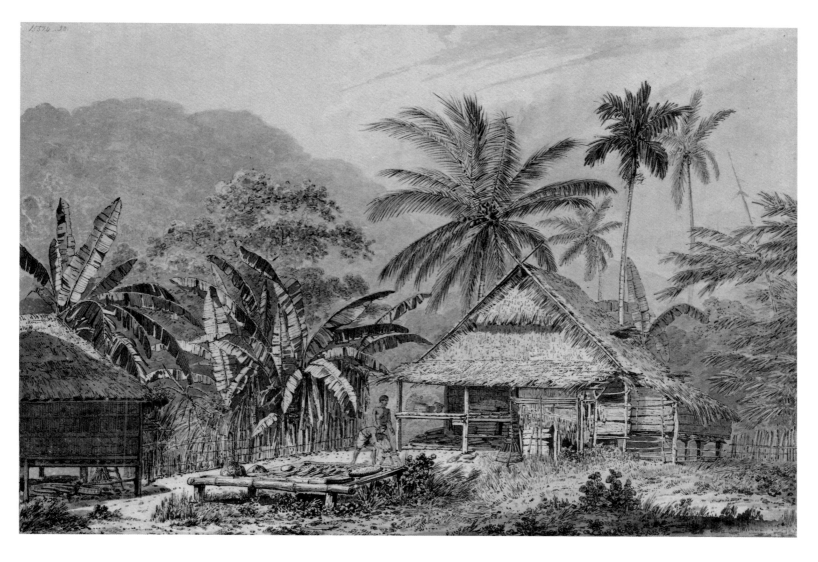

JOHN WEBBER

**3.408   A View in the Island of Cracatoa [Krakatau]
          [plate 177]   [Feb 1780–]**
pen, wash and water-colour, 14½ × 21 : 368 × 534,
unsigned.

Inscribed 'View at Krakatoa in . . . Straits of Sunda' in pencil
on the mount below drawing, and no. '157' (u.l.), which identifies this drawing with the painting so numbered and titled 'A
View of the Natives Habitations', in the 'Caracatoa' section of
Webber's Catalogue.

A large hut containing stores at centre right; at left centre an
open-air trestle with objects. Another hut at extreme left. Coconut palm at right, plantains at left. Large tree-clad hill in
background.

Cracatoa in the Sunda Straits disappeared on 27 August 1883
during the greatest volcanic explosion known to history.

ver: Similar composition to 3.409 and 3.410, except for dif-
        ferences in the arrangement of figures.

British Library, London. Add MS 15514, f.50.

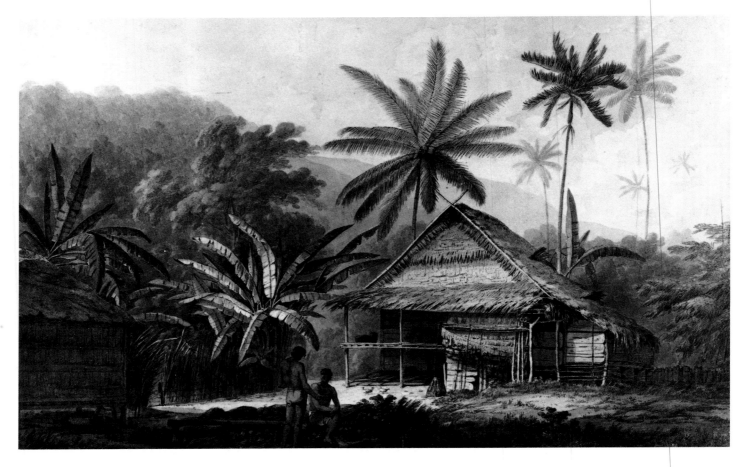

JOHN WEBBER

3.409   A View in the Island of Cracatoa   [Feb 1780–]
pencil, pen, grey wash and water-colour, 14 × 22 :
356 × 558, unsigned.

A large hut under palm trees in middle ground; another hut cut
by the frame on the left; two men in the foreground, one seated,
the other standing in front of him.

ver: For other versions of this view see 3.408 and 3.410.

Collection of L. G. Duke, Sotheby's, 21 May 1970 (188); Messrs.
Sanders of Oxford; Christie's 10 July 1984.

Private collection, England.

JOHN WEBBER

3.410   A View in the Island of Cracatoa   [1784]
oil on canvas, 44 × 56 : 1118 × 1422, signed and
dated 'J. Webber pinxt 1784'.

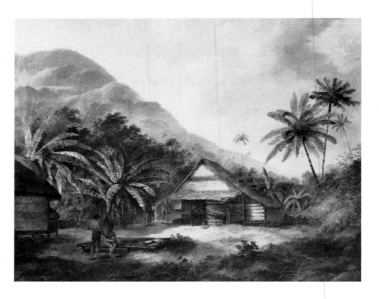

A house among plantains at left, another at centre. Two natives,
one sitting on a low trestle in an open space in the foreground;
a third native in the central mid-distance. Coconut palms at
right.

The date suggests that this was the painting Webber exhibited
at the R.A. in 1785 (211) 'View at Cracatoa, an island in the
China Seas'.

ver: Similar to Webber's composition of a 'View in the Island
of Cracatoa' (3.410A).
ref: Listed as 'View at Cracatoa, an island between Sumatra and
Java' in the Admiralty *Cat.* (1911) no. 49; *Exh. Cat.* London
(1951/52) 32 (42).

Admiralty House, London.

614

JOHN WEBBER

3.410A   **a. 'View in Cracatoa, near China'**
hand-coloured etching, the title in pencil along lower edge, mounted on cardboard, 13¼ × 18¾ : 337 × 476 (10³⁄₁₆ × 15¾ : 259 × 400), signed 'J. Webber fec.' in pencil (l.l.).

On verso, four small chalk studies of the leaves of 'plantain', 'Cocos', 'Cabage' and 'Bambo' with inscriptions probably in Webber's hand. Inscribed in brown ink: 'Drawings by Webber'.

ver: For Webber's original drawing see 3.408.

British Museum, Department of Prints and Drawings, London. C. 6*.

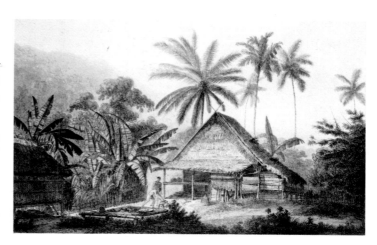

b. 'View in the Island of Cracatoa' (with slight alterations in the figures)
softground etching, tinted in brown and grey wash, or hand-coloured, 13 × 17¹³⁄₁₆ : 329 × 452 (11¼ × 16½ : 286 × 419). 'J. Webber fecit'. 'London Pubᵈ July 1. 1789 by J. Webber Nº 312 Oxford Street'. 'Vide Cook's last Voy. Vol III Ch. XI'.

British Museum, Department of Prints and Drawings, London. 246* a.2. and C. 6*.

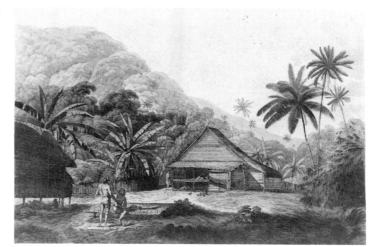

c. 'View in the Island of Cracatoa'
coloured aquatint. 'J. Webber fecit'. 'London Pubᵈ April 1 1809 by Boydell & Compᵞ Nº 90 Cheapside'. 'Vide Cook's last Voy. Vol III, Ch. XI'.

Issued as J. Boydell, *Views in the South Seas* (London, 1808) pl. XV.

National Maritime Museum, London; Bernice P. Bishop Museum, Honolulu.

3.410   **d. A copy of 'View in the Island of Cracatoa'**
pen, wash and water-colour, measuring 14⅜ × 19½ : 365 × 496.

Inscribed in ink on verso as above by an eighteenth century copyist.

The drawing shows some greatly extended areas on the right and shows additional foliage to the original composition.

National Library of Australia, Canberra. Rex Nan Kivell Collection 6788/B.

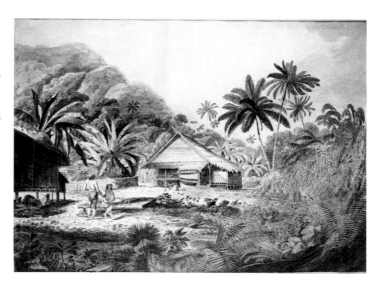

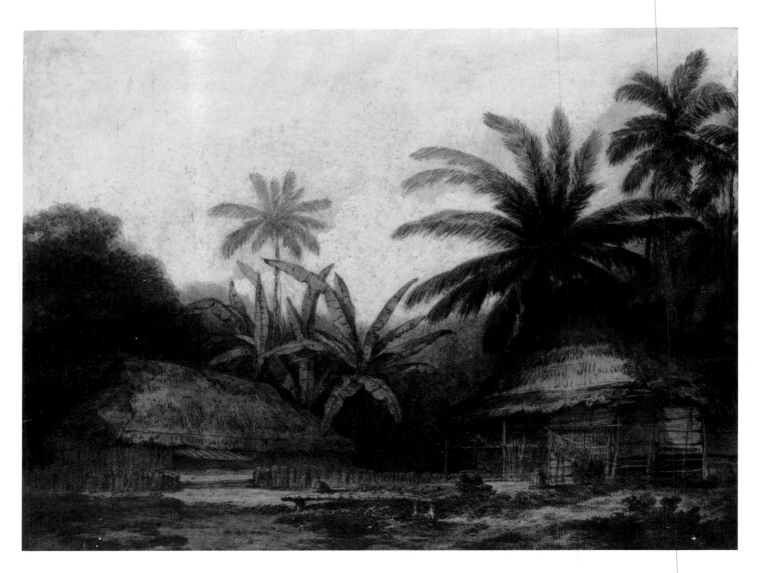

JOHN WEBBER

3.411   [A View in the Island of Cracatoa]   [c. 1785]
pen with wash and oil paint on paper, varnished over,
9¹⁄₁₆ × 11¹¹⁄₁₆ : 230 × 297, unsigned; w/m: 'C
Paine'.

Titled in sepia 'View in Otaheite' on verso in an eighteenth
century hand and in black ink '2nd Act/Sc 5'.

The painting is based on Webber's view in Cracatoa (cf. the
house at right with the similar house in 3.408), but is most
probably a stage design for P. J. de Loutherbourg's Pantomime
'Omai, or, a Trip Round the World', Covent Garden (20 December 1785). The painting is thus of the same category as 3.174.
Though a great many dresses and stage sets were based on third
voyage material, these were used with much artistic licence. Scene
5 of act 2 demanded 'A village in Tongataboo, the most beautiful
and considerable of the Friendly Islands', and it is possible that
because of its village character this scene was used instead of a
proper Tongan view.

Attributed to Webber in Goodison (1977); formerly attributed
to William Hodges (Mesman) and to the portrait painter C. H.
Hodges (Earp), see ibid., 276-7.

Bequeathed by Daniel Mesman in 1834.

Fitzwilliam Museum, Cambridge. Acc. no. 276.

616

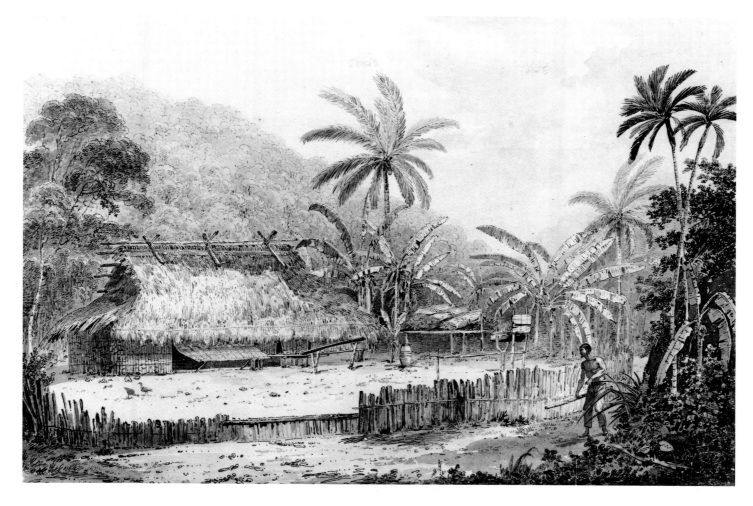

JOHN WEBBER

3.412   [A View in Cracatoa]   [Feb 1780]
pen, wash and water-colour, $14\frac{5}{8} \times 21\frac{1}{4}$: 371 $\times$ 540, unsigned.

Inscribed 'Pulau Condore' in pencil on the mount below drawing.

A large native hut enclosed by a palisaded fence. Natives at right carrying a log. Coconut palms and banana trees.

The structure of the house and the palisaded fence suggest that this drawing was taken in Cracatoa (cf. the house with the one at left in 3.410) and not in Pulau Condore.

British Library, London. Add MS 15514, f. 52.

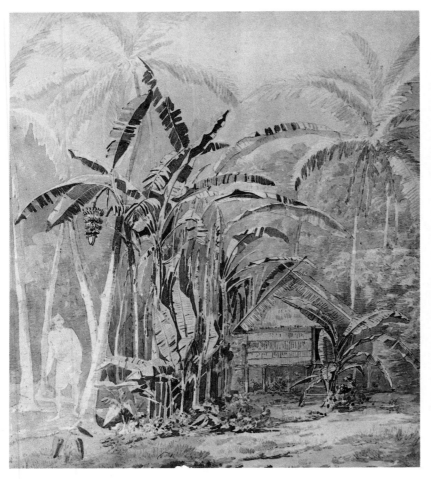

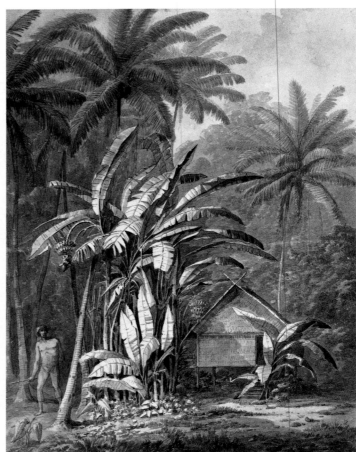

JOHN WEBBER

3.413   **The Plantain Tree [plate 178]**   [Feb 1780]

    pen, pencil, wash and water-colour, 16⅜ × 14⅛ : 416 × 359, unsigned.

Laid down on card within sepia framing lines with '180' in pencil at centre of lower margin. A pencil inscription cut off, along the lower edge with 'Cracatoa' and 'by Webber' discernible. On verso in brown ink 'Drawn by Webber who accompanied Cap. Cook, in the island of Caracacoa' and the lot no. in pencil '180/1'.

A bamboo hut at centre surrounded by palms and plantains. A standing fully-clothed figure at left, unfinished.

'The town [. . . was] surrounded with trees of various kinds, among which were the coco nut and plaintain trees; the latter were the largest we had seen before. All the houses were elevated upon posts, about two feet from the ground and were built upon the same plan as those of Prince's Island.' Ellis (1782) II, 344.

ver: For a more developed version, see 3.414.

ref: Smith (1960) pl. 62.

National Library of Australia, Canberra. Rex Nan Kivell Collection. NK 52/0.

JOHN WEBBER

3.414   **The Plantain Tree**   [c. 1788]

    pencil and wash with tints of blue water-colour, 14 × 10⅝ : 351 × 270, traces of the signature 'J. Webber' (l.r.).

ver: Similar to 3.413 but more developed and reduced in size. The figure at left is here however half-stripped. The drawing served as model, in reverse, for Webber's etching 3.414A.

British Museum, Department of Prints and Drawings, London. Inv. no. 1957-7-5-54.

618

3.414A   **a. 'The Plantain Tree, in the Island of Cracatoa'**
softground etching, tinted in brown and grey wash, or hand-coloured, 17⅛ × 12⅜ : 435 × 315 (14⁹⁄₁₆ × 10⁹⁄₁₆ : 370 × 269). 'J. Webber fecit 1788'. 'London Pub.ᵈ Nov.ʳ 1 1788 by J. Webber N.º 312 Oxford Street'. 'Vide Cooks last Voyage Vol 3. Chap. 10'.

ver: For Webber's original drawing see 3.414.

British Museum, Department of Prints and Drawings, London. 246* a.2 and C. 6*.

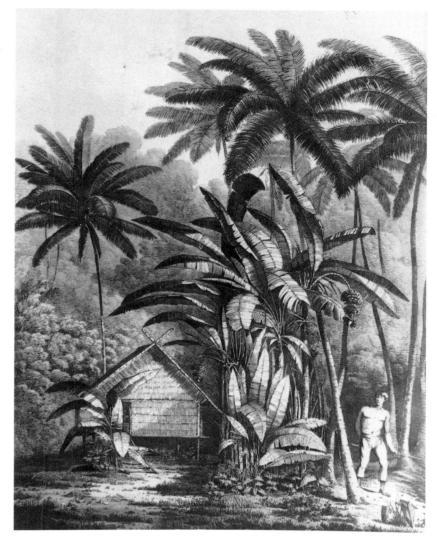

b. 'The Plantain Tree in the Island of Cracatoa'
coloured aquatint. 'J. Webber fecit, 1788'. 'London Pub.ᵈ April 1 1809 by Boydell & Comp.ʸ N.º 90 Cheapside'. 'Vide Cooks last Voyage Vol 3. Chap. 10'.

Issued as J. Boydell, *Views in the South Seas* (London, 1808) pl. IV.

National Maritime Museum, London; Bernice P. Bishop Museum. Honolulu.

JOHN WEBBER

3.415   A Fan Palm [plate 179]   **[Feb 1780]**
pencil, pen, wash and water-colour, 20¼ ×
14½ : 514 × 368, signed 'J. Webber del.'.

Inscribed 'Fan Palm, Cracatoa' in pencil on the mount below
drawing. This drawing is probably the one referred to in Webber's
Catalogue as '152 A plant called the Fan Palm' where it is however
listed under the section 'Pulo Condore'.

A view in a clearing with palms and other trees.

ver: For Webber's etching of this composition with the addition
of a half-naked girl, published as 'The Fan Palm, in the
Island of Cracatoa', see 3.415A.

British Library, London. Add MS 15514, f. 51.

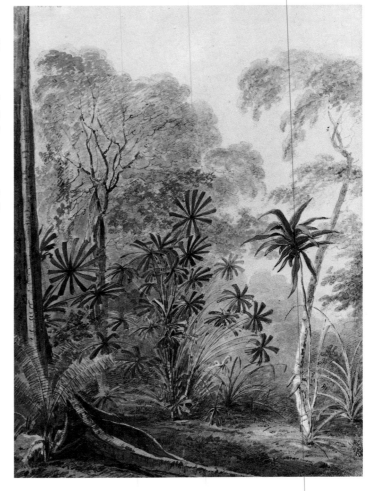

JOHN WEBBER

3.415A   a. 'The Fan Palm, in the Island of Cracatoa'
softground etching, finished in brown and grey wash,
or hand-coloured, 16⅞ × 12⅜ : 428 × 314
(14⁵⁄₁₆ × 10¾ : 363 × 273). 'J Webber fecit
1788'. 'London Pub. Aug.ᵗ 1. 1788 by J. Webber N°.
312 Oxford Street'. 'Vide Cooks last Voyage Vol. 3.
Chap. 10'.
ver: For Webber's original drawing see 3.415.
ref: Smith (1960), pl. 63; Kaeppler (1978a) fig. 4 (7), repro-
ducing a brown and grey coloured copy from the Fuller
Collection, Bernice P. Bishop Museum, Honolulu.

British Museum, Department of Prints and Drawings, London.
246* a.2 and C. 6*; Bernice P. Bishop Museum, Honolulu, Fuller
Collection.

b. 'The Fan Palm, in the Island of Cracatoa'
coloured aquatint. 'J. Webber fecit. 1788'. 'London
Pub.ᵈ April 1 1809 by Boydell & Comp.ʸ N°. Cheapside'.
'Vide Cooks last Voyage Vol. 3. Chap. 10'.

Issued as J. Boydell, *Views in the South Seas* (London,
1808) pl. XVI.

National Maritime Museum, London. Bernice P. Bishop
Museum, Honolulu.

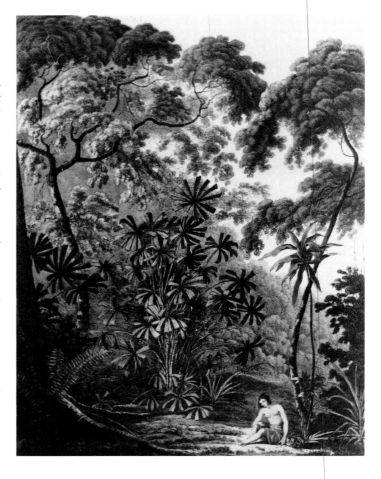

JOHN WEBBER

3.416   [A portrait of a man]   [1780]
          pencil, 9 × 9 : 228 × 228, unsigned.

On verso two studies of Chinese vessels and a Chinese man with
a pigtail (3.383).

Plump face of an elderly man with protruding cheek-bones, turning right. The sitter wears a cloth around his head. Probably a
Malayan or Chinese man.

British Library, London. Add MS 17277. no. 42 (verso).

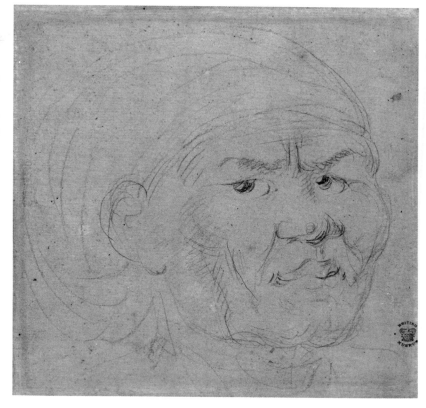

JOHN WEBBER

3.417   A portrait of a woman   [1780]
          red crayon, 15⅞ × 11⅞ : 404 × 302, unsigned.

Portrait of head and shoulders of a woman with curly hair, wearing
a piece of cloth around the back of her head. She is possibly
Malayan.

British Library, London. Add MS 17277, no. 48.

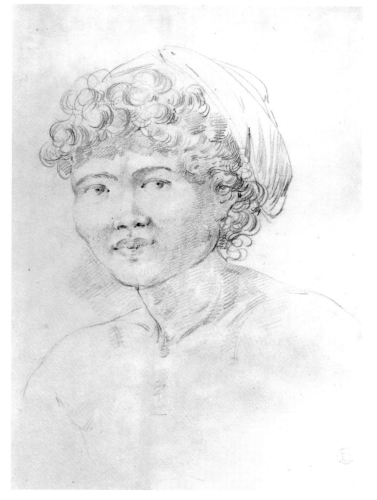

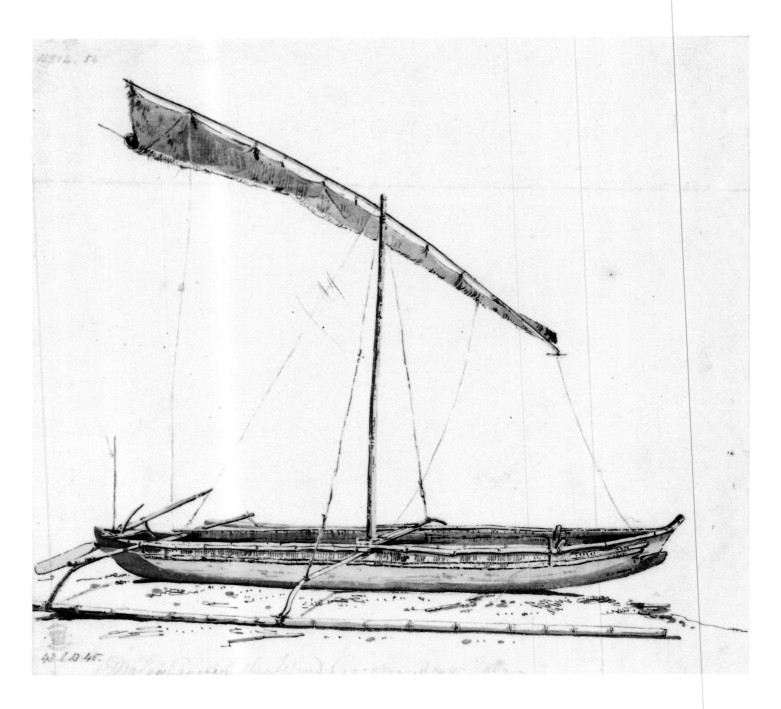

JOHN WEBBER

3.418   Canoe of Cracatoa   [1780]
pen and wash, $13\frac{5}{8} \times 14\frac{1}{2}$: 346 × 368, unsigned.

Inscribed 'A Malay Canoe of the Island Cracatoa near Java' on
drawing in Webber's hand in pencil and '156' (u.l.), identifying
it as '156 a Canoe' in the section Caracatoa in Webber's Catalogue. Another inscription 'iii 471' in pencil (u.l.).

A canoe beached, with long bamboo outriggers on both sides.

British Library, London. Add MS 15514, f. 54.

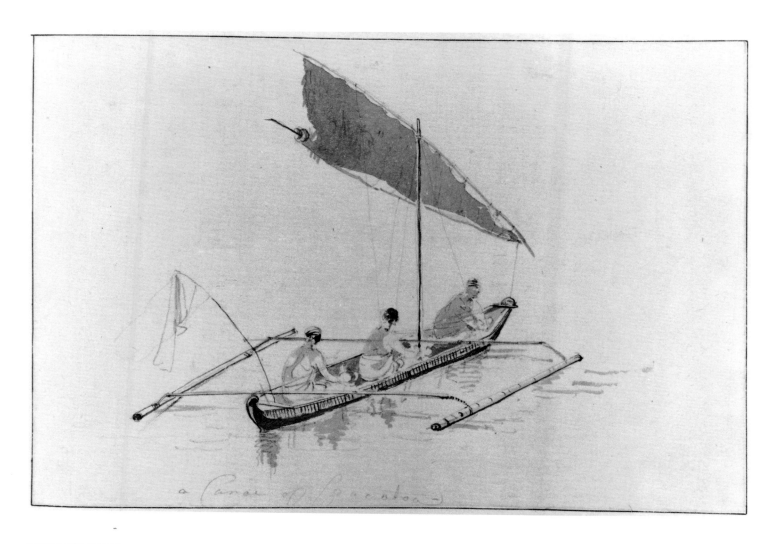

a Canoe of Cracatoa

JOHN WEBBER

3.419   A Canoe of Cracatoa   [1780]
        pencil, pen and wash, 6⅝ × 9⅞ : 168 × 251, unsigned.

The title above in pencil at lower centre in Webber's hand.

A canoe with two outriggers and a sail, manned by three natives.

National Maritime Museum, London. (In volume of plates to Cook's Voyages.)

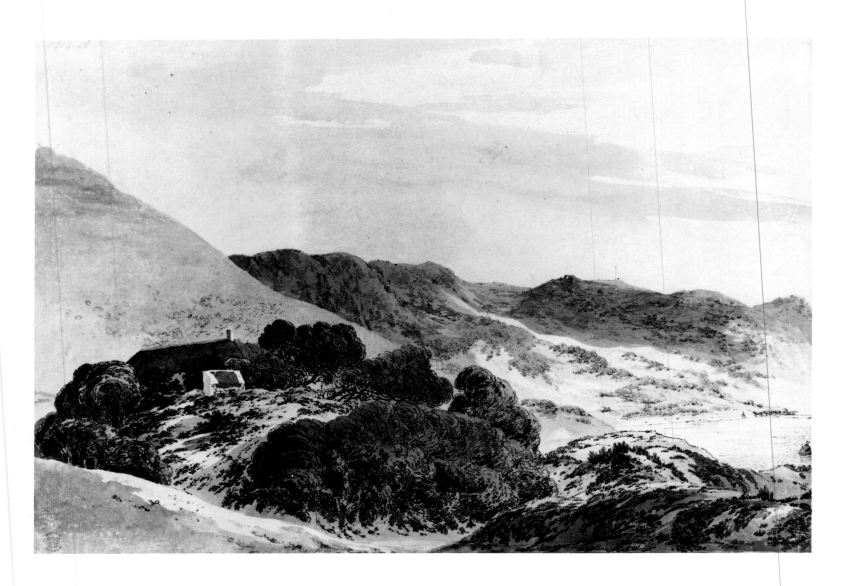

JOHN WEBBER

3.420a **A View of the North Part of False Bay — Cape of Good Hope [plate 184]**   **[Apr-May 1780]**
pen, wash and water-colour, $14\frac{3}{8} \times 21 : 365 \times 533$, unsigned.

Inscribed on mount in pencil below drawing: 'Scenery — Cape of Good Hope'.

A cottage at left behind white outhouses, amid rolling hills. At extreme right a bay with a team of oxen on the shore. This view is a continuation to the right of 3.420b, in the form of a panorama.

'False Bay, situated to the Eastward of the Cape of Good Hope, is frequented by shipping during the prevalence of the North West winds, which begin to blow in May and make it dangerous to lie in Table Bay. It is terminated on the West by the Cape of Good Hope, and on the Eastward by False Cape.' Cook/King (1784) III, 485.

British Library, London. Add MS 15514, f. 57.

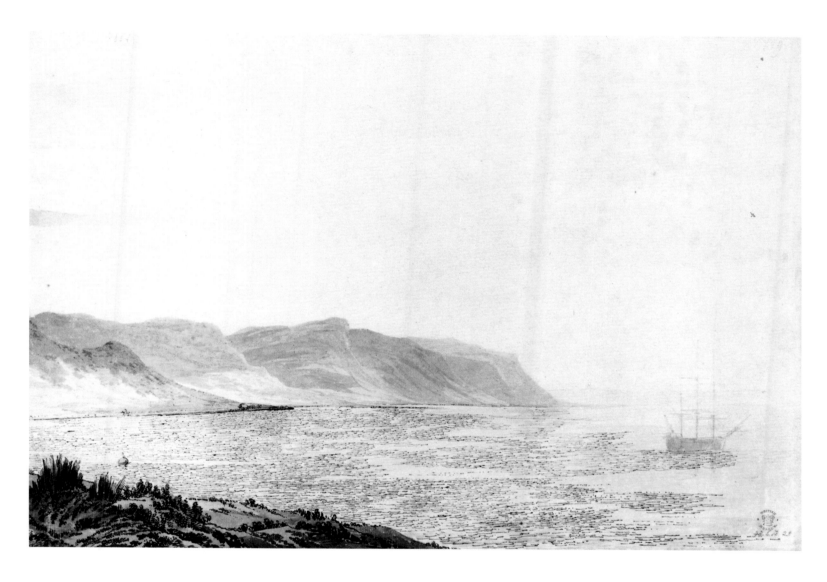

JOHN WEBBER

3.420b   A View of the North Part of False Bay — Cape of Good Hope [plate 184]   [Apr-May 1780]
pen, wash and water-colour, 14⅜ × 20⅝ : 365 × 524, unsigned.

The title inscribed as above in pencil on mount below drawing; traces of inscription 'North . . .' at top centre and '159' (u.r.): thus corresponding with Webber's Catalogue, in which no.159 is 'A view of the North Part of False Bay'.

View of the bay with a ship at right. This view is continued to the left by 3.420a.

From Paterson's 'Map of the Southern Extremity of Africa' at the end of his *Narrative* (1789), which gives a topographical survey of False Bay, it appears that Webber's drawing of 3.420a,b was taken from Simon's Bay (a part of False Bay) looking towards Eerste River.

British Library, London. Add MS 15514, f. 56.

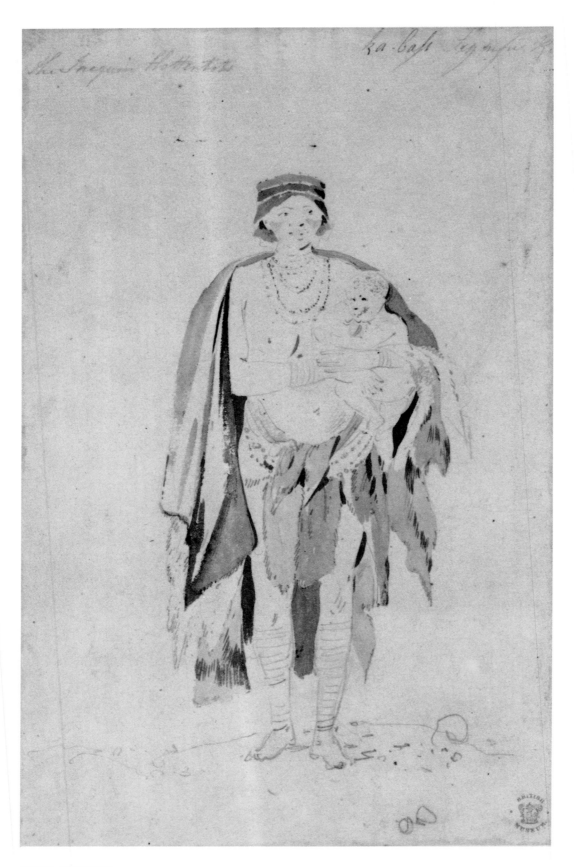

JOHN WEBBER

3.421   Hottentot Woman [plate 183]   [Apr-May 1780]
pencil, pen and wash, 12¹⁵/₁₆ × 7½ : 329 × 190,
unsigned.

The title as above in pencil on lower edge also inscribed 'ka-bass'
in Webber's hand followed by indecipherable script (u.r.) and
'the Inequin Hottentots' (u.l.).

Full-length figure of a woman holding a child in her left arm.

British Library, London. Add MS 17277, no. 49.

626

MISCELLANEOUS

WILLIAM ELLIS

3.422   **Three Studies of a Man (from Pulo Condore?) [1780]**
pencil, 10⁷⁄₁₆ × 7¹⁄₁₆ : 265 × 179, unsigned.

Inscribed 'Chinese' in brown ink (u.l.); unidentified w/m: 'EB/I' surrounded by leaves in a circle.

Three studies of a man wearing a turban; (a) at top right, in profile; (b) at centre, en face; (c) at bottom, full-figure, standing and facing left.

Tipped into a copy of Captain George Dixon, *A Voyage Round the World* (London, 1789) fp. 311.

National Library of Australia, Canberra. Rex Nan Kivell Collection. NK 7402.

WILLIAM ELLIS (?)

3.423   **A man reading**
pencil and grey wash, 12⅛ × 7⅞ : 308 × 200, unsigned; w/m: 'Pro Patria'.

Profile view of a bearded man reading. He is seated on the ground, with his left arm resting on his knee, and his waist covered by a piece of cloth. Above, the study of a hand.

ref: Murray-Oliver (1977), 34.

Alexander Turnbull Library, Wellington. A 264.26B.

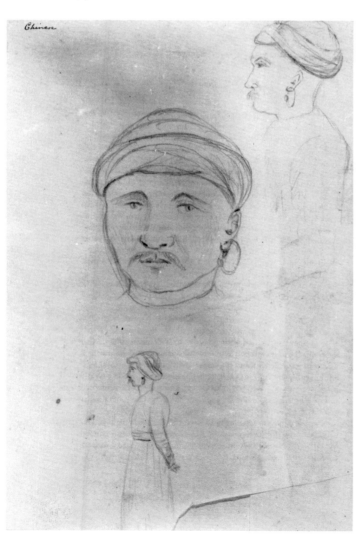

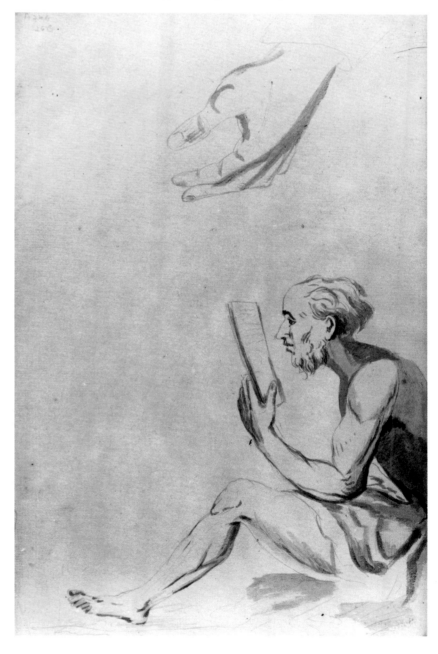

WILLIAM ELLIS

3.424   Drawings of faces and a hand
Six pencil drawings on one sheet, 11½ × 7⁵/₁₆ :
292 × 186, unsigned; w/m: 'GR' under a crown, surrounded by wreaths, in a circle.

On recto are two portraits of natives of the Friendly Isles, see
3.77.

Drawings of four faces, three of women, one of a child; also a
nose and an arm. They appear to be European, except possibly
one of a young woman who appears to wear flowers in her hair.
They may be copies from a book on figure drawing.

ref: Murray-Oliver (1977) 32.

Alexander Turnbull Library, Wellington. A264.15B.

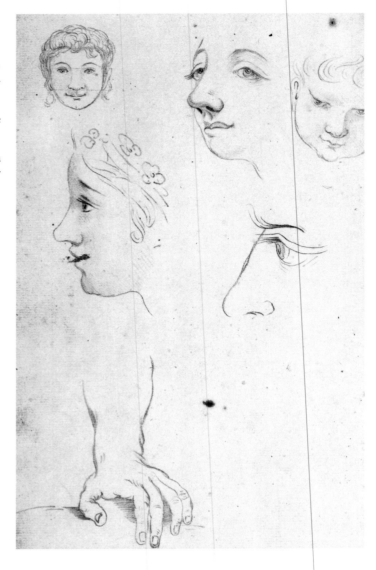

WILLIAM ELLIS

3.425   Drawing of trees and a rock
water-colour, 11⅛ × 10⅜ : 281 × 263, unsigned;
w/m: 'ALCV', colour testing brush strokes (l.r.).

Recto is a drawing of a portrait of a native of the Sandwich
Islands, see 3.315.

(a) trees at shoreline, with a hut (?)
(b) a thick stand of trees
(c) a branch of leaves of a bread fruit tree
(d) a large, sheer, basaltic-type rock.

ref: Murray-Oliver (1977) 36.

Alexander Turnbull Library, Wellington. A264.44B.

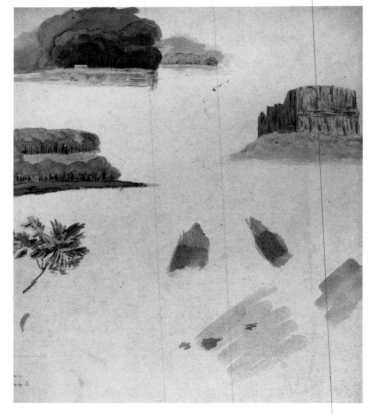

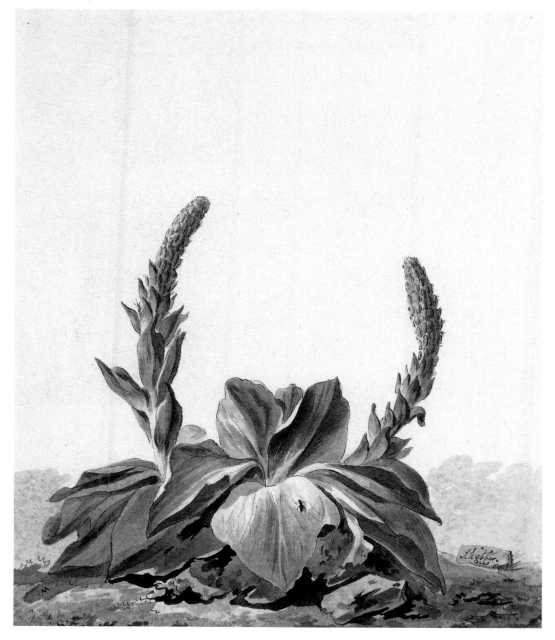

JOHN WEBBER

3.426a **Kerguelen Island cabbage, (*Pringlea antiscorbutica*)**
[plate 9]   **[Dec 1776]**
pen, wash and water-colour, 9 × 7½ : 228 × 190,
signed 'J. Webber delin.'

Listed in Webber's Catalogue as no. 3.

See Anderson's description of this plant in Cook, *Journals* III, 2,
771-2.

ref: Sawyer (1971) 197; Hulton/Smith (1979) 42.

British Museum (Natural History), Botanical Library, London.

JOHN WEBBER

3.426b   Kerguelen Island cabbage, (*Pringlea antiscorbutica*)
[Dec 1776]
water-colour and wash, 6¼ × 6¼ : 160 × 160, signed
and dated in ink 'J.W. 1777'; w/m: C. TAYLOR.

Inscribed in ink: 'This which grows on the Rocks is the only
vegetable except Moss that we saw on Kerguelen's Land'. The
drawing is pasted into volume I of the log of James Burney.

ver: The drawing is another version of 3.426a.

Mitchell Library, State Library of New South Wales, Sydney.
Log of James Burney, vol. I, f. 12 (Safe 1/64).

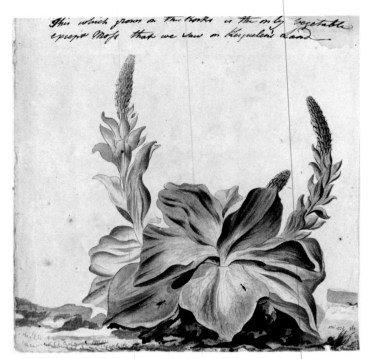

WILLIAM ELLIS

3.427   A Study of trees by a small sheet of water in Adventure
Bay, Tasmania [plate 11]   [Jan 1777]
pencil, wash and water-colour, 10⁷⁄₁₆ × 14½ : 265
× 368, unsigned; w/m: partly cut off, with a cross,
perhaps J. Villedary.

Inscribed in pencil '281' (u.r.) and on the back in ink 'V.
Diemen's Land?' in brown ink.

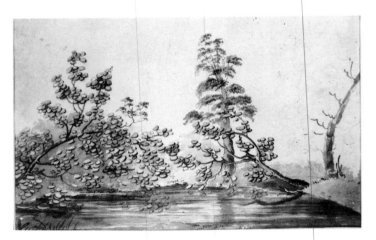

We are indebted to W. D. Jackson, Professor of Botany, University of Tasmania, for the following comments:

'I would think it highly likely that both the plants represented
in the drawing are in fact eucalypts, and could well be those
present at Adventure Bay, Bruny Island.

'The two adults are probably *E. globulus* (Tasmanian Blue Gum),
the one on the right fire damaged or dead. The two shrubby forms
in the foreground with large wide elliptical leaves are also likely
to be *E. globulus* in juvenile foliage after fire damage, or just because they are growing in an exposed situation near the shoreline.
The form of the tree in the background with its foliage in discrete
branch clusters is characteristic of eucalypts and would be most
unusual in a northern hemisphere tree. The artist's use of small,
vertical strokes for the foliage also leads me to assume that he is
trying to show the hanging leaves. This is particularly noticeable
on the branches in the upper crown.

'The decussate leaf arrangement of large, oblong, glaucous leaves
on juvenile *viminales* groups of eucalypts would seem very remarkable to northern hemisphere observers. The sketch is not
an unfair representation of the visual impact of these plants. The
foliage is most likely to be juvenile *E. globulus*, although it is
possible that it is *E. cordata*. *E. globulus* juvenile and adult is common along the foreshore of Adventure Bay, especially near the
creeks. *E. cordata*, which has rounder, cordate leaves, is recorded
in the literature from the Adventure Bay area but seems to be
absent now.

'The natives frequented the area near the creeks and would have
burnt the coastal scrub and vegetation frequently. Thus one would
expect that most low trees would be frequently clothed in the
heteroblastic juvenile leaf form because of flame scorch. The tree
on the left appears to have one branch where the artist clearly
shows what I take to be some adult foliage with vertical strokes.
This I take to be a branch which escaped the hot flames.'

ref: Lewis (1976) 6; W. D. Jackson to B. Smith, *in litt.* 8
November 1985.

La Trobe Library, State Library of Victoria, Melbourne. M. 5405.

3.428   **Two plants**

(a) pencil, pen, wash and water-colour, 15¾ × 10¾ : 400 × 273; signed in brown ink (l.l.) 'W. Ellis'; w/m: shield with fleur-de-lis, under a crown, below the initials 'VDL'.

Inscribed in pencil on recto by a later hand 'Mimulus comes very near to M. Lutens' and 'Chelsea'. Inscribed on verso along lower margin in pencil 'North West America' and 'Ellis'.

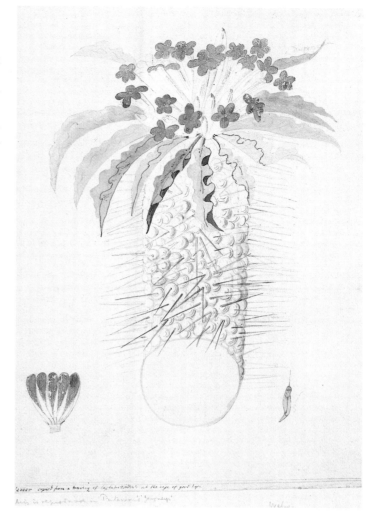

(b) wash and water-colour, 6¼ × 7¼ : 159 × 184. Inscribed on recto in pencil (l.r.) 'Ellis', as well as 'Trillium erectum Linn.' Inscribed on verso in pencil along lower margin 'Kamshatka' and 'Ellis'.

ref: Sawyer (1971) 125.

British Museum (Natural History), Botanical Library, London.

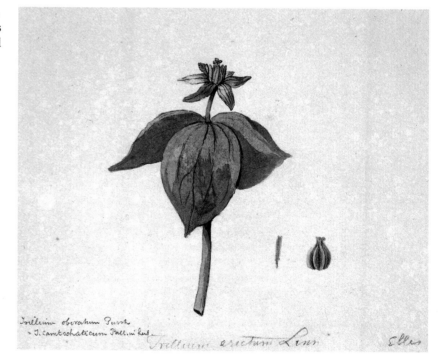

631

3.429 Two flowers

(a) Stapelia Gordoni (*Hoodia gordoni*)

pencil, pen and water-colour, with touches of lead white, $14^{15}/_{16} \times 10^{5}/_{8}$: 380×270.

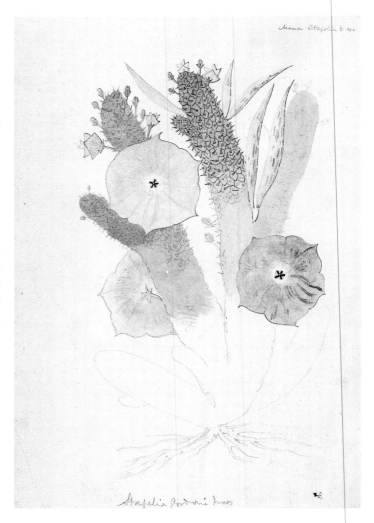

Inscribed on recto in black ink (l.l) 'Webber', also in pencil at lower centre by a later hand 'Stapelia gordoni Mass.' and (u.r.) 'Masson Stapelia, t.40', which is a reference to Francis Masson's *Stapeliae Novae: or a collection of several new species of that genus, discovered in the interior parts of Africa*, London (1796) [-97] pl. 40, inscribed 'Stapelia Gordoni. Publish'd as the Act directs, June 20 1797 by F. Masson', the plate is a softground etching by Mackenzie.

On page 24 of his *Stapeliae Novae* Masson, who in his capacity as collector of plants for the Royal Gardens at Kew stayed at the Cape of Good Hope between 1772-74/75 and 1786-96, states that he did not examine this plant and that he owed the drawing to the favour of Captain Gordon. It would thus appear that Webber based his drawing on one of Gordon's or was commissioned by Gordon. See also 3.429b.

(b) Pentandra Monogynia (*Pachypodium namaquanum*)

pencil, pen and water-colour, $15^{1}/_{16} \times 11$: 383×280.

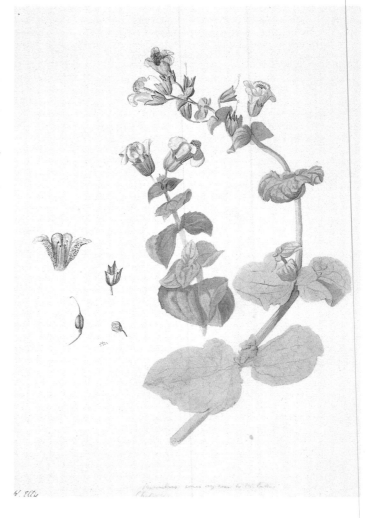

Inscribed on recto in brown ink along lower margin: 'Webber copied from a Drawing of Captain Gordon's at the Cape of good hope' (not in Webber's hand). On the folio in pencil by a later hand: 'This is reproduced in Paterson's Journeys facing p.124', also 'Pachypodium namaquanum'. The reference to Paterson's Journeys concerns Lieutenant William Paterson, *A narrative of four journeys into the country of the Hottentots and Caffraria in the years 1777, 1778 and 1779*, (London, 1789), where this flower is published as 'Pentandra Monogynia. From the Great Nemiqua Land', hand-coloured engraving, f.p. 124. In October 1779, during his fourth journey into the interior of Africa, which was partly conducted with Captain Gordon, Paterson wrote: 'I found here [near the Lions River] the most beautiful plant I ever saw of the Petandria Monogynia class. It grows to six feet high, and is full of long spines from the ground to the tops, and forms a large crown of crisped leaves, and reddish tubelar flowers, tinged with yellow and green.' Ibid., 124.

For other drawings which Webber copied from Gordon, see also 3.444 and 3.445.

Both drawings are stuck into folios of a volume *Collection of Drawings by Francis Masson*, fols. 26 and 40.

ref. Sawyer (1971) 197.

British Museum (Natural History), Botanical Library, London.

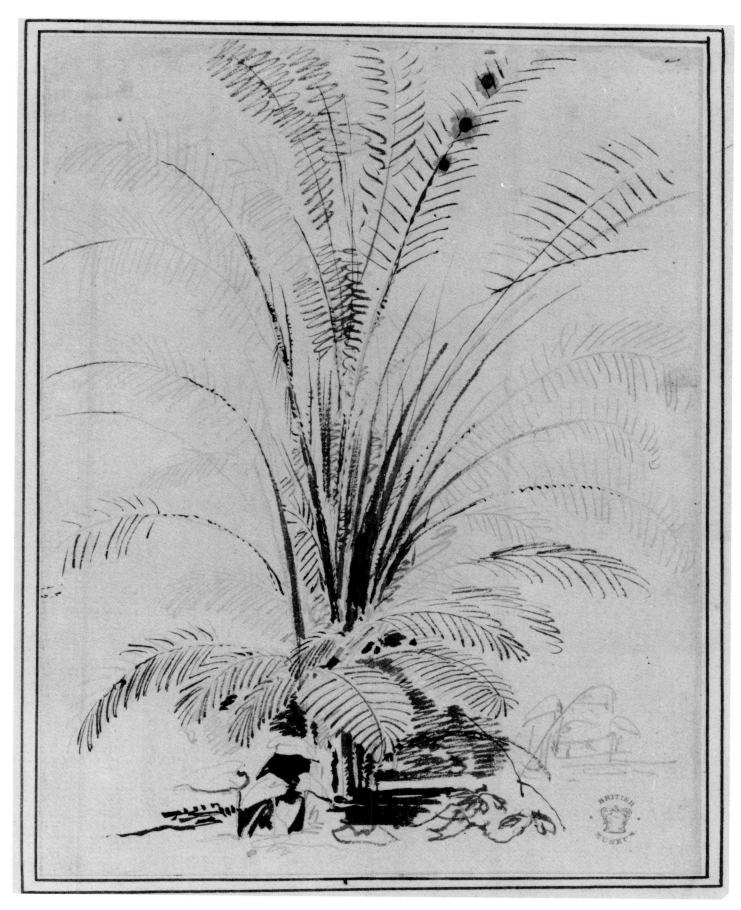

JOHN WEBBER

3.430   A Study of a Palm Tree
    pencil, pen and wash, 9¼ × 7⅛ : 235 × 181.

A brilliant and spirited rendering of a palm, probably a field-
sketch.

British Library, London. Add MS 17277, no. 51.

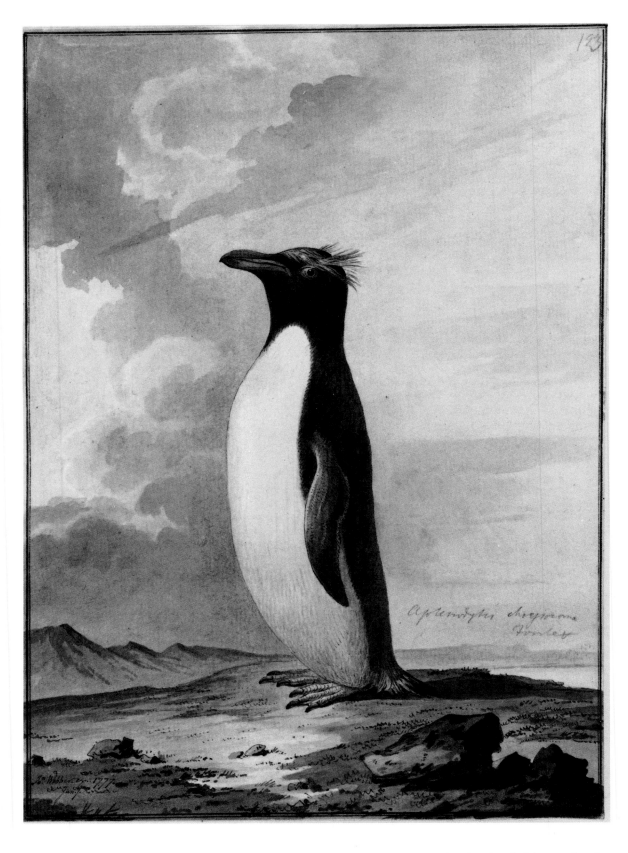

JOHN WEBBER

3.431   **Album of forty-six natural history drawings [plates 6, 8, 23]**

pencil, pen, water-colour, wash and gouache representing thirty-eight birds, from the Cape of Good Hope, Kerguelen's Island, Adventure Bay, Van Diemen's Land, Palmerston Island, the Friendly Islands, the Society Islands, Christmas Island, the Sandwich Islands, King George's Sound, north-west coast of America, Alaska, Bering Strait, Siberian Coast, Japan and Princes Island; also seven fishes mostly of the Palmerston Island and the Sandwich Isles, and a drawing of a lizard of Adventure Bay.

The penguin representing this album is a King penguin (*Aptenodytes patagonicus*) which Webber saw and drew at Christmas Harbour. The drawing was obviously used in two views of Christmas Harbour, compare especially the second bird from the right (3.3 and 3.4). Cook describes the King penguin in his *Journals* III, 1, 46, and Anderson in ibid., 2, 773.

ref: Lysaght (1959) 339-44.

British Museum, Department of Prints and Drawings, London. 199* b.2.

634

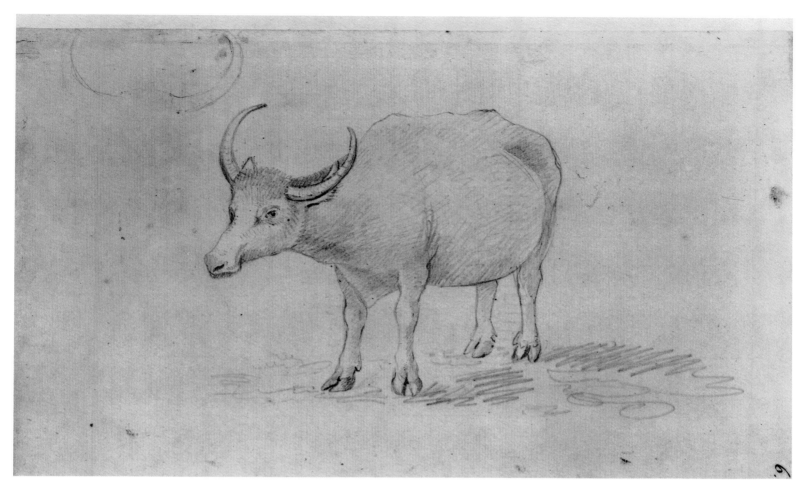

WILLIAM ELLIS

3.432 **Album of 115 natural history drawings [plates 203, 204]**

water-colour and pencil, representing ninety birds from the Cape of Good Hope; Kerguelen Land; Adventure Bay, Van Diemen's Land; New Zealand; Atiu (Cook Island); Palmerston Island; the Friendly Islands; the Society Islands; Christmas Island; Sandwich Islands; King George's Sound; Sandwich Sound; Alaska; Norton Sound; Bering Strait; Arctic; Kamchatka; Japan; Pulau Condore, Princes Island; moreover fifteen drawings of fishes and ten drawings of mammals and crustaceans, including a walrus.

The collection is here represented by a buffalo of Pulau Condore (f. 6). There is a close similarity between this animal and the representation of a buffalo in Webber's drawing 3.397 and his etching 3.397 A.

ref: Sharpe (1906), 199-208; Stresemann (1949, 1950, 1953); Lysaght (1959) 322-39; Whitehead (1968); Sawyer (1971) 125.

British Museum (Natural History), London. Zoological Library, 88q E.

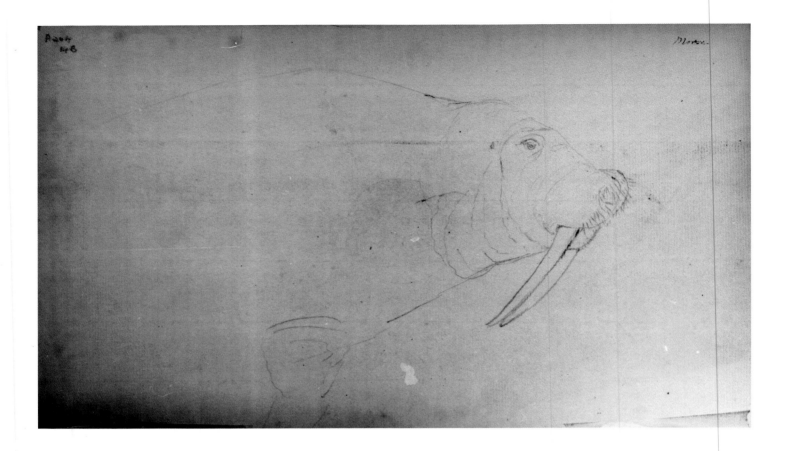

WILLIAM ELLIS

3.433   **Eight folios of natural history drawings [plate 204]**
water-colour and pencil representing birds from the
north-west coast of America (Nootka to Bering Strait)
and of Kamchatka, as well as a sketch of the head of
a walrus.

The drawing represented here, the head of a walrus (f. 14B)
compares with the animals depicted in Webber's drawings and
paintings of 'Shooting Sea Horses' (3.278-3.282). It seems to be
a study for Ellis's more finished drawing in his album in the British
Museum, Natural History, London.

For another illustration from this collection see plate 204.

ref: Medway (1977) 23-7; Murray-Oliver (1977).

Alexander Turnbull Library, Wellington. A. 264.14B.

JOHN WEBBER

3.434   **An Opossum of Van Diemen's Land**
[plate 16]   **[Jan 1777]**
pencil, pen, wash and water-colour, 12¼ × 19⅜ :
312 × 494, signed and dated in ink 'Johⁿ. Webber f.
1777'.

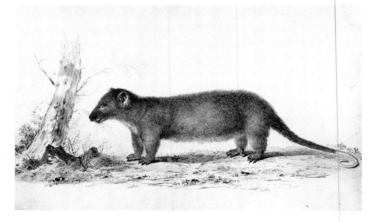

Inscribed in ink on verso: 'Lot No 13' and 'No 3'. Probably the
drawing listed in Webber's Catalogue, as no. 6.

This drawing was probably used for engraving the furred body of
the animal (3.435A) with 3.435 being used for engraving the
landscape setting.

A reference to the opossum is made by Anderson in Cook, *Journals*
III, 2, 792.

ver: For another version see 3.435.

Dixson Library, State Library of New South Wales, Sydney.
Pf 55.

636

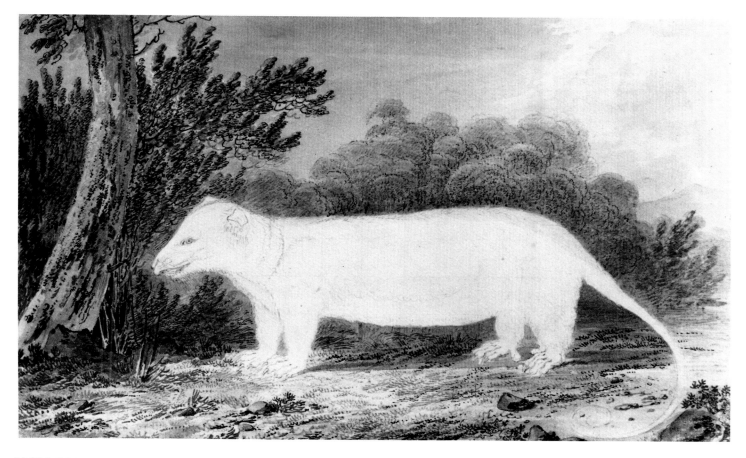

JOHN WEBBER

3.435   **An Opossum of Van Diemen's Land**   [c. 1781-3]
pencil, pen, wash and water-colour, 6⅜ × 10¹/₁₆ :
162 × 256; w/m: 'T. FRENCH'.

Inscribed in pencil on verso 'An Opossum — New Ṣ Wales'.

ver: This drawing is another version of 3.434 and probably
served for the landscaping and positioning of the tail for
the engraving 3.435A.

National Library of Australia, Canberra. Rex Nan Kivell Collection. NK 52/I.

JOHN WEBBER (after)

3.435A   'An OPOSSUM of VAN DIEMAN'S LAND'
Engraving. 'J. Webber' — 'P. Mazell sculp.'

Published in Cook/King (1784) pl. 8, I, 109.

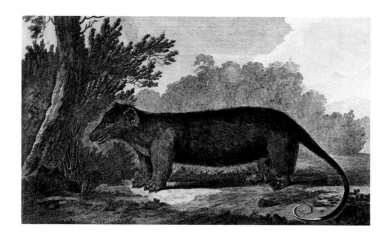

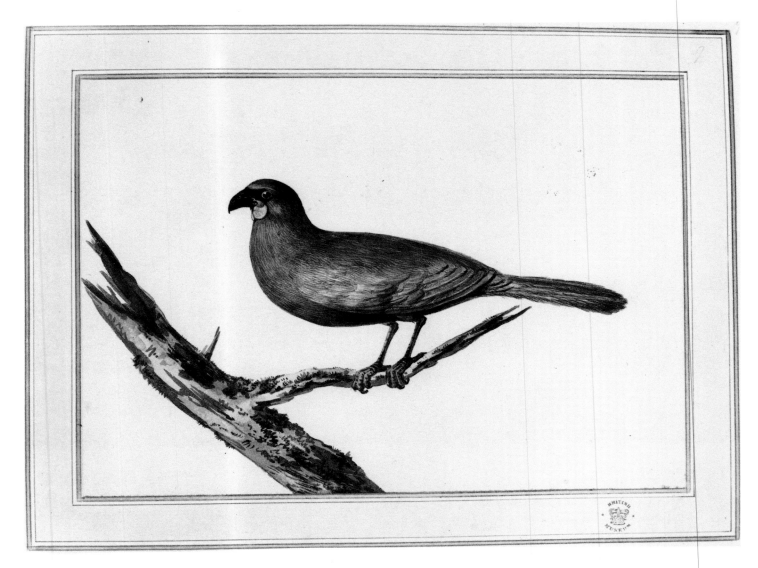

JOHN WEBBER

3.436   The Wattle Bird   [Feb 1777]
pen, wash and water-colour, $7\frac{3}{16} \times 10\frac{1}{16}$:
182 × 256.

Inscribed as above on lower mount in pencil probably in Webber's hand, with 'New Zeeland' added.

For a description of the wattle bird see Anderson in Cook, *Journals* III, 2, 806.

British Library, London. Add MS 17277, no. 9.

JOHN WEBBER

3.437   A Tropic or Frigate Bird *(tachypetes aquilus)*
[1777]
pen, wash and water-colour, $12\frac{1}{4} \times 19\frac{1}{2}$: 312 × 496,
signed and dated in ink 'Jo^n. Webber f. 1777'.

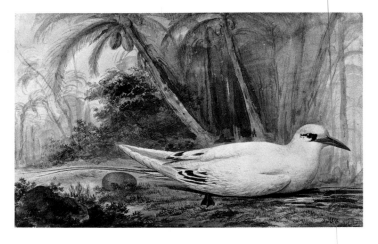

Inscribed in ink 'lot no. 19', and 'no. 2', as well as in pencil 'Cap^n. Campbell'.

The tropic bird from which the feathers of the precious Tongan feather caps were derived (see Cook, *Journals* III, 1, 117). A drawing of the tropic bird is listed in Webber's Catalogue as no. 17 and since he lists it in the Friendly Island section, he probably drew it in Tonga.

ref: Exh. Cat. Auckland (1964) pl. 36.

Dixson Library, State Library of New South Wales, Sydney. Pf 53.

638

JOHN WEBBER

3.438   The Humming Bird
pen, wash and water-colour, 8³⁄₁₆ × 6³⁄₈ : 208 × 162.

Inscribed on lower mount as above, followed by 'Trochylus colibris from California'.

British Library, London. Add MS 17277, no. 23.

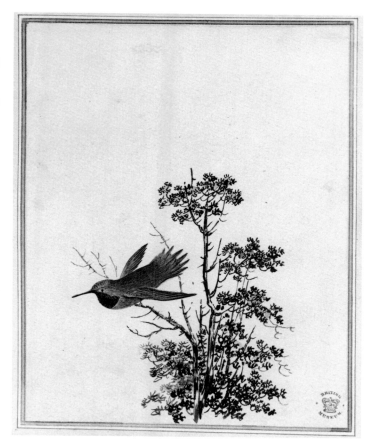

JOHN WEBBER

3.439   A Sea Otter   **[Apr 1778]**
pencil, wash and water-colour, 8⁷⁄₈ × 17⁵⁄₈ : 226 × 448, numbered '66' in pencil (u.l.), and on verso '18'.

Inscribed in pencil 'The Sea Otter call'd by the Natives of King Georges Sound . . .'. Listed in Webber's Catalogue as no. 66.

A description of the sea otter probably based upon Anderson's (lost) journal is provided in Cook/King (1784) II, 295.

ver: Engraved by P. Mazell for Cook/King (1784) pl. 43.

ref: Cook, *Journals* III, 1, pl. 78a.

Francis Edwards, *Cat.* 416 (London, July 1921) as no. 769 'A Sea Otter (17½ by 9 in) in sepia and colour'.

National Library of Australia, Canberra. Rex Nan Kivell Collection. NK 52/A.

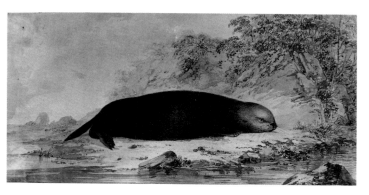

JOHN WEBBER (after)

3.439A   'A Sea Otter'
Engraving. 'J. Webber del.' — 'Mazell sculp.'

Published in Cook/King (1784) pl.43, II, 295.

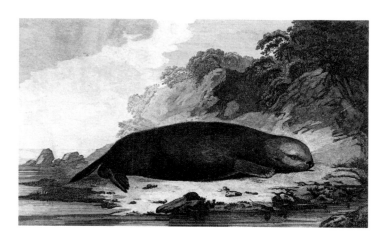

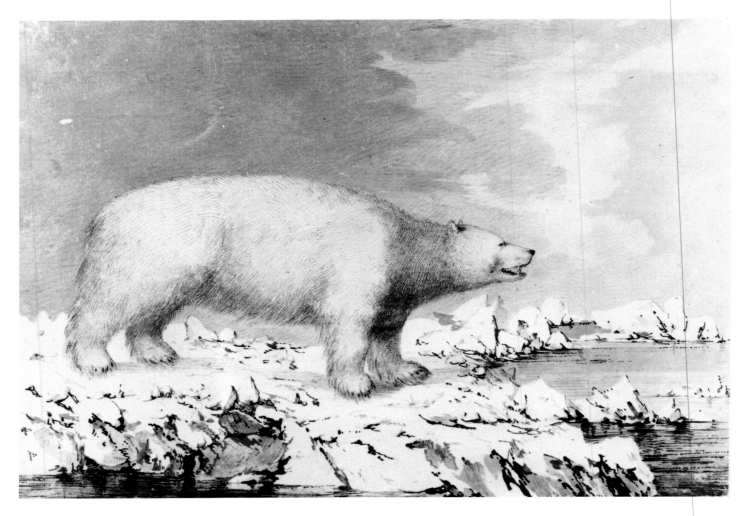

JOHN WEBBER

3.440 **A White Bear** [1779]
pencil and wash, 12³⁄₁₆ × 17¹¹⁄₁₆ : 310 × 450,
signed and dated in ink 'Jnº. Webber del. 1779'.

Inscribed on verso in pencil 'White Bear'. Listed in Webber's
Catalogue as no. 85 'A White Bear'.

A description of the ships' encounter with polar bears on 20 July
1779 is given by Clerke, in Cook, *Journals* III, 1, 695-6. See also
Ellis (1782) II, 266-7.

ver: Engraved by P. Mazell for Cook/King (1784) pl. 73.

ref: Cook, *Journals* III, pl. 78b.

Francis Edwards, *Cat.* 416 (London, July 1921) as no. 769 'A
White Bear (17½ by 12 in) in sepia'.

National Library of Australia, Canberra. Rex Nan Kivell Collection. NK 52/D.

JOHN WEBBER (after)

3.440A **'A White Bear'**
Engraving. 'J. Webber del.' — 'Mazell sculp.'

Published in Cook/King (1784) pl. 73, III, 252-3.

A proof-state inscribed in pencil 'A White Bear — upon the Ice
Lat. 71 Nº.' in Webber's hand is kept in the National Library
of Australia, Canberra in a folio of plates from the Skottowe Hall
Library.

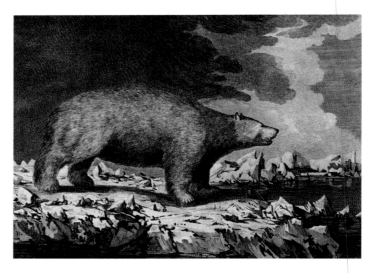

JOHN WEBBER

3.441   **A White Bear**   **[c. 1778-9]**
pencil, pen and wash, 7 × 9¾ : 177 × 248.

ver: The drawing is probably a sketch for the more finished version of 3.440.

Formerly owned by the British naturalist Thomas Pennant and interleafed into his copy of Cook/King, *Voyage*, 2nd edn, Nicoll and Cadell (London, 1785) fp. 252.

Dixson Library, State Library of New South Wales, Sydney. Q.77/37.

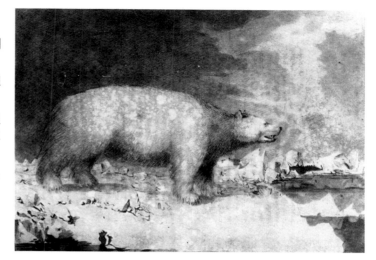

JOHN WEBBER

3.442   **A Deer of Princes Island (Sunda Strait)**
[plate 181]   **[Feb 1780]**
pencil, wash and water-colour, 11¹¹⁄₁₆ × 18¹⁵⁄₁₆ : 297 × 469.

Inscribed ' . . . Isles' as well as on verso in pencil 'No 1'. '18' (?) and 'Cap.ᵗ Campbell'. Listed in Webber's Catalogue as no. 158 'A Hog Deer of Princes Island.'

An 'Animal of the Deer Tribe', measuring '10½ by 11½ in' listed in Francis Edwards, *Cat.* 416 (London July 1921) as no. 769.

National Library of Australia, Canberra. Rex Nan Kivell Collection. NK 52/K.

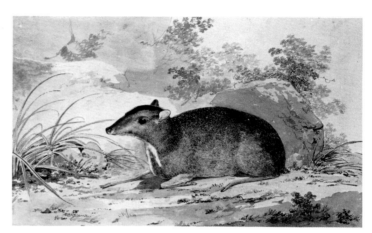

JOHN WEBBER

3.443   **A Gnu of the Cape of Good Hope**
[plate 182]   **[Apr, May 1780]**
water-colour and pencil, 10³⁄₁₆ × 14⁹⁄₁₆ : 258 × 370.

Inscribed in pencil 'Animal in the Menagerie — Cape of Good Hope'.

British Library, London. Add MS 17277, no. 50.

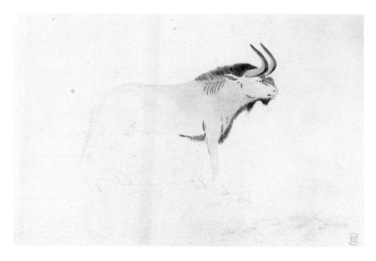

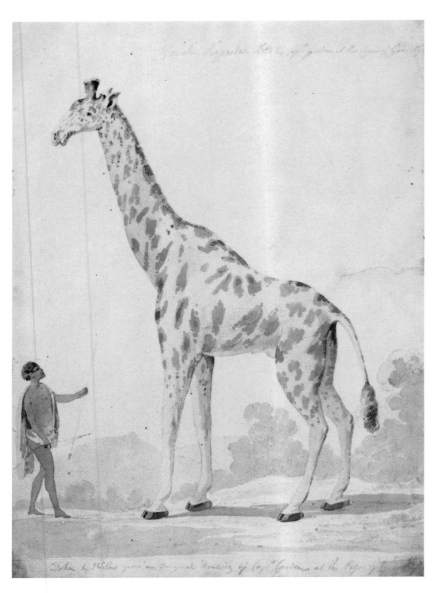

JOHN WEBBER

3.444   **A Giraffe of the Cape of Good Hope**
[Apr–May 1780]
pencil and wash, $19^{11}/_{16} \times 13^{15}/_{16} : 500 \times 354$.

Inscribed in pencil below 'Kamela Leoparda. Killed by Cap.ᵗ Gordon of the Cape of Good Hope' and 'Taken by J. Webber from an Original Drawing by Cap.ᵗ Gordon at the Cape of Good Hope', 'The animal 16 feet', '5 feet Rylands measure'.

A similar representation — but without the native boy — appears as an engraving in Paterson (1789), opposite p.125 under the title 'Camelopardalis'. A camelopardalis was shot on 18 October 1779 by a travelling party which included Captain Gordon and Lieutenant Paterson. The shot animal was a male and its skin and skeleton were preserved. 'The skin is now stuffed and in the possession of John Hunter, Esq. Leicester Square.' Paterson (1789) 127. It is possible that this is identical with the animal which Webber copied from Captain Gordon's drawing.

British Museum, Department of Prints and Drawings, London. 1914-5-20-692.

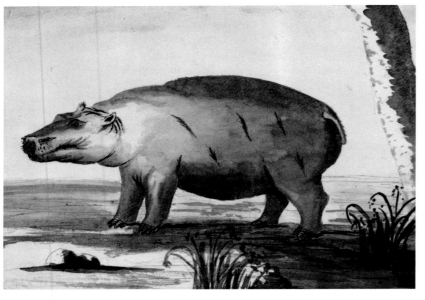

JOHN WEBBER

3.445   **A Hippopotomos of the Cape of Good Hope**
pencil and wash, $13^{15}/_{16} \times 19^{5}/_{8} : 354 \times 498$.

Inscribed in brown ink in Webber's hand on verso: '. . . attacked Cap.ᵗ Gordon, was shot by him at the Cape of Good Hope — the size of the drawing is about one Inch to a Foot'. The beginning of the inscription has been cut off.

British Museum, Department of Prints and Drawings, London. 1914-5-20-689.

OTHER DRAWINGS AND PAINTINGS
BY JOHN WEBBER

Including drawings of ships and canoes and portraits of
the Commanders of the *Resolution* and *Discovery*.

3.446–3.456a

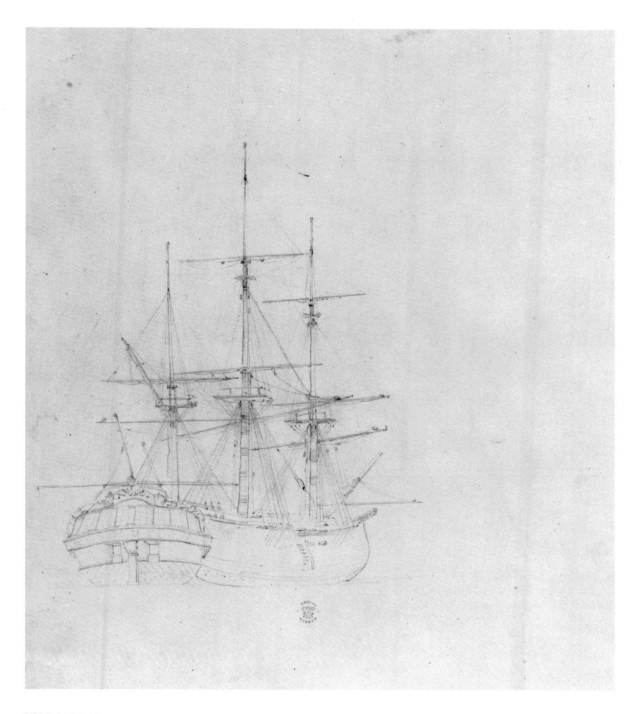

JOHN WEBBER

3.446   **The *Resolution***
        pencil, 17 × 14⁹/16 : 432 × 370, unsigned.

A study for the *Resolution* as depicted in 3.3.

ref: Cook, *Journals* III, 1, pl. 4; Murray-Oliver (1969a) pl. 94;
        idem. (1975) pl. 9; Cobbe (1979) pl. 15.

British Library, London. Add MS 17277, no. 1.

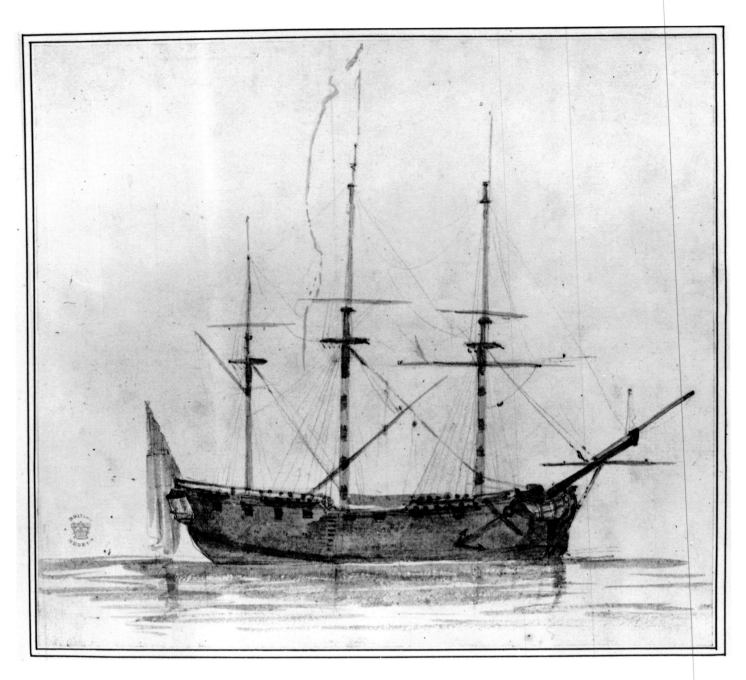

JOHN WEBBER

3.447   **The *Resolution***
Pencil and wash, 10¼ × 11¹⁄₁₆ : 260 × 281, unsigned.

Similar to the *Resolution* as depicted in 3.3 and 3.240. The figure-head of a sea-serpent identifies this ship as the *Resolution*.

British Library, London. Add MS 17277, no. 2.

JOHN WEBBER

3.448   **European Vessel under Sail**
pen and wash, 10³⁄₈ × 11¹³⁄₁₆ : 264 × 275, unsigned.

Probably not one of Cook's ships. Probably sketched on the out- or ingoing voyage.

British Library, London. Add MS 17277, no. 3.

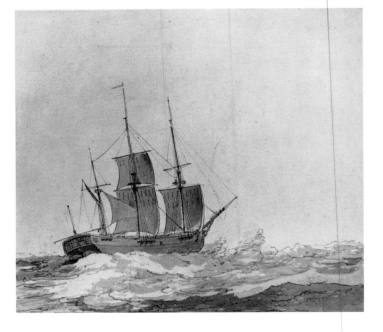

644

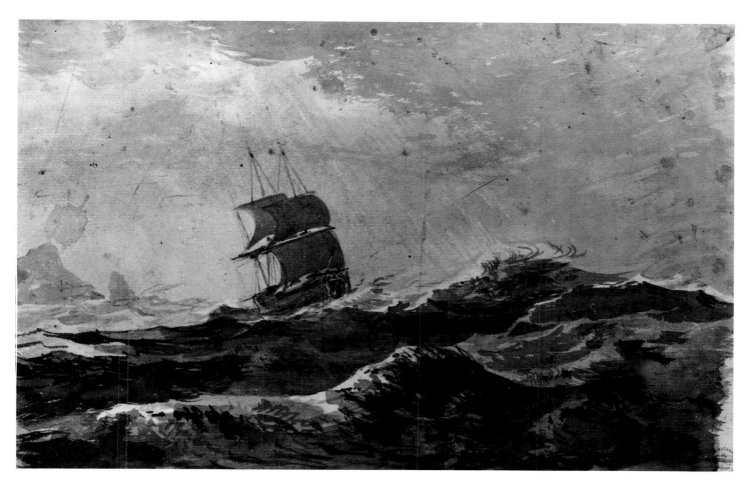

JOHN WEBBER

3.449   **European Vessel under Sail in heavy Seas**
wash, 8⅞ × 13⅝ : 225 × 346, unsigned.

For another version in lighter wash see 3.450.

British Library, London. Add MS 17277, no. 4.

JOHN WEBBER

3.450   **European Vessel under Sail in heavy Seas**
wash, 10¼ × 13⅝ : 260 × 346, unsigned.

ver: Similar to 3.449 but more faintly washed, probably a study for it.

ref: Cobbe (1979) pl. 24, where titled 'The *Discovery* in rough weather'.

British Library, London. Add MS 17277, no. 5.

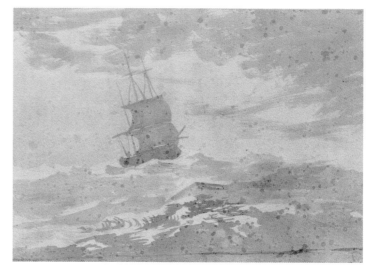

3.451 **Portrait of Captain James Cook** [1776]
oil on canvas, in oval spandril, 14½ × 11½ : 368 × 292, unsigned.

Head and shoulders, turned towards the right, wearing a dark blue captain's uniform, painted in 1776 on the outward going voyage.

ver: For the engraving by F. Bartolozzi see 3.451A.

ref: Scharf (1888) 119-20; Warner, September 1952, 86; Hill (1970) 56 (26); *Exh. Cat.* Portland (1974) no. 2, there identified as a copy after Webber by Sir Lionel Cust, however, according to Mr Jacob Simon, Curator at the National Portrait Gallery, London: 'It was the Webber which was shown in the 1974 Oregon exhibition. We do not have a Cust copy.' *In. litt.* 9 July 1984.

Purchased in 1858 from the dealer G. H. Burn, 29 Bow Street, Covent Garden, London.

National Portrait Gallery, London. 26.

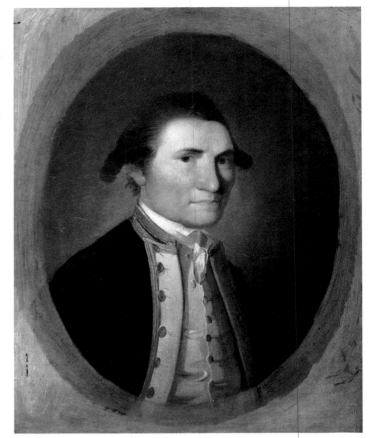

3.451A **'Captⁿ James Cook F.R.S.'**
Stipple engraving. 'Painted at the Cape of Good Hope, by J. Webber' — 'F. Bartolozzi R.A. sculp.' 'Publish'd as the Act directs, June 4th 1784, by J. Webber Nº. 312, Oxford Street'.

ref: Rienits (1968) f/piece; Schoenherr (1977) f/piece.

Copies of this print are in the Department of Prints and Drawings, British Museum, London (C. 17*), the Mitchell Library, Sydney (PXD 59⁻¹, f. 4 a) and The Public Archives of Canada, Ottawa.

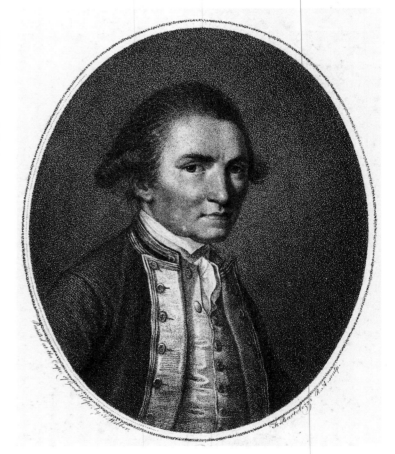

JOHN WEBBER

3.452 **Portrait of Captain James Cook [plate 198] [1782]**
oil on canvas, 45 × 36 : 1143 × 914, signed and dated
(l.r.) 'J. Webber / pinx. 1782'.

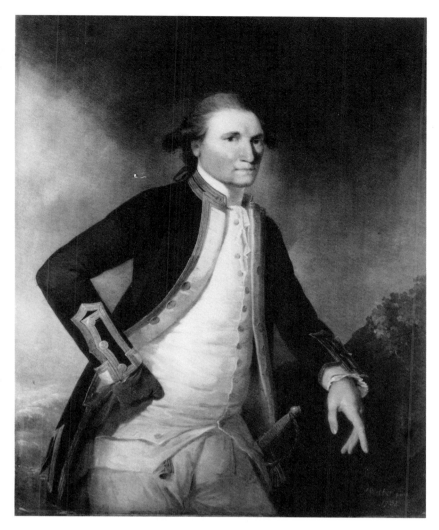

Three-quarter figure, standing to the right, the sea to the left.
Wearing a captain's uniform and a sword, the right hand with
glove. Hanging down from below the waistcoat a gold chain with
a seal.

ver: In the conception of the figure the portrait is similar to
3.453, but lacks the hat and the telescope.

ref: *Exh. Cat.* Sydney (1970) f/piece; Cobbe (1979) cover and
pl. 1, opp. 72; Sotheby's, *Cat. of Australian and European
Paintings*, Regent Hotel (Sydney, 23 March 1983) no. 45,
28-31, entry by J. Kerslake.

The first known reference to the painting is that given in the
sale catalogue of Webber's estate on 14/15 June 1793, by Christie's.
The entry says: 'Captain Cook's Portrait and a small ditto'. A
copy of the sale catalogue in the possession of Messrs Christie's,
London is annotated 'Bt. Segr.' This probably refers to William
Seguier, first Keeper of the National Gallery. When Seguier died
in 1843 the two pictures were possibly sold on the market. Shortly
afterwards this portrait is referred to in an order of the Board of
Trinity House, Hull, of 6 July 1844: 'that the portrait of the late
Captain James Cook the celebrated navigator which is now on
sale be purchased for the purpose of being hung in this House'.
The picture was bought by Trinity House, Hull, Yorkshire, from
which it was sold by Sotheby's Australia, Sydney, on 23 March
1983. It was bought by the London dealer Angela Neville for an
Australian client.

Private collection, Australia.

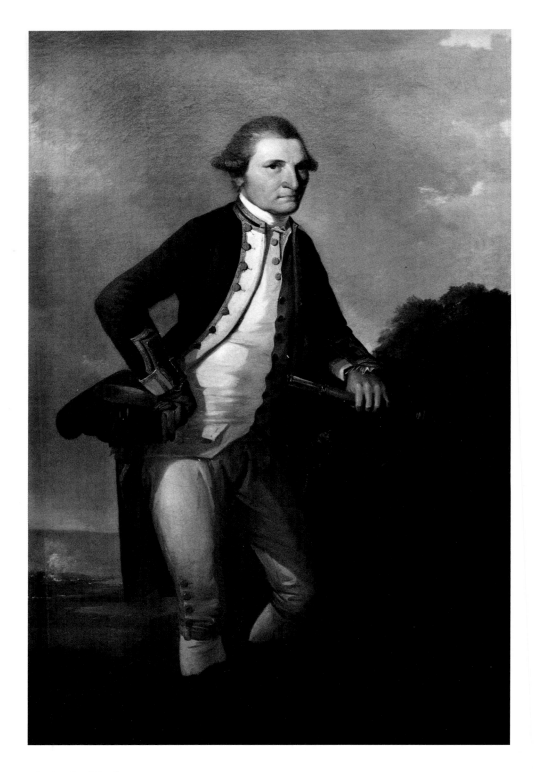

JOHN WEBBER

3.453   **Portrait of Captain James Cook**
          oil on canvas, 43½ × 27½ : 1105 × 698, unsigned.

Almost full-length representation of Cook in captain's uniform, leaning against a rock in front of the sea, holding a telescope in his left hand and his hat in his right.

Concerning Webber's depiction of Cook a letter by Molesworth Phillips to William Brockendon (5 April 1826) may be quoted: 'He was certainly six feet. I should rather guess that he exceeded that height. He was raw (?) boned, with a very small head, and capable of enduring the greatest fatigue.' (Icon Notes; *Cook*, National Portrait Gallery, London, Brockendon Album I, 4).

ref: *Exh. Cat.* Auckland (1964), pl. 1; Cook, *Journals* III, 1, f/piece; Rienits (1968) 18; Beaglehole (1974) pl. 44; Murray-Oliver (1975) pl. 2 (all in col.).

In the possession of Mrs Cook; in 1829 given to John Fleck, nephew of Captain Cook, to his daughter Mrs Stevenson, to Mrs John Gibson (sister of Mrs Stevenson), in 1864 bought from the family of John Gibson by the family of Mr Bolckow (documentary evidence in the Captain J. Cook file in the National Portrait Collection). In 1929 in the possession of H. W. F. Bolckow, Esq. of Brackenhoe, Morton, Yorkshire, later in the collection of Canon T. Harrison Park, Marton-in-Cleveland, Yorkshire, in 1960 acquired by the New Zealand Government.

National Portrait Collection at the National Art Gallery, Wellington.

3.454 Portrait of Captain James Cook
oil on canvas.(?)

Now lost or destroyed. When Webber completed the portrait of Tu he in turn requested a portrait of Cook (see 3.113).

'When the portrait was finished it was framed, and with a box, lock, and key, by which it was secured, was delivered to Otoo; who received it with inexpressible satisfaction. He readily, and, as the event has proved, most faithfully promised that he would preserve it always with the utmost care; and would show it to the commanders of such ships as might in future touch at the Society Islands.' Phillip (1789) 294.

Eleven years after Cook's visit Lieutenant John Watts, in command of the *Lady Penhryn*, from Sydney, was greatly surprised, on arriving in Tahiti on 14 July 1788, 'to see a man carrying the portrait of Captain Cook drawn by Webber in 1777'.

'Notwithstanding so much time had elapsed since the picture was drawn, it had received no injury, and they were informed that O'too always carried it with him wherever he went. After the first salutations were over, Mr. Watts asked O'too to accompany him to the ships, to which he readily agreed; but previously to his entering the boat he ordered the portrait in, and when he got alongside the ship he observed the same ceremony.' Ibid., 233-4.

On 27 October of the same year Captain William Bligh was shown the portrait, when he touched at Tahiti: 'Captn. Cook's Picture which was left by him in 1777 and drawn by Mr. Webber was brought to me, With a request to repair it. They said it came from Otoo, that it was Toote Errie no Otaheite [Cook Chief of Otaheite]. They said Toote told Otoo when he gave it him, that when his son came out he must show it to him, and they would always be good Friends. Excepting a little of the background [of] the Picture being eat off, it was not at all defaced. The Frame wanted a little repair and as all came within my abilities I assured them it should be done and they left it.' Bligh (1936) I, 372-3. See also Bligh (1792), 64, and Mackaness (1952) 46.

Cook's portrait was again sighted in March 1791 by Captain Edwards of H.M.S. *Pandora* and his surgeon George Hamilton (see Thomson (1915) 118) who refer to the high veneration in which the picture was then held.

George Tobin who accompanied Bligh on the second breadfruit voyage (1791-1792) wrote to his brother in July 1792: 'I can not refrain from remarking with what friendly care and reverence a picture of Captain Cook by Webber (painted while at O'tahytey in his last voyage) was preserved by Pomaurey. Nothing, I suppose, could tempt this amiable chief to part with it . . . [it] was said by those who knew him, to be a most striking resemblance. It has been customary for the different commanders of vessels visiting the island to note on the back of this picture the time of their arrival and departure. Some other tablet must now be found, as visits have been so frequent, no more space is left.' Mackaness (1951) 263. See also Lee (1920) 79-80.

Finally, Captain George Vancouver noted the existence of the portrait during his voyage round the world: 'Amongst the several chiefs who visited us, was Poeno, chief of Matavai, who brought with him a portrait of Captain Cook, drawn by Mr. Webber, in the year 1777. This picture is always deposited in the house of the chief of Matavai, and is become the public register. On the back of it was written, that the Pandora had quitted this island the 8th of may 1791.' Vancouver (1798) I, 104, entry for 2 January 1792.

After that the portrait fades from knowledge.

ref: Cook *Journals* III, 1, cxi; Smith (1984) 310-12.

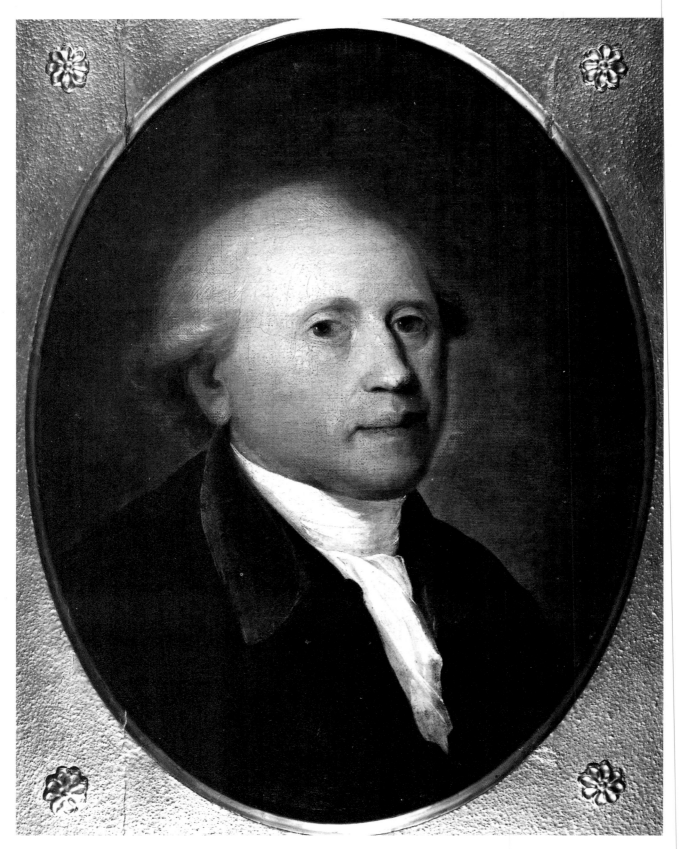

JOHN WEBBER

3.455   A Portrait of Captain John Gore   [1780]
oil on canvas, oval 17 × 12½ : 432 × 317, signed and
dated on back of canvas 'J.ⁿ Webber pinx. 1780'.

Breast portrait with the head facing right.

ref: Beaglehole (1974) pl. 30 b; Murray-Oliver (1975) pl. 16
(col.).

National Library of Australia, Canberra. Rex Nan Kivell Collection. NK 3680.

650

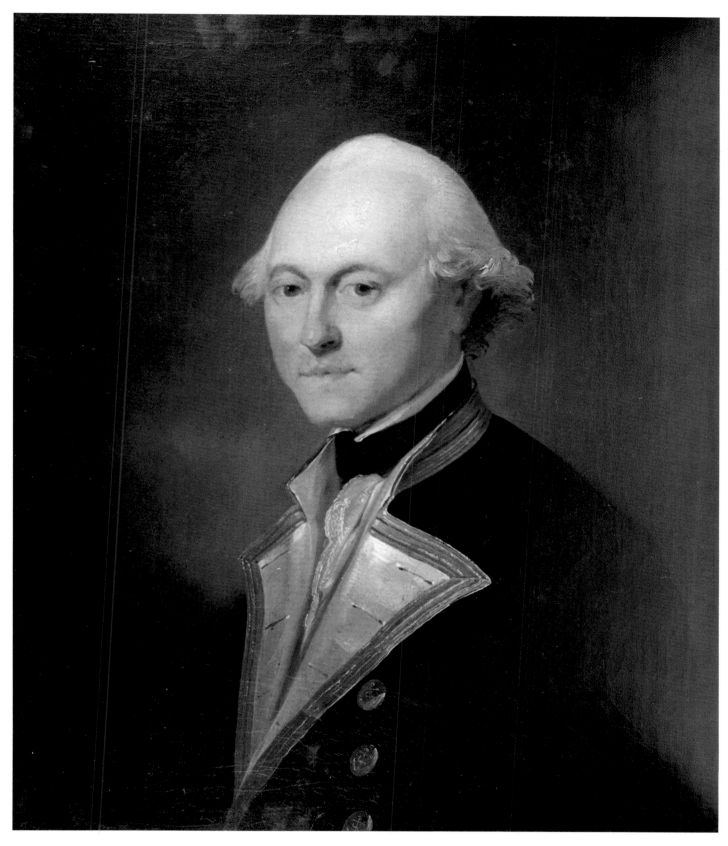

JOHN WEBBER

3.456   **A Portrait of Captain James King**
         [plate 199]   [1782]
         oil on canvas, 24 × 20 : 609 × 508, signed and dated
         'J. Webber del 1782' (l.l).

Breast portrait in captain's uniform, head facing left.

ref: Murray-Oliver (1975) pl. 17 (col.).

National Library of Australia, Canberra. R 3631.

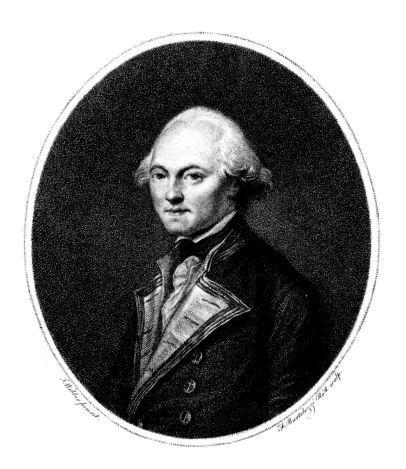

3.456A   Captain James King, L.L.D., F.R.S.
Stipple engraving. 'J. Webber pinxit' — 'F. Bartolozzi R.A. sculp.' 'Publish'd as the Act directs, June 4th 1784, by J. Webber N.º 312 Oxford Street'.

Copies of this print are in the National Library of Australia, Canberra; in the Mitchell Library, State Library of New South Wales, Sydney, PXD 59⁻¹ f. 4 b.; in the Alexander Turnbull Library, Wellington.

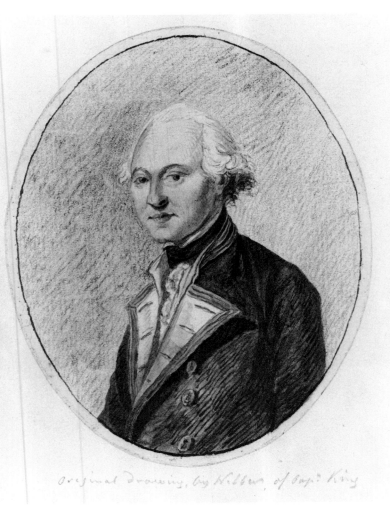

3.456a   Captain James King
pencil, wash and water-colour, $4\frac{3}{4} \times 3\frac{7}{8}$: 120×99. Inscribed in pencil on recto 'original drawing by Webber of Capt. King'. A copy after the engraving.

ref: Long (1984) 27.

Alexander Turnbull Library, Wellington.

BIBLIOGRAPHY

Documents and published works consulted in the preparation of this volume

ABBEY, J. R. *Travel in aquatint and lithography, 1770-1860, from the library of J. R. Abbey. A bibliographical Catalogue*, 2 vols. London, 1956-57 = Abbey (1957).

ADHÉMAR, JEAN and SEZNEC, JEAN. *Diderot, Salons*, 4 vols. Oxford, 1957-67 = Adhémar/Seznec (1957-67).

ADMIRALTY HOUSE, LONDON. *Catalogue of Pictures*, Presentation Plate, Figureheads, Models, Relics and Trophies at the Admiralty, pt. 1. The property of the Admiralty, London 1911 = Admiralty *Cat.* (1911).

ALLODI, MARY. *Canadian Watercolours and Drawings in the Royal Ontario Museum*. 2 vols. Toronto, 1974 = Allodi (1974).

ANCHORAGE. Historical and Fine Arts Museum. *With Captain Cook in the North Pacific. Views of Alaska in 1778 by John Webber*. Anchorage, 1978 = Exh. *Cat.* Anchorage (1978).

ANTROPOVA, V. V. 'The Itel'mens', in *The Peoples of Siberia*, ed. M. G. Levin and L. P. Patapov (Chicago/London, 1964) 876-83 = Antropova (1964).

ANTROPOVA, V. V. and KUZNETSOVA, V. G. 'The Chukchi' in *The Peoples of Siberia*, ed. M. G. Levin and L. P. Patapov (Chicago/London, 1964) 799-835 = Antropova and Kuznetsova (1964).

ARCHIBALD, E. H. H. *Dictionary of Sea Painters*. Suffolk, 1980 = Archibald (1980).

ARNOLDI-LIVIE, Galerie. *Vom Manierismus bis in die Goethezeit*. München, 1982 = Arnoldi-Livie Exh. *Cat.* (1982).

AUCKLAND CITY ART GALLERY. *Captain James Cook: his Artists and Draughtsmen*. Auckland, New Zealand, Oct-Dec 1964 = Exh. *Cat.* Auckland (1964).

AUCKLAND CITY ART GALLERY. *Two Worlds of Omai*. Auckland, New Zealand, 1977 = *Exh. Cat.* Auckland (1977).

BACOU, ROSELINE et al. *French Landscape Drawings and Sketches of the 18th century*. Exh. Cat., British Museum, Department of Prints and Drawings, London, 1977 = Bacou (1977).

BALSTON, THOMAS. 'John Boydell, Publisher, The Commercial Maecenas', *Signature*, VIII, n.s. (1949) 3-22 = Balston (1949).

BANKS, SIR JOSEPH. *The Endeavour Journals of Joseph Banks 1768-1771*, ed. J. C. Beaglehole. 2 vols. Sydney, 1962 = (Banks 1962).

BAKER, GEORGE. *A Catalogue of the very choice and select library of the late George Baker, Esq. of St. Paul's Churchyard*. Sold by auction by Mr. Sotheby, Monday, June 6 1825 and two following days. London, 1825 = Baker (1825a).

BAKER, GEORGE. *A Catalogue of the highly valuable collection of prints and drawings, the property of the late George Baker, Esq. of St. Paul's Church Yard* . . . which will be sold by auction by Mr. Sotheby . . . London, 1825 = Baker (1825b).

BANDI, H. G. 'Einige Gegenstände aus Alaska und British Kolumbien, gesammelt von Johann Wäber (John Webber) Bern / London, während der dritten Forschungsreise von James Cook, 1776-1780', *International Congress of Americanists* (Copenhagen, 1956) 214-20.

BASSY, ALAIN-MARIE. 'Typographie, topographie "outopo-graphie". L'illustration scientifique et technique au XVIIIᵉ Siècle', *Die Buchillustration im 18. Jahrhundert*, Colloquium der Arbeitsstelle 18. Jh. Wuppertal (Heidelberg, 1980) 206-33 = Bassy (1980).

BEAGLEHOLE, J. C. *The Life of Captain James Cook*. London, 1974 = Beaglehole (1974).

BEALL, KAREN. *Kaufrufe und Strassenhändler. Cries and Itinerant Trades*. Hamburg, 1975 = Beall (1975).

BEDDIE, M. K. (ed.). *Bibliography of Captain James Cook, R.N., F.R.S., Circumnavigator*. The Library of New South Wales (2nd edn) Sydney, 1970 = Cook *Bibl.* (1970).

BEGG, A. CHARLES and BEGG, NEIL C. *James Cook and New Zealand*. Wellington, New Zealand, 1969 = Begg (1969).

BELL, C. F. *Annals of Thomas Banks, Sculptor, Royal Academician*. Cambridge, 1938 = Bell (1938).

BENISOVICH, MICHAEL N. 'A French artist in Mexiko in 1769. A contribution to the Biography of A. J. Noël', *The Art Quarterly*, XVII (1954) 138-44 = Benisovich (1954).

BERN, Kunstmuseum. *Führer durch die Sammlungsausstellung. Gemälde und Plastik*. Bern, 1936 = Cat. Bern (1936).

BERNT, W. *Die Niederländischen Maler des 17 Jahrhunderts*. 4 vols. München, 1948 = Berndt (1948).

BINYON, LAURENCE. *Catalogue of Drawings by British Artists of Foreign Origin working in Great Britain preserved in the Department of Prints and Drawings in the British Museum*. (4 vols, London 1898-1907) vol. IV. London, 1907 = Binyon (1907).

BLIGH, WILLIAM *The Log of the Bounty*. 2 vols. London, 1936 = Bligh (1936).

BLIGH, WILLIAM. *A Voyage to the South Sea* . . . London, 1792 = Bligh (1792).

BOERLIN-BRODBECK, YVONNE. 'Johann Caspar Füssli und sein Briefwechsel mit Jean-Georges Wille', *Beiträge zur Kunst des 17. und 18. Jahrhunderts in Zürich*, Jahrbuch 1974-77, Schweizerisches Institut für Kunstwissenschaft (Zürich, 1978) 77-178 = Boerlin-Brodbeck (1978).

BOERLIN - BRODBECK, YVONNE. *Zeichnungen des 18. Jahrhunderts aus dem Basler Kupferstichkabinett*, Basel, 1979 = Boerlin-Brodbeck (1979).

BORLASE. W. *Observations on the Antiquities, Historical and Monumental of the County of Cornwall*, consisting of several essays on the first inhabitants, druid-supersticion, customs and remains of the most remote antiquity in Britain and the British Isles. Oxford, 1754 = Borlase (1754).

BOSWELL, JAMES. *Boswell's Life of Johnson*. London, 1953 = Boswell (1953).

BRAILSFORD, BARRY. *The Tattooed Land: The Southern Frontiers of the Pa Maori*. Wellington, New Zealand, 1981.

BREWINGTON, M. V. and BREWINGTON, DOROTHY. *The Marine Paintings and Drawings in the Peabody Museum*. Salem, Mass., 1968 = Brewington (1968).

BUKDAHL, ELSE MARIE. *Diderot, Critique d' Art, II, Diderot, Les salonniers et les esthéticiens de son temps*, Copenhagen, 1982 = Bukdahl (1982).

BURNEY, FANNY. *Diary and Letters of Madame D'Arblay*, ed. Charlotte Barrett, with preface and notes by Austin Dobson, 6 vols. London, 1904-05 = Burney (1904-05).

BURNEY, JAMES, Journal of the proceedings of His Majesty's Sloop, the *Discovery*, Chas. Clerke, Commander, in company with the *Resolution*, Captn James Cook . . . 1776-1779. (See also under Inventory of Collections, Mitchell Library, Sydney.)

BUSHNELL JR, DAVID I. 'Drawings by John Webber of Natives of the Northwest Coast of America, 1778', *Smithsonian Miscellaneous Collections*, 80, 10, (24 March 1928) 1-12 = Bushnell, Jr. (1928).

BUTLIN, MARTIN and JOLL, EVELYN. *The Paintings of J. M. W. Turner*, 2 vols. New Haven/London, 1977 = Butlin/Joll (1977).

CATALOGUE OF MANUSCRIPTS OF WESTERN AMERICANA IN THE YALE UNIVERSITY LIBRARY. New Haven, 1952 = Cat. Western Americana (1952).

CHAPPE d' AUTEROCHE, JEAN. *Voyage en Sibérie fait . . . en 1761*. 3 vols. Paris, 1768 = Chappe d'Auteroche (1768).

COBBE, HUGH. 'The Voyages and their Background', *Cook's Voyages and Peoples of the Pacific*, ed. Hugh Cobbe (London, 1979) 13-46 = Cobbe (1979).

COLE, DOUGLAS. 'John Webber: Etchings and Aquatints', *The Turnbull Library Record*, 8, 2, (October 1975) 25-7 = Cole (1975).

COLE, DOUGLAS. 'Cook at Nootka — the Engraved Record', *Canadian Antiques Collector*, XI, 3 (May/June 1976) 27-9 = Cole (1976).

COLE, DOUGLAS. 'John Webber: A Sketch of Captain James Cook's artist', *B. C. Historical News*, 12, 5, (1979) 18-22 = Cole (1979a).

COLE, DOUGLAS. 'John Webber', *Dictionary of Canadian Biography*, IV (1771-1800) (Toronto, 1979) 762-3 = Cole (1979b).

COLE, DOUGLAS and TIPPETT, MARIA. 'Pleasing Diversity and Sublime Desolation. The 18th Century British Perception of the Northwest Coast' *Pacific Northwest Quarterly*, LXV, January 1974, 1-7 = Cole/Tippett (1974).

COLNAGHI'S. *Masters of Maritime Art* . . ., exh. cat., London, March 1936 = Colnaghi *Exh. Cat.* (1936).

COLNAGHI'S. *English Drawings, Watercolours and Paintings*, exh. cat., November-December 1973. (London, 1973) = Colnaghi *Exh. Cat.* (1973).

CONISBEE, PHILIP. *Claude-Joseph Vernet, 1714-1789*, exh. cat., Kenwood, Greater London Council. (London, 1976) = Conisbee (1976).

654

CONISBEE, PHILIP. 'Pre-Romantic Pleinair Painting', *Art History*, 4 (December 1979) 422-8 = Conisbee (1979).

Cook *Bibl.* (1970), see BEDDIE

COOK, JAMES, *The Journals of Captain James Cook*, ed. J. C. Beaglehole, *The Voyage of the Resolution and Discovery, 1776-1780*, 2 vols. Cambridge, 1967 = Cook, *Journals* III (1967).

COOK, JAMES and KING, JAMES. *A Voyage to the Pacific Ocean . . . performed under the direction of Captains Cook, Clerke, and Gore, in His Majesty's Ships the Resolution and Discovery. In the Years 1776, 1777, 1778, 1779 and 1780 . . .* 3 vols and folio of plates. London, 1784 = Cook/King, *Voyage* (1784).

CORNEY, BOLTON GLANVILL. *The Quest and Occupation of Tahiti by emissaries of Spain, during the Years 1772-76.* 3 vols. London, 1913-19 = Corney (1913).

CROSTHWAITE, DANIEL. *A Catalogue of Crosthwaite's Museum*, undated ms. catalogue in the Keswick Museum, c. 1800 = Crosthwaite (c. 1800).

DANCE, PETER. *Shell Collecting. An Illustrated History.* London, 1966 = Dance (1966).

DAVIDSON, JANET. 'The Ellis drawings: an ethnographical viewpoint', *The Turnbull Library Record*, 10, 2 (October 1977) 20-2 = Davidson (1977).

DAWSON, WARREN R. *The Banks Letters*, A calendar of manuscript correspondence of Sir Joseph Banks. London, British Museum, Natural History, 1958 = Dawson (1958).

DENING, GREG. 'Sharks that walk on the Land. The Death of Captain Cook', *Meanjin* 4 (1982), 427-37.

DEUSCH WERNER R. 'Der Kupferstecher Johann Georg Wille und sein Pariser Tagebuch. Ein Beitrag zu den deutsch-französischen Kunstbeziehungen im 18. Jahrhundert', *Imprimatur*, N.F., II (1960) 100-13 = Deusch (1960).

DIDEROT, DENIS and d'ALEMBERT, JEAN. *Encyclopédie ou Dictionaire raisonné des sciences, des arts et des métiers.* 17 vols. Paris, 1751-65 = Diderot/d'Alembert (1751-65).

DIXON, GEORGE. *A Voyage Round the world but more particularly to the North-West Coast of America, performed in 1785, 1786, 1787 and 1788.* London, 1789 = Dixon (1789).

DOCKING, GIL. *Two Hundred Years of New Zealand Painting.* Wellington, New Zealand, 1971 = Docking (1971).

DUCLAUX, LISE and PRÉAUD, TAMARA. *L'atelier de Desportes. Dessins et esquisses conservés par la Manufacture nationale de Sèvres*, exh. cat. Musée du Louvre, Paris, 1982 = Duclaux/Préaud (1982).

DUPLESSIS GEORGES (ed.). *Mémoires et Journal de J. G. Wille Graveur du Roi*, Publiés d' après les manuscrits autographes de la Bibliothèque Impériale. 2 vols. Paris, 1857 = Duplessis (1857).

DURRANS, BRIAN. 'Ancient Pacific Voyaging: Cook's Views and the Development of Interpretation', *The British Museum Yearbook*, 3 (London, 1979) 137-66 = Durrans (1979).

DUTTON, GEOFFREY. *White on Black. The Australian Aborigine portrayed in art.* Melbourne, 1974 = Dutton (1974).

EARP, F. R. *Descriptive Catalogue of the Pictures in the Fitzwilliam Museum.* Cambridge, 1902 = Earp (1902).

EBERSTADT, EDUARD. 'The William Robertson Coe Collection of Western Americana', *Yale University Library Gazette*, 23 (1948) 41-130 = Eberstadt (1948).

EDWARDS, EDWARD. *Anecdotes of Painters who have resided or been born in England.* London, 1808 = Edwards (1808).

EDWARDS, FRANCIS. *Captain James Cook (1928-1929).* London, 1929 = Edwards (1929).

EDWARDS, FRANCIS. *Catalogue of the Australasian Collection of Books and Pictures, formed by the late James Edge-Partington.* London, 1934 = Edwards (1934).

EGERTON, JUDY. 'William Day, 1764-1807', *Connoisseur* (July 1970) 176-85 = Egerton (1970).

ELLIS, WILLIAM. *An authentic narrative of a voyage performed by Captain Cook and Captain Clerke in His Majesty's Ships Resolution and Discovery.* 2 vols. London, 1782 = Ellis *Narrative* (1782).

FAGAN, LOUIS. *A Catalogue Raisonné of the Engraved Works of William Woollett.* London, 1885 = Fagan (1885).

FALLET, EDUARD M. *Der Bildhauer Johann August Nahl der Ältere, seine Berner Jahre von 1746 bis 1755*, Archiv des Historischen Vereins des Kanton Bern, 54, Bern, 1970, = Fallet (1970).

FANNING, PAULINE. 'A tribute to Sir Rex de Charambac Nan Kivell', *Art in Australia* 15, 3 (March 1978) 252 = Fanning (1978).

FARINGTON, JOSEPH. *The Diary of Joseph Farington*, ed. Kenneth Garlick and Angus MacIntyre, vols. 1,2 (1978), vols. 3,4,5,6 (1979), vols. 7,8,9,10 (1982), vols. 11,12 (1983). New Haven and London = Farington (1978-83).

FISCHER, HERMANN von. *Die Kunsthandwerker-Familie Funk im 18. Jahrhundert in Bern*, Berner Heimatbücher 79/80, Bern, 1961, = Fischer (1961).

FISHER, ROBIN. 'Cook and the Nootka', *Captain James Cook and His Times* ed. Robin Fisher and Hugh Johnston, (Vancouver/London, 1979) 81-98 = Fisher (1979).

FOLAN, WILLIAM and DEWHIRST, JOHN T. 'Yuquot: Where the wind blows from all Directions', *Archaeology*, 23, 4 (October 1970) 276-86 = Folan/Dewhirst (1970).

FORCE, ROLAND W. and FORCE, MARYANNE. *The Fuller Collection of Pacific Artifacts, the Man and his Collection.* New York, 1971 = Force and Force (1971).

FORSTER, GEORGE (JOHANN GEORGE ADAM). *A Voyage round the world in His Britannic Majesty Sloop* Resolution, *commanded by Captain James Cook, during the years 1772, 1773, 1774 and 1775.* 2 vols. London, 1777 = Forster (1777).

FORSTER, GEORG. *Werke in vier Bänden*, ed. Gerhard Steiner. Leipzig, 1971 = Forster (1971).

FRIEDMAN, WINIFRED. *Boydell's Shakespeare Gallery*, New York, 1976 = Friedman (1976).

FRYE, HOWARD T. *Alexander Dalrymple.* London, 1970 = Frye (1970).

GAUS, JOACHIM. 'Die Urhütte. Über ein Modell in der Baukunst und ein Motiv in der bildenden Kunst', *Wallraf-Richartz-Jahrbuch*, XXXIII (Köln, 1971) 7-70 = Gaus (1971).

GEISER, BERNHARD. 'Johann Ludwig Aberli und sein graphisches Werk', *Das graphische Kabinett*, no. 3, Winterthur 1923 = Geiser (1923).

GEISER, BERNHARD. *Johann Ludwig Aberli, 1723-1786, Leben, Manier und graphisches Werk.* Belp, 1929 = Geiser (1929).

GEISSLER, H. *Deutsche Landschaftszeichnungen des 18. Jahrhunderts.* Stuttgart, 1985 = Geissler (1985).

GENGA, BERNARDINO. *Anatomy improv'd and illustrated with regard to the uses thereof in designing . . .* First published in Rome by Dome di Rossi, and now re-engraven by the ablest hands in England and republished by John Senex . . . London [1723] = Genga (1723).

GOODISON, J. W. *Fitzwilliam Museum, Cambridge, Catalogue of Paintings*, vol. III, *British School*, Cambridge, 1977 = Goodison (1977).

GOULD, RUPERT T. 'Bligh's Notes on Cook's last voyage', *The Mariner's Mirror*, XIV, 4 (October 1928) 371-85 = Gould (1928).

GRANT, M. H. *A Chronological History of the Old English Landscape Painters.* 8 vols. Leigh-on-Sea 1957-61 = Grant (1957).

GRASELLI, M. MORGAN and ROSENBERG, PIERRE. *Watteau 1684-1721.* Washington, 1984 = Graselli/Rosenberg (1984).

GRAVES, ALGERNON. *The Royal Academy of Arts, a complete dictionary of contributors and their work from its foundation 1769 to 1904.* 8 vols. London, 1905-06 = Graves (1906).

GRAVES, ALGERNON. *The Society of Artists of Great Britain, 1760-1791.* London, 1907 = Graves (1907).

GRAVES, ALGERNON. *Art Sales from early in the Eighteenth Century to early in the Twentieth Century.* 3 vols. London, 1918-21 = Graves (1918).

GREYERZ, LINA von. 'Christian Fueter, 1752-1844', *Sammlung Bernischer Biographien*, IV (Bern, 1902) 384-95 = Greyerz (1902).

GRUNER, ERICH. *Die Bürgerliche Gesellschaft zu Kaufleuten in Bern.* Bern, 1944 = Gruner (1944).

GUNNIS, RUPERT. *Dictionary of British Sculptors (1660-1851).* London, 1953 = Gunnis (1953).

HADDON, A. C. and HORNELL, JAMES. *Canoes of Oceania* (3 vols., Honolulu 1936-38) I: The canoes of Polynesia, Fiji and Micronesia, by James Hornell. Honolulu, 1936 = Haddon and Hornell (1936); III: Definition of terms, general survey and conclusions, by A. C. Haddon and James Hornell, Honolulu, 1938 = Hadden and Hornell (1938).

HARDIE, MARTIN. *English Coloured Books.* London, 1906 = Hardie (1906).

HAWCROFT, FRANCIS. *Watercolours by John Robert Cozens*, exh. cat. Whitworth Art Gallery, Manchester and Victoria and Albert Museum (London, 1971) = Hawcroft (1971).

HENKING, KARL H. 'Die Südsee- und Alaskasammlung Johann Wäber', *Jahrbuch des Bernischen Historischen Museums*, XXXV and XXXVI (1955/56) 325-89 = Henking (1955/56).

HENRY, JOHN FRAZIER. *Early Maritime Artists of the Pacific Northwest Coast, 1741-1841.* Seattle/London, 1984 = Henry (1984).

HENRY, TEUIRA. *Ancient Tahiti*, Bernice P. Bishop Museum, Bulletin, 48 (Honolulu, 1928) = Henry (1928).

HERMANN, LUKE. *British Landscape Painting.* London, 1973 = Hermann (1973).

HERMANNSSON, HALLDÓR. 'Sir Joseph Banks and Iceland', *Islandica*, XVIII, Ithaca, New York, 1928 = Hermannsson (1928).

HILL, M. *Concise Catalogue, 1856-1969*. National Portrait Gallery, London, 1970 = Hill (1970).

HIRSCHFELD, CH. C. L. *Theorie der Gartenkunst*. 2 vols. Leipzig, 1779-80 = Hirschfeld (1779-80).

Historical Records of New South Wales, Sydney, 1893 = HRNSW.

HOARE, MICHAEL E. 'William Webb Ellis, Cook's scientific artist; Problems and Possibilities', *The Turnbull Library Record*, 10, 2 (October 1977) 10-19 = Hoare (1977).

HOCKEN, T. M. *A bibliography of the literature relating to New Zealand*. Wellington, New Zealand, 1909 = Hocken (1909).

HOLMES, MAURICE G. *Captain James Cook, R.N., F.R.S. A Biographical Excursion*. London, 1952 = Holmes (1952).

HONOUR, HUGH. *The European Vision of America*. Cleveland Museum of Art (exhibition also held in Washington and Paris 1776/77), Cleveland, 1975 = Honour (1975).

HUGGLER, MAX. 'Johann Ludwig Aberli und die Malerei des 18. Jahrhunderts in Bern', *Festgabe Hans von Greyerz*. Bern, 1967 = Huggler (1967).

HUGGLER, MAX. *Sigmund Freudenberger, Der Berner Kleinmeister*. Bern, 1976 = Huggler (1976).

HULTON, PAUL and QUINN, DAVID BEERS. *The American Drawings of John White 1577-1590*. A catalogue raisonné and a study of the artist, London and Chapel Hill, North Carolina 1964 = Hulton/Quinn (1964).

HULTON, PAUL and SMITH, LAURENCE. *Flowers in Art*. London, 1979 = Hulton/Smith (1979).

HUTCHINSON, SIDNEY C. 'The Royal Academy Schools, 1768-1830', *The Walpole Society*, 38, (London, 1960-62) 123-91 = Hutchinson (1962).

INGAMELLS, JOHN. *The English Episcopal Portrait 1559-1835. A Catalogue*. London, 1981 = Ingamells (1981).

JOPPIEN, RÜDIGER. *Philippe Jacques de Loutherbourg, R.A.*, exh. cat. Kenwood, Greater London Council, London, 1973 = Joppien (1973).

JOPPIEN, RÜDIGER. *Drawings from Captain Cook's Voyages. An unrecorded collection of fourteen ethnographical and natural history drawings relating to the second and third voyage*. London, 1976 = Joppien (1976a).

JOPPIEN, RÜDIGER. 'A visitor to a ruined churchyard — a newly discovered painting by P. J. de Loutherbourg', *Burlington Magazine* (May 1976) 294-301 = Joppien (1976b).

JOPPIEN, RÜDIGER. 'John Webber's South Sea Drawings for the Admiralty. A Newly Discovered Catalogue among the Papers of Sir Joseph Banks', *The British Library Journal*, 4, 1, (Spring 1978) 49-77 = Joppien (1978).

JOPPIEN, RÜDIGER. 'Philippe Jacques de Loutherbourg's Pantomime "Omai, or, a Trip round the World" and the Artists of Captain Cook's Voyages', *The British Museum Yearbook*, 3, (London, 1979) 81-136 = Joppien (1979).

JOPPIEN, RÜDIGER. 'Cataloging the Drawings from Captain Cook's Voyages: A Task Completed', *Australian Journal of Art*, 3 (1983) 59-78 = Joppien (1983).

JOPPIEN, RÜDIGER. *John Webber's Views in the South Seas. An unpublished group of related drawings*, typescript, London, 1984 = Joppien (1984).

KAEPPLER, ADRIENNE L. 'Eighteenth century Tonga: new interpretations of Tongan society and material culture at the time of Captain Cook', *Man*, 6, 2 (June 1971) 204-20 = Kaeppler (1971).

KAEPPLER, ADRIENNE. *Artificial Curiosities*. An exposition of Native Manufactures. Collected on the Three Pacific Voyages of Captain James Cook, R.N., Bernice P. Bishop Museum, Honolulu, 1978 = Kaeppler (1978a).

KAEPPLER, ADRIENNE. *Cook Voyage Artifacts in Leningrad, Berne and Florence Museums*, Honolulu, Hawaii 1978 = Kaeppler (1978b).

KAEPPLER, ADRIENNE. 'Tracing the History of Hawaiian Cook Voyage Artefacts in the Museum of Mankind', *The British Museum Yearbook*, 3 (1979) 167-97 = Kaeppler (1979).

KING, JONATHAN C. H. 'The Nootka of Vancouver Island', *Cook's Voyages and Peoples of the Pacific*, ed. Hugh Cobbe (London, 1979) 89-108 = King (1979).

KING, JONATHAN C. H. *Artificial Curiosities from the North-west Coast of America*. Native American Artefacts in the British Museum collected on the Third Voyage of Captain James Cook and aquired through Sir Joseph Banks. London, 1981 = King (1981).

KITSON, ARTHUR. *Captain James Cook*. London, 1907 = Kitson (1907).

KRASHENINNIKOV, STEPAN PETROVICH. *The History of Kamtschatka and the Kurilski Islands with the countries adjacent illustrated with maps and cuts . . .* translated into English by James Grieve, M.D. Printed for T. Jefferys geographer to His Majesty, London MDCCLXIV = Krasheninnikov (1764).

KRÖNIG, WOLFGANG. 'Vesuv-Ausbrüche von 1774 und 1779 gemalt von Philipp Hackert',

Medicinae et artibus. Festschrift für Professor Dr. phil. Dr. med Wilhelm Katner, Düsseldorfer Arbeiten zur Geschichte der Medizin, Beiheft 1 (Düsseldorf, 1968) 51-60 = Krönig (1968a).

KRÖNIG, WOLFGANG. 'Kehrtwendung der Blickrichtung in Vedutenpaaren von Philipp Hackert', *Wallraf-Richartz-Jahrbuch*, XXX (1968) 253-74 = Krönig (1968b).

KRÖNIG, WOLFGANG. 'Sepia-Zeichnungen aus der Umgebung Neapels von Philipp Hackert', *Wallraf-Richartz-Jahrbuch*, XXXIII (Köln, 1971) 175-204 = Krönig (1971).

KUTHY, SANDOR. *Die Gemälde*, cat. Kunstmuseum Bern, 1983 = Kuthy (1983).

LANGDON, ROBERT. *The Lost Caravel*. Sydney, 1975 = Langdon (1975).

LAUTERBURG, LUDWIG. 'Biographische Literatur enthaltend eine Sammlung gedruckter, biographischer Quellen aus dem Zeitraume von 1785 bis 1840 über das Leben und Wirken hervorragender verstorbener Berner und Bernerinnen des alten deutschen Kantonstheils', *Nachtrag zum Berner Taschenbuch* (Bern, 1853) 305-6 = Lauterburg (1853).

LE BLANC, CHARLES. *Catalogue de l'Oeuvre de Jean Georges Wille, Graveur*. Leipzig, 1847 = Le Blanc (1847).

LEE, IDA. *Captain Bligh's Second Voyage to the South Seas*. London, 1920 = Lee (1920).

LESSEPS, J. B. B. de. *Journal historique du voyage de M. de Lesseps, consul de France, employé dans l'expedition de M. le comte de la Pérouse en qualité d'interprète du Roi, depuis l'instant ou il a quitté les fregattes Françoises au port Saint-Pierre & Saint Paul du Kamtschatka jusqu'a son arrivée en France, le 17 octobre 1788*. 2 vols. Paris, 1790 = Lesseps (1790).

LEVEY, MICHAEL. 'Some Paintings by Dietrich for J.-G. Wille', *Gazette des Beaux-Arts* (January 1958) 33-40 = Levey (1958).

LEWIS, MARY. 'The Cook Exhibition', *La Trobe Library Journal*, 2, 5 (April 1970) 4-10 = Lewis (1970).

LONDON. Royal Academy of Arts, *The First Hundred Years*. London, 1951/52 = Exh. Cat. London (1951/52).

LONDON. Arts Council, *Royal Academy Diploma Pictures*. London, 1961/62 = Exh. Cat. London (1961/62).

LONDON. Royal Academy of Arts, *Catalogue of the Royal Academy of Arts Bicentenary Exhibition*. London, 1968/69 = Exh. Cat. London (1968/69).

LONG, MOIRA. 'Samuel Daniell and John Webber: some recently identified drawings', *The Turnbull Library Record*, XVII, 1 (May 1984) 24-7 = Long (1984).

LONGCHAMP. F. C. J. L. *Aberli Catalogue Complet*. Paris/Lausanne, 1927 = Longchamp (1927).

LÖSCHNER, RENATE. 'Humboldt's Naturbild und seine Vorstellung von künstlerisch — physiognomischen Landschaftsbildern', *Mythen der Neuen Welt. Zur Entdeckungsgeschichte Lateinamerikas*, ed. Karl-Heinz Kohl (Berlin, 1982) 245-53 = Löschner (1982).

LYLE, I. F. 'Thomas Martyn's The Universal Conchologist: An early copy and a theory', *Journal of the Society for Bibliography of Natural History*, 5, 2 (1969) 142-3 = Lyle (1969).

LYSAGHT, AVERIL. 'Some Eighteenth Century Bird Paintings in the Library of Sir Joseph Banks (1743-1820)', *Bulletin of the British Museum* (Natural History) Historical Series, 1, 6 (London, 1959) 253-371 = Lysaght (1959).

LY-TIO-FANE, MADELEINE. *Pierre Sonnerat, 1748-1814*. Mauritius, 1976 = Ly-Tio-Fane (1976).

MACKANESS, GEORGE. *The Life of Vice-Admiral William Bligh*. 2nd edn. London, 1951 = Mackaness (1951).

MACKANESS, GEORGE. *A Book of the Bounty and selections from Bligh's writings*. London, 1952 = Mackaness (1952).

MAGGS BROS. LTD. *Australia and the South Seas*, Cat. no. 491. London, 1927 = Maggs Bros. Cat. (1927).

MARTYN, THOMAS. *The Universal Conchologist exhibiting the Figure of every known Shell accurately drawn and painted after Nature with a New Systematic Arrangement by the author Thomas Martyn. Sold at his House No. 26, King Street, Covent Garden*. London, 1784 = Martyn (1784).

MARTYN, THOMAS. *A Short Account of the Nature, Principle and Progress of a Private Establishment instituted for the Purpose of Instructing Youth in the Art of illustrating, and painting, Subjects in Natural History: at his House, No. 16, Great Marlborough Street*. London, 1789 = Martyn (1789).

MASSIN. *Les Cris de Paris*. Paris, 1978 = Massin (1978).

MATSCHE-VON WICHT, BETKA. 'Das Grabmal im Landschaftsgarten', *Wie die Alten den Tod gebildet. Wandlungen der Sepulkralarchitektur 1750-1850*, Kasseler Studien zur Sepulkralkultur. (Mainz, 1979) 45-56 = Matsche-von Wicht (1979).

MAXTED, IAN. *The London Book Trades, 1775-1800. A preliminary checklist.* Folkestone, 1977 = Maxted (1977).

MEDWAY, DAVID G. 'The Ellis bird drawings', *The Turnbull Library Record*, 10, 2 (October 1977) 23-7 = Medway (1977).

METEYARD, ELIZA. *The Life of Josiah Wedgwood from his private correspondence and family papers.* 2 vols, London, 1866 = Meteyard (1866).

MILET-MUREAU, M. L. A. *Voyage de la Pérouse autour du Monde*, publié conformément au décret du 22 Avril 1791 et rédigé par M. L. A. Milet-Mureau, 4 vols in 2 pts, Paris, 1797 = Milet-Mureau (1797).

MITCHELL, CHARLES. 'Zoffany's Death of Captain Cook', *Burlington Magazine* (March 1944) 56-62 = Mitchell (1944).

MONTREAL MUSEUM OF FINE ARTS. *The Painter and the New World.* Montreal, 1967 = Exh. Cat. Montreal (1967).

MÜNSTER. Westfälisches Landesmuseum. *Frankreich vor der Revolution. Handzeichnungen aus dem Musée des Beaux Arts, Orléans.* Münster, 1973 = Exh. Cat. Münster (1973).

MURRAY-OLIVER, A. A. ST. C. M. *Captain Cook's Artists in the Pacific, 1769-1779.* Christchurch, 1969 = Murray-Oliver (1969a).

MURRAY-OLIVER, A. A. ST. C. M. 'John Webber and his Aquatints', *The Turnbull Library Record*, 2, 2 (October 1969) 74-9 = Murray-Oliver (1969b).

MURRAY-OLIVER, A. A. ST. C. M. *Captain Cook's Hawaii, as seen by his artists.* Wellington, New Zealand, 1975 = Murray-Oliver (1975).

MURRAY-OLIVER, A. A. ST. C. M. 'The Ellis Drawings: An Inventory', *The Turnbull Library Record*, 10, 2 (October 1977) 28-37 = Murray-Oliver (1977).

MURRAY-OLIVER, A. A. ST. C. M. 'Portrait of Tu, Pomare I of Tahiti, by John Webber', *The Turnbull Library Record*, 11, 2 (October 1978) 112-14 = Murray-Oliver (1978).

NICOLSON, BENEDICT. *Joseph Wright of Derby. Painter of Light.* 2 vols. London, 1968 = Nicolson (1968).

NAN KIVELL, REX and SPENCE, SYDNEY. *Portraits of the Famous and Infamous.* Australia, New Zealand and the Pacific, 1492-1970. London, 1970 = Nan Kivell/Spence (1970).

OLIVER, DOUGLAS L. *Ancient Tahitian Society.* 3 vols. Honolulu, 1974 = Oliver (1974).

PANOFSKY, ERWIN. 'Et in Arcadia ego: Poussin and the Elegiac Tradition', *Meaning in the visual arts.* (Harmondsworth, 1970) 340-67 = Panofsky (1970).

PARKINSON, SYDNEY. *A Journal of a Voyage to the South Seas.* London, 1773 = Parkinson (1773).

PATERSON, WILLIAM. *A narrative of four journeys into the country of the Hottentots and Caffraria in the years 1777, 1778 and 1779.* London, 1789 = Paterson (1789).

PEE, HERBERT. *Johann Heinrich Schönfeld.* Berlin, 1971 = Pee (1971).

PENFOLD, P. A. *Maps and Plans in the Public Record Office*, 2, *America and West Indies.* London, 1974 = Penfold (1974).

PHILLIP, ARTHUR. *The Voyage of Governor Phillip to Botany Bay.* London, 1789 = Phillip (1789).

PICART, BERNARD. *Les Cérémonies et coutumes religieuses de tous les peuples du monde*, 8 vols. Amsterdam, 1723-43 = Picart (1723).

PINAULT, MADELEINE. *Dessin et Sciences XVIIe-XVIIIe siècles*, exh. cat. Cabinet des Dessins, Musée du Louvre, Paris, 1984 = Pinault (1984).

PORTLAND. Oregon Historical Society, *Captain Cook, R.N., The Resolute Mariner. An International Record of Oceanic Discovery.* Thomas Vaughan and A. A. ST. C. M. Murray-Oliver. Portland, 1974 = Exh. Cat. Portland (1974).

PORTLAND. Oregon Historical Society, *Soft Gold. The Fur Trade & Cultural Exchange on the Northwest Coast of America.* Thomas Vaughan and Bill Holm. Portland, 1982 = Exh. Cat. Portland (1982).

PRIDEAUX, SARAH T. *Aquatint Engraving.* London, 1909 = Prideaux (1909).

RÉAU, L. 'L'exotisme russe dans l'oeuvre de Le Prince', *Gazette des Beaux-Arts*, I (1921) 147-65 = Réau (1921).

REYNOLDS, GRAHAM. 'British Artists Abroad. I. Captain Cook's Draughtsmen', *Geographical Magazine*, XIX, 10 (February 1947) 457-66 = Reynolds (1947).

REYNOLDS, JOSHUA. *The Letters of Sir Joshua Reynolds*, ed. F. W. Hilles, Cambridge, 1929 = Reynolds (1929).

RICHMOND. Virginia Museum of Fine Arts, *Painting in England 1700-1850.* The Collection of Mr and Mrs Paul Mellon. 2 vols. Richmond, Virginia, 1963 = Richmond (1963).

RIENITS, REX and THEA. *The Voyages of Captain Cook.* London, 1968 = Rienits (1968).

ROBELS, HELLA. *Niederländische Zeichnungen vom 15.-19. Jahrhundert im Wallraf-Richartz-Museum.* Köln, 1983 = Robels (1983).

ROBERTS, HENRY. *A Log of the proceedings of His Majesty's Sloop Resolution on discoveries, towards the North Pole. James Cook, Esq.*, *Commander.* Dixson Library, State Library of New South Wales, Sydney. (See also under Inventory of Collections, Dixson Library.)

RODT, BERNHARD EMANUEL von. 'Die Gesellschaft von Kaufleuten in Bern. Ein Beitrag zur Geschichte des Stadtbernischen Gesellschafts- und Zunftwesens', *Berner Taschenbuch*, (Bern, 1862) 1-171 = Rodt (1862).

ROJAS-MIX, MIGUEL. 'Die Bedeutung Alexander von Humboldts für die künstlerische Darstellung Lateinamerikas', *Alexander von Humboldt, Werk und Weltgeltung*, ed. Heinrich Pfeiffer (München, 1969) 97-130 = Rojas-Mix (1969).

ROMANG, FRIEDRICH. 'Johann Wäber', *Sammlung Bernischer Biographien*, vol II, Bern, 1896 = Romang (1896).

ROSENBLUM, ROBERT. *Transformations in late Eighteenth Century Art.* Princeton, 1967 = Rosenblum (1967).

ROUCHÈS, GABRIEL. 'Documents figurant au fond d'archives de la Bibliothèque de l'Ecole de Beaux-Arts', *Bulletin de la Société de l'Histoire de l'art Français*, Année 1913. Paris, 1913 = Rouchès (1913).

SAHUT, MARIE-CATHERINE, VOLLE, NATHALIE et al. *Diderot & Art de Boucher à David, les Salons 1759-1781*, exh. cat., Editions de la Réunion des Musées Nationaux, Hôtel de la Monnaie, Paris, 1984 = Sahut/Volle (1984).

SAVOURS, ANN. 'The younger Cleveley and the Arctic, 1773-74', *The Mariner's Mirror*, 69 (August 1983) 301-4 = Savours (1983).

SAWYER, FREDERICK C. 'A short History of the Libraries and list of Manuscripts and original drawings in the British Museum (Natural History)', *Bulletin of the British Museum (Natural History)*, Historical series, 4, 2 (London, 1971) 79-204 = Sawyer (1971).

SCHARF, G. *Catalogue of the National Portrait Gallery.* London, 1888 = Scharf (1888).

SCHILLING, EDMUND. *Katalog der deutschen Zeichnungen*, Städelsches Kunstinstitut, Frankfurt a.M., 2 vols., München, 1973 = Schilling (1973).

SCHOENHERR, DOUGLAS E. *Captain Cook's Last Voyage 1776-80. Portraits and Views from the Northwest Coast by John Webber.* Ottawa, 1977 = Schoenherr (1977).

SCHOUMAN, AERT. *Art Schouman*, exh. cat. Rijksprintenkabinett, Rijksmuseum Amsterdam, 1961 = Schouman (1961).

SCHOUMAN, AERT. *La Volière Imaginaire. Aquarelles d'oiseaux par Aert Schouman (1710-1792)*, exh. cat. Fondation Custodia, Institut Néerlandais, Paris, 1982 = Schouman (1982).

SCHULZE-ALTCAPPENBERG, HEIN-TH. *Jean Georges Wille und seine Schule. Zeichnungen und Druckgraphik-Studien zur Künstlergenese, zum "Hollandismus" und zur bürgerlichen Wahrnehmungsästhetik der Aufklärung*, doctoral dissertation, not yet published Philosophical Faculty, University of Bonn, 1985 = Schulze-Altcappenberg (1985).

SENDEY, JOHN. *The Nootkan Indian. A Pictorial.* Port Alberni, B.C. 1977 = Sendey (1977).

SHARPE, R. BOWDLER. 'Birds', *The History of the Collections contained in the Natural History Department of the British Museum*, II, London, 1906 = Sharpe (1906).

SHORTER, A. *Paper Mills and Paper Makers in England, 1479-1800.* Hilversum, 1957 = Shorter (1957).

SKELTON, R. A. *The Journals of Captain James Cook on his Voyages of Discovery, Charts & Views.* Cambridge, 1955 = Skelton (1955).

SKELTON, R. A. *Captain James Cook after two hundred years.* London, 1969 = Skelton (1969).

SKOTTOWE, PHILIP F. *The Leaf and the Tree.* London, 1963 = Skottowe (1963).

SLATKIN, REGINA SHOOLMAN. 'Abraham Bloemaert and François Boucher: Affinity and relationship', *Master Drawings*, XIV, 3 (Autumn 1976) 247-60 = Slatkin (1976).

SMITH, BERNARD. 'European Vision and the South Pacific', *Journal of the Warburg and Courtauld Institutes*, XIII (1950), 65-100 = Smith (1950).

SMITH, BERNARD. *European Vision and the South Pacific 1768-1850.* Oxford, 1960 = Smith (1960). 2nd edn, New Haven/London, 1985 = Smith (1985).

SMITH, BERNARD. *The Rex Nan Kivell Room.* Canberra, 1974 = Smith (1974).

SMITH, BERNARD. *Art as Information. Reflections on the Art from Captain Cook's Voyages.* Sydney, 1979 = Smith (1979a).

SMITH, BERNARD. 'Cook's Posthumous Reputation', *Captain James Cook and His Times*, eds Robin Fisher and Hugh Johnston (Vancouver/London 1979) 159-85 = Smith (1979b).

SMITH, BERNARD. 'William Hodges and English Plein-air Painting', *Art History*, VI, 2 (1983) 143-52 = Smith (1983).

SMITH, BERNARD. 'Captain Cook's artists and the portrayal of Pacific peoples', *Art History*, VII, 3 (September 1984) 295-312 = Smith (1984).

SMITH, EDWARD. *The Life of Sir Joseph Banks.* London, 1911.

SONNERAT, PIERRE. *Voyage à la Nouvelle Guinée.* Dans lequel on trouve la description des Lieux, des Observations physiques & morales, & des détails relatifs à l'Histoire Naturelle dans le Regne Animal & le Regne Végétal, Paris, 1776 = Sonnerat (1776).

SPENCER, JEREMY. 'The New Zealand Charts compiled on H.M. Bark *Endeavour* by Cook, Molyneaux and Pickersgill, 1769-1770', *Archifacts*, 39 (March 1985).

STAFFORD, BARBARA MARIA. 'Toward romantic landscape perception: illustrated travels and the rise of "Singularity" as an aesthetic Category', *Art Quarterly*, Autumn 1977, N.S. I, 1 (1977) 89-124 = Stafford (1977).

STAINTON, LINDSAY. *British Landscape Watercolours, 1600-1860.* London, 1985 = Stainton (1985).

STARZECKA, DOROTA C. 'Society Islands, New Zealand, Hawaii', *Cook's Voyages and Peoples of the Pacific,* ed. Hugh Cobbe (London, 1979) 47-70, 71-88, 109-128 = Starzecka (1979).

STEINER, GERHARD and BAEGE, LUDWIG. *Vögel der Südsee, 23 Gouachen und Aquarelle nach Zeichnungen Georg Forsters, entstanden während seiner Weltumsegelung 1772 bis 1775.* Leipzig, 1971 = Steiner/Baege (1971).

STEINITZ, WOLFGANG. *Les Cris de Paris und die Kaufrufdarstellungen in der Druckgraphik bis 1800.* Salzburg, 1971 = Steinitz (1971).

STRESEMANN, E. 'Birds collected in the North Pacific Area during Capt. James Cook's last voyage (1778 and 1779)', *Ibis,* 91 (1949) 244-55 = Stresemann (1949).

STRESEMANN, E. 'Birds collected during Capt. James Cook's last expedition (1776-80)', *Auk,* 67 (1950) 66-88 = Stresemann (1950).

STRESEMANN, E. 'Additions and correction to "Birds collected in the North Pacific Area during Capt. James Cook's last voyage" (*Ibis,* 1949: 244-255).', *Ibis,* 95 (1953) 371 = Stresemann (1953).

STRICKLER, J. 'Die Berner Münzstatt und ihr Direktor Christian Fueter, 1789-1803', *Neues Berner Taschenbuch* (1905) 15-62 = Strickler (1905).

SYDNEY, Mitchell and Dixson Galleries, State Library of New South Wales, *The Opening up of the Pacific.* Sydney, 1970 = Sydney (1970).

TATTERSALL, BRUCE. 'Henry Webber. Art at the Service of Industry', *Apollo* (July 1985) 36-42 = Tattersall (1985).

THIEME, U. and BECKER, F. *Allgemeines Lexikon der bildenden Künstler.* 37 vols. Leipzig, 1907-50 = Thieme/Becker.

THOMSEN, THOMAS. *Albert Eckhout ein niederländischer Maler und sein Gönner Moritz der Brasilianer.* Copenhagen, 1938 = Thomsen (1938).

THOMSON, BASIL. George Hamilton. *Voyage of H.M.S. Pandora,* with an introduction and notes by Basil Thomson. London, 1915 = Thomson (1915).

TIPPETT, MARIA and COLE, DOUGLAS. *From Desolation to Splendour. Changing Perceptions of the British Columbia Landscape.* Toronto/Vancouver 1977 = Tippett/Cole (1977).

TOOLEY, R. V. *English Books with Coloured Plates, 1790-1860.* London, 1954 = Tooley (1954).

TÜRLER, H. 'Wäber', *Schweizerisches Künstler-Lexikon,* ed Carl Brun, 4 vols. Frauenfeld, 1905-17, reprint 1967 = Türler (1967).

URBAN, MANFRED. *200 Jahre Göttinger Cook-Sammlung,* Göttingen, 1982 = Urban (1982).

VANCOUVER, GEORGE. *A Voyage of Discovery to the North Pacific Ocean and round the World . . . performed in the years 1790, 1791, 1792, 1793, 1794, and 1795 in the Discovery . . . and Chatham under the command of Captain George Vancouver.* 3 vols. London, 1798 = Vancouver (1798).

VENN, JOHN ARCHIBALD. *Alumni Cantabrigiensis. A biographical list of all known students, graduates and holders of office at the University of Cambridge, from the earliest times to 1900.* Cambridge, 1944 = Venn (1944).

WÄBER, HARALD. *Die Familie Wäber von Bern,* typed ms., privately bound, a copy is kept in the Staatsarchiv des Kantons Bern, (Bern 1979) 57-70 = Wäber (1979).

WAGNER, SIGMUND von. 'Leben Johann Webers von Bern', *Siebenzehntes Neujahrsstück,* herausgegeben von der Künstler-Gesellschaft in Zürich auf das Jahr 1821 = Wagner (1821).

WAGNER, SIGMUND. *Verzeichnis der von Herrn Sigmund Wagner sel. hinterlassenen Kunstsachen.* Bern, 1836 = Wagner (1836).

WAGNER, HUGO and WYSS, ROBERT L. *Die Bildnisse im Bernischen Historischen Museum.* Bern, 1957 = Wagner/Wyss (1957).

WALLIS, HELEN. 'Publication of Cook's Journals: Some New Sources and Assessments', *Pacific Studies,* 1, 2 (Spring 1978) 163-94 = Wallis (1978).

WARNER, OLIVER. 'John Webber', *Apollo,* LVI (September 1952) 84-6 = Warner (1952).

WEBBER, JOHN. *A Catalogue of the Genuine and Valuable Collection of Drawings and Prints, a few Pictures, Books, & Late the Property of the Ingenious Mr. Webber, R.A. . . .* which will be sold by auction by Mr. Christie . . ., on Friday, June 14th 1793, and following day. London, 1793 = Webber (1793).

WEBBER, JOHN. *Catalogue for the Admiralty:* see Joppien (1978).

WEBSTER, MARY. *Francis Wheatley.* London, 1970 = Webster (1970).

WHINNEY, MARGARET. *Sculpture in Britain, 1530 to 1830.* Harmondsworth, 1964 = Whinney (1964).

WHITE, CHRISTOPHER. *English Landscape 1630-1850.* Drawings, Prints & Books from the Paul Mellon Collection, New Haven, 1977 = White (1977).

WHITEHEAD, PETER J. P. *Forty Drawings of Fishes made by Artists who accompanied Captain James Cook on his three voyages to the Pacific, 1768-71, 1772-75, 1776-80,* London, 1968 = Whitehead (1968).

WHITEHEAD, PETER. 'Zoological specimens from Captain Cook's voyages', *Journal of the Society for Bibliography of Natural History,* 5, 3 (1969) 161-201 = Whitehead (1969).

WHITEHEAD, PETER. 'A Guide to the Dispersal of Zoological Material from Captain Cook's Voyages', *Pacific Studies* (Fall 1978) 52-93 = Whitehead (1978a).

WHITEHEAD, PETER. 'The Forster collection of Zoological drawings in the British Museum (Natural History)', *Bulletin of the British Museum (Natural History). Historical Series,* 6, 2 (30 March 1978) 25-47 = Whitehead (1978b).

WILSON, S. C. and BORROW, K. T. *The Bridge over the Ocean, Thomas Wilson (1787-1863), Art Collector and Mayor of Adelaide.* Adelaide, 1973 = Wilson/Borrow (1973).

WILTON, ANDREW. 'William Pars and his work in Asia Minor', Richard Chandler, *Travels in Asia Minor 1764-1765,* ed. Edith Clay, London, 1971 = Wilton (1971).

WORCESTER, G. R. G. *The Junks and Sampans of the Yangtze. A Study in Chinese Nautical Research.* 2 vols. Shanghai, 1947-48 = Worcester (1947).

WORTLEY, CLARE STUART. 'Amateur Etchers', *Print Collector Quarterly* (July 1932) = Wortley (1932).

INDEX